or you don't

Egon Ronay's Guides
35 Tadema Road
London SW10 0PZ

Editorial Director **Andrew Eliel**
Publishing Director **Angela Nicholson**
Sales & Marketing Director **Stephen Prendergast**

Chairman **Roy Ackerman**
Leading Guides Ltd
Part of the Richbell Group of Companies

The contents of this book are believed correct at the time of printing. Nevertheless, the publisher can accept no responsibility for errors or omissions or changes in the details given.

ISBN 1 898718 85 7

Designed and typeset in Great Britain by Paul Fry, Bookman Projects Ltd.

First published 1995 by Bookman Projects Ltd.
Floor 22
1 Canada Square
Canary Wharf
London E14 5AP

Establishments are independently researched or inspected. Inspections are anonymous and carried out by Egon Ronay's Guides team of professional inspectors. They may reveal their identities at hotels in order to check all the rooms and other facilities. The Guide is independent in its editorial selection and does not accept advertising, payment or hospitality from listed establishments.

This year's award winners are presented here. Full details of the recipients can be found on the pages indicated.

12 The Grand Hotel
Stockholm, Sweden
**Hotel of the Year,
Western Europe**

14 Hotel Bristol
Warsaw, Poland
**Hotel of the Year,
Eastern Europe**

16 Residenz Heinz
Winkler
Aschau, Germany
**Restaurant
of the Year,
Western Europe**

18 Vinárna v Zátiší
Prague, Czech
Republic
**Restaurant
of the Year,
Eastern Europe**

EGON
RONAY'S
GUIDES
1996

CONTENTS

Foreword by Seagram   6

C O N T E N T S

Sponsor's Foreword

International gourmets and travellers will be delighted to see the new *Egon Ronay's Seagram Guide 1996 Europe*. This definitive guide to good eating and fine living reveals some of today's best restaurants and hotels. It covers a broad range of establishments and is designed to meet differing budgets, occasions and individual tastes.

The association between Egon Ronay's Guides and Seagram stems from a simple and shared belief that fine cuisine and premium spirits and wines enhance the quality of life and are best appreciated and enjoyed in the right environment.

Seagram has an unrivalled portfolio of prestigious distilled spirits and wines, suitable for any such occasion. Chivas Regal, the world's leading premium Scotch whisky, continues to win international acclaim, while our two very distinctive single malt Scotch whiskies, The Glenlivet and Glen Grant, remain favourites among whisky connoisseurs. We also have Four Roses Bourbon, with its distinctive, all-American whisky style and flavour. From Martell, the oldest of the major Cognac Houses, we offer a fine range of quality Cognacs, including Martell's unique flagship marque, Cordon Bleu. We are also extremely proud to be able to offer Absolut Vodka, the world's number one premium vodka.
Our choice of wines is equally extensive. From The House of Sandeman we have a selection of Ports and Sherries, while classic French Wines are available from Barton & Guestier. Finally, should your occasion require added sparkle, Seagram has the perfect answer with two of France's best known Champagnes, Mumm and Perrier-Jouët.

Welcome to *Egon Ronay's Seagram Guide 1996 Europe*. As it divulges, there are many wonderful hotels and restaurants to be found throughout Europe. It simply remains for you to explore this Guide and savour some of the delights it has to offer.

Getting about

With the opening of the Channel Tunnel, access to parts of Europe has been made easier – not that venturing outside these islands has ever been difficult. Maybe it just seems that the boundaries have moved nearer – no longer are we separated by the sea, nor are there such clear-cut divisions between East and West. Travelling has never been easier, prices are competitive, and our quest for new experiences remains undiminished. Avenues of opportunity beckon, whether it's business in Prague or a fling in Finland. Whereas years ago we would have been satisfied with a holiday, say, in the Algarve; today, we are more becoming more adventurous and setting off for pastures new, experiencing and discovering cultures that previously we have only read about or heard and seen on the news.

Sans frontières

Britain may be a long-time member of the European Union, but the fact is that the majority of British do not yet feel European, and it will be a long time before they do. It will take some time for our island to shed its insular attitude, and while the world may be shrinking in terms of communications, prejudices and opinions take longer to change. This Guide, the second edition, has no such constrictions – we've dined in Moscow (not, I hasten to add, at the newly opened Maxim's de Paris, part-owned by Pierre Cardin, where the astronomical cost of a meal is way beyond the depth of our inspectors' pockets!), lunched in Brussels (3½ hours door to door by Eurostar), slept in Rome and partied (not overly so!) in Budapest. Everywhere we've been, standards (and prices) are rising, and though the East will inevitably take longer to catch up with the very best standards in the West, the gap is already closing. Joint ventures are now commonplace, whether it's an international hotel corporation linking with a national government, or an established French chef cooking in, say, St Petersburg. Decent facilities, good service and good food know no boundaries; good manners and a smile cost nothing; a positive attitude alone is often enough to satisfy.

Coverage

We set out with a purpose: to introduce you to a taste of the best that Europe has to offer. We are as selective and as comprehensive as we believe it's necessary to be. The Guide has been prepared very much with business travellers in mind, and therefore concentrates on the major cities across 30 European countries. Of course, we have not covered *every* establishment whose standards match our own; that would be impossible and beyond even our means, since everywhere we go we pay. There is no charge for an entry in our Guides – it is achieved purely on merit. Within these covers, you will find something suitable, whether it's a luxury hotel in a major city or a fine restaurant in the country and therefore worth a special detour. However, as in all walks of life it pays to do your homework first – always check that prices and opening times are correct; they were when the Guide went to press, but they do change, particularly in the East, where the US dollar is often the preferred currency to their own; in several instances we quote prices in US $.

Awards

During the year, in association with Seagram, we embarked on a whistle-stop tour to present our annual awards, a tangible achievement that sets the very best apart. We travelled by plane and train, hosting receptions as far afield as St Petersburg and

See over

8

Introduction

From page 7

Vienna, Budapest and Brussels, Sofia and Paris. Everywhere we went we were received with warm hospitality, not only by hoteliers and restaurateurs, but also by burghers and mayors keen to promote their own cities. As a public relations exercise our trips were triumphant, but more importantly they showed us that success brings out the best in everyone – there is no substitute for quality. Our awards (see pages 12-19), are selected on the basis of an establishment's consistent excellence and outstanding enterprise, by our own team of visiting inspectors and contributors, and we look forward to making presentations in the Czech Republic, Germany, Poland and Sweden.

Support

Our continued association with Seagram is of double benefit since, through the local knowledge of their representatives in areas covered by this Guide, we are able to check out first hand establishments we might otherwise not have known about. We particularly acknowledge the contribution of our colleague Charles Florman, an experienced septuagenarian of unbounded enthusiasm, energy and expert tastebuds, and someone who has eaten more often in Europe's top restaurants than even some of our own indefatigable inspectors. Others deserving a mention are Joseph Berkmann, Phil and Aña Diment, Mario Dix, Zoltan Halasz, Robin Lodge and Ian Wiesnieski.

The Scotch Beef Club

We are glad once again to welcome the Scotch Beef Club. Originally started in Italy, the Scotch Beef Club has spread throughout Europe with members in France, Germany, Belgium, Holland, Luxembourg and the UK. Scotland is justifiably proud of the reputation of its beef industry and only the finest, genuine Scotch Beef is served in member establishments.

Your views

As ever, we rely just as much on you, the reader, as well as our own team, to let us know of places worthy of inclusion in subsequent editions. We also welcome your comments (favourable or otherwise) on establishments that we already recommend, and should you ever have cause to complain about somewhere within these pages, please make the nature of your complaint known to them before writing to us; and don't forget compliments and words of praise are always well received.

How to use this Guide

Egon Ronay's Seagram Guide 1996 Europe covers 30 countries throughout Europe, listed in the order shown on the contents page. Each country is preceded by a title page containing useful information for the traveller. Within each country, major towns are listed in alphabetical order. Establishments within a reasonable distance of major locations are listed after those locations, and at the end of some countries is a section 'Elsewhere in .....', listing worthy establishments perhaps not near a major town or city. A 4-page map of locations included in the Guide begins on page 362.

Order of Entries

Within each location hotels with recommended restaurants (HR), hotels (H) and restaurants (R) are listed in alphabetical order; (RR) denotes a restaurant with rooms. An index to each country's entries will be found at the end of the book.

Prices

Hotel prices given are per night for a double room with en-suite facilities and continental breakfasts; prices will often vary considerably according to the season and the length of stay. Meal prices are for two people – three courses (à la carte where offered), a modest bottle of wine, and coffee. In some Eastern European countries prices are listed in US dollars, following local practice. Opening times and closures are liable to alteration, and it's always best to book.

Symbols

The star ★ symbol denotes the pick of the restaurants throughout the Guide. The quality of cooking is not the only consideration (though this is the major factor), as we also take into account factors such as ambience, comfort and service.

A star followed by a plus sign ★+ denotes the best cooking in the country.

The symbol 🐄 at the end of an entry denotes an establishment that is a member of the Scotch Beef Club. A full list of Club members appears at the end of participating countries.

Starred Restaurants, 1996

The plus sign + denotes the best cooking in the country.

Hanover — Landhaus Ammann
Munich — Aubergine
Tantris +

HUNGARY
Budapest — Gundel Restaurant
Mátyàs Pince
Robinson Restaurant

IRELAND
Cork — Arbutus Lodge
Cliffords
Dublin — Le Coq Hardi
Patrick Guilbaud
La Stampa
Shangarry — Ballymaloe House

ITALY
Abbiategrasso — Antica Osteria
del Ponte +
Castrocaro Terme — La Frasca +
Costiglione d'Asti — Da Guido
Erbusco — Gualtiero Marchesi +
Florence — Don Chisciotti
Enoteca Pinchiorri +
Milan — L'Ami Berton
Bistrot di Gualtiero
Marchesi +
Calajunco +
Rome — Checchino dal 1887
Lord Byron Hotel

LUXEMBOURG
Geyershaff — La Bergerie
Kockelscheuer — Patin d'Or

MALTA
Valetta — The Carriage

MONACO
Monte Carlo — Hotel de Paris +

NETHERLANDS
Amsterdam — Christophe
Hoorn — De Oude Rosmolen
Leidschendam — Villa Rozenrust
Overveen — De Bokkedoorns

NORWAY
Oslo — Bagatelle +
Le Canard
Continental Hotel
D'Artagnan
Feinschmecker

POLAND
Warsaw — Bazyliszek
Hotel Bristol

PORTUGAL
Lisbon — Casa da Comida

ROMANIA
Bucharest — Sofitel

RUSSIA
Moscow — Pirosmani
St Petersburg — Grand Hotel Europe

SPAIN
Barcelona — Jaume de Provença
Reno
Via Veneto
Madrid — El Amparo +
Bajamar
Cabo Mayor
Casa Lucio
Las Cuatras
Estaciones
Jockey
El Pescador
Principe de Viana
La Trainera
Zalacáin +
Marbella — La Fonda
La Hacienda
La Meridiana
Rosas — El Bulli +
San Sebastian — Arzak +
St Celoni — El Racó de Can
Fabes +
Valencia — Oscar Torrijos
Rías Gallegas

SWEDEN
Gothenberg — Sjömagasinet
Westra Piren
Stockholm — Eriks +
Grand Hotel
Operakällern
Paul & Norbert
Wedholms Fisk

SWITZERLAND
Basle — Stucki
Crissier — Girardet +
Gattikon — Sihlhalde
Geneva — L'Arlequin
L'Orangerie de la
Perle du Lac
Parc des Eaux-Vives
Küsnacht — Restaurant
Kunststuben +
Unterengstringen — Witschi's
Vufflens-le-Chateau — Hotel de l'Ermitage +
Zürich — Restaurant Agnès
Amberg
Dolder Grand Hotel

UNITED KINGDOM
Belfast — Roscoff
Bray — Waterside Inn +
Bristol — Restaurant Lettonie
Great Milton — Le Manoir aux
Quat'Saisons +
London — Alastair Little
Aubergine +
Chez Nico at 90
Park Lane +
The Dorchester +
Four Seasons Hotel
Le Gavroche +
Inter-Continental +
Langan's Brasserie
Restaurant Marco
Pierre White +
Les Saveurs +
The Square
La Tante Claire +
Longridge — Paul Heathcote's +
Shinfield — L'Ortolan +

Awards

Hotel of the Year
Western Europe

Grand Hotel
Stockholm, Sweden

Grand in every sense, this privately-owned hotel, which plays host to the annual Nobel prize-winners, is located on the harbour quayside opposite the Royal Palace. Opened towards the end of the last century, renovated and rebuilt some ten years ago, it retains many of its original features, notably the marble staircase

leading to The Winter Garden banquet hall and the frescoed ceiling of The Hall of Mirrors, two of the finest banqueting and meeting rooms in Europe; others are housed in the Bolinder Palace, which also belongs to the hotel. Gilt plasterwork, glittering chandeliers, antiques and works of art complete the picture, which, allied with standards of comfort and service of the highest calibre, gives you a truly world-class hotel.

Congratulations

Seagram is delighted to congratulate
the Hotel of the Year, Western Europe.

THE GRAND HOTEL
STOCKHOLM, SWEDEN

Hotel of the Year
Eastern Europe

Hotel Bristol
Warsaw, Poland

A joint venture between the State Tourist Agency Orbis and Forte plc, this magnificently restored hotel, originally built at the turn of the century, is managed, and has been since its re-opening, by the distinguished Michael Goerdt. One of Forte's Exclusive Hotels (there are only around twenty world-wide) this stylish, characterful and historic hotel is once again at the forefront of Warsaw's social and cultural life – indeed it sponsors the most famous festivals of classical music in Poland. It is truly grand, and demonstrates the best that eastern Europe can now offer as a result of the dramatic political changes in recent times.

PAST WINNER	
1995	**Grand Hotel Europe** St Petersburg, Russia

Congratulations

**Seagram is delighted to congratulate
the Hotel of the Year, Eastern Europe.**

HOTEL BRISTOL
WARSAW, POLAND

Restaurant of the Year Western Europe

Residenz Heinz Winkler
Aschau im Chiemgau, Germany

Respected and appreciated by Bocuse when he worked with him in France, and previously a success in Munich, Heinz Winkler now gives full rein to his talents here. The beautifully situated 15th-century building, originally a post house, combines hotel and restaurant; the latter, with a touch of Venice about it, has stunning views (sit out on the magnificent terrace). There is no better chef in

Germany (and he's German!); he's certainly the equal of the best in Europe, his cooking soundly based on classical French principles with Bavarian touches. Look out for dishes such as marinated foie gras served with a summer salad and nuts; emincé of turbot with chives and caviar; roast duckling with a grain mustard sauce; iced Grand Marnier soufflé with strawberries. Well worth the journey from Munich, though it's actually closer to Salzburg (60km).

Past Winner	
1995	**'t Laurierblad**
	Berlare, Belgium

Congratulations

**Seagram is delighted to congratulate
the Restaurant of the Year, Western Europe.**

Residenz Heinz Winkler
Aschau im Chiemgau, Germany

Restaurant of the Year
Eastern Europe

Vinárna v Zátiší
Prague, Czech Republic

A truly international restaurant (one of several, including the excellent *Parnas,* owned by Sanjiv Suri) serving a variety of dishes from around Europe with many Czech specialities. With a change of decor, a newly-arrived Swedish chef Kenneth Askenberg, and knowledgable staff with a genuine desire to please, you're guaranteed the best food in town – look out for crispy roast duck leg served with red cabbage and herb dumplings; salmon marinated in sea salt and dill; and the legendary chocolate mousse served with vanilla ice cream.

PAST WINNER	
1995	**Gundel** Budapest, Hungary

Congratulations

**Seagram is delighted to congratulate
the Restaurant of the Year, Eastern Europe.**

VINÁRNA V ZÁTIŠÍ
PRAGUE, CZECH REPUBLIC

You either have it

or you don't

ABSOLUT ROME.

ABSOLUT VODKA IS THE SUPREME CHOICE ANYWHERE IN EUROPE
ENJOYED NEAT, ON THE ROCKS, OR IN DRINKS AND COCKTAILS

Mellow but never tame.

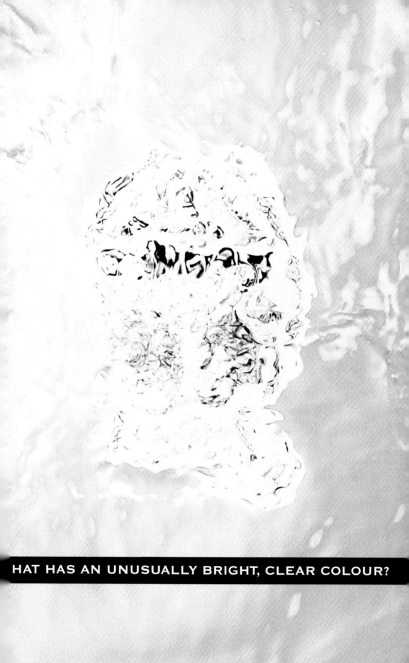

HAT HAS AN UNUSUALLY BRIGHT, CLEAR COLOUR?

ABSOLUT AMSTERDAM.

ABSOLUT VODKA IS THE SUPREME CHOICE ANYWHERE IN EUROPE,
ENJOYED NEAT, ON THE ROCKS, OR IN DRINKS AND COCKTAILS

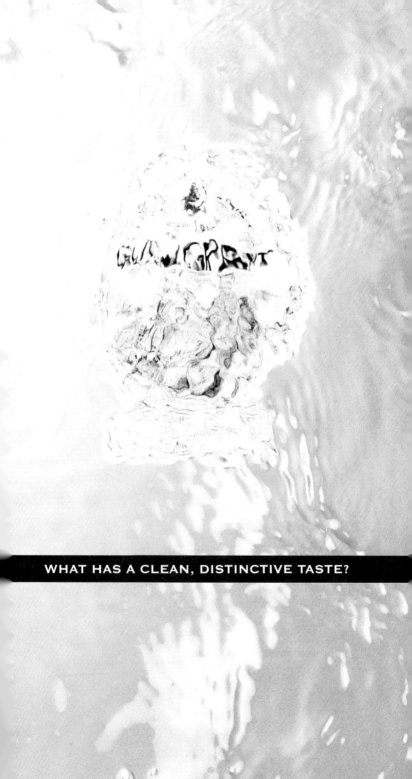

WHAT HAS A CLEAN, DISTINCTIVE TASTE?

THE ART OF DISTINCTION.

Those who appreciate quality enjoy it responsibly.

Many are called V.S.O.P., but only one bears the rare seal of Louis XIV and offers a distinctive marriage of our most exquisite cognacs: Martell Medallion V.S.O.P.

MARTELL

SINCE 1715

COGNAC. L'ART DE MARTELL.

GLEN GRANT. DIFFERENT BY TRADITION SINCE 1840.

ABSOLUT BRUSSELS.

ABSOLUT VODKA IS THE SUPREME CHOICE ANYWHERE IN EUROPE,
ENJOYED NEAT, ON THE ROCKS, OR IN DRINKS AND COCKTAILS

PASSPORT SCOTCH. A STYLE OF IT'S OWN.

12 years ago my daughter was born. She breezed into my life like a miniature hurricane. I celebrated with something new: Malt Whisky.

Has she changed my life? I'll say. (You try standing in a hurricane for twelve years.) One thing hasn't changed: I still like that Whisky.

The **GLENLIVET** *Single Malt Scotch Whisky*. **AGED *12* YEARS.**
Definitive Speyside character, remarkably flowery, clean and soft. BODY: *Medium, firm, smooth.*
PALATE: *Fruity, flowery, notes of vanilla. Delicate balance between sweetness and malty dryness.* FINISH: *Long, subtle, gently warming.*
COLOUR: *Pale gold.*

SPECIALLY SELECTED SCOTCH BEEF

THE TRUE TASTE OF QUALITY

Scotland's world-wide reputation for producing prime beef cattle owes much to nature. Favoured with the ideal stock-rearing conditions of a temperate climate, an abundance of grass and pure water, and vast tracts of unspoiled countryside, generations of Scottish farmers have used their skills to produce beef for the discerning tables of the world.

300 YEARS OF TRADITION AND DEVELOPMENT

As far back as the 17th century, the beef from Scottish cattle was in demand, and each year tens of thousands were exported - on foot - to eager English markets.

A century later agricultural improvements enabled whole herds to be fed through the winters, and attention was then turned to improving native cattle breeds. The result, by the early 19th century, was beef breeds which were to become renowned throughout the world.

Until the 19th century Scotch beef cattle continued to be walked to markets in the south, but the introduction of steam navigation, then railways, brought the cattle droving tradition of generations to an end. Prime Scotch beef could now travel to London in peak condition, and the modern meat industry began.

Now, one hundred years on, fleets of refrigerated vehicles daily transport Specially Selected Scotch Beef to markets throughout the UK and continental Europe.

REPUTATION FOR EXCELLENCE

Like other products with a reputation for excellence - such as vintage red wine and famous malt whiskies - it takes time and skill to produce Specially Selected Scotch Beef.

Generations of experience in cattle rearing, backed by the quality assurance schemes of today, means that Specially Selected Scotch Beef is produced to the highest farming standards throughout. The Scotch meat industry has its own expertise, and Specially Selected Scotch Beef is matured in the traditional, time-honoured way to maximise the flavour and tenderness for which it is world renowned.

EUROPEAN QUALITY BEEF

The EC recognises the contribution of the Scottish meat industry in setting standards of quality. The use of the European Quality Beef logo signifies that strict EC standards for quality

control and product traceability from farm to consumer have been adhered to - further enhancing the reputation of Specially Selected Scotch Beef for consistent product quality.

A WHOLE NEW EATING EXPERIENCE

Specially Selected Scotch Beef is recognised as a popular choice for caterers around the world and many top class restaurants have enhanced their reputations with the quality of the Scotch beef they serve.

For the true taste of quality and a whole new eating experience, discover the flavour and tenderness of Specially Selected Scotch Beef at one of the many Scotch Beef Club restaurants, highlighted throughout this Guide.

This advertorial is partially funded by the EC.

WELCOME TO THE SCOTCH BEEF CLUB

An elite club with over 600 members throughout the UK and continental Europe - each one a distinguished restaurant with an international reputation for excellence.

This Guide, recognised for the quality of its listed establishments and an indispensable aid to the discerning diner, features many of the Scotch Beef Club members.

Chefs demand exacting standards of quality in the beef they buy. Scotch Beef Club members purchase not only one of the world's finest meat products, but a true taste of quality.

This, together with their culinary expertise produces Specially Selected Scotch Beef dishes that enhance their international reputations and confirms their listing in the Guide.

D.S. Cameron

"At Turnberry we cater for the most discerning of both national and international clientele, and are proud to feature the finest of Scotch beef throughout the hotel's three restaurants. The Scotch Beef Club ensures that the highest standards are constantly maintained and protected for the future. Turnberry Hotel is proud to be a founder member of this prestigious Club".

**D.S. Cameron,
Executive Chef de Cuisine,
Turnberry Hotel.**

Look for the Black Bull symbol to identify members of the Scotch Beef Club.

So whether you favour a succulent steak, a tender roast or a more exotic international recipe, visit a Scotch Beef Club member and experience the flavour and tenderness of Specially Selected Scotch Beef for yourself.

The Scotch Beef Club operates in Belgium, France, Germany, Great Britain, Holland, Italy and Spain - and each member restaurant is identified by a distinctive door sticker or plaque.

MEMBER OF THE
SCOTCH BEEF CLUB

European Quality Beef

Specially Selected
SCOTCH BEEF

Partially funded by the EC.

For a full list of all Scotch Beef Club members, please contact the Scotch Quality Beef and Lamb Association on

0131•333 5335

or write to: Scotch Quality Beef and Lamb Association, Rural Centre, West Mains, Ingliston, Newbridge, Midlothian EH28 8NZ, Scotland.

This advertorial is partially funded by the EC.

SEAGRAM'S 7 CROWN.
THE BEST OF AMERICA.

IT WAS THE whiskey which grew up with America. And the real thing is still available today. 7 Crown American Whiskey is made in the traditional way using the finest ingredients for a full bodied taste. A taste which was America's favourite for 40 years.

America's No. 1 selling *whiskey*.

Austria

Currency Austrian Schilling **Exchange Rate** £1=approx AS 15.65
International dialling code: 00 43 (Vienna+1 Salzburg+662)
Passports/Visas No visa required by British passport holders.
British Consulate in Vienna Tel 1-713 1575 Fax 1-712 7316

TRANSPORT
Airports
Flughafen Wien (Vienna) Tel 1-711 100
Salzburg Flughafenbetriebesgesmbh Tel: 662-80 550
Railway Stations
Vienna Westbahnhof/Südbahnhof/Franz-Josef-Bahnhof Tel 1-1717
Salzburg Hauptbahnhof Tel 662-1717
Car hire in Vienna
Tel Nos. **Avis** 1-587 62 41 **Budget** 1-71 46 565 **Europcar** 1-505 42 00
Hertz 1-713 15 91-0 **Rent-A-Car** 1-544 7151 **Trans hire** 1-714 6717
Speed limits: 100km/h on trunk roads, 130km/h on motorways, 50km/h
in towns.

OPENING TIMES
Banks 8am-12.30pm & 1.30-3pm Mon-Wed & Fri, 8am-12.30pm
& 1-5.30pm Thur. Closed Sat, Sun. Money changes are open at
airports/main railway stations.
Shops 8am-6.30pm weekdays, 8am-1pm Sat, 8am-5pm first Sat every
month. Many shops closed 2hrs midday.

NATIONAL HOLIDAYS
New Year's Day, 6 Jan, Easter Monday, 1 May, Ascension Day,
Whit Monday, Corpus Christi, 15 Aug, 26 Oct, 1 Nov, 8 Dec,
Christmas Day & Boxing Day.

Tourist Offices
Austrian Tourist Board in **London** Tel 0171-629 0461
In Austria **Vienna** Tel 1 211 140 **Salzburg** Tel 662 88 9 87
American Express Travel Service Offices or Representative (R)
Vienna   AETS
             21/23 Kaerntnerstrasse
             A-1015
             PO Box 28
             Tel 1-51540 #
Salzburg AETS
             5 Mozartplatz
             A-5010
             PO Box 244
             Tel 622 842501 #

Salzburg

SALZBURG **Hotel Altstadt Radisson SAS** S2500

Tel: (662) 848 57 10   Fax: (662) 848 57 16
Judengasse 15, 5020 Salzburg   H

An elegant international hotel set in a 14th-century building that has a rich and varied history, having been a college, synagogue and brewery in its past lives. The whole hotel was renovated three years ago but no two rooms are alike and all retain the original exposed beams or elegant stucco ceilings and all have traditional furniture and the expected mod cons. Whether you choose a room with a view over the Salzach or one overlooking the now pedestrianised narrow lanes and alleys of the old town, the surroundings are equally charming. *Rooms 60. Room service 24hr. Private garage S280. Banqueting facilities 150. Conference facilities 50. Secretarial services on request. Safe. Satellite TV. Amex, Diners, Mastercard, Visa.*

SALZBURG **Hotel Dorint** S1530

Tel: (662) 88 20 31   Fax: (662) 88 20 319
Sterneckstrasse 20, 5020 Salzburg   H

A modern business hotel ten minutes walk from the old town. Bedrooms are equipped with satellite TV and mini-bar but no air-conditioning. The hotel was recarpeted last year and a new restaurant opened serving traditional Austrian food. *Rooms 140. Room service 24hr. Private parking. Banqueting facilities 200. Conference facilities 260. Sauna. Solarium. Amex, Diners, Mastercard, Visa.*

SALZBURG **Hotel Gasthof Brandstätter** S1350

Tel: (662) 43 45 35   Fax: (662) 43 45 35 90
Münchner Bundesstrasse 69, 5020 Salzburg   HR

A warm countrified place in an old farmhouse on the outskirts of Salzburg, quiet but still glamorous enough to attract the Austrian television station, ORF, for regular meetings. The rooms are in keeping with the style of the building, and are decorated with traditional farmhouse furniture. The hall is lined with rich warm Persian carpets. The garden is quiet and a real sun-trap in summer. *Rooms 36. Room service limited. Private parking. Banqueting facilities 40. Conference facilities 40. Satellite TV. Sauna. Solarium. Indoor swimming pool. Closed 23-26 Dec. Amex, Diners, Mastercard, Visa.*

Restaurant   S1400

Karl Paller in the kitchen trained in Vienna and has been here for three years. His food is devotedly Austrian (a combination of German and Czech influences). Marinated crab and trout are firm favourites and there is also a daily fresh-fish option dictated by the market. Heartier fare might include beef bouillon with liver dumplings (note the Czech influence here) or one of a range of meat cutlets served with salads and potatoes. Set menus start at S260 per person and there's a *feinschmecker* menu for true gourmets at S650. Note that booking is almost always essential. *Seats 60 (terrace 50). Open 1130-1400, 1830-2130. Closed last 2 weeks Jun, 1st week Jul, 23-26 Dec, 3-15 Jan. No credit cards.*

SALZBURG **Hotel Mercure** S1400

Tel: (662) 881 43 80   Fax: (662) 871 111 411
Bayerhamerstrasse 14, 5020 Salzburg   H

This modern hotel, 15 minutes walk from the old town, is part of the Accor Group which also owns Ibis and Novotel. The area is pleasant and quiet with a small park around the building. Bedrooms are decorated in white and red and are equipped with cable TV and mini-bars. *Rooms 121. Room service limited. Private parking S80. Banqueting facilities 100. Conference facilities 150. Amex, Diners, Mastercard, Visa.*

> Opening times are often liable to change at short notice, so it's
> always best to book.

SALZBURG   Hotel Österreichischer Hof   S2500

Tel: (622) 88 9 77   Fax: (622) 88 9 77 551
Schwarzstrasse 5-7, A-5020 Salzburg

On the quieter bank of the Salzach river, this hotel has a pedigree dating back to 1866 and was taken over in 1988 by the same family that owns Hotel Sacher in Vienna. The public rooms retain their 19th-century grandeur. The magnificent central staircase with its rich, red carpeting and the glass-covered roof create quite an impression. The bedrooms are tastefully furnished, and discreetly incorporate all the mod cons. The traditional coffee-house, *Cafe ÖH*, with its watercolours of famous Salzburg conductors, is the ideal place to sample the famous *Sachertorte* and the hotel also boasts three restaurants, a *Theaterkeller* wine cellar and a Wintergarten piano bar. *Rooms 120. Room service 24hr. Private garage S300. Banqueting facilities 120. Conference facilities 80. Secretarial/translation services on request. Air-conditioning. Cable TV. Disabled room. Laundry service. Safe.*
Amex, Diners, Mastercard, Visa.

SALZBURG   Hotel Rosenberger   S1750

Tel: (662) 43 55 46   Fax: (662) 43 95 10 95
Bessarabierstrasse 94, 5020 Salzburg

Built in 1989, this family-run chain hotel is located opposite the Exhibition Centre, 15 minutes drive from the centre of Salzburg. As might be expected, facilities are aimed at business guests – notably eight fully-equipped conference rooms. *Rooms 120.*
Room service limited. Private parking S55. Banqueting facilities 250. Conference facilities 400. Sauna. Amex, Diners, Mastercard, Visa.

SALZBURG   Hotel Schloss Mönchstein   S3000

Tel: (662) 8 48 55 50   Fax: (662) 84 85 59
Mönchsburg Park 26, 5020 Salzburg

Set in its own 25-acre park and commanding wonderful views over Salzburg, this fairy-tale castle dates from the 14th century and has been run as a hotel by the Von Mierka family for the last 40 years. The traditionally decorated interior is filled with antiques, chesterfield-style sofas, chandeliers and ornate mirrors. Air-conditioning, though not found in the bedrooms, has recently been installed in the restaurant where harp concerts entertain diners at weekends. *Rooms 17. Room service limited. Private parking. Banqueting facilities 72. Conference facilities 30. Tennis. Amex, Diners, Mastercard, Visa.*

SALZBURG-PARSCH   Hotel Villa Pace   S4100

Tel: (662) 64 15 01   Fax: (662) 64 15 01 22
Sonnleitenweg 9, 5020 Salzburg-Parsch

A lovely sweeping lawn leads up to the 400-year-old main building of this elegant hotel, surrounded by fields and forests at the foot of the Gaisberg, 5km from Salzburg. Service is friendly and efficient with guests pampered from the moment of arrival with champagne, flowers and a fruit basket in their rooms. The decor is as traditional as the warmth of the welcome with heavy wooden furniture, antiques and rich fabrics throughout. Three new suites in the house next to the hotel (connected by a passage) were completed in 1995. The Villa previously closed from November to February but may remain open all winter in future; phone to check. *Rooms 16. Room service 24hr. Private parking. Banqueting facilities 25. Outdoor swimming pool. Sauna. Solarium. Amex, Diners, Mastercard, Visa.*

Around Salzburg

HOF   Hotel Schloss Fuschl   S3700

Tel: (6229) 2 25 30   Fax: (6229) 22 53 531
5322 Hof

Located on a peninsula in an 85-acre park overlooking Lake Fuschl, 20km from Salzburg, this luxurious hotel was once the residence of the city's archbishops. Leisure facilities are as superb as the setting. Hunting is popular in the surrounding forests (the hotel has its own hunting museum) and there is also a private beach, rifle range, 9-hole golf course, tennis court and horse-riding centre at the disposal of guests. Those who prefer indoor activities can visit the beauty farm or work up a sweat in the gym and sauna. Decor is comfortingly traditional, with fine antiques in many rooms. *Rooms 84. Room service 24hr. Private parking. Conference facilities 250. Sports facilities. Gym. Sauna. News kiosk. Amex, Diners, Mastercard, Visa.*

MONDSEE — Hotel Seehof — S1960

Tel: (6232) 50 31   Fax: (6232) 50 31 51   H
Loibichl, 5311 Mondsee

A lovely lakeside location is the major attraction of this fine country house hotel surrounded by acres of parkland. Facilities are aimed at the leisure rather than the business market with excellent waterskiing and windsurfing possible on the lake and tennis courts, sauna and gym available in the grounds. *Rooms 35. Closed end Sep–mid May.*
Room service limited. Private parking. Conference facilities 18. Tennis. Gym. Sauna. Solarium. Beauty treatment. No credit cards.

Vienna

VIENNA — Altes Presshaus — S450

Tel: (1) 32 23 93   Fax: (1) 32 23 42 85   R
Cobenzlgasse 15, 1190 Wien

Grinzing is Vienna's answer to Montmartre, and the Altes Presshaus, a traditional Heurige or vintner's garden, is, like its French counterpart, a place for pleasure-seekers. This vast place comprises a large dining-room with an open fireplace, a trophy-filled room and a historic wine vault, where regular wine tastings are organised. The building itself is a 16th-century convent and a national monument; and the food inside is as much a monument to traditional Viennese cooking as one can find anywhere in this city. Country-style sausages are served with whipped cream and horseradish sauce; weinhauer, another favourite, is a mixed platter of beef and sausages. A popular feature is the buffet (a typically hearty Viennese offering of cured meats, dumplings and sauerkraut). Follow up with the sweet curd cheese strudel with custard sauce. There is a wine list but most people traditionally drink the *Heurige* or latest house vintage in copious quantities whilst serenaded by Viennese singers. *Seats 500 (garden 500). Open 1600-2400.*
Closed Jan, Feb. Public parking. Amex, Diners, Mastercard, Visa.

VIENNA — Hotel Biedermeier — S1400

Tel: (1) 71 67 10   Fax: (1) 71 67 15 03   H
Landstrasser Haupstrasse 28, 1030 Wien

Two handsome 19th-century Biedermeier-style buildings, ten minutes from the Cathedral, are home to this traditional hotel. The original stone floors and cherrywood fittings remain but the interior has been modernised and all bedrooms have satellite TV and mini-bars. Five conference rooms are available for meetings. *Rooms 203. Private parking S170.*
Banqueting facilities 300. Conference facilities 150 Hair salon. Amex, Diners, Mastercard, Visa.

VIENNA — Hotel Bristol — S4140

Tel: (1) 51 51 60   Fax: (1) 51 516 550   HR
Kärntner Ring 1, 1015 Wien

The turn-of-the-century Bristol won our Award for Best Business Hotel in Western Europe in 1995 and, although ownership recently passed from the CIGA Group to ITT Sheraton, it continues to provide a superb level of service. Business customers can stay on the club floor at preferential room rates and have the VIP lounge at their disposal. The Global Business Center can supply full secretarial and translation services, laptops, audio-visual equipment, up-to-date world financial and travel information, desk-top publishing, mobile phones and even complimentary refreshments. All this is provided in an atmosphere of luxury and style with sumptuous antique-filled public rooms, a burnished brass staircase and stylishly-decorated air-conditioned bedrooms. Guests have free use of a nearby health club. *Rooms 146. Room service 24hr. Public parking. Banqueting facilities 104. Conference facilities 180. Business centre. Amex, Diners, Mastercard, Visa.*

Restaurant Korso bei der Oper — ★ — S2000

Chef Reinhard Gerer has made a major impact on Austria's gastronomic scene with his superb interpretations of traditional Austrian and international dishes. A typical Viennese meal might start with spinach and cream cheese dumplings with brown butter, followed by Tafelspitz (traditional Viennese boiled beef), and a strudel to finish, while a more international dinner might consist of gnocchi with seafood *à la Korso*, followed by roasted

sole and a tomato and olive sauce, and then a sorbet. Look out also for the daily menu. If you have special dietary requirements, the restaurant is happy to tailor a menu to your needs. Some of the vintages on the lengthy wine list date back to 1945.
Set menus from S380 (lunch) and S680 (dinner). *Seats 65. Open 1200-1400, 1900-2300. Closed L Sat (L Sun Jul-Aug), 3 weeks Aug.*

Tel: (1) 32 32 18   Fax: (1) 32 66 60
Sieveringer Strasse 46, 1190 Wien

Maria Zarl-Eckel cooks traditional Austrian and international dishes in the old farmhouse built by her grandfather north west of the centre of Vienna. Veal and venison dishes, served with potatoes or noodles, are prominent on the carte but fish-lovers are also provided for with trout and anglerfish fried in butter or baked and served with potato salad. Eating under the chestnut and linden trees in the garden is delightful in warm weather. *Seats 120. Open 1200-1430, 1800-2230. Closed Sun, Mon, last 2 weeks Aug, 3 weeks at Christmas. Public parking. Amex, Diners, Visa.*

Tel: (1) 50 11 00   Fax: (1) 50 11 04 10
Kärntner Ring 16, 1015 Wien

This grand building in the centre of Vienna near the Opera House was built as the residence of the Duke of Würtemberg in 1867 but became a hotel only six years later. The facade has recently been reconstructed and repainted and the lobby enlarged but the atmosphere inside remains splendidly regal. Bedrooms are elegantly and comfortably furnished and all have air-conditioning, cable TV and mini-bar. Guests can use a nearby fitness centre free of charge. Daily piano concerts take place in the Imperial Café where you can sample the hotel's famous Imperial Torte which is exported around the world. *Rooms 128. Room service 24hr. Valet parking. Banqueting and conference facilities 200. Beauty treatment. Hair salon. Amex, Diners, Mastercard, Visa.*

Tel: (1) 512 88 43   Fax: (1) 513 81 30
Mahlerstrasse 9, 1010 Wien

A Turkish chef cooks for both the unpretentious Kervansaray downstairs and the more elegant Hummerbar upstairs. Traditional Austrian dishes such as medallion of veal with goose liver in a herb sauce served with fresh asparagus appear alongside doner and mixed kebabs on the downstairs carte while the Hummerbar specialises in fish and lobster. Scallops with sauce mornay, roasted turbot with parsley potatoes and poached fillet of sole with a champagne sauce are typical dishes. Flambéed Turkish figs are a fine way to finish a meal. *Seats 50 (Kervansaray), 80 (Hummerbar). Open 1200-2330. Closed Sun, 24-26 Dec. Public parking. Amex, Diners, Mastercard, Visa.*

Tel: (1) 533 93 81   Fax: (1) 533 93 814
Schottengasse 7, 1010 Wien

Located near the university, this elegant restaurant is famed for its wienerschnitzel. Another speciality dish is beef tenderloin stuffed with goose liver and served with a herb cream sauce and *serviettenknödel* (dumpling boiled in a napkin and then sliced). The more informal Zum Leopold bistro upstairs serves excellent goulash soup with beer, and apple strudel. The closure times below apply only to Kuperferdachl; *Zum Leopold* is open seven days a week throughout the year. *Seats 350. Open 1200-1500, 1800-2300 (Sat till 0000). Closed L Sat, all Sun, 3 weeks Aug. Public parking. Amex, Diners, Mastercard, Visa.*

Tel: (1) 798 45 15   Fax: (1) 798 47 14
Schwarzenbergplatz 9, 1030 Wien

Enjoying one of the most spectacular settings in Vienna, the hotel in this 18th-century baroque castle is set in a 15-acre park behind the State Opera in the centre of the city. The public rooms, furnished with antiques and fine carpets, are warm and welcoming while banqueting rooms, with their painted ceilings, ornate mirrors and chandeliers, retain a palatial splendour. Bedrooms and similarly luxurious. The energetic can play tennis while the sedate try their hand at croquet. *Rooms 38. Room service 24hr. Private parking. Banqueting facilities 450. Conference facilities 250. Tennis. Amex, Diners, Mastercard, Visa.*

Tel: (1) 515 170   Fax: (1) 512 22 16
Parkring 16, A-1010 Wien

If you can sleep easy in the knowledge that this was the headquarters of the Luftwaffe during World War I, then this hotel is hard to fault. Incorporating two adjacent 19th-century *palais* opposite the city Stadtpark, it is only 5 minutes away from the main railway station. Catering largely for the business traveller the Royal Club lounge has all up-to-date business facilities and there are several palatial state rooms for functions. The building was completely renovated in 1993 but the original facade and state rooms have been restored to their former glory. Bedrooms are decorated in a simple Biedermeier style. The fitness room is available for a daily supplement of S150. *Rooms 246.*
Room service 24hr. Private parking S350. Air conditioning. Business centre. Sauna. Solarium. Fitness room. Disabled rooms. Satellite TV. Amex, Diners, Mastercard, Visa.

Tel: (1) 51 4 56   Fax: (1) 51 4 57 810
Philharmonikerstrasse 4, A-1010 Wien

A veritable institution like the Viennese State Opera opposite, Hotel Sacher is renowned for its famous Sachertorte cake, the production of which incidentally requires no less than 50 tons of chocolate a year, and which is sold throughout the world. Privately owned since 1934 by the Gürtler family, it retains the traditional Viennese elegance with its Ringstrasse-style rich, velvety decor and long-serving staff. The hotel boasts a fine collection of furniture and paintings and the even the rooms and suites are full of old masters and valuable carpets. The kaffeehaus has long been one of Vienna's most fashionable spots for drinking coffee and swapping gossip. *Rooms 116. Room service 24hr. Private parking. Banqueting facilities 100. Conference facilities 120. Secretarial/translation services on request. Private garage. Air-conditioning. Satellite TV. Amex, Diners, Mastercard, Visa.*

Restaurant Anna Sacher   S1600

Named after the cigar-smoking wife of Eduard Sacher, the hotel's founder, this is the sine qua non of power-lunching venues in Vienna. Here, underneath Austria's oldest electric chandeliers, you can dine on perfectly prepared traditional Viennese dishes. The house speciality is *tafelspitz* (boiled beef) served with roast potatoes, horseradish, apple and chive sauces but other Viennese specialities abound like *Wiener Schnitzel* (of course), *Gerostete Kalbsleber "Wiener Art"* (calf's liver with marjoram and mushrooms) and *Altwiener Zwiebelrostbraten* (rib of beef sautéed with onions, Viennese-style potatoes and gherkins. Desserts are a must here: the ubiquitous *Sachertorte* topped with whipped cream or perhaps an iced *Marmorgugelhupf* raisin cake with sour cherries. *Seats 60.*
Open 1200-1430, 1800-2330. Closed last 2 weeks Jul, 1st week Aug.

Tel: (1) 727 77   Fax: (1) 727 77 199
Handelskai 269, A-1020 Wien

This functional hotel opened in 1988 in a converted dockland grain store on the Danube and has all the facilities one would expect from a large Swedish hotel chain from its state-of-the-art conference facilities to the Scandic Active Club sports facilities. The bedrooms are surprisingly large and well equipped and there are even anti-allergic rooms. It's just 15 minutes from the centre of town, but still very much in Vienna and the airport is a mere 13km drive away. If you are tired of Austrian cooking, the restaurant serves a Swedish smörgasbord on Sundays. *Rooms 367. Room service limited. Free parking for 200 cars. Conference facilities 300. Secretarial/translation services on request. Air-conditioning. Cable TV. Disabled rooms. Fitness equipment. Sauna. Solarium. Heated outdoor swimming pool. Tennis. Amex, Diners, Mastercard, Visa.*

Meal prices for 2 are based on à la carte menus. When set menus are available, prices will often be lower.

Tel: (1) 713 31 68   Fax: (1) 713 516 82
Rasumofskygasse 2, A-1030 Wien

The chef of 16 years, Helmut Österreicher, is a man with lofty international culinary ambitions, some original Royal menus and even a regular television slot. He certainly provides a welcome change from the uniformity of most Viennese restaurants. Lightly smoked veal sweetbreads, pike-perch roasted with cardamon and fennel and *Wildhasensteak mit Vogelbeersauce* (a wild hare steak with rowanberry sauce). *Granatapfel-Soufflé mit weissem Pfeffereis* (pomegranate mousse with white-pepper ice cream) is a signature dessert. The kitchen is very friendly and if a particular dish appeals, Österreicher will give you a copy of the not-so-secret recipe. A visit to the wine cellar brings the impressive wine list to life. *Seats 65 (Winter Garden 25). Open 1130-1430, 1900-2330. Closed Sat, Sun. Private parking. Amex, Diners, Mastercard, Visa.*

Tel: (1) 87 74 74 70 Fax: (1) 87 76 05 0
Auhofstrasse 76-78, A-1130 Wien

The former home of actor Hans Moser, this villa was totally rebuilt recently as a restaurant, with only the original outer walls surviving. All three floors, each with various different dining rooms have undoubtedly retained their glamorous appeal with fine old paintings on the walls, plush green carpets on the floor, silver cutlery and crystal glasses. Both meat and fish dishes feature on the daily-changing menus: some interesting interpretations of the sweet-and-sour theme are evident, for example pike-perch served with mango and breast of duckling with caramelised apples and ratatouille. Game is prominent in season and served traditionally, often with dumplings and red cabbage. There is a set 5-course dinner menu at S350 per head and a 7-course gourmet menu at S750. *Seats 180 (terrace 50, garden 50). Open 1200-1400, 1900-2200. Closed Sun, Mon, 24 Dec-9 Jan. Private parking. Amex, Diners, Mastercard, Visa.*

Opening times are often liable to change at short notice, so it's always best to book.

Your **Guarantee** of
Quality and **Independence**

- Establishment inspections are anonymous
- Inspections are undertaken by qualified Egon Ronay's Guides inspectors
- The Guides are completely independent in their editorial selection
- The Guides do not accept advertising, hospitality or payment from listed establishments

Titles planned for 1996 include

Hotels & Restaurants ● Pubs & Inns ● Europe
Ireland ● Just A Bite
And Children Come Too ● Paris
Oriental Restaurants

Belgium

Currency Belgian Franc **Exchange Rate** £1=approx BFr 46
International dialling code 00 32 (Antwerp+3 Brussels+2
   Bruges+50)
Passports/Visas No visa required by British passport holders.
British Embassy in Brussels Tel 2-287 6211   Fax 2-287 6360

TRANSPORT
Airports
Brussels National Airport Tel 2-753 2111
Deurne Airport Antwerp Tel 3-218 1211
Railway Stations
Brussels Central Tel 2-203 2880 **Antwerp Central** Tel 3-204 2040
Bruges Tel 50-38 23 82
Car hire in Brussels
Tel Nos **Eurodollar** 2-735 6005 **Avis** 2-730 6211 **Budget** 2-721 5097
Europcar 2-640 94 00 **Luxauto** 2-538 33 21
Speed limits 90 km/h outside built-up areas, 120 km/h on motorways,
50 km/h in towns.

OPENING TIMES
Banks 9am-12, 2-4pm Mon-Fri.
Shops 9am-6pm Mon-Sat. Shops in the main cities are open until
9pm on Fridays.

NATIONAL HOLIDAYS
New Year's Day, Easter Monday, 1 May, Ascension Day, Whit Monday,
21 Jul, 15 Aug, 1 Nov, 11 Nov, 15 Nov, Christmas Day & Boxing Day.

Tourist Offices
Belgian Tourist Board in **London** Tel 0891 887799
In Belgium **Brussels** Tel 2-504 0300/2-504 0200 / Antwerp Tel 3-232
0103 / **Bruges** Tel 50-44 86 86
American Express Travel Service Offices or Representative (R)
Antwerp AETS
            Frankrijklei 21
            2000
            Tel 3-232 5920
Brussels AETS
            2 Place Louise
            1050
            Tel 2-676 2727

Antwerp

Tel: (3) 234 01 35   Fax: (3) 232 39 70
66-70 De Keyserlei, 2018 Antwerp

Leisure facilities are excellent at this eight-storey hotel next to the Diamond Centre and the railway station. A gym, solarium, Turkish bath and whirlpool bath are at the disposal of guests, although business provisions are more limited with three meeting rooms able to accommodate a total of 120 people. Decor is no-fuss modern and bedrooms are equipped with air-conditioning and cable TV. A shuttle service to Zaventem airport runs from just opposite the hotel. *Rooms 123. Room service 24hr. Public parking 400FB. Banqueting facilities 120. Conference facilities 50. Secretarial/translation services on request. Indoor swimming pool. Gym. Sauna. Solarium. Turkish bath. Amex, Diners, Mastercard, Visa.*

Tel: (3) 237 02 60   Fax: (3) 238 11 68
6 Karel Oomsstraat, 2018 Antwerp

Located in a quiet, central neighbourhood, this hotel is a refreshing change from the characterless chains. It opened in 1986 but the art deco building dates from 1929. Chandeliers and stained glass give character to the entrance hall while bedrooms are individually decorated in a mix of old and contemporary styles. A new wing was constructed in 1993 and all rooms have recently been refurbished. There is no restaurant but light meals can be arranged. *Rooms 17. Closed 22 Jul-13 Aug, 23 Dec-8 Jan. Room service limited. Valet parking. Secretarial/translation services on request. Patio. Amex, Diners, Mastercard, Visa.*

Tel: (3) 233 62 70   Fax: (3) 233 99 03
24 Reynderstraat, 2000 Antwerp

Exuberant owner-chef Johann Segers bursts out of his kitchen to explain his menu and offer advice to diners in this wonderful rustic restaurant. His cooking is as vivacious as his manner. Specialities include fillet of sole with rhubarb, scallop salad with foie gras, calf's sweetbreads (*ris de veau*) with truffles, and beef *à la bordelaise* (cooked in butter, red pepper, brandy, red wine and cream). Although there is no vegetarian menu, Segers will be happy to reel off a spontaneous list of suggested dishes or will fulfil any requests. *Seats 30. Open 1200-1500, 1900-2200. Closed Sat, Sun, 3 weeks in Aug, New Year. Public parking. Amex, Diners, Mastercard, Visa.*

Tel: (3) 233 59 69   Fax: (3) 233 11 49
22 Grote Pieter Potstraat, 2000 Antwerp

Opulence and intimacy are combined in this tiny restaurant (it only has nine tables) very near Grand Place. Chef and owner Yves Michiels trained under the best, Joël Robuchon and Roger Vergé, and their influence is evident in his nouvelle-légère cooking. The carte is seasonal and the menu changes monthly but certain signature dishes are likely to be available all year. These include *pigeonneau laqué au miel* (baby pigeon coated in honey) and *ris de veau aux asperges et chicons* (calf's sweetbreads with asparagus and Belgian endives). The *menu gourmand en dégustation* is excellent value at 1950FB (or 2850FB with wines). Southern French wines from Languedoc are particularly popular in Belgium at the moment and are well represented on the list. *Seats 30. Open 1200-1400, 1900-2200. Closed L Mon & Sat, all Sun, 2 weeks before Easter, 2nd/3rd weeks Jul. Public parking. Amex, Diners, Mastercard, Visa.*

Tel: (3) 225 01 40   Fax: (3) 231 41 11
21-23 Rosier, 2000 Antwerp

A warm welcome is assured in this small family-run hotel with the atmosphere of a private home. The building dates from 1627 and is centrally located a few minutes from the cathedral. Rooms have names rather than numbers ("Blue Angel", "Flying Dutchman" for example) and are individually decorated, filled with fresh flowers and furnished with English and French antiques, some of which are for sale. An indoor swimming pool and

Boechout   49

sauna add a touch of modern luxury. **Rooms** *12. Closed 24-25 Dec, 1-2 Jan. Private parking 350FB. Room service all day. Conference facilities 12. Garden. Indoor swimming pool. Sauna. Spa bath. Amex, Diners, Mastercard, Visa.*

Tel: (3) 238 72 52   Fax: (3) 238 25 88
31 Van Putlei, 2018 Antwerp

Vateli opened 33 years ago in a quiet residential suburb ten minutes drive south of the city centre. For the last 20 years, Chef Jacques Slap has presided over the kitchen and produces a seasonal menu of excellent classic French food. Among his specialities are salmon marinated *à l'ancienne* in dill, and pan-fried duck liver with a sprinkling of cinnamon. Tempting main dishes include turbot grilled en chemise with a mustard sauce, and duckling, cooked twice, *à la rouennaise*. The wine list will not disappoint, with over 500 bottles from which to choose. **Seats** *65. Open 1200-1430, 1800-2100. Closed L Sat, all Sun, 18- 31 Jul, National Holidays. Valet parking. Amex, Diners, Mastercard, Visa.*

Tel: (3) 457 95 86   Fax (3) 458 13 68
78 Kontichsesteenweg, 2630 Aartselaar

This restored 17th-century Flemish farmhouse by Groeninghe Castle has only seven rooms (mainly to accommodate those dining in the first-rate restaurant), but these too have their attractions, being well equipped and furnished with antiques. The house is full of attractive features like leaded windows and exposed beams and, interestingly, the staircase which leads up to the rooms is made out of the original stone steps of Antwerp Cathedral, 6km away, which were salvaged and brought here after its restoration a couple of years ago. Though limited in accommodation space the hostellerie can, rather surprisingly, host a conference for up to 250 people. **Rooms** *7. Room service none. Private parking.*
Banqueting facilities 180. Cable TV. Mini-bar. Amex, Diners, Mastercard, Visa.

To describe the cooking here as nouvelle (and they do) is rather misleading. The food is certainly light, well-balanced and French-based, with a healthy choice of meat, fish and vegetables. Typical dishes are *supreme de turbot à l'infusion de persil et sabayon de moutarde* (turbot cooked with parsley in a whipped mustard sauce) and *canard sauvage au sang et nouilles fraiches au lardons* (wild duck served with noodles and lardons). Scottish salmon is grilled with celery and served with a mustard sauce; escalope of goose liver is sautéed with mangos. There is a *dégustation* menu at 2750FB per person. Loire wines are the best-sellers amongst the 300 French labels on offer but the owners also bottle their own Bordeaux house wine. During the summer, meals are served on the terrace. **Seats** *30 (terrace 30). Open 1200-1430, 1830-2130. Closed L Sat, all Sun. Private parking.*

Tel: (3) 454 19 31
10 Appelkanstraat, 2530 Boechout

Open for just two years, this small, family-run restaurant is only 15 minutes drive from Antwerp, yet as you sit outside on the terrace with its ornamental pool, the city is but a distant memory. The menu is traditional and sticks to classics like *rognon de veau grillé aux champignons et oignons* (grilled veal kidneys with mushrooms and onions), *consommé de pieds de porc, foie d'oie et lentilles* (consommé with pigs' trotters, goose liver and lentils) and a fresh fish dish of the day, simply prepared. The choice though is extensive, with a *menu dégustation*, a set menu and the à la carte menu to choose from. Desserts are light and refreshing mousses, fruit compotes and sorbets. **Seats** *28. Open 1200-1500, 1900-2200. Closed Sun, Mon, last 2 weeks Aug, first 2 weeks Sep. Amex, Mastercard, Visa.*

Bruges

Tel: (50) 33 79 26   Fax: (50) 34 19 68
41 Wollestraat, 8000 Brugge

A 15th-century house, by the canal and near the Markt, which has been a restaurant for the past 15 years. The owners, M and Mme de Flandre, describe the cooking as *à découvrir* and most of the dishes contain highly individual touches. The ever-popular *foie d'oie* is pan-fried in a port and juniper berry sauce and served with caramelised apple and red sorrel, spiced breaded veal sweetbreads come with a saffron and ginger sauce. The house speciality is fish and shellfish, sometimes prepared elaborately, as in red mullet cooked in olive oil with *zestes de citron confits, fondue de tomates au basilic et pates fraiches*, sometimes simply, as with turbot, cooked with the juice of wild mushrooms and served with *chips de pommes nouvelles*. Set menus start at 1550FB (lunch) and 2000FB (dinner). *Seats 40. Open 1200-1430, 1900-2130. Closed Tue, Wed, 15 Nov-15 Dec. Public parking. Amex, Diners, Mastercard, Visa.*

Tel: (50) 34 41 73
18 Ezelstraat, 8000 Brugge

Bruges is a living museum of wonderful architecture and this restaurant, decorated in the manner of an English sitting-room, is in a typical 1620s house near the Belfry. It is owned by M and Mme Dryepondt and Monsieur cooks traditional French dishes such as magret of duck with a cream of Puy lentils and tarragon, and ragout of langoustine tails with fennel. Desserts include *millefeuille glacé au coulis de fruits. Seats 24. Open 1900-2130. Closed Sun, Mon, Jul. Public parking. Diners, Mastercard, Visa.*

Tel: (50) 31 19 07   Fax: (50) 31 77 66
Zandstraat 2, 8200 Bruges

A friendly and informal hotel, most of whose staff have been here almost 20 years. It's surrounded by a large garden and seven of the bedrooms look out over it; four of these even have a private terrace. Whatever room you stay in, you will find it peaceful and secluded, despite being only 500m from the city centre. The rooms are decorated in a very cosy English style, and have all the necessary mod cons. One room is equipped for disabled guests. ***Rooms** 18. Room service limited. Closed last 2 weeks Jan. Private parking. Banqueting facilities 80. Conference facilities 25. Secretarial/translation services on request. Cable TV. Mini-bar. Safe. Amex, Diners, Mastercard, Visa.*

Restaurant   4000FB

Chef Verhaeghe, another long-standing member of staff, has a real passion for fish. His speciality is monkfish cooked with leeks, bone marrow and green beans. But for those less keen on fish, the menu also has some traditional meat dishes like the saddle of lamb which is roasted with fresh tarragon and thyme from the garden and carved in front of diners. Zabaglione is also prepared at the table. *Seats 60. Open 1200-1345, 1845-2045. Closed D Tue, all Wed, last 2 weeks Jan, 2 weeks Jul.*

Tel: (50) 33 82 59   Fax: (50) 33 10 11
19 Langestraat, 8000 Brugge

Geert Van Hecke converted this house, once the weekend home of a local Baron, into a restaurant in 1983. His menu is largely cuisine recherché, owing much to his time working with the Roux brothers and Alain Chapel. A typically elaborate starter is *salade tiède de pintadeau de Bresse à l'huile de noisettes, croustillant de ses cuisses, pousses d'épinards à l'orange séché* (warm salad of Bresse guinea fowl with hazelnut oil, a crisp pastry case of leg meat, with spinach and dried oranges). Main courses are similarly complex, for instance, *navarin de turbot et homard aux champignons des bois, gésiers de canard confits et pommes grenailles au thym citron* (stew of turbot and lobster with wild mushrooms, duck gizzards, apples and lemon thyme). Belgian ingredients surface in desserts such as *les cérises pochées à la bière 'Kriek', crème glacée à la bière, madeleine tiède aux épices* (cherries poached in Kriek, a Belgian cherry-flavoured beer, with beer ice cream and warm, spicy madeleine cake). Set menus start at 2100FB and, for those with gargantuan appetites, 3300FB will buy you eight courses. *Seats 65. Open 1200-1400, 1900-2130. Closed D Sun, all Mon, 18- 31 Jan, 24 Jun- 7 Jul. Private parking. Amex, Diners, Mastercard, Visa.*

De Snippe

Tel: (50) 33 70 70   Fax: (50) 33 76 62
53 Nieuwe Gentweg, 8000 Brugge

A fine 17th-century house, by the canal and a few minutes walk from the Markt, has been home to Luc Huysenstruyt's fish restaurant for the past 17 years. His seasonal menu is dictated by the market but might include langoustine tails with chives, and fried goujons of sole. A Flemish speciality is *waterzooi* of turbot: a type of fish soup with white wine, thyme, bay leaf, sage and parsley. In summer it is possible to eat on the terrace or in the Winter Garden. The restaurant also has nine bedrooms priced from 5000FB. *Seats 60. Open 1200-1500, 1900-2200. Closed L Mon, all Sun, mid Feb-mid Mar. Private parking. Amex, Diners, Mastercard, Visa.*

Die Swaene

Tel: (50) 34 27 98   Fax: (50) 33 66 74
1 Steenhouwersdijk, 8000 Brugge

Three 15th-century houses by the canal and next to the fish market were converted into a hotel in 1981 and provide an idyllic retreat in the centre of Bruges. The decor is delightful. Silk wall hangings, walnut bookcases and fine chandeliers give the public rooms a rich but comfortable air, while bedrooms are furnished with antiques, canopied four-posters and (in some rooms) open fires. An indoor swimming pool, fitness centre and sauna are currently being built and are due to open in 1996. *Rooms 22. Room service 24hr. Private parking 250FB. Banqueting facilities 45. Conference facilities 20. Garden. Amex, Diners, Mastercard, Visa.*

Restaurant

Chef Peter de Pauw cooks French haute cuisine of a high standard. The carte is short but tempting and is particularly strong on fish and shellfish dishes: Zeeland oysters with garden sorrel and curry sauce, and spicy crusted fillets of sole with black pasta and basil sauce, for instance. Two set dinner menus are available: Die Swaene at 1850FB and the more luxurious Romeo et Juliette (2550FB) which may include lobster grilled with Isigny butter and Malines asparagus, roulade of young lamb filled with fresh goose liver, and a 'crisp purse' of Belgian brie and gingerbread and an apple coulis. Set business lunches start at 1050FB. *Seats 40. Open 1200-1400, 1900-2115. Closed L Thu, all Wed, 2 weeks Jan, 9-28 Jul.*

Vasquez

Tel: (50) 34 08 45   Fax: (50) 33 52 41
38 Zilverstraat, 8000 Brugge

When Isabelle of Portugal came to Flanders in the second half of the 15th century, she was accompanied by her private secretary, Jean Vasquez, who built this house in 1468. It was converted into a restaurant in 1987. Chef Guy Deerlinck has been influenced by the time he spent in California and, although his cooking is French-based, he is particularly interested in unusual spice and herb mixtures. He blends his own spices, often 10 to 20 together, in different combinations to give each dish a unique flavour. Examples are salmon marinated in beetroot juice with five spices, fillets of red mullet *au parfum des Indes* with a compote of mangoes and apples, and veal fillet roasted in cinnamon and rosemary. Two set menus, the *menu Jean Vasquez* and *menu la route des épices*, are excellent value at 1980FB and 2800FB respectively. The Californian influence extends to the wine list. *Seats 50 (garden 40). Open 1200-1400, 1900-2130. Closed L Sun & Thu, all Wed, 1-14 Jul. Public parking. Amex, Mastercard, Visa.*

Brussels

Tel: (2) 547 47 47   Fax: (2) 513 52 77
1-3 rue de l'Amigo, 1000 Bruxelles

Although only dating from the late 1950s, the rooms at this hotel feel far older, with their Flemish tapestries and oak furniture. Facilities are up to date following three years of renovations and conference provisions are excellent. The location, by the Grand Place and near the Gare Centrale, is ideal for both business and pleasure. *Rooms 183*.
Room service 24hr. Private parking. Banqueting facilities 200. Conference facilities 100. Amex, Diners, Mastercard, Visa.

Tel: (2) 217 511 55 50   Fax: (2) 514 33 81
13 rue des Bouchers, 1000 Bruxelles

The rue des Bouchers is full of restaurants but few can compete with the Armes, run by the Veulemans family since 1921, for quality of food and atmosphere. The three dining-rooms are decorated in different styles: one in minimalist white with modern paintings, another with banquette seating down the sides, wood panelling and brass chandelier, and the main room with 1920s glass and chrome fittings and copious plants. As you would expect in any Belgian restaurant, mussels appear on the menu in a wide variety of preparations. Another speciality of chef-patron Jacques Veulemans is *waterzooi* dishes, which are (usually) a type of fish soup with white wine and herbs. Chicken waterzooi is more sophisticated with the stock thickened with cream and flavoured with lemon juice. Note that the restaurant is closed during June and July. *Seats 180. Open 1200- 2315. Closed Mon, Jun/Jul. Amex, Diners, Mastercard, Visa.*

Tel: (2) 217 62 90   Fax: (2) 217 11 50
103 rue Royale, 1000 Bruxelles

This grand art deco-style hotel, located in Brussels' business district, was built in 1908 and thoroughly renovated in 1968. Air-conditioning has recently been installed in all bedrooms and many have been redecorated in a classical style with antiques and leather sofas. The Pullman Bar is furnished with original wooden panelling and seats from the Golden Arrow train and there is also a piano bar. *Rooms 125. Room service 24hr (food until 2200). Private parking 600FB. Banqueting facilities 150. Conference facilities 200. Terrace. Amex, Diners, Mastercard, Visa.*

The lovely Louis XVI decoration of the dining-room is a fitting backdrop for excellent French food. The menu changes daily but house specialities include lobster ravioli, terrine of Landes goose foie gras with a port jelly, and double-filtered consommé of free-range wild fowl *aux fines herbes*. The house speciality menu is particularly good value at 1550FB (including aperitif, wine and coffee). The wine list is not long but includes some choice Margaux and Pauillac. Look out for the occasional 'Gastronomic weeks'. *Seats 40. Open 1200-1500, 1900-2200. Closed D Sun.*

Tel/Fax: (2) 479 67 32
70 avenue Jean Sobieski, 1020 Bruxelles

Self-taught cook Madame Ma has been preparing authentic Vietnamese cuisine in this restaurant for 22 years. Specialities of the house include a Vietnamese fondue (order 24 hours in advance), sea bass browned with lime and ginger, crispy lobster pancakes and six different preparations of duckling. The restaurant is a ten-minute drive north of the centre but worth the journey for those tiring of rich French food and endless plates of mussels. *Seats 60 (garden 30). Open 1200-1500, 1900-2230. Closed D Sun, all Tue, 5- 12 Jan, 15 days at Easter, all Aug. Public parking. Amex, Diners, Mastercard, Visa.*

Tel: (2) 512 78 40   Fax: (2) 514 17 59
135 rue du Midi, 1000 Bruxelles

This privately-owned hotel enjoys a central location three minutes walk from Grand Place. The hall and breakfast rooms have recently been renovated and bedrooms are decorated in a comfortable, if unexciting, modern style. All are equipped with satellite TV, direct-dial phone, mini-bar and hairdryer. The hotel also has a restaurant, piano bar and gift shop. **Rooms** 296. *Room service limited. Private parking 350FB. Banqueting facilities 250. Conference facilities 250. Amex, Diners, Mastercard, Visa.* 🐂

Tel: (2) 427 69 78   Fax: (2) 425 97 26
73 avenue Broustin, 1080 Bruxelles

Close to the Sacré Coeur Basilica in the north-western suburb of Ganshoren is where you will find Jean-Pierre Bruneau's excellent restaurant. Following a major renovation in 1992, it now has a 1920s-style decor, air-conditioning and a pretty terrace. Jean-Pierre has travelled widely and experimented with so many styles of cuisine that he now considers his cooking to be "freestyle", although it is still clearly French-based. Goose liver is a speciality and comes in a variety of guises from au naturel to accompanied by a chicory and truffle salad. Main dishes include *fricassée de homard breton aux chicons confits au gingembre et citron vert* (fricassee of Brittany lobster with a chicory confit, ginger and lime) and *rognon de veau en croute de sel aux échalotes confites* (calf's kidneys in a salt crust with a shallot confit). A fine selection of French and Belgian cheeses makes a satisfying end to a meal. The *menu découverte* (2750FB for four courses) and the *menu surprise* (3750FB for six courses) are popular choices, with the market dictating which dishes are on offer. Wines are of the highest quality. **Seats** 80. *Open 1200-1400, 1900-2200. Closed D Tue, all Wed, 15 May- 5 Jun, 24 Dec-3 Jan. Public parking. Amex, Diners, Mastercard, Visa.* 🐂

Tel: (2) 426 00 00   Fax: (2) 426 65 40
46 avenue Vital Riethuisen, 1080 Bruxelles

In the shadow of the Koekelberg Basilica, ten minutes to the northwest of the city centre, stands this restaurant in a smart townhouse. Claude Dupont's fine cooking is classical French with some light, modern touches and he specialises in *produits de la chasse*: game. In addition to the carte, there is a *menu au marché aujourd'hui*, a *menu de saison* (2150FB) and a *menu relais gourmand* (3200FB) which may contain such delicacies as medallion of goose liver with muscat grapes in a Sauternes jelly, *noisette de faon rotie au poivrade au thym frais* (noisette of fawn, roasted with pepper and fresh thyme) and passion fruit coulis. **Seats** 30. *Open 1200-1430, 1900-2130. Closed Mon, Tue, one week in Feb, early Jul-early Aug. Public parking. Amex, Diners, Mastercard, Visa.* 🐂

Tel: (2) 512 29 21   Fax: (2) 511 80 52
23 place Rouppe, 1000 Bruxelles

Chef Pierre Wynants has made this fabulous restaurant a place of pilgrimage for gourmets and other cooks all over the world for the last 40 years. The plush art nouveau decor lends an appropriately grand atmosphere in which to sample some of Wynants' classic dishes, such as pan-fried veal kidneys with sautéed mushrooms and juniper berries, fillet of beef with black truffles, and fillets of sole with medallions of lobster *en cardinal*. Set menus range from 1975FB to the exquisite 4350FB menu which might include roast langoustines and asparagus *petite flamande* with smoked ham, cutlet of minced pigeon with celery and balsamic vinegar, and noisettes of milk-fed pork in white truffle oil *croustillant de fins légumes*. Among the delicious desserts are crème brulée with gin, crepes of caramelised orange and Gascony peaches flambéed in their juice. **Seats** 40. *Open 1200-1400, 1900-2200. Closed Sun, Mon, Jul, Christmas, New Year. Valet parking. Amex, Diners, Mastercard, Visa.*

Tel: (2) 542 42 42   Fax: (2) 542 42 00
71 avenue Louise, 1050 Bruxelles

Avenue Louise is one of Brussels' grandest boulevards and the building which is now the Conrad was formerly one of the Royal residences. It opened as a hotel in 1992 but the decor is shamelessly nostalgic, from the pristine elegance of the vast, marble-floored lobby to the reproduction period furniture and restrained colour schemes of the bedrooms. Business facilities are excellent, with a staffed business centre and 18 rooms available for conferences and functions. A shopping arcade containing more than 30 exclusive boutiques is adjacent to the hotel. **Rooms** 269. *Room service 24hr. Private parking 360FB. Banqueting facilities 440. Conference facilities 600. Business centre. News kiosk. Shop. Amex, Diners, Mastercard, Visa.* 🐂

Tel: (2) 512 87 51   Fax: (2) 511 99 50
18 rue Bodenbroek, 1000 Bruxelles

Ecailler means 'oyster-   seller' and both the menu and the decor of this restaurant,
500m from the Palais Royal, are inspired by the sea. The building dates from the 17th
century and was a private house before being converted to a café around 1920, and then
into a splendid
restaurant in 1967. The original wooden panelling and bar from the café (with its blue and
green fish scale-shaped tiles) survive. Chef Attilio Basso brings all his 45 years of cooking
experience to bear on the superb food. Try pan-fried John Dory (Saint-Pierre) with *pommes
boulangère* (potatoes and onions cooked in stock and butter), grilled turbot with a vegetable
purée, or *barbue soufflée avec beurre de cresson* (brill soufflé with watercress butter). Only
the choicest ingredients are used: lobsters from Norway, wild Scottish salmon, sea urchins
from France. For the perfect accompaniment, select a bottle of champagne or white
burgundy from the fine list. *Seats 60. Open 1200-1430, 1900-2230. Closed Sun, Aug, Easter
week, National Holidays. Public parking. Amex, Diners, Mastercard, Visa.*

Tel: (2) 504 11 11   Fax: (2) 504 21 11
38 boulevard de Waterloo, 1000 Bruxelles

Next to Egmont Park, the 28-floor Hilton is ideally placed for the up-market shops and
museums in this area of Brussels. Guests staying on the Executive floors at the top of the
tower enjoy particularly fine views over the city, as well as their own lounge with
complimentary drinks and snacks and a separate check-in desk. Meeting and business
facilities are first-rate. *Rooms 450. Room service 24hr. Private parking 490FB.
Banqueting facilities 580. Conference facilities 550. Business centre. Sauna. Solarium.
Beauty treatment. News kiosk. Coffee shop. Amex, Diners, Mastercard, Visa.*

Michel Theurel has been cooking at the Hilton since it opened in 1967, specialising in
modern French and Belgian cuisine. Some of the dishes feature local ingredients, such as
creamy Ostend shrimp croquettes with fried vegetables, while others make use of
international fare, for instance, prime rib of US beef roasted in a salt crust, sautéed Breton
lobster and roasted pigeon from the Vendée with a summer salad and wild mushrooms.
Set menus at 1590FB (three-course lunch) and 1990FB (four-course dinner). *Seats 95.
Open 1200-1430, 1900-2230.*

Tel: (2) 511 82 44   Fax: (2) 514 31 48
9 Grand Place, 1000 Bruxelles

Grand Place is one of the most spectacular squares in Europe. Book a table at this first-floor
restaurant and enjoy the wonderful view. The building has a colourful history: constructed
in 1528, it was a cabaret venue before burning down in 1695 and being rebuilt as the
headquarters of the Butchers Guild. It became a restaurant in 1958 and has a great
atmosphere with beamed ceilings, wooden panelling and fine paintings, including two
originals by Pieter Brueghel the Younger. Chef Richard Hahn's classic French cooking
matches the richness of the surroundings. Caviar, foie gras, smoked salmon, lobster bisque
and French oxtail soup are typical starters. Main dishes include sautéed lobster in tarragon,
and milk-fed veal roasted in sherry with a fondue of mushrooms à la crème. Strawberry
soup with strawberry sorbet is a refreshing way to end a meal. Set menus from 2450FB to
2800FB. The wine list is short but includes some good Bordeaux. *Seats 100.
Open 1200-1430, 1930-2200. Closed L Sat, all Sun, 1st 3 weeks Aug, 23 Dec-2 Jan.
Valet parking. Amex, Diners, Mastercard, Visa.*

Tel: (2) 539 02 50   Fax: (2) 537 57 29
28 chaussée de Charleroi, 1060 Bruxelles

The 19th-century building that houses this elegant hotel is a 20-minute walk from the
centre of the city. Formerly a medical clinic, it was converted four years ago and is
decorated in a rich Louis XV style with lots of gilt and rococo fixtures. All rooms have
marble bathrooms and are equipped with cable TV and mini-bar. Only small conferences
can be accommodated. *Rooms 55. Room service limited. Private parking 280FB.
Conference facilities 15. Garden. Amex, Diners, Mastercard, Visa.*

Tel: (2) 649 95 86   Fax: (2) 649 22 49
381 avenue Louise, 1050 Bruxelles

This Japanese-owned hotel on elegant Avenue Louise is near the Bois de la Cambre park and a short walk away from the city's major art galleries. The style of the decor in most bedrooms is unfussily modern although some are designated "Lady rooms", the assumption being that women are happier with Laura Ashley-style furnishings. Larger Executive rooms come complete with jacuzzis. The small, shady garden is lovely in the summer. *Rooms 99. Room service limited. Valet parking. Banqueting facilities 200. Conference facilities 150. Amex, Diners, Mastercard, Visa.*

Tel: (2) 217 23 00   Fax: (2) 218 02 20
31 place de Brouckère, 1000 Bruxelles

This hotel on the busy Place de Brouckère, a few minutes from the Grand Place, celebrated its centenary in 1995. Its lavish decor is breathtaking, from the long, marble French Renaissance entrance hall to the Corinthian columns, deep leather sofas and palm trees of the *19ième Bar*. Bedrooms are less ornate than the public rooms but equally stylish and comfortable. Business and leisure facilities are extensive. *Rooms 410. Room service 24hr. Public parking. Conference facilities 600. Business centre. Secretarial/translation services on request. Gym. Sauna. Solarium. Massage. Amex, Diners, Mastercard, Visa.*

Tel: (2) 466 65 91   Fax: (2) 466 90 07
31 Schepen Gossetlaan, Groot-Bijgaarden, 1720 Bruxelles

Michel and Helda Coppens' restaurant is in a detached house in a residential suburb west of the centre, near the junction of the motorway ring road and the E40. The decor is light and airy and a small patio is used for dining in the summer. Michel's cooking is refreshingly free of the elaboration some chefs feel is compulsory in good French food. Instead, the quality of the ingredients is allowed to shine through in dishes such as pan-fried scallops with shallots, and steamed langoustines with vinaigrette. Fish such as turbot, sole and brill are grilled or steamed and served with, perhaps, a simple sauce mousseline or mustard sauce. Meat is treated with similar respect: for example, grilled *cotes d'agneau* with seasonal vegetables. The *menu d'affaires* (1570FB) changes daily while the *menu dégustation* (3350FB) alters monthly. A few Italian wines fight it out with the largely French list. *Seats 45. Open 1200-1430, 1900-2130. Closed Sun, Mon, last 3 weeks Aug. Private parking. Amex, Diners, Mastercard, Visa.*

Tel: (2) 741 85 11   Fax: (2) 741 85 00
134 avenue de Tervueren, 1150 Bruxelles

The Montgomery is located in a quiet, leafy residential district near the Cinquantenaire Park and a short walk from Berlaymont. Although only three years old, the hotel has the atmosphere of a cosy English club, from the wood-panelled library with its big armchairs and open fire, to the friendliness and personalised service offered by the staff. Bedrooms are decorated in one of three styles: 'elegant' dark blues and mahogany, 'romantic' red and green floral patterns, or 'Chinese' bright blues and whites. In the past year, the hotel restaurant La Duchesse moved from the library to its own space on the ground floor. *Rooms 64. Room service 24hr. Private parking. Banqueting facilities 30. Conference facilities 25. Secretarial/translation services on request. Fitness centre. Sauna. Amex, Diners, Mastercard, Visa.*

Tel: (2) 725 30 50   Fax: (2) 721 39 58
1830 Olmenstraat, Diegem, Bruxelles

The hotel is easier to see than to reach – follow the Zaventem signs (with the aeroplane symbol) off the ring road then right at the lights and right again at the first crossroads. Dating from the 70s, it was the first Novotel to be built outside France and offers the familiar good value and facilities with a minimum of frills and fuss. The garden has just been landscaped and the entire hotel is in the process of being refurbished. A free minibus runs to the airport every 20 minutes. *Rooms 206. Room service 24hr. Private parking. Conference facilities 110. Garden. Outdoor swimming pool. Amex, Diners, Mastercard, Visa.*

BRUSSELS   Radisson SAS Hotel Brussels   13,180FB

Tel: (2) 219 28 28   Fax: (2) 219 62 62
47 rue du Fossé-aux-Loups, 1000 Bruxelles

Formerly called the SAS Royal, this hotel opened in 1990 but its art deco design harks back to more glamorous times. Bedrooms are decorated in one of four styles: Italian, Scandinavian, Oriental and 'Royal Club'. The SAS service centre offers full business facilities and conference provisions are excellent. Guests can work out in the well-equipped fitness centre or relax with a drink in the Bar Dessiné which celebrates the work of Belgium's cartoonists. The hotel's location is in the historical, cultural and commercial centre of Brussels, only five minutes from Central Station. *Rooms 281. Room service 24hr. Valet parking 600FB. Banqueting facilities 280. Conference facilities 450. Business centre. Gym. Sauna. Spa bath. Beauty treatment. Amex, Diners, Mastercard, Visa.*

Sea Grill J Le Divellec   6000FB

Chef Yves Mattagne honoured his culinary guru Jacques Le Divellec in the name of this restaurant but he has proved himself to be an excellent cook in his own right. Among his specialities are line-caught bass, roasted in a sea-salt crust, and the unusual pressed Brittany lobster: a live lobster is chosen from the tank, cooked and then pressed in front of diners in a lobster press. Other dishes range from the simple *tourteau* (large crab) with aïoli or *vinaigrette aux fines herbes*, to richer fare like smoked langoustine ravioli with tomato butter and a *'caviar'* of aubergines, and pan-fried tournedos of red tuna and foie gras with a *périgourdine* (truffle) sauce. Five set menus are available from 2050FB to 3550FB. *Seats 80. Open 1200-1430, 1900-2230. Closed L Sat, all Sun, Easter week, 21 Jul-15 Aug.*

BRUSSELS   Royal Crown   8300FB

Tel: (2) 220 66 11   Fax: (2) 217 84 44
250 rue Royale, 1210 Bruxelles

A firm favourite with Eurocrats, the Royal Crown is situated in a quiet district of the city, next to the Botanical Gardens, near the Gare du Nord, and a 15-minute drive from the airport. The decor is resolutely modern and all rooms have air-conditioning and cable TV. As might be expected, conference facilities are excellent, with 19 meeting rooms accommodating between 25 and 550 delegates. *Rooms 315. Room service 24hr. Private parking 250FB. Banqueting facilities 400. Conference facilities 550. Secretarial/translation services on request. Gym. Sauna. Solarium. Beauty treatment. Amex, Diners, Mastercard, Visa.*

BRUSSELS   Royal Windsor   10,250FB

Tel: (2) 505 55 55   Fax: (2) 505 55 00
5 rue Duquesnoy, 1000 Bruxelles

Located in the heart of Brussels, the Royal Windsor is more personal and friendly than might be expected for a hotel of this size. Bedrooms are individually decorated in a mix of classic and contemporary styles. Executive rooms have faxes, while the spacious Royal Suite comes with its own sauna. Business facilities are excellent with a staffed business centre and extensive conference provisions. Guests can unwind in the evening with a drink in the Waterloo piano bar or the 'English pub' atmosphere of the Windsor Arms, before dancing the night away at Griffin's night club. *Rooms 275. Room service 24hr. Private parking 490FB. Banqueting facilities 220. Conference facilities 230. Business centre. Fitness club. Bureau de change. Amex, Diners, Mastercard, Visa.*

Les Quatres Saisons   4600FB

André Smit cooks refined and creative French food in this elegant restaurant. His *menu d'affaires* is excellent value at 1390FB and includes dishes such as crab bisque perfumed with aniseed, escalope of salmon pan-fried with noodles and creamed morel mushrooms, and a classic *tarte tatin à la vanille*. Richer fare is available on the *menus gourmands*. A typical meal might start with magret of smoked duck and salad with truffle juice, followed by tournedos of veal *à la crème de moutarde*, and topped off with *bavarois à la pistache*. The extensive wine list includes some superb *premier grands crus*. *Seats 50. Open 1200-1430, 1930-2330. Closed L Sun, 20 Jul-19 Aug.*

BRUSSELS   Sheraton Brussels Airport   12,080FB

Tel: (2) 725 10 00   Fax: (2) 725 11 55
1930 Zaventem, Bruxelles

The unapologetically modern Sheraton boasts of being only "39 steps from the airport door" and is firmly pitched at business custom. From the flight arrivals and departures screen in the lobby to the excellent conference facilities and fully equipped 24-hour business centre, the staff aim to anticipate every requirement of the harassed executive. A pleasant way to unwind on a Sunday is to enjoy the jazz brunch in the Atrium. The room rate drops by half at weekends. *Rooms 298. Room service 24hr. Valet parking 830FB. Banqueting facilities 400. Conference facilities 600. Business centre (24hr). Fitness centre. Amex, Diners, Mastercard, Visa.*

Tel: (2) 506 91 11   Fax: (2) 512 17 08
9 rue du Commerce, 1040 Bruxelles

The restrained elegance of an English country house has been successfully recreated in the Stanhope. Heavy curtains, thick carpets, huge beds, choice wallpapers and tasteful antiques all help to convey a luxurious but relaxed atmosphere. The reception rooms are furnished with big sofas and old books while the gym and sauna provide an alternative way to relax. Conference facilities, formerly very limited, have been greatly improved by the construction of two new boardrooms since last year, each with a capacity of 60. *Rooms 50. Room service 24hr. Valet parking 200FB. Conference facilities 14. Garden. Keep-fit equipment. Sauna. Amex, Diners, Mastercard, Visa.*

Brighton Restaurant   5000FB

The famous Royal Pavilion in Brighton inspired the decor of the restaurant and paintings of the seaside town line the walls. However, the cooking is firmly rooted over the other side of La Manche. A new chef, Yves Cavelier, arrived in January 1995 and, in addition to the carte and a daily menu, he offers a monthly menu dégustation which might include creamed cold asparagus with caviar, *filet de rouget, sauce aux olives noires parfumées* (fillet of red mullet in a perfumed black olive sauce) and a soup of red fruits with sorbet. If you are uncertain about your choice of wine, the Maître D' will be pleased to offer a recommendation. In summer, lunch and dinner can be taken in the private walled garden. *Seats 70. Open 1200-1430, 2000-2200. Closed Sat, Sun, 21 Jul, 25 May, Easter Monday, National Holidays.*

Tel: (2) 512 07 15   Fax: (2) 514 23 33
30 rue de la Paille, 1000 Bruxelles

The quiet, up-market Le Sablon district with its exclusive antique shops is the location of André Martiny's restaurant. He is a self-taught cook and, although French-based, his style is highly individual. *Salade de mer, terre et rivière* is a wonderful combination of ingredients from sea, land and river, while another speciality is a platter of roast pigeon wing, smoked quail, foie gras and duck liver covered in truffle juice. Desserts are equally spectacular: gratinée of seasonal fruits in little baskets of spun sugar with a mango coulis, for instance. When he is not cooking, Martiny makes dioramas and the split-level restaurant contains several of his models of Egypt, Spain and Greece, complete with little lights. They are so well known that Eurodisney has placed an order for one. *Seats 45. Open 1200-1430, 1900-2330. Closed Sat, Sun, Jul, Christmas, New Year. Public parking. Amex, Diners, Mastercard, Visa.*

Tel: (2) 640 44 22   Fax: (2) 647 97 04
12 boulevard de la Cambre, 1050 Bruxelles

Water-colours by Belgian artists line the walls of an elegant restaurant in a mansion on the edge of the Bois de la Cambre woods. The pedigree of chefs Aziz Bhatti and Erik Lindelauf, formerly at *Comme Chez Soi* (qv), is impeccable and they offer a diverse and imaginative menu with plenty of light touches. Starters include a butterfly (*papillon*) of smoked salmon and crayfish with *crème de caviar,* and hot duck foie gras in sherry vinegar. Salmon is braised with shiitake mushrooms, red wine, potatoes and saffron, while a *grappe* (cluster) of melon and tomato with a red pepper sorbet is a striking dish from the 2100FB *menu dégustation.* Truffles, black and white, are the house speciality and are showcased in the 3475FB menu diamant: with turbot, petits pois and morel mushrooms; *à la julienne,* with a *potée* of vegetables and crayfish; in a champagne vinaigrette over Bresse chicken. In addition to the excellent French wines on the list, there are classic, full-bodied Italians, such as Brunello di Montalcino: a perfect accompaniment to truffles. *Seats 50. Open 1200-1415, 1900-2300. Closed L Sat, all Sun, 1-15 Aug. Valet parking. Amex, Diners, Mastercard, Visa.*

Tel: (2) 374 31 63   Fax: (2) 372 01 95
75 avenue du Vivier d'Oie, 1180 Bruxelles   R

The setting of this restaurant is lovely: near to the huge Forêt des Soignes in a residential area of Brussels, with lanterns hanging in chestnut trees in the garden. Inside, the decor is smart Regency-style. The great chef Marcel Kreusch once held sway here and he has passed his metaphorical apron into the able hands of Henri Van Ranst and chef Freddy Vandecasserie. Cold crab soup with basil, scrambled eggs with morel mushrooms, and crayfish salad with nut oil are tempting starters. Bresse pigeon in truffle juice, grilled sole with shellfish butter, and *carré d'agneau aux jeunes légumes* are equally enticing main courses, while *soufflé au citron* and *crepelines* with orange honey and lime are fine desserts. **Seats** 100. *Open 1200-1400, 1900-2130. Closed Sun, last 3 weeks Jul. Valet parking. Amex, Diners, Mastercard, Visa.*

Around Brussels

Tel/Fax: (2) 672 81 85
2041 chaussée de Wavre, 1160 Auderghem   R

On the edge of the Soigné forest, 8km from the centre of Brussels, and surrounded by a flower garden, Augustin Chanson's small restaurant is a delight. He admits to being greatly influenced by his internationally-renowned friend, Pierre Wynants of *Comme Chez Soi* (qv), but his cooking has a personal lightness of touch. Chanson's sons, Serge and Marc, now assist him in the kitchen to produce dishes such as open lobster ravioli with red curry, monkfish *(lotte)* with creamed red peppers, and cheese and nut terrine. The carte offers three courses for 1750FB, while the dégustation menu is 1900FB. Most of the wines on the list are red Bordeaux. **Seats** 30. *Open 1200-1430, 1900-2130. Closed 1-15 Aug, Christmas, New Year. Private parking. Amex, Diners, Mastercard, Visa.*

Tel: (2) 655 63 11   Fax: (2) 655 64 55
4 avenue Hoover, 1332 Genval   H

The Manoir, formerly the private home of a notary, is a peaceful haven from the outside world with plain wooden furniture, floral curtains and carpets. Only the Turkish bath, sauna and solarium lend hints of modernity. Seminars and conferences can be held at the nearby Villa du Lac while food is available at the Chateau du Lac, 100m away (see below). **Rooms** 13. *Room service limited. Private parking. Banqueting facilities 60. Conference facilities 40. Garden. Outdoor swimming pool. Sauna. Solarium. Turkish bath. Amex, Diners, Mastercard, Visa.*

Tel: (2) 654 07 98   Fax: (2) 653 31 31
Chateau du Lac, 87 avenue du Lac, 1332 Genval   R

This former Schweppes bottling factory, 20 minutes drive from Brussels, is owned by John Martin Hotels, but the superb cooking of chef Michel Haquin is highly individual. Langoustines are served with toasted sesame seeds, goose liver and muscat raisins are wrapped in a galette; brill and shrimps come with *croquettes de beurre au riz basmati*. Desserts are simple but exquisite: vanilla ice cream with strawberries and raspberries, charlotte of lime and wild strawberries. The *menu gastronomique* is 2450FB and the *menu dégustation* costs 2950FB. The "Rapid Business Lunch" menu is excellent value at 1450FB. Over 500 wines are listed. The restaurant is part of the luxurious Chateau du Lac. **Seats** 60. *Open 1200-1430, 1900-2130. Closed Mon, Tue, 8 Jan-10 Feb. Private parking. Amex, Diners, Mastercard, Visa.*

Meal prices for 2 are based on à la carte menus. When set menus are available, prices will often be lower.

Elsewhere in Belgium

Tel: (52) 42 48 01   Fax: (52) 42 59 97
4 Dorp, 92 T Berlare

Guy Van Cauteren's family have deep roots in Berlare. His grandfather ran a community theatre-cum-brasserie here, his father was a butcher, and now Guy has taken a jumble of old buildings and created one of the country's best restaurants. The bare brick walls and exposed timbers of the old galleried theatre stand on one side of a lovely water garden, while opposite is a linseed oil mill. Joining the two sides is a modern section which features regular art exhibitions. The stylish, harmonious whole is appropriately analogous to Guy's cooking which, with dash and bravura, combines luxury and sophistication with no-nonsense gout du terroir. Potato gnocchi and lobster with puréed leeks and truffles, and hot or cold oxtail (queue de boeuf) consommé with manzanilla sherry are typical starters. Beer is one of Belgium's greatest glories and it is used in some quirky dishes, such as turbot and calf's foot braised in *Lambic* (beer fermented by wild yeast) with leek fritures and asparagus tips. More conventionally French are sole with fresh shrimps, and Pauillac lamb roasted in aromatic herbs with new vegetables and parsley potatoes. Desserts include some interesting ice creams (rhubarb jam, chocolate and Ceylon tea) and delicacies like *chocolat soufflé parfumé à l'orange*. There are also set menus from 1515FB to 3135FB. The largely French wine list features some fine champagnes. The restaurant is very much part of the community (locals buy their bread here and it is also a *salon de thé* during the day), and Guy is a well-known character: "All my friends call me the village idiot, happily living in my own world". Berlare is 30 minutes drive west of Brussels. *Seats 65. Open 1200-1430, 1900-2130. Public parking. Amex, Diners, Mastercard, Visa.*

Five delightful bedrooms have recently been completed. Although the price of the cheapest is as indicated above, four of the rooms cost 3900FB per night. Breakfast is extra but guests have free use of bicycles.

Tel: (12) 23 60 96   Fax: (12) 26 32 07
Grimmertingenstraat 24, 3724 Kortessem

In 1982 Christian and Denise Denis bought this 17th-century chateau-farmhouse and converted it into a restaurant. The setting is sublime, surrounded by trees and plants and a stone terrace stretching around the house. It's very much a family affair: Christian is helped in the kitchen by his daughter Véronique, while Nathalie, his other daughter, works *en salle* with her mother. Nathalie's husband is the in-house wine expert. The food is wonderfully inventive and subtle. Young Bresse pigeon is cooked with exotic spices and served with a mint salad, John Dory comes with a potato and sweet garlic mousseline and *vinaigrette aromatisée*, lamb is coated in *persillade* (a mixture of parsley and other chopped herbs) and served with a lasagne of vegetables and rosemary. Desserts are of a similar standard and the house patisserie is superb. Set dinner menus at 3500FB and 3950FB. *Seats 50. Open 1200-1400, 1900-2130. Closed Mon, Tue, Christmas to New Year, 17-31 Jul. Private parking. Amex, Diners, Mastercard, Visa.*

Scotch Beef Club Members: Belgium

ANTWERPEN
ANTWERP: Country Grill
ANTWERP: Holiday Inn
ANTWERP: Petrus
ANTWERP: La Rade
ANTWERP: La Sirena
ANTWERP: Ten Carvery
ANTWERP: Vateli
BRASSCHAAT: De Notelaar
HERENTALS: Snepkenshoeve
KONTICH: Careme
MOL: Hippocampus
SCHOTEN: Kleine Barreel

BRABANT
ASSE: De Pauw
BLANDEN: Chateau de Namur
BRUSSELS: Aux Pavés de Bruxelles
BRUSSELS: Bécasse Blanche
BRUSSELS: Hotel Bedford
BRUSSELS: Belle Maraichère
BRUSSELS: Boerenhesp
BRUSSELS: Brasseries Georges
BRUSSELS: Bruneau
BRUSSELS: Café du Dome
BRUSSELS: Cambrils
BRUSSELS: Claude Dezangre
BRUSSELS: Conrad Hotel
BRUSSELS: Critérion
BRUSSELS: Dupont Claude
BRUSSELS: La Farigoule
BRUSSELS: I Trulli
BRUSSELS: 't Kelderke
BRUSSELS: Le Medicis
BRUSSELS: Meiser
BRUSSELS: 't Misverstand
BRUSSELS: Pergola
BRUSSELS: Les Petits Oignons
BRUSSELS: Prince de Liège
BRUSSELS: Roma
BRUSSELS: La Réserve
BRUSSELS: La Roue d'Or
BRUSSELS: Les 4 Saisons (Royal Windsor)
BRUSSELS: Serge et Anne
BRUSSELS: Sterkerlapatte
BRUSSELS: Les 3 Tilleuls
BRUSSELS: Vieux Boitsfort
BRUSSELS: Le Vieux Pannenhuis
BRUSSELS: La Villa Loraine
BRUSSELS: La Villette
BRUSSELS: Le Wine Bar
CORROY LE GRAND: Le Pin Pignon
DIEGEM: Holiday Inn (Airport)
GENVAL: l'Argentine
GENVAL: Le Trèfle à 4
GROOT-BIJGAARDEN: De Bijgaarden
GROOT-BIJGAARDEN: Michel
HALLE: Les Eleveurs
HALLE: Mario
HERNE: Kokejane
HOEILAART: Le Bollewinkel
HUIZINGEN: Terborght
ITTRE: La Valette
KESSEL LO: In Den Mol
KOBBEGEM: Chalet Rose
LIMELETTE: Chateau de Limelette
MELSBROECK: Kasteel Boetfort
OPHAIN: Cheval Fou
OVERIJSE: Barbizon
VILVOORDE: 't Riddershof
VLEZENBEEK: Philippe Verbaeys
WATERLOO: La Maison du Seigneur
WAVRE: Le Bateau Ivre
WEMMEL: De Kam
WEZEMBEEK: l'Auberge Saint-Pierre

HAINAUT
CHARLEROI: Chateaubriand
CHARLEROI: Le Saint Louis
CHARLEROI: Square Sud
DOTTIGNIES: La Chaumière de l'E3
FELUY: Les Peupliers
FLEURUS: Les Tilleuls
GOSSELIES: Saint-Exupéry
MAFFLE: Le Chauffour
MONS: Chez John
MONS: Devos
MOUSCRON: L'Escapade
TORTRE: Vieux Colmar

LIEGE
FRAIPONT: Auberge de Halinsart
HAMOIR: Hotel Restaurant du Commerce
LIEGE: Au Vieux Liège
LIEGE: Chez Max
LIEGE: Le Duc d'Anjou
LIEGE: Le Lion Dodu

MARCHE EN FAMENNE: Au Menu
    Plaisir
ST VITH: Zur Post
SPA: L'Auberge
VIEUXVILLE: Au Vieux Logis

LIMBOURG
BOCHOLT: Kristoffel
DIEPENBEEK: De Baenwinning
HOUTHALEN: De Barrier
KORTESSEM: Clos Saint-Denis

NAMUR
CRUPET: Les Ramiers
DINANT: La Couronne
DINANT: Le Grill
DINANT: Le Moulin de Lisogne
GEMBLOUX: St Guibert
LAVAUX ST ANNE: Lavaux
PHILIPPEVILLE: La Cote d'Or
ROCHEFORT: Le Luxembourg
SOMME-LEUZE: Le Charolais

OOST-VLAANDEREN
AVELGEM: Alta Ripa
BERLARE: 't Laurierblad
DEINZE: d'Hulhaeghe
DEINZE: Wallebeke
DE PINTE: Te Lande
GENT: Amadeus
GENT: Caphorn
GENT: Reinaert
KRUISHOUTEM: Yzerberghoeve
LAARNE: Gasthof van het Kasteel
LOCHRISTI: De Lozen Boer

MASSEMEN: Geuzenhof
MERENDREE: De Waterhoeve
NINOVE: De Hommel
OOSTAKKER: Sint-Bavo
ST NIKLAAS: Begijnhofke
SINT-MARTENS-LATEM: Auberge
    du Pecheur
WAASMUNSTER: Zilverberk
ZAFFELARE: Kasteel van Saffelaere

WEST-VLAANDEREN
BRUGES: Die Swaene
DAMME: Gulden Kogge
DE PANNE: De Braise
HOLLEBEKE: Golf & Country Club
    Ieper
IEPER: Rallye Grill
IEPER: Regina
IEPER: Yperley
KNOKKE: Ter Dycken
KOKSIJDE: Le Régent
KORTRIJK: Broel Central Hotel
NIEUWPOORT: Bistro du Port
OOSTENDE: 't Genoegen
OOSTDUINKERKE: Bécassine
ROESELARE: Savarin
ST IDESBALD: l'Aquilon
TIELT: De Wildeman
VEURNE: Croonhof
VEURNE: De Kloeffe
WESTENDE: Mercator
WINGENE: De Moorkens
ZWEVEGEM: De Muishond
ZWEVEGEM: Gambrinus

THE INDEPENDENT

INDEPENDENT
ON SUNDAY

Your truly
independent
guides to life

Bulgaria

Currency: Bulgarian Lev   **Exchange Rate:** £1=approx Lev 96
International dialling code: 00 359 (Sofia+2)
Passports/Visas: Visa required by British passport holders, except those on pre-booked package holidays.
(Bulgarian Embassy in London - 186 Queensgate SW7 8NA
Tel 0171-584 9400)
British Embassy Sofia Tel 2-88 53 61

TRANSPORT
Airports
Sofia Airport Tel 2-84 44 33
Railway Stations
Central Railway Station Tel 2-31 111
Car hire in Sofia
Tel Nos **Avis Varco Rent-a-Car** 2-813 569 **Budget** 2-706 148
Hertz 2-791 506 (airport) 2-723 957 (Hotel Pliska)
Speed limits 80km/h on trunk roads, 120km/h on motorways, 60km/h in towns.

OPENING TIMES
Banks 8am-12.30pm & 1-3pm Mon-Fri, 8am-2pm Sat.
Shops 8am-5pm (some shops until 8pm) Mon-Fri, 8am-2pm Sat.

NATIONAL HOLIDAYS
New Year's Day, 3 Mar, May Day, 24 May, Christmas Day.

Tourist Offices
In Sofia Balkantourist Tel 2-43 331
American Express Travel Service Offices or Representative (R)
Sofia   Megatours (R)
           Levski Str.1
           Tel 2-872567/808889 #

Sofia

Tel: (2) 442 581
Oborishete Str 18, Sofia

R

Quite a smart little galleried restaurant with pink upholstery, white walls, brass fittings and air-conditioning. Hot towels arrive with the menu, which has a meze section (nibbles such as salami, cheese and smoked pork, served with drinks tapas-style). Starters as such include the usual salads plus omelettes, pasta and stuffed vine leaves. Cosmopolitan main dishes range from chicken à la paysanne and Provençal-style mussels to steak béarnaise. There are also some Bulgarian specialities; *kavarma* (pork cooked in a special earthenware dish) and *giuveche* (tongue in butter with mushrooms and cooked cheese). Desserts include *mlechna banitza* (sweet egg custard in filo pastry). In the summer there are a couple of pavement tables. *Seats 35. Open 1200-2300. Closed 25 Dec & 2 days at New Year. Amex, Diners, Mastercard, Visa.*

Tel: (2) 442 948
27 Veliko Tamovo, Sofia

R

Formerly the preserve of the diplomatic community (it's in the heart of the embassy district), this restaurant is now open to all but particularly attracts the new movers and shakers from both government and business. The menu reflects the restaurant's origins by offering a globe-trotting selection of dishes including onion soup and beefsteak *provençale* from France, wiener schnitzel from Austria, langoustines Americano, chicken wings in 'Chinese sauce' and cutlet 'à la Moscow', prepared with varying degrees of authenticity. Bulgarian specialities like brain fritters and deep-fried stuffed peppers in batter add some local colour. Several separate rooms allow for discreet business lunches. In summer there are tables set out under an awning in the courtyard. *Seats 60 (courtyard 20). 1200-2300. Amex, Diners, Mastercard, Visa.*

Tel: (2) 62 518   Fax: (2) 68 12 25
100 James Bourchier Boulevard 1407 Sofia

HR

Formerly the Vitosha, this modern, high-rise hotel on the Southern outskirts of the city changed ownership during the summer of 1995 but for the moment there are no major changes other than the name. The spacious, comfortable, air-conditioned bedrooms have every modern amenity (international direct dialling was installed last summer) and good-sized bathrooms, all with showers over the tub. The public areas are smart and extensive with a sunken marble day-bar in the vast lobby area, numerous restaurants including a hard-currency-only Japanese timber affair sitting on its own ornamental lake, and first-rate facilities for the business traveller: business centre, bank, travel agency, Hertz and Avis car rental desks. Room prices are fixed in US dollars ($211 – including a 3% service charge-for a standard double in mid-1995) so the local currency price quoted above is liable to vary. *Rooms 266. Room service 24hr. Free garage parking. Conference facilities 450. Indoor swimming pool. Gymnasium. Sauna. Steam room. Sun-beds. Hairdressing. Beauty salon. Shops. Ten-pin bowling (8 lanes). Night club. Casino. Amex, Diners, Mastercard, Visa.*

Restaurant Lozenetz   LEV4000

The decor may be rustic Bulgarian but the cooking is authentically Italian with chef Martino's short menu offering dishes such as carpaccio, gnocchi, minestrone, spaghetti carbonara, rigatoni bolognese, veal stewed with gin and juniper berries and salmon with mustard and cream. Desserts include traditional tiramisu. In summer dine outside to the accompaniment of a folk music group that plays each evening on the terrace of the hotel's main restaurant next door. Italian wines at fair prices. *Seats 80. Open 1800-2330.*

Tel: (2) 437 679
47 Tcherkovna St, 1505 Sofia

R

In a leafy suburb to the south of the city centre, the restaurant is rather chic, with mauve damask-upholstered French reproduction chairs sitting genteelly on marble floors in a galleried interior. What was a pretty courtyard, with more marble and a fountain, has now been covered to create a conservatory area. Both lunch and dinner are accompanied by a just slightly out-of-tune upright piano. The menu is mainly Bulgarian, with a few more Western dishes. *Seats 80. Open 1200-0100. Amex, Diners, Mastercard, Visa.*

Tel: (2) 87 65 41   Fax: (2) 87 10 38
5 Sveta Nedelya Square, 1000 Sofia

HR

Right in the centre of town, this imposing, 50s-built, neo-classical pile has been a Sheraton hotel for nearly a decade. It's equally grand inside with huge chandeliers, lots of pillars and much marble, including a broad marble staircase reaching right up to the top of the building. Good-sized, high-ceilinged bedrooms feature darkwood furniture and all modern conveniences like air-conditioning but, oddly, only the de luxe rooms and suites get a remote control to go with the multi-channel TV. At breakfast, in addition to the breakfast buffet, there's a short-order cook on hand to prepare eggs freshly just as you like them. Winner of our Best Business Hotel Eastern Europe award 1995, the Sheraton offers everything the modern business traveller needs, from fully-fledged business centre, bank and travel agency to the local British Airways office which is located within the hotel. There's also a choice of dining, ranging from the formal Preslav restaurant to a Viennese café with pavement tables, providing for all levels of entertaining. A night club with floor show and a fitness centre cope with off-duty hours. Room prices are fixed in US dollars ($285 for a standard double in mid-1995) so the local currency price quoted above is liable to vary. *Rooms 188. Room service 24hr. Open parking. Conference facilities 250. Sauna. Spa bath. Gymnasium. Sun beds. Hairdressing. Night club. Amex, Diners, Mastercard, Visa.*

The most formal of several dining choices, the Preslav provides an opulent setting with glittering chandeliers, rich red decor, pianist at a grand piano, and tail-coated waiters offering correct, if somewhat cold, service. A short (about eight main dishes) à la carte of fairly straightforward French-inspired dishes does not change much over time: terrine of goose liver with a sweet pepper parfait, pan-fried perch with a herb crust, fillet of lamb on a bed of boulangère potatoes, pork tenderloin with apple and prunes in a brandy sauce, baba au rhum. Local wines, which are very drinkable, offer the best value on the wine list. *Seats 50. Open (D only) 1900-2330. Closed Sat & Sun.*

Tel: (2) 44 29 81
14 Prof Asen Zlatarov, 1504 Sofia

R

Set in a period house in the diplomatic district of town, this restaurant has exactly 33 chairs (plus a couple of tables in the courtyard in summer), so reservations are essential. It is smart, fashionable and popular with local `celebrities'. The chef boasts a repertoire of some 1000 different dishes of which a good selection appears on each daily-changing menu written using the Cyrillic alphabet (invented by two Bulgarians), but thankfully with accurate English translations. Hors d'oeuvre offer a variety of sausages and cheeses plus a couple of dozen salads (the traditional start to a Bulgarian meal) such as lettuce with sprats and capers; `Cleopatra' with orange, walnuts and cream; Chinese with celery, bamboo shoots and shrimps; and African with maize, beans, leeks and tomatoes. Hot starters include a rather good soufflé with shrimps and globe artichokes. Main dishes come along the lines of chicken grilled with honey, a roulade of pork filled with ham, cheese and herbs, and grilled Black Sea herrings. Desserts are mostly variations on the theme of fruit and ice cream; for the really sweet-toothed there's a dish of three different kinds of Turkish baklava. *Seats 33 (courtyard garden 14). Open 1200-2400. Street parking. No credit cards.*

Your Guarantee of Quality and Independence

- Establishment inspections are anonymous
- Inspections are undertaken by qualified Egon Ronay's Guides inspectors
- The Guides are completely independent in their editorial selection
- The Guides do not accept advertising, hospitality or payment from listed establishments

Titles planned for 1996 include

Hotels & Restaurants ● Pubs & Inns ● Europe
Ireland ● Just A Bite
And Children Come Too ● Paris
Oriental Restaurants

Cyprus

Currency Cyprus Pound **Exchange Rate** £1=approx CY£ 0.7
International dialling code 00 357
(Larnaca+4 Nicosia+2 Paphos+6 Limassol+5)
Passports/Visas No visa required by British passport holders.
UK British High Commission in Nicosia Tel 2-473131/7
Fax 2-367198

TRANSPORT

Airports
Larnaca International Tel 4-643000 **Paphos** Tel 6-422833
Car hire: Tel Nos. **Avis** Larnaca 4-657132 (airport 4-643120)
Nicosia 2-472062 **Budget** Larnaca (airport) 4-643350
Nicosia 2-462042 Paphos (airport) 6-245146 Limassol 5-323672
Speed limits 100km/h on motorways, 50km/h (min) 65 km/h (max) on
other roads unless a lower one is indicated.

OPENING TIMES

Banks 8.15am-12.30pm Mon-Fri, centrally located banks provide
'afternoon tourist services' Tue-Fri.
Shops 8am-1pm, 2.30-5.30pm (4-7pm in summer) Mon, Tue, Thur, Fri,
8am-1pm Wed & Sat.

NATIONAL HOLIDAYS

New Year's Day, 6 Jan, 26 Feb, 1 Apr, Easter, 1 May, 3 Jun, 15 Aug, 1
Oct, 28 Oct, Christmas Day & Boxing Day.

Tourist Offices

Cyprus Tourist Board in **London** Tel 0171-734 9822
In Cyprus **Nicosia** Tel 2-444264 **Limassol** Tel 5-362756, 5-323211,
5-343868 **Larnaca** Tel 4-643000 (24 hrs service)
Paphos Tel 6-232841, 6-422833 **Agia Napa** 3-721796
Platres 5-421316
American Express Travel Service Offices or Representative (R)
Nicosia   A.L Mantovani & Sons Ltd (R)
              2E Agapinou Str
              PO Box 1127
              Tel 2-443777 #
Larnaca   A.L Mantovani & Sons Ltd (R)
              King Paul Square
              PO Box 1045
              Tel 4-652024

Limassol

Tel: (5) 32 11 00   Fax: (5) 32 43 94
Amathus Avenue, Limassol

Wishing to develop a holiday rather than a corporate image, the owners have not renewed their Sheraton franchise and the hotel will be known as St Raphael Resort from November 1995. Conference facilities are still good with three large meeting rooms and several small syndicate rooms available, but it is the leisure amenities which are truly first-class. Four restaurants, two bars, a private marina, water sports, tennis courts and a health club are a few of the many types of amusement on offer. *Rooms 215. Room service 24hr. Private parking. Banqueting facilities 325. Conference facilities 525. Business centre. Indoor and outdoor swimming pools. Tennis. Children's pool and play area. Gym. Sauna. Jacuzzi. Beauty treatment. News kiosk. Amex, Diners, Mastercard, Visa.*

Nicosia

Tel: (2) 37 67 37
2 Agaphons Street, Nicosia

Classic Cypriot dishes are prepared at this popular restaurant in a busy part of Nicosia. Lamb and beef casseroles, served with fresh okra, green beans or artichokes, simply-prepared local fish, and, of course, meze are house specialities. The quality and handling of ingredients, attentiveness of service and smartness of the decor are a cut above the normal and have earned Date Club a deservedly high reputation. A fixed price meze lunch is CY£12.50 for two. *Seats 120 (terrace 80). Open 1200-1500, 1930-2300. Closed Sun, Christmas. Public parking. Amex, Diners, Mastercard, Visa.*

Tel: (2) 36 85 85   Fax: (2) 47 67 40
4 Photiou Stavrou Pitta Street, Nicosia

A simple, five-storey hotel in the bustling centre of Nicosia. The lounge is decorated in 70s' brown and orange but the smallish bedrooms, clad in paler colours, are easier on the eye. Most rooms have a balcony and all have air-conditioning, TV and mini-bar. *Rooms 36. Room service limited. Amex, Diners, Mastercard, Visa.*

Tel: (2) 45 90 59
1 Goudiou Street, Nicosia

This handsome sandstone building with its high ceilings and tiled hall stands on a hill overlooking Nicosia, but is only five minutes walk from the city centre. Inside, the decor is plush and pictures of 50s film stars gaze down on diners feasting on steaks (the house speciality), king prawns in ouzo, grilled fish and salads. The glamorous piano bar is one of the best in Cyprus. *Seats 90 (terrace 110). Open 2100-2330. Closed Sun, Aug, 9 days at Easter, Christmas, National Holidays. Public parking. Amex, Diners, Mastercard, Visa.*

Tel: (2) 47 45 66
3 Menandros Street, Nicosia

Owner and chef Thassos Ioannou is an acknowledged expert on Cypriot cooking, with several books on the subject to his credit. He used to specialise in vegetarian food, but its popularity has been waning of late and trade generally has dropped off so that only the upstairs room and the garden of his restaurant are currently open. The old taverna with its rustic decor and furniture is still a lovely setting in which to sample traditional meat and bean stews, salads and meze. The eminently drinkable Keo wines from Limassol are a good bet from the solely Cypriot list. *Seats 60 (outside 40). Open 2000-2330. Closed Sun. Public parking. No credit cards.*

Tel: (2) 37 77 77   Fax: (2) 37 77 88
Archbishop Makarios III Avenue, Nicosia

For many Cypriots, the Hilton is a symbol of their island's international standing and extensive redevelopment has recently increased its capacity and facilities. A new wing was completed in early 1995, adding a further 84 bedrooms, 7 function rooms and a staffed business centre. All bedrooms are air-conditioned, with balconies giving views over the pool and the city or towards the Troodos mountains. In the basement, the Hiltonia Club has a fully-equipped gym where aerobics, yoga and other exercise classes are run. At the time of going to press, The Orangery restaurant had closed and will be replaced by an eating complex with three restaurants and a bar, due to open in February 1996. The hotel is located on a hill overlooking Nicosia but is only five minutes walk from the Venetian Walls and the city centre. *Rooms 298. Room service 24hr. Private parking.*
Conference facilities 1000. Business centre. Indoor swimming pool. Tennis. Squash. Gym. Sauna. Jacuzzi. Hair salon. News kiosk. Amex, Diners, Mastercard, Visa.

Tel: (2) 47 51 31   Fax: (2) 47 33 37
70 Regaena Street, Nicosia

This family-owned Holiday Inn franchise manages to combine a friendly welcome and relaxed atmosphere with top-class facilities. It re-opened in April 1995 after substantial building work and refurbishment and is now particularly attractive to business people with its six fully-equipped meeting rooms, staffed business centre and excellent support services. Two restaurants, a brasserie with live music and a cocktail bar provide good options for relaxing in the evening. *Rooms 140. Room service limited. Public parking.*
Banqueting facilities 500. Conference facilities 500. Business centre. Indoor swimming pool. Fitness equipment. Sauna. Massage. Amex, Diners, Mastercard, Visa.

Tel: (2) 35 20 86   Fax: (2) 35 19 18
Grivas Digenis Avenue, Engomi, Nicosia

Located in a quiet suburb, five minutes drive from the centre, the five-floor Ledra's lack of aesthetic appeal is balanced by its extensive facilities and lovely gardens. Bedroom decor is still stuck firmly in the 70s but the ten-pin bowling alley, shopping arcade, gym, swimming pool, bars, coffee shop and children's pool and playground mean that guests will probably be out enjoying themselves most of the time. The hotel's tennis courts are popular with Nicosian residents. *Rooms 103. Room service 24hr. Private parking. Conference facilities. Garden. Outdoor swimming pool. Tennis. Children's play area. Gym. Ten-pin bowling. Hair salon. Amex, Diners, Mastercard, Visa.*

Take your pick from typical Cypriot dishes or à la carte French food. Somewhat incongruously, stuffed vine leaves sit alongside chateaubriand with béarnaise sauce, and grilled meatballs appear with *escalope de veau Hoffman* (veal escalope) with ham and cheese). Wednesday nights are entirely devoted to Cypriot food with a fine meze spread and folk-dancing. *Seats 150 (terrace 50). Open 1200-1500, 1900-2300.*

Tel: (2) 49 97 00   Fax: (2) 49 80 38
Eylandjia Avenue, Nicosia

Owned by the Cypriot Ministry of Commerce, the somewhat stark Philoxenia is designed for business rather than pleasure. Most guests are attending conferences or seminars in the five well-equipped meeting rooms (two of which offer theatre-style seating). Renovations to add a further 40 bedrooms and redecorate the public rooms are due to start in early 1996. *Rooms 36. Room service limited. Private parking. Banqueting facilities 1000. Conference facilities 600. Outdoor swimming pool. Tennis. Sauna. Amex, Diners, Mastercard, Visa.*

Meal prices for 2 are based on à la carte menus. When set menus are available, prices will often be lower.

Tel: (2) 44 64 98
6 Makarios Square, Nicosia

This is the place to try Cypriot meze in all their glory. George Frangeskides has been cooking here for over 20 years and is so proud of his speciality that no other dishes appear on the menu, but with 30 different meze to choose from this is not a problem. Familiar dishes such as tsatsiki, houmus and taramasalata appear alongside grilled mushrooms, courgettes with scrambled egg and tahini (crushed sesame seeds in olive oil). Prices are a little higher than in most tavernas but the service is speedy and friendly and the quality of the food high. *Seats 300 (outside 200). Open 1900-2400. Closed Sun. Private parking. Diners, Mastercard, Visa.*

Tel: (2) 35 09 90
No. 59 28th October Street, Nicosia

George Constantinou's purpose-built restaurant specialises in finely prepared Mediterranean fish. Bream, ink fish, swordfish, and snapper, most of which are caught off Larnaca, come lightly grilled, Greek-Cypriot style, with a rich Provençal-style cream sauce and tend to be priced by the kilo. Specialities are the *saganaki* (a Greek dish of fish, mussels or shrimps with feta cheese), baked king prawns or traditional meze at CY£6.60 per person. A sumptuous fish buffet is laid out for dinner Wednesday to Saturday. A smattering of German, Italian and French wines appear alongside the 100 or so Cyprus labels available. *Seats 250 (terrace 150). Open 1100-1500, 1800-2400. Private parking. Amex, Diners, Mastercard, Visa.*

Tel: (2) 46 49 95   Fax: (2) 36 08 29
4 Nikokreontos Street, Nicosia

In the centre of a commercial district, the 1930s sandstone house is dwarfed by surrounding office blocks. It is set back from the road in its own grounds and has a smart, high-ceilinged interior with linen table-cloths, napkins and upholstered chairs. The four chefs cook mainly seafood – bream, red mullet, lobster, cuttlefish, squid, sea bass – some of which diners can pick fresh from the fish tank and then have prepared in a manner of their choice, often simply grilled with herbs, olive oil and lemon juice. There is also a selection of fish meze (CY£8.50 per person). As the majority of its clientele are businessmen, dress tends to be formal. *Seats 100 (outside 140). Open 1230-1530, 1930-2330. Closed Sun, 25 Dec. Private parking. Amex, Diners, Mastercard, Visa.*

Tel: (2) 44 59 50
3 Stassinos Street, Nicosia

Established almost 30 years ago, this elegant restaurant's pride in its cuisine and high class clientele can result in a lack of attention to the less important. However, the French and international cooking is excellent, and features dishes such as steak tartare, shrimps in a whisky sauce, and pork cooked in wine with coriander. Local specialities, like chicken kebab with garlic, are not entirely shunned. Local wines are the most popular on the list. *Seats 80 (terrace 50). Open 1200-1500, 1900-2400. Closed Sun, Aug. Private parking. Amex, Diners, Mastercard, Visa.*

Meal prices for 2 are based on à la carte menus. When set menus are available, prices will often be lower.

Paphos

Tel: (6) 62 17 11   Fax: (6) 62 17 42
Coral Bay, Paphos

Although only two years old, the Coral Beach has been designed with rather more respect for traditional materials and design than is typical of many modern Cypriot hotels.
All bedrooms have balconies with views of the sea or the mountains plus air-conditioning, satellite TV and mini-bar. Facilities are superb with four conference rooms, five restaurants, four bars and a wealth of leisure activities available including a fully-equipped health and beauty spa. *Rooms 304. Room service 24hr. Private parking. Banqueting facilities. Conference facilities. Secretarial services. Indoor and outdoor swimming pools. Gym. Squash. Solarium. Beauty treatment. Children's play area. News kiosk. Amex, Diners, Mastercard, Visa.*

Tel: (6) 62 10 52
Coral Bay, Paphos

This atmospheric stone restaurant has a lovely terrace entwined with grape vines, old-fashioned woven table cloths and baskets decorating the walls. Owner Panicos Charalambous personally supervises or prepares every dish, many using ingredients grown in his garden. Veal and fresh fish, such as grilled swordfish with tomato and garlic, are his specialities. One of the red wines on the list is made locally by Panicos's father-in-law. *Seats 55 (terrace 45). Open 1200 - 1500, 1800 - 2330. Private parking. Amex, Diners, Mastercard, Visa.*

THE INDEPENDENT

INDEPENDENT
ON SUNDAY

Your truly independent guides to life

Czech Republic

Currency: Czech Crown **Exchange Rate** £1=approx KC 43
International dialling code 00 42 (Prague+2)
Passports/Visas No visa required by full British passport holders.
British Embassy in Prague Tel: 2-24 51 04 39

Airports:
Ruzyne airport, Prague Tel 2-36 77 60
Railway Stations
Prague Main station Tel 2-24 21 76 54
Car hire Tel nos. **Avanticar** 2-316 5204 **Hertz** 2-297 836
(airport 2-312 0717) **Europcar** (airport) 2-316 7849
Speed limits 90km/h on trunk roads, 110 km/h on motorways, 60km/h
in towns.

Banks 8am-4pm Mon-Fri, (a few are open 8-12 on Sat)
Shops Hours vary, but most shops are open 7am-6pm Mon-Fri, 8am-
noon Sat (some department stores open until 4pm Sat).

New Year's Day, Easter Monday, 1 May, 5 & 6 July, 28 Oct, Christmas
Eve, Christmas Day & Boxing Day.

Czech Tourist Centre in **London** Tel 0171-794 3263
In **Prague** Information Service Tel 2-242 12 212
American Express Travel Service Offices or Representative (R)
Prague   AETS
           Vaclavske Namesti 56
           11000-1
           Tel 2-443777 #

Prague

Tel: (2) 24 39 41 11 Fax: (2) 24 39 42 15
Evropská 15, 16000 Praha 6

Modern, mid-rise hotel on the road to the airport (it's much favoured by flight crews) but close to a metro station with frequent trains to the city centre just a few stops away. Spacious, marble-floored public areas are matched by good-quality, standard bedrooms each with a couple of good armchairs and all the usual amenities plus air-conditioning, mini-bar and satellite TV. One floor is reserved for non-smokers. Facilities include a night club with dancing to live music and a fitness centre that is bright and inviting although without a swimming pool. Under the same Austrian management as the top-of-the-market *Savoy Hotel* (qv). Room prices are fixed in Austrian schillings (S2700 for a standard double in mid-1995) so the local currency price quoted above is liable to vary. ***Rooms 382.***
Room service limited. Garage parking kc300 per day. Conference facilities 400. Keep-fit equipment. Sauna. Spa bath. Hairdressing. Florist. Amex, Diners, Mastercard, Visa.

Tel: (2) 24 21 17 15 Fax: (2) 24 22 93 06
Washingtonova 19, 11000 Praha 1

Part art deco and part Italianate, the public areas of this 1920s-built hotel have just been restored to their former glory to complement bedrooms that were previously refurbished, also in art deco style. Rooms have all the usual modern facilities including room-safe and mini-bar. In the summer of 1995 work was under way to add air-conditioning to 20 of them. Half the smart marble bathrooms have shower and WC only. Room service operates from early morning until 2am. The hotel is located close to the main railway station and only a few steps away from the Museum at the top of Wenceslas Square. ***Rooms 64.***
Room service all day. Free open parking (monitored overnight) for 15 cars. Conference facilites 45. Coffee shop (0600-0200). Amex, Diners, Mastercard, Visa.

Tel: (2) 61 19 11 11 Fax:(2) 61 21 16 73
Kongresová 1, 14063 Praha 4

Late 80s' glass tower a couple of metro stops out from the city centre to the south-east – next to the Palace of Culture conference centre. Standardised bedrooms are fairly functional in style but come with air-conditioning, mini-bars, room safes and all the usual large hotel facilities like 24hr room service. 15 floors of bedrooms are reserved for non-smokers. Business travellers are well catered for with good work space and second telephone line (for fax) in the rooms and a business centre associated with the conference rooms, of which there are 15 of various sizes. Best place for meeting and greeting is the large lobby area which offers lots of easy seating, a cocktail bar and no less than three decorative water features. At the top of the hotel, on the 25th floor, the leisure centre has panoramic views. In the basement there's a 'beer and bowling' bar (ten-pin, four-lane). ***Rooms 531. Room service 24hr. Parking kc200 (outside) kc300 (garage) per 24hr.***
Conference facilities 300. Indoor swimming pool. Sauna. Gymnasium. Sun bed. Squash. Ten-pin bowling. Hairdressing. Beauty salon. Casino. Amex, Diners, Mastercard, Visa.

Tel: (2) 23 23 417   Fax: (2) 23 29 545
Králodvorská 4, 11000 Praha 1

Tucked away in a side street just off Republic Square, the Grand was built as a private hotel in the 1920s and later became the headquarters of the KGB in Prague. The facade remains, but Austrian owners have rebuilt the interior to create an exclusive, air-conditioned haven for the business traveller (there's a fax/telephone-answering machine in every room) and well-heeled tourist. Only the stunning neo-baroque 'Boccaccio' ballroom is untouched, except for the addition of modern conference facilities. Public areas have been given a subtle 20s' flavour as also have the bedrooms with their lightwood furniture and restful green and blue decor. A single fresh flower adds a dash of colour to otherwise clinically white bathrooms that are appointed to a very high standard. Beds are turned down at night. Room prices are designated in Austrian schillings (S6300 for a standard double in mid-1995) so the local currency price quoted above is liable to vary. ***Rooms 78.***
Room service all day. Valet parking kc550 per 24hrs. Conference facilities 140. Amex, Diners, Mastercard, Visa.

Restaurant   KC1800

Smart, airy restaurant with well-spaced tables and a favourable price/quality ratio. Chef Michal Prasek's menu includes a section of Bohemian specialities – Prague tripe soup, braised beef in a cream sauce with cranberries and dumplings, Bohemian yeast cake with blueberries and whipped cream – but generally the selection reflects a cosmopolitan clientele: beef carpaccio, smoked trout *sauce ravigote*, escalope of veal Viennese style, marinated lamb cutlets in red wine sauce with Basmati rice. Interesting vegetarian options and a good-value business lunch (kc190 Mon-Fri). *Seats 60. Open 1200-1430, 1900-2230 (1800-2130 in winter).*

PRAGUE   Inter-Continental   KC8200

Tel: (2) 24 88 11 11   Fax: (2) 24 81 00 71
Nám Curieových 43/5, 11000 Praha 1

Near the river, but just a couple of minutes walk from the city centre, this medium-rise hotel has just benefited from a multi-million pound refurbishment. Public areas are smart and spacious and there is now a fully-fledged leisure centre. Air-conditioned bedrooms feature cool marble surfaces and all sorts of facilities from room safes to mini-bars and no less than three telephones (in the bathroom, at the desk and by the bed); suites, of which there are 58 'junior' and 39 'full', also have fax machines. Splendid marble bathrooms have hand as well as power showers over the tub. For those on a working trip there's a fully-equipped business centre and various conference and meeting rooms. *Rooms 365.*
Room service 24hr. Garage parking kc160 per 24hrs. Conference facilities 400.
Indoor swimming pool. Spa bath. Sauna. Steam room. Gymnasium. Sun beds. Hairdressing.
Beauty salon. Mini-golf (indoor). Amex, Diners, Mastercard, Visa.

PRAGUE   Palace Hotel   KC8900

Tel: (2) 24 09 31 11   Fax: (2) 24 22 12 40
Panská 12, 11121 Praha 1

The 1989 refurbishment of the Palace only hints at the original (1906) art nouveau style in public areas that are not notably spacious. Huge crystal chandeliers make a good first impression in the lobby, off which the lower-ceilinged reception area provides the only lounge seating other than that in the piano (live nightly) bar. Good-quality international-standard bedrooms come with air-conditioning, free mini-bar (soft drinks and beer), multi-channel TV and white marble bathrooms boasting towelling robes, huge bathsheets and lots of toiletries. 25 bedrooms (and 5 of the 10) suites have in-room fax machines and 50 are reserved for non-smokers. High levels of service begin with the top-hatted doorman and extend to 24hr room service and the turning down of beds in the evening. Breakfast includes an outstanding cold buffet selection. *Rooms 124. Room service 24hr.*
Garage parking (30 spaces) kc130 per 24hrs. Conference facilities 60. Sauna. Coffee shop (1200– 0000). Amex, Diners, Mastercard, Visa.

PRAGUE   Parnas   KC2500

Tel: (2) 24 22 76 14   Fax: (2) 24 22 89 32
Smetanovo Nâbřezi 2, Praha 1

Overlooking the river on the National Theatre side of the Legü Bridge, the Parnas has been established since the 1920s – note the marquetry panelling – but there are such modern-sounding dishes as carpaccio with fresh herbs and parmesan, grilled fillet of swordfish, and salmon with pineapple in a dill sauce to be found on a varied menu that also includes classics like lobster bisque and lobster thermidor, a range of home-made pastas, Bohemian specialities and some good vegetarian options. Decent French bread is served, but you have to ask for it. Pear crème brulée (made with milk rather than cream) makes a nice light conclusion or there are some French cheeses. Polite, efficient service and well-spaced tables attract local business people so booking is advisable (if the above number is busy try 24 22 92 48). Twelve wines available by the glass. Set L from kc495 Set D from kc795. Sunday buffet brunch (with live jazz) kc595. *Vinárna V Zátiší* (qv) is in the same ownership as are three new restaurants: Avalon Bar and Grill; Circle Line Brasserie – with Prague's only oyster bar – (both at Malostranské nám 12 Tel: 53 02 63 and 53 03 08 respectively); and U Patrona (Drazické nám 4 Tel: 53 15 12). *Seats 75. Open 1200-1500 (Sun from 1100), 1730-2330. Closed 24 Dec. Amex, Mastercard, Visa.*

Opening times are often liable to change at short notice, so it's always best to book.

Tel: (2) 24 84 11 11 Fax: (2) 24 81 18 96
Pobřenžní, 18600 Praha 8

Built in the form of a square enclosing a vast atrium, overlooked by many of the bedrooms, this is the Republic's largest hotel. Standardised rooms offer all the comforts of a mid-range international hotel including air-conditioning, although the latter only works, like all the electrics, when you insert your key card into a slot in the room so that in summer, when Prague can get quite hot, it may take a while for the room to cool down after a day out. The big plus is that there's lots to do within the hotel (should you get bored with one of the most beautiful and lively cities in Europe) with everything from a casino with floor show and a leisure centre with indoor tennis to an outdoor putting green. Much reduced room rates in July and August. Acquired by Hilton in the summer of 1995. *Rooms 788. Room service 24hr. Garage parking kc200 per 24hrs. Conference facilities 1500. Putting green. Indoor swimming pool. Gymnasium. Squash. Indoor tennis. Sauna. Spa bath. Sun bed. Hairdressing. Beauty salon. Casino/night club. Amex, Diners, Mastercard, Visa.*

Tel: (2) 24 81 03 96 Fax (2) 23 13 133
V Celnici 7, 11000 Praha 1

Modern hotel with fine central location just off the Republic Square – one entrance to the Metro station is under the hotel. The spacious marble-floored lobby has a useful little café area; the main bar is part of a rustic-themed, informal restaurant. Well-designed, air-conditioned bedrooms greet guests with a personalised welcome message on a TV screen which also offers hotel information and numerous television channels in various languages. New since last year are voice-mail facilities and safes in every room plus the creation of a Club Floor (the 9th) whose guests enjoy various extra services and amenities including an exclusive lounge where complimentary canapés and champagne are served in the afternoon. *Rooms 309. Room service all day. Garage parking kc400 per 24hrs. Conference facilities 370. Indoor swimming pool. Sauna. Steam room. Keep-fit equipment. Amex, Diners, Mastercard, Visa.*

Tel: (2) 24 34 11 11 Fax: (2) 24 31 12 18
Suïká 20, 16635 Praha 6

Out towards the airport, in Prague's poshest suburb, the Praha was built in the early 80s (but the decor has a 70s' feel) as a secure hotel for Communist Party bigwigs. An unusual serpentine, terraced design means that every single room has its own verdant terrace and fine views of the city. All the air-conditioned bedrooms are spacious, if somewhat functional, with their own entrance lobby and loos separate from large bathrooms, all with bidets. The decor is rather dated but in good condition. Nearly a third of rooms are full suites with the eight largest, designed for Party Secretaries, absolutely vast. Public areas are also on a grand scale with broad marble steps leading down from the lobby to an echoey main lounge with water garden and nightly dancing to live music. One of several conference rooms is a very comfortable theatre/cinema with simultaneous translation facilities. The hotel is owned by the City of Prague. *Rooms 124. Room service 24hr. Ample parking (some covered) kc100 per 24hrs. Conference facilities 200. Garden. Tennis. Indoor swimming pool. Sauna. Hairdressing. Beauty salon. Amex, Diners, Mastercard, Visa.*

Tel: (2) 24 30 21 11 Fax (2) 24 30 21 28
Keplerova Ul 6, 11800 Praha 1

Discreet and luxurious, this new hotel in the government and embassy district has been created behind an original art nouveau facade. Intimate in character, the public areas include marble-floored lobby, elegant library-lounge and cosy bar with red banquette seating. Air-conditioned bedrooms are furnished and equipped to a high standard with fax and video machines (the hotel has a library of films) and no less than four telephones, including one in the separate loo and one in the coloured bathroom with walk-in shower in addition to the tub. Beds are turned down at night. Two floors of rooms are reserved for non-smokers. Room prices are fixed in Austrian schillings (S2950 for a standard double in mid-1995) so the local currency price quoted above is liable to vary. *Rooms 61. Room service 24hr. Valet parking kc250 per 24hrs. Conference facilities 35. Terrace. Gymnasium. Sauna. Steam room. Spa bath. Hairdressing. Beauty salon. Amex, Diners, Mastercard, Visa.*

At the touch of a button it is possible to make the roof slide open and the windows sink into the floor to create a semi-alfresco environment at this comfortable and otherwise fairly formal hotel restaurant. Multi-lingual menus have a distinct Austrian/Czech flavour with main dishes like fillet of pork in garlic cream sauce with mushroom dumplings and mashed potatoes; baby chicken with wild mushrooms, Madeira sauce and home-made noodles, fillet of beef with Bohemian sauce, potato cake and mashed apple, and plaice with bacon and mushrooms, but the preparation of dishes in chef Vidovich's kitchen is quite refined and dishes often turn out to be quite delicate. Starters might include a tomato consommé with mozzarella ravioli and lobster stew with kohlrabi, and the desserts, some gratinated fruits with an amaretto sabayon, and a vanilla parfait with marinated strawberries. Set menus: L kc380 D kc760. *Seats 80. Open 1200-1600, 1800-2300.*

Tel: (2) 53 84 22   Fax: (2) 53 84 98
Janský Vršek 328-3, Mala Strana 11800 Praha 1

A small, functionally modern hotel built behind a period facade, near the US Embassy, across the river from the city centre. Public rooms are limited to a bar counter in the atrium reception area and a breakfast room where a decent cold buffet, plus bacon and eggs, is served. Bedrooms are simple and uncluttered. Doubles (two single beds pushed together) have tubs in their pristine bathrooms, while the singles (just two) have shower and WC only. All have mini-bars and multi-channel TV. Three suites are in similar style. Helpful staff speak good English. *Rooms 22. No room service. Street parking for 5 cars kc200 per 24hrs. Amex, Diners, Mastercard, Visa.*

Tel: (2) 53 22 51   Fax: (2) 53 33 79
U Lužického Semianáre 106, Praha 1

The name means Peacock, and a small inn-like sign depicting the bird hangs over the door of this mid-19th-century house (built in an older style and completely renovated in 1991) on the Lesser Town side of the river not far from the Charles Bridge. Small, intimate and with considerable charm, it has just eleven rooms, of which five are full suites. All are well appointed, with rug-strewn tiled floors, timber ceilings, crystal chandeliers, tapestry upholstery and stained-glass windows from which the suites have views of the Castle. Facilities include mini-bars and good bathrooms but telephones are not direct-dial. The entrance hall features a couple of old stone pillars and a marble-topped bar counter. Other public areas are limited to a small restaurant and separate breakfast room. Delightful staff. *Rooms 11. Room service all day. Free parking for three cars (reserved spaces in street). Amex, Diners, Mastercard, Visa.*

Tel: (2) 531 133
Nový Svět 3, Hradčany Praha 1

This 17th-century restaurant in the Castle district has several panelled dining-rooms on two floors. The long menu (some 30 main dishes) seems even longer with each dish translated into five languages: tripe in five guises, four different soups, three snail dishes, game, fish and poultry. There's even a special section of dishes 'suitable for gentlemen' and another section 'suitable for ladies'. New this year is a daily-changing market menu. Choice rather than subtle cooking is the order of the day and there's an emphasis on show with several flambéed items and dishes served sous cloche. A courtyard on the opposite side of the lane has a cheaper menu for alfresco diners. Set L kc300. *Seats 95. Open 1130-1500, 1800-2400. Parking difficult. Closed 24 & 25 Dec. Amex, Diners, Mastercard, Visa.*

> Meal prices for 2 are based on à la carte menus. When set menus are
> available, prices will often be lower.

Tel: (2) 47 25 511   Fax: (2) 47 29 426   **H**
K Novému Dvoru 124/54, 14200 Praha 4-Lhotka

In a leafy suburb, a good 15-minute taxi ride south of the city centre (more if the driver doesn't know the way), the house was built in 1912 and restored to its original art nouveau glory in 1992. Engraved glass and period light-fittings feature in the reception area, where there is some café-style seating, and in the bar with its marble-topped counter. In summer there is a bar and barbecue out in a pretty garden. Bedrooms are also decorated in art nouveau style, comfortably furnished with proper armchairs and/or sofas and gold-plated (we were assured) brass bedsteads. All boast air-conditioning, mini-bar, room safe and multi-channel TV. Bathrooms, of which four have shower and WC only, are smart. *Rooms 13. Room service 24hr. Free parking for 10 cars. Garden. Amex, Diners, Mastercard, Visa.*

Tel: (2) 24 22 89 77   Fax: (2) 24 22 89 32   **R**
Liliová 1, Betlémské Náměstí, Praha 1

Winner of this year's Best Restaurant Eastern Europe Award, the name means 'still life' and this theme is picked up in pictures and foody displays that form part of the new Provençal decor of three of the four dining-rooms. There are a couple of Bohemian specialities on the menu but this is essentially an up-market establishment with sophisticated modern cooking from new chef Kenneth Akenberg. Try warm duck liver sautéed with white wine and cognac and served on a bed of fresh greens, carpaccio with mature parmesan, salmon marinated in dill and sea-salt with melon, vegetable-stuffed sole with lobster sauce, medallions of lamb in puff-pastry with garlic sauce, chateaubriand with sauce choron. Chocolate mousse is the most popular dessert or try the likes of hot banana and chocolate soufflé, crème brulée, and Amaretto sabayon. If you intend a full three-course meal go for the 'deluxe menu' which allows a full choice from the à la carte but at a saving from the individual dish prices; the price of the meal depends on the main dish chosen ranging from kc495 (vegetarian main dish) to kc795 (with lobster). Several Czech wines on the list that contains English tasting notes. Booking advisable (24 23 11 87 is an alternative number). To find the restaurant ask for directions to Bethlehem Square. Sister restaurant to *Parnas* (qv). *Seats 110. Open 1200-1500 (Sun from 1100), 1730-2300. Closed 24 Dec. Amex, Mastercard, Visa.*

Denmark

Currency Danish Krone **Exchange Rate** £1=approx DKR 8.71
International dialling code: 00 45
Passports/Visas No visa required by British passport holders.
British Embassy in Copenhagen Tel: 35-264600 Fax: 35-38 1012

TRANSPORT

Airports
Copenhagen Tel 32-50 9333 **Aarhus** Tel 86-36 3611
Billund Tel 75-33 8022
Railway Stations
Copenhagen Tel 33-14 1701 **Odense** Tel 66-12 1013
Aarhus Tel 86-18 1778
Car hire
Tel nos. **Copenhagen Avis** 31-31 5020 (airport 31-51 2299)
Budget 33-13 3900 (airport 32-52 3900)
Aarhus Budget (airport) 86-36 3999
Billund Budget (airport) 75-35 3900
Speed limits 80 km/h on trunk roads, 110 km/h on motorways, 50 km/h
in towns.

OPENING TIMES

Banks Mon-Wed & Fri 9.30am-4pm, Thu till 6pm.
Shops Mon-Wed 9am-5.30pm, Fri till 7/8pm, Sat till 1/2pm (first and
last Saturday of each month, some shops stay open till 4/5pm).

NATIONAL HOLIDAYS

New Year's Day, 4 Apr, Good Friday, Easter Sun & Mon, 3, 16, 26, 27
May, 5 Jun, Christmas Eve, Christmas Day & Boxing Day, New Year's
Eve (from noon).

Tourist Offices

Danish Tourist Board in **London** Tel 0891 600109 (answerphone
service), 0171-259 5959 11am-4pm.
In **Denmark Copenhagen** Tel 33-11 1325 **Aarhus** Tel 86-12 1600
Odense Tel 66-12 7520 **Aalberg** Tel 98-12 6022
American Express Travel Service Offices or Representative (R)
Copenhagen   AETS
                        Amagertov 18 (Stroget)
                        DK 1146
                        Tel 33-122301 #

Copenhagen

Tel: 33 12 11 36   Fax: 33 15 00 31
Tivoli Vesterbrogade 3, 1620 København V

In the middle of the Tivoli Gardens, so when the weather's fine go for the balcony tables overlooking the lake. The Belle Terrasse offers a good variety of dishes from a high-class menu executed with skill and flair by chef Steen Berthelsen. Starters like foie gras-stuffed ravioli in chicken consommé, green and white asparagus with sauce mousseline, Danish langoustines baked with mushrooms and herbs, and smoked salmon with a tomato stew and caviar mousse are followed by such main dishes as tournedos Rossini, salted duck breast with spring leeks and horseradish sauce, veal roasted with rosemary and served with a mushroom ratatouille, fillet of turbot with a clam mousseline on poached chicory with lime butter and, from the charcoal grill, veal with morel sauce, Riesling- and tarragon-marinated breast of chicken with sugar-peas and tarragon sauce, and beefsteak with béarnaise and bordelaise sauces. Desserts might include apple pie with prunes and armagnac and a marbled chocolate mousse with crisp nut-cakes. In addition to the à la carte there is a three-course set lunch, which varies in price (according to the ingredients) from Dkr375 to Dkr445, and a similar four-course set dinner Dkr465-Dkr545. *Seats 250 (+ 60 balcony).*
Open 1200-2230. Closed mid Sept-late Apr. Parking difficult. Amex, Diners, Mastercard, Visa.

Tel: 33 14 68 47   Fax: 33 14 60 06
Bernstorffsgade 5, 1577 København V

In the middle of the Tivoli amusement park (the 1995 admission fee was Dkr40), La Crevette is predominatly a seafood restaurant, with daily deliveries ensuring the very freshest of raw materials for the kitchen, where former sous-chef Stig Anderson has now taken over the top job. The menu remains largely unchanged with starters like half a freshly-boiled lobster served with tomato and herbs in a Provençal sauce, terrine of vegetables with Bayonne ham and a mild mustard dressing, and duck foie gras with apples and a Sauternes jelly before mains like salmon with crispy potatoes, garlic and a beurre blanc sauce, paupiettes of sole stuffed with scallops and served with tomato lasagne and coral sauce, and grilled red mullet with fried celery, sautéed spinach and parsley purée. A special section of 'classic' dishes includes sole meunière, fried plaice with lemon and parsley sauce and salmon hollandaise. There are always a couple of meat dishes on the menu. More whites (appropriately) than reds on a good wine list that majors on France but has other European and a few New World representatives. *Seats 60 (+ 35 terrace).*
Open 1200-2230. Closed mid Sept-mid Apr. Parking difficult. Amex, Diners, Mastercard, Visa.

Tel: 33 12 51 51   Fax: 33 91 08 82
Tivoli Gardens Vesterbrogade 3, 1620 København V

Surrounded by the Tivoli Gardens, this house overlooks the lake and enjoys a view of the fairy-tale Hans Andersen Castle. It was built in the early 19th century when the gardens were first laid out. Chef Jens Andersen's varied, and various, menus come bound, along with the good French wine list, into a stylish booklet produced each year. Dishes might include carpaccio of beef with truffle vinaigrette and Tete de Moine and Grana cheese; terrine of lobster and turbot with herb cream and trout roe; chicken salad with fresh asparagus, crisp bacon and toast; whole plaice with parsley sauce; beef tartare; fillet of veal with braised root vegetables, truffle sauce and buttery spinach; Danish meat-balls with potato salad and pickled cucumber, and a Danish meat hash with fried egg, beetroot and sauce béarnaise. *Seats 200. Open 1200-2230. Closed mid Sept-late Apr. Parking difficult. Amex, Diners, Mastercard, Visa.*

Tel: 33 14 13 41   Fax: 33 91 07 00
Store Strandstrøde 3, 1255 København K

Overlooking the Nyhavn canal, this establishment opened as a coffee shop in the early 19th century and was immortalised in a poem by Hans Christian Andersen, a regular customer. With traditional Danish decor, complete with a proud moose head pinned to the wall, it is now a Danish-cum-French restaurant. There are two limited-choice set menus to choose from, one priced for one, two or three courses. Frogs' legs with chanterelle sauce, mussel flan with smoked shrimps on crispy salad, consommé with quail's eggs and *fines herbes*, breast of chicken with vegetables and a mild mustard sauce, and summer venison with mushrooms and a tarragon sauce demonstrate the style. The menus change frequently but Sevruga caviar, lobster and paté de foie gras (listed in a separate box) are more or less permanent fixtures. The European wine list is dominated by France. Set meals Dkr217/276 & Dkr346. *Seats 60. Open 1200-1500, 1730-2200. Closed 24-26 Dec & 2 Jan. Meter parking. Amex, Diners, Mastercard, Visa.*

Tel: 33 91 36 55   Fax: 33 11 36 55
Store Kongensgade 70, København K

Few restaurants in the world manage to be genuinely original; but this one does. In existence for over a century (in its present building since 1974), it was started by Oskar Davidsen with his wife Petra and has since passed down through the female side of the family; the present owner, Ida, is Oskar's great-granddaughter. The female-only kitchen produces no fewer than 177 different open sandwiches (smørrebrød); the list is over 140cm long, the longest in the world according to the Guinness Book of Records. Puréed smoked salmon with raw egg yolk, horseradish and onion; hot fried eel; roast beef with cold béarnaise sauce; half a pigeon with stewed mushrooms, and tongue with fried egg hardly begin to show the range. They smoke their own duck, salmon and lamb, so those sandwiches are also worth looking out for. Drink the draught beer. *Seats 85. Open 0900-1700. Closed Sat, Sun, July, Good Fri-Easter Mon & 23 Dec-1 Jan. Public parking. Amex, Diners, Mastercard, Visa.*

Tel: 33 12 09 90   Fax: 33 93 12 23
Ny Adelgade 7, 1104 København K

Built by an old Danish commander (hence the name) in 1698, this house has been a restaurant since the 1930s. Old wooden beams and a timber floor contrast with Andy Warhol prints on the walls and fine Royal Copenhagen china on the tables. The à la carte (lunchtime it's a shorter version of the evening carte) ranges from carpaccio of scallops with vegetables, summer truffles and parmesan; terrine of duck foie gras; and rack of lamb with leeks, capers and small new potatoes to braised turbot with olive sauce and lemon thyme; poached chicken breast with a tomato and morel stock, and oxtail and lobster with a purée of parsley and tomato with a sauce lyonnaise. Desserts include mixed berries with junket, and strawberry tart with white wine jelly and vanilla ice cream. At lunchtime there's also a three-course set menu (Dkr275) and at night chef Francis Cardenas' special five-course menu at Dkr490 (with a selection of different wines for an extra Dkr320). A mostly French wine list includes some good wines available by the glass. *Seats 45. Open 1200-1430, 1730-2200. Closed L Sat, all Sun & Christmas-New Year. Parking difficult. Amex, Diners, Mastercard, Visa.*

Tel: 33 12 59 02   Fax: 33 93 59 01
Vester Voldgade 25, 1552 København V

Two hotels, rebuilt in the late 1900s, were amalgamated in 1973 to create the Kong Frederik. The location is ideal, being just two minutes from the Tivoli Gardens and the Town Hall Square and five minutes from the main railway station. Bedrooms, which are furnished in classical British style, all have mini-bars and some have room safes. *Rooms 110. Room service all day. Hotel has reserved spaces in nearby public car park, Dkr100 per 24hrs. Conference facilities 100. Amex, Mastercard, Visa.*

Tel: 33 11 68 68   Fax: 33 32 67 68
Vingardsstraede 6, 1070 København K

King Hans of Denmark used to own this cellar, one of the oldest in Denmark, which is now a typically French restaurant, complete with French chef Daniel Letz, who has been here for 15 years. They offer dishes like mussel soup laced with saffron, warmed goose liver with raspberry vinaigrette, confit of duck and coq au vin, rounded off with crème brulée. The wines are exclusively French, except for one lone Spanish bottle. The Gothic-style, arched dining-room is just off the main Kongens-Nytoru Square, near the Royal Theatre. *Seats 40. Open D only 1800-2200. Closed Sun, Jul & 24 Dec-1 Jan. Amex, Diners, Mastercard, Visa.*

Tel: 31 31 48 01   Fax: 31 23 96 86
Helgolandsgade 3, 1653 København V

Family-run bed-and-breakfast hotel in a peaceful side street in the city centre near the main railway station. Decor has an Eastern slant, particularly in the ten de luxe rooms on the fifth floor. There are also four full suites. Rooms all have mini-bars, safes and beverage-making kit but about half have shower and WC only. Reception is open 24hrs but there is no restaurant, although *Divan 2 Tivoli* (qv) is in the same ownership. *Rooms 106.*
Closed 23 Dec-2 Jan. Room service limited. Meter parking. Amex, Diners, Mastercard, Visa.

Tel: 33 13 89 00   Fax: 33 14 12 50
Sankt Anna Plads 14-20, 1250 København K

In a small side street near the harbour, not far from the shops, this hotel is run along very environmentally-conscious lines by owner Bente Noyons with various policies in effect to save electricity (room keys activate the lights) and water (special taps) and to recycle waste (each room has two wastepaper baskets, one for burnable and one for non-burnable items). Bedrooms are decorated in pale restful colours and come with multi-channel TVs, mini-bars and safes; some have air-conditioning. About half the bathrooms have tubs, the remainder shower and WC only. (In the same ownership, to the north of the city centre, is the no-frills, 160-room Esplanaden Hotel (Dkr865), Tel: 33 91 32 00). *Rooms 133.*
Closed Christmas-New Year. Room service 24hrs. Street parking (meters). Conference facilities 70. Amex, Diners, Mastercard, Visa.

This is just the place to sample some real Danish regional cooking. The shortish menu changes with the seasons and brings the specialities from different areas at different times of the year. A recent menu from Samsø, one of the smaller islands, included chicken soup with potato balls; pork with white cabbage, potatoes and carrots in butter; roast leg of venison with apples and thyme; vegetable-stuffed cabbage with mustard and a dill beurre blanc, and a special Madeira cake served with blackcurrant jam. There is also a café menu: fishcakes, smoked salmon, soup, sandwiches, beers. The atmosphere they like to engender is that of *hygge*, a vague Danish concept to do with warmth, friendliness and companionship. Set meals Dkr190/240. **Seats 40. Open 1200-1500, 1800-2130.**
Closed Sun, Jul & Christmas-New Year.

Tel: 33 13 50 18   Fax: 33 32 07 97
Gammel Strand 34, 1202 København K

Alongside the canal and right opposite the parliament buildings, there has been a restaurant here since 1830. Chef Lars Kyllesbeck's brilliant cooking is Danish-orientated and a perfect complement to the elegant, luxurious interior. The à la carte includes terrine of smoked salmon and eel, a starter of herrings served as several small hot and cold dishes, asparagus soup with Brittany oysters, fricassee of lobster with watercress and green apple, lightly-salted pigeon with glazed vegetables and horseradish, passion fruit bavarois, and a 'caramel fanfare' consisting of several small caramel delicacies. In addition to the carte there is a daily-changing, three-course set lunch (Dkr250) and two no-choice set dinners (both Dkr 465) including the fish menu that begins with their signature starter in which a hen's eggshell is filled with lobster mousseline and Sevruga caviar and served with toast 'soldiers'. The wine list offers a breathtaking array of clarets and an exceptional selection of burgundies from Romanée Conti, not to mention a huge list of ports including some of the fine 1970 vintage. Lunchtimes only, an informal and much less expensive menu is served in the basement Thorvaldsen restaurant. **Seats 50. Open 1130-1500 (till 1600 in Thorvaldsen), 1730-2200. Closed Sun, Jul (except Thorvaldsen), Public Holidays & Christmas-New Year. Meter parking. Amex, Diners, Mastercard, Visa.**

Tel: 33 14 92 62   Fax: 33 93 93 62
Bernstorffsgade 4, 1577 København V

Early 20th-century hotel built in art deco style right in the centre of Copenhagen, opposite the main railway station. Air-conditioned bedrooms are traditionally furnished and decorated with Laura Ashley-style prints. Rooms vary in size from Standard (the smallest) through Medium to Deluxe. Public rooms include two restaurants and the Library Bar. *Rooms 93. Closed 10 days Christmas. Room service all day. Garage parking Dkr120 per 24hrs. Conference facilities 40. Amex, Diners, Mastercard, Visa.*

COPENHAGEN   Radisson SAS Royal   DKR2135   H

Tel: 33 14 14 12   Fax: 33 14 14 21
Hammerichsgade 1, 1611 København V

Designed by avant-garde architect Arne Jakobfen, this 60s building is simple but sophisticated, with public areas featuring tall mirrors and marble floors. Twenty storeys high, the hotel is right in the middle of the city, close to the Tivoli Gardens. Air-conditioned bedrooms are in clean-cut, uncluttered Scandinavian style; all have multi-channel TV, mini-bar and room safe. Two floors are reserved for non-smokers and seven floors of de luxe Royal Club rooms share their own lounge, where complimentary breakfast is available. Business class SAS passengers can check in for their flight before leaving the hotel. *Rooms 255. Room service 24hrs. Garage parking Dkr125 per 24hrs. Conference facilities 200. Gym. Sauna. Sun bed. Massage. Business centre. Amex, Diners, Mastercard, Visa.*

COPENHAGEN   71 Nyhavn Romantik Hotel   DKR1350   H

Tel: 33 11 85 85   Fax: 33 93 15 85
Nyhavn 71, 1051 København K

Created out of a 200-year-old warehouse by the harbour, this hotel is full of rustic charm with Pomeranian beams (they gain a particular character from having been towed here by the old sailing ships), terracotta tiles and white walls. All rooms are well equipped but go for the Superior rooms to enjoy the best views of the harbour with its sailing boats. There are three L-shaped 'junior' and six 'full' suites. The hotel also owns an old lightship moored opposite in the harbour and used for banquets. *Rooms 82. Room service 24hrs. Free parking (un-reservable) for just seven cars or valet parking to nearby public park Dkr100 per 24hrs. Conference facilities 25. Amex, Diners, Mastercard, Visa.*

Around Copenhagen

HOLTE   Søllerød Kro   ★ DKR1100   R

Tel: 42 80 25 05   Fax: 42 80 22 70
Søllerødvej 35, 2840 Holte

Some 15km north of Copenhagen, in the pretty village of Søllerød, this charming 16th-century thatched inn is to be found opposite the church down a winding street. The old-fashioned dining-rooms are filled with antiques, Danish paintings and objets d'art and there are two sitting-rooms to retire to for coffee after dinner. In addition to the delightful setting, the attraction here is the outstanding cooking of Steen Eis Thomsen. Veal terrine, foie gras, vichyssoise and lobster salad à la Søllerød feature amongst the starters on the à la carte before main dishes such as fillet of lemon sole baked with Brittany oysters; a simple sole meunière; suckling lamb with saffron ravioli, dandelions, fennel sauce and sun-dried tomatoes, and breast of guinea fowl with summer truffles and fried aubergine. Desserts include vanilla profiteroles with lime cream and wild strawberries, and meringue with caramel parfait and seasonal berries; the really sweet-toothed can choose the Grand Dessert. An impressive wine list boasts many fine vintage clarets, and suitably priced for deep pockets. Set L Dkr275, Set D Dkr395 (three courses) & Dkr575 (six courses). *Seats 50. Open 1130-2200. Closed Sun & Public Holidays. Ample own parking. Amex, Diners, Mastercard, Visa.*

Elsewhere in Denmark

EBELTOFT   Mellem Jyder   R DKR220

Tel: 86 34 11 23
Juulsbakke 3, 8400 Ebeltoft

Way up on the east coast of Jutland, this characterful, black-and-white timbered, early-17th-century house specialises in hearty Danish fare. It's family run and homely, and tables are piled high with boiled hams, open sandwiches, roasted partridges, herrings and rye bread. In addition to this smørrebrød there is an à la carte offering wiener schnitzel with sauté potatoes, entrecote with salad and fries, and their unique speciality of eel fried in butter and served in a cream sauce with new potatoes. About 20 mainly French wines or beer to drink. *Seats 70. Open 1000-2100. Closed Tue & Feb. Public parking. Mastercard, Visa.*

FREDENSBORG   Store Kro Hotel   DKR1150

Tel: 42 28 00 47   Fax: 42 28 45 61
Slotsgade 6, 3480 Fredensborg

Built next to Fredensborg Castle in 1723 by King Frederick IV to house his guests, this lovely old inn is now open to all. Individually decorated bedrooms are traditional in style, with open fireplaces and fine paintings, while incorporating modern comforts such as mini-bars and multi-channel TVs. The hotel is located about 40km north of Copenhagen close to Denmark's biggest lake, Esium. *Rooms 49. Closed Christmas-New Year. Room service 24hrs. Ample free parking. Conference facilities 80. Amex, Diners, Mastercard, Visa.*

SNEKKERSTEN   Scanticon Hotels   DKR1250

Tel: 42 22 03 33   Fax: 42 22 03 99
Nørrevej 80, 3070 Snekkersten

The hotel is located on the northern tip of Zealand, a slim stretch of water away from Sweden, close to Elsinore and Hamlet's castle of Kromborg. Opened in 1989, the hotel is surrounded by a public park. Scandinavian simplicity combines with modern facilities in bedrooms whose bathrooms mostly have showers rather than tubs. Conferencing is important, with 33 fully-equipped conference and meeting rooms available, the main ones air-conditioned. *Rooms 149. Room service all day. Ample free parking. Conference facilities 300. Tennis. Boules. Indoor swimming pool. Sauna. Spa bath. Gym. Table tennis. Amex, Diners, Mastercard, Visa.*

VEJLE   Munkebjerg   DKR1025

Tel: 75 72 35 00   Fax: 75 72 08 86
Munkebjergvej 125, 7100 Vejle

Just outside Vejle, the hotel, family-run since the 1960s, enjoys an idyllic location surrounded by a beech forest with grazing deer and glimpses of the fjord glistening through the trees. Their main business is conferences in the winter (they have 18 fully-equipped meeting rooms) and tourists and holidaymakers in the summer. Leisure facilities include a 2km illuminated jogging track around the hotel and both golf and riding are available nearby. *Rooms 148. Closed 10 days Christmas. Room service all day. Ample free parking. Conference facilities 400. Garden. Tennis. Indoor swimming pool. Gym. Sauna. Sun bed. Billiard room. Darts room. Amex, Diners, Mastercard, Visa.*

THE APARTMENT SERVICE

Tel in UK (0181) 748 4207   Fax (0181) 748 3972

The Apartment Service will find you the right apartment worldwide to suit your needs, whether you are on a short or long-term stay. A 96-page colour catalogue is free on request. All budgets are catered for.

Currency: Estonian Kroon **Exchange Rate:** £1=approx EEK 19.25 Amounts equal to or exceeding 80,000 EEK must be declared. For amounts over 200,000 EEK, a document proving the legal origin is required.
International dialling code: 00 372
Passports/Visas: No visa required by British passport holders for stay of less than 30 days. British Visitor's passports are not accepted.
British Embassy in Tallinn Tel: 6-313 462/3 or 6-313 353

TRANSPORT

Airports
Tallinn Airport Tel 6-388 888
Railway Stations
Tallinn Main Station ("Baltijaam") Tel 2-624 958 (general) 2-446 756 (international)
Car hire in Tallinn
Hertz Tel 6-388 923 (airport) / Avis Tel 6-315 930 (Hotel Olümpia), 2-215 602 (airport)
Speed limits 90 km/h on trunk roads, 50 km/h in towns.

OPENING TIMES

Banks Hours vary, but banks are generally open between 9am & 4pm. Exchange bureaux may stay open later.
Shops Hours vary, but shops are generally open between 9am & 6pm (some later).

NATIONAL HOLIDAYS

New Year's Day, 24 Feb, Good Friday, 1 May, 23 & 24 Jun, 16 Nov, Christmas Day & Boxing Day.

Tourist Offices

Estonian Embassy in **London** Tel 0171-589 3428 (general information)
Tourist Board in Tallinn Tel 2-601 700
American Express Travel Service Offices or Representative (R)
Tallinn   Estravel Ltd (R)
             Suur-Karja 15
             (Box 3727)
             EE0090 Tallinn
             Tel 6-313 313

Tallinn

Tel: (02) 640 73 00   Fax: (02) 640 72 99
Vabaduse Valjak 3 EE0001 Tallinn

Enjoying a central location, the hotel dates back to the days of Estonia's previous independence in the 30s. The whole place was renovated in 1989, and a night club opened on the seventh floor. Some of the rooms are air-conditioned, and most have showers only (ten have just baths). Two of the suites have their own sauna. All the bedrooms have satellite TV and mini-bar. *Rooms 91. Room service all day. Conference facilities for 100. Bureau de change. Lobby bar (1000-2300). Free parking. Amex, Diners, Mastercard, Visa.*

THE APARTMENT SERVICE

Tel in UK (0181) 748 4207   Fax (0181) 748 3972

The Apartment Service will find you the right apartment worldwide to suit your needs, whether you are on a short or long-term stay. A 96-page colour catalogue is free on request. All budgets are catered for.

Finland

Currency Finnish Marks **Exchange Rate** £1=approx FIM 6.8
International dialling code 00 358 (Helsinki+0)
Passports/Visas No visa required by British passport holders.
British Consulate in Helsinki Tel 0-66 1293

Airports
Finnair 600-18100
Railway Stations 0-707 4085
Car hire
Tel nos **Avis** 0-859 841 **Budget** 0-685 3311 **Europcar** 0-755 6133
Hertz 0-7001 9000 **Toyota Ren** 0-8518 2585
Speed limits If no signposts 80km/h. 120km/h on motorways in
summer, 100km/h in winter. 50/60km/h in towns.

Banks 9.15am-4.15pm weekdays. Closed Sat, Sun.
Shops 9am-6pm weekdays (9am-8pm department stores weekdays),
9am-2pm Sat

New Year's Day, 6 Jan, Good Friday, Easter Sun & Mon, 30 Apr, 1, 16 &
26 May, 21 & 22 Jun, 2 Nov, 6 Dec, Christmas Eve, Christmas Day &
Boxing Day.

Finnish Tourist Board in **London** Tel 0171-839 4048
In **Helsinki** Tel 0-403 011
American Express Travel Service Offices or Representative (R)
Helsinki Area Travel Agency Ltd (R)
              Mikonkatu 2 D 2krs
              00100 Helsinki
              Tel 0-33 6055 #

Helsinki

Tel: (0) 639610   Fax: (0) 63 14 35
Pohjoisesplanadi 17, 00170 Helsinki

With marble floors and stone walls, this 19th-century former Tsarist nobleman's house makes an appropriately grand setting for some classical Russian cooking. In addition to the à la carte there is the fixed-price, no-choice Romanov menu with marinated salmon Stolichnaya before the main dish of reindeer à la stroganoff and Countess Likhachova's halva parfait to finish. Some 15 wines available by the glass. Set meal FIM250. *Seats 100. Open 1200-0000 (Sun in winter from 1800). Closed National Holidays. Street parking. Amex, Diners, Mastercard, Visa.*

Tel: (0) 626676   Fax: (0) 63 60 64
Sofiankatu 4, 00170 Helsinki

A two-storey 18th-century hall is the setting for a menu that includes both traditional Finnish fare and international dishes. The former might include herb-marinated fillet of elk with shallot and fennel compote, juniper-smoked reindeer with arctic cloudberry sauce and baked salmon with creamed morels; the latter game paté with cumberland sauce, escargots bourguignon, and roast lamb with pesto. Finish with meringue plum tart or gratinated berries with vanilla ice cream. There are about 150 bottles on the wine list. Set L FIM140 & FIM180. *Seats 99. Open 1100-2400 (Sat from 1700). Closed L Sat (all Sat in Jul), all Sun & National Holidays. Public parking. Amex, Diners, Mastercard, Visa.*

Tel (0) 179560   Fax (0) 63 69 85
Rahapajankatu 3, 00160 Helsinki

The oldest Russian restaurant in Helsinki, dating back to 1917, the Bellevue is located down a quiet old street in the city centre. Fillet of beef Novgorod (with sauerkraut and barley) and shashlik (lamb on a skewer) are particular specialities; other dishes include blini with fish roe, salted cucumber with honey and sour cream, snow grouse souvarov, beef stroganoff and cabbage rolls à la Moscow. On the wine front there are a dozen reds and a similar number of whites (from France and the New World) on offer with a couple of each available by the glass. Set L FIM70/FIM110 for 2 and 3 courses respectively. *Seats 100. Open 1100-2400 (Sat & Sun from 1700). Closed Christmas & Midsummer Holiday. Amex, Diners, Mastercard, Visa.*

Tel: (0) 666882   Fax: (0) 63 14 35
Unioninkatu 23, 00170 Helsinki

In the same building (and under the same management) as the *Alexander Nevski* (see above), the Havis Amanda is separate from it and specialises in seafood. Assorted Finnish fish roes, cold-pickled Baltic herrings, poached perch with a ragout of vegetables and butter sauce, chargrilled salmon with creamed morels and warm-smoked sea trout with red berries show the variety. For an unusual starter try herring ice cream with marinated herrings. There is always one meat dish on the menu. Desserts include almond cake with wild strawberry sauce and a saffron pear with lemon sorbet. Set meals FIM 225 & FIM 250 plus à la carte. *Seats 95. Open 1200-2400 (Sun from 1800). Closed Sun in winter. Amex, Diners, Mastercard, Visa.*

Tel: (0) 43101   Fax: (0) 43 10 995
Mannerheimintie 50, 00260 Helsinki

Conveniently located close to Töölö Bay and handy for both the main shopping streets and tourist sights (Congress Hall, National Museum, Opera House), the hotel was built in 1972 and has since numbered Elizabeth Taylor, Sammy Davis Jr, Pavarotti and Domingo among its more famous guests. Air-conditioned bedrooms are light, airy and well equipped, with mini-bars, room safes and good modern bathrooms. *Rooms 376. Closed 1 week Christmas. Room service all day. Garage parking FIM50 overnight, FIM7 per hr during the day. Conference facilities 450. Indoor swimming pool. Plunge pool. Sauna. Massage. Sun beds. Gymnasium. Golf simulator. Night club (Wed-Sun). Amex, Diners, Mastercard, Visa.*

Tel: (0) 6949446   Fax: (9) 88 86 760
Lapinlahdenkatu 12, 00180 Helsinki

No longer the only place in Helsinki where you can sample sushi but chef-owner, Mr Takayama, was the first to bring this particular delicacy to the people of Finland. Other Japanese specialities include tofu soup, fried squid with ginger, and sliced grilled fillet of beef with vegetables. Tuna is a particular house speciality, served as sashimi as well as sushi. Traditional sakés and Japanese beer are served along with a couple of French and Australian wines. Booking is advisable as there are just seven tables, of which two are very low (you sit on cushions) in the traditional Japanese style. *Seats 36. Open 1130-1400, 1700-2300 (Sun 1400-2300). Closed Sat & National Holidays. Street parking. Amex, Diners, Mastercard, Visa.*

Tel: (0) 440833   Fax: (0) 49 34 08
Mechelininkatu 39, 00250 Helsinki

At Tölöö Bay, ten minutes from the centre of Helsinki, this long-established restaurant serves both Finnish and international dishes from a longish à la carte which varies according to the seasons. Starters like pickled herring with cheese, salted salmon with mustard sauce, oysters mornay and game paté precede such mains as pike-perch with a shrimp sauce, breast of pheasant with game sauce, *coeur de filet provençale* (a speciality), and escalope of veal with a mushroom cream sauce. Nicely varied desserts range from deep-fried brie with raspberry jam to meringue cake with blackcurrant sauce. Set L FIM98 (buffet) & FIM125 plus the carte. Wines from all over the world on a shortish list. *Seats 120. Open 1100-2400 (Sat from 1600, Sun 1300-2100). Closed Christmas & Midsummer Holiday. Parking difficult. Diners, Mastercard, Visa.*

Tel: (0) 615815   Fax: (0) 68 01 315
Lönnrotinkatu 29, 00180 Helsinki

Built in 1903, the castle-like, greystone Lord Hotel is considered to be one of the finest examples of the Finnish Jugendstil. Public areas include groin-vaulted ceilings, some bold patterned frescos and numerous fascinating architectural features. All but one of the bedrooms are in a separate block built in the courtyard in the late 1980s. Comfortable and stylish with lightwood furniture and soft colour schemes, the rooms all have mini-bars and multi-channel TVs. *Rooms 48. Room service all day. Garage parking FIM60 per 24hrs. Conference facilities 200. Sauna. Spa bath. Amex, Diners, Mastercard, Visa.*

Tel (0) 134561   Fax: (0) 65 47 86
Eteläranta 10, 00130 Helsinki

Built for the Helsinki Olympics of 1952, this city-centre hotel was completely renovated just a couple of years ago. The first eight floors of the building are occupied by offices with the hotel bedrooms all on the ninth, main public rooms on the tenth and the sauna suite and American Bar enjoying the best of the views from the top floor. Air-conditioned bedrooms all have mini-bars and multi-channel TVs; Club rooms get various extras like bathrobes. A particular attraction is the afternoon tea (complete with little sandwiches and even scones on occasion) served free to guests from 4.30 to 5.30. *Rooms. 50. Room service 24hrs. Garage parking FIM55 per 24hrs. Conference facilities 200. Sauna. Amex, Diners, Mastercard, Visa.*

Tel: (0) 69580   Fax: (0) 69 58 71 00
Runberginkatu 2, 00100 Helsinki

Formerly the SAS Royal, this early-90s' hotel is ideally situated between the park, the beach and the centre of town. Bedrooms come in one of four decorative styles: Oriental, Italian, Scandinavian and art deco, but all share the same up-to-date facilities including air-conditioning. Some rooms are reserved for non-smokers and there are special rooms for disabled guests and those suffering from allergies. *Rooms 260. Room service all day. Conference facilities 300. Garage parking FIM80 per 24hrs. Sauna. Sun bed. Massage. Gymnasium. Amex, Diners, Mastercard, Visa.*

See over

Restaurant Johan Ludvig   FIM650

The dining-room features a chargrill from which come various steaks with a choice of sauces – béarnaise, choron, red wine-and grilled fillet of reindeer with a pepper sauce. Other dishes from a shortish, mainly international, menu include gravlax with dill mustard sauce, snails in garlic, French onion soup and roast rack of lamb with thyme sauce. Desserts from the trolley plus home-made apple pie, cheesecake with melba sauce and ices. No smoking. *Seats 66. Open 1130-1430, 1800-2300. Closed Sun, National Holidays and several weeks in midsummer.*

HELSINKI   Ramada Presidentti   FIM1178

Tel: (0) 6911   Fax: (0) 69 47 886
Eteläinen Rautatiekatu 4, 00100 Helsinki

Eight-storey hotel right in the centre of town. Air-conditioned bedrooms, all recently renovated, are modern, simply decorated and well equipped. In addition to some designed for wheelchair-bound guests there are special rooms for people with allergies (parquet floors, special fabrics), some brand new 'environmental' rooms that incorporate various energy saving devices, and one floor of rooms reserved for non-smokers. The hotel also houses a state-owned casino from which all the profits go to charity. *Rooms 495. Room service all day. Parking FIM96 per 24hrs. Conference facilities 400. Indoor swimming pool. Saunas. Physiotherapy. Massage. Casino. Amex, Diners, Mastercard, Visa.*

HELSINKI   Rivoli   FIM350

Tel: (0) 643455   Fax: (0) 64 77 80
Albertinkatu 38, 00180 Helsinki

Several venues under one roof here with a choice of eating and surroundings. Kala is a fish restaurant done out to resemble an old Atlantic liner with lots of polished wood and brass portholes, offering the likes of crispy-fried Baltic herrings with mashed potatoes, perch fillets stuffed with dill and onions, and grilled salmon with spinach. In the Bistro Rivoli the cooking is French in style-steak tartare, chateaubriand steak with a choice of sauces, sweetbreads with mustard sauce and ratatouille – and the decor art nouveau. A pizzeria provides yet another option and, new this year, the Last Hope Bar offers snacks and drinking till the early hours. *Seats 200. Open 1100-2400 (Sat & Sun from 1800). Closed Sat & Sun (Jun & Jul), Christmas, Easter & Midsummer Holiday. Street parking. Amex, Diners, Mastercard, Visa.*

HELSINKI   Sipuli   FIM650

Tel: (0) 179929   Fax: (0) 63 06 62
Kanavaranta 3, 00160 Helsinki

Models of old sailing boats form part of the decor at this traditional restaurant set in a turn-of-the-century former store-house. A sensibly short but high-class carte might include slightly-salted Arctic char with a roe and chive mousse and green asparagus; Parma ham, melon and papaya savarin, and sweetbread terrine with braised red cabbage among the starters and mains like scallops and scampi au gratin with champagne sauce, sautéed veal with lentils and a truffle sauce, and grilled reindeer fillet with puréed cranberries and a mushroom pasty. Finish with Arctic bramble ice cream or a selection of cheese, fruit and biscuits. *Seats 140. Open D only 1800-2400. Closed Sat, Sun, National Holidays & 24 Jun-8 Aug. Amex, Diners, Mastercard, Visa.*

HELSINKI   Sokos Hotel Vaakuna   FIM1140

Tel: (0) 131181   Fax: (0) 13 11 82 34
Asema-aukio 2, 00100 Helsinki

Sharing a building with a popular department store, City Sokos, the hotel occupies the fifth to eighth floors. Despite being in the city centre, and only 80m from the main railway station, rooms are surprisingly quiet; all are air-conditioned and about 25% are reserved for non-smokers. Two saunas were being built during the summer of 1995. *Rooms 288. Conference facilities 10. Parking in nearby public car parks. Amex, Diners, Mastercard, Visa.*

Meal prices for 2 are based on à la carte menus. When set menus are
available, prices will often be lower.

HELSINKI   Hotel Strand Inter-Continental   FIM1517

Tel: (0) 39351   Fax: (0) 39 35 255
John Stenbergin Ranta 4, 00530 Helsinki

The hotel is on Siltasaari, the former island turned peninsula, right by the waterfront alongside the old city centre and with great views over the harbour and up to the Gulf of Finland. The rooms are equipped with every facility one would expect in an international hotel from air-conditioning to mini-bars and there are jacuzzis in five of the eight suites. Birch bedheads are an elegant touch, as is the Lapland marble and Finnish stone that features in the public areas. *Rooms 200. Closed Christmas & Easter. Room service 24hrs. Conference facilities 250. Valet parking FIM80 per 24hrs. Amex, Diners, Mastercard, Visa.*

Restaurant Pamir   FIM750

The à la carte offers just three or four choices at each stage-warm duck liver with morel mousse, fillet of reindeer with sea buckthornberry sauce, breast of pheasant with cloudberry sauce and beetroot pie, apple pudding with cinnamon ice cream-but if even that represents too much decision-making to face after a hard day go for the five-course, no-choice Chef Recommends menu (FIM490 inclusive of wine); tartar of Arctic char with horseradish mousse followed by sea buckthornberry sorbet before a main dish of herb-marinated breast of snow grouse with cress sauce, and then a selection of Finnish cheese with Arctic brambleberry ice cream to finish was the offering one day last summer. Most wine-growing regions are represented on a longish list. *Seats 65. Open D only 1800-2400. Closed Sat, Sun & mid Jul-mid Aug.*

Opening times are often liable to change at short notice, so it's always best to book.

HELSINKI   SVENSKA TEATERN   FIM750

Tel: (0) 1354706   Fax: (0) 13 54 896
Maurinkatu 6, 00170 Helsinki

Close to the sea, just over a kilometre from the town centre, this restaurant is set in a turn-of-the-century former private house. There are several function rooms capable of coping with quite large numbers (200 in one room, 700 in total) but independent diners head for the A la Carte Room to enjoy traditional Finnish cuisine: marinated filet of beef with mustard sauce, baked salmon with a morel sauce, pike-perch with horseradish sauce. In addition to a short carte there are three no-choice set menus at FIM120, 180 & 240. *Seats 50 Open 1200-2400. Closed Sun, mid Jun-mid Aug & National Holidays. Street parking. Amex, Diners, Mastercard, Visa.*

HELSINKI   TORNI HOTEL   FIM750

Tel: (0) 131131   Fax: (0) 13 11 361
Yrjönkatu 26, 00100 Helsinki

The name means 'Tower' and this 30s' hotel is the tallest building in Helsinki-you can see five cities from the top. In the 80s the turn-of-the-century, art nouveau building next door was annexed by the hotel and the rooms in this part have just been refurbished in an appropriate art nouveau style. Rooms in the tower favour the art deco look. Whichever takes your fancy all rooms are air-conditioned and come with mini-bars and multi-channel TVs. There are special rooms for the disabled and for those suffering from allergies. Reception is an elegant glass-roofed hall. *Rooms 152. Closed 2 weeks Christmas. Room service during restaurant hours. Conference facilities 10. Parking in adjacent public car park, concessionary rate of FIM40 between 1600 and 1000 to hotel guests. Saunas. Amex, Diners, Mastercard, Visa.*

Ritarisali means knights' hall; modern-day guests are treated to a menu of largely Finnish delicacies such as tartare of slightly salted salmon and fish roe, fillet of reindeer marinated in herbs with balsamic vinegar, tournedos of hare with ceps and, for afters, a soup of buckthornberries with honey ice cream. The menu is well balanced between game, meat and fish. There is a special game menu in season. *Seats 120. Open 1130-1430, 1800-2400.*

Tampere

Tel: (31) 2441111   Fax: (31) 22 33 375
Pyynikintie 13, 33230 Tampere

Conference-orientated, 70s-built hotel about ten minutes out from the city centre, next to a lake, and surrounded by a national park. Air-conditioned bedrooms are simple and functional in style but all come with mini-bar and multi-channel TV. Three single rooms are specially adapted for the disabled and one floor of rooms is designated for non-smokers. *Rooms 213. Room service all day. Conference facilities 700. Free open parking. Tennis. Indoor swimming pool. Sauna. Sun beds. Squash. Golf simulator. Amex, Diners, Mastercard, Visa.*

The same straightforward menu is shared by the hotel's main restaurant and the smaller Cantina Rosa (located in the hotel lobby). White fish in onion cream sauce with dill potatoes, grilled escalope of pork with mushroom sauce, chicken breast with apricot sauce and pasta, and entrecote with garlic butter typify the main dishes. *Seats 280 (+ 75 in Cantina Rosa). Open 1200-2400 (from 0900 in Cantina Rosa).*

Tel: (31) 2121191   Fax: (31) 21 21 192
Satamakatu 7, 33200 Tampere

Finnish dishes and those from other European climes mix happily on the menu here. Slightly salted white fish tartare and mozzarella toast both appear among the starters and mains include feta cheese ravioli, fried breast of chicken with cherry sauce, smoked chateaubriand with juniper berry sauce, and calf's liver and bacon. Just 25 wines on the list selected from around the world. *Seats 95. Open 1100-1500, 1700-2400 (till 2300 in summer). Closed Sun in summer, Christmas, Easter & 4-24 July. Street parking. Amex, Diners, Mastercard, Visa.*

Tel (31) 2121220   Fax: (31) 212 12 19
Kauppakatu 10, 33210 Tampere

Set in brick cellars under the art nouveau-style halls of residence of the old Tampere University, this antique-furnished, family-run restaurant is very atmospheric. The menu ranges from cold-smoked, slightly-salted salmon with beetroot purée; grilled goat's cheese; fennel cream soup; guinea fowl with honey and walnut sauce; fillet of lamb grilled on a skewer with herb aïoli; fried Finnish perch with crayfish sauce, and smoked duck breast with mango sauce to desserts like chocolate cake with chocolate ice cream and marinated orange with pistachio. The wine list features France and the New World. Set L FIM65. *Seats 160. Open 1100 -1500, 1700-2400 (Sat 1200-2400). Closed L for 2 weeks mid-Jul, all Sun & National Holidays. Amex, Diners, Mastercard, Visa.*

Currency: French Franc **Exchange Rate** £1=approx 7.68F
International dialling code 00 33 (Paris+1)
Passports/Visas No visa required by British passport holders.
British Consulate in Paris Tel 1-42 66 91 42 Fax 1-40 76 02 87

Airports Roissy Charles de Gaulle Tel 1-48 62 22 80;
Orly Tel 1-49 75 15 15; **Le Bourget** Tel 48 62 12 12,
Lyon-Satolas Tel 72 22 72 05; **Marseilles-Provence** Tel 42 78 21 00;
Nice-Cote d'Azur Tel 93 21 30 12; **Strasbourg** Tel 88 64 67 67.
Rail
SNCF Paris Tel 1-45 65 60 60. French Railways Ltd, 179 Piccadilly,
London W1 Tel 0891 515477.
Car hire Contact UK international branches for information
Tel nos. **Avis** 0181-848 8733 **Budget** 0800 181181 **EuroDollar**
0895 233300 **Hertz** 0181 679 1799/1777.
Speed limits 130km/h on toll motorways, 110km/h on dual
carriages/motorways without tolls, 90km/h on other roads, 50km/h in
towns. 50km/h on motorways in foggy conditions, when visibility is less
than 50m, also special speed limits on wet roads.

Banks 9am-noon, 2-4pm weekdays. Closed either Sat or Mon, and
early the day before a National Holiday.
Shops 9/10am-6.30/7pm Mon-Sat. Many closed all day or half day Mon.

New Year's Day, Easter Sun & Mon, 1, 8, 16, 26 & 27 May, 14 Jul, 15
Aug, 1 & 11 Nov, Christmas Day.

French Tourist Board in **London** Tel 0891-244 123
In **France** Paris Tel 1-49 52 53 54 Bordeaux Tel 56 44 28 41
Lille Tel 20 30 81 00 Lyons Tel 78 42 25 75 Nice Tel 93 87 07 07 Reims
Tel 26 47 25 69 Strasbourg Tel 88 52 28 22
Toulouse Tel 61 11 02 22/61
American Express Travel Service Offices or Representative (R)
        Tel 78 37 40 69 #

Paris	11 Rue Scribe 75009 Tel 1-47 77 70 07/47 77 79 79 #	**Lyons**	6 Rue Childebert 69002
Paris-City	5 Rue De Chaillot 75116 Tel 1-47 23 72 15 #	**Marseilles**	Canebiere Voyages (R) 39 La Canebiere 13001 Tel 91 13 71 21
Paris-Reg	91 Avenue Pierre Grenier Boulogne-Billancourt 92100 Tel 1-46 20 48 06	**Nice**	11 Promenade Des Anglais 06048 Tel 93 16 53 53 #
Bordeaux	14 Cours Intendance 33000 Tel 56 81 70 02/56 44 47 57 #	**Strasbourg**	31 Place Kleber 67000 Tel 88 75 78 75

Aix-en-Provence

Tel/Fax: 42 27 21 06
10 rue de la Couronne, 13001 Aix-en-Provence

R

There is a reassuringly traditional feel to this centrally-located restaurant with its stone floor and wood panelling. Chef Jean-Marc Taillefer previously worked at the *Petit Nice Passédat* (qv) in Marseilles and has kept his seasonal menu simple, based on fresh, local ingredients. *Marinade de saumon aux tomates confites, pot-au-feu et foie gras à la marjolaine* (boiled beef and vegetables in a broth with foie gras and marjoram) and *ris de veau* (calf's sweetbreads) aux courgettes are typical dishes. Desserts, such as coulis of red fruits, are also refreshingly straightforward. Set menus start at 125F and the *menu dégustation* is 280F. The wine list features some good local bottles. *Seats 50. Open 1200-1400, 1930-2300. Closed L Thu, all Wed (during Jul & Aug open D every night, closed L Sat, Sun & Mon). Amex, Diners, Mastercard, Visa.*

Around Aix-en-Provence

Tel: 42 58 68 54   Fax: 42 58 68 05
Le Canet de Meyreuil, 13590 Meyreuil

R

Gabriel Astouric's restaurant is located a few kilometres south-east of Aix in a lovely rural setting. The appearance of the place is as typically Provençal as the food, which is assembled from a wonderful profusion of specialities to be found in this region. Courgette flowers stuffed with salmon in a lightly vinegared dressing, red mullet of a bed of jellied ratatouille and lamb smoked with thyme and rosemary drizzled with local olive oil are typical of the starters. Fish dishes could include a splendid panaché of the day's market selection flavoured with verbena and carrot juice, or codling with multicoloured noodles and a fennel sauce, while for meat the choice could be lamb fillet with pan-fried noodles and a curry sauce, rabbit leg with a herb crust served with puréed potato or sliced duck breast with wild mushrooms and a red berry sauce. For dessert, try the local speciality – *calisson* – an almond pastry, here served with melon preserve. Private parking. *Seats 50. Open 1200-1400, 2000-2200. Closed D Tue, all Wed, 2 weeks Feb. Private car park. Amex, Diners, Mastercard, Visa.*

Les Baux-de-Provence

Tel: 90 54 33 21   Fax: 90 54 45 98
13520 Les Baux-de-Provence

H

In a secluded location, with a flower garden and rockeries, this hotel is owned by the same family as *Oustau de Baumanière* (qv). Reception and the restaurant are in one building, bedrooms in another, plus more rooms, in a third. Most of the air-conditioned rooms were redecorated in 1995 and the bedrooms are furnished with reproduction antique furniture, the apartments with the real thing. Breakfast can be taken on the main terrace or, in the case of 12 rooms, on their own balconies. *Rooms 22. Room service limited. Private parking. Banqueting facilities 100. Conference facilities 100. Outdoor swimming pool. Tennis. Children's play area. Amex, Diners, Mastercard, Visa.*

Tel: 90 54 33 07   Fax: 90 54 45 29
13520 Les Baux-de-Provence

HR

A 500-year old mas and its annexes, beautifully surrounded by trees, rocks and vines, offers luxurious and charming rustic accommodation (canopy beds, beams, fireplaces, and period furniture). Continental breakfast only. Tennis, horse-riding and golf nearby. *Rooms 20. Conference facilities. Swimming pool. Closed mid Jan-Mar, also Wed Nov-mid Jan. Amex, Diners, Mastercard, Visa.*

Restaurant   ★ ★ ★   1800F

Created by the legendary Raymond Thuilier, the restaurant used to be one of the 16th-century outbuildings attached to the Chateau des Baux, 100m up the road, and it still retains most of the original features, like the impressive vaulted ceiling, stone walls and wood panelling, offset by colourful tablecloths designed by the owners. Carrying on his grandfather's proud tradition, chef-patron Jean-André Charial and his team have adopted a strong Mediterranean/Southern style of cooking, which, added to the Provençal ingredients readily available, gives subtle and inventive flavours: *salade de homard dans sa gelée au safran*; swordfish brochette with liquorice; *fricassée de sole et palourdes au beurre leger de romarin*, fillet of beef with anchovies or Gers duckling roasted with peaches. Not to be missed are desserts such as hot pistachio soufflé with an almond syrup, *plie au chocolat aux fruits rouges* and a super selection of sorbets. Massive wine list, including a wine (Chateau de Romarin) from their 50-acre vineyard nearby. *Seats 100. Open 1200-1430, 1930-2130. Closed as above, also L Thu.*

LES BAUX-DE-PROVENCE   La Riboto de Tavern ★   900F

Tel: 90 54 34 23   Fax 90: 54 38 88
Les Baux de Provence 13520

Jean-Pierre Novi's parents started this restaurant in an 18th-century Provençal farm and he himself has been cooking since he was tall enough to reach the table. After a successful period at *Le Provence*, Bournemouth, and a short stint at *Gordleton Mill*, Lymington, he returned here to live and work. This is a delightful restaurant situated right on the edge of a cliff in the centre of Les Baux village (65km from Aix); the two dining-rooms, simply furnished in Provençal style, are actually built into the rock. The cooking is as unusual as the decor, with lively interpretations of traditional regional dishes. Lobster could appear in various guises – in lasagne with finely diced vegetables, in a salad with basil, or sautéed with *hyringus* (an intriguing decoction of ginger, carrots and honey) and finished with muscat de Beaumes-de-Venise. Note also sea bass with a kumquat vinaigrette, saddle of Provence lamb with thyme and *soupe au pistou*, and chicken breast with girolles. Besides the carte, there are various fixed-price menus: 198F at lunchtime only including wine and coffee; 295F; and, for the whole table only, 420F (580F with appropriate wines by the glass). *Seats 40. Open 1200-1400, 1930-2130. Closed D Tue (Oct-Jun), all Wed, 10 Jan-mid Mar. Private parking. Amex, Diners, Mastercard, Visa.*

Bordeaux

BORDEAUX   Burdigala   990F

Tel: 56 90 16 16   Fax: 56 93 15 06
115 rue Georges Bonnac, 33000 Bordeaux

Burdigala is the Latin name for Bordeaux and this hotel is situated on the edge of the Mériadeck business district, a few minutes walk from Place Gambetta and the main shopping area. Although built in 1988, its external architecture is typically Bordelais while the interior is modern but cosy. The air-conditioned, individually-decorated bedrooms are spacious and well designed and have luxurious marble or granite bathrooms. Service is particularly friendly. *Rooms 83. Room service limited. Private parking 45F. Banqueting facilities 100. Conference facilities 100. Amex, Diners, Mastercard, Visa.*

BORDEAUX   Le Chapon Fin   ★   900F

Tel: 56 79 10 10   Fax: 56 79 09 10
5 rue Montesquieu, 33000 Bordeaux

Catalan Francis Garcia and his French wife, Geraldine, have established a formidable reputation in Bordeaux for imaginative, colourful cooking. Their specialities include *lamproie à la bordelaise* and saddle of young wild rabbit with a tartlet of snails. Inevitably, Garcia's Spanish background comes through strongly in some dishes, such as lobster gazpacho and *piquillos farcis d'homard* (baby peppers stuffed with lobster). Even in some typically French dishes, he introduces exquisite (if cosmetic) Spanish touches, witness the *terrine de ris de veau et foie gras* decorated like a miniature Miro painting. The well-priced and stocked wine cellar is particularly good on half bottles. The interior of their restaurant resembles a grotto, with rock walls, masses of plants and a skylight in the ceiling. Set menus from 140F to 400F. *Seats 50. Open 1200-1400, 2000-2200. Closed Sun, also Mon in Jul & Aug). Public parking 8F. Amex, Diners, Mastercard, Visa.*

BORDEAUX   Jean Ramet   ★   500F   R

Tel: 56 44 12 51   Fax: 56 52 19 80
7/8 place Jean Jaurès, 33000 Bordeaux

Located on the quayside of La Garonne, between the Stock Exchange, the theatre and the Quinconces, the restaurant is as typically Bordelais as any in the city. The building dates from the 18th century and was a fishmonger's shop before being converted into a restaurant in 1982. Inside, it is sturdily rustic in decor with wood panelling and plenty of bare stone. Jean Ramet trained under the Troisgros brothers and considers his cooking to be classic in style and free from culinary acrobatics. He prides himself on the purity and simplicity of his dishes and, as a trained patissier, his *feuilleté* dishes, such as *feuilleté d'huitres au caviar*, are a particular treat. Another fine speciality dish is *escalope de foie frais de canard au vinaigre de framboises* (fresh duck liver with raspberry vinegar). His methods may be straightforward and his ingredients basic, but the end result is often decidedly unusual, for instance, *gaspacho de homard à la vanille* (lobster gazpacho with a vanilla sauce). Desserts include peaches and morello cherries with a spiced ice cream. Set menus from 155F (lunch) and 240F (dinner). Wines are from all over France and include the excellent Graves, Chateau Chantegrive. *Seats 35. Open 1215-1400, 1945-2200. Closed Sat & Sun (open L Sat Oct-Mar). Public parking. Closed Amex, Mastercard, Visa.*

BORDEAUX   Hôtel de Normandie   600F   H

Tel: 56 52 16 80   Fax: 56 51 68 91
7 cours du Trente Juillet, 33000 Bordeaux

A friendly, comfortable hotel looking out on to Place de Quinconces in a pleasantly old-fashioned area of the city. The building, with its original brick facade, is 300 years old and has been run as a hotel by the same family for three generations. Bedrooms are air-conditioned and double-glazed. There is a bar but no restaurant. *Rooms 100. Room service limited. Conference facilities 50. Amex, Diners, Mastercard, Visa.*

BORDEAUX   Le Pavillon des Boulevards   950F   R

Tel: 56 81 51 02   Fax: 56 51 14 58
120 rue Croix de Seguey, 33000 Bordeaux

Monsieur and Madame Franc bought this typical Bordelais house and converted into a restaurant ten years ago. The majority of the clientele are locals who appreciate the quality and adventurous nature of the cooking, which often uses unusual (and sometimes startling) combinations of ingredients: for instance, *les Saint-Jacques au jus d'herbes, artichauts sautés aux pieds et oreilles de porc* (scallops cooked in herbs and served with sautéed artichokes, pig's trotters and pig's ears). More conventional dishes include the popular *foie gras de canard aux épices douces, marmelade de pommes* (lightly spiced duck foie gras served with an apple compote). The wine list does not ignore bottles from outside Bordeaux and the sommelier can be relied upon to recommend the best wines to suit individual tastes and pockets. Set menus 200F (lunch) and from 270F to 420F (dinner). *Seats 45 (garden 30). Open 1200-1345, 2000-2215. Closed L Sat, all Sun, 1-10 Jan, 11-19 Aug. Amex, Diners, Mastercard, Visa.*

Cannes

CANNES   Carlton Inter-Continental   1750F   HR

Tel: 93 06 40 06   Fax: 93 06 40 25
58 bd La Croisette, 06400 Cannes

The Carlton today is still the place to stay and be seen in Cannes. Its location at the centre of La Croisette and its likeness to a huge wedding cake, with the famous cupolas, ensures that its very presence dominates the seafront. Its rooms and apartments have all been refurbished in elegant style to match the wonderful high ceilings of most of the rooms, which are fully air-conditioned. Furnishings match the elegance in all rooms, but the suites in particular have, in addition, some lovely antique furniture. The best rooms and suites are situated on the front of the building overlooking the sea, and the higher up the better the views. Bathrooms are in marble with elegant fittings: the bigger rooms, again generally on the front elevation, have enormous bathrooms with double basins and separate shower. Towels are luxurious and plentiful and valeting facilities for guests are first class and provided as fast as one could hope for in any hotel. There is even the choice of having your starched shirts hung or folded! Among the public rooms the entrance lobby is particularly impressive with its double-height ceiling and marble floors and columns. Adjacent to this are the listed banqueting rooms with wonderful gilded ceilings and ornate mirrors. The Café Carlton and Piano Bar are situated at the far end of the lounge and open on to the famous Carlton Terrace which overlooks La Croisette. There is also a small lobby Caviar Bar called Le Petit Bar, which is near the main reception area. On the penthouse seventh floor is the Carlton Casino Club with its Casino Restaurant and terrace overlooking the sea. Additionally there are a number of shops within a small arcade, and the hotel has its own garage for 100 cars at the rear of the building. *Rooms 349. Amex, Diners, Mastercard, Visa.*

La Belle Otéro   1000F

Tel: 93 68 00 33   Fax: 93 39 09 06

A restaurant in classic style near the top of the hotel, La Belle Otéro takes its name from a celebrated 19th-century courtesan who loved gambling and Spanish dancing. Chef Chauveau's cooking is Mediterranean with a particular penchant for seafood and an emphasis on interesting sauces and stylish presentation. Dishes to note include *loup roti au parmesan*, purée of petits pois with morels, langoustines and smoked bacon, blue lobster roasted with broad beans and purple asparagus, and *croustillant de fruits rouges à l'anis*. *Seats 80. Open 1200-1400, 1930-2300. Closed L mid Jun-mid Sep, all Sun & Mon mid Sep-mid Jun, also 1st 2 weeks Nov, 3 weeks Jun/Jul.*

CANNES   Hotel Martinez   920F

HR

Tel: 92 98 73 00   Fax: 93 39 67 82
73 bd La Croisette, 06400 Cannes

Built in the 1920s, when the area attracted starlets and paparazzi like bees to a honeypot, many celebrities and would-be stars have since stayed here. The Concorde Hotel group now own it and have recently renovated the older, more traditional wing (with 144 rooms) and 286 more modern rooms. The art deco entrance, which looks over the waterfront, and the old Waring and Gillow English furniture undoubtedly add glamour, but the real attractions here are the excellent amenities: theatre-style conference facilities for up to 750 people, a swimming pool, private beach and tennis courts. The large bar opens on to a little garden and the pool. *Rooms 430. 24hr room service. Satellite TV/fax. Secretarial/translation/valet services on request. Private/valet parking. Amex, Mastercard, Visa.*

Restaurant La Palme d'Or   1400F

Owned by the same company as the Hotel de Crillon in Paris, this restaurant, and menu, owes much to the quirkiness of the chef, Christian Willer: customers can even ask for a table for five in the kitchen. His menu has been strongly influenced by his love of Mediterranean cooking and its heavy emphasis on fish and creative use of vegetables: *salade de rouget* (red mullet served in a chilled salad), *langouste rose de mediterranée* (pink Mediterranean crayfish salad) and *loup de mer bouché aux petits légume*s (sea bass served in a vol-au-vent with fresh mixed vegetables). The à la carte menu also has some delicate pigeon, veal and chicken dishes. The dégustation at 550F offers the best value. *Seats 80. Open 1200-1400, 1930-2230. Closed Mon & Tue.*

> Meal prices for 2 are based on à la carte menus. When set menus are
> available, prices will often be lower.

Around Cannes

AURIBEAU-SUR-SIAGNE   Auberge de la Vignette Haute   1090F

HR

Tel: 93 42 20 01   Fax: 93 42 31 16
370 route du Village, 06810 Auribeau-sur-Siagne

Situated on the edge of the Massif Central, in blissfully peaceful countryside but only 15km north of Cannes, this small, friendly hotel offers first-class comforts in rustic surroundings. The original buildings burned down in a fire in 1986, but the current owner, Jean-Jacques Meyer, bought the charred ruins and rebuilt it, using as many of the original materials as could be salvaged. With its stone walls and floors, old beams and individually decorated bedrooms, furnished with antiques, the auberge still feels wonderfully old. *Rooms 12. Room service limited. Private parking. Banqueting facilities 180. Conference facilities 50. Secretarial services on request. Amex, Mastercard, Visa.*

See over

Restaurant   1000F

Not many restaurants can boast a stable, complete with donkey and other animals, to
entertain diners. One of the three rooms in the restaurant features just such an attraction
(behind a glass wall) while the other rooms have a 'medieval' and a 'sheepfold' theme. The
decor is as warmly rustic as the hotel and oil-lamps add to the feeling of intimacy. Belgian
chef Bernard Peeters cooks traditional and updated Provençal dishes with great style and his
seasonal menu might include fricassee of lobster tails with a Sauternes sauce, noisettes of
lamb with a sweet garlic purée and sautéed courgettes, and a classic *aïoli à l'huile d'olive
douce*. The set menus at 145F and 200F (lunch) and 390F and 500F (dinner) all include
wine. In summer, you can eat on the terrace, which commands marvellous views of the
surrounding countryside. *Seats 130 (terrace 70). Open 1200-1400, 2000-2230.
Closed 15 Nov-5 Dec.*

JUAN-LES-PINS   Juana   1980F

Tel: 93 61 08 70   Fax: 93 61 73 60
La Pinède, avenue Gallice, 06160 Juan-les-Pins   HR

In a town overrun with pizzerias, the Juana is one of the last bastions of F Scott Fitzgerald-
style charm. Built in 1931, it is now in the third generation of the friendly Barache family,
and, although facilities are modern, it still has a feeling of carefree, pre-war glamour which
has made it a popular haunt of showbiz stars. The hotel has an outdoor heated swimming
pool within its gardens and is separated from the sea by a pine grove. Although meeting
facilities are limited, there is a major conference centre next door. *Rooms 51.
Room service 24hr. Private parking. Conference facilities 20. Garden.
Outdoor swimming pool. Mastercard, Visa.*

Restaurant La Terrasse   1400F

On taking over from the famed Alain Ducasse in 1987, the current chef, Christian
Morisset, must have been apprehensive, but he has more than preserved the high
reputation of the restaurant with his imaginative interpretations of traditional Provençal
dishes. Seafood plays a major role on the seasonal carte, and dishes include *Saint-Pierre du
pays roti sur l'arete, cannelloni d'aubergine à l'origan, gastrique au rosmarin frais* (John
Dory roasted on the bone with aubergine cannelloni flavoured with fresh rosemary).
Alternatively, diners can choose the fish, such as gilt-head bream or sea bass, and the
method of cooking: roasted in basil butter or grilled with olive oil and lemon, for instance.
Set menus from 260F. *Seats 80 (terrace 80). Open 1230-1400, 1930-2200 (2230 in high
season). Closed Wed (except 1 Jul-1 Sep).*

MOUGINS   Le Moulin de Mougins   ★+ 1500F

Tel: 93 75 78 24   Fax: 93 90 18 55
Quartier Notre Dame de Vie, 06250 Mougins   R

A 16th-century olive oil mill, 6km from Cannes but in the depths of the countryside, is
where you will find Roger and Denise Vergé's internationally renowned restaurant. The
lovely setting, surrounded by palms and mimosa, is matched by the splendid interior, which
makes use of the original wood and stone and displays a fine collection of contemporary art
from the likes of César, Farhi and Folon. Roger and his trusty right-hand man in the
kitchen, Serge Chollet, have been working together for 21 years and continue to produce
some stunning examples of traditional French *cuisine modernisé*. They are renowned for
their extraordinary attention to detail in both preparation and presentation of food, as in
*consommé double au parfum de morilles et son oeuf cuit en vapeur de truffe noire de
Vaucluse* (double-filtered consommé perfumed with morel mushrooms and served with
a egg scented with black Vaucluse truffles). The menu changes with the seasons but might
include *blanc de loup de ligne en matignon de légumes truffés cuit à la feuille, courte
sauce au vin de Madère* (fillet of line-caught bass wrapped and cooked in cabbage or
spinach leaves and served with a Madeira sauce) and *fricassée de homard breton au poivre
rose et crème de Sauternes* (lobster fricasseed with pink pepper and a creamy Sauternes
sauce). If you have problems choosing between the equally fine desserts (such as bitter
chocolate mousse with a coffee bean sauce), why not try a little of each with the plate of
mini-desserts, or perhaps simply settle for a selection of Savoie cheeses. The wine list
balances grand crus against excellent local bottles. Set menus at 315F (lunch) and 615F and
740F (dinner). The restaurant has five very popular rooms from 950F per night including
breakfast. *Seats 120. Open 1230-1430, 1930-2230. Closed L Thu, all Mon (open D Mon
15 Jul-30 Aug), 12 Feb-12 Mar. Valet parking. Amex, Diners, Mastercard, Visa.*

Nice   Négresco   1540F
HR

Tel: 93 88 39 51   Fax: 93 88 35 68
37 promenade des Anglais, 06000 Nice

When impoverished Romanian Henri Négresco came to France to seek his fortune as a young man he could little have imagined that he would one day build one of the grandest hotels in the south of France, on Nice's most famous boardwalk. The hotel opened in 1912 and the list of illustrious guests reads like a Who's Who of the 20th century: Winston Churchill, Ernest Hemingway, Jean Cocteau, The Beatles, Bardot, Brando... Its vibrant decor is a mix of highly-stylised Belle Epoque and almost everything else imaginable. For instance, the landing of the fifth floor is in Napoleon III style, on the fourth it's Empire, on the third, Louis XV. Numerous exquisite antiques decorate the public rooms: 17th-century tapestries, a 19th-century Baccarat crystal chandelier commissioned by the Tsar of Russia, and some superb stained glass from the workshops of Gustav Eiffel. The air-conditioned bedrooms are also furnished with beautiful period pieces. Service combines respectful formality with super-efficiency. *Rooms 150. Room service 24hr. Valet parking. Banqueting facilities 400. Conference facilities 600. Terrace. Amex, Diners, Mastercard, Visa.*

Restaurant Chantecler   1100F

Chef Dominique Le Stanc may be from Alsace but here he has taken full-blooded Provençal cuisine to his heart with wonderful results. In addition to two set menus (430F and 490F) the maitre d' can suggest a special selection of the chef's specialities at 550F per person, or you can choose from the carte (written in English as well as French). Starters include salad of langoustines, diced veal cheek and orange slices, served on a bed of fresh spinach, chilled soup of local white beans with smoked pigeon slices and spring onions, and red mullet terrine with courgettes, tomatoes, basil and aïoli. Most of the tempting mains are roasted dishes, such as roast fillet of sea bass, served with *socca* (chick pea-flour pancakes), fennel and olive oil flavoured with aniseed, and roast pigeon with cumin, garnished with young potatoes and red onions. Unusually for France, there is always a good selection of vegetarian dishes, such as fresh pasta with wild mushrooms and sautéed courgettes. Desserts match the quality of the rest of the dishes. House specialities include warm chocolate tart with almond-flavoured ice cream, and layers of liquorice-flavoured meringue, whipped cream and raspberry sorbet. *Seats 50. Open 1230-1430, 1930-2230. Closed mid Nov-mid Dec.*

Tel: 92 00 72 00   Fax: 92 04 18 10
30 boulevard Maurice Maeterlinck, 06300 Nice

Originally a private club, the hotel opened five years ago, although part of the building dates back to the beginning of the century. It enjoys a secluded location, set in its own gardens and wonderful views out to sea. Bedrooms are individually decorated with light, plain colours and modern furniture. Leisure amenities are good: there's a swimming pool, fitness centre and private beach, but business facilities are limited to two small conference rooms. The hotel also has its own helipad. Note that the hotel and restaurant are closed throughout the winter. *Rooms 28. Closed Nov-Feb. Room service limited. Valet parking. Banqueting facilities 160. Conference facilities 25. Swimming pool. Gym. Amex, Diners, Mastercard, Visa.*

Traditional Provençal cuisine is cooked with a refreshing lightness of touch here and, given the location, it's no surprise to find fish a firm favourite. The menu changes weekly but often includes specialities such as courgette flowers stuffed with salmon, red mullet tapénade and *turbot en écaille de courgettes* (turbot wrapped in ribbons of courgettes). Desserts such as *moelleux de chocolat et sorbet framboise* are also excellent. You can eat in either of the two large dining-rooms, one with thick burgundy carpets and sober wood panelling, the other marble-floored, on an enclosed veranda overlooking the sea. Set menus at 140F (buffet lunch) and 240F for the dinner *menu gastronomique*. *Seats 80 (terrace 50). Open 1200-1430, 1930-2200. Closed as hotel.*

Meal prices for 2 are based on à la carte menus. When set menus are available, prices will often be lower.

Lille

LILLE   A l'Huîtrière   1000F

Tel: 20 55 43 41   Fax: 20 55 23 10
3 rue des Chats Bossus, 59800 Lille

The gracious and friendly owner, Monsieur Proye, was born in the house that is now his restaurant. In his grandfather's time, it was a snail and oyster shop (hence the name) and seafood remains the core of the menu. Chef François Fovassier has been here for 25 years and his seasonal carte features dishes such as fillet of John Dory, roasted with thyme flowers, *fricassée de sole et de homard au coulis du crustacés* and a parmentier of milk-fed lamb's sweetbreads and kidneys. Set menus start at 250F. The restaurant has a restful decor of pale oak panelling and mirrors and there is a wonderful mosaic in the original fish shop at the front. *Seats 80. Open 1200-1430, 1900-2200. Closed D Sun, 22 Jul-25 Aug. Amex, Diners, Mastercard, Visa.*

Around Lille

VERLINGHEM   Château Blanc   300F

Tel: 20 40 71 02   Fax: 20 40 99 40
20 route de Lambersart, 59237 Verlinghem

Set in its own park a ten-minute drive from Lille, this impressive house was once home to a wealthy textile merchant. The dining-room is elegantly decorated, with a large fireplace, wooden floors and crystal chandeliers. Chef Philippe Fumoux cooks largely traditional dishes with an emphasis on fish, but also likes to introduce subtle Oriental spices as, for instance, in *émincé de saumon cru en marinade de neuf parfums* (thinly sliced raw salmon marinaded in nine 'perfumes'). Other dishes are decidedly more rustic, such as *pavé de pied de cochon et confit de canard au jus de foie gras* (slices of pig's trotter with a confit of duck and a foie gras jus). Set menus from 160F to 300F. *Seats 80 (garden 35). Open 1200-1330, 1930-2130. Closed D Sun, all Mon, 2 weeks in Aug. Private parking. Mastercard, Visa.*

Lyons

LYONS   L'Alexandrin   ★   650F

Tel: 72 61 15 69   Fax: 78 62 75 57
83 rue Moncey, 69003 Lyon

Located on a pedestrianised street near the *cité judiciaire*, chef-patron Alain Alexanian's restaurant has built a fine reputation for serving adventurous interpretations of traditional French country dishes. Experimentation and change are vital components of Alexanian's culinary philosophy and he never repeats a dish from one year to the next. If you visit in 1996 your meal might start with *blinis fourrées d'un caviar d'aubergine et caviar ocietre, crème de saumon fumé,* followed by lobster and summer truffle lasagne with *jus de veau sur crème de mousserons* (wild mushrooms) or, perhaps, *filet de boeuf au jus de truffes avec paillassons lyonnais* (lattice of grated potato) *et champignons des bois,* and conclude with *entremets chocolat amer servi avec sauce à l'infusion de verveine fraiche* (a speciality bitter chocolate dessert served with a verbena sauce). The wine list features a particularly good selection of Cotes du Rhone. The charming Véronique Alexanian works *en salle,* where the simple decor provides an unpretentious setting for an excellent meal. *Seats 40. Open 1200-1330, 1930-2130. Closed Sun, Mon, last 3 weeks Aug, 23 Dec-2 Jan, National Holidays. Amex, Mastercard, Visa.*

LYONS   Auberge de l'Ile   900F

Tel: 78 83 99 49   Fax: 78 47 80 46
Quartier St Rambert, Ile Barbe, 69009 Lyon

Occupying part of a 17th-century monastery on the tiny residential island of Ile Barbe north of the centre of Lyons, the restaurant has been serving traditional French food for nigh on 30 years. The interior is appropriately plain, with wooden beams and stone floors, although there are plans to refurbish the dining-rooms to give them a fresher atmosphere. Jean-Christophe Ansanay-Alex took over in the kitchen from his father three years ago, but has continued to cook classic dishes like shank of lamb en croute with black olives, and delicious desserts such as *soupe de peche aux épices douces et muscat frappé*. Set menus from 130F (lunch) and 135F (dinner). ***Seats 55. Open 1200-1400, 1930-2200. Closed D Sun, all Mon, 6-20 Aug. Private parking. Amex, Diners, Mastercard, Visa.***

Tel: 78 37 38 64   Fax: 78 38 20 35
8 place des Célestins, 69002 Lyon

Local Lyonnais styles inspire Christian Bourillot's cooking and the place itself. The building was constructed out of old bricks from the Célestins convent and the wine cellars are the convent's original ones. Inside, the two dining-rooms are simple, with wooden floors. Christian concentrates his efforts on re-interpreting local dishes like *rouget à la purée de poivrons au jus de romarin* (red mullet served on a purée of peppers with a rosemary-infused sauce) and *quenelles de brochet* (pike dumplings in a lobster sauce). His old grandmother's recipe has been a longstanding favourite: *volaille de Bresse 'Marie' et pommes aux truffes* is local Bresse fowl served with potatoes cooked in thick cream and truffles. Naturally, most of the wines are French, but there are some Spanish and Californian bottles. Anne-Marie Bourillot leads the team *en salle*. ***Seats 35. Open L 1200-1400, 1930-2200. Closed L Mon, all Sun, Jul. Amex, Diners, Mastercard, Visa.***

Tel: 78 42 75 75   Fax: 72 40 93 61
6 rue du Boeuf, 69005 Vieux Lyon

A collection of 14th-century Jesuit buildings was modernised back in 1987 and converted into a hotel. The beamed bedrooms, with parquet floors and bright, modern furniture, attract young artistes to stay; and the classical evening concerts have become so popular that they are now a regular feature. A large Renaissance glass-covered courtyard leads through to a small garden. 24hr room service. Theatre-style conference facilities for up to 200. Private parking. ***Rooms 63. Garden. Indoor swimming pool. Sauna. Amex, Diners, Mastercard, Visa.***

Tel: 78 69 46 26   Fax: 72 73 38 80
249 rue Marcel-Mérieux, 69007 Lyon

The art-deco facade of this restaurant, slightly out of the centre of the city, leads into two dining-rooms, one decorated traditionally, one in a contemporary style, and then out to a large, shady flower garden. Although chef Daniel Judéaux is a Breton, the influence of his native region only really shines through in some of his seafood dishes which include the unusual *homard en os à moelle*. In this dish, bone marrow is removed and placed on top of the bones which are then stuffed with mushrooms and surrounded by lobster. Another curious speciality is wheat and barley flambéed in malt whisky and served with lightly grilled sardine fillets. Set menus from 139F to 290F. The selection of Cotes du Rhone on the wine list is particularly good. ***Seats 55 (garden 55). Open 1200-1400, 1945-2145. Closed L Sat, all Sun, 23 Dec-4 Jan, National Holidays. Amex, Diners, Mastercard, Visa.***

Tel: 78 52 02 52   Fax: 78 52 33 05
14 place Jules Ferry, 69006 Lyon

Formerly the railway buffet in the Gare de Brotteaux, this restaurant is still part of the old station buildings but also has a lovely terrace and garden. The recession has hit trade hard and prices have fallen, meaning that food is particularly good value here at the moment. Cooking is traditional and changes with the seasons, with *produits de la chasse* particularly popular, as in dishes such as *rable de lapereau confit aux girolles* (saddle of young rabbit pickled with chanterelle mushrooms). Lobster ravioli is another excellent speciality. The 128F set menu is available for lunch and dinner and includes a glass of wine. ***Seats 150 (terrace 150). Open 1200-1345, 2000-2145. Closed L Sat, all Sun. Private parking. Amex, Diners, Mastercard, Visa.***

> Opening times are often liable to change at short notice, so it's
> always best to book.

LYONS   Léon de Lyon   ★+   1200F

Tel: 78 28 11 33   Fax: 78 39 89 05
1 rue Pléney, 69001 Lyon

Four adjoining dining-rooms, clad in dark wood and featuring a collection of culinary paintings and bronze statues, make up this fine restaurant. It has been owned by the Lacombe family since 1904 and the present chef, Jean-Paul Lacombe, grew up in the restaurant, taking over from his father in the kitchen almost 50 years ago. He now owns several restaurants (including the cheaper *Bistro de Lyon*) but this place, located in the old Place des Teurreaux quarter, remains the jewel in his crown. Lyonnais cooking is traditionally rather fatty and heavy but Jean-Paul has made his name by lightening and refining classic dishes such as *pomme de terre farci au pied de porc* (potato stuffed with pig's trotter) and *terrine du cochon de lait* (terrine of suckling pig). Other specialities include *pavé de foie de veau* (roasted calf's liver with a herb sauce) and pheasant soup with kidney beans. The delights of praline are celebrated in six desserts *sur le thème de la praline de St-Genix*, six desserts inspired by almonds from the village of St-Genix. *Seats 80. Open 1200-1345, 2000-2145. Closed Sun, one week mid Aug. Valet parking. Amex, Mastercard, Visa.*

LYONS   La Mère Brazier   700F

Tel: 78 28 15 49   Fax: 78 28 63 63
12 rue Royale, 69001 Lyon

The original Mère Brazier, grandmother of the current owner, opened this restaurant in an 18th-century merchant's house in 1921. A faithful clientele eats in its low-ceilinged, panelled rooms and enjoys the solidly traditional food that emerges from the kitchen. Dishes such as *fond d'artichaut au foie gras* and *volaille de Bresse au demi-deuil* remain as popular now as ever. The latter means 'Bresse chicken in semi-mourning' and refers to the black patches on the otherwise white meat caused by the truffles placed under the skin prior to cooking. *Seats 100. Open 1200-1400, 1930-2200. Closed L Sat, all Sun, Aug. Private parking. Amex, Diners, Mastercard, Visa.*

LYONS   Nandron   900F

Tel: 78 42 10 26   Fax: 78 37 69 88
26 Quai Jean Moulin, 69002 Lyon

The restaurant, looking out on to the quays of the Rhone in the heart of the city, is something of an institution. Gérard Nandron has been cooking here for 40 years and his smiling wife, Odette, has been working *en salle* for the same time. The first floor dining-room has an appropriately nostalgic atmosphere and many of the earthy Lyonnais dishes on the menu have hardly changed since the restaurant opened. Examples are calf's kidneys cooked *en cocotte, volaille de Bresse au vinaigre* and *quenelles de brochet à la Nantua*. The all-French wine list is on the pricy side. *Seats 50. Open 1200-1400, 1930-2200. Closed Sat, Aug. Valet parking. Amex, Diners, Mastercard, Visa.*

LYONS   Paul Bocuse   ★+   1500F

Tel: 72 42 90 92   Fax: 72 27 85 87
Pont de Collonges au Mont d'Or, 69660 Lyon

The red and green banded exterior walls are the distinctive decoration of this substantial 1920s' house located on the banks of the Saone, about three miles from the city centre. The interior is a stylish and refined blend of rich colours, beautiful fabrics, antique furniture and soft lighting. Well-spaced tables gleam with fine silverware, creating a sublime setting for food that is nowadays prepared by head chef Roger Jaloux, a *meilleur ouvrier de France*, along with general manager Jean Fleury. The second chef is Christian Bonravel and the three of them make sure the operation is as polished as befits a world-renowned restaurant. Dishes such as *canette rotie à la broche* (local duckling roasted on a spit over an open fire in the restaurant), *poulet de Bresse* and *carré d'agneau persillé à la fleur de thym* are among the specialities. Other local influences can be seen in *soupe aux truffes noires VGE* (a black truffle soup with a pastry lid, created for Valéry Giscard d'Estaing at the Elysée Palace in 1975); *soupe de cuisses de grenouilles aux champignons de bois; foie gras maison cuit en terrine, gelée au porto; riz et filet mignon de veau à la crème et aux champignons; filets de St Pierre à la tomate fraiche et au basilic;* and *loup en croute à la mousse de homard, sauce Choron*. There are several fixed-price menus ranging from 450F for four courses to the magnificent seven-course Menu Gourmand which commands a hefty 740F. Sommelier Yann Eon, who sports a remarkable moustache, is on hand to offer expert oenological advice. *Seats 120. Open 1200-1400, 1900-2200. Amex, Diners, Mastercard, Visa.*

LYONS   Pierre Orsi   1200F   R

Tel: 78 89 57 68   Fax: 72 44 93 34
3 pl Kléber 69006 Lyon

Having trained with Paul Bocuse and then at Maxim's in Paris, Orsi brought a wealth of culinary experience to his Lyonnais restaurant, which opened in 1975. He has continued to expand and develop his menu and repertoire with dishes that take their inspiration from all over France: *les trois foies gras des Landes* from the South-West, *saucisson* from Lyons (of course), red mullet from the Mediterranean with risotto and a tomato confit, snails from Burgundy. Particular specialities include ravioli of foie gras and truffles with a port jus, *barigoule de homard et rouget, aiguillette* of duck with *sauce bigarade* and roast peach, and cherries jubilee. Lots of choice with various set menus (L 200F, L&D 400F, 500F & 600F) in addition to the carte. For a cheaper meal try his other restaurant in Lyons, Cazenove (75 rue Boileau). *Seats 120. Open 1200-1400, 2000-2200. Closed Sun. Amex, Mastercard, Visa.*

LYONS   Tour Rose   1240F   HR

Tel: 78 37 25 90   Fax: 78 42 26 02
22 rue du Boeuf, 69005 Lyon

Each of the suites in the hotel is unique in that it has been individually and stylishly decorated by a different Lyonnais silk manufacturer and the finished suite bears the decorator's name. Rich rugs, restoration art and high beamed ceilings decorate all the suites, from the restoration rooms to the textile designers' salons. The 15th- to 17th-century hotel buildings are as stunningly irregular as the rooms: painted in rich burnt siennas and ochres, they rise up like Roman buildings around a long, narrow courtyard. The place is very informal and in the evenings an arty crowd of guests start in the bar and soon proceed to the restaurant. Conference facilities for up to 50. *Suites 12. Private parking. Amex, Diners, Mastercard, Visa.*

Restaurant   1400F

Having previously worked with Paul Bocuse, Philippe Chavent moved here in 1987 and has developed his own highly distinctive style of cooking. This is a successful blend of the creative together with a few traditional dishes. Begin with a chillled cream of oyster soup with tiny poached meringues and caviar, a tartare of tuna with beetroot crisps and little onion fritters, *bouillabaisse* of monkfish with a poached egg and toast spread with a paste of dried fish roe, or skate wing roasted with garlic and served with saffron-flavoured olive-mashed potatoes. Main dishes are no less innovative, ranging from pan-fried red mullet with lentils and sea urchins, or crisply cooked pigeon with truffles and rocket and wild mushroom salad, to rib of milk-fed veal studded with morels and accompanied by a sauté of artichoke bottoms and bacon pieces. Set menus begin at 295F; the 500F one includes a glass of wine chosen to accompany each course. *Seats 70. Open 1230-1430, 1930-2230. Closed Sun.*

LYONS   Villa Florentine   1660F   H

Tel: 72 56 56 66   Fax: 72 40 90 56
25 Monté Saint Barthelemy, 69005 Lyon

A former orphanage dating back to the 17th century, the Villa Florentine was converted into a hotel around 1970. Although it was modernised at this time, the old parquet floors and some of the heavy, sombre furniture were retained; the original chapel is now the reception. In the old part of town, the hotel is surrounded by peaceful gardens. Two rooms have their own terrace. *Rooms 19. Room service 24hrs. Ample free parking. Conference facilities 30. Outdoor swimming pool. Amex, Diners, Mastercard, Visa.*

Around Lyons

CALUIRE EUT CUIRE   Auberge de Fond-Rose   700F

Tel: 78 29 34 61   Fax: 72 00 28 67
23 quai George Clémenceau, 69300 Caluire eut Cuire

On the banks of the Saone, surrounded by a large garden, this restaurant enjoys a wonderfully peaceful location, and yet is only a 15-minute drive from Lyons. Chef Michel Brunet has been cooking here for 30 years and, as a disciple of Paul Bocuse, produces traditional dishes of a high quality. His menu changes with the seasons. In winter, you will find simply cooked pigeon, lamb, beef and venison, while summer is the best time for fish dishes, such as *bar grillé au fenouil* (bass grilled with fennel) and *marinade de rougets aux oranges* (red mullet marinated with oranges). The fixed-price lunch menu at 140F (weekdays only) is excellent value, as are the other set menus, ranging from 185F to 460F. *Seats 100 (terrace 120). Open 1200-1400, 1930-2200. Closed D Sun, L Mon (all Mon Oct-Easter). Private parking. Amex, Diners, Mastercard, Visa.*

DARDILLY-LE-HAUT   Le Panorama   600F

Tel: 78 47 40 19   Fax: 78 43 20 31
place Général Brosset, 69570 Dardilly-le-Haut

Ten minutes north of Lyons, the tiny village of Dardilly is home to Daniel Léron's refreshingly unpretentious restaurant. He is known particularly for the quality of his sauces, as demonstrated in dishes such as *homard grillé entier, sauce béarnaise* and *filet de loup braisé à la moutarde douce* (fillet of sea bass braised in mild mustard). Other simple specialities include *filet de porc avec des raisins, lapin en gelée* and the perennial favourite *foie gras de canard*. Set menus from 145F to 320F. Beaujolais wines are a feature of the list. *Seats 90 (terrace 90). Open 1200-1400, 1930-2200. Closed D Sun, all Mon. Private parking. Amex, Diners, Mastercard, Visa.*

MIONNAY   Alain Chapel   ★+   2000F

Tel: 78 91 82 02   Fax: 78 91 82 37
1 route Nationale, 01390 Mionnay

Alain Chapel was one of France's most celebrated chefs until his death in 1989. Happily, his eponymous restaurant has not become a museum to a culinary master. Chapel himself said that "pleasure is not born of habit" and his successor, Philippe Jousse, who worked alongside him for ten years, has taken this as licence to develop further the exquisite, eclectic dishes for which Chapel was famed. Examples are *langoustines et gros ravioli de fromage frais en infusion de coriandre* (langoustines and large ravioli of fromage frais infused with coriander) and *carré d'agneau roti, salade tiède d'artichauts violets et d'échalotes nouvelles à l'huile d'olive* (roast rack of lamb, warm salad of violet artichokes and new-season shallots in olive oil). One of Jousse's specialities is the savoury jelly, as in *crème de primeurs à l'estragon, en gelée de crustacés*, and another house favourite is *salade de homard, de gorges de pigeonneaux au pourpier et truffes noires* (salad of lobster and pigeon throats with purslane and black truffles). Almond strudel with roast figs is a typically delicious dessert. A special business lunch menu is excellent value at 310F (Wednesday to Friday only) and other set menus start at 570F. The light and airy dining-rooms, with their antique furniture and traditional beams, make a fitting setting for the superb food. Located in a tiny village 20km from Lyons, the restaurant has a lovely flower-garden and also 14 luxurious bedrooms from 970F per night. *Seats 50 (terrace 15). Open 1200-1300, 1900-2100. Closed L Tue, all Mon, Jan. Private parking. Amex, Diners, Mastercard, Visa.*

MONTROND-LES-BAINS   Hostellerie La Poularde   640F

Tel: 77 54 40 06   Fax: 77 54 53 14
2 route de Saint-Etienne, 42210 Montrond-les-Bains

Although only 8km from St Etienne airport, this 18th-century coaching inn is located in a sleepy little village, occasionally enlivened by tourists visiting the nearby thermal spa in high season. The Etéocle-Randoing family restored the old buildings and furnished the comfortable bedrooms with antique furniture and paintings by local artists. There are also three appartments, more modern in decor, which overlook an internal courtyard garden. *Rooms 14. Room service limited. Private parking. Banqueting facilities 40. Conference facilities 40. Amex, Diners, Mastercard, Visa.*

Restaurant   1200F

Everything about the restaurant is reassuringly traditional, from the silverware and wooden panelling of the dining-room to the familiar dishes on the menu. Chef Gilles Etéocle's seasonal menu may offer few surprises but this is more than made up for by the consistently high quality of his cooking. Luxury ingredients such as lobster, truffles and foie gras feature heavily on the carte, as in *salade de homard tiède, saumon mariné et foie gras frais de canard* and *chausson aux truffes noires de Saint Donat, escalope de foie gras chaud poelée* (a puff pastry case filled with black Saint Donat truffles and served with a slice of warm foie gras). A variety of set menus is offered, priced between 200F and 550F, offering simple dishes such as *choisi de veau de lait, son jus de cuisson, rattes aux lardons 'cocotte'* (choice cut of milk-fed veal, cooked in its own juices, served with rattes potatoes and lardons cooked en cocotte) and desserts mysteriously described as *impromptu des desserts de l'artisan*. Cotes du Rhone, Bordeaux, Burgundy and Alsace wines are well represented on the long list. *Seats 140. Open 1200-1400, 1930-2200. Closed L Tue, all Mon, 2-11 Jan.*

Tel: 78 50 11 36   Fax: 78 51 99 47
35 quai Jean-Jacques Rousseau, 69350 La Mulatière

Roger Roucou and his daughter are just in the process of building a hotel, which will make this restaurant (founded in 1759) an all the more appealing place to stop, near the banks of the Saone, and eat. The menu is classical, which suits the 18th-century interior filled with Louis XV furniture. Most of his ingredients come fresh from the different regions: foie gras from Quercy, volaille de Bresse and other poultry and meat. The three set menus run every lunch and dinner starting at 200F. *Seats 150. Open 1200-1400, 1900-2100. Closed D Sun, all Mon, Aug. Amex, Diners, Visa.*

Tel: 78 55 28 72   Fax: 78 55 01 55
7 rue de l'Eglise, 01700 Neyron-le-Haut

Located in a tiny village 12km from Lyons, this 19th-century farmhouse offers comforting cuisine bourgoise with strong Lyonnais roots. René Champin opened the restaurant in 1982 and cooks fine dishes such as *salade de rouget et de homard poelé à l'huile de noisette* (salad of red mullet and lobster pan-fried in hazelnut oil), or cassoulet of sautéed frogs' legs with parsley, and langoustines en chemise in a lobster sauce. The cluttered decor – bookcases, ornaments, pictures – is simultaneously homely and elegant. Set menus from 175F to 350F. *Seats 30. Open 1200-1315, 1930-2045. Closed D Sun, all Mon, 1st 2 weeks Jan, 1st 3 weeks Aug. Mastercard, Visa.*

Tel: 78 88 50 92   Fax: 78 88 35 22
Chemin des Iles, 39140 Rilleux-la-Pape

This pretty restaurant near the Rhone was opened by Monsieur Larivoire in 1860 and has been in the Constantin family for more than 90 years. The current chef-patron Bernard Constantin has worked in some of Paris's top restaurants as well as *The Savoy* in London and has an eclectic and personalised style of cooking. His specialities include *deux oeufs en cocotte aux langoustines et morilles* (two eggs cooked en cocotte with langoustines and morel mushrooms), *courgette fleurs farcies et jeunes légumes sur une sauce anchoïade* (stuffed courgette flowers with young vegetables on an anchovy paste sauce), and *canard de Dombes laqué poivre et miel en deux services* (Dombes duck basted with pepper and honey). Set menus 200F, 310F and 410F. *Seats 80 (terrace 80). Open 1200-1400, 1900-2200. Closed D Mon, all Tue. Private parking. Mastercard, Visa.*

Meal prices for 2 are based on à la carte menus. When set menus are
available, prices will often be lower.

Tel: (1) 77 42 30 90   Fax: (1) 77 42 30 95
7 rue de la Richelandière, 42100 St Etienne

Pierre Gagnaire converted this 30s-built house into a restaurant four years ago and designed the stylish art deco interior himself. His cooking is wonderfully idiosyncratic. Starters from the carte include *nage glacée d'écrevisses aux artichauts salambo, parfumée de macis; crémeux de tourteau au suc d'étrille* (iced crayfish soup with salambo artichokes perfumed with mace, served with a cream of crab and a crab jus). Main courses are equally extraordinary: *joue de cochon "à la cuillère" braisée à la lie de vin; jus d'abricot à la cannelle; paillasson croustillant au cerfeuil; l'oreille en salade aux pousses d'epinards* (pig's cheeks braised with wine lees, served with apricot juice and cinnamon, on a crunchy chervil base with pig's ear in a spinach salad), for instance, or the possibly even more bizarre *coffre de pigeon gauthier roti aux cosses de chocolat torréfiées, navets confits à la rhubarbe; velouté de brebis aux noisettes* (gauthier pigeon breast roasted with a casing of roasted chocolates, served with turnip and rhubarb confit and a purée of ewe's milk cheese and hazelnuts). Desserts such as *biscuit moelleux au caramel parfumé à la folle blanche, sabayon de fraises des bois; un verre d'hydromel givré* (smooth caramel biscuit with a sabayon of wild strawberries, served with a glass of frosted mead) are only marginally more conventional. Set menus 300F (lunch, weekdays only) and 660F and 860F (dinner). *Seats 80. Open 1200-1430, 2000-2200. Closed D Sun, 28 Jul-16 Aug. Private parking. Amex, Mastercard, Visa.*

Tel: 74 53 01 96   Fax: 74 85 69 73
14 boulevard Fernand Point, 38200 Vienne

Opened by the legendary chef Fernand Point in 1923, this superb restaurant is named after the adjacent Roman monument, which is said to have marked the start of chariot races. Romanesque columns in the spacious, light dining-room overlooking a flower garden and ancient urns and jars on the terrace continue the theme. Current chef-patron Patrick Henriroux took over the restaurant from the Point family in 1989 and has maintained the highest of standards in his imaginative and complex interpretations of Lyonnais and Mediterranean cooking. Duck foie gras is cooked *à l'ancienne* (rolled in muslin, boiled in duck stock, left to cool and sliced) and served with a *Beaumes-de-Venise* jelly, rhubarb compote and dried crystallised apples, while langoustines and asparagus are browned with bacon and served on a salad of golden purslane and watercress with a duck stock perfumed with toasted peanuts. Another interesting dish is *rissolée de grenouilles à la poudre d'ail, artichauts violets farcis d'escargots de Tupin, beurre battu à la sariette* (frog's legs browned with garlic powder, purple artichokes stuffed with snails and a whipped savory herb butter). Desserts are utterly mouthwatering: try the piano of chocolate and praline with almonds and hazelnuts, a roasted coffee sauce and a bitter cocoa sorbet. An excellent selection of dessert wines from the huge cellar (around 30,000 bottles) is available by the glass. Set menus at 420F, 520F and 620F. The restaurant also has 25 rooms overlooking the garden and costing from 1040F for a double including breakfast served in the conservatory. *Seats 70 (terrace 70). Open 1200-1330, 1930-2130. Closed L Thu, all Wed, Feb. Private parking. Amex, Diners, Mastercard, Visa.*

Marseilles

Tel: 91 59 25 92   Fax: 91 59 28 08
Anse de Maldormé, Corniche J F Kennedy, 13007 Marseille

There are wonderful views out to sea from this white colonial-style hotel on the harbour. Architect-designer Eric Klein remodelled and refurbished the entire building in 1989 and all bedrooms and suites are open-plan, decorated in pastel colours, with pear and sycamore wood, and sunken baths. Palm trees and lush plants surround the swimming pool. *Rooms 18. Room service 24hr. Private parking. Garden. Outdoor swimming pool. Solarium. Amex, Diners, Mastercard, Visa.*

The Passédat family built this stone-floored, wood-panelled restaurant by the harbour in 1917. Current chef Gérald, the third generation Passédat to have cooked here, has received a superb training all over the world, including a stint at Paul Bocuse, and produces top-class local dishes. His starters include *salade de la mer antiboise* and prawns cooked in carrot juice and ginger, while mains might be roast lamb with aubergine confit and sea bass cooked with his grandmother Lucie's sauce (a closely guarded secret). *Seats 70 (terrace 70). Open 1200-1400, 1930-2130. Closed D Sun, all Mon (open L Mon in Jul/Aug).*

Around Marseilles

CARRY-LE-ROUET   L'Escale   ★   1000F

Tel 42 45 00 47   Fax 42 44 72 69
Promenade du Port, 13620 Carry-le-Rouet

In this picturesque fishing village setting with wonderful views of the harbour and the ocean, seafood is the obvious choice and most definitely chef Gérard Clor's speciality. It's a wonderful Provençal restaurant, colourfully decorated with murals and art deco paintings, with a garden and terrace built literally into the cliff face. Fishermen bring him fresh catches of sea bass, red mullet, lobsters, prawns and clams, which in turn become dishes such as *casserole de poissons "Cote Bleue"* (Cote Bleue being the section of the Cote d'Azur between Marseilles and Montpellier), pan-fried langoustines or a classic *bouillabaisse*. However, if fish does not appeal, there are some good lamb and duckling dishes to choose from. The menu changes every month, reflecting the variety of fish available at different times of the year. Many local wines feature on the list: Cassis, Bandol and Coteaux d'Aix en Provence. The light, crisp rosé wines complement the style of food ideally, a traditional style based on regional produce with new and interesting approaches in both cooking and presentation. *Seats 70 (Terrace 70). Open 1200-1400, 1930-2130. Closed D Sun, all Mon (except D Jul & Aug), Nov-Feb. Amex, Visa.*

THE APARTMENT SERVICE
Tel in UK (0181) 748 4207   Fax (0181) 748 3972
The Apartment Service will find you the right apartment worldwide to suit your needs, whether you are on a short or long-term stay. A 96-page colour catalogue is free on request. All budgets are catered for.

Paris

PARIS   L'Ambroisie   ★   1800F

Tel: (1) 42 78 51 45
9 place des Voges, 75004 Paris

A beautiful 17th-century square in the narrow streets of the Marais district is a fitting setting for Bernard Pacaud's elegant and exclusive restaurant. The interior maintains the period atmosphere with a hanging tapestry, Thonet chairs, stone floors and dark wood. Bernard's charming wife Danielle works *en salle* while her husband produces consistently superb food in the kitchen. Dishes change with the seasons: in summer you might find *feuillantine* of langoustines with sesame seeds and a curry sauce, *dos de Saint-Pierre à la feuille de laurier, barigoule d'artichauts* (John Dory on a bay leaf with artichoke stuffed with mushrooms, shallots, butter and parsley) and *millefeuille léger à la crème citronée, compote de mangue* (light millefeuille of lemon cream with a mango compote). Sommelier Pierre Le Moullac's excellent cellar includes the heart-stoppingly expensive burgundy Romanée-Conti 1972 at 6900F. *Seats 35. Open 1200-1330, 2000-2130. Closed Sun & Mon, 2 weeks in Feb, 1st 3 weeks Aug.Amex, Mastercard, Visa.*

PARIS   Amphyclès   ★   1800F

Tel: (1) 40 68 01 01   Fax: (1) 40 68 91 88
78 avenue des Ternes, 75017 Paris

Chef-proprietor Philippe Groult's cooking is a marvellous mixture of traditional and modern, inventive and often light, with many dishes featuring subtle use of herbs and spices. Much of the menu involves intriguing combinations: brochette of partridge, wild duck and wild pigeon with truffled juices, grilled scallops and chestnuts with a salad flavoured with white Piedmont truffles, and slice of turbot with vanilla-flavoured fleur de sel. There are also some more familiar favourites (ox cheek with confit of carrots and fillet of Lozère lamb with a persillade of orange and lavender are specialities), plus fine cheeses and superb desserts – try the *tarte fine aux pommes, raisins et noix de pécan* or *crêpes Suzette*, the latter served to the whole table. Three fixed-price menus are available for everyone at a table – *'menu des nos terroirs'*, *'menu crustacés aux saveurs d'autrefois'* and *'menu prestige'*. Private room 5/20. Set lunch 260F. Also *menu dégustation* L&D 580F/680F/920F. *Seats 42. Open 1200-1430, 1900-2230. Closed L Sat, all Sun. Amex, Diners, Mastercard, Visa.*

PARIS · **Apicius** · ★+ · **1400F**

Tel: (1) 43 80 19 66   Fax: (1) 44 40 09 57
122 avenue de Villiers, 75017 Paris

A firm grounding in French culinary classics has given chef Jean-Paul Vigato a solid platform from which to experiment with more contemporary and individual ideas. His carte changes twice a year and includes dishes as varied as tempura-style langoustines, *foie gras de canard poelé en aigre doux aux radis noirs confits* (duck foie gras sautéed in a sweet and sour sauce with a confit of black radishes) and turbot cooked with thyme and rosemary and served with an émulsion of shellfish. Desserts are equally good, particularly those involving chocolate, such as *soufflé au chocolat noir, chantilly sans sucre et glace vanillée*. All the major French wine regions are represented on the 400-strong list, as well as some Spanish, Italian and American bottles. Set menus at 380F and 520F. *Seats 60. Open 1230-1400, 1930-2215. Closed Sat, Sun, Aug. Valet parking. Amex, Diners, Mastercard, Visa.*

PARIS · **L'Arpège** · ★ · **2400F**

Tel: (1) 45 51 47 33   Fax: 44 18 98 39
84 rue de Varenne, 75007 Paris

There are few better restaurants in Paris than L'Arpège, but food this good does not come cheaply. The minimalist decor (bare pink stuccoed plaster, white napery, charcoal grey furniture) seems designed to distract the diner's attention as little as possible from Alain Passard's cooking. He has spent time with Boyer in Reims and Senderens at Lucas Carton but shows a distinctive originality in his interpretations of traditional dishes. Typical starters from the carte are *crème de cèpes du pays de Brive aux oeufs et parmesan* (cream of ceps mushroom soup with eggs and parmesan) and *homard de Bretagne et navets en vinaigrette aigre-douce au romarin* (lobster and turnips in a sweet and sour dressing with rosemary). Tempting mains include *sole de l'ile d'Yeu farcie au gingembre, jus d'oignon blanc* (Ile d'Yeu sole stuffed with ginger and served with white onion jus) and *dragée de pigeonneau vendéen à l'hydromel* (young pigeon cooked in mead). Desserts include the decidedly strange *tomate confite farcie aux douze saveurs* (baked tomato stuffed with 12, mainly citrus, 'flavours'). Set menus at 390F (lunch) and 790F (dinner). *Seats 40. Open 1230-1330, 1930-2230. Closed L Sun, all Sat, 5-21 Aug. Amex, Diners, Mastercard, Visa.*

PARIS · **Le Bellecour** · ★ · **1000F**

Tel: (1) 45 55 68 38   Fax: (1) 45 50 30 11
22 rue Surcouf, 75007 Paris

Located near the Esplanade des Invalides, south of the Quai d'Orsay, this restaurant is renowned for its earthy Lyonnais specialities such as *andouillette au vin de Macon* and *salade de clapotons* (lamb's trotters). A second carte lists more refined dishes like lobster salad with white peaches, French beans and lobster egg vinaigrette, and fillet of beef with a confit of shallots and potato gratin. Set menu 160F and 250F (lunch) and 250F and 420F (dinner). *Seats 35. Open 1200-1400, 1930-2230. Closed L Sat (all day in Jun/Jul), all Sun, Aug. Amex, Diners, Mastercard, Visa.*

PARIS · **Benoit** · ★ · **1000F**

Tel: (1) 42 72 25 76   Fax: (1) 42 72 45 68
20 rue Saint-Martin, 75004 Paris

With its parquet floors, red velvet banquettes, white napery and plants, this elegant bistro has a refined but relaxed atmosphere. The cooking is blissfully simple, with classic dishes prepared slowly and lovingly, such as calf's head with sauce ravigote, roast pigeon with petit chou farci and monkfish steaks au poivre. *Gigot d'agneau* is cooked in Pauillac wine, chicken roasted with chanterelle mushrooms in a salt crust, and supreme of turbot poached and served with a Noilly sauce. Set menu 200F. *Seats 55. Open 1200-1400, 2000-2200. Closed Aug. No credit cards.*

PARIS · **Bistrot d'à Coté** · **500F**

Tel: (1) 43 54 59 10   Fax: (1) 43 29 02 08
16 boulevard St-Germain, 75005 Paris

Michel Rostang's tremendously successful restaurant has spawned three other branches, all following the same formula of serving modern versions of traditional dishes in a lively atmosphere. House specialities include *brochettes de moules poelées, salade de champignons, rognon de veau à la compotée de pieds de porc, gratin macaroni* (veal kidneys with a compote of pig's trotters and macaroni cheese) and *pot de crème au chocolat à l'ancienne.* There is a choice of seven or eight dishes for each course: two cost 139F, three are 185F. The other *Bistrots d'à Coté* are at 16 avenue de Villiers, 75017 Paris (tel: 47 63 25 61), 10 rue Gustave Flaubert, 75017 Paris (tel: 42 67 05 81), and 4 rue Boutard at Neuilly 9200 (tel: 47 45 34 55). *Seats 65 (roadside 45). Open 1200-1400, 1900-2300. Closed L Sat, all Sun (all Sat in Aug). Amex, Diners, Mastercard, Visa.*

Tel: (1) 48 04 88 44   Fax: (1) 48 04 00 59
2 rue de la Bastille, 75004 Paris

An offshoot of the renowned Brasserie Dome and a sister restaurant to the Montparnasse Bistrot (14th arr, see below), with the same effective decor mix of rag-painted walls, fish tiles and plastic grapes as table lights and on the vine overhead, and the same à la carte ideas on the blackboard menu. The menu is all fish, the cooking skilful and relatively unembellished: an excellent dish of pepper stuffed with brandade lapped by a thick tomato sauce, fillet of St Pierre with aubergine purée, *tartare de saumon, friture d'éperlans*, grilled sardines, skate salad, *St Jacques provençale*, rascasse with olive oil potato purée, *bourride, solettes meunière*, whole bream buttery-braised with new potatoes and cloves of garlic in their skins. St Nectaire farmhouse cheese, or simple sweets like dark chocolate tart, pineapple or gratin of pears round off a good, reasonably priced meal. *Seats 80. Open 1200-1430, 1930-2330. Amex, Mastercard, Visa.*

Tel: (1) 43 35 32 00
1 rue Delambre, 75014 Paris

Very near the famous Brasserie Le Dome, the Bistro is solely fish-orientated. The menu is renewed daily according to availability and written on slate boards which are passed around the tables. All is simply cooked – open with a tuna and salmon tartare or pan-fried shrimps, move on to roasted John Dory with herbs or skate with a vinaigrette sauce (hot) and finish with *pommes miettes* (apple crumble). *Seats 60 (+ 16 outside). Open 1215-1430, 1930-2300. Closed Sun & Mon in Aug only. Amex, Mastercard, Visa.*

Tel: (1) 43 25 45 94   Fax: (1) 43 25 23 07
53 quai des Grands Augustins, 75006 Paris

Decor is a stylish 'designer-distressed' blend of soft creamy hues with small colourful highlights gouged out of the plaster on the walls. Napery is a summery pale yellow and with minimalist black chairs and cleverly diffused lighting the ambience complements the short, modish menu. A blackboard lists a further brief but enticing selection of the day's specials. Both this and the menu proper feature innovative and well-prepared dishes that are composed with attention to detail. A carpaccio of paper-thin slices of raw tuna comes with raw baby vegetables dribbled with anchovy essence and topped with a crisp round of fine parmesan-flavoured pastry, chicken liver terrine is accompanied by an apple chutney and pumpkin soup has a garnish of potato rissoles, ham and tapénade. Main dishes could be milk-fed veal braised with mushrooms served with a gratin of marrows, or breast of young chicken marinated in spices and roasted with cabbage and a confit of lemons. *Seats 70. Open 1200-1430, 1900-2400. Closed L Sat, all Sun. Amex, Mastercard, Visa.*

Tel: (1) 47 05 45 42   Fax: (1) 45 55 75 54
111 avenue de la Bourdonnais, 75007 Paris

This turn-of-the-century building in the 7th arrondissement offers comfortable accommodation in traditional Parisian style. *Rooms 60. Room service limited. Garden. Amex, Diners, Mastercard, Visa.*

Tel: (1) 47 05 47 96   Fax: (1) 45 51 09 29

Next door to Le Bordonnais at no 113, this restaurant is not only one of the most popular in the city, but also one of the friendliest. Philippe Bardau's cooking is firmly rooted in Provence, as can be witnessed by starters such as *confit d'aubergines au basilic, tartines de maïs à l'ail doux* (confit of aubergines with basil, served with small garlic-flavoured corn tartlets) and *millefeuille de Saint-Pierre au concassé d'olives et de fenouil* (millefeuille of John Dory with olives and fennel). Main courses are also blessedly simple and evocative of the sun-drenched south-east. For example, Lozère lamb with ratatouille, and pan-fried red mullet with *spaghetti pimentés et aromates*. Desserts include *macaron glacé choco-caramel* with toasted hazelnuts. Set menus at 180F and 220F (lunch) and 280F and 380F (dinner). *Seats 60. Open 1200-1430, 2000-2400. Closed 1 May, 25 Dec.*

Tel: (1) 42 66 91 45

HR

112 rue du Faubourg St Honoré, 75008 Paris

If you want exclusivity and luxury, and money is no object, then Le Bristol is the place to stay. The elegant public rooms blend antiques with top-quality reproductions and are hung with fine tapestries. Most bedrooms are decorated in a traditional style, although one wing, formerly a Carmelite monastery, is more modern in design. The peaceful garden is an unexpected pleasure in a city-centre hotel and there are great views over the Paris rooftops from the sixth-floor swimming pool. Service is impeccable and business facilities, including five conference rooms and a direct link to the Bourse, are excellent. *Rooms 193*.
Room service 24hr. Private parking. Conference facilities 180. Business centre. Garden. Indoor swimming pool. Gym. Amex, Diners, Mastercard, Visa.

Restaurant   ★   1600F

The beautiful circular dining-room is wood-panelled from floor to ceiling, where four paintings of the four seasons look down on small round tables with Louis XV armchairs and vases of fresh flowers. Chef Emile Tabourdiau's seasonal menu (written in English as well as French) lists superb dishes such as sardines and red mullet in a thin pastry case with a garlic and anchovy filling, rack of lamb in a mustard and black olive crust with courgette flowers, and iced bitter almond cracknel with peaches and *Beaumes-de-Venise zabaglione*. Set menus at 340F (lunch) and 450F (dinner). *Seats 60. Open 1200-1430, 1900-2230.*

Tel: (1) 47 27 88 88   Fax: (1) 47 04 85 70

R

112 avenue Kléber, 775116 Paris

Owned by Guy Savoy, this restaurant is located on the ground floor and basement of a luxurious modern development in the 16th arrondissement. The decor makes effective use of iron girders and columns, and the turquoise of the seats matches the colour of the waiters' shirts. Provençal and Mediterranean influences are conspicuous on the short carte which includes *carpaccio de magret de canard au basilic*, *carré d'agneau au thym et à la tapénade* and simple desserts such as *tarte fine aux pommes*. Set menu at 210F. *Seats 90 (outside 40). Open 1200-1430, 1900-2400. Amex, Diners, Mastercard, Visa.*

Tel: (1) 42 86 82 82   Fax (1) 42 86 07 71

R

14 rue de Castiglione, 75001 Paris

Charming restaurant in an arcade off Rue de Rivoli with three elegant bourgeois-style dining-rooms and a glass-covered courtyard. Adding to the comfort this year is newly installed air-conditioning. Alain Dutournier's brilliant cooking is firmly based in his native Gascony with a strong awareness of the seasons, as in the six-course no-choice "Ideas of the Season" menu which, for an extra 180F, comes with glasses of four different wines chosen to complement the various courses; this menu is only available if taken by the whole table. Typical dishes from the main carte might be cassolette of girolle mushrooms with foie gras, poached eggs on a chaud-froid of asparagus and caviar, turbot with grilled vegetables, *tete de veau à la navarraise*, slices of veal kidney with black truffle coulis and a fricassee of baby artichokes, and roast duck with white peaches and fresh almonds. Amongst the desserts (most of which need to be ordered at the beginning of the meal) there might be *brioche perdue* (like bread-and-butter pudding) with red berries, a croustade of apricots with nougat ice cream, millefeuille of rhubarb, and a cardamom-flavoured mango tart. The huge wine list (over 1300 bins) is mostly French but other European and some New World producers are also represented. Set L 280F Set L&D 580F (dégustation). *Seats 70. Open 1200-1430, 19.30-2230. Closed L Sat, all Sun & Aug. Amex, Diners, Mastercard, Visa.*

Tel: (1) 42 60 07 11

R

1 rue du Mail, 75002 Paris

Almost 70 years old, this classic bistro-brasserie near the Place des Victoires is as popular now as it ever was. Bernard Brouillet and Alain Devouges have been cooking simple, comforting dishes here for a quarter of a century and their menu rarely changes. Starters include *poelée de girolles fraiches* and *oeufs mayonnaise*, while main courses such as *cotes d'agneau grillées*, *haricot verts* and *andouillette de Troyes grillée* (grilled chitterling sausage) are equally straightforward and satisfying. Bottles of wine are left on the tables and you pay for what you drink. *Seats 60. Open 1200-1400, 1900-2130. Closed Sun, 1st 2 weeks Aug, National Holidays. Amex, Mastercard, Visa.*

Tel: (1) 40 68 50 68   Fax: (1) 40 68 50 43
3 place Général Koenig, 75017 Paris

The top six of the 33 floors of this building are called 'Le Top Club', where 157 executive bedrooms (supplement) have butler service and use of a business suppport centre as well as a health club located in the basement of the hotel (not part of the establishment). It has its own check-in area and private lounge. The hotel is part of the Palais des Congrès, where exhibitions, conventions, congresses, trade fairs and concerts are held, and where 80 shops and four cinemas are located. The conference room, divisible into smaller sections, has a capacity of 2000 (7000 in the Palais). The business centre is fully equipped and staffed, with translation and secretarial services available. The view across Paris from the standardised, comfortable and well-equipped bedrooms is exceptional. It can be even more appreciated from the panoramic bar *'Plein Ciel'* on the 33rd floor. The coffee shop, *'Les Saisons'*, is open from 6am to midnight. **Rooms 970.** *Amex, Diners, Mastercard, Visa.*

Tel: (1) 40 68 51 28

On the first floor of the hotel is a modern, comfortable restaurant with lightwood panelled walls and ceiling and claret-coloured carpet and chairs. Diners are serenaded by a harpist in the evenings while enjoying Jean-Claude Lhonneur's classic but inventive cuisine: broad bean and savory cream soup; risotto with frogs' legs; sea bream pan-fried with fresh herbs; roast Challans duck with baby turnips; wild strawberry tartlet; hot chocolate soufflé. Set menu 290F. **Seats 80.** *Open 1200-1400, 1900-2230. Closed Sat, Sun, Aug, National Holidays except 1 Jan.*

Tel: (1) 43 20 14 20   Fax: (1) 43 35 46 14
102 boulevard du Montparnasse, 75014 Paris

Good, honest food is served by very professional staff in this vast air-conditioned brasserie, beloved of Parisians and visitors alike, and busy since the day it opened in 1927. Reservations are only taken up to 2030 so should there be a wait for a table, order a drink at the bar to the left of the entrance and watch the comings and goings to pass the time. If you've arranged to meet friends, allow plenty of time just to find their table, so big is the place! Oysters, choucroute, snails and onion soup, grills and steak tartare are favourite choices along with cold leg of lamb with ratatouille niçoise, grilled lobster flamed with whisky, and cassoulet of goose. Starters range from melon (plain, with port, or italienne), rabbit terrine with cider jelly, and Welsh rarebit to Sevruga caviar with blinis and crème fraiche. A simpler menu is available on the terrace. Fish and shellfish are delivered daily. Set menus: 87F (till 1500, not Sat or Sun) & 109F (before 1800 & after 2200). **Seats 450.** *Open 0730-0200 (lunch served from noon). Closed D 24 Dec. Amex, Diners, Mastercard, Visa.*

Tel: (1) 44 71 15 00   Fax: (1) 44 71 15 02
10 place de la Concorde, 75008 Paris

This fabulous palace, owned by the Taittinger family, continues to uphold the high standards which made its reputation. The central hall of Siena and Portor marble manages to maintain intimate proportions and the salons have been carefully restored to their former glory. Many of the spacious, quiet, air-conditioned bedrooms have been tastefully decorated in traditional style by Sonia Rykiel and all have lavish marble bathrooms. The hotel's first floor, dedicated to conferences and receptions, has a series of linked historic rooms: salon Marie-Antoinette with its pretty terrace, *salon des Aigles* and *salon des Batailles*, all looking out on to the famous obelisk. **Rooms 163.** *Room service 24hr. Public parking. Banqueting facilities 200. Conference facilities 440. Amex, Diners, Mastercard, Visa.*

Tel: (1) 44 71 16 16   Fax: (1) 44 71 15 00

Everything about this magnificent restaurant radiates quality and refinement, from its chequered floors to its *trompe l'oeil* skies. The gilded mirrors, painted friezes of cherubs, night-blue curtains and tables sparkling with crystal and silver might seem overwhelming in their opulence if the classical proportions of the room were not perfect. Instead, the atmosphere is of intimacy and comfort; a feeling which the impeccable but friendly service enhances. The setting is perfect for chef Christian Constant's outstanding cooking.

See over

Although classically-trained, he is continually experimenting and prides himself on rarely repeating a dish from one seasonal menu to the next. Examples of his best dishes are starters like *confit de foie gras d'oie, poivre et sel, purée de figues et pruneax* (confit of foie gras with salt and pepper and puréed figs and prunes), and *moelleux de pommes rattes, médaillons de homard à la civette* (lobster medallions with rattes potatoes and chives) and mains such as *darne de bar clouté aux anchois, meunière de poivrons et aubergines à l'huile d'olive* (roast fillet of bass studded with anchovies, served with aubergines and bell peppers 'meunière' in olive oil) and *carré d'agneau de Pauillac roti sous la cendre, tomate farcie de pied et épaule d'agneau* (rack of Pauillac lamb roasted in embers with tomatoes stuffed with lamb shoulder and trotters). Constant's desserts are of an equally high quality, as in *macaron au fenouil frais glacé, fruit rouges et noirs dans leur jus* (iced fresh fennel macaroon with red and black fruits in their juice). The wine list is heftily-priced but includes some of the best bottles in France. Set menus at 340F (lunch) and 610F (dinner). **Seats 60. Open 1200-1430, 1900-2230.**

L'Obélisque   600F

Different in style and atmosphere from Les Ambassadeurs, the hotel's second restaurant feels more like a club, with its low ceilings, panelled walls and Lalique chandeliers. It has a separate entrance on the Rue Boissy d'Anglas and is invariably packed at lunchtimes. Christian Constant supervises the kitchen and offers a good-value set menu at 270F. A typical meal might consist of *mousseline d'avocat aux crabes, coeur de laitue vinaigrette* (mousseline of avocado and crab served with a dressed lettuce heart), *daurade roti* (roast fillets of sea bream) *à l'huile d'olive avec ratatouille niçoise*, and *crème brulée à la vanille Bourbon*. Look out for the occasional fortnights of foreign cooking. At the time of writing, chefs from the Peninsula restaurant in Hong Kong had been flown over to cook Chinese food. Set menu at 270F. **Seats 90. Open 1200-1430, 1900-2230.**

PARIS   Le Dome   700F

Tel: (1) 43 35 25 81   Fax: (1) 42 79 01 19   R
108 boulevard du Montparnasse, 75014 Paris

Bouillabaisse, oysters and lobster remain among the traditional specialities at this most durable of Montparnasse institutions, but Franck Graux's menu also moves with the times. Carpaccio of tuna fish with aubergine purée, Saint-Pierre sautéed with potatoes and courgette 'spaghetti', and *sole de l'Ile de Yeu à la meunière* show the contemporary side. Fruit is put to excellent use in many desserts, including baked figs, apple tart and a gratin of red fruits. **Seats 130. Open 1200 -1500, 1900-0030. Open for coffee and snacks from 8am. Closed Mon, also Sun in Aug. Amex, Diners, Mastercard, Visa.**

PARIS   Drouant   ★+   1600F

Tel: (1) 42 65 15 16   Fax: (1) 49 24 02 15   R
18 place Gaillon, 75002 Paris

A short stroll from Place de l'Opéra with a restaurant as well as a café, Drouant started out as a simple café-tabac back in 1880 but soon had a reputation for its good seafood and a strong literary following; the first Prix Goncourt was awarded here and the literary tradition continues with the Prix Apollinaire (for poetry) presented here each June. Being close to the Paris Bourse, it's also popular with the business community. Louis Grondard's cooking is of extremely well-thought-out dishes prepared in a style that's modern but retains a clear classical pedigree. Particular specialities from the carte include a cassolette of girolle mushrooms made with the distinctively flavoured *vin jaune* from the Jura, charlotte of langoustines with an aubergine confit, veal kidneys roasted with rosemary, and turbot roasted in a clay mould with truffles. Set L 300F Set D 650F. **Seats 70. Open 1200-1430, 1900-2230. Closed D 25 Dec & all 1 Jan. Amex, Diners, Mastercard, Visa.**

PARIS   Duquesnoy   ★+   1200F

Tel: (1) 47 05 96 78   Fax: (1) 44 18 90 57   R
6 avenue Bosquet, 75007 Paris

Jean-Paul Duquesnoy prepares haute cuisine dishes for a smart, civilised clientele in his handsomely decorated, wood-panelled restaurant just south of Pont d'Alma. His skill, finesse and light touch are evident throughout an exceptionally enticing carte: *soupe crémeuse de girolles au cerfeuil et grosses langoustines*, crab-stuffed courgette flowers, line-caught turbot with a fine 'minestrone' of vegetables and *sauce pistou, rouelles d'abats de la "Saint Cochon"*, beef with truffles in a Graves wine sauce with quenelles of bone marrow and ethereal pommes soufflées, and a spectacular dessert of four different chocolate creations. Choosing is a delightful, but difficult task, and Jean-Paul will do it for you if you (and all at your table) order the *menu dégustation* of four specialities served in small portions. The 250F lunchtime menu provides great value for money. Classic wines accompany the classic food. Françoise Duquesnoy is a charming and knowledgable hostess. Set L 250F, Set L & D 450F & 520F (dégustation) **Seats 45. Open 1200-1400, 2000-2200. Closed L Sat, all Sun, 1st 2 wks Aug, 25 Dec & 1 Jan. Amex, Mastercard, Visa.**

PARIS   Faugeron   ★+   1200F

Tel: (1) 47 04 24 53   Fax: (1) 47 55 62 90
52 rue de Longchamp, 75116 Paris

It was in 1972 that Henri Faugeron first put puréed truffles together with a simple soft boiled hen's egg, added brioche 'soldiers', and created his now famous signature dish *oeufs coque Faugeron*; as popular now as it was then to judge by the number being eaten all around us on a recent lunchtime visit. But there are many other wonderful dishes to be enjoyed here: tournedos of lobster with ravioli of ceps was stunning and a dish of fresh foie gras with figs and caramelised butter lacked only "the sound of trumpets" – both from the day's *Grand Menu Dégustation*. What you will not find here is asparagus in autumn or strawberries in winter as Henri is a stickler for using ingredients only in their natural season when they are at their very best. Game is a particular speciality in season – noisettes of venison with autumn fruits, *croustillant et salmis de faisan aux jus de truffes* – and amongst the desserts a *mille-feuille 'Amadéus' en duo de chocolats*, the creation of Gerlindé Faugeron, who is the charming hostess overseeing the discreetly cosseting service. The immaculately hand-written wine list is outstanding and wine waiter Jean-Claude Jambon was voted the 'best sommelier in the world' a couple of years ago. Each month there is a selection of three or four wines by the glass, usually including a 1st-growth claret. Set L 290F Set L & D 650F (dégustation) Set D 550F (with wine). **Seats 50. Open 1200-1400, 1930-2200. Closed Sat (except D Oct-Apr), Sun, Aug & 23 Dec-2 Jan. Parking: valet at lunchtime, in street at night. Amex, Mastercard, Visa.**

PARIS   Gallopin   460F

Tel: (1) 42 36 45 38   Fax: (1) 42 36 10 32
40 rue Notre Dame des Victoires, 75002 Paris

With its moulded ceilings, brass and mahogany fittings, and air of comforting permanence, little seems to have changed in this famous old restaurant since it opened in 1876. The classic seasonal menu lists old favourites such as entrecote Gallopin, steak tartare and *foie de veau au poivre vert*. The set dinner menu (150F) might consist of escargots de Bourgogne, followed by sole meunière and then *plateau de fromages*, and comes with a kir royal aperitif and half a bottle of Cotes du Rhone. **Seats 120 (terrace 30). Open 1130-1500, 1930-2330. Closed Sat & Sun. Amex, Diners, Mastercard, Visa.**

PARIS   George V   3200F

Tel: (1) 47 23 54 00   Fax: (1) 47 20 40 00
31 avenue George V, 75008 Paris

Named after an English king, designed by an American (in the late 1920s) and run by the international Forte group, the George V is the one Parisian hotel that most people will have heard of. Grand, high-ceilinged public rooms boast antique furniture, 17th-century tapestries, objets d'art and even a Renoir plus lots of fresh flowers, all helping to create an atmosphere of elegance and luxury. Whether staying in one of the many sumptuous suites or in an individually designed bedroom one can expect the same high standards of service. Numerous private function rooms include the wood-panelled Louis XIII salon with its massive stone fireplace and the Chantilly room with cool, stylised classical murals. Parking 140Fa day. Ten conference rooms. **Rooms 260. Access, Amex, Diners, Visa.**

Les Princes Restaurant   ★   900F

Chandeliers above widely spaced tables with elegant place settings and a huge floral centrepiece – this is a truly grand hotel dining-room with a suitably expansive menu. Long-standing chef Joyeux's main carte is supplemented by a limited choice fixed-price menu and, in season, a special game menu. Specialities include pan-fried langoustines, St Pierre and crab in a light green onion sauce, and miniature pompoms of fowl, truffles and foie gras with an asparagus salad. If you want to go the whole hog try the no-choice tasting menu that consists of eight suitably small-sized courses. A large terrace can seat up to 70 and when in use the dining-room itself is not. Set menus 240F/450F. **Seats 60. Open 1200-1430, 1900-2230.**

Tel: (1) 42 33 14 74   Fax: (1) 42 33 85 71
5 rue Coq-Héron, 75001 Paris

Silver carafes in display cases, old paintings and immaculate settings at well-spaced tables are all part of the elegant scenery, but it's Gérard Besson's superb cooking which takes centre stage at this outstanding restaurant in the old Les Halles area. The marriage of traditional cuisine with innovative flair delights in dishes like hot foie gras tartlet with a truffle coulis; Brittany lobster on a bed of artichoke, mushroom and fennel; roast zander with turnip and anchovy confits; veal sweetbreads meunière with champagne sauce, and Bresse chicken cooked with a gratin of macaroni and foie gras and a classical *sauce albuféra*. Desserts are equally tempting with such creations as a white-cheese *bavarois* with melon balls and crushed black peppercorns, and a fresh fruit cocktail with almond milk and zest of lime. Classy French wine list with just a handful of foreign interlopers. Set L 260F Set L&D 480F & 780F *(dégustation)* **Seats** *40. Open 1200-1430, 1915-2230. Closed L Sat & all Sun. Amex, Diners, Mastercard, Visa.*

Tel: (1) 40 07 32 32   Fax: (1) 42 66 12 51
2 rue Scribe, 75009 Paris

Built during the Napoleon III era, this luxurious and elegant hotel is located on a corner of Place de l'Opéra, opposite the Opera House. The cental reception room, the Cour d'Honneur, is a marble-floored lounge under a huge steel and glass dome. Business facilities are particularly impressive with 18 conference rooms available for meetings of between eight and 500 people. **Rooms** *514. Room service 24hr. Private parking 150F. Conference facilities 500. Secretarial/translation services on request. Gym. Sauna. Solarium. Amex, Diners, Mastercard, Visa.*

Restaurant Opéra   800F

Tel: (1) 40 07 30 10   Fax: (1) 40 07 33 75
5 place de l'Opéra

This fabulously opulent restaurant, decorated in blue and gold, with its famous ceiling painted with stylised cherubs and clouds, is an appropriate setting for luxury eating. Truffles, lobster, foie gras and other such ingredients dominate the list of starters which includes Périgord chestnut cream and foie gras flan, and warm fillet of squab and truffle pie. Fish dishes are particularly fine: sea bass roasted with almonds and served with fennel purée flavoured with coriander, and crispy fillet of pike-perch with green olive cream. Surprisingly, the restaurant has recently halved the prices of all the wines on its extensive list in order to make good wine more accessible. An excellent bottle can now be had for around 100F. **Seats** *75. Open 1200-1500, 1900-2300. Closed Sat & Sun, Aug, one week in Jan.*

Brasserie Café de la Paix   400F

Tel: (1) 40 07 30 20
12 boulevard des Capucines

Guests take breakfast in the brasserie which runs along two sides of the hotel. It has been a popular meeting place since it opened 130 years ago and is decorated with fine 19th-century wall and ceiling frescoes. In season, oysters are a speciality on the traditional menu which also includes dishes such as steak tartare and grilled salmon with béarnaise sauce. The glass-roofed pavement terrace is a great place for eating, drinking and people watching. Set menu 138F. **Seats** *220. Open 1200-1315.*

Tel: (1) 42 96 56 27   Fax: (1) 42 86 80 71
17 rue de Beaujolais, 75001 Paris

The origins of this historic restaurant stretch back to 1784 when a café opened in a wing of the (then new) Palais Royal. The current owners, Taittinger, restored the ornate interior a few years ago and chef Guy Martin has established a top-class kitchen, producing classic cuisine. Frogs' legs with garlic, foie gras ravioli with creamed truffles and egg in an aspic of pepper, Sichuan pepper and caviar are typical summer starters on his seasonal carte. Main dishes are also stunning yet relatively simple: *rouget barbet cuit entier, jus avec son foie* (whole red mullet accompanied by a jus flavoured by its liver), parmentier of oxtail with truffles, and *cote de veau de lait poelée aux cèpes* (milk-fed veal chops, pan-fried with ceps mushrooms). Chocolate is a feature of the dessert menu, as in the enigmatic-sounding *evanescence en noir et blanc* and the extraordinary *déclinaison sur le thème du chocolat au thé vert 'Fuji-Yama', au café d'Ethiopie, à la bière 'pur malt'*. If you have trouble making up your mind, the chef's choice of the day, the *menu plaisir*, can be sampled by your whole table. Set lunch at 305F. **Seats** *60. Open 1230-1415, 1930-2215. Closed Sat & Sun, Aug. Amex, Diners, Mastercard, Visa.*

Tel: (1) 43 80 40 61   Fax: (1) 46 22 43 09
18 rue Troyen, 75017 Paris

Guy Savoy's air-conditioned restaurant, close to the Arc de Triomphe, is one of the gastronomic temples of Paris. The atmosphere is intimate and sophisticated, with pastel colours, bold wallpaper, modern paintings, exquisite china, copious flowers and lightwood screens sectioning off eating areas. Since the restaurant opened in 1986, Savoy has established an enviable reputation as one of the city's top chefs and the secret of his success lies in his refreshingly simple style. The pleasure he takes in his cooking is evident in every dish, from deceptively straightforward starters such as *supreme de volaille de Bresse, foie gras et artichauts* (breast of Bresse chicken with foie gras and artichokes), and *thon et petits pois marinés aux herbes* (tuna and peas marinated in herbs) to main courses like *Saint-Pierre roti, parmentier d'herbes à l'huile d'olive et roquette poelée* (pan-fried John Dory with a herb and olive oil parmentier and rocket) and pigeon poché-grillé with new vegetables and a giblet vinaigrette. Desserts are equally superb: *terrine de pamplemousse, sauce au thé* (grapefruit terrine with tea sauce) and chaud-froid of peach and blackcurrant, for example. Unusually, a reasonable selection of wines from Spain, Italy and California is available as well as some excellent French wine by the glass. The *menu dégustation* is 820F. **Seats** *100. Open 1230-1430, 1930-2330. Closed L Sat, all Sun. Valet parking. Amex, Mastercard, Visa.*

Tel: (1) 42 73 92 00   Fax: (1) 47 83 62 66
18 avenue de Suffren, 75015 Paris

Only a few yards from the Eiffel Tower, the 11-storey Paris Hilton overlooks the Palais de Chaillot and Trocadero Gardens. All rooms are equipped with air-conditioning, cable TV (18 channels) in stereo with remote control, radio, mini-bar and direct-dial telephone. Fourth-floor bedrooms are designated non-smoking, and there are also non-smoking sections in the hotel's two restaurants. The Toit de Paris on the 10th (rooftop) floor has a panoramic view of Paris and is a good spot for de luxe seminars. Up to 1000 can be accommodated theatre-style in the conference and banqueting area, where the business centre is located. **Rooms** *456. Amex, Diners, Mastercard, Visa.*

Tel: (1) 43 55 44 34   Fax: (1) 47 00 32 34
10 place de la République, 75011 Paris

Most Holiday Inns are purpose-built modern blocks, but the building housing this hotel is a listed historic monument dating back to 1850. All rooms are air-conditioned and equipped with satellite TV and mini-bar. The original courtyard is an attractive place to relax. Business facilities are excellent, with nine conference rooms. **Rooms** *318. Room service 24hr. Conference facilities 280. Amex, Diners, Mastercard, Visa.*

La Belle Epoque   700F

The recently renovated restaurant offers a three-course 'Discovery' menu (printed in English as well as French) at 195F. A meal might consist of salmon and sole terrine with cream of chives, followed by pan-fried angler fish with cream of saffron and sautéed fennel, and ice cream nougat with kiwi fruit sauce to finish. A lunchtime buffet is available at 95F and a full dinner buffet at 155F. **Seats** *200. Open 1200-1430, 1930-2230.*

Meal prices for 2 are based on à la carte menus. When set menus are available, prices will often be lower.

Tel: (1) 44 77 11 11 Fax: (1) 44 77 14 60
HR
3 rue Castiglione, 75001 Paris

Situated off Place Vendome and facing the landscaped Tuileries Gardens, this extremely elegant hotel is a listed historic monument. Of the 450 air-conditioned rooms, 70 are spacious suites, and all offer the highest standards of luxurious accommodation. Eleven function rooms (max 900 for a banquet, 1200 for a theatre-style conference) – two with elaborately mouldings and painted ceilings, chandeliers and columns. *Rooms 450. Bureau de change. Café (0630-2300). Amex, Diners, Mastercard, Visa.*

Tel: (1) 44 77 10 44

A stylish and attractive restaurant whose best feature is the glass-ceilinged and columned central courtyard which has been designed with a winter garden theme. Chef Raoul Gaiga serves modern French cuisine with dishes such as fillet of young mackerel served with a refreshing minty tabbouleh, finely sliced duck breast served with a pea salad, garlic broth and snail-filled ravioli and sole goujons prepared with grilled noodles as starters, followed by a millefeuille of calf's sweetbreads with artichoke, beef casserole with chanterelle mushrooms and onions or free-range cockerel in red wine. In the mornings they serve a splendid breakfast. Set menus: L & D 310F. *Seats 40 (+ 90 outside). Open 1200-1430, 1900-2200. Closed 25 Dec-1 Jan.*

Tel: (1) 43 26 49 39 Fax: (1) 43 54 54 48
R
14 rue des Grands-Augustins, 75006 Paris

A discreet doorway on a narrow, ancient street in the St Germain area near the Seine, leads up to this charming first-floor restaurant. The 16th-century decor of heavy beams and partially oak-panelled walls hung with old oil paintings contrasts with Jacques Cagna's energetic, eclectic cooking. He prides himself on the freshness of his ingredients and on rarely repeating a dish from one menu to the next, but examples of typical starters are *salade tiède de homard breton, légumes de Provence aux aromates* (warm lobster salad with Provençal vegetables and aromatic herbs) and *carpaccio de dorade rose, rémoulade de céleri et caviar Sévruga* (carpaccio of sea bream with a rémoulade of celery and Sevruga caviar). Mains include *canard de Challans aux zestes d'orange et citron* (Challans duck cooked with orange and lemon zest, served with a red burgundy sauce) and roast chicken with wild mushrooms. For chocolate addicts, the plate of five different chocolate desserts is a must. Set menus at 270F (lunch) and 490F (dinner). *Seats 60. Open 1200-1400, 1930-2230. Closed L Sat, 3 weeks in Aug, Christmas/New Year. Public parking. Amex, Diners, Mastercard, Visa.* 🐂

Tel: (1) 45 55 61 44 Fax: (1) 47 05 29 41
R
2ème Etage Tour Eiffel, 75007 Paris

Situated on the second floor of the Eiffel Tower, this restaurant enjoys a truly unique view and location. A private lift takes diners up to the stylish modern dining-room, decorated in severe blacks and greys. Chef Alain Reix's cooking focuses on seafood: sole braised whole with a sabayon infused with a shellfish jus and served with noodles; lobster with veal jus and clarified butter. Terrine of foie gras might come *au naturel, au caramel* or smoked, with a walnut salad. Book well in advance. Set menus 300F (lunch, Monday to Friday) and 680F (dinner *menu dégustation* – for the entire table only). *Seats 100. Open 1200-1345, 1900-2145. Valet parking. Amex, Diners, Mastercard, Visa.* 🐂

Tel: (1) 44 05 75 00 Fax: (1) 44 05 74 74
H
81 avenue Kléber, 75016 Paris

Located in the 16th arrondissement, near the Palais de Chaillot, this plush, ultra-modern *résidence hotelière* opened in October 1993. All bedrooms are air-conditioned and have kitchenettes (sometimes only a sink and hob in a cabinet) and overlook either the hotel's plant-filled atrium or the street. Leisure facilities are good: the fitness centre in the basement has a mini-gym, sauna, Turkish bath, solarium and a huge jacuzzi. Three conference rooms are available for hire. *Rooms 83. Room service limited. Private parking 60F. Conference facilities 60. Gym. Sauna. Spa bath. Amex, Diners, Mastercard, Visa.*

Tel: (1) 43 59 53 43   Fax: (1) 45 63 72 23
17 avenue Franklin D Roosevelt, 75008 Paris

René Lasserre, at the age of 12, came to Paris from Bayonne between the wars to seek his fortune and went on to found this much loved restaurant. Customers and staff are equally loyal. Regulars have their own 'Club de la Casserole' and ex-staff have their own organisation, 'Les Anciens de Lasserre', which includes such illustrious members as Gérard Boyer, Guy Savoy and Marc Haeberlin. Attention to detail, in decor, service and cooking, is the cornerstone of the restaurant's success. The surroundings are splendid, from the specially commissioned chandeliers to the famous sliding roof which retracts on summer evenings. Current chef Bernard Joinville still cooks timeless Lasserre classics like "Le Ragout 74" and *sole soufflée au salpicon de crustacés* as well as other traditional dishes such as *grenadins de veau de lait poelées au cidre* (small slices of veal pan-fried in cider), turbot poached with hollandaise sauce or grilled with Choron sauce (béarnaise sauce with tomato purée) and *chateaubriand*. Desserts are also splendidly simple: *trois sorbets de saison and soufflé chaud à la liqueur d'Amaretto*, for instance. And to drink? It has to be Champagne Lasserre. *Seats 100. Open 1230-1430, 1930-2230. Closed L Mon, all Sun, Aug. Valet parking. Amex, Mastercard, Visa.*

Tel: (1) 42 25 00 39   Fax: (1) 45 62 45 21
41 avenue Gabriel, 75008 Paris

Built in the 1840s, Laurent is one of the 'pavilion' restaurants in the gardens at the Place de la Concorde end of the Champs Elysées. Chef Philippe Braun is a protégé of Joël Robuchon and an exquisite chef in his own right. His seasonal menu lists deceptively simple-sounding dishes whose subtle combinations of taste and texture are masterly. Sardines marinaded in thyme and *araignée de mer* (spider crab) *en gelée* are typically straightforward starters. Mains include grilled turbot with *artichauts à la barigoule* (artichokes stuffed with finely chopped mushrooms, shallots, parsley and butter) and superbly roasted rack of lamb with a spiced aubergine purée. Finish with a plate of French and Swiss cheeses or a dessert such as the speciality *deux soufflés Laurent*. Virtually every French wine can be found on the superb list. The terrace is a wonderful setting for summer dining. Set menu 380F. *Seats 100 (terrace 100). Open 1230-1500, 1930-2300. Closed L Sat, all Sun, National Holidays. Valet parking. Amex, Diners, Mastercard, Visa.*

Tel: (1) 47 42 35 98   Fax: (1) 47 42 55 01
Carré des Champs-Elysées, 75008 Paris

Patronised by Robespierre, painted by Tissot, written about by Maupassant – Ledoyen's claim to be the "most legendary gastronomic address in Paris" is no idle boast. It opened in 1792 (as Chez Doyen) and the setting, in a pavilion near the Petit Palais in the Jardin des Champs Elysées, is incomparable, with the most elegant first-floor dining-room looking out over the gardens. Restaurants are all about food, however, and husband and wife team Jean-Paul and Ghislaine Arabian (the former as ebullient manager, the latter to take charge of the kitchen) moved from their highly acclaimed restaurant in Lille to reinvigorate the cuisine here. Deceptively simple dishes concentrate on taste and flavour rather than spectacular presentation: scallops in a fluffy liquor flavoured with beer (something of a signature ingredient – it also appears as a flavouring for the eel in aspic, turbot is roasted in it and it crops up again in a hot sabayon served with the chicory parfait for dessert); ravioli of lobster and girolle mushrooms. Game in season might include a terrine of hare with rhubarb chutney, and noisettes of venison flavoured with juniper berries and served with figs cooked in red wine. Prices are not totally astronomic and one can even find a 50F half bottle of Cotes de Blaye rubbing shoulders with Ch Petrus on the wine list. On the ground floor, and also under the supervision of Ghislaine Arabian (although she is very much 'at the stove' in the gastronomic restaurant above), is Le Cercle Ledoyen (also open on Saturday, Tel (1) 47 42 76 02 for reservations) where all the main dishes are priced at 100F. Set menus 480F. *Seats 50. Open 1200-1400, 1900-2200. Closed Sat, Sun, Aug. Amex, Diners, Mastercard, Visa.*

Lipp 560F

Tel: (1) 45 48 53 91   Fax: (1) 45 44 33 20   R
151 boulevard Saint-Germain, 75006 Paris

Perhaps the capital's most famous brasserie, founded in 1880 by Léonard Lipp. It now has a 20s decor of ceramics, mirrors and painted ceiling (it's classed as a historic monument). It was, and is, the haunt of the famous, from Malraux to Speilberg, from Hemingway to Tom Cruise. Throughout its long opening hours it serves a classic brasserie menu, and listed as specialities are *cervelas rémoulade*, Bismarck herrings, grilled stuffed pig's trotters, and choucroute with pork knuckle. The choice is extensive and each day there are additional dishes such as poached haddock beurre blanc, navarin of lamb and Provençal stuffed vegetables. Set menu 195F. **Seats 150. Open 1000-0100. Amex, Mastercard, Diners, Visa.**

Lucas Carton ★+ 2600F

Tel: (1) 42 65 22 90   Fax: (1) 42 65 06 23   R
9 place de la Madeleine, 75008 Paris

Bertrand Guénon has been chef de cuisine since 1980, but it is still Alain Senderens who inspires the kitchen of this stunning Belle Epoque restaurant with its blond wood panelling and etched glass. Among his renowned dishes are *raviolis de pétrouches* (baby scallops) *aux courgettes, foie gras au chou, canard Apicius roti au miel et aux épices* and *tarte aux zestes d'oranges*. The carte is unique in giving the option of a glass of wine individually chosen to complement each and every dish, including the puds – a truly wonderful idea. A glass of '86 Jurançon with the cabbage-wrapped foie gras, for example, a grand chablis with a dish of langoustines, ginger and fried oysters; Pomerol with the wild duck and the Ch Latour '87 with the noisettes of lamb. Desserts are all prepared individually to order so it is necessary to order them along with the starter and main dish, unless leaving all decisions to the kitchen by going for the no-choice 'Menu Lucas Carton' – served only to the whole table. Valet parking. **Seats 100. Open 1200-1430, 1800-2230. Closed L Sat, all Sun, 21 Dec-7 Jan, most of Aug. Access, Visa.**

Hotel Lutétia 1280F

Tel: (1) 49 54 46 46   Fax: (1) 49 54 46 00   HR
45 boulevard Raspail, 75006 Paris

This grand old hotel opened in 1910 and is one of the most famous on the Left Bank. In 1983, Sonia Rykiel oversaw a major refurbishment which restored it to its full art deco glory. Public rooms are well proportioned, decorated in marble, gilt and velvet and furnished with Taki's sculptures, Lalique and elegant glass screens. The Bar Lutèce, overlooking the huge reception area, is still a favourite meeting place for the chic set who gossip, sip cocktails and listen to live piano or jazz. Bedrooms are equipped with air-conditioning and all modern amenities but, with their mahogany wardrobes, octagonal bedheads and ornate furnishings, have an elegant period atmosphere. Business needs are not overlooked and 12 conference rooms are available for meetings and receptions. **Rooms 271. Room service 24hr. Public parking 120F. Conference facilities 450. Amex, Diners, Mastercard, Visa.**

Le Paris ★ 1000F

As a disciple of Escoffier, chef Philippe Renard has a classical pedigree but loves to experiment. His seasonal carte includes *cannelloni de foie gras de canard à la truffe noire du Périgord, tournedos de boeuf à la moutarde de Brive, palet de pommes aux amandes* (tournedos of beef in Brive mustard, served with apple and almond rings) and *petit coeur sablé au coco et aux framboises, violettes cristallisées* (heart-shaped cocoa and raspberry shortbread with crystallised violets). Set menus at 250F and 350F (lunch) and 350F, 495F and 550F (dinner). Brasserie Lutétia, the hotel's informal second restaurant, is also open from 0730 for breakfast and, later, serves excellent seafood platters as well as other light dishes. **Seats 43. Open 1200-1400, 1930-2230. Closed Sat & Sun, Aug.** 🐂

Residence Maxim's de Paris 2490F

Tel: (1) 45 61 96 33   Fax: (1) 42 89 06 07   H
42 avenue Gabriel, 75008 Paris

Enjoying a superb position overlooking the Champs-Elysées, Maxim's is a supremely stylish hotel. When Pierre Cardin acquired this grand building a few years ago he completely redesigned and redecorated every room to create some of the most elegant and luxurious bedrooms and suites in Paris. All are different: some are relatively plain, in cool blues and whites, while others are painted in sunny oranges with patterned carpets. The suite with wood panelling and huge wall paintings is particularly magnificent. Bathrooms feature highly polished fossil stones and stunning murals. Service is equally impressive. **Rooms** *33. Room service 24hr. Valet parking. Conference facilities 80. Secretarial and translation services. Amex, Diners, Mastercard, Visa.*

Tel: (1) 44 36 44 36   Fax: (1) 44 36 49 00
19 rue Cdt-Mouchotte, 75014 Paris

This being one of the few skyscraper buildings (25 floors and eight lifts) in the centre of Paris, the view from the upper floors is exceptional. In the heart of Montparnasse guests here are perfectly located for a stay in Paris, whether on business or pleasure. The comfortable bedrooms include 33 suites and six 'pied à terre' rooms with offices. All rooms are air-conditioned and soundproofed, and room equipment includes 20-channel television, radios and mini-bars. There's a business centre offering multi-lingual secretarial services and the hotel is well geared-up for conferences and banquets. **Rooms** *953. Room service 24hr. Parking in public park beneath the hotel 95F per 24hr. Conference facilities 2000. Amex, Diners, Mastercard, Visa.*

Tel: (1) 44 36 44 25 Fax (1) 44 36 49 03

The hotel's gastronomic dining option, where the classically orientated carte includes some fairly elaborate dishes such as frogs' legs meunière with wild mushroom purée and foie gras, marinated mackerel with herbs and deep-fried langoustines on a salad of purslane, roast monkfish tail with a confit of young vegetables and a saffron jus, saddle of milk-fed Pauillac lamb flavoured with thyme, and roast *chapon* (a Mediterranean fish) garnished with ratatouille-stuffed squid. Desserts are just as interesting: pastilla of rhubarb with honey, a sabayon of mead and verbena ice cream; cassolette of apricot en croute with almond ice cream; warm feuilleté of nectarines poached in vin de Maury. Decor is 1920s with photos of stars of stage and screen from the period hanging on the walls next to reproduction Modigliani paintings. Tables are well spaced and service is discreetly efficient. California, Italy and Spain are represented on the wine list, as well as France. Set L 240F Set D 300F & 390F. **Seats** *70. Open 1200-1430, 1930-2230. Closed Sat, Sun, Aug, 25 Dec-1 Jan & National Holidays.*

Tel: (1) 44 36 44 00

On the first floor of the hotel, overlooking a 100 square metre terrace garden with trees, plants, shrubs and flowers, this brasserie resembles an enclosed verandah. The day starts with breakfast (till 1030), the main à la carte coming on stream at midday and being available till closing. This might include such modish offerings as tomato millefeuille with fromage frais and pistou; beef carpaccio with parmesan shavings, and curried fricassee of tuna with lime-flavoured risotto, along with sole (grilled or meunière), steak with tomato provençale, béarnaise sauce and 'matchstick' fries, and calf's liver with mashed potatoes. Lemon crème brulée, chocolate tart and caramelised pear to finish. A special Sur le Pouce section of the menu lists quick bites like croque monsieur, club sandwich, cheeseburger and omelettes. Lunch (1200-1430) and evening (1900-2230) there is also a fixed-price buffet. On Sundays, the 'Bébé Brunch' menu (adults 220F, children 4-12 110F, under 4s free) is especially geared towards families. Set L & D 295F (buffet). **Seats** *250. Open 0700-2230.*

Tel: (1) 44 58 10 10   Fax: (1) 44 58 10 17
228 rue de Rivoli, 75001 Paris

Dating from the time when Préfect Haussmann was replanning Paris, the Meurice, with its location overlooking the Tuileries Gardens, quickly established itself as a favourite of the Imperial Court. More recently it has become a haunt of the literati with the jury of a new literary prize 'Le Jury Du Prix Novembre' making its home here. Following the hotel's acquisition by the Ciga group in 1988 considerable refurbishment has returned the sparkle to the stunning Salon Pompadour with its elaborate gilt decoration, and other public rooms and restored the hotel's position amongst the best in Paris. Antique furniture, fresh flowers, original paintings and the occasional marble fireplace are among the elements that bring individuality and luxury to both the bedrooms and the 37 suites. Bathrooms are marble and standards of service high. **Rooms** *180. Amex, Diners, Mastercard, Visa.*

See over

Le Meurice   ⭐ 1100F

Marc Marchand's menu changes with the seasons in this exquisitely appointed restaurant, but on Wednesdays you might get all four seasons at once, as Vivaldi is often included in the musical *'saveurs lyriques'* evenings. Cannelloni of lobster in a Jura wine-flavoured stock, terrine of eel with blinis and sevruga caviar, fillet of whiting with a lemon butter and asparagus sauce, calf's liver with aged vinegar, roast goose, fillet of lamb with prunes, preserved lemons and Oriental spices, and filet mignon poached in consommé with vegetables from the pot-au-feu are typical choices. Palette of chocolate tastes and mandarin soufflé with a cocoa-flavoured iced cream is a speciality dessert. Set menus: L 330F D (inclusive of wine) 410F. *Seats 60. Open 1215-1430, 1930-2230.*

PARIS   Michel Rostang   ★+ 1600F

Tel: (1) 47 63 40 77   Fax: (1) 47 63 82 75   R
20 rue Rennequin, 75017 Paris

Despite his far-flung culinary interests, Michel Rostang still cooks full time in his eponymous restaurant in north-west Paris. The striking interior has an almost Oriental atmosphere, with dark red lacquered woodwork, matching walls, carpets and chairs, and a cream and red ceiling. Michel's cooking is bursting with life and invention, although his classic dishes such as *soufflé de quenelle de brochet au homard and volaille de Bresse à la crème d'estragon* are admirably unfussy. The carte offers starters such as terrine of veal sweetbreads and duck foie gras with a compote of onions and raw wild mushroom salad. Tempting mains are pan-fried red mullet with a purée of peas and olive oil and a red mullet liver jus, and *pigeon en crapaudine* (spatchcocked) roasted in a garlic crust with beetroot juice and chards pan-fried with parmesan. The cheese selection is excellent and desserts include the intriguing *risotto de peches blanches aux aromes de vanille tuiles aux pralines* and a marvellous cold raspberry soufflé. Service is effortlessly efficient. Set menus 298F (lunch), 540F and 720F (lunch and dinner). *Seats 65. Open 1200-1400, 2000-2215. Closed Sat (but open D Sat Jun-Sep), all Sun, 1st 3 weeks Aug. Valet parking. Amex, Diners, Mastercard, Visa.*

PARIS   Hotel Nikko de Paris   1950F

Tel: (1) 40 58 20 00   Fax: (1) 45 75 42 35   HR
61 quai de Grenelle, 75015 Paris

On the banks of the Seine between the Eiffel Tower and Mirabeau Bridge, the Nikko is a tall, strikingly modern Japanese-owned hotel. Public areas are bright, cool, smart and spacious. La Seine Bar shows a more classic side with well-upholstered light wood furniture, splendid Japanese murals and a nightly pianist. The majority of the bedrooms offer good views and are modern in style and design, each with cable TV and mini-bar among the up-to-date facilities provided. Buffet, American and Japanese breakfasts are served, but no Continental breakfast. Banqueting and conference facilities for up to 600; Coffee Shop/Brasserie Pont Mirabeau (open 0700-2400). *Rooms 764. Amex, Diners, Mastercard, Visa.*

Les Célébrités   1200F

Tel: (1) 40 58 21 29

A table by the window looking out over the Seine must be the best location to sit in this spacious, modern restaurant. Duck galantine with foie gras, cream of asparagus soup with watercress, scallops and langoustines are two of the starter suggestions and pan-fried red mullett with a *Niçoise tapénade* or roast Pauillac lamb with a rice and liver galette could be offered as main courses. Open for breakfast 0700-0930. Set menus: L & D 290F, 390F. *Seats 70. Open 1200-1430, 1900-2200. Closed Aug.* 🐂

Benkay   900F

The decor may be contemporary but essentially this is a traditional Japanese restaurant offering a variety of set meals as well as a short but comprehensive carte. Lunchtime is best for lower-priced set menus: L from 140F, D from 350F. *Seats 120. Open 1200-1400, 18.30-2200.*

Opening times are often liable to change at short notice, so it's
always best to book.

Tel: (1) 40 02 02 12
15 place Lachambeaudie, 75012 Paris

A smart modern restaurant with picture windows opening on to the terrace. The chairs and banquette seating are furnished in bold fabrics and copper cooking pans, jars of home-made preserves, plants and flowers decorate the interior. The *menu du marché* (150F) changes daily and offers simple but delicious dishes such as *salade de queue de boeuf aux oignons nouveaux* (oxtail salad with onions) and veal braised with olives. Southern French dishes are also prominent on the carte: *tarte fine croustillante aux sardines fraiches, tomates et parmesan* and fillet of gilthead pan-fried with pipérade, for instance. Desserts include flambéed peaches with honey and rosemary, and *parfait glacé aux noisettes caramélisées*. The four-course menu de saison (230F) includes wine. *Seats 45 (terrace 30). Open 1200-1415, 2000-2215. Closed L Sat, all Sun. Amex, Diners, Mastercard, Visa.*

Tel: (1) 46 33 31 31   Fax: (1) 46 33 07 60
44 boulevard St-Germain, 75005 Paris

Designed to resemble a rather smart private dining-room-pictures, shelves of books, crystal chandeliers-Roland Magne's restaurant has enormous charm as well as fine food. The cuisine is classically-based but interpreted with Roland's own inventiveness: *raviolis d'escargots à la crème d'ail*, fricassee of lobster with girolle mushrooms, stuffed pig's trotter, escalope of salmon in a pesto sauce, *tarte au chocolat, crème brulée aux parfums des iles*. In addition to the à la carte there's a set five-course *menu gourmand* (279F) and a limited-choice business lunch (285F). There's a public car park across the street. *Seats 48. Open 1215-1430, 1900-2230. Closed L Sat, 1 May, 24 & 25 Dec. Amex, Mastercard, Visa.*

Tel: (1) 42 60 56 22   Fax: (1) 42 36 55 50
9 rue d'Argenteuil, 75001 Paris

Promoting foreign food in the capital of French gastronomy might seem like an uphill struggle, but Paolo Petrini's classic Italian cooking has proved very popular in this tiny restaurant near the Palais Royal. His seasonal menu might include starters like *taccole alla marinara* (salad of mangetout, squid and prawns) and carpaccio with rocket, lemon, olive oil and parmesan. Pasta dishes are mainly simple although *tagliatelle nere con ragù di calamari, scampi, gamberi e vongole* (octopus ink tagliatelle with a squid, scampi, prawn and clam sauce) is more unusual. A speciality is *filetto di bue al sale grosso con intingolo di erbe aromatiche* (fillet of beef cooked in green salt with herbs). The wine list manages to stay as purely Italian as the menu. *Seats 30. Open 1200-1430, 2000-2300. Closed L Sat, all Sun, Aug. Amex, Diners, Mastercard, Visa.*

Tel: (1) 44 05 66 66   Fax: (1) 44 05 66 00
55 avenue Raymond Poincaré 75016 Paris

Nina Campbell masterminded the renovation of this handsome hotel, which tries to combine British refinement with French hospitality. It comprises five buildings set around an interior courtyard garden (not quite a park!) set with trees and flowers, a feature which emphasises the country-house style. Among the day rooms are a cosy bar, a library with tartan upholstery and a number of salons accommodating up to 350 for functions or conferences. Bedrooms combine the Campbell style with all the expected up-to-date facilities, including fax/computer points, two telephones, electronic safes and Bang & Olufsen cable TVs. 24hr room service. One floor of rooms is designated non-smoking. Parking 150F a day. *Rooms 120. Amex, Diners, Mastercard, Visa.*

Tel 47 27 12 27

As we went to press, our information from Le Parc was that Joël Robuchon would be leaving at the end of 1995. Acknowledged as one of the greatest chefs in the world, he made an enormous impact during his years in Paris, and a seat at one of his tables was always the result of booking months, not just weeks, ahead. Specialities such as *gelée de caviar à la crème de chou-fleur, tarte friande de truffes aux oignons et lard fumé* and *lièvre à la royale* earned superlatives in these and other pages, and in Robuchon's hands even the humble *pommes purées* was elevated to almost regal status. If he happens to stay for another season, get on the phone now. The hotel's own restaurant, **Le Relais du Parc (Tel: (1) 44 05 66 10),** produces a touch of Robuchon style at very un-Robuchon prices – about 700F for two. *Seats 45. Open 1215-1415, 1930-2215. Closed Sat, Sun, 4 wks Jul/Aug. Access, Visa.*

Tel: (1) 42 77 96 40   Fax: (1) 42 77 63 06
28 place des Vosges, 75003 Paris

Located on one of the city's most beautiful squares, this hotel offers elegant and
comfortable accommodation. The entrance hall has huge exposed beams and a stone-tile
floor and is furnished with antiques. Bedrooms are all air-conditioned and pleasantly
decorated, with views over the garden or the courtyard with its attractive flowers.
No restaurant. *Rooms 55. Room service 24hr. Private parking. Secretarial services on
request. Amex, Diners, Mastercard, Visa.*

Tel: (1) 43 80 28 54   Fax: (1) 44 40 04 29
42 rue des Acacias, 75017 Paris

Bernard Fournier's provincial-style auberge has remained for 60 years a bastion of classic
French cooking. Amid the woodwork and the flowers and the copper ornaments an
appreciative clientele tucks into terrine of foie gras with brioche, confit de canard and rib
of beef with bone marrow and two sauces. Pigeon roasted in a salt crust with truffle juice is
a speciality along with a kebab of eggs with fresh truffles. Equally appreciated are dishes
such as roast turbot with fresh pasta and woodland mushrooms or casserole of suckling calf
with ceps and girolle mushrooms. There's a great cellar, with bottles selected from all
round the world, and every month sees a special promotion, with a red and a white on
offer by the glass. The 200F four-course menu carte offers remarkable value for money; the
set dinner is 350F. *Seats 80. Open 1215-1430, 1930-2230. Closed L Sun, all Sat,
1st 2 weeks Aug. Amex, Mastercard, Visa.*

Tel: (1) 43 31 58 59
9 boulevard du Port-Royal, 75013 Paris

The three Cousin brothers, Michel, Jacques and Alain, create a very friendly ambience at
this genuine Parisian bistro. Michel and Jacques spend most of their time in the kitchen,
occasionally coming out to greet customers or join in the conversation. Alain makes sure all
runs smoothly in the two dining-rooms with their ancient tiled floors and aged pink walls
covered with mirrors. The brothers specialise in game, offal, fresh fish and regional dishes,
and among their most popular are various terrines with foie gras (hare, pheasant, partridge
with juniper berries), *escargots de Bourgogne*, warm salad of scallops and langoustines, and
rosette of lamb with basil and an aubergine gateau. Set menus only: 165F at lunch, lunch
and dinner 205F, 325F, 455F. Special game menu in season. *Seats 80 (+ 20 outside).
Open 1200-1415, 1930-2230. Closed Sun, Mon, Aug & 24 Dec-2 Jan. Amex, Diners,
Mastercard, Visa.*

Tel: (1) 42 33 64 33   Fax: (1) 42 36 61 09
52 bis rue Notre-Dame-des-Victoires, 75002 Paris

A warm, cosy restaurant on two floors with burgundy red walls and a small bar/greeting
area near the entrance. Everything is made on the premises, including bread (two bakings
a day), petits fours and the chocolates served with coffee. Normandy farms supply much of
the produce, and typifying the dishes on the carte menu are scrambled eggs with a purée of
morels, rabbit terrine with rosemary and thyme, pigeon roasted in truffle oil with pan-fried
foie gras, and oxtail pot-au-feu. For dessert, perhaps frozen yoghurt with crumbled biscuits
and blackcurrant compote, or apples pan-fried in butter served with cinnamon ice cream.
Lunch is a fixed-price affair of four courses (including cheese) of dishes taken from the
evening menus with about eight choices at each stage. Set menus from 235F (lunch) and
280F (dinner) to 320F. *Seats 40. Open 1200-1400, 2000-2200. Closed Sat, Sun, Aug,
24 Dec-1 Jan, National Holidays. Mastercard, Visa.*

Tel: (1) 47 23 78 33   Fax: (1) 47 20 20 70
25 avenue Montaigne, 75008 Paris

Surrounded by the great haute-couture houses, the Plaza has its own inimitible sense of style and has long been a haunt of the famous-and sometimes infamous; Mata Hari was arrested in the hotel's darkwood and leather English bar. Other public areas include a large circular lobby, vaulted Galerie de Gobelins with pairs of columns down each side, and a verdant courtyard garden with fountains and red umbrellas that match the awnings of the balustraded bedroom windows that overlook it. There are four splendid conference rooms. Bedrooms in Louis XV, Louis XVI or Regency style are elegant and comfortable, with air-conditioning and ultra-modern bathrooms. There are 443 suites. Services include 24-hour room service, hairdressing salon, perfume boutique and theatre desk. Guests have free access to a fitness club, and transport to it (but not back). Parking for about a dozen cars (150F a day). Forte. *Rooms 253. Access, Amex, Diners, Visa.*

An elegant dining-room with fluted pilasters supporting an elaborate gilded frieze, and widely spaced tables displaying silver place settings. The menu is very much Grand Hotel in both style-separate sections for grills, fish etc-and content; the starters include oysters, caviar, smoked salmon and foie gras. Amongst the other, perhaps less standard, dishes are a lobster soufflé, curried monkfish with shellfish, green noodles and sweet peppers, and breast of chicken simmered with lemon and peppermint. From a good varied choice of desserts this would be just the place to enjoy the spectacle that is crepe Suzette flambée. Menu gourmande 490F. Over 2000 references on the wine list, including a champagne de la maison. *Seats 75 (+ 80 outside) Open 1230-1430, 1930-2230.*

Informal, all-day eatery with 1930s' decor and entrance direct from the street as well as from within the hotel. It's breakfast till 11am after which the full menu runs through until the early hours. With something to suit all appetites the choice ranges from club sandwiches and croque monsieur, via pasta, salads and egg dishes to lamb curry, sole meunière and grills. Set lunch 225F, set dinner 260F. *Seats 103. Open 0800-0130.*

Tel: (1) 45 24 55 58 Fax: (1) 45 24 43 25
route de Suresnes, Bois de Boulogne, 75016 Paris

Enjoying a wonderful location in the Bois de Boulogne, this beautiful restaurant has been restored to its full 18th-century glory by Christian Benais. The grand dining-rooms and summer terraces are a fine setting for Roland Durand's superb cooking, which he describes as "neo-classic with rustic tendencies and light touches of the Orient". Among the imaginative starters on his seasonal carte are *cervelle d'agneau en marinade citronée aux épices, tomate confite et coeur de laitue* (lamb's brains marinated in lemon and spices, served with tomato confit and lettuce hearts), and *soupe rafraichissante de carottes au parfum de cumin* (cold carrot soup perfumed with cumin). Main dishes are equally delicious: *risotto noir* of langoustines and Thai basil, and rack of lamb scented with rosemary and served with courgettes and stuffed aubergines. Nectarine crumble with a vanilla sabayon and pastis ice cream makes a fine end to a meal. The wine list includes some good Italian and Californian bottles. Set menus from 270F (weekday lunch) and 550F (dinner). *Seats 80 (terrace 80). Open 1200-1430, 1930-2230. Closed D Sun, all Mon, 2 weeks in Feb. Private parking. Amex, Diners, Mastercard, Visa.*

Tel 45 48 86 58   Fax 42 22 84 76
4 rue Recamier 75007 Paris

A really splendid place for late spring and summer when Recamier's open-air terrace comes into its own. Extending into a delightful, pedestrianised street awash with flowers long-established, the restaurant majors on solid classics from the Burgundy region as in beef bourguignon with fresh noodles and *jambon persillé*. Modern influences also appear as in an escalope of tuna with pesto or fillets of red mullet with basil and mashed potato. *Gratin dauphinois* is a favourite accompaniment, appearing with the likes of rack of lamb, Auvergne-style calf's liver and various steaks. The wine list is phenomenal, particularly strong on Bordeaux and champagne. Set lunch 300F (also 230F on Saturday, when there's no à la carte). *Seats 80. Open 1200-1430, 1945-2230. Closed Sun. Amex, Diners, Mastercard, Visa.*

Tel: (1) 43 16 30 30   Fax: (1) 43 16 31 78
15 place Vendome, 75001 Paris

HR

Since being opened by César Ritz in 1898, this hotel, and his name, have become
a synonym for opulence and luxury. Still in private hands, and unconnected with other
hotels bearing the name, the Ritz continues to live up to its own legend. Day rooms in the
18th-century former private residence retain their authentic period atmosphere but today
are joined by facilities such as the Ritz Health Club with its hi-tech fitness centre and
romanesque pool and the Ritz Club for dancing until the small hours; for the less energetic
high tea is served in the Vendome garden to the sound of a harp. The Vendome Bar is
spacious and overlooks the gardens while the Hemingway Bar, panelled and more intimate,
has books and letters of the great man and other literary giants, and cocktails shaken by an
Englishman. Antique-furnished bedrooms include nearly 50 full suites, some especially
luxurious named after such notables as the Duke of Windsor, Coco Chanel and Scott
Fitzgerald. Air-conditioning and all the usual up-to-date amenities combine with the sort of
service that runs to a 24hr valet-all in all making you feel well and truly pampered.
Own parking. *Rooms 187. Amex, Diners, Mastercard, Visa.*

A Second Empire room of delicate elegance, where the exact shade of turquoise in
a *trompe l'oeil* sky is picked up in the trimmings for the elaborate drapes that adorn high
windows (which open on to the Vendome gardens for summer dining) and matching
mirrored 'windows' that surround the room, giving it a satisfying symmetry. Add Venetian
glass 'flower vase' lights set on sconces around the walls and you have a setting into which
the wing-collared, be-tailed waiters fit perfectly. A typically thoughtful Ritz touch is the
little gilt hook discreetly tucked away on the side of each chair to accommodate handbags.
The first chef at the Ritz was the great Auguste Escoffier, who also designed the original
kitchens, and it is from his classic tradition that long-serving chef Guy Legay has developed
his own style, taking into account modern trends. *Menus dégustation* (590F) are where
a chef generally likes to 'show off' but here it is perhaps the safe choice with such dishes as
foie gras fried with vine peaches and a Médoc sauce or coeur de filet with a panaché of
mushrooms, fried herbs and sauce périgourdine. The main menu is somewhat more
adventurous: here the foie gras (goose in this case) might be served cooked pink with red
onions and honey or in ravioli (back to duck) with a bouillon of herbs and pearl barley.
A respectable cheese trolley comes with their own excellent bread. The impressive wine list
is full of classic names from Bordeaux and Burgundy. *Seats 60. Open 1200-1500,
1900-2300.*

Tel: (1) 44 71 24 24   Fax: (1) 42 65 39 97
1 rue Scribe, 75009 Paris

HR

A major corner site, formerly the Jockey Club, whose Napoleon III facade today conceals
a busy cosmopolitan hotel. Refurbishment over recent years has extended from the
spacious lobby with its Baccarat crystal chandeliers and the luxurious, softly-lit cocktail bar
to the bedrooms. Things like air-conditioning, double-glazing (for streetside rooms) and
endless TV channels provide the modern comforts for rooms that are mostly furnished in
Louis Philippe or Louis XVI style, although some rooms are in 'English' style and there are
some suites, featuring mezzanine bedroom floors, that are more contemporary in concept.
One floor of rooms is designated non-smoking. Two conference rooms. *Rooms 217.
Amex, Diners, Mastercard, Visa.*

Tel: (1) 44 71 24 26

Guests at this sophisticated restaurant sit at round tables in sombre surroundings of wood
panelling, black lacquer, mirrors and bouquets of flowers. The cooking is a mix of classic
and modern: warm salad of sea bass in a watercress-infused oil; prawns in puff pastry with
herbs and satay; lamb 'en crépinette' with savory, young carrots and mushrooms; mignons
of veal with asparagus and candied tomato; cinnamon-flavoured crème brulée; peanut crisp
with peaches and rhubarb served with wild strawberries. Set menus at lunch and dinner:
210F and 270F. *Seats 40. Open 1200-1430, 1930-2230. Closed Sat, Sun, Aug & Bank
Holidays.*

Tel: (1) 43 71 65 30   Fax: (1) 40 09 79 75
35 rue Faidherbe, 75011 Paris

One of the culinary delights of the little town of Souseyrac in the Lot region of France is its cassoulet. This dish therefore features as one of the South-Western specialities served in this typical 1920s-30s bistro with its tiled floors, wood panelling and diplomas on the walls. Others are their home-made foie gras (goose or duck), hare *à la royale* (in season) and coquilles St Jacques with sorrel, which you might follow with an apple feuilleté with armagnac or *crème brulée maison*. 260-long wine list. Set menu: L & D 175F.
Seats 60. Open 1200-1400, 1930-2200. Closed L Sat, all Sun & Aug. Amex, Diners, Mastercard, Visa.

Tel: (1) 44 95 15 01   Fax: (1) 42 25 95 18
15 rue Lammenais, 75008 Paris

A most civilised and refined of restaurants presided over by the urbane second-generation owner Jean-Claude Vrinat. Wood-panelled walls and discreet, polished service help to create an almost club-like atmosphere relished by the good and the great of the capital's establishment. Philippe Legendre continues in the tradition of his predecessor (who was head chef here for 30 years) of acknowledging modern trends but only gradually and from a solidly classical base. Boudin of Brittany lobster, terrine of sweetbreads and mushrooms, langoustines with fresh pasta and truffled pig's trotter andouillette are among the classics, and some of the specialities are available for 2 or more diners: *poulette de Bresse en cocotte lutée, selle d'agneau de lait aux herbes, cote de boeuf grillé au deux sauces. Farandole de desserts* gets you a tasting of several delights. The legendary wine list is supported by their own wine shop, one of the best in Paris, in the nearby Rue du Faubourg Saint-Honoré.
Seats 120. Open 1200-1330, 1930-2200. Closed Sat, Sun, last week Jul, 1st 3 wks Aug. Amex, Diners, Mastercard, Visa.

Tel: (1) 42 85 05 15   Fax: (1) 40 16 13 98
23 rue Dunkerque, 75010 Paris

Directly across from the imposing facade of Gare du Nord this classic 20s' brasserie is the perfect first or last stop on a Eurostar train journey or a longer, more exhausting channel port trip. There's something for everyone on the splendidly traditional, daily-changing menus. There's even one for children (main dish, dessert and a drink 62F). The fixed price menus represent good value, too, with a choice of starter and main or main and dessert with an inclusive half-bottle of wine. House specialities are numerous, including tarama with toasted country bread and goose foie gras with riesling jelly among the starters, and as a main dish, choucroute several ways or lamb's sweetbreads in puff pastry with a champagne sauce. Classic dishes include a 300gm entrecote steak or chateaubriand, both with béarnaise sauce, and lamb noisettes with tarragon. The selection of seafood (shellfish make an eye-catching and mouthwatering display outside) is superb – ask for the separate menu. Prepared fish dishes could include warm oysters in a champagne sauce, Scottish salmon with crisply cooked skin accompanied by wild mushrooms, and monkfish medallions with baby vegetables. Service from well-drilled, smartly attired staff is serious and attentive. Set menus 112F and 189F. Also open for breakfast, teas and coffees. Pavement terrace. *Seats 200. Open 1100-0030. Amex, Diners, Mastercard, Visa.*

Tel: (1) 43 25 44 42
35 quai de la Tournelle, 75005 Paris

A charmingly decorated restaurant by the Seine. Chef-patron Philippe de Givenchy has an eclectic, refined style of cooking, and the influence of the Mediterranean is evident on the seasonal carte in dishes such as *grosse tapénade aux anchois et mozzarella en salade de basilic*, roasted sweet pepper ravioli and stuffed aubergines. Tempting main courses include *dorade rotie à l'estragon et piment et son jus de matelote reduit* (gilthead roasted with tarragon and chilis served with its own jus) and pig's trotters stuffed with Spanish peppers and serrano ham and roasted in olive oil. Desserts are simple: *crepes aux fraises* and *tarte fine au chocolat*, for instance. Set menu 230F (lunch). *Seats 20. Open 1200-1430, 1930-2230. Closed L Mon, all Sun, 3 weeks Aug, 2 weeks Feb. Mastercard, Visa.*

La Tour d'Argent   ★+   2400F

Tel: (1) 43 54 23 31   Fax: (1) 44 07 12 04
15 quai de la Tournelle, 75005 Paris

Almost a historic monument, this is the restaurant that once-in-a-lifetime visitors to Paris head for – if their pockets are deep enough. Even their speciality dish, a duck à la presse with cherries, has been on the menu for over 100 years and comes with a numbered certificate; they are currently up to around 800,000. Duck is what the Tour d'Argent is best known for, but there are other specialities, too, including *quenelles de brochet* and *peches flambées à l'eau de vie de framboise*. There are also some lighter dishes on an essentially traditional carte that competes with luxurious surroundings, spectacular views of the Seine and Notre Dame from the coveted window tables and a fabulous cellar which also contains a museum of wine. If the prices are beyond your reach (unless you choose the more manageable set lunch menu at Fr375) head for their shop opposite, *Comptoirs de la Tour d'Argent*, where souvenirs bearing the restaurant's logo are sold–tinned foie gras, tableware, silk ties and the like. *Seats 110. Open 1200-1430, 2000-2230. Closed Mon. Amex, Diners, Mastercard, Visa.*

Le Train Bleu   600F

Tel: (1) 43 43 09 06   Fax: (1) 43 43 97 96
Gare de Lyon, 75012 Paris

Named after the legendary luxurious Paris-Cote d'Azur express of the 1920s, the buffet of the Gare du Lyon (classified as a historic monument) is truly unique. In 1900, thirty artists were commissioned to paint the most beautiful parts of France crossed by the Paris-Lyon-Marseille rail network. These paintings (41 of them) now cover the restaurant's ornate ceilings and walls and provide a wonderful backdrop to food of a high quality. Starters include duck terrine with pistachios and *saucisson lyonnais* with parsley potatoes, while typical main dishes are grilled rack of lamb with Provençal herbs and brill (barbue) soufflé with wild mushrooms. Set menu 250F. *Seats 200. Open 1200-1430, 1900-2200. Amex, Diners, Mastercard, Visa.*

Hotel Vernet   2190F

Tel: (1) 47 23 43 10   Fax: (1) 44 31 85 69
25 rue Vernet, 75008 Paris

Built at the turn of the century and completely refurbished in 1989, the Vernet combines period style with modern comforts. Antique–furnished bedrooms and suites are all air-conditioned and the splendid marble bathrooms all have jacuzzi tubs. Day rooms include an elegant lounge with panelled walls where afternoon tea and cocktail hour are accompanied by the piano. Guests have use of the health and beauty centre of the nearby Royal Monceau Hotel. 24hr room service (cold food only after 11pm). *Rooms 57. Private parking (110F a day) Amex, Diners, Mastercard, Visa.*

Les Elysées du Vernet   ★   1000F

The magnificent, glass-roofed Belle Epoque dining room provides a really splendid setting for some fine cooking with a sunny Mediterranean slant: *filets de rougets de roche poelés aux olives et tomates confits; langoustine royale rotie au sel de Guérande, mesclun niçoise; cote de boeuf de Chalosse, grosses frites à la graisse d'oie, sauce bordelaise à la moelle et poivre noir* (for two), *petites brioches toastées aux fruits noirs, sorbet noix de coco.* Farmhouse cheeses, good choice of coffees and teas and a comprehensive French wine list. 24 of the seats are in a non-smoking covered terrace. Set lunch 400F, dinner 370F and 490F. *Seats 40 (+ 15 outside). Open 1200-1430, 1930-2200. Closed Sat, Sun, Aug, 1 week Christmas.*

La Villa Maillot   1900F

Tel: (1) 45 01 25 22   Fax: (1) 45 00 60 61
143 avenue de Malakoff, 75116 Paris

This former embassy near the Porte Maillot has been converted into a refreshingly understated and stylish art deco hotel. The striking public rooms include the lovely Le Jardin conservatory where a meal, snack or cocktail can be enjoyed while gazing at the lush trees and shrubs outside. The light and airy bedrooms are equipped with air-conditioning, soundproofing, satellite TV and mini-bar and have luxurious rose-coloured marble bathrooms. The hotel's three suites are named after Picasso, Chagall and Modigliani while a motoring theme runs through the Bugatti, Maserati and Ferrari meeting rooms. *Rooms 42. Room service limited. Private parking 100F. Conference facilities 20. Amex, Diners, Mastercard, Visa.*

Tel: (1) 45 04 04 31   Fax: (1) 45 03 09 84
192 avenue Victor Hugo, 75016 Paris

Chef-patron Claude Peyrot has been here since 1970 and is acknowledged as being one of the finest in the city. If the interior of the restaurant is nothing to enthuse over, his classical cooking certainly is, though opinions are divided whether you can actually attribute a style to his cuisine. The menu has changed little over the years, with but minor reworkings of the classic themes. *Galettes de pommes de terre aux truffes* is a renowned seasonal speciality, and other dishes of note are *barbue rotie au jus de viande et au lard* and *canard au miel et aux épices*. In addition to the carte, there's a three-course *menu déjeuner* (345F) featuring many dishes that will require translation and explanation since they are often idiosyncratically described, for instance *ravioli Rastellini, bar antiboise* and *plaisir d'agneau*. For dessert try the more explicable *tarte fine au chocolat*. Claude's wife Jacqueline charmingly marshals the staff, who are unobtrusively professional and efficient, greatly enhancing the enjoyment of a meal here. *Seats 50. Open 1200-1400, 2000-2200. Closed Sat, Sun, Aug & National Holidays. Amex, Diners, Mastercard, Visa.*

Around Paris

Tel: (1) 30 84 38 00   Fax: (1) 39 49 00 77
1 boulevard de la Reine, 78000 Versailles

Situated on the edge of the Royal Park, a short walk from the Palace of Versailles, and ten miles from the centre of Paris, the hotel has welcomed a long and distinguished line of guests. Monarchs and generals, oil magnates and film stars have walked the long, marble-columned corridors and stayed in the elegant, high-ceilinged bedrooms, which are furnished with antiques. The building dates from 1910 and was thoroughly renovated four years ago when it was bought by a Japanese company. Old-fashioned luxury is matched by the most up-to-date amenities, including an international conference centre in the neighbouring Trianon Hotel (linked by a landscaped walkway) with its six conference and five committee rooms. Leisure facilities are equally splendid. In addition to a fully-equipped gym and health spa, guests can also swim, play tennis and relax in a traditional Moroccan hammam. *Rooms 98. Room service 24hr. Valet parking. Banqueting facilities 250. Conference facilities 250. Business centre. Indoor swimming pool. Tennis. Gym. Sauna. Hair salon. Amex, Diners, Mastercard, Visa.*

Les Trois Marches
Tel: (1) 39 50 13 21

Chef Gérard Vié prides himself on the research and invention behind his cooking. Some of his dishes are fiendishly complicated, while others are nearer the peasant simplicity of the food of his youth. Examples are *galette de pomme de terre, lard et caviar* (potato, bacon and caviar pancake), *ragout d'abats caramélisés* (caramelised offal stew) and *langouste rose aux épices, figues, navet confits* (spiny lobster with spices, figs and turnip confit). Portions are not huge. A special dietetic menu is available. Set menus 260F (lunch) and 495F and 595F (dinner). The excellent sommelier is particularly good at discovering 'petits vins' from areas such as Languedoc/Roussillon. *Seats 60 (terrace 60). Open 1200-1400, 1930-2200. Closed Sun, Mon.*

Reims

Tel: 26 82 80 80   Fax: 26 82 65 52
64 boulevard Henry-Vasnier, 51100 Reims

A few minutes from the centre of Reims, this turn-of-the-century chateau situated in its own 17-acre park formerly belonged to Louise Pommery, "la grand dame de Champagne". Gérard and Elyane Boyer spent two years converting it into a stylish and comfortable hotel. Bedrooms are decorated in a variety of period styles and furnished elegantly. *Rooms 19. Closed 22 Dec-12 Jan. Room service limited. Private parking. Helipad. Garden. Tennis. Amex, Diners, Mastercard, Visa.*

See over

Restaurant   ★ ✦ 1600F

Two of the three dining-rooms are wood-panelled and display a fine collection of 16th,
17th and 18th-century original oil paintings alongside contemporary works by local artists.
Seats in the English-style bar overlook the sweeping lawns of the chateau's grounds. The
setting is a suitably grand one for Gérard Boyer's magnificent and lavish cooking, prepared
with an extraordinary attention to detail. There are no set menus, only a carte offering such
delicacies as pig's trotters stuffed with foie gras and ceps mushrooms, and mussel soup with
saffron and orange. Roasted Breton lobster flavoured with Sauternes and served with fennel
and flat-leaf parsley is superb, while *tete de cochon mitonée aux légumes, croustillant
d'oreille, toast de cervelle* (pig's head simmered with vegetables with crispy pig's ears and
brains on toast) is perhaps more of an acquired taste – apart from sounding much better in
French than in English! Chocolate addicts will go for the assiette tout chocolat for dessert
but there are plenty of other tempting dishes: *abricots blonds rotis en croustillant aux
fleurs de lavande, une glace au lait d'amande* (white apricots baked in a crispy pastry case
with lavender flowers and served with almond milk ice cream), for instance. It is
no surprise to find a cellar containing one of the finest champagne collections in France.
Seats 80. Open 1200-1430, 1915-2230. Closed as hotel plus L Tue, all Mon.

REIMS   Le Chardonnay   700F

Tel: 26 06 08 60 Fax: 26 05 81 56   R
184 avenue d'Epernay, 51100 Reims

Purpose-built in the 1930s, this place is still as traditional as it has always been, with
a well-spaced dining-room and local art on the walls. In the kitchen, haute cuisine meets
traditional regional cooking, with splendid results. The chef, Jean-Jacques Lange, worked
with Gérard Boyer before coming here and closely follows his culinary largesse: *poelée de
morilles et riz d'agneau à la crème, fricassée de homard aux pates fraiches, filet d'agneau
grillé à la fleur de thym*. The business lunch, *dégustation* and also champagne menus – the
latter is for two people and naturally includes a bottle of bubbly – all change seasonally.
For dessert, don't try to resist the soufflés, flavoured with Cointreau, Poire William or
Grand Marnier. *Seats 70. Open 1200-1400, 1930-2000. Closed L Sat, D Sun.*
Amex, Diners, Mastercard, Visa.

REIMS   Hotel Reims   520F

Tel: 26 40 01 08 Fax: 26 40 34 13   HR
37 boulevard Paul Doumer, 51100 Reims

Although the hotel was only built in 1990, it was recently taken over by Choice Hotels
and thoroughly renovated. The lobby has been remodelled in marble and all bedrooms are
now air-conditioned and have been repainted in smart blue, orange, yellow or pink. The
location, in the heart of Reims backing onto a canal, is central but can be a little noisy.
*Rooms 80. Room service limited. Private parking. Banqueting facilities 100. Conference
facilities 100. Amex, Diners, Mastercard, Visa.*

Restaurant Orphée   450F

Portuguese chef Jean-Paul Fernandès has added a Mediterranean element to the classic
French cooking served in the restaurant's splendid round dining-room. Typical dishes from
his seasonal carte include *cassoulet de langoustines, jus de volaille à la truffe noire*
(cassoulet of langoustines with a poultry and black truffle sauce), *filet de Saint-Pierre roti et
son gratiné d'herbes* (filet of John Dory roasted with a gratin of herbs), and *carpaccio de
canard à la vinaigrette d'oeuf mollet* (carpaccio of duck with a soft-boiled egg vinaigrette).
Desserts include *moelleux tiède du chocolat* (warm fondant of chocolate). Set menus at
95F, 150F and 195F. *Seats 80 (terrace 35). Open 1200-1400, 1900-2200. Closed L Sat,
all Sun.*

Around Reims

CHAMPIGNY SUR VESLE   La Garenne   850F
R

Tel: 26 08 26 62   Fax: 26 84 24 13
route de Soissons, 51370 Champigny sur Vesle

The tiny village of Champigny is 5km north-west of Reims on the N31, a couple of minutes from the A4 autoroute. The restaurant's two dining-rooms have recently been redecorated in a light beige and are furnished in a sleek modern style. Chef-patron Laurent Laplaige worked with Boyer in Reims before taking over here nine years ago and his cooking is solidly grounded in tradition. Typical dishes on his market-based menu are *poitrine de pigeon et cuisse confits* (confit of deboned pigeon breast and leg meat) and *marmite de turbot, homard et langoustines*. Service is friendly and efficient. A fine selection of champagnes, many reasonably priced, can be found among the 12,000 bottles in the cellar. Set menus at 150F and 205F. *Seats 70. Open 1200-1400, 1930-2200. Closed D Sun, all Mon, 1st 3 weeks Aug. Amex, Diners, Mastercard, Visa.*

Strasbourg

STRASBOURG   Hotel Baumann   690F
HR

Tel: 88 32 42 14   Fax: 88 23 03 92
16 place de la Cathédrale, 67000 Strasbourg

Owner Guy Pierre Baumann opened the hotel in 1990 to complement the already successful restaurant. It enjoys a splendid location, looking out over the square to the cathedral, although it can be a little noisy. Bedrooms are decorated in plain greys and blues with contemporary furniture and marble bathrooms. **Rooms** 9. *Room service limited. Banqueting facilities 360. Conference facilities 150. Amex, Diners, Mastercard, Visa.*

Restaurant Maison Kammerzell   600F

This wonderful three-storey wooden building dates from the 15th century and contains twelve dining-rooms hung with Alsatian folk art. A team of chefs cook traditional fare with a strong regional accent. The Germanic influence on the area's cuisine is evident in dishes such as *salade de cervelas sur pommes de terre tièdes* (saveloy and warm potato salad) and in the many different types of sauerkraut on offer. Other dishes such as *supreme de pintade aux légumes croquants, crème de brocolis* (guinea fowl breast with crunchy vegetables and creamed broccoli) are more mainstream French. The modest wine list predictably features a good selection of local bottles. Set menus at 190F and 260F. *Seats 350 (terrace 250). Open 1200-1500, 1900-2400. Closed 24 Dec.*

STRASBOURG   Buerehiesel   ★   1300F
R

Tel: 88 61 62 24   Fax: 88 61 32 00
4 parc de l'Orangerie, 67000 Strasbourg

This 17th-century Alsatian farmhouse has been transported and reconstructed on its present site, in a park ten minutes from the city centre, only a few steps away from the European parliament. Chef-patron Antoine Westermann has been cooking deceptively simple Alsatian food here for more than a quarter of a century. His longevity has not made him complacent, though, and he continues to look for new inspiration by taking long cycle trips into the countryside around Strasbourg. Starters from his seasonal carte include *foie gras d'oie frais des Landes fait maison, pain de campagne grillé et gelée au Gewürztraminer* (home-made foie gras with grilled country bread and Gewürztraminer aspic) and *Schniederspäetle et les cuisses de grenouille poelées, au cerfeuil* (noodles with pan-fried frogs' legs and chervil). Mains such as *turbot poelé, tomate et fenouil aux aromates* (pan-fried turbot with tomato, fennel and aromatic herbs) and *poitrine de pintadeau rotie aux mousserons et aux girolles, gratin de poireaux* (breast of guinea fowl, roasted with wild mushrooms, served with a gratin of leeks) are equally splendid. A fine way to finish a meal is with the gourmandise of melted chocolate with a bitter chocolate sorbet. You can eat in the cosy dining-rooms or the light and airy conservatory and aperitifs can be taken on the terrace. Set menus from 290F (lunch) and 330F (dinner) to 640F. *Seats 100. Open 1200-1430, 1900-2130. Closed Tue & Wed, 2 weeks school holidays Feb/Mar, 2 weeks mid Aug, 2 weeks Christmas/New Year. Private parking. Amex, Diners, Mastercard, Visa.*

Tel: 88 22 12 12   Fax: 88 23 28 00
12 place de la Cathédrale, 67000 Strasbourg

This small, friendly hotel is well placed on the pedestrianised Cathedral square, ten minutes from the railway station and a 20-minute drive from the airport. Bedroom decor and furnishings are modern and comfortable but business and leisure facilities are limited. A new annexe, 100m away, was completed in early 1995, adding a further five rooms with kitchenettes. Expect to pay more if you want a room with a view of the cathedral. **Rooms** 40. Room service 24hr. Private parking 100F. Conference facilities 20. Amex, Diners, Mastercard, Visa.

Tel: 88 32 13 02   Fax: 88 75 72 01
10 rue de l'Outre, 67000 Strasbourg

Legend has it that General Kléber's aide-de-camp, Captain Ackermann, brought back the crocodile which hangs outside this restaurant from Napoleon's Egyptian campaign. The charmingly decorated building, originally a farmhouse, enjoys a central location near the cathedral and the town square. Chef Emile Jung trained in several top restaurants including Paul Bocuse before buying Le Crocodile in the early 70s and establishing his own distinct version of Alsatian cooking with wine as the key ingredient: for example, *foie gras d'oie au naturel en gelée de Gewürztraminer* and fillet of beef pan-fried in red Graves with slivers of fried garlic, puréed potatoes, carrots and black olives. A typical meal from the carte might commence with caviar of aubergines and fried courgettes with basil, followed by red mullet pan-fried with rosemary and served with *fondue provençale*, with *crème brulée au malt d'Orge torréfié* (toasted malt) to finish. The magnificent wine list is widely recognised as offering the finest selection of Alsace wines in the world. Set menus 295F and 395F (lunch) and 395F and 620F (dinner). **Seats** 80. Open 1200-1430, 1900-2130. Closed Sun, Mon, 8-29 July, 22 Dec-1 Jan. Amex, Diners, Mastercard, Visa.

Tel: 88 36 01 54   Fax: 88 35 40 14
22 quai des Bateliers, 67000 Strasbourg

On the quays, five minutes from the cathedral square, this 17th-century building stands opposite the Chateau des Rohan. Inside, the dining-room is decorated with lamps and other pieces of original art deco, with reproduction paintings on the walls. The cooking is traditionally Alsatian, and tends to be lighter in the summer, using plenty of fish and herbs, and the rest of the year, more filling, with vegetable and meat dishes. From a summer menu come terrine of goose foie gras with pressed vegetables, vol-au-vent of boned frogs' legs and asparagus, roast fillet of bass with thyme flower and courgettes with a tomato butter, and Limousin beef with marrow, pinot noir and potato quenelles. **Seats** 35. Open 1200-1400, 1900-2200. Closed Sun, Mon, 7-31 Aug, 25 Dec-1 Jan. Mastercard, Visa.

Around Strasbourg

Tel 89 71 89 00   Fax 89 71 82 83
68970 Illhaeusern, Strasbourg

Sixty kilometres from Strasbourg, the restaurant, particularly popular with Germans just across the border, has been in the Haeberlin family's hands since it was built at the end of the 19th century. Originally a farmhouse with a small restaurant attached to it, the building was reconstructed after the war, having been virtually razed to the ground. In an idyllic garden setting with the grounds sloping down to the banks of the River Ill, the restaurant is filled with silver and crystal ornaments, antique tables, chairs and rugs on the floor. In the kitchen, Haeberlin father (Paul) and son (Marc) create an imaginative modern French menu (note the Haeberlin cover painting) featuring plenty of interesting fish dishes: *salade de langoustines et son beignet en croute de riz basmati, parfumé au curry doux; homard farci à la créole et son jus aux épices; filets de carpes et d'anguilles roties au coulis de petits pois et légumes printaniers* or one of the house specialities *saumon soufflé 'Auberge de l'Ill'* (salmon surrounded by a fish mousse and encased in a soufflé). If your fancy is for something non-fishy, try the *salade de tripes panées au foie d'oie et aux fèves, supreme de pigeon au chou en crépinette et sa petite pastilla d'abats au foie d'oie, jus au vieux porto,* or their version of roast beef and Yorkshire pudding rather enchantingly titled *filet de boeuf*

'Black Angus' et la petite chartreuse de queue de boeuf à la moelle (oxtail and bone marrow), Yorkshire pudding. Cheese-lovers should order a plate of local Munster at the start of the meal – it is served in a variety of ways both hot and cold. Fixed-price inclusive lunch menus are priced at 500/600F, and the *menu dégustation*, a series of dishes (depending on what's fresh and available from the markets) is available for an entire table only at 710F per head. The almost biblical wine list includes Rieslings, Gewerztraminers and Sylvaners by the truckload, featuring all the best growers (Théo Faller, Trimbach, Léon Beyer, Lorentz, Hugel etc). The family also owns the *Hotel des Berge*s, once a tobacco-drying shed, at the bottom of the garden (11 great big air-conditioned rooms with wood floors and picture windows, including two suites and the *maison de pecheur*; double rooms from 1400 to 2600F, Tel 89 71 87 87, Fax 89 71 87 88). Bedroom amenities include satellite TV, mini-bar and safe. ***Seats** 100. Open 1200-1400, 1900 -2100. Closed D Mon, all Tue, Feb. Ample underground parking. Amex, Diners, Mastercard, Visa.*

Toulouse

TOULOUSE — Brasserie Beaux Arts — 300F — R

Tel 61 21 12 12   Fax 61 21 14 80
1 quai de la Daurade, 31000 Toulouse

Part of the Flo group, this is a vast Belle Epoque restaurant with walnut panelling and lots of mirrors. A daily-changing menu offers the likes of foie gras de canard, gelée au riesling; soupe de poissons, sa rouille et ses croutons; cassoulet au confit de canard; cote de boeuf grillé, sauce béarnaise, and desserts such as *feuilleté tiède aux framboises, nougat glacé au miel, coulis de framboise or ile flottante et ses pralinnettes*. The fixed-price menus (lunch 101F, dinner 145F, and *menu faim de nuit* 97F served after 2200) are great value and include a ½ of wine in carafe. ***Seats** 140. Open 1200-1530, 1900-0100. Amex, Diners, Mastercard, Visa.*

TOULOUSE — Les Jardins de l'Opera — 1200F — R

Tel: 61 23 07 76   Fax: 61 23 63 00
1 place du Capitole, 31000 Toulouse

Diners can sip aperitifs in the Florentine-style, ivy-clad courtyard before moving inside to sample Dominique Toulousy's refined cooking. Only the freshest ingredients are used for specialities such as tartare of salmon and oysters served with blinis and lemon cream with chives, *raviolis de foie gras frais au jus de truffes* and *cassoulet toulousain*. Set menus 290F and 480F. ***Seats** 80. Open 1200-1400, 2000-2200. Closed Sun, 5-21 Aug, National Holidays. Public parking. Amex, Diners, Mastercard, Visa.*

TOULOUSE — Mermoz — 550F — H

Tel: 61 63 04 04   Fax: 61 63 15 64
50 rue Matabiau, 31000 Toulouse

Toulouse is the aviation capital of France and Jean Mermoz was one of the city's most famous aviators. This small, friendly hotel, owned by the Ponsot family, is filled with flying memorabilia and offers comfortable accommodation. Although it is in the centre of town, a few minutes walk away from the main railway station, the hotel is surprisingly quiet. ***Rooms** 52. Room service 24hr. Private parking 35F. Conference facilities 40. Amex, Diners, Mastercard, Visa.*

TOULOUSE — Les Ombrages — 600F — R

Tel: 61 07 61 28   Fax 61: 06 42 26
48 bis route St Simon 31100 Toulouse

This warmly decorated restaurant stands in a peaceful suburban setting, a gentle 10km from the city centre. Monsieur Zagot, the chef-manager, like many others in his profession, loves cooking fish and the three set and à la carte menus are clearly biased in favour of dishes like fillet of sole cooked in champagne, fillet of pike-perch in a light sorrel sauce and ragout of spring lobster (in season only). Other meat and fowl dishes are simple and traditional: baby pigeon is roasted with cloves of fresh garlic. ***Seats** 60. Open 1200-1400, 2000-2230. Closed Mon. Amex, Diners, Mastercard, Visa.*

Around Toulouse

VIGOULET-AUZIL   Auberge de Tournebride   560F

Tel 61 73 34 49   Fax 62 19 11 06

R

31320 Vigoulet-Auzil

An old wooden house with a flower-bedecked terrace and great views across to the Pyrenees, in an even older country village ten minutes south of Toulouse near the equestrian club, was turned into a relaxed bistro before becoming a fully-fledged restaurant. The chef, Mark Cain is English, a nationality not usually popular in a traditional French kitchen. He has, however, managed to make his special mark, notably with a number of fish dishes, which he loves to cook: *tartare de saumon à la marinade d'épices; gigot de lotte roti aux pommes caramélisées; médaillons de thon poellés à l'escabèche*. His cooking may not be distinctively Mediterranean, but it also bears no trace of his English culinary heritage – dishes such as *filet mignon de porc à la crème de pleurotes* or *rable de lapin farci aux olives, à l'infusion d'estragon*. Splendid cheeses, pleasing desserts (*bavarois aux framboises; tarte sablée aux fraises*). Fixed-price weekday lunch menu 115F, dinner 155/195F. **Seats** *60 (Terrace 40). Open 1230 -1330, 2000-2130. Closed L Sat, D Sun, all Mon, 1 week Feb, 1st 2 weeks Aug. Private parking. Amex, Mastercard, Visa.*

Tours

TOURS   Charles Barrier   ★   1200F

Tel 47 54 20 39   Fax 47 41 80 95

R

101 avenue de la Tranchée, 37100 Tours

Chef-patron Barrier and his wife Nicole have been in situ for over fifty years, yes 50, at this stylish air-conditioned restaurant which has its own enclosed flowery terrace overlooking lush green lawns. His style of cooking has changed little during this time, sticking very much to *cuisine traditionelle* with many different regional specialities with a nod towards fish dishes-pike-perch *(sandre)* cooked in its skin with a *mousseline de poireau*, fillets of John Dory *au chou frisé*, or *homard breton entier, roti au beurre blanc*. He has neither lost his enthusiasm nor taken his hands off the reins in the kitchen, where he leads a small team of some half dozen chefs. Whether you choose from the fixed-price menus (230/470/560F) or à la carte (the menus change four times a year in accordance with the seasons), look out for dishes such as *foie gras frais des Landes en terrine; soupe de moules légèrement fumées; canette de Challans au suc d'ananas, miel et pommes de reinettes; pied de cochon farci aux ris d'agneau et aux truffes, pommes purée.* Home-smoked salmon with blinis and chive cream is a favourite, so too roast pigeon with cabbage and baby onions and farmhouse goat's cheeses. Desserts such as *coffret léger feuilleté aux poires caramélisées* and *soufflé chaud au chocolat amer ou au Grand Marnier.* Bread is baked daily in the kitchen's real baker's oven. The Loire valley is well-represented on the French-only wine list, which also has a decent Bordeaux showing. **Seats** *45. Open 1200-400, 1900-2200. Closed D Sun. Private parking. Mastercard, Visa.*

TOURS   Jean Bardet   900F

Tel 47 41 41 11   Fax 47 51 68 72

HR

57 rue Groison, 37100 Tours

Sophie and Charentes-born Jean Bardet's magnificent 19th-century colonnaded house in white Touraine stone is set in its own park on the banks of the Loire. Some of the elegant bedrooms boast verandah balconies (which make the perfect spot for breakfast). Charmingly designed by Sophie in light combinations of flowery quilts and pale curtains, with antiques, decent paintings and splendid marble bathrooms providing exquisite toiletries, they are variously in English, Louis XV or XVI style. Parked proudly outside the house are a Rolls Royce Silver Shadow (available for hire with a chauffeur) and a vintage Citroën. **Rooms** *21. Garden. 24hr room service. Conference facilities for up to 35. Secretarial/translation services on request. Outdoor swimming pool. Amex, Mastercard, Visa.*

Restaurant   1800F

The herb and kitchen garden and magnificent greenhouse play an important role for the self-taught, flamboyant, cigar connoisseur Bardet (ask about his wine/cigar combinations, eg white Chateauneuf-du-Pape with a Chateau Margaux Davidoff cigar). He produces his own interpretations of traditional French cooking with a variety of menus to choose from: *menu du terroir* 270F, *menu fascination* 750F that ends with four 'tasting' desserts, and a 300F business lunch or 450F Sunday menu, the last two inclusive of wine. Try the *menu dégustation* (for an entire table and priced at 620F per person or 750F if you wish to substitute one of the dishes with lobster), where you are likely to encounter dishes such as *velouté de coquillages; langoustines poelées; nage de sole et d'écrevisses aux aromates; pigeon au caramel d'épices*, ending with a plate of farmhouse cheeses, and a couple of desserts, perhaps warm honey-caramelised apricots with lavender ice cream. Foie gras is a popular choice here, specialities being *terrine et lobe de foie gras de canard confit dans sa graisse* or *foie gras de canard poelé aux épices, figues noires*. Fish-lovers might try curried John Dory, carnivores, roast saddle of lamb with a herb jus and broccoli mousse. Leave room for excellent desserts such as a plate of exotic fruits served with a China tea and jasmine-scented sorbet. A carefully compiled wine list – there are some 30,000 bottles in the cellar – of mainly Loire wines perfectly complements the style of food, and being able to eat out on the terrace in summer or at tables scattered around the grounds in shady places is a further bonus. Inside, the tables are prettily decorated with dark cerise tablecloths, pale yellow overlays and large white flower arrangements. Relax in one of the lounges after your meal and choose one of the many Havana cigars, cabinet-kept in perfect condition. *Seats 140. Open 1200-1400, 1900-2200. Closed D Sun (but open Apr-Oct), all Mon (but open L Nov-Mar, D Apr-Oct).*

Tours   La Roche Le Roy   800F   R

Tel 47 27 22 00   Fax 47 28 08 39
55 route de Saint-Avertin, 37200 Tours

The restaurant is a converted 17th-century chateau with Louis XV furniture blending with the heavy, ornate curtains and old paintings, a renaissance-style setting for chef Alain Couturier's classic cuisine with a hint of nouvelle. The family have been here nine years, and Alain's wife Marilyn is English, so translating menus presents no problems. Start perhaps with a cold terrine of foie gras served with a glass of sweet Montlouis, or a slice served warm with apricots, followed by Loire perch roasted in spices and butter served as a house speciality or sautéed veal kidneys with three mustards and fresh pasta. Marvellous cheeses and super desserts, especially from the patissier, such as strawberry *millefeuille* or a gratin of raspberries with its own coulis. Only France gets a look-in on the wine list, with Loire wines obviously to the fore. *Seats 50 (Terrace 40). Open 1200-1400, 1930-2130. Closed D Sat, L Sun, all Mon, 1 week Feb, 1-24 Aug. Private parking. Amex, Mastercard, Visa.*

Around Tours

Onzain   Domaine des Hauts de Loire   1070F   HR

Tel: 54 20 72 57   Fax: 54 20 77 32
Route de Harbault 41150 Onzain-en-Touraine

Originally a hunting lodge built in 1860 and surrounded by many acres of secluded parkland and two lakes, the Bonnigal's ivy-clad hotel with white shutters is a restful spot with a relaxed setting. The wood-panelled reception is as welcoming as the long-serving staff, the lounge furnished with 19th-century antiques, antique brass pots with wonderful floral displays and rich blue curtains. A spiral staircase leads to charming and well-maintained bedrooms with painted beams and oak bathrooms; some of the best rooms are in the annexe. *Rooms 35. Closed Dec and Jan. Tennis. Outdoor swimming pool. Fishing. Secretarial/fax services on request. Private parking. Amex, Diners, Mastercard, Visa.*

Restaurant   800F

Candlelight dining in the pretty restaurant where chef Rémy Giraud only uses top-quality ingredients for his fixed-price menus or à la carte. Look out for dishes such as *crépinette* of crab and lobster with a small salad dressed in a mango vinaigrette and roasted sesame seeds; red mullet with chicken livers and a *barigoule* of fennel and artichokes; baked pike-perch with a tomato cream, parsley and garlic; chateaubriand with girolles, an oxtail jus and parsley purée. There's a good selection of French cheeses, while desserts are not to be missed: lime soufflé with a pina colada sorbet, *crème caramelisée au café* with a roasted fig coated in maple syrup. *Seats 75. Open 1230-1400, 1930-2100. Closed as accommodation, also L Tue & all Mon in Nov, Feb, Mar.*

ROCHECORBON   Les Hautes Roches   1185F

Tel: 47 52 88 88   Fax: 47 52 81 30

H

86 quai de la Loire, 37210 Rochecorbon

Built into a cliff overlooking the Loire, this unique hotel was formerly a monastery. Parts of the building date back to the 11th century and eight of the rooms are actually built into the rock. The decor in these is appropriately minimalist, while the other three bedrooms, located over the hotel restaurant, have warmer colour schemes and wooden furniture. Tours is a 15-minute drive away. *Rooms 11. Room service limited. Private parking. Banqueting facilities 80. Conference facilities 25. Secretarial services on request. Amex, Diners, Mastercard, Visa.*

Elsewhere in France

BRACIEUX   Bernard Robin   1200F

Tel 54 46 41 22   Fax 54 46 03 69

R

1 avenue de Chambord, 41250 Bracieux

The restaurant, a 19th-century post house with a shady terrace, is situated on the edge of the Chambord forest some 20km from Blois in the Loire valley. Chef-patron Bernard Robin has stuck throughout more than 20 years here to classical cooking principles, using regional produce wherever possible, presenting a number of fixed-price menus (from 195F during the week to 595F for the *menu de la mer*) alongside the à la carte that changes with the seasons. For instance, when the hunting season starts, he concentrates on game dishes, which are extremely popular with locals. Look out for typical dishes such as *salade de pigeon et homard; filet de bar avec des oeufs en neige et du caviar* and *queue de boeuf en hachis parmentier, jus au truffes.* Note the excellent selection of local cheeses. A huge wine list features wines from the Loire, but no house wine. *Seats 60 (Terrace 20). Open 1200-1345, 1930-2100. Closed D Tues, all Wed, end Dec-mid Jan (but open all week Jul & Aug). Public parking. Amex, Mastercard, Visa.*

CHAGNY   Lameloise   ★ +   700F

Tel 85 87 08 85   Fax 85 87 03 57

RR

36 place d'Armes, 71150 Chagny

An elegant 15th-century restaurant with rooms (17 charming, spacious and well-kept bedrooms from 700F to 1500F) situated on the town square in a village surrounded by vineyards in the heart of Burgundy. It has been in the family for three generations and is now run by chef-patron Jacques Lameloise, once the great chef Lenotre's star pupil, and his wife Nicole – note her wonderful fresh flower arrangements. The food is traditionally French with some notable Lyonnais influences, specialising in game and fish: *rable de lapin et sa cuisse rotis en fine chapelure de noisettes; blanc de turbot et sa marmelade d'herbes fraiches dans une nage beurrée de tomates; pigeonneau en vessie et ses pates fraiches au foie gras.* End with delicious desserts (some need to be ordered at the start of the meal) such as *griottines au chocolat noir et leur sorbet sur une marmelade d'oranges* or *soufflé chaud au citron.* The 590F seven-course *menu dégustation* served in slightly smaller portions has choices in both the starter and main course, as well as in between: palate-cleansers of either a red wine granité or cold melon soup. Best value, perhaps, is the 360F menu with three choices in the starters and main courses, followed by cheeses and desserts. A large and impressive wine list puts the emphasis on local burgundies. Twice a year Monsieur Lameloise, sometimes accompanied by his son, makes guest cooking trips, one usually to Bangkok, and this year (1995) to London's Savoy Hotel. *Seats 80. Open 1200-1430, 1930-2130. Closed L Thu, all Wed (but open Wed D 6 Jul-18 Oct), 21 Dec-26 Jan (rooms also closed Wed, 1 May). Garage parking. Amex, Mastercard, Visa.*

Meal prices for 2 are based on à la carte menus. When set menus are available, prices will often be lower.

Tel: 58 05 06 07   Fax: 58 51 10 10
40320 Eugénie-les-Bains

Tucked away in a little spa village in Gascony, this is a spacious, palatial, colonial house, built for Napoleon III's wife Eugénie, and surrounded by extensive scented gardens and trees. Over the years it has become a magnet for those seeking healthy food and a rest in Christine Guérard's individually designed rooms of impeccable taste, which are large, yet intimate, bright and luxurious. 35 are in the original house, the rest in the converted 18th-century Couvent des Herbes (dogs allowed) that opens out onto the herb garden. Fantastic leisure facilities including an outdoor heated swimming pool, spa and hot springs, sauna, beauty salon, and tennis. *Rooms 42. 24hr room service. Conference facilities. Ample parking. Amex, Diners, Mastercard, Visa. Closed Dec-Mar.*

Author of the highly acclaimed books Cuisine Minceur and Cuisine Gourmande, Michel Guérard has been instrumental in changing the cooking styles of a generation of chefs. He has espoused healthy eating, embracing it with an artistic and aesthetic presentation of food. Since the dishes that he creates are balanced from a calorific and health point of view, you can eat royally and lose weight into the bargain. Fixed-price menus from 390F-530F, or à la carte, feature truffles, wild mushrooms and lots of vegetables, the emphasis always on the freshest products. The *demi-homard grillé et fumé à la cheminée* (grilled and smoked over hot coals) is one of the specialities, along with *turbot grillé au pain blanc, piqué d'ail roussi et la mousseline aux feuilles de fenouil* (with a topping of breadcrumbs and lightly cooked garlic crisps and served with a fennel leaf mousseline). *L'oreiller moelleux de mousserons et de morilles aux asperges* (a soft 'pillow' of field mushrooms with morels and asparagus) is another speciality. Other dishes could be *la tourte sauvagine de lapin*: a pie filled with wild rabbit, duck and an escalope of foie gras, *pot-au-feu* of ox-cheek and quail in a *truffled bouillon*, and sensational desserts, a particular forte of Guérard, who started his career as a pastry chef: *la peche blanche de Gascogne et la glace verveine du jardin* (verbena) or *le dessert du roi 'tout en chocolat'*, a hot chocolate soufflé, chocolate sorbet and chocolate pot. Service in the chic and relaxing dining-room is beyond reproach, the wine list classically French, strongest in Bordeaux with quite hefty prices, but try perhaps the Baron de Bachen, a well-respected wine from Guérard's own vineyard a few miles down the road. *Seats 80. Open 1200-1400, 2000-2200. Closed L Thu, all Wed (except in summer) and as for hotel.*

Tel: 58 45 18 80   Fax: 58 45 16 57
7 place des Tilleuls, 40270 Grenade sur l'Adour

The house is typically Gascon, but the food served in the restaurant has a decided Provençal slant. Chef-patron Philippe Garret's menus are full of appeal, and typical dishes include a starter of lobster salad and a spicy artichoke chutney with aniseed and mustard vinaigrette and a splendid main course of *grosse cote de veau de lait rotie, mousserons et légumes du pays cuisinés au jambon*. A plate of local cheeses is an alternative (or indeed addition) to a dessert. Wines of south west France are well respresented on the list. Set menus from 175F to 400F. *Seats 70 (terrace 80). Open 1200-1430, 2000-2230. Closed D Sun, all Mon (open D Mon in Jul & Aug). Private parking. Amex, Diners, Mastercard, Visa.*

Tel 86 62 09 70   Fax 86 91 49 70
14 faubourg de Paris, 89304 Joigny

Created almost 40 years ago, Michel and Jacqueline Lorain's lovely hotel and restaurant lies on the banks of the River Yonne, about an hour-and-half's drive from Paris. The original building, which houses the restaurant and ten bedrooms, is on the main road, but by entering a 'secret' underground tunnel, strikingly decorated with Roman artefacts, you access the modern building (la Résidence) with its bar and luxurious bedrooms overlooking the river. These air-conditioned rooms have their own terrace or balcony, as do two in the Villa Camille. All rooms provide satellite TV, mini-bar and safe, have sumptuous marble bathrooms and are individually decorated in great style. There's an indoor heated swimming pool, sauna and tennis, a large and beautifully maintained garden, not to mention the hotel's launch, available for hire – start the day with a cruise and brunch! Price quoted is for a room in the main house; those in the residence and villa are more expensive. *Rooms 29. Garage/ample parking. Room service: breakfast only. Conferences 45. Amex, Diners, Mastercard, Visa.*

See over

Restaurant ★ ✦ 1600F

Though Michel Lorain remains in overall charge, it is his son Jean-Michel who is responsible for the very fine kitchen, which produces some of the best food in France. Emphasising that this is very much a family business, Jacqueline is a charming hostess, overseeing the three elegant dining-rooms, as well as looking after the comprehensive wine list (they have their own vineyard producing a white chardonnay), while other members of the family are also active here and at La Rive Gauche, a 42-bedroomed hotel and restaurant on the other side of the river. Helpfully, dishes on the menu have English translations, though the latter do not always do justice to what actually appears in front of you! Whether you choose à la carte, daily specials, 'musts' that have earned the restaurant such an excellent reputation over the years, the weekday *lunch du marché* at 380F or *le menu gourmand* (six tasting courses, choice of starter only, for 720F), you'll be sampling a mixture of old and new, dishes of exceptional brilliance and artistry. This is cooking at the top of its class, typically, *huitres bretonnes en petite terrine océane; bar de ligne* (sea bass) *poelé, accompagné de petites aubergines farcies aux encornets* (squid), *jus d'étrilles* (baby crab) *corsé à la moutarde violette; grosse raviole de homard au persil plat et à la truffe; pigeon fermier et artichauts poivrades, chutney aux pommes acides et aux épices; suite de desserts et friandises*, perhaps a *feuilleté* of caramelised pears with ginger ice cream or passion fruit soufflé. Alternatively, an entire table can plump for *le menu surprise*, five dishes at 750/840F, depending on the seasonal produce used. There's a special children's menu charged at half the cost of a main dish from the carte: starter, main course (half portion) and sweet. ***Seats*** 80. *Open 1200-1345, 1915-2145.*

PONT-DE-L'ISÈRE **Michel Chabran** ★ 1200F

Tel 75 84 60 09   Fax 75 84 59 65   RR
avenue du 45ème parallèle, 26600 Pont-de-l'Isère

In 1935 Michel Chabran's grandfather opened a small roadside village bistro in this 19th-century building, some ten miles from Valence on the N7, and over the years it has gradually expanded into today's restaurant (with 12 comfortable air-conditioned rooms for overnight diners from 640F per double), which Michel and Rose-Marie took over in 1973. Exposed stonework and original wood are used to good rustic effect in the light and airy dining-room with a large fireplace, decent pictures and lots of flower arrangements (from their patio garden perhaps?). Candle-lit at night, it's a romantic and quiet setting in which to enjoy Chabran's artistry, based on local ingredients wherever possible, such as Bresse poultry, Charolais beef and Rémuzat lamb. The à la carte menu offers some choice combinations: *millefeuille de foie gras de canard aux artichauts et courgettes; risotto de langoustines aux champignons des bois; aiguillettes de boeuf du Charolais au vieil Hermitage* – dishes that also appear on the various fixed-price menus ranging from the menu gourmand at 475F to the *menu dégustation* at 625F. There are cheaper menus at lunchtime, and one (765F) featuring several Brittany lobster dishes, cheese and a couple of desserts, perhaps *trilogie de citron au coulis de fruits rouges* and *gelée de fraises des bois, granité à la menthe fraiche*. A very fine selection of Rhone wines is a feature of the comprehensive wine list. ***Seats*** 100. *Open 1200-1430, 2000-2200. Ample parking. Amex, Diners, Mastercard, Visa.*

PUYMIROL **L'Aubergade** ★ 900F

Tel 53 95 31 46   Fax 53 95 33 80   RR
52 rue Royale, 47270 Puymirol

Also known as Les Loges de l'Aubergade since there are ten exquisite bedrooms starting at 950F for a double with breakfast. And, what bedrooms! Most of the furniture and fittings come from Italy, complementing the bare walls of this 13th-century white-stoned medieval country house, originally built for the counts of Toulouse. Maryse Trama was instrumental in the large bedrooms' design, while her self-taught, Havana cigar-loving, scuba-diving chef-patron husband Michel Trama is a creative cook, as well as being a superb patissier. During the week there's a fixed-price 'business' lunch at a very reasonable 180F, other fixed-price *menus de marché* and *gourmand* priced at 280F and 580F respectively, plus of course à la carte. Ingredients are always the freshest in the market with plenty of herbs and spices added, as in *salade de homard aux épices douces; foie gras de canard cuit au naturel, sa gelée de poivre; poisson du marché poelé simplement à l'huile d'olive vierge; pied de cochon aux champignons; cuisse de pintade en cocotte aux petits légumes*. And, those desserts, which should be ordered at the start of the meal: club sandwich aux fruits, sauce passion; *millefeuille de nougatine glacé au pralin; biscuit de chocolat chaud, sauce acidulée*. Good wine list – drink cuvée Michel Trama, his personal selection. In fine weather you can dine outside under white parasols. Conferences up to 50. Garden with plunge pool. Garage (70F) for hotel guests, ample parking next door. ***Seats*** 60 *(Terrace 60). Open 1200-1330, 1930 - 2130. Closed Mon (out of season), 2 weeks Feb/Mar (school holidays). Amex, Diners, Mastercard, Visa.*

Roanne   Troisgros   1000F
HR

Tel 77 71 66 97   Fax 77 70 39 77
place Jean Troisgros, 42300 Roanne

The hotel, centrally situated opposite the railway station, is painted pink and green to reflect one of the restaurant's specialities of salmon with sorrel (see below). The hotel has two wings, the old one completely renovated with bedrooms now very modern and well equipped, and the new wing also luxuriously decorated in contemporary style. The air-conditioned rooms, with huge bathrooms, overlook either the garden or the square with its famous statue (by Arman) of a hundred interlinking forks, dedicated to the memory of the deceased Troisgros. The hotel does not aim to cater for conferences, but there is a meeting room for up to 30. Note the hotel is closed on Tuesday and Wednesday nights.
Rooms 19. Garden. 24hr room service. Secretarial/translation services on request. Closed Tue, Wed, 3 weeks Feb/Mar, 1st 2 weeks Aug. Ample parking. Amex, Diners, Mastercard, Visa.

Restaurant   ★★   1200F

The dynasty began in 1930 when grandfather Troisgros opened a small café, in turn becoming a respected restaurant, expanding in the early 70s when Jean and Pierre introduced their own ideas that eventually blossomed into what most of us associate with nouvelle cuisine. Decor is contemporary, with two of the dining-rooms featuring the work of specific artists, and the huge trademark plates, made fashionable here, still in use. The cooking, under the direction of Michel Troisgros (Pierre's son), continues on its consistent path – no risks, but occasional surprises, witness some dishes from a recent *menu dégustation: foie gras chaud aux choux chinois à l'arachide grillée; poelée de grenouilles aux herbes fines; loup au Gamay et à la moelle; cassolette de queues d'écrevisses à la nage et gingembre; opaline aux framboises; crèmes glacées, sorbets et fruits de saison.* Fixed-price menus at 560F (280F weekday lunch only) and 680F (as above) are offered along with a 'spontaneous' menu, which aims to produce whatever customers desire. Several dishes have been passed down the Troisgros generations, like *saumon à l'oseille* (pan-fried escalope of salmon served in a sorrel sauce) and *chateau au Fleurie à la moelle* (poached fillet of local Charolais, arguably the world's greatest beef, with a sublime Fleurie-based sauce with bone marrow). Desserts are no less enticing: a lime and acacia honey soufflé, or raspberry *norvégienne*, a sort of baked Alaska, while the hand-made goat's cheese comes with its own glass of Sancerre. One of the most comprehensive wine lists in France includes the local red Cote Roannaise as the house wine. *Seats 100. Open 1200-1330, 1930-2130. Closed D Tue, all Wed and as above.*

Romorantin   Grand Hotel Lion d'Or   1000F
HR

Tel 54 76 00 28   Fax 54 88 24 87
69 rue Georges Clemenceau, 41200 Romorantin-Lanthenay

The aristocratic credentials of this private hotel are impeccable; it was built by a friend of François I in the 16th century and remained in the same family's hands up until the Revolution. The present proprietors (Colette and Alain Barrat, their daughter Marie-Christine and son-in-law Didier Clément) have been here for well over 30 years and are used to welcoming many important guests, who fly into the private airport 4km away and come to relax. It's right in the centre of the town, but most of the rooms look out onto a medieval courtyard with tall trees and a herb garden. The air-conditioned bedrooms, with satellite TV, mini-bar and safe, are decidedly luxurious with king-size beds and striking furniture, some with antique 18th-century bedheads. Smart granite and terracotta-tiled bathrooms. *Rooms 16. Closed 20 Feb-20 Mar. Room service. Conference facilities for up to 40. Secretarial/translation/fax services on request. Private parking. Amex, Diners, Mastercard, Visa.*

Restaurant   1100F

The dining-room with predominantly blue decor, wood panelling and pretty watercolours also boasts lovely flower arrangements. Chef Didier Clément loves dredging up old recipes (many can be found in his and Marie-Christine's books Colette/Sologne Gourmande) and the use of spices with local produce. Most of the dishes can be served in half portions, ie starter or main course, a novel and welcome idea: perhaps courgette flowers stuffed with crabmeat; langoustine risotto; red mullet béarnaise with a friture of tomatoes and artichokes or tournedos of sweetbreads with fresh girolles. Finish with cherry brochettes with vanilla-scented crème caramel or peach soufflé with a redcurrant sauce. Fixed-price menus are priced at 420F (three courses) or 620F (five courses, including a green salad). House champagne is Perrier-Jouët Grand Brut at a not unreasonable 320F, otherwise seek advice on the wine list from Madame Colette, a real connoisseur of Loire wines. *Seats 50. Open 1200-1400, 1930-2100.*

Tel 59 37 01 01   Fax 59 37 18 97
19 place du Général de Gaulle, 64220 St-Jean-Pied-de-Port

Situated in the heart of a Pyrenean village, some 60km from Biarritz, with cobblestone streets and pink sandstone buildings, Anne-Marie and Firmin Arrambide's restaurant, built in 1728, was once a post house where stage coaches stopped en route to Spain. The restaurant has two terraces, one overlooking the main street where you can watch the local Basques coming and going, the other, with a heated outdoor swimming pool, looking on to the lovely garden that slopes down to the River Adour. There are twenty comfortable bedrooms, though they don't enjoy the fabulous mountain views, with a double room starting at 700F with breakfast. The dining-room is classically decorated in light peach colours with antique furniture; the cooking, by third generation self-taught Firmin (well actually he learnt from his grandmother and father) is traditional Pays Basque with his own original touches. The raw ingredients are mostly local: the cèpes, lobster, the fresh salmon that he catches, the game which he personally shoots, and the Spanish cod from over the border. Typical examples of his dishes: *soupe aux écrevisses; salade de haricots verts frais au foie gras; fricassée de homard aux champignons des bois; filet d'agneau de lait du pays roti à l'ail, petites fèves et légumes farcis; gateau moelleux et croustillant au chocolat praliné, glace à l'Izarra verte; grande assiette aux cinq gourmandises*, the last to be ordered at the start of the meal. There are several fixed-price menus to choose from, starting at 220F, up to the *grand menu* at 500F. The wine list includes the local red and white Irouléguy made by the neighbouring Brana family, and a page of Spanish wines. *Seats 90 (Terrace 30). Open 1215-1400, 1945-2115. Closed Tue (except Jul, Aug, Sep), 5-28 Jan, 20 Nov-20 Dec. Garage (50F). Amex, Mastercard, Visa.*

Tel 86 33 20 45   Fax 86 33 26 15
89450 Saint-Père-sous-Vézelay

A native of this sleepy little village, Marc Meneau converted the family grocery shop into today's hotel and restaurant some twenty-five years ago. With his charming wife Françoise, they have created something very special: a stylish restaurant with two glassed-in dining-rooms and terrace overlooking the delightful garden, and lovely bedrooms: there are forty to choose from, either in the main house, at the Pré des Marguerites (with terraces here) or more rustically decorated suites in the converted mill. Wherever you sleep, it's worth waking up to the excellent breakfasts. Large conferences and banquets catered for.
Rooms 40. *Garden, outdoor heated swimming pool. Ample parking. Amex, Diners, Mastercard, Visa.*

Meneau is a fine chef, influenced by some great names of the past, following their eclectic approach to cooking, flitting between bourgeois and classical styles. His fixed-priced menus, ranging from a weekday lunch at 360F to 650F/870F, available both at lunch and dinner, or à la carte, change consantly reflecting what's available from the markets. This is cooking of the highest order; no long and fancy menu descriptions here, but just a simple down-to-earth approach, maximising the quality of ingredients and their flavours such as his famous dishes of jellied oysters, and grilled spatchcock pigeon. Look out too for: *homard breton en vinaigrette de crustacés aux peches; poelée d'écrevisses aux gnocchis; poulet de Bresse farci de truffes roti à la broche; filet de féra à la purée de citrons confits; turbotin poché au lait, sauce hollandaise.* Desserts are no less exciting, perhaps *le grand dessert d'été* to be ordered at the start of the meal, chocolate tart with vanilla ice cream or caramel soufflé served with a fresh fruit salad. Red or white Vézelay burgundies from his own vineyard are featured on the huge and impressive wine list. *Seats 80. Open 1200-1430, 1930-2200. Closed L Wed, all Tues, Feb.*

Tel 80 64 07 66   Fax 80 64 08 92
2 rue d'Argentine, 21210 Saulieu

Situated half way between Paris and Lyons on the N6, this has always been a stop-over for travellers going to (or coming from) the south of France – it became really famous under chef Alexandre Dumaine in the 50s (his portrait, old menus and pictures of his era hang in the breakfast room). Bernard Loiseau arrived here in 1982, since when the restaurant has gone from strength to strength with the help of his wife Dominique, who looks after front-of-house. 1995 was a particularly momentous year for Bernard with his election to the Legion of Honour (President Mitterrand dubbed him at the Elysée Palace) and the opening of his boutique next to the hotel restaurant selling regional products. Three attractive dining-rooms overlook the English garden; the building itself retains old beams and fine wood panelling and there are some good 18th-century paintings. Bernard has developed a healthy cooking style using local produce and little or no fat. His (water-based) sauces are the subject of an amusing story attributed to another equally well-known chef, Paul Bocuse, whose restaurant lies on the River Saone. Gazing into the water flowing past his restaurant Bocuse said "there my friends you see the sauce of Bernard Loiseau". Various fixed-price menus from a 390F weekday lunch menu to the *menu dégustation* at 890F (four half-portion courses, cheese and three desserts for an entire table only) are offered, though it is perhaps the *légumes en fete* menu at 450F (four courses, goat's cheese, and two desserts) that best shows off his mastery and understanding of vegetables – an aspect of cooking that many other French chefs ignore. Typical à la carte dishes might feature *terrine de foie gras de canard et sa gelée; petits rougets farcis et sa sauce à l'olive liée aux foies de rougets; poularde de Bresse à la vapeur 'Alexandre Dumaine' au riz truffé; parfait glacé au caramel et son feuilleté croustillant.* Chocolate desserts, incidentally, are something of a speciality here. Burgundy wines are naturally to the fore on a fine wine list. **Seats** *100. Open 1230-1430, 1930-2200. Amex, Diners, Mastercard, Visa.*

Rooms   1220F

Fifteen luxurious double rooms and suites overlook the garden and the five newest rooms are air-conditioned. Garage. Room rates increase at weekends.

VALENCE   Pic   ★★   1700F
RR

Tel 75 44 15 32   Fax 75 40 96 03
285 avenue Victor Hugo, 26001 Valence

The Pic family have been restaurateurs for four generations, serving their classic and contemporary cuisine in an elegant, wood-panelled, beamed dining-room with culinary and landscape paintings scattered around. An added attraction is the courtyard that's a most agreeable spot for a drink, before or after a meal. They are hoteliers as well, since there are five very comfortable and luxuriously furnished air-conditioned bedrooms (from 900F), providing cable TV, mini-bar and exceptional breakfasts. However, with demand for rooms high, a new annexe of a further 12 deluxe rooms is due to be constructed in 1996. Since the death of Jacques Pic in 1992 (note that one or two dishes are attributed to his name), at which time the entire village rallied round in support of his wife Suzanne, his son Alain has run the kitchen, cooking in fine style with a particular emphasis on fish on the menus (there are four of them and an à la carte: a business lunch menu at 290F, and others ranging from 560F to 920F). Your choice might be a *salade des pecheurs au Xérès; filet de loup au caviar; blanc de turbot roti, courgettes fleurs au jus de langoustines* or *feuillantine de homard, vinaigrette basilic.* Non-fish choices might include *escalopes de foie de canard aux raisins* or *crépinette d'agneau aux morilles dauphinoise.* Finish with splendid cheeses and fantastic desserts, perhaps an iced orange soufflé. Wonderful selection of Rhone wines, including Condrieu, Cote-Rotie, St-Joseph, Hermitage, Cornas and Chateauneuf-du-Pape with great growers like Jaboulet, Chapoutier and Guigal to the fore. The house Cotes-du-Rhone Pic is a bargain. **Seats** *150. Open 1200-1400, 2000 -2200. Closed D Sun, all Wed, 2 weeks in Aug. Conferences for up to 100. Ample parking. Amex, Diners, Mastercard, Visa.*

VEYRIER-DU-LAC   Auberge de L'Eridan   2500F
HR

Tel: 50 60 24 00   Fax: 50 60 23 63
13 Vieille route des Pensières, 74290 Veyrier-du-Lac

On the shores of Lake Annecy, surrounded by a park and with the mountains as a backdrop there could not be a more beautiful location for a small country hotel. If you then combine it with one of the top restaurants in France, you have the perfect place to visit. The creator of this is Marc Veyrat, the renowned *fils de l'Haute Savoie.* With only eleven elegant rooms, all with terraces, you are sure of being well looked after. Bathrooms are very large and luxurious and some feature jacuzzis. There is also a small conference room. A private boat is available for excursions and from the lake, the hotel, which is painted in Savoy blue, is unmissable. ***Rooms*** *11. Private parking. Conference facilities 20. Air-conditioning. Amex, Diners, Mastercard, Visa.*

Restaurant Marc Veyrat   1200F

In the last couple of years, Marc Veyrat has emerged as one of the premier chefs in France. Always wearing his black mountain hat, he and his team stalk the countryside, carefully picking the herbs and plants that form the basis of many of his dishes and have become his trademark. Veyrat has made herb-picking a way of life and it has become a source of inspiration for many of his dishes. As he says, "if one touches nature, it takes command". In fine weather, meals are served under parasols on the terrace overlooking the lake. Appointments and service are of the highest order with the blue theme followed faithfully

See over

in the linen and napery. Wherever possible the menu will feature one of the most delicate and least-known offerings of Lake Annecy, the *omble chevalier du lac*. Its delicate pinkish-white flesh simply must be tasted when you visit. It is almost the only dish served without herbs but with a simple sauce. Other notable dishes such as *soupe de melons glacée aux aromes, ravioli de légumes sans pate* and *saumon au gros sel à la vinaigrette de rumex verveine* all feature on the *dégustation* menus – the eight-course Sonate or the nine-course Symphonie. We also liked the marmite de carré d'agneau on a bed of herbs. Desserts arrive in several servings and include *les trois crèmes brulées* and *tarte aux framboises* as well as an assortment of sorbets and ices. **Seats** 50.

VONNAS   Georges Blanc   1300F

Tel 74 50 90 90   Fax 74 50 08 80   HR
place du Marché, 01540 Vonnas

Jacqueline and Georges Blanc (here since 1968) are the third generation of the family at this informal hotel, built in 1872 on the banks of the River Veyle. The hotel, actually named "la Mère Blanc", is just an hour's drive from Lyons and only a little longer from Geneva, and despite being in the centre of the village, is situated in its own lovely gardens with a heated swimming pool, tennis and helipad. Smart bedrooms have antique furniture collected over many years; the majority, several with balconies, including suites and two apartments, are situated in the main house, with the rest (a little cheaper) in a new building across the road, accessible via a pretty covered wooden bridge. There, you will also find *La Boutique Gourmande*, which exclusively sells Blanc's charcuterie, wines from his own vineyard and gourmet food. For large receptions and cocktail parties, Blanc will open up his nearby chateau. He also owns several other enterprises, (including an old auberge serving *cuisine du terroir*), La Cour aux Fleurs and La Résidence des Saules, providing further accommodation. **Rooms** *38. Theatre-style conference facilities for up to 100. Secretarial/translation/fax services on request. Closed 2 Jan-10 Feb. Own garage. Amex, Diners, Mastercard, Visa.*

Restaurant   ★✚   2000F

The rustic and timbered dining-room with lots of local antiques is situated on the river (drinks on the terrace). With a classical and traditional training, Monsieur Blanc's influences come from a long line of family restaurateurs including his grandmother, many of whose recipes have been handed down. He remains loyal to them, adding a few Mediterranean touches, his own interpretation and perhaps more modern techniques. The several set menus (from 450F to 790F) and à la carte are seasonal: an extensive *terre et mer* menu offers such dishes as *blanquette de grenouilles au mariage d'épices et poudre d'ail* and *homard à la coque à l'endive et au basilic*. His *poularde de Bresse aux gousses d'ail et foie gras* (Bresse capon stuffed with cloves of garlic and foie gras) is a classic, indeed the commercial success of Bresse poultry is probably largely attributable to him! Other favourites are *crepe parmentière au saumon et caviar* and *turbot à la compote d'aubergines et au caviar*. Before the real dessert, there's a 'tasting' dessert, while cheese lovers will appreciate, amongst others, the many local goat varieties. Exquisite petits fours, own-label champagne and wines on an extensive list (note the Macon and Chiroubles), and caring service under the Jacqueline's direction. **Seats** *120. Open 1230-1400, 1930-2130. Closed Mon, Tue (open D Tue 15 Jun-15 Sep).*

Scotch Beef Club Members: France

PARIS
PARIS 75001: Le Grand Louvre
PARIS 75001: Hotel St James &
    Albany
PARIS 75002: Drouant
PARIS 75006: Jacques Cagna
PARIS 75006: Le Jules Verne
PARIS 75006: Hotel Lutetia
PARIS 75008: La Couronne
PARIS 75008: Hotel George V
PARIS 75008: Le Jardin des
    Cygnes/Regency
PARIS 75008: Le Pub Saint-Lazare
PARIS 75009: Café de la Paix
PARIS 75009: La Taverne
    Kronenbourg
PARIS 75011: Hotel Holiday Inn
PARIS 75014: Chez François & Fils
PARIS 75014: Ciel de Paris
PARIS 75014: Hotel Méridien
    Montparnasse
PARIS 75015: Hotel Adagio
PARIS 75015: Hotel Hilton
PARIS 75015: Hotel Nikko
PARIS 75015: Le Relais de Sèvres
PARIS 75016: Bertie's
PARIS 75016: La Petite Tour

SEINE ET MARNE
COUBERT: à l'Escargot d'Or
LOUAN VILLEGRUIS FONTAINE:
    Le Restaurant
LE MESNIL AMELOT:
    Le Montparnasse

YVELINES
MAISONS-LAFITTE: Le Tastevin
VERSAILLES: La Fontaine Trianon
    Palace
VERSAILLES: Le Potager du Roi

ESSONNE
EVRY: Académie Accor

VAL DE MARNE
ORLY: Maxim's

VAL D'OISE
ROISSY-EN-FRANCE: La Dime
ROISSY-EN-FRANCE:
    Saint-Exupéry
ROISSY-EN-FRANCE: Hotel Sofitel

ALSACE
BUSCHWILLER: A la Couronne
COLMAR: Schillinger
MULHOUSE: La Boucherie

AQUITAINE
BIARRITZ: Hotel du Palais
BORDEAUX: Baud et Millet
BORDEAUX: Hotel Chateau
    Chartrons
BORDEAUX: Sofitel Aquitania
CREON: Hostellerie Chateau
    Camiac
St EMILION: Restaurant Francis
    Goullee

BOURGOGNE
CUISEAUX: Hotel du Nord
TOURNUS: Le Rempart

FRANCHE-COMTE
CUBRY: Le Maugre
SOCHAUX: Arianis

LANGUEDOC-ROUSSILLON
PERPIGNAN: Brasserie Vauban

LIMOUSIN
VARETZ: Chateau de Castel Novel

MIDI-PYRENEES
SAINT-FELIX: Auberge du Poids
    Public

NORD
AMIENS: Barsserie Jules
AMPLIER: Le Val d'Hautie
ANNAY: Le Sabayon
BETHUNE: Le Vieux Beffroi
BOULOGNE SUR MER: Le Matelot
HARDELOT: Hotel du Parc
LILLE: Brasserie André
LUMBRES: Auberge du Moulin de
    Mombreux
MARQ EN BAROEUL: Hotel Sofitel
    Lille
MAUBERGE: Hostellerie de
    Remparts
MONTREUIL SUR MER: Chateau
    de Montreuil
WIMILE: Le Relais de la Brocante

PAYS DE LA LOIRE
MONTRAND-LES-BAINS: Hotellerie
   la Poularde
PORNICHET: Le Sunset
VILLARS: Aberdeen Brasserie

PROVENCE/ALPES/COTE D'AZUR
AIX-EN-PROVENCE: Gu & Fils
BEAULIEU-SUR-MER: Hotel
   Metropole
CANNES: Le Grill d'Alex
CANNES: La Palme d'Or
CANNES: La Palmyre
CAVALIAIRE-SUR-MER: Bon Plaisir
CUERS: Le Lingousto
EZE: Chateau de la Chèvre d'Or
FUVEAU: Le Sainte Victoire
LES ISSAMBRES: Restaurant Saint
   Elme
MANDELIEU LA NAPOULE:
   La Brocherie II
MOUGINS: Le Terrasse
NICE: Flo Brasserie
NICE: Hotel Nice Arenas
ROQUEBRUNE CAP MARTIN: Cala
   Azzura
ROQUEBRUNE CAP MARTIN: Vista
   Palace
ST RAPHAEL: L'Excelsior
ST TROPEZ: Restaurant du Bistrot
   des Lices
SOPHIA ANTIPOLIS: L'Arlequin
VALBONNE: Le Reve de Grasse
   (Hotel Mercure)
VILLENEUVE LOUBET: Biovimer
VIEUX FREJUS: Chez Vincent

RHONE/ALPES
ALBERTVILLE: Restaurant Million
GLEIZE: Calad'Inn
LYON: L'Alexandrin
LYON: Bistrot de Lyon
LYON: Fedora
LYON: Bouchon aux Vins

LYON St RAMBERT: Auberge
   de l'Ile
MEGEVETTE: L'Auberge de
   Megevette
MERIBEL: Allodis
MIRIBEL CEDEX: Restaurant
   Jacques Marguin
NEYRON: Le Saint-Didier
LA PLAGNE: Eldorador
ST JEAN D'ARDIERES: Chateau
   de Tizay
ST MARTIN DE BELLEVILLE:
   La Bouitte
LE SAPPEY EN CHARTREUSE:
   Le Pudding
TARARE: Restaurant Jean Brouilly
THOISSEY: Au Chapon Fin
VILLEFRANCHE-SUR-SAONE:
   L'Epicerie
VILLEFRANCHE-SUR-SAONE:
   Le Faison Doré
VOUGY: Le Capucin Gourmand

NORMANDIE
DEAUVILLE: L'Augeval
DEAUVILLE: Casino de Deauville
DEAUVILLE: La Flambée
DEAUVILLE: Hotel du Golf
DEAUVILLE: La Potinière
DEAUVILLE: Hotel Royal
DEAUVILLE: Le Spinnaker
DEAUVILLE: Le Yearling
PONT L'EVEQUE: Restaurant
   de L'Aeroport Deauville
TROUVILLE: Les Roches Noires

Germany

Currency Deutschmark **Exchange Rate** £1=approx DM 2.24
International dialling code 00 49
(Berlin+30, Bonn+228, Hamburg+40, Düsseldorf+211, Frankfurt+69,
Hanover+511, Munich+89, Stuttgart+711, Cologne+221)
Passports/Visas No visa required by British passport holders.
British Embassy in Bonn Tel 228-234061Fax 228-234070/237058

Airports
Berlin-Tegel Tel 30-41011 **Berlin-Tempelhof** Tel 30-69510
Düsseldorf Tel 211-4210 **Frankfurt** Tel 69-690 30511
Hamburg Tel 40-50750 **Hannover** Tel 511-9770 **Munich** Tel 89-97500
Stuttgart Tel 711-9480
Railway Stations
Berlin Zoo Tel 30-297 61131 **Berlin Hauptbahnhof** 30-297 22256;
Central train information Tel 30-19419
Car hire
Contact UK international branches for information.
Tel nos. **Avis** 0181-848 8733 **Budget** 0800 181181
EuroDollar 01895 233300 **Hertz** 0181 679 1799/1777.
Speed limits 100 km/h on trunk roads, 130 km/h on motorways, km/h
as indicated in towns.

Banks 8.30am-1pm, 2.30-4pm Mon-Fri (Thur to 5.30pm).
Shops 9am-6.30pm Mon-Fri (some shops to 8.30pm Thur), to 2pm
Sat. Closed Sun. (On the first Saturday of the month, shops may
remain open until 6pm).

New Year's Day, 6 Jan, Good Friday, Easter Monday, 1, 16 & 27 May,
6 Jun, 15 Aug, 3 & 31 Oct, 1 & 20 Nov, Christmas Day & Boxing Day.

German Tourist Board in **London** Tel 0891 600100
In **Germany** Berlin Tel 30-21234 Cologne Tel 2-213345
Hamburg Tel 40-300510 Frankfurt Tel 69-21238800
Munich Tel 89-2330300 Stuttgart Tel 7-1122280
American Express Travel Service Offices or Representative (R)

Berlin	Uhlandstr 173 D-10719 Tel 30-8827575 #	**Hanover**	Georg Strasse 54 D-3000 Tel 511-363428 #
Cologne	Burgmauer 14 D-5000 PO Box D-50667 Tel 221-2577484 #	**Munich**	Promenadeplatz 6 Im Bayerischen Hof 80333 PO Box 100120 Post Code 80075 Tel 89-290900 #
Düsseldorf	Heinrich-Heine-Allee 14 D-4000 Tel 211-82200 #		
Frankfurt	8 Kaiserstrasse PO Box 100146 Tel 69-21051 #	**Stuttgart**	Lautenschlagerstrasse 3 D-7000 Tel 711-20890 #
Hamburg	Rathausmarkt 5 D-2000 Tel 40-331141 #		

Berlin

Tel: (30) 323 87 30   R
Windscheidstrasse 31, 10627 Berlin

Since the advent of the new Germany, this area, Charlottenburg, has become fashionably bohemian, so Ingrid and Karl Wannemacher's endearingly old-fashioned restaurant, with antique lamps hanging from the ceiling, dark wooden-panelled, mirrored walls and some banquette seating, fits in well with the community. Like many German restaurants, they have been quite heavily influenced by French cuisine, even offering a fixed-price menu, the cost determined by the number of dishes chosen (three courses DM95 to five, with sorbet and cheese DM135). Select from starters such as ravioli stuffed with rabbit, served with kohlrabi and chanterelles, or millefeuille of lobster and tomato with gazpacho sauce, followed by fillet of pike-perch with shallots and red wine butter or saddle of venison with mushrooms, cabbage and potato noodles and an elderberry sauce. Filling desserts, perhaps apricot dumplings with peach ice cream or raspberry strudel accompanied by a raspberry parfait, should send you home quite content. *Seats 35. Open 1900-2300. Closed Sun, Mon. Amex, Diners, Visa.*

Tel: (30) 323 30 94   Fax: (30) 324 62 28   R
Damaschkestrasse 17, 10711 Berlin

In a quiet corner of the city, the Bufacchi family have been running their Italian restaurant for more than twenty years, though today both the interior and style of cooking are modern. They serve a variety of dishes – their house speciality is baked fish – such as sea bream with rosemary, sliced tomatoes and plenty of garlic. During the day, the restaurant is frequented by the business community, while at night the setting is more romantic: the oil lamps are lit and customers are serenaded by Spanish singers, warbling Italian songs! Private garage. *Seats 80. Open 1200-2400. Closed Sun & 23-28 Dec. Amex, Mastercard, Visa.*

Tel: (30) 88 44 70   Fax: (30) 88 44 77 00   H
Joachimstaler Strasse 29, 10719 Berlin

Most of us equate modern hotels with comfortable but bland chains. The Art Hotel Sorat shows that 'modern' can mean exciting. From its gold-coloured corrugated iron ceilings to Wolf Vostell's abstract paintings and Philippe Starck's humorous, sculptural furniture, this is designer paradise. Although the hotel has no restaurant, breakfast can be taken on the terrace in sunny weather and meals can be ordered from the restaurant next door. The location, a couple of minutes away from the Kurfürstendamm and close to the station and zoological gardens, is excellent. *Rooms 75. Room service limited. Private parking DM18. Conference facilities 12. Terrace. Solarium. Amex, Diners, Mastercard, Visa.*

Tel: (30) 218 42 82   Fax: (30) 214 23 48   R
Regensburgerstrasse 7, 10777 Berlin

In the Schöneberg district, down a quiet side street in the centre of Berlin, the restaurant is elegant and chic in a grand rustic style, and acknowledged as one of the best in town. Run by chef-patron Franz and Dorothea Raneburger, originally from Austria, the cooking is best described as classical with light touches, featuring dishes from their native country, as well as regional Italian and German ones. Typical examples include lobster on a pearl barley risottto with green asparagus, rabbit and foie gras terrine with summer truffles, sea bass served with chive potatoes, pigeon served with artichokes and stuffed courgette flowers. Classic plum tart to finish. Many Austrian wines on a comprehensive list. There's also a bistro attached, which is cheaper (around half the above price), offering a simpler version of the same menu. *Seats 40 (Bistro 30). Open 1800-2200. Closed Sun, Mon & 2 wks Jan, 3 wks Aug. Amex, Diners, Visa.*

Tel: (30) 88 43 40   Fax: (30) 883 60 75   HR
Kurfürstendamm 27, 10719 Berlin

Right in the city centre, this recently refurbished hotel is grand in every sense with lofty, columned public areas and stylish air-conditioned and double-glazed bedrooms that are classically elegant, one of their main features being impressive marble bathrooms. Some rooms are now equipped with fax machines, complementing the staffed business centre. Theatre-style conference facilities for up to 500 – this is one of Berlin's main venues for state visits and galas. **Rooms 315.** *Indoor swimming pool, sauna, solarium, steam room, gym. Amex, Diners, Mastercard, Visa.*

Restaurant Eck · DM160

There other restaurants in the hotel, but perhaps it's this all-day brasserie that best typifies their cosmopolitan approach to cooking. Chef Schubert orchestrates the kitchen to produce an eclectic menu with starters such as chicken satay and spicy peanut butter, carpaccio of beef with basil, red peppers and mushrooms, or even a selection of dim sum. Fish-lovers can enjoy the likes of steamed salmon with noodles and sorrel butter, while carnivores can choose Germanic dishes such as tafelspitz with savoy cabbage, hash browns and chive sauce or a classic *Wiener schnitzel*. For desserts, there are home-made pastries, dark and white chocolate mousse with fresh mango, or an orange terrine with Campari sauce. Plenty of local beers, and wines by the glass to supplement an impressive and international wine list. Sunday music brunch (DM49, children under 4 free, otherwise half-price). **Seats 90** *(Terrace 100). Open 1200-2400.*

BERLIN · Ephraim Palais · DM120

Tel: (30) 242 51 08   Fax: (30) 32 19 29 2
Spreeufer 1, 10178 Berlin

R

Many museums, galleries and exhibition halls throughout Europe now offer very good food in their restaurants. This one in the famous Ephraim Palais Museum, built in the 18th-century, is no exception and, helpfully, dishes on the menus are translated into English and French. Alongside the à la carte (perhaps a cream of leek and potato soup with bacon croutons, fillet of sole with a crab ragout, saddle of veal in a pepper sauce, assorted sorbets with fresh summer berries) there are several 3/4-course fixed-price menus from DM48 to DM75 offering mainly the same dishes at reduced prices. **Seats 50.** *Open (lunch by arrangement), 1800-2400. Amex, Diners, Mastercard, Visa.*

BERLIN · Forsthaus Paulsborn · DM160

Tel: (30) 813 80 10   Fax: (30) 814 11 56
Hüttenweg 90, 14193 Berlin

RR

Situated in the Grunewald forest (just outside the city centre), this is an old-style rustic restaurant, which in the old days would have displayed the results of a successful hunt hanging from the rafters! Today, it's rather more sophisticated, offering light German cooking with some French classics, regional dishes and game in season. Starters might include lobster bisque, beef consommé with marrow dumplings or pheasant terrine with an orange sauce; fish dishes: perhaps poached turbot with tarragon sauce and risotto or medallions of sole on a nest of saffron noodles. For a main course, saddle of veal in a pastry case with calvados sauce, timbale of spinach and potato cakes or loin of pork with a Dijon mustard sauce and croquette potatoes. End with cinnamon parfait and rum-laced fruit, chocolate mousse or strawberry charlotte. Fixed-price menus range from DM35to 83. Several private dining-rooms; eat in the garden in fine weather. 10 charming and well-maintained bedrooms up to DM235 per couple per night. **Seats 110.** *Open 1100-1500, 1800-2300. Closed Mon. Amex, Diners, Mastercard, Visa.*

BERLIN · Frühsammers Gasthaus · DM300

Tel: (30) 803 80 23   Fax: (30) 803 77 36
Matterhornstrasse 101, 14129 Berlin

R

The Frühsammer family run this gasthaus, situated in a beautiful suburb, overlooking the Schlachtensee lake. Chef-patron Peter Frühsammer spends as much time as he can on their 300-acre farm, where they breed Galloway cattle – beef being the restaurant's main speciality, as in ragout of oxtail served with red wine and shallots, beef bourguignonne with mashed potatoes and carrots, and offal served with herbs and tomatoes. The daily-changing menu is mostly German with a distinct French and Italian influence, utilising market-fresh produce. Fixed-price dinner menu (six courses) DM110 offers good value. Some French and Italian wines alongside Germany on an extensive list; around a dozen available by the glass. Several tables in the garden in fine weather. **Seats 40.** *Open 1800-2200. Closed 2 weeks Jan, 2 weeks Jul. Amex, Mastercard, Visa.*

Tel: (30) 25 47 80   Fax: (30) 265 11 71
Lützowufer 15, 10785 Berlin

Bauhaus minimalism inspired the decor of this large, modern but individual hotel opposite Berlin's largest park, the Tiergarten. Rooms are spacious, comfortable and equipped with sound-proofing and air-conditioning. Business facilities are excellent, with nine meeting rooms, and the hotel even owns its own conference ship, able to accommodate up to 120 people while cruising the capital's extensive waterways. *Rooms 402. Room service 24hr. Private parking DM20. Banqueting facilities 450. Conference facilities 450. Indoor swimming pool. Gym. Sauna. Solarium. Amex, Diners, Mastercard, Visa.*

Tel: (30) 825 38 10   Fax (30): 826 63 00
Gottfried-von-Cramm-Weg 47-55, 14193 Berlin

As the name implies, the restaurant, decorated in English country-house style, is situated in a (very prestigious) tennis/sports club, only ten minutes walk from the city centre – a seemingly unlikely location for some of the best cooking in Berlin. Owner-chef Johannes King uses local and seasonal ingredients, producing dishes of modern German style with French influences. Specialities include stuffed sole with kohlrabi and a champagne sauce or marsh lamb (reared on salt meadows) with sliced green beans. Fixed-price menus from DM125 to 175. *Seats 45. Open 1830-2200. Closed Sun, Mon, 2 weeks Jan & 3 weeks Aug. Amex, Diners, Mastercard, Visa.*

Tel: (30) 26 02 13 9   Fax: (30) 26 02 80 760
Budapester Strasse 2, 10787 Berlin

Located in the heart of the city, the huge Inter-Continental enjoys views over the Tiergarten and the zoo, and is only a few minutes walk from Berlin's main thoroughfare, the Kudamm. As might be expected, decor is sleek and modern and all rooms have air-conditioning, satellite TV, mini-bar and safe. With a staffed business centre and fully-equipped conference facilities able to accommodate 1500 people, it is no surprise that the majority of guests are business executives. *Rooms 511. Room service 24hr. Private parking DM24. Banqueting facilities 1000. Conference facilities 1500. Business centre. Terraces. Indoor swimming pool. Gym. Sauna. Massage. Shop. Amex, Diners, Mastercard, Visa.*

Tel: (30) 23 27 45 00   Fax: (30) 23 27 33 62
Friedrichstrasse 158-164, 10117 Berlin

A purpose-built corner hotel, offering every conceivable facility in the centre of a city geared to attracting new business, be it conferences, business travellers or tourists. The strylish and comfortable air-conditioned bedrooms (incidentally, around fifty rooms in the Linden wing have just been refurbished) overlook the new unified centre of Berlin and are equipped with fax, VCR, satellite TV and mini-bar. 24hr room service. Theatre-style conference facilites for up to 100. Secretarial/translation services. Private/valet parking. *Rooms 349. Garden, indoor swimming pool, spa bath, gym, sauna, solarium, massage, hair salons, beauty salon. Amex, Diners, Mastercard, Visa.*

A very grand dining-room in which executive chef Rolf Schmidt, a well-known gastronomic figure in Berlin, presents a menu that is flamboyantly modern German, though somewhat influenced by luxury French ingredients and classical dishes. Look out for starters such as caviar potatoes with marinated wild salmon; terrine of foie gras with truffle vinaigrette and roasted langoustines on Japanese noodles with a tandoori sauce, followed perhaps by sea bass with tapénade and tomato butter or French lamb with either a confit of aubergines or a ragout of artichokes. Desserts are a real highlight: whitte peaches with blueberries and peach sorbet, a trio of sorbets with their own fresh fruits or blueberry pancakes with a frothy vanilla sauce. Two fixed-price menus (DM130 for four courses and DM189 for the `tasting' menu, eight mini-courses) are also available if chosen by an entire table. *Seats 90. Open 1800-2230. Closed Sun, Mon & Jul/Aug (school holidays).*

Tel: (30) 280 71 21
Bergstrasse 22, 10115 Berlin

New and expanded premises for the owners, three musicians originally from Bremen (Werner, Martina and chef Uwe Popall). Seasonal menus with daily specials, offering a good variety of modern and traditional German dishes: starters such as veal kidneys in a port wine jus and confit of shallots; king prawns with a red paprika mousse, or salmon in pastry with mussels and leeks, followed by a main course of, perhaps, pot-roast beef with a rosemary sauce, kohlrabi and dumplings or chicken in a pink peppercorn jus with spinach and rice cakes. Finish with a nougat soufflé, served with white chocolate ice cream and blackberries or raspberry parfait and fresh figs. Bargain business lunch at DM20, fixed-price dinner menus from DM45 to 85. Short list of carefully-chosen wines. Free parking near the cemetery, otherwise public car parks nearby. *Seats 80. Open 1200-1400, 1800-2330. Amex, Mastercard, Visa.*

Tel: (30) 20 26 83   Fax: (30) 200 44 38
Unter den Linden 5, 10117 Berlin

The Opernpalais, a protected historic monument, completely renovated in the early 1990s, is now a sort of gastrodome with several eateries (Henry's Treff, Fridericus). The original Palais was built in 1733, serving firstly as a royal residence, later as an exhibition room for the Schinkel Museum, and, rebuilt after World War II, site of the *Operncafé*, still operating today and well worth a visit, if only for the choice of some 50 different home-made pastries and cakes. Königin Luise, with fine views of the Unter den Linden avenue, offers an imaginative menu with plenty of modern German dishes, chef Dirk Heinz utilising market-fresh regional produce. Look out for carpaccio of beef served with asparagus tips and a herb cream; pan-fried scallops with a rucola sauce; breast of Barbary duck with a honey and ginger sauce or rack of lamb in a herb and mustard crust with rosemary sauce. For dessert there are seasonal fruit mousses with their own compote or a yoghurt and mint timbale with fresh strawberries. Cheeses, incidentally, are from France, whose wines feature strongly on the list, alongside a good showing from the New World. Fixed-price menus from DM58 to 75. Nearby parking (mostly free after 1900). *Seats 80. Open 1800-2400. Closed Sun, Mon & 1st 3 weeks Aug. Amex, Mastercard, Visa.*

Tel: (30) 25 02 0   Fax: (30) 262 65 77
Im Europa-Center, 10789 Berlin

Built in the late 60s, the hotel was thoroughly renovated in 1993 in a plush Italian style, with lots of marble, gold and swirling lines. The huge lobby is particularly grand, built of "the costliest materials nature has to offer" as the brochure boasts. Bedrooms are more restrained in decor but very comfortable and all are air-conditioned. The hotel is in the Europa-Center shopping mall, 500m from the railway station, and guests have free use of the swimming pools, gym and sauna in the Therman im Europa-Center next door. *Rooms 321. Room service limited. Private parking 20DM. Banqueting facilities 300. Conference facilities 580. Solarium. Amex, Diners, Mastercard, Visa.*

Tel: (30) 342 19 99
Spielhagenstrasse 3, 10585 Berlin

Down a quiet residential street in the centre of Berlin, Valter Manza's restaurant has earned a trusted reputation over a number of years. The menu, offering modern Italian dishes, is as cosy and comfortable as the Italian furniture and simple tablecloths, which makes it feel like a small country trattoria. Specialities include a spinach salad; baked sea bream with olives and tomatoes; fillet of turbot; rack of lamb or stuffed rabbit. Mascarpone mousse is a must for all lovers of that rich Italian cheese. Wines by the glass available from a decent Italian list. *Seats 40. Open 1830-2300. Closed Tue, 1 month Jul/Aug (school holidays). Diners.*

Meal prices for 2 are based on à la carte menus. When set menus are available, prices will often be lower.

BERLIN — Radisson Plaza Hotel Berlin — DM360

Tel: (30) 238 28   Fax: (30) 23 82 75 90   H
Karl-Liebknechtstrasse 5, 10178 Berlin

Ten minutes walk from Friedrichstrasse railway station, this hotel is typical of the modern, efficient Radisson chain. A major renovation of the imposing marble-floored lobby and the pastel-hued bedrooms was completed in 1994 and all rooms are now air-conditioned, with cable TV and mini-bars. One floor is reserved for non-smokers and there are two bedrooms specially equipped for disabled guests. *Rooms 560. Room service 24hr. Private parking 24DM. Banqueting facilities 350. Conference facilities 350. Secretarial/translation services on request. Indoor swimming pool. Gym. Sauna. Solarium. Beauty treatment. Amex, Diners, Mastercard, Visa.*

BERLIN — Hotel Riehmers Hofgarten — DM200

Tel: (30) 78 10 11   Fax: (30) 78 66 059   H
Yorckstrasse 83, 10965 Berlin

Located on one side of a courtyard, off a pedestrianised street, this cosy, family-run hotel offers a warm welcome to guests. The 19th-century building is decorated in soothing pastel tones with lots of wood and plants, and the bedrooms are comfortable and homely. There is a breakfast room but no restaurant and business facilities are limited to one conference room. *Rooms 21. Room service limited. Private parking DM16. Conference facilities 35. Amex, Diners, Mastercard, Visa.*

BERLIN — Rockendorf's Restaurant ★ DM400

Tel: (30) 402 30 99   Fax: (30) 402 27 42   R
Düsterhauptstrasse 1, 13469 Berlin

Siegfried Rockendorf has made quite a name for himself over the years, managing to lure diners to his Jugendstil (German art nouveau) restaurant, whose walls are decorated by young German artists, in the suburbs of Berlin. One of the reasons for all this attention is because he continues to modernise regional German cooking, adding his own imaginative flair to dishes, using only market-fresh produce: salmon terrine with a watercress vinaigrette and artichoke salad; lobster in a champagne sauce with field mushrooms and a julienne of celery; rack of lamb with a balsamic jus and gnocchi or venison with a blackcurrant and pepper sauce, served with potato dumplings. Desserts could include an elderberry sorbet or caramelised strudel of cherry mousse. Fixed-price menus (lunch from DM110-175, dinner DM175 to 225) offer several courses. Extensive wine list. *Seats 40. Open 1200-1400, 1900-2130. Closed Sun, 1 month Jul/Aug (school holidays), 22 Dec-6 Jan, Bank Holidays. Amex, Diners, Mastercard, Visa.*

BERLIN — Savoy Hotel — DM350

Tel: (30) 31 10 30   Fax: (30) 31 10 33 33   H
Fasanenstrasse 9, 10623 Berlin

This 1930s building used to be the British Embassy and was converted into a hotel in 1987. Since then, the Savoy has attracted a veritable galaxy of stars and high-powered political figures as well as the paparazzi that inevitably follow them. The hotel, like all other Savoys, is right in the city centre, only 500m from the zoological gardens, and within walking distance of the main shopping streets and banking district. The bedrooms have been modernised, with cable TV installed, but only the sixth floor has air-conditioning. *Rooms 131. Garden, sauna. Theatre-style conference facilities for up to 100. Secretarial/translation services. Amex, Diners, Mastercard, Visa.*

BERLIN — Schlosshotel Vier Jahreszeiten — DM685

Tel: (30) 89 58 40   Fax: (30) 89 58 4800   H
Brahmstrasse 6-10, 14193 Berlin

Originally built between 1912 and 1914 for Walter von Pannwitz, lawyer and adviser to Wilhelm II, the last kaiser of Germany, this grand palace has recently been renovated, its interior design (not to mention hotel stationery, menus, tableware and uniforms) being the responsibility of celebrated fashion designer Karl Lagerfeld. Set in its own grounds in Grunewald, just a few minutes away from the city centre, the building retains all its original features including a carved staircase, fireplaces and stuccoed ceilings. Air-conditioned bedrooms are, naturally, individually furnished with antiques, lovely rich silks and fine bed linen, each providing two telephones, a fax machine, stereo, video, cable TV, mini-bar and safe, as well as a luxuriously equipped marble bathroom with underfloor heating and Chanel toiletries. The Karl Lagerfeld suite, furnished with his own belongings, is his for the rest of his life; in his absence, it's available to (vetted) guests at around DM3500 a night! The garden terrace and leisure centre have direct access to the park, and there are two restaurants and bars. Several meeting rooms can accommodate up to 100. Underground car park. *Rooms 52. Garden. Indoor swimming pool. Sauna. Spa bath. Gym. Massage. Limousine. Amex, Diners, Mastercard, Visa.*

Cologne

COLOGNE   Ambiance am Dom   DM250

Tel: (221) 139 19 12
Domplatz, 50677 Köln

Located within the *Excelsior Hotel Ernst* (see below – turn left on entering the foyer) but privately owned and quite separate from it. Classic French food is delightfully presented whether you choose the à la carte or, at night, the five-course set dinner. A recent example of the latter began with a lobster salad before turbot in white wine sauce and then a choice of main dish between saddle of lamb, wild boar fillet and salmon lasagne. Dessert of gratinated peaches with a champagne sauce and its ice cream came an excellent French cheese trolley sporting about 25 different French cheeses. Many concert connoisseurs eat two courses, go to hear the Philharmonic Orchestra round the corner, then come back for their dessert. Set L DM60 Set D DM110 (*dégustation*) *Seats 30. Open 1200-1500, 1800-2300. Closed Sat, Sun, 5 days Easter, National Holidays, last 2 weeks Jul & 1st week Aug.*

COLOGNE   Antik Hotel Bristol   DM245

Tel: (221) 12 01 95   Fax: (221) 13 14 95
Kaiser-Wilhelm-Ring 48, 50672 Köln

The Hummel family are keen antique collectors and their acquisitions are scattered throughout this elegant but cosy hotel. All bedrooms are decorated differently in styles ranging from regal to rustic, some featuring ornate chandeliers, some with old oil paintings, and others with particularly fine carved wooden beds. Access from the autobahn is easy yet all Cologne's sights are in comfortable walking distance. *Rooms 44. Closed 23 Dec-2 Jan. Room service 24hr. Conference facilities 30. Amex, Diners, Mastercard, Visa.*

COLOGNE   Die Bastei   DM193

Tel: (221) 12 28 25   Fax: (221) 139 01 87
Konrad Adenauer Ufer 80, 50668 Köln

Within an octagonal watch tower (part of the old city walls and very much on the tourist circuit) overlooking the Rhine, this restaurant is itself a splendid sight with shimmering chandeliers and slab-stone walls. The chef, Jochen Blatzheim, mostly cooks fish and game (in season), with dishes like home-marinated salmon served with potato cakes, baby turbot baked in a Riesling sauce and scampi in port sauce. In addition to the à la carte (a shorter version of the evening carte is offered at lunchtime) there are several set menus for lunch (DM43 (Sun), DM52.50 (business) & DM65) and dinner (DM83 & DM95). *Seats 180. Open 1200-1500, 1900-2230. Closed L Sat, all 23 & 24 Dec. Own parking (7 spaces). Amex, Diners, Mastercard, Visa.*

COLOGNE   Börsen-Restaurant Maître   DM230

Tel: (221) 13 30 21   Fax: (221) 13 30 40
Unter-Sachsenhausen 10-26, 50667 Köln

In the Stock Exchange building, this French restaurant serves classic dishes using regional German raw ingredients. Home-made goose liver terrine, bouillabaisse and fillet of salmon in a black pepper sauce are all regular dishes on the menu but the house speciality is fillet of veal served in a creamy white wine sauce. In addition to the carte there are set lunch (DM65) and dinner (DM100) menus and a list of daily specials. The wine list sticks mainly to Bordeaux, burgundy and Chablis in France and Rieslings and Mosel wines from Germany. *Seats 55. Open 1200-1430, 1800-2200. Closed Sun, National Holidays & Aug. Amex, Diners, Mastercard, Visa.*

Opening times are often liable to change at short notice, so it's always best to book.

Tel: (221) 27 01   Fax: (221) 13 51 50
Trankgasse 1-5, 50667 Köln

The Swiss Kracht family have been running this exquisite 19th-century hotel for over 100 years. The location, opposite the cathedral right in the centre of Cologne and only 300m from the main railway station, is ideal (unless travelling by car as they have no parking of their own). Up-to-date facilities include air-conditioning, mini-bars, room safes and satellite television while marble brings a touch of old-fashioned luxury to the bathrooms. A fitness centre including steam room, sun beds, spa bath and exercise equipment was due to open in October 1995. *Rooms 160. Room service 24hr. No parking. Conference facilities 150. Hairdressing. Amex, Diners, Mastercard, Visa.*

This imaginative, internationl menu truly departs from the heavy German restrictions of traditional regional cooking, with starters like a light tomato carpaccio served with tempura of prawns and light main courses such as poached turbot and crayfish served with a bouillabaisse sauce. For dessert, try the perfect blend of lemon and honey parfait with caramel strudel. Open bottles are served as house wines from the international, but heavily French and German-biased wine list. *Seats 80. Open 1200-14.30, 1800-2300.*

Tel: (221) 203 40   Fax: (221) 203 47 77
Magnusstrasse 20, 50672 Köln

Located in the centre of Cologne, near the Cathedral and 1km from the railway station, this modern hotel is part of the worldwide Renaissance group and offers excellent facilities. Relax in the swimming pool, boil in the Turkish bath, sip drinks in the winter garden or on the summer terrace. The ten air-conditioned function rooms can accommodate anything from a private dinner for six to a conference for 350. *Rooms 236. Room service limited. Private parking DM24. Banqueting facilities 350. Conference facilities 350. Business centre. Terrace. Indoor swimming pool. Sauna. Solarium. Turkish bath. Massage. Amex, Diners, Mastercard, Visa.*

Tel: (221) 72 11 08   Fax: (221) 72 80 97
Ebertplatz 3-5, 50668 Köln

Established for nearly 30 years, this restaurant is still serving some of the best Italian food to be found in Germany. Cooking is modern in style with starters like home-made goose liver terrine, carpaccio and fillet of veal in truffle sauce making a delicious prelude to some of their home-made pasta, perhaps fettuccine with truffle sauce, black noodles in a rich lobster sauce. This is also home to probably the largest selection of Italian wines in Germany (about 1500), plus some excellent champagnes. Set meals DM98 (4-course) & DM115 (5-course). *Seats 70. Open 1200-1400, 1800-2330. Closed Sun & Mon. Amex, Diners, Mastercard, Visa.*

Tel: (221) 162 30   Fax: (221) 162 32 00
Turinerstrasse 9, 50668 Köln

This family-run hotel (no relation to its more illustrious namesake) enjoys a central location, close to the Rhine and the Cathedral, and only 200m from the railway station. It was built ten years ago and bedrooms (all with TV, mini-bar and safe) are decorated in bright, cheery colours. An unusually high proportion (50%) of rooms are singles and there are five fully-equipped meeting rooms, making it a good choice for businessmen. *Rooms 100. Closed 23 Dec-2 Jan. Room service limited. Private parking DM15. Conference facilities 80. Sauna. Steam room. Solarium. Amex, Diners, Mastercard, Visa.*

Tel: (221) 200 80   Fax: (221) 200 88 88
Kaygasse 2, 50676 Köln

This extraordinary hotel in the largest water tower in Europe opened in 1990. The building is 125 years old and is set in its own park, 1.5km from the main railway station. A wonderful variety of materials has been used – powdered glass, African hardwoods, corroded metal – to harmonise with the brickwork and create a unique designer modernism. The luxurious interior furnishings are the work of French designer Andrée

Putman, and works of art by the likes of Vaserely, Baselitz and Warhol are among the 350 original paintings which line the walls. With over 100 members of staff, service is of the highest order. *Rooms 90. Room service 24hr. Private parking. Conference facilities 90. Translation/secretarial services on request. Terrace. Sauna. Solarium. Massage. Amex, Diners, Mastercard, Visa.*

Tel: (221) 257 78 79   Fax: (221) 258 08 61
Salzgasse 13, 50667 Köln

Elegant restaurant (wood panelling, an impressive collection of oil paintings, antique furniture) set in a 17th-century building in the pedestrianised heart of the old town. Urbane owner Karl-Heinz Steinbüchel presides front of house while chef Dirk Schneider produces a happy mix of modern German and traditional French cooking. Start with the likes of pan-fried sweetbreads with herb risotto in advance of a main such as salmon with a shrimp ragout or Walfisch topf (a trio of veal, lamb and beef fillets with a morel sauce and home-made noodles) before trying to resist the sweet trolley. The wine list runs to some 250 different bottles (80% German, 20% French) with about 10 house wines available by the quarter-litre carafe. *Seats 90. Open 1200-1400, 1800-2300. Closed L Sat, all Sun, National Holidays & 23 Dec-5 Jan. Amex, Diners, Mastercard, Visa.*

Around Cologne

Tel: (221) 49 23 23   Fax: (221) 497 28 47
Olympiaweg 2, 50933 Köln-Müngersdorf

With its tranquil location in the middle of the Stadtwald city park this restaurant is just the spot for a romantic *diner à deux*, especially in summer when the large terrace comes into its own. It's not just the setting that brings folk here though but chef Stefan Sold's attractive modern style of cooking which utilises only the freshest of ingredients. Dishes like home-smoked fillet of gurnard with ratatouille salad and pesto, carpaccio of beef and veal with pine kernels and tarragon cream, fish soup with crème fraiche, lobster-stuffed guinea fowl with champagne sauce and herb noodles, saddle of Scottish lamb with an olive and onion crust, leg of rabbit stuffed with vegetables and served with coriander sauce and duchess potatoes typify the style. In addition to the carte there are daily-changing lunch (DM65) and dinner (DM100) menus. Desserts from the trolley or French cheeses to finish. About a dozen wines from the French-German list are served by the glass. *Seats 45. Open 1200-1415, 1800-2115. Closed 10 days Feb/Mar (during Carnival). Public parking next door. Amex, Diners, Mastercard, Visa.*

Dresden

Tel: (351) 864 20   Fax: (351) 864 27 25
An Der Frauenkirche 5, 01067 Dresden

Built in 1989, the Hilton is located on a quiet side street in the historic centre of the city near the Elbe. The decor is resolutely contemporary – plain colours, black furniture – and facilities are good, with shops, swimming pool and an athletic club to keep guests occupied. Hunger is never likely to be a problem: the hotel contains eight restaurants. *Rooms 330. Room service limited. Private parking DM23. Conference facilities 300. Indoor swimming pool. Gym. Sauna. Solarium. Beauty treatment. Hair salon. Amex, Diners, Mastercard, Visa.*

Tel: (351) 566 20   Fax: (351) 559 97
Grosse Meissner Strasse 15, 01097 Dresden

The core of this ten-year-old hotel, set in a park near the Elbe and the town centre, is a fine 17th-century townhouse. It is decorated in a mix of contemporary and classical styles designed to create a formal yet cosy atmosphere. Facilities are good and include a fitness club, three bars and five restaurants. The railway station is 500m away and the airport 10km. *Rooms 340. Room service limited. Banqueting facilities 140. Conference facilities 300. Secretarial/translation services on request. Indoor swimming pool. Gym. Sauna. Solarium. Amex, Diners, Mastercard, Visa.*

Tel: (351) 37 48 10   Fax: (351) 374 81 18   H
Stechgrundstrasse 2, 01324 Dresden

One of many hotels which opened in the former East Germany in the wake of reunification, the Villa Emma manages to be more personal, homely and friendly than many of its competitors. The house was built in 1914 and features many delightful Jugendstil touches. Facilities are limited but, with a forest on its doorstep, the hotel's location, 5km from the city centre and 20 minutes drive from the railway station and airport, is blissfully quiet. *Rooms 21. Closed Christmas, New Year. Room service limited. Private parking. Sauna. Amex, Diners, Mastercard, Visa.*

Düsseldorf

Tel: (211) 130 30   Fax: (211) 130 38 30   H
Heinrich-Heine Allee 36, 40213 Düsseldorf

The neo-classical Breidenbacher Hof is proud to be Germany's oldest luxury hotel (opened in 1806). Its location is certainly choice: in the centre of the city, behind the fashionable tree-lined Königsallee and the cobbled streets of the Altstadt. Inside, the decor skilfully blends the ancient and modern. Most bedrooms are decorated in a restrained contemporary style and have air-conditioning and all the usual amenities. The public rooms are altogether grander, with Gobelin tapestries, antiques, old paintings and elaborate chandeliers. *Rooms 130. Room service 24hr. Private parking DM25. Banqueting facilities 100. Conference facilities 100. Secretarial/translation services on request. Beauty treatment. Amex, Diners, Mastercard, Visa.*

Tel: (211) 621 60   Fax: (211) 621 66 66   H
Nördlicher Zubringer 6, 40470 Düsseldorf

Close to the trade fairgrounds, ten minutes away from the Königsallee, and with easy access from the autobahn, this is a typical international chain hotel. Facilities are exemplary, particularly for business people, with a staffed business centre, executive offices for hire, a luxurious 'Club' floor, and eleven meeting rooms. It is 4km from the airport and 5km from the railway station. *Rooms 245. Room service limited. Public parking 20DM. Banqueting facilities 348. Conference facilities 520. Business centre. Indoor swimming pool. Sauna. Solarium. Amex, Diners, Mastercard, Visa.*

Tel: (211) 37 50 10   Fax: (211) 37 40 32   H
Fürstenplatz 17, 40215 Düsseldorf

Although situated in a quiet area south of the centre, the railway station, Königsallee and the Altstadt are only ten minutes walk away. Bedrooms are comfortably furnished with mahogany furniture and a predominantly white decor and all are equipped with satellite TV and mini-bar. Leisure facilities include an indoor swimming pool. The hotel is part of the German Günnewig Group. *Rooms 81. Room service 24hr. Private parking DM17. Banqueting facilities 40. Conference facilities 60. Garden. Terrace. Indoor swimming pool. Fitness centre. Sauna. Solarium. Bureau de change. Amex, Diners, Mastercard, Visa.*

Tel: (211) 59 44 02   Fax: (211) 597 97 59   R
Bonifatiusstrasse 35, 40547 Düsseldorf

Since the mid-1980s, Sybille and Peter Nöthel have been running this modern German restaurant on the outskirts of the city, near the Rhine, with great success. Peter, who learnt his culinary skills in various German and Austrian establishments, has gone on to develop his own style and a most interesting menu. In addition to the à la carte there is a six-course tasting menu and a most unusual daily-changing, six-course menu consisting entirely of lobster (there's no dessert) that might include lobster cream soup with champagne, Asian-style lobster spring rolls, grilled lobster with sugar peas and nutmeg butter among its courses. Other tempting dishes could be US beef fillet with polenta and cumin jus and grilled turbot covered with potato scales and a lemon jus. Desserts are equally adventurous: coconut soufflé sitting in an iced raspberry sauce for example. The wine list includes New World bottles. Set D DM165 (*dégustation* & lobster menus). *Seats 45. Open D only 1800-2200. Closed Sun, Mon & 1 week Jan. Own parking. Amex, Diners, Mastercard, Visa.*

Tel: (211) 40 10 50   Fax: (211) 40 36 67
Kaiserwerther Markt 9, 40489 Düsseldorf

Established in 1733 and located on the first floor, this has long been one of Düsseldorf's leading restaurants – actually it's about ten miles north in one of the city's oldest suburbs on the Rhine. Since the 70s it has been run by Jean-Claude Bourgeuil (visible with his chefs in the kitchen), who combines French nouvelle cuisine with modern German cooking to great effect: tapénade of Breton lobster with courgettes and balsamic vinegar, artichoke or asparagus charlotte, wild mushrooms in a light garlic jus, seafood in Oriental spices, tart of Bresse pigeon with pepper sauce. Finish with crisp pancakes, served with quark cream on a passionfruit coulis, or Black Forest gateau with wild cherries. The wine list runs to some 500 bins from all over the world but with an emphasis on the major French wine-growing regions. Set D DM179 & DM196. Cheaper dishes available on the ground floor (Aalschokker, Tel: 40 39 48). *Seats 45. Open D only 1900-2130. Closed Sun & Mon. Valet parking. Amex, Visa, Mastercard, Diners.*

Tel: (211) 36 70 30   Fax: (211) 367 03 99
Cantadorstrasse 4, 40211 Düsseldorf

This quiet hotel is well located, near the Hofgarten park and five minutes walk from the railway station. The lobby is awash with marble and mirrors but bedroom decor is more unobtrusively modern and facilities are good. *Rooms 52. Closed 23 Dec-2 Jan. Room service limited. Private parking 25DM. Conference facilities 30. Fitness club. Sauna. Amex, Diners, Mastercard, Visa.*

Tel: (211) 36 03 36   Fax: (211) 35 66 42
Oststrasse 128, 40210 Düsseldorf

The dynamic German Rema chain currently have 21 hotels and bought the venerable early-19th-century Savoy in 1994. Much renovation has taken place since then to restore the Jugendstil decor. Bedrooms are individually appointed with old mahogany furniture and bright colours, and leisure facilities include swimming pool, gym, sauna and sunbeds; there is no restaurant. The hotel's location, between the main railway station and the Königsallee, is excellent. *Rooms 123. Private parking. Conference facilities 120. Indoor swimming pool. Fitness centre. Sauna. Solarium. Amex, Diners, Mastercard, Visa.*

Tel: (211) 39 39 31   Fax: (211) 39 17 19
Stromstrasse 47, 40221 Düsseldorf

Italian restaurant with art deco interior down by the harbour. Inside, the light coming from the Murano glass lamps is deep red and dark green, a truly Italian setting. The menu is also Italian, but with innovative touches: tartare of salmon with avocado and dill, *spaghettini alla marinara*, grilled salmon steak with pesto sauce, breast of Bresse chicken with truffles, tournedos of Angus beef with green peppercorn sauce. Finish with the richly delicious mascarpone cream, served with fresh fruit and warm cherry sauce. The menu changes daily. Wines from all over the world. Set L & D DM66 (for min 2 persons). *Seats 100. Open 1200-1500, 1800-2300. Closed L Sat & all Sun (except during Düsseldorf Fair) Amex, Mastercard, Visa.*

Tel: (211) 32 68 32   Fax: (211) 32 83 37
Königsallee 14, 40212 Düsseldorf

Wood-panelled dining-room with a relaxed, discreetly traditional atmosphere much appreciated by a clientele drawn from the surrounding business district. It's been a going concern for over 80 years, and in its current ownership for the last ten. The cooking is Italian with the likes of carpaccio dressed in truffle oil, black spaghetti with seafood, gnocchi with mushrooms and king prawns, tortellini with tomato and fresh basil, turbot in a white wine sauce and the standard range of Italian desserts. Everything on the all-Italian wine list is available by the glass as well as the bottle. Set L DM60 Set D DM75, DM85 & DM100. *Seats 60. Open 1200-1430, 1830-2300. Closed Sun & 22 Dec-5 Jan. Amex, Diners, Mastercard, Visa.*

Tel: (211) 32 02 22   Fax: (211) 13 10 13
Königstrasse 3a, 40212 Düsseldorf

Chef-patron Günther Scherrer has been here since 1984 and continues to please with his refined modern French cooking: tomato consommé with basil ravioli, medallions of John Dory with truffles and leeks, lamb cutlets with lemon thyme, crème brulée, cold Grand Marnier soufflé with raspberry coulis, summer pudding. A large selection of French cheeses rounds off the menu. Set L DM55/DM85 Set D DM135/DM165. *Seats 50. Open 1200-1500, 1900-2230. Closed Sun & National Holidays. Amex, Diners, Mastercard, Visa.*

Tel: (211) 46 90 00   Fax: (211) 46 90 06 01
Blumenthalstrasse 12, 40476 Düsseldorf

Built as an orphanage in 1914, this unusual hotel is situated in a very quiet part of the city, ten minutes from the central railway station. All rooms are suites (except for one maisonette), varying in size from 35 to 100 square metres, and decorated in a variety of styles from chintzy flowery fabrics to rich Oriental tones. Staff are friendly and helpful and the large garden at the back with its duck pond is an added attraction. *Rooms 40. Closed 23 Dec-2 Jan. Room service 24hr. Private parking 50DM in garage, free outside. Banqueting facilities 15. Conference facilities 15. Garden. Sauna. Solarium. Amex, Diners, Mastercard, Visa.*

Tel: (211) 13 11 63   Fax: (211) 13 29 74
Andreasstrasse 2, 40213 Düsseldorf

A 16th-century Jesuit chapel, now on a pedestrian-only walkway in the old city, has been converted into this regional German and French restaurant. A gratin of snails in a garlic butter might appear alongside more traditional North German dishes like white herrings served in a beer sauce on a well-balanced menu that might also include medallions of veal and roasted fillets of pike-perch. There's always an interesting vegetarian option like courgette and tomato soufflé served with rice, fresh basil and grated truffles. Most of the wines are German, with 220 different bottles. Set L DM60 Set D DM120 plus à la carte. *Seats 135 (+ 40 outside). Open D only 1800-2400. Closed Sun (except during Düsseldorf Fair). Amex, Diners, Mastercard, Visa.*

Around Düsseldorf

Tel: (201) 100 70   Fax: (201) 100 77 77
Huyssenallee 55, 45128 Essen

Early 1980s hotel built in a quiet park on the outskirts of the city. Air-conditioned bedrooms, of which about 80 are reserved for non-smokers, are well equipped, with satellite televisions, in-house video channel, mini-bar and, in some rooms, fax points. Although the hotel's in-house conference facilities are limited to 150 (theatre-style), they have an arrangement with the Saalban Conference Centre in Essen where up to 1600 delegates can be accommodated. *Rooms 205. Room service 24hr. Ample parking. Conference facilities 150. Indoor swimming pool. Sauna. Solarium. Gym. Amex, Diners, Mastercard, Visa.*

A large restaurant with an international menu that ranges from T-bone steak with freshly grated horseradish and 'surf and turf' with crayfish and fillet steak with lime garlic butter (the menu reassuringly states that "we only serve German, American, French and Argentinean beef"!) to medallions of angler fish with chanterelles, wild rice and chive sauce, sole meunière and veal kidneys in sherry mustard sauce. Desserts include a "dream of champagne rosé sorbet" and gratinated citrus fruits with white coffee ice cream or choose something from the sweet trolley. Set L DM58. *Seats 150. Open 1200-1500, 1800-2400.*

Meal prices for 2 are based on à la carte menus. When set menus are
available, prices will often be lower.

MEERBUSCH BÜDERICH   Landhaus-Mönchenwerth   DM230

Tel: (2132) 779 31   Fax: (2132) 710 99
Niederlörickerstrasse 56, 40667 Meerbusch-Büderich

This family restaurant, in a 17th-century former monastery 50km from Düsseldorf, has been passed down from father to son as, to some extent, has the menu with its happy mix of Italian and French dishes. Jellied meatloaf with herb vinaigrette and sautéed potatoes, half a lobster with creamed tagliatelle, pike-perch and crayfish in a dill cream sauce with rice, escalope of veal with chanterelles and casseroled duck with cabbage and duchess potatoes demonstrate the style. Finish with perhaps fresh berries and semolina or iced soufflé with Grand Marnier and summer berries. The location is superb: the terrace, which is surrounded by gardens, looks out over the Rhine. Set L & D DM52/DM58 & DM95/DM125. *Seats 60. Open 1200-1430, 1830-2130. Closed Sat (except by arrangement for parties over 15), 23 & 24 Dec. Own parking. Amex, Diners, Mastercard, Visa.*

Frankfurt

FRANKFURT   Arabella Grand Hotel   DM525

Tel: (69) 298 10   Fax: (69) 298 18 10
Konrad-Adenauer-Strasse 7, 60313 Frankfurt am Main

The German Arabella chain, based in Munich, has 13 hotels around the country and opened the luxurious Grand six years ago. Ten minutes walk from the main railway station, it offers a wide range of facilities from 13 fully-equipped conference rooms to air-conditioned bedrooms with three telephones and marble bathrooms with floor heating. There are also seven restaurants offering every type of cuisine from German to Japanese and Chinese. *Rooms 378. Room service 24hr. Private parking 28DM. Banqueting facilities 500. Conference facilities 500. Indoor swimming pool. Gym. Sauna. Solarium. Massage. Amex, Diners, Mastercard, Visa.*

FRANKFURT   Bistrorant Die Leiter   DM150

Tel: (69) 29 21 21   Fax: (69) 29 16 45
Kaiserhofstrasse 11, 60313 Frankfurt am Main

A place for seeing, and being seen: right opposite Yves Saint Laurent in a chic shopping street, this brasserie is the meeting place for businessmen, artists and actors. The decor is black and white with chrome fittings and the food reliably good. A Mediterranean-influenced menu sticks largely to the tried and tested with such dishes as Caesar salad, grilled lobster and roasted guinea fowl. *Seats 40. Open 1200-0100. Closed Sun. Amex, Diners, Mastercard, Visa.*

FRANKFURT   5 Continents   DM160

Tel: (69) 690 53 901   Fax: (69) 69 47 30
Abfhughalle B Frankfurt Airport, 53901 Frankfurt am Main

It is quite alien to the British, but airport restaurants on the Continent are often very good, and this one certainly is. The seasonally-changing, French-inspired menu might include cold cucumber soup with dill, vegetables and shrimps marinated in champagne vinegar and hazelnut oil, guinea fowl with chanterelles and tortelloni, and John Dory on a lobster mousseline with dill and saffron rice. Short list of French and German wines. *Seats 220. Open 1200-1500, 1800-2130. Amex, Diners, Mastercard, Visa.*

FRANKFURT   Die Gans   DM160

Tel: (69) 61 50 75   Fax: (69) 62 26 25
Schweizerstrasse 76, 60594 Frankfurt am Main

Located in a trendy shopping street, Die Gans' appealing menu shows considerable Italian influence in dishes such as home-made tagliatelle with chanterelles and Romana salad with apple wedges and gorgonzola vinaigrette among the starters, saltimbocca of angler fish with leeks and potatoes, mozzarella-gratinated veal with gnocchi and stuffed tomatoes and chicken breast with a ragout of mushrooms among the mains. For afters there's exotic fruit salad with passion fruit sorbet and mocha charlotte with vanilla sauce or a selection of Italian cheeses served with grapes. There's a terrace for summer eating. Set menus DM68-DM78. *Seats 34 (+ 20 outside). Open D only 1800-300. Closed Sun (except during trade fairs), 23 Dec-5 Jan & 2 weeks Feb. Amex, Diners, Mastercard, Visa.*

Tel: (69) 754 00   Fax: (69) 754 09 24

Friedrich-Ebert-Anlage 40, 60325 Frankfurt am Main

The position of this hotel, opposite the main entrance to the international exhibition centre and five minutes walk from the railway station, ensures its continuing popularity. Bedrooms are furnished with antiques and decorated in French, Roman or Chinese style. In addition to the standard facilities, there are safes in all rooms and also, unusually, fitness equipment. *Rooms 117. Room service 24hr. Private parking 25DM. Banqueting facilities 120. Conference facilities 220. Business centre. Amex, Diners, Mastercard, Visa.*

Tel: (69) 23 25 41   Fax: (69) 23 78 25

Kaiserstrasse 67, 60329 Frankfurt am Main

Part of a small chain of excellent Chinese restaurants (quite rare in Germany, though there are plenty of Indonesian establishments). Most of the dishes are Cantonese, with wonton soup, crispy duck in spicy sauce, veal and broccoli in oyster sauce and sweet and sour pork. The house speciality is a bird's nest of egg noodles with fried seafood. *Seats 170. Open 1200-2300. Closed 24 & 25 Dec. Private parking. Amex, Mastercard, Visa.*

Tel: (69) 29 800 70   Fax: (69) 29 60 68

Schützenstrasse 6 60311 Frankfurt am Main

German cuisine, both traditional and modern, is the forte of this restaurant set in a 16th-century cellar. Rabbit with green asparagus, crayfish and yellow pea soup with cumin, John Dory roasted with fennel (for two), roast black-feather chicken flavoured with vanilla, saddle of venison with spätzle cake and crépinette of veal with baked mushrooms show the style. For afters try semolina dumplings with a ragout of elder blossom or a 'gazpacho' of seasonal fruits with orange saffron ice cream. The wine cellar is about half German (particularly strong in whites) and half French (including all the famous names) with many available by the glass – so do ask. *Seats 200. Open D only 1900-2300. Closed Sun (except during major trade fairs) & 24 Dec-2 Jan. Own parking for 50 cars. Amex, Diners, Mastercard, Visa.*

Tel: (69) 74 67 02   Fax: (69) 74 53 96

Westendstrasse 15, 60325 Frankfurt am Main

When so many Frankfurt hotels are faceless modern chains, it comes as a welcome surprise to find a small, friendly hotel offering comfort and character. Antiques, grandfather clocks, old paintings and carved wooden chairs and beds all help to create the atmosphere of a private house. The price you pay for style is limited facilities: there is no restaurant and conferences are not possible here. The hotel is located in a quiet district west of the centre but only five minutes walk from the railway station. *Rooms 20. Closed 22 Dec-5 Jan. Room service 24hr. Private parking. Secretarial/translation services on request. Garden. Terrace. Amex, Diners, Mastercard, Visa.*

Around Frankfurt

Tel: (6102) 300 00   Fax: (6102) 30 00 55

Hofgut Neuhof, 63303 Dreieich-Götzenhain

Eighteen kilometres from Frankfurt, this restaurant was opened by the Schumacher family back in the 1940s and sits opposite the club house of a golf course also owned by the family. The menu is fairly international - mutton broth with pearl barley, home-made jellied pork with a green herb sauce, prawn cocktail, fillet of beef béarnaise, medallions of pork in blue cheese sauce with noodles, duck with orange – the wine list sticks to German and French bottles. *Seats 200. Open 1200-1430, 1800-2200. Closed 2 weeks Feb. Own parking. Amex, Diners, Mastercard., Visa.*

Tel: (69) 67 59 96   Fax: (09) 87 39 28
Kelsterbacherstrasse 66, 60528 Frankfurt-Niederrad

It's well worth the 10km trip out from the centre of Frankfurt to find this elegant late 19th-century restaurant surrounded by old chestnut trees. Inside, glistening crystal and crisp, pale yellow table-cloths set the scene for cooking that is inspired by France and whatever is best and freshest from the day's markets. The wine list is both extensive and wide ranging with New World offerings alongside comprehensive European listings that include vintage ports dating back to 1890. Six wines available by the glass. Set L DM51 (business) Set D DM98 (5-course) & DM108 (7-course). *Seats 60. Open 1200-1500, 1800-2230 Closed L Sat, all Sun. Own parking. Amex, Diners, Mastercard, Visa.*

Tel: (6173) 701 01   Fax: (6173) 70 12 67
Hainstrasse 25, 61476 Kronberg

Built towards the end of the last century by Empress Friedrich, this splendid schloss, set in parkland a few miles to the north-west of Frankfurt, is a haven of peace and tranquillity. The grounds include a fine Italianate rose garden and they have their own 18-hole golf course. Beamed ceilings, grand stone fireplaces, polished panelling, chandeliers, a well-stocked library, original oil paintings and numerous antiques feature in the public area that have the ambience of a bygone era. All the individually decorated bedrooms also boast antique furniture and period features along with modern touches like mini-bars and 20-odd channels on the TV. The seven full suites also have fax points. *Rooms 58. Room service all day. Private parking. Conference facilities 120. Golf. Golf driving range. Amex, Diners, Mastercard, Visa.*

Chef Günther Ledermüller's distinctively modern style is exemplified by starters like sweetbreads on a Jerusalem artichoke rösti, carpaccio of beef with truffle marinade and parmesan, and fried crayfish with roasted vegetables. Mains are no less up-to-date: monkfish with lemon grass, corn-fed chicken larded with truffles, best end of lamb tandoori, fillet of beef gratinated with Pommery mustard and bone marrow. Finish with the likes of plum ragout with poppy-seed ice cream and iced marzipan dumplings on Amaretto 'pulp'. Set L DM65, Set D DM135 (*dégustation*). *Seats 40. Open 1200-1400, 1830-2200.*

Tel: (621) 203 26
R7 34, 68161 Mannheim

The chef's culinary pedigree includes spells at both *Aubergine* and *Tantris* in Munich. Here, however, the menu is Italian/Mediterranean with such dishes as seafood salad, sea bass cooked in salt and olive oil with marinated vegetables, lasagne layered with salmon and mushrooms and roast pigeon served in a black olive sauce typifying the regularly changing carte. The wine list is exclusively Italian. *Seats 40. Open 1200-1400, 1830-2130. Closed Mon & 14-31 Jul. Amex, Mastercard.*

Hamburg

Tel: (40) 44 29 05   Fax: (40) 44 98 20
Abteistrasse 14, 20149 Hamburg

For those wanting a change from huge, characterless chain hotels, the Abtei will come as a welcome relief. This turn-of-the-century villa, down a quiet suburban street, offers a personal, friendly welcome and cosy, antique-furnished rooms. Facilities are necessarily limited but, unusually for such a small place, the hotel has its own restaurant. The railway station and the airport are both a 20-minute drive away. *Rooms 11. Closed 1 week in summer, 1 week in Jan. Room service limited. Garden. Amex, Diners, Mastercard, Visa.*

Opening times are often liable to change at short notice, so it's always best to book.

HAMBURG — Anna & Sebastiano ★ DM300

Tel: (40) 422 25 95   Fax: (40) 420 80 08
Lehmweg 30, 20251 Hamburg

A team effort with Anna Sgroi in the kitchen and partner Sebastiano looking after front of house and taking responsibility for the outstanding Italian wine list. Anna's modern Italian cooking was informed by a spell with Gualtiero Marchesi at his restaurant outside Milan but her inspiration comes from all the Italian regions from Piedmont to Sicily. Risottos are a particular speciality on the daily-changing menu that might also include a Tuscan salad of warmed langouste and white beans and perhaps a dish of oven-baked baby goat. Located in a residential part of the city there is a choice between two dining-rooms, one in modern Milanese style the other making elegant use of rustic Tuscan furniture. The all-Italian wine list provides a comprehensive tour of that country's wine growing regions with nearly 300 different wines on offer. Set D DM100 (4-course) & DM110 (5-course). *Seats 48.*
Open D only 1900-2200. Closed Sun, Mon, 3 weeks summer (school holidays) & 3 weeks from 23 Dec. Amex, Diners, Mastercard, Visa.

HAMBURG — L'Auberge Française DM220

Tel: (40) 410 25 32   Fax: (40) 410 58 57
Rutschbahn 34, 20146 Hamburg

Owner Jacques Lemercier, who also acts as maitre d', has been presiding over this little French enclave for a quarter of a century providing, with the help of his totally French team, a genuine Gallic experience to the people of Hamburg. From chef Pierre Hervet's kitchen come dishes like scampi provençale, goose liver terrine, fillet of sole with puréed potatoes and truffle jus, magret of duck with green peppercorn sauce, sweetbreads with Cassis, roast rabbit with tarragon cream sauce, crepe normande (filled with apples and calvados and served with vanilla ice cream) and crème brulée. The wines, about 130 bins, are all French too, with a red bordeaux and white Sauvignon as the house wines. The restaurant is located in the centre of the old city. Set menus DM65, DM85 & DM110
Seats 45. Open 1200-1430, 1830-2230. Closed L Sat (all Sat Jun-Aug), all Sun & Christmas-New Year. Amex, Diners, Mastercard, Visa.

HAMBURG — Le Canard DM350

Tel: (40) 880 50 57   Fax: (40) 47 24 13
Elbchaussee 139, 22763 Hamburg

Northern German cooking heavily influenced by more aesthetic French cuisine is at the heart of Herr Viehhauser's menu at this restaurant set in an extraordinary post-modern building that looks out over the River Elbe. A starter of lobster with potato salad might be followed by fillet of char with "Ingwersauce" and a white bean purée or duck with red cabbage and bordeaux wine sauce. Among the desserts look out for the Salzburger nockerl (for two), dumplings with a filling involving egg white, vanilla, lemon and cream. An extensive wine list majors on Germany, Austria and France. In summer there are tables set out in the garden. Set L DM135 Set D DM180 & DM225. *Seats 50 (+ 30 outside).*
Open 1200-1430, 1900-2230. Closed Sun. Own parking. Amex, Diners, Mastercard, Visa.

HAMBURG — Elysée Hotel DM360

Tel: (40) 41 41 20   Fax: (40) 41 41 27 33
Rothenbaumchaussee 10, 20148 Hamburg

The Elysée is the first venture into the hotel world for the owner of a successful chain of German steakhouses (a second is opening in Leipzig in 1997). Built in 1985, it offers every facility expected in a luxury hotel, from the swimming pool and fitness centre to ten conference rooms. The mahogany and leather furnishings of the library aim to create the atmosphere of an English club. Bedrooms are decorated in unobtrusive light tones with sleek modern furniture and triple glazing to ensure absolute quiet. The location is central and Dammtor railway station is three minutes walk away. *Rooms 305. Room service 24hr. Private parking 16DM. Banqueting facilities 500. Conference facilities 500. Secretarial/translation services on request. Indoor swimming pool. Gym. Sauna. Solarium. Amex, Diners, Mastercard, Visa.*

Opening times are often liable to change at short notice, so it's always best to book.

Tel: (40) 11 40 40   Fax: (40) 41 40 420
Magdalenenstrasse 60, 20148 Hamburg

Just out of the centre of Hamburg (15 minutes from the airport and 10 minutes from the main railway station), this hotel has particularly well-equipped bedrooms. All have modern, stylish furniture, but have kept the charm of the original early 20th-century Patrichia houses. There's a conservatory, where up to ten people can meet for an informal meeting, but no other more structured conference facilities. It is also important to note that it is a hotel garni (bed and breakfast) so there is no restaurant and room service is limited to drinks and sandwiches. *Rooms 60. 24hr room service. Private parking for 6 cars. Amex, Diners, Mastercard, Visa.*

Tel: (40) 880 13 25   Fax: (40) 880 62 60
Elbchaussee 130, 22763 Hamburg

The Scherrens opened this restaurant between Elbchaussee and the fashionable quarter of Hamburg, Blankenese, in the 70s. Since that time the menu has evolved with the emphasis now on lighter, more modern dishes and away from the heavier, more traditional German cooking. Starters like terrine of foie gras with cherry chutney and monkfish carpaccio with crème fraiche and caviar might precede crayfish *à la nage* with herbs, roast monkfish with a mangetout purée and tandoori sauce, and roast breast of guinea fowl with mushrooms and fine noodles. The house speciality is crispy whole roast duck, carved at the table, served with a light black pepper sauce. Look out for some interesting rustic regional dishes as well. Afters include simple sorbets with fruit and French cheeses from Philippe Olivier along wiht more elaborate creations like gratinated lemon parfait with apple compote and basil. *Seats 50. Open 1200-1400, 1830-2200. Closed Sun. Own parking. Amex, Diners, Mastercard, Visa.*

Tel: (40) 24 83 30   Fax: (40) 24 83 35 88
Kirchenallee 34, 20099 Hamburg

Centrally located right opposite the main railway station (but very efficiently double-glazed to eradicate any possibility of noise disturbance) with the main shopping area just the other side of the station, and close to theatres and, of course, the lake. The entrance is very grand – marble pillars, gilded mirrors, polished reception desk, glittering chandeliers – but the atmosphere is not in any way stuffy or overpowering. Staff throughout are friendly and helpful. Standards of housekeeping are very high throughout and although the bedrooms vary in size and view potential, all are excellently equipped. One floor is reserved for non-smokers. There is only one lift point, so that rooms furthest from this central area might involve a longish baggage haul. Snacks (sandwiches and rolls, cakes and ices, coffee and tea) are available all day in Bistro Schampus; extensive buffet breakfasts (including Buck's Fizz!) are served in the main restaurant. Excellent leisure facilities. *Rooms 303. Garage parking. Conference facilities 200. Sauna. Solarium. Steam room. Indoor swimming pool. Amex, Diners, Mastercard, Visa.*

The restaurant is designed to resemble a grand liner at the pinnacle of turn-of-the-century style: those seated on the galleried area can enjoy watching the hustle and bustle below as waiters in gold-braided white coats glide smoothly between the tables. The food style varies between classic and modern, as shown in starters like a smoked fish platter (salmon, eel and halibut) with horseradish cream, or light tomato broth with basil dumplings. Main courses range from fillet of turbot steamed in Riesling and served with sliced mixed vegetables, or plain grilled and served with a mousseline sauce, to fillet of veal Vienna-style with fried potatoes, or grilled calfs' liver Berlin-style with sliced apples and onions and mashed potato. Puddings include the much-loved Hamburger Rote Grütze served with vanilla cream. *Seats 100. Open 1200-1500, 1800-2330.*

Meal prices for 2 are based on à la carte menus. When set menus are available, prices will often be lower.

Tel: (40) 24 17 26   Fax: (40) 28 03 851
HR
An der Alster 9, 20099 Hamburg

A fairly small but much-loved hotel, named after the family which founded it. The white-painted building commands lovely views of the tree-lined lake, and the small garden feels surprisingly secluded given the potentially busy location. Bedrooms are well equipped, immaculately maintained, individually designed and named after former "honoured guests". Although the style is mostly set by the exquisite antiques which the family accumulated and which are now carefully positioned throughout the hotel, there are also touches like the ultra-modern bathrooms, or the tiny Stuberl bistro which is themed like a Tyrolean hut. The large dining-room is 17th-century in style, while the smaller specialist restaurant (see below) is also modern in style. This mixture, however, somehow seems cohesive rather than disparate as the friendly and efficient staff are all working as a team to ensure a comfortable visit. *Rooms 56. Sauna. Garden. Amex, Diners, Mastercard, Visa.*

This specialist seafood restaurant has attracted much acclaim, and it's easy to see why. The coolly modern decor epitomised by a laminate ceiling housing recessed lighting is offset by traditionally luxurious napery and drapery, and traditionally correct service at all times. The cooking is delicate and delicious, with everything made in house and the focus of extreme attention to detail. A light, smooth starter of lobster mousse was accompanied by very very fine green and white asparagus spears, while a (potentially similar) terrine of scallops was in fact an altogether different creation, with chunks of scallop scattered throughout and a tomato and basil salsa to accompany it. Typical main courses might be S*eeteufel und Meerasche* served with a red pepper coulis and rice; or sole, boned at the table and served with leaf spinach and yellow, waxy potatoes. Desserts are exquisitely presented on black plates and sprinkled with icing sugar whenever this best displays their potential, as in mixed sorbets with seasonal berries, and mocha parfait with fresh apricots. Good, strong coffee is accompanied by hand-made petits fours. An extensive wine list rewards investigation, and there is good advice available from a very knowledgeable sommelière. *Seats 40. Open 1900-2200, Closed Sun.*

Tel: (40) 89 27 60   Fax: (40) 899 33 24
R
Holstenkamp 71, 22525 Hamburg

Tafelhaus is located in a busy area of the city that is filled with thundering traffic during the day, but quiet at night. The entrance can be difficult to find: down a small lane and through their front garden, but it is well-worth discovering this modern German kitchen. The menu has some well-chosen and well-executed meat and fish dishes. Particular specialities include langoustines with potatoes and herb butter and *crépinette* of lamb. Unlike many traditional German restaurants, this place also has some great desserts like a rich, warmed chocolate tart served with Cointreau ice cream. Set D DM95. *Seats 55 (+ 45 outside). Open 1200-1400, 1900-2130. Closed Sun, Mon, 3 weeks Jan & 3 weeks Jul. Own parking. No credit cards.*

Hanover

Tel: (511) 83 16 71   Fax: (511) 837 98 11
R
Hildesheimerstrasse 230, 30519 Hannover

In a 19th-century farmhouse south of the city centre, the owner-chef combines regional French recipes with traditional German dishes to good effect. Mango and melon salad; mushroom terrine; cucumber salad with shrimps; monkfish with a tomato fondue, noodles and spinach, and calf's liver with apple sauce were all to be found on a recent menu. Desserts are traditionally German. Large international wine list. Garden for alfresco dining in summer. *Seats 100 (+ 100 outside). Open 1200-1400, 1800-2300. Closed Sun (Jul & Aug), 25 & 26 Dec. Own parking. Amex, Mastercard, Visa.*

Opening times are often liable to change at short notice, so it's always best to book.

Tel: (511) 304 40   Fax· (511) 304 40 07
Luisenstrasse 1-3, 30159 Hannover

In the heart of Hanover, between the Opera and the central railway station, this hotel has been in the Kasten family since it opened in 1856. Not surprisingly, the emphasis on tradition is strong with many rooms decorated in an elegant baroque style, plain colours and antique furniture. A newer extension features a Jugendstil decor. Guests have ranged from German Presdents to Andy Warhol. *Rooms 160. Room service limited. Private parking 15DM. Banqueting facilities 140. Conference facilities 200. Secretarial/translation services on request. Amex, Diners, Mastercard, Visa.*

Tel: (511) 83 08 18   Fax: (511) 843 77 49
Hildesheimerstrasse 185, 30173 Hannover

Surrounded by the Eilenriede forest, the Landhaus Ammann looks and feels like a country hotel with extensive gardens and a sunny summer terrace but in fact it is only 10 minutes by car from the main railway station and was built, in country-house style, only about ten years ago. Bedrooms are simply decorated with old-fashioned chairs, sofas and standard lamps. Facilities are not extensive but it's a great place to stay if you are in Hanover, particularly in the summer. *Rooms 16. Room service all day. Own parking. Conference facilities 150. Amex, Diners, Mastercard, Visa.*

The owner of the hotel, Helmut Ammann, is also the chef and, with his relatively large kitchen team is responsible for the excellence of the cooking here, bringing a lightness of touch to an essentially German cuisine. Dishes such as venison paté with apple and celery salad and a red onion compote; consommé of venison with dumplings; lobster hot-pot; sole, lobster and salmon with spinach on a saffron sauce; roast saddle of lamb with rosemary and, for dessert, a lemon cream with tea sauce and mangoes demonstrate the style. With its mahogany furniture and elegant silverware the dining-room is in keeping with the overall style of the hotel: there's a garden terrace for summer dining Set meals DM128 & DM168 in addition to the carte. Long wine list with a bias towards Bordeaux and a good selection of half bottles. *Seats 45 (+ 100 outside). Open 1200-1400, 1900-2200.*

Tel: (511) 349 50   Fax: (511) 349 51 23
Hinüberstrasse 6, 30175 Hannover

Privately-run 80s' hotel in the city centre, only 500m from the central railway station. Modern rooms come with mini-bars, satellite television and all the usual amenities except that only about half the hotel is air-conditioned. Rooms on the `1st class' floor all have their own fax machines. 90 of the rooms are decorated in modern art deco style, while the lobby is lined with marble and warmed by open fireplaces. *Rooms 200. Room service all day. Valet parking DM20 for 24 hours. Conference facilities 450. Amex, Diners, Mastercard, Visa.*

Tel: (511) 349 52 52

Art deco-cum-rococo-style dining-room where the chef is constantly experimenting within his Mediterranean-influenced menu. One of the house specialities is the `catch-of-the-day' from the fish market served with a light white butter sauce on a bed of mixed salad (priced for either a larger or smaller portion). Other dishes might include double consommé with mushroom ravioli, pan-fried king prawns on a lollo rosso and chicory salad, sweetbreads with home-made vegetable noodles, roasted pike-perch on balsamico lentils with thyme potatoes and sliced fillet of beef with a wild mushroom cream sauce and more of the home-made noodles. Another speciality (subject to availability) is a Provençal-style fish casserole incorporating braised vegetables, garlic and herbs. To conclude try a semolina flummery on jellied berries with vanilla ice drops. New World and European wines. *Seats 75. Open D only 1800-2400. Closed Aug.*

Meal prices for 2 are based on à la carte menus. When set menus are available, prices will often be lower.

HANOVER — Titus Restaurant — DM200

Tel: (511) 83 55 24   Fax: (511) 838 65 38

Wiehbergstrasse 98, 30519 Hannover

Chef-patron Dieter Grubert's frequently-changing menu is market driven with only the freshest of ingredients used in his modern German creations. Dishes like chanterelles tossed in fresh noodles and herbs, and turbot baked in a champagne sauce are house specialities. The light French cheese soufflé served with fresh rhubarb must be tried. The wine list runs to about 50 bottles (half French and half German with the exception of just a few Italians) with about ten available by the glass. Set L DM42 Set D DM89 (dégustation) plus à la carte. *Seats 36 (+ 20 outside). Open 1200 -1400, 1800 - 2200. Street parking. Amex, Diners, Mastercard, Visa.*

Around Hanover

BENTHE-HANOVER — Hotel Benther Berg — DM180

Tel: (5108) 640 60   Fax: (5108) 64 06 50

Vogelsangstrasse 18, 30952 Benthe-Hannover

The major attraction of this century-old hotel is its location: on the edge of a forest, in its own 15 hectares of gardens, yet only 15 minutes drive south-west of Hanover. The German national football team are among the guests who have enjoyed the tranquillity of the setting and the friendliness of the service. Bedrooms are decorated in a very simple, plain style although those in the original house have older furniture than those in the new extension. *Rooms 67. Room service limited. Private parking. Banqueting facilities 110. Conference facilities 80. Indoor swimming pool. Sauna. Amex, Diners, Mastercard, Visa.*

GARBSEN — Landhaus am See — DM150

Tel: (5131) 468 60   Fax: (5131) 46 86 66

Seeweg 27, 30827 Garbsen

This typical north German country house is 20km south of Hanover and in a lovely location in a park on the edge of the Berenbostelersee. It was opened as a hotel three years ago by the Löhmann family. The main building is 75 years old and is decorated in a homely style with restrained colours and wooden furniture, while two newer buildings have modern furnishings. Hanover airport is 40 minutes away by car. *Rooms 36. Room service 24hr. Private parking. Conference facilities 45. Secretarial/translation services on request. Sauna. Amex, Diners, Mastercard, Visa.*

LAATZEN — Treff-Hotel Britannia — DM285

Tel: (511) 878 20   Fax: (511) 86 34 66

Karlsruher Strasse 26, 30880 Laatzen

Situated in the small town of Laatzen, 6km south of the centre of Hanover but only a minute's walk from the Messe (fair site), this hotel is part of the 50-strong German Treff chain. Bedrooms are decorated in a functionally modern style. The hotel has its own sauna and tennis courts and guests can use a nearby fitness centre free of charge. *Rooms 100. Room service limited. Private parking. Conference facilities 250. Secretarial/translation services on request. Tennis. Sauna. Amex, Diners, Mastercard, Visa.*

Munich

MUNICH — Aubergine — ★ DM320

Tel: (89) 59 81 71   Fax: (89) 550 43 53

Maximiliansplatz 5, 80333 München

There have been major changes at the Aubergine. Eckart Witzigmann, the most acclaimed chef in Germany in recent years, is no longer in residence. After going through a much-publicised personal crisis he is now "visiting chef" from his base in Düsseldorf. Chef Patrik Jaros has taken over at the stoves, and happily standards have remained quite high. The restaurant, formerly the Regina Palace Hotel, built in the 30s, is coolly luxurious and was redecorated in 1995. It now features very attractive trompe l'oeil murals of Italian lakes by Rainer Maria Latzke. The cooking can be described as modern French-inspired German and is best experienced by trying one of the gourmet menus: four courses for DM132, five courses for DM164 or the full six-course menu for DM198. We tried a cassolette of shellfish followed by wild salmon with spinach and morels. Other dishes worth noting are

Steinbutt auf provenzalischem Gemüse (turbot on a bed of Provençal vegetables) and medallions of venison with glazed apples. An excellent dessert is mango tart with coconut ice. Some reasonably-priced wines are suggested to accompany this menu: let manager Guido Wenzel guide you. Parking difficult. *Seats 40. Open 1200-1500, 1900-2400. Closed Sun, Mon. Amex, Diners, Mastercard, Visa.*

Tel: (89) 212 00   Fax: (89) 212 09 06
Promenadeplatz 2-6, D-80333 München

This hotel has been attracting the rich and famous since 1841 and is now in its fourth generation of the Volkhardt family. Well over a century after it was built, the family acquired the adjacent Palais Montgelas which is now transformed into a conference and banqueting centre. The rooms are sumptuous and lavish, in a choice of styles, and have been totally refurbished since the days when the hotel could accommodate up to 1000 guests. Even now, it is one of the smartest places in town, with its own jazz club and theatre. It is five minutes from the main railway station and 50 minutes from Munich Airport. In addition to the restaurant, there is also the jovial, beery Palais-Keller and a branch of the Polynesian restaurant chain, Trader Vic's. *Rooms 428. Room service 24hr. Private parking. Banqueting facilities 1200. Conference facilities 1500. Secretarial/translation services on request. Hairdressing. Massage. Sauna. Solarium. Steam bath. Swimming pool. Amex, Diners, Mastercard, Visa.*

This light, elegant restaurant with its winter gardens and summer terrace serves a modern German menu, with plenty of fish dishes. Fillet of sole is served in a butter cream sauce and salmon soufflé comes with mashed potatoes. Two meat dishes on offer at the time of our last visit were *kleine Blutwürsten auf Semmelknödelsalat* (mini black-puddings served on a bed of bread dumplings) and *Rinderschmorbäckchen in Rotweinsauce* (braised beef in a red wine sauce). Regional wines are particularly well represented on the eclectic wine list, stretching from excellent Cotes du Rhone to strong burgundies. *Seats 108. Open 1200-1500, 1800-2330.*

Tel: (89) 55 10 40   Fax: (89) 55 10 49 05
Schillerstrasse 8, 80336 München

Despite being right next to the main railway station, this is a tranquil spot since most of the bedrooms look down on to an inner courtyard and the rest of the rooms are double-glazed. They are all decorated in traditional German style, chintzy fabrics and solid wooden furniture, and come with mini-bars and satellite TV. Long-serving staff maintain a friendly, cosy atmosphere. However, this is very much a business hotel, with few tourists. *Rooms 82. Room service 24hr. Parking in nearby public car park at concessionary rate of DM12 for 24 hours. Conference facilities 40. Amex, Diners, Mastercard, Visa.*

Tel: (89) 55 13 70   Fax: (89) 55 13 71 21
Schützenstrasse 11, 80335 München

Sister hotel to the nearby Königshof (see below), and with similarly high standards of service and accommodation including the air-conditioning of all bedrooms. Located just around the corner from the main railway station. *Rooms 113. Room service all day. Garage parking (at Königshof) DM16 for 24 hours. Conference facilities 30. Amex, Diners, Mastercard, Visa.*

Tel: (89) 212 09 58   Fax: (89) 212 09 79
Hartmannstrasse 8, 80333 München

Forget the clichés about German food when you sample the top restaurants in Munich. Otto Koch, chef-patron at Le Gourmet, is a fine example of the high standards Munich restaurateurs are capable of achieving. His small, traditionally decorated restaurant offers many refined dishes such as hot foie gras with ginger or smoked pigeon breast. Another starter is a fennel flan topped with thin slices of bone marrow, coarse salt and chives. You might also want to try a mushroom cake of thin layers of crepes interspersed with a rich mushroom purée. A dish more related to Munich is a version of the famous Munich white sausage made with seafood and served, surprisingly, with a mustard sauce. After that, try a typical Bavarian cheese. For dessert there are soufflés and an apple dessert with thinly sliced apples marinated in red wine and served with an apple sorbet. Truly fine wines accompany this excellent food. *Seats 35. Open 1200-1430, 1900-2300. Closed Sun, Mon. Amex, Diners, Mastercard, Visa.*

Tel: (89) 28 59 09   Fax: (89) 28 27 86
Schönfeldstrasse 22, 80539 München

Down a quiet street between the city centre and the heart of Munich's caféland, Schwabing, this restaurant (the name means Tally Ho), is stacked with hunting trophies. Everything here is traditional, from the meat-laden menu to the Wagner playing discreetly in the background. As one might expect, game is a big speciality during the hunting season, with dishes like medallions of venison with mushrooms, the meat being cooked pink. Other dishes tend to be more international and might include rack of lamb with a basil crust, stuffed aubergine and a potato gratin and, among the desserts, mascarpone ice cream with a compote of cherries and vanilla cream. Set L DM35 Set D DM85. *Seats 60. Open 1200-1400, 1800-2200. Closed L Sat, all Sun, 24-27 Dec, 5 days Easter & 2 weeks Aug. Amex, Mastercard, Visa.*

Tel: (89) 416 82 47   Fax: (89) 416 86 23
Schumannstrasse 1, 81679 München

For casual but elegant dining in an attractive setting, Michael Käfer's first-floor suite of dining-rooms above the very popular gourmet shop is a favourite haunt. Müncheners like to spend an evening in his relaxed restaurant, where the standard of cooking is high without the seriousness of the gastronomic temples. The menu ranges far and wide and includes both Italian and French specialities. On a recent visit we enjoyed seafood starters such as crayfish tails simmered in a delicate bouillon with thyme, dill and parsley and a rolled crepe filled with moist smoked salmon and salmon caviar with a cream sauce. Black grouper, dorade and sea bass featured among the fish courses. The meat dishes on offer included lamb chops Munich-style (braised in a herb-rich broth). There are many ice cream desserts such as the famous German Rote Grütze (red fruit jelly) with sorbet and ice cream. *Seats 180. Open 1130-2400. Closed Sun, National holidays. Public parking. Amex, Diners, Mastercard, Visa.*

Tel: (89) 864 41 63   Fax: (89) 86 43 85
Waidachanger 9, 81249 München

Werner Böswirth, the owner and head chef, has created an international menu here but still with a German flavour. Fish, meat and poultry are all served with plenty of fresh vegetables from the local market. Summer salad with bacon and croutons, tomato soup with ricotta ravioli, sea bass and lobster in saffron, fricassee of veal and apple cake with macadamia nuts show the style. The restaurant is just outside Munich. Set D DM85 (4 course) & DM125 (6 course) plus à la carte. *Seats 25. Open D only 1830-2200. Closed Sun, Mon & 2 weeks from Whit Sunday. Amex.*

Meal prices for 2 are based on à la carte menus. When set menus are available, prices will often be lower.

Tel: (89) 55 13 60   Fax: (89) 55 13 61 13
Karlsplatz 25, 80335 München

First class hotel, in the classic 'grand hotel' mould, conveniently located on the Stachus Plaza in the city centre; just five minutes from the main railway station. All rooms and suites are air-conditioned and soundproofed and come with every modern convenience from mini-bar to cable television. High levels of service include the hand polishing of shoes and an eight-hour laundry service. *Rooms 103. Room service all day. Garage parking DM18 for 24 hours. Conference facilities 100. Amex, Diners, Mastercard, Visa.*

Tel: (89) 36 00 20   Fax: (89) 36 00 22 00
Berlinerstrasse 93, 8000 München 40

You could be excused for mistaking this hotel for an ultra-modern airport terminal. Located at the edge of the city in Schwabing, one of Munich's main business districts, the Marriott is within short walking distance of the Englischer Garten. Like other hotels in the group, its range of sports and conference facilities is comprehensive, with a fully-equipped fitness club and 13 state-of-the-art function rooms including the vast Grand Ballroom. The bedrooms are simply furnished with pastel colours and floral bedspreads and there are special facilities for the disabled as well as separate non-smoking rooms. In addition to the hotel restaurant, there is a lobby café serving lighter fare and a piano cocktail bar. *Rooms 349. Room service 24hr. Banqueting facilities 420. Conference facilites 500. Underground parking DM22. Gym. Laundry service. Satellite TV. Sauna. Solarium. Spa bath. Indoor swimming pool. Amex, Diners, Mastercard, Visa.*

Tel: (89) 419 710   Fax: (89) 419 71 819
Trogerstrasse 21, 81675 München

It is an art to combine modernity with traditional elegance, but owner Klaus Lieboldt has done just that at this hotel built during the late 80s. The new building is filled with Louis XVI-style furniture and old oil paintings while white and beige linen-clad sofas are the very latest designs. The two duplex suites are particularly spectacular with graceful spiral staircases leading up to the bedrooms and personal saunas in the bathrooms. Regular rooms, (there is a premium for those overlooking the garden), come with cable television, mini-bar and safe. The rooms are not air-conditioned but portable units can be requested when booking. Good central location and the garden offers a secluded retreat in a busy city. *Rooms 71. Room service 24hr. Garage parking DM18 for 24 hours. Conference facilities 42. Sauna. Gym. Amex, Diners, Mastercard, Visa.*

Tel: (89) 38 45 0   Fax: (89) 38 45 1845
Am Tucherpark 7, 80538 München

Right by the English Garden and just 10 minutes from the railway station, this 14-floor 70s tower with its extraordinary large number of rooms is an exemplary member of the Hilton group. Every imaginable facility is available and expertly organised and with its 14 function rooms this is the first-choice venue for big conferences and galas in the city. DM40 million was recently spent upgrading and modernising the comfortable bedrooms and some feature handsome pieces of original old furniture. Rooms are available for disabled guests. As well as the first-rate Grill, there is also a Chinese restaurant (Tse-Yang) and one featuring vegetarian dishes, not to mention the Biergarten and piano bar. *Rooms 477. Room service 24hr. Garage parking. Conference facilities 1500. Secretarial/translation services on request. Beauty treatment. Cable TV. Gym. Hairdressing. House doctor. Massage. Beach club. Sauna. Solarium. Indoor swimming pool. Amex, Diners, Mastercard, Visa.*

With its deep leather seats, darkwood panelling and fresh flower arrangements, this restaurant feels rather like an English club. The menu has a number of daily-changing specialities with plenty of grilled fish and seafood dishes always available: *Lachstatar mit kleinen Kartoffelbällchen* (aromatic salmon tartare served with little potato balls filled with caviar) and *Hummerterrine mit tatar und Wachtelei* (terrine of lobster tartare and quail's eggs) being two examples. Meat dishes are often ceremoniously carved at your table. A long list of different set menus starts at around DM85. Petits fours are served with coffee. The wine list is international but quite pricy. *Seats 80. Open 1200-1430, 1900-2230. Closed L Sat.*

Tel: (89) 23 70 30   Fax: (89) 23 70 38 00
Sparkassenstrasse 10, 80331 München

H

The original family-run hotel was knocked down in the early 80s and the present one was built on the same site. It is right in the centre of the historic old part of the city, near the main railway station. Rooms are traditional in their furnishings, but more up-to-date in their amenities: cable TV and mini-bars in all rooms, fax and room safe in some. *Rooms 170. No room service. Garage parking DM20 for 24 hours. Conference facilities 180. Fitness room. Sauna. Steam room. Sun bed. Amex, Diners, Mastercard, Visa.*

Tel: (89) 45 84 50   Fax: (89) 45 84 54 44
Innee Wiener Strasse 6, 81667 München

HR

Friendly Anneliese Würbser owns and runs this 70s hotel next to the English Garden and Deutsches Museum. Bedrooms come with air-conditioning, safes, mini-bars, and satellite television, are filled with mahogany furniture, fresh flowers and fruit, while the rest of the hotel is invitingly decorated with plants and small trees. *Rooms 71. Room service during restaurant hours. Garage parking DM18 per 24hr. Conference facilities 50. Indoor swimming pool. Sauna. Spa bath. Closed Christmas. Amex, Diners, Visa.*

Despite this appearing to be a typical German cellar restaurant the atmosphere is as refined as the cooking, which is now in the hands chef Sonnen: foie gras with red wine and apple, veal carpaccio marinated with lemon, sea bream with roasted onion and yellow pepper sauce, peppermint parfait with pineapple and a strawberry coulis. The menu changes weekly utilising fresh market produce. The restaurant shares the 300-year-old vaulted cellars with some 30,000 bottles of wine. *Seats 70. Open D only 1800-0100. Closed Sun, National Holidays & 23 Dec-7 Jan.*

Tel: (89) 29 09 80   Fax: (89) 22 25 39
Neuturmstrasse 1, 80331 München

H

This is the most exclusive and quietly elegant hotel in Munich. It is ideally located in the heart of the old town and next to the famous Hofbräuhaus where every visitor drops in for a glass of beer. The building, a former antique market, has been beautifully renovated in neo-renaissance and opened as a hotel six years ago. Rooms are very luxurious with under-floor heating, marble bathrooms and attractive prints and engravings. Some of the rooms have private terraces and all boast four telephones and fresh flower arrangements. In the reception areas are Biedermeier furniture and a sumptuous blend of panelling and precious marble. Guests can also enjoy breathtaking views of Munich from the Roof Terrace, with its heated outdoor pool. *Rooms 73. Room service 24hr. Private parking. Banqueting/conference facilities 100. Heated outdoor swimming pool. Amex, Diners, Mastercard, Visa.*

Tel: (89) 22 03 13   Fax: (89) 22 91 95
Marienplatz 8, 80331 München

R

Deep in the 19th-century cellars of the former town hall, this cavernous restaurant has served traditional *Bayerisch* (Bavarian) cooking since 1868, now with a few more international dishes on the menu. Smoked trout, potato soup, sauerkraut and suckling pig with potato dumplings are the hearty regional staples. The splendid decor includes 19th-century frescoes on the intersecting vaults, old carved wooden panelling and antique pew-like benches. In addition to the restaurant there is an equally characterful wine tavern with live music nightly and, in summer, a garden café in the courtyard. Set L DM25, DM45 & DM75 Set D DM45, DM55 & DM85 plus à la carte. *Seats 450. Open 1000-2400. Closed 24 Dec. Amex, Mastercard, Visa.*

Tel: (89) 36 20 61   Fax: (89) 361 84 69
Johann-Fichte Strasse 7, 80805 München

R

The extraordinary, ultra-modern decor of Tantris, very different from almost every other gastronomic temple, continues to shock and surprise but it does not overshadow the high cooking standards of Hans Haas, who is now well established in the kitchen. Seafood is prepared in a variety of ways, from a simple fish and vegetable terrine or salmon marinated in herbs and caviar, to Breton lobster served with fresh noodles and a cream of white truffle sauce. For those who prefer to sample a variety of the chef's creations there are two *feinschmecker* gourmet menus: a larger one of eight courses for DM218 or the more modest five-course one which we tried. At a cost of DM215 it includes two wines, one of which is a quality red burgundy. Our lobster salad with marinated asparagus was followed by gilthead with a tomato coulis and baby veal in a truffle sauce. For dessert were crepes with a traditional cherry filling. Restaurant manager Peter Kluge will advise if you choose to go à la carte. The wines come from a cellar of 70,000 bottles, one of the best in Germany. *Seats 70. Open 1200-1400, 1830-2300. Closed Sun, Mon, National Holidays, 1-10 Jan. Private parking. Amex, Diners, Mastercard, Visa.*

Tel: (89) 21 25 0   Fax: (89) 21 25 20 00
Maximilianstrasse 17, 80539 München

Standing proudly on Maximilianstrasse, this classic and traditional 19th-century palais is Munich's leading luxury hotel. Several new wings were added in 1972 and although the rooms have been recently renovated, many are still traditionally decorated. Just two minutes walk from the Opera house and 35 minutes by car to the airport. With ten function rooms to choose from, catering for every conceivable meeting, big business conferences and jet-setters' balls is a major part of the operation. *Rooms 322. Room service limited. Private garage. Banqueting facilities 400. Conference facilities 600. Secretarial/translation services on request. Gym. Hairdresser. Indoor swimming pool. Massage. Sauna. Solarium. Private garage. Amex, Diners, Mastercard, Visa.*

The chef in this timelessly elegant restaurant has been serving a diverse international menu here since the 1970s with some reliably good combinations: *Tranche vom Steinbutt pochiert mit Tomaten und Blattspinat* (turbot poached with tomatoes and leaf spinach), roasted medallions of monkfish with a butter sauce served with sliced courgettes and carrots, seafood in a shellfish sauce on a bed of linguine with fresh ricotta and tournedos of beef in a pepper sauce. The menu is extensive, with a good choice of seafood, fish, game and poultry dishes. The usual mouthwatering desserts – fresh fruit sorbets, chocolate mousse and lime parfait – end the meal nicely. Wines are predominantly German, with a few French offerings. *Seats 65. Open 1200-1430, 1800-2300. Closed Aug.*

Around Munich

Tel: (8052) 179 90   Fax: (8052) 17 99 66
Kirchplatz 1, 83229 Aschau im Chiemgau

Some 80km south-east of Munich just off autobahn E52 (actually Salzburg airport across the Austrian border is much nearer) the charming village has a romantic castle and baroque churches. The hotel too is almost medieval in style with white arcades, vivid orange roof tiles, bright red-and-white shutters and a large paved patio. Inside, there are comfortable lounges and luxurious bedrooms, many with fantastic views across to the foothills of the Alps. Conferences for up to 60. *Rooms 32. Garden. Sauna. Beauty Therapy. Amex, Diners, Mastercard, Visa.*

Without doubt Heinz Winkler is one of the best chefs in Germany today. He has already demonstrated his abilities at in Munich, but now that he is here, his talents have really blossomed. The elegant dining-room allows for space between the tables and has a pleasant view of the garden. On a recent visit we chose the five-course *dégustation* menu. It offered lobster medallions with avocado vinaigrette and lasagne of scallops in a delicious truffle oil sauce followed by breast of pigeon and parsley ragout. Other noteworthy dishes from the à la carte menu are salmon carpaccio lightly warmed in a lemon vinaigrette and courgette flowers baked in Madeira sauce. There are several excellent fish courses such as sea bass baked in sea salt with tarragon sauce. Venison, a German favourite, and young rabbit with prunes and noodles are served in season. Unusual desserts are quark soufflé with pear sauce and rhubarb savarin with a strawberry mousse. There are several set menus ranging in price from DM39 for three courses to DM198 for eight courses. The wine list is extensive and worth a detailed study. Service, atmosphere and decor are all what you can, and should, expect of one of Germany's finest country restaurants, a worthy winner of our Restaurant of the Year Award, Western Europe. *Seats 150. Open 1200-1330, 1830-2200.*

Stuttgart

Tel: (711) 640 17 62   Fax: (711) 649 24 05
Böheimstrasse 38, 70178 Stuttgart

Horst Plassmann's restaurant, right in the centre of Stuttgart, offers a mix of French cuisine and regional German dishes. Asparagus hollandaise or marinated salmon could be followed by roast rack of lamb served with green beans and gratin potatoes or their special roast goose dish (in season) that comes with fried apples, cranberry sauce, sauerkraut made with 'blue' cabbage, and steamed potatoes. For dessert try the pancakes steeped in Jack Daniels with a bitter orange sauce. The menu changes seasonally. *Seats 80. Open 1130-1430, 1800 -2230. Closed L Sat, all Mon & school holidays. Own parking for 30 cars. Amex, Mastercard, Visa.*

Tel: (711) 456 00 37   Fax: (711) 456 00 38
Am Schloss Hohenheim, 70599 Stuttgart

From 1770, German citizens used to make representations to Duke Karl Eugen of Würtemberg in these rooms; since 1993 it has been a restaurant, with marquee-like interior, where chef Martin Öxle has been making his mark. Daily-changing menus emphasise fresh fish dishes - fillet of pike-perch served as a soufflé on a lentil cream sauce, monkfish resting on a bed of pesto noodles - although meat and poultry also appear with dishes like calf's head salad with green asparagus and lobster. Tempting desserts like white wine mousse wrapped in filo pastry and served with fresh peaches. *Seats 45. Open 1200-1400 (Sun only), 1830-2400. Closed D Sun, all Mon & 1-15 Jan. Own parking. No credit cards.*

Tel: (711) 204 80   Fax: (711) 204 85 42
Amulf-Klett-Platz 7, 70173 Stuttgart

Only 3km away from the trade fair centre and central railway station, and very near the Palace Gardens, this hotel is part of the Steigenberger chain. Since it opened in the 30s, Kissinger, Gorbachov and Yeltsin have all visited and many EU meetings have been hosted here. Pastel colour schemes feature in bedrooms that are equipped with air-conditioning, cable TV and mini-bars. One floor of rooms are reserved for non-smokers. *Rooms 240. Room service 24hr. Valet parking DM25 for 24 hours. Conference facilities 460. Indoor swimming pool. Sauna. Amex, Diners, Mastercard, Visa.*

Tel: (711) 948 21 37   Fax: (711) 797 92 10
Flughafen, 70621 Stuttgart

This stylish art deco restaurant is actually inside the airport. The menu combines light modern German cooking with regional dishes. Grilled turbot and sea bass are served alongside rump steak served in miso and basil sauce. Other dishes lean towards more international cuisine, with cannelloni filled with lobster and fresh tarragon and salmon, sturgeon and artichoke carbonara. Set L DM54 Set D DM100, DM120 & DM150 plus à la carte. *Seats 30. Open 1145-1400, 1745-2200 (Sat 1800-2400). Closed L Sat & 3 weeks Aug. Amex, Diners, Mastercard, Visa.*

Tel: (711) 236 70 01   Fax: (711) 236 70 07
Hohenheimerstrasse 30, 70184 Stuttgart

Despite being only five minutes from the main railway station, just off a main road in the centre of the city, this family-run hotel is relatively quiet inside with plenty of protection and comfort given by air-conditioning and double-glazing. Although constructed in the 1940s the building incorporates old beams, doors, wrought-iron work and some ornate frescoed ceilings that are over 400 years old. Bedrooms are furnished with old, heavy oak furniture and decorated with bronze-forged ornaments. All have cable television. *Rooms 26. Room service all day. Closed 20 Dec-6 Jan. Amex, Diners, Mastercard, Visa.*

Set in a 19th-century former wine cellar with timbered ceiling, ornately carved doors and heavy wooden tables, Zur Weinsteige offers a typical Southern German menu with fresh trout (something of a speciality) and Black Forest venison among other things. On the main menu, sausages are accompanied by creamed mushrooms and noodles and medallions of veal and pork are cooked with chanterelles and baby vegetables. There's a garden patio for summer dining. Long, mostly regional German, wine list. Set L DM16 (business) Set L & D DM45 & DM78 Set D DM98 (*dégustation* – DM150 with recommended wines). *Seats* 60 (+ 30 outside). *Open 1200-1400, 1800-2200. Closed Sun, Mon, National Holidays & 20 Dec-6 Jan.*

Tel: (7221) 90 00   Fax: (7221) 387 72
Schillerstrasse 6, 76530 Baden-Baden

A quiet, walkable distance from Baden-Baden, which has been famous for its spas since the 1600s, this privately-owned hotel in the Black Forest has been in existence for over 120 years. It has been the scene of several momentous political decisions, as well as accommodating such notables as de Gaulle, Adenauer, the Duke and Duchess of Windsor and the Aga Khan. Inside, the rooms have great style, with classic period decor and interesting antiques. Visitors still come to this very fashionable and luxurious hotel, specifically for its own Brenner's Spa and Black Forest Clinic, the latter providing everything from dentistry to plastic surgery. *Rooms 100. Room service all day. Valet parking. Conference facilities 200. Indoor swimming pool. Sauna. Steam room. Gym. Beauty salon. Health clinic. Amex, Diners, Mastercard, Visa.*

Tel: (7442) 49 20   Fax: (7442) 49 26 92
Tonbachstrasse 237, 72270 Baiersbronn

Deep in the Black Forest, Baiersbronn is reached from the Karlsruhe-Basel motorway by a 45km scenic route. The hotel is beautifully situated in a green valley above the town. More than a hotel, it is one of Germany's finest resorts, fully equipped to offer guests a range of health and beauty treatments second to none. Rooms are large and luxuriously furnished, and many have balconies. The Finkbeiner family has been here for over 200 years. *Rooms 300. Own parking. Conference facilities 60. Garden. Tennis. Squash. Boules. Indoor & outdoor swimming pools. Salt water pool. Medicinal baths. Spa bath. Sauna. Gym. Sun beds. Beauty treatment. Hairdressing. Billiard room. Children's playroom. No credit cards.*

Tel: (7442) 492 665

The jewel in the crown of the Traube Tonbach is their gourmet restaurant in the *Schwarzwaldstube* (Black Forest Room). The basement room was refurbished in the summer of 1995 and is most elegant in its new blue and gold livery. Under head chef Harald Wohlfahrt, the kitchen has gone from strength to strength over the last 15 years, making advance booking highly advisable, especially for dinner. The style is refined with dishes like a galantine of veal sweetbreads and goose foie gras in a port aspic, *petite langouste aux fines herbes sur un risotto au safran et à la tomate parfumé au pistou* (a speciality), pike-perch cooked with a crispy skin and served on a red-wine butter sauce, medallions of venison on a bed of ceps with caramelised red cabbage and a creamy pepper sauce, ballontine of guinea fowl on a potato purée with glazed vegetables and desserts such as *millefeuille au chocolat farcie d'une ganache truffée et ses poires caramélisées* and a hot banana and lime soufflé served with pistachio ice cream appearing on the daily-changing carte. Set meals DM160 & DM200 (dégustation). *Seats 85. Open 1200-1400, 1900-2200. Closed Mon, Tue, 9-31 Jan & 31 Jul-22 Aug.*

Meal prices for 2 are based on à la carte menus. When set menus are available, prices will often be lower.

FRIEDRICHSRUHE — Wald und Schlosshotel — DM295

HR

Tel: (7941) 608 70   Fax: (7941) 614 68
74639 Friedrichsruhe

Set in magnificent parkland about 90km from Stuttgart (a 20-minute drive from Heilbronn), the Wald und Schlosshotel offers peace and quiet in abundance. Bedroom accommodation is either in a hunting lodge built by a German prince in 1712 - traditional in style with antique furniture; the 19th-century Torhus - Laura Ashley decor, mostly suites but including a couple of double rooms; or the main building which was totally refurbished in 1989. *Rooms 49. Room service all day. Own parking. Conference facilities 80. Golf. Tennis. Outdoor and indoor swimming pools. Sauna. Amex, Diners, Mastercard, Visa.*

Restaurant — DM400

There's a choice of dining here. In the main restaurant chef Lother Eiermann's menu is largely French inspired - goose liver terrine, lobster consommé, sea bass on a bed of watercress with salsify, entrecote with an onion crust on a ragout of cabbage and potato, mushroom-stuffed poussin - while in the less formal, bistro-like Jägerstube the emphasis is more on the cooking of the local region. A large terrace encourages alfresco eating in summer. Set meals (restaurant) DM140 & DM198 *(dégustation). Seats 85 (+ 70 outside). Open 1200-1415, 1845-2130. Closed Mon & Tues (except for residents).*

LEIPZIG — Kempinski Hotel Fürstenhof — DM450

H

Tel: (341) 980 5005   Fax: (341) 980 5006
Tröndlinring 8, 04105 Leipzig

After three years of renovation, the hotel is due to open in March 1996. Built two hundred years ago as a private house, it became a hotel at the end of the 19th century - now, it's destined to become a luxurious boutique establishment, providing exceptional service and quality. The air-conditioned and individually-designed bedrooms, with PC and fax connections (secreterial services available at reception), offer satellite TV, mini-bar, and safe. *Rooms 92. 24hr room service. Conference/banqueting facilities 80/60. Covered parking. Patio. Indoor swimming pool. Spa bath. Sauna. Steam room. Solarium. Gym. Hair salon. Beauty treatment. News kiosk.*

PASSAU — Holiday Inn — DM280

H

Tel: (851) 590 00   Fax: (851) 590 05 29
Bahnhofstrasse 24a, 94032 Passau

Situated right on the Bavarian border, Passau is 170km from Munich and 100km from Linz. The hotel is located in the Donaupassage shopping mall. Despite the hotel being part of an international chain, the decor is typically Bavarian. Standard bedrooms come with everything one would expect - satellite TV, in-house movies, air-conditioning, queen-size beds, mini-bars - while the Executive Club rooms, aimed at the business traveller, get a second telephone at the desk and various little extras. **Rooms 129.** *Room service all day. Garage parking DM17 for 24 hours. Conference facilities 300. Indoor swimming pool. Sauna. Sun bed. Amex, Diners, Mastercard, Visa.*

THE APARTMENT SERVICE

Tel in UK (0181) 748 4207   Fax (0181) 748 3972

The Apartment Service will find you the right apartment worldwide to suit your needs, whether you are on a short or long-term stay. A 96-page colour catalogue is free on request. All budgets are catered for.

Scotch Beef Club Members: Germany

BADEN-BADEN: Privathotel
  Quissiana
BADEN-BADEN: Hotel Brenner's
  Park
BIELEFELD: Zum Mauseteich
BRAUNSCHWEIG: Mövenpick
BREMEN: Hotel Havenhaus
  Restaurant
BREMEN: Maritim Hotel Congress
  Centrum Bremen
COLOGNE: DOM-Hotel
COLOGNE: SAS Royal Hotel
CUXHAVEN: Silencehotel Deichgraf
DARMSTADT: Maritim Hotel
  Rhein-Main
DORTMUND: Mövenpick
DUSSELDORF: Mövenpick
EGLOFFSTEIN: Gasthaus Krone
ESSEN: Sheraton-Hotel
FRANKFURT: Bettina Eck
FRANKFURT: Mövenpick
GOTTINGEN: Gebhards Hotel
HAMBURG: Mövenpick
HAMBURG: SAS Royal Hotel
HAMELN-WESSER: Klütturm

KEITUM/SYLT: Beef und Lobster
LINDAU/BODENSEE: Hotel Bad
  Schachen
LINNESTADT OEDIGEN: Hotel
  Restaurant Haus Buckmann
LILENTHAL: Alte Posthalterei
MANNHEIM: Hotel Pfalz
MUNICH: Marriott Hotel
MUNICH: Park Hilton
MUNICH: Hotel Bayerischer Hof
MUNSTER-HANDORF: Hotel
  Deutscher Vater
NORDSEEINSEL JUIST:
  Hotel Worch
NURNBERG: Grand Hotel Nürnberg
PASSAU: Holiday Inn
PORTA WESTFALICA:
  Porta Berghotel
SIEGEN: Queens Hotel
STUTTGART: Mövenpick
WEGBERG: Molzmühle
WEINSTADT/BEUTELSBACH:
  Krone
ZEIL AM MAIN: Zeiler Bürgerstube

Your Guarantee of Quality and Independence

EGON RONAY'S GUIDES 1996

- ● Establishment inspections are anonymous
- ● Inspections are undertaken by qualified Egon Ronay's Guides inspectors
- ● The Guides are completely independent in their editorial selection
- ● The Guides do not accept advertising, hospitality or payment from listed establishments

Titles planned for 1996 include

Hotels & Restaurants ● Pubs & Inns ● Europe
Ireland ● Just A Bite
And Children Come Too ● Paris
Oriental Restaurants

Currency Greek Drachma **Exchange Rate** £1=approx Dr 362
International dialling code 00 30 (Athens+1)
Passports/Visas No visa required by British passport holders.
British Embassy & Consulate Tel 1-723 6211/19 Fax 1-724 1872

Airports
Athens West Air Terminal (Olympic Airways and domestic flights)
Tel 1-936 3363 (fligh arr/dep information)
Athens East Air Terminal (International and charter flights)
Tel 1-969 9466
Railway Stations
(Central information & tickets)
1 Karolou Street Tel: 1-524 0601 or 6 Sina Street Tel 1-362 4404-6
Car Hire
Tel nos. **Avis** 1-322 4951 **Budget** 1-921 4771 **Eurodollar** 1-922 9672
Europcar 1-921 5788 **Hertz** 1-961 3625

Banks 8am-2pm Mon-Fri.
Shops 9am-5pm Mon & Wed, 9am-7pm Tues, Thur, Fri, 8.30am-3.30pm Sat.

New Year's Day, 6 Jan, 26 Feb, 25 Mar, Easter, 1 May, 3 Jun, 15 Aug, 28 Oct, Christmas & Boxing Day.

Greek Tourist Board in **London** Tel 0171-734 5997
In **Athens** Greek National Tourist Organization Tel 1-322 3111
American Express Travel Service Offices or Representative (R)
Athens   2 Hermou Street
             Syntagma Square
             GR 10225
             PO Box 3325
             Tel 1-3244976 #

Athens

Tel: (1) 64373025   Fax: (1) 6466361
Timoleontos Vassou Street 22, 115 21 Athíni

With a very high staff to guest ratio, you are assured excellent service at this quiet, relaxed hotel five minutes drive from the centre of Athens. The lobby has big comfortable armchairs and Persian rugs while the decor of the air-conditioned bedrooms is more modern with stucco walls and pale colours. Two restaurants – one Chinese, one Italian – are at the disposal of guests. A shuttle service operates to the airport. *Rooms 30. Room service 24hr. Valet parking. Banqueting facilities 160. Conference facilities 110. Business centre. Amex, Diners, Mastercard, Visa.*

Tel: (1) 9023666   Fax: (1) 9243000
Syngrou Avenue 89-93, 117 45 Athíni

This immense hotel on a noisy street five minutes from the centre is a product of the early-80s building boom in Athens. The grand lobby is awash with marble and mirrors while bedrooms are furnished with modern furniture and decorated in pastel colours. Four restaurants provide a wide choice of eating options and the ballroom is the biggest in the city, able to accommodate 2000 people. One floor is designated for non-smokers and six bedrooms are specially equipped for disabled guests. ***Rooms** 551. Room service 24hr. Private parking 2500drs. Banqueting facilities 2000. Conference facilities 2000. Secretarial/translation services on request. Swimming pool. Gym. Sauna. Amex, Diners, Mastercard, Visa.*

Tel: (1) 9414824   Fax: (1) 9425082
Syngrou Avenue 385, 175 64 Athíni

The hotel is situated near the sea, between the airport and Piraeus. Although the city centre is ten minutes drive away, a free shuttle bus runs every hour, and the location is ideal for exploring landmarks such as Sounion or nipping over to the island of Hydra. A massive renovation plan is currently under way. All the bathrooms were refurbished in early 1995, the public areas will be redecorated in the middle of 1996 and the last phase, due in 1997, will be to replace all the bedroom furniture and give the exterior a face lift. This will not, we are assured, affect guests in any way. ***Rooms** 366. Room service 24hr. Private parking. Banqueting facilities 500. Conference facilities 500. Business centre. Outdoor swimming pool (on roof). News kiosk. Amex, Diners, Mastercard, Visa.*

Tel 01 7250 201   Fax 01 7253 110
46 Vassilissis Sofias Avenue, 115 28 Athíni

In a commanding location on a hill near the US Embassy, this ten-storey Hilton has impressed many a VIP with its magnificent, pillared marble lobby and gallery of exclusive shops. All the rooms are spacious, with good views and smart new marble bathrooms. There is a fully-equipped room for disabled guests. The two uppermost floors are reserved for the Executive Club guests and two of the function rooms have recently been renovated. There is an independently-owned business centre in the building for the use of guests. The poolside terrace, once part of the Ta Nissia restaurant is now a traditional Beer Garden and there is also the Byzantine restaurant for lunch and dinner all year round. ***Rooms** 453. Room service 24hr. Private parking. Banqueting facilities 1500. Conference facilities 800. Secretarial/translation services on request. Air-conditioning. Sauna. Swimming pool. Amex, Diners, Mastercard, Visa.*

The traditional taverna-style interior of the restaurant with its hand-carved wooden walls and porcelains and bronze relics is the ideal setting for this mélange of traditional Greek taverna grilled food, with some fancier French dishes. The specialities are a platter of different meats, either roasted or barbecued and char-grilled T-bone steak and plenty of fresh fish is also available. A large wine list stretches to some good French and Italian bottles. ***Seats** 120. Open 1900-2400. Closed mid Jul-mid Sep.*

Tel: (1) 7210093   Fax: (1) 7223598
Alsos Evangelismou, 106 76 Athíni

Located in a small park opposite the Hilton in the centre of Athens, this old summer house was converted from a simple taverna to an Italian restaurant eight years ago. Greek chef George Tsiahtsiras, who was previously at *Precieux Gastronomie* (qv), cooks straightforward dishes such as pasta, gnocchi, skewered swordfish and salmon marinated in herbs. *Seats 80 (courtyard 120). Open 1300-1600, 2030-0030. Closed L Sat, all Sun, 5-20 Aug, 1 Jan, Easter. Public parking. Amex, Visa.*

Tel: (1) 8949454
Zisimopoloulou Glifatha 10, 166 74 Athíni

The interior of this cosy restaurant, south of the centre and near to the sea, is decorated with hand-made tiles and furnished with simple wooden tables and chairs. It serves simple Italian food with fish and fresh pasta the specialities. Typical dishes are langoustines wrapped in pasta, and chicken grilled with saffron, served with zucchini. Set lunch 4500drs. *Seats 90 (outside 150). Open 1300-1600, 2000-0130. Closed 10 days at Easter. Valet parking. Amex, Diners, Mastercard, Visa.*

Tel: (1) 3314 444   Fax: (1) 3228 034
Constitution Square, 105 63 Athíni

Built in the mid-19th century, this imposing mansion occupies a prime position in the city's business district, opposite the Parliament building and near the National gardens. Grand public areas include stained-glass-ceilinged halls, mirrored salons and a ballroom, all carefully restored with hand-carved furniture, large chandeliers and fine brocade curtains. Elegantly proportioned bedrooms are traditionally furnished and boast every modern convenience from mini-bar and satellite television to air-conditioning. Marble features in up-to-date bathrooms. Sheraton. *Rooms 364. Room service 24hrs. Free parking outside the hotel. Conference facilities 1100. Hair salon. News kiosk. Amex, Diners, Mastercard, Visa.*

Tel: (1) 9347711   Fax: (1) 9358603
Syngrou Avenue 115, 117 45 Athíni

The swish, modern Marriott is located in a business district between the sea and the city centre. Bedrooms, decorated in pastel shades, are equipped with air-conditioning, satellite TV and mini-bar. Business facilities are good but leisure amenties are more limited. The roof-top terrace with swimming pool is a pleasant spot to relax with a drink, but note there is no restaurant. Service is efficient and friendly. *Rooms 255. Room service 24hr. Private parking. Banqueting facilities 350. Conference facilities 500. Secretarial/translation services on request. Terrace. Outdoor swimming pool. Hair salon. News kiosk. Amex, Diners, Mastercard, Visa.*

Athens is not renowned for its range of foreign restaurants, so it is refreshing to find not just one, but two exotic cuisines under the same roof. The main restaurant specialises in Polynesian food, and serves dishes such as beef fried in sesame oil, egg and spring rolls and also the appetising 'seafood dragons' (pancakes filled with crabmeat and cream cheese). There is also a smaller Japanese teppanyaki section. *Seats 96 (Polynesian), 24 (teppanyaki). Open 1930-0045. Closed Sun, Easter week.*

Tel: (1) 7012276   Fax: (1) 9247181
Trivonianou 32, 116 36 Athíni

As traditional as a Greek taverna can be, this is a good place to sample classic dishes such as moussaka and minced veal pies. More unusual dishes include baby lamb in lemon sauce, oven-baked pigeon with potatoes and mussels cooked on a spit. The restaurant has a cosily rustic atmosphere, being decorated with old plates and vases and furnished with simple wooden chairs and tables. *Seats 170. Open 2000-0100. Closed Sun, 15 Jul-28 Aug. Private parking. Amex, Diners, Mastercard, Visa.*

ATHENS   Park Hotel   28,000DRS

Tel: (1) 8832711   Fax: (1) 8238420
Alexandras Avenue 10, 106 82 Athíni

Built in the 1970s, this centrally-located hotel is five minutes walk from the train station in a noisy, bustling part of the city. The decor is modern and standard throughout all bedrooms have air-conditioning, satellite TV and mini-bar. *Rooms 143. Room service 24hr. Valet parking. Banqueting facilities 500. Conference facilities 500. Garden. Terrace. Outdoor swimming pool. Beauty treatment. Hair salon. News kiosk. Coffee shop. Amex, Diners, Mastercard, Visa.*

ATHENS   Pentelikon Hotel   70,400DRS

Tel: (1) 8080311   Fax: (1) 8019223
Deligianni Street 66, Kifissia, 145 62 Athíni

Located in a quiet, residential area out of the city centre, this 1920s neo-classical building was thoroughly renovated and converted into a hotel in the 1980s. It has retained its grandeur, with sweeping marble floors, frescoed ceilings and deep leather chesterfields in the halls. The air-conditioned bedrooms are equally splendid, with traditional wooden furniture and marble bathrooms. Major refurbishment of the ballroom and banqueting rooms was due to start at the end of 1995. The shady gardens around the hotel can accommodate up to 1000 people for an outdoor buffet. *Rooms 43. Room service 24hr. Valet parking. Banqueting facilities 300. Conference facilities 250. Garden. Outdoor swimming pool. Amex, Diners, Mastercard, Visa.*

Vardi's   24,000DRS

One of the most popular restaurants in Athens, Vardi's has recently been revamped with a lighter decor and lighter dishes on the menu. Marinated fish, lobster and splendid salads are perfect for a sultry Mediterrean evening. A particular speciality is foie gras salad with grapes marinated in dark, sweet Mavrodaphne wine from Patras. During the summer the restaurant decamps to marquees in the garden. *Seats 70. Open 1930-0130. Closed Aug.*

ATHENS   Precieux Gastronomie   19,000DRS

Tel: (1) 3608 616   Fax: (1) 3608 619
14 Akadimias, 10671 Athini

The Greek chef at this popular restaurant is regularly sent to gastronomic seminars in France, where he has developed a penchant for lightly cooked fish dishes. His specialities, more delicately presented than traditional Greek food, are fillet of sea bass steamed with parsley and garlic and grilled salmon served in a mushroom sauce or with hollandaise. There is a traditional menu entitled From the Greek Kitchen. Dim lighting, a pretty skyscape mural and soulful guitar and piano music give a touch of romance to the elegant dining- room. As well as a good choice of Greek wines, there are around 24 French labels supplied by Maison Fauchon in Paris. *Seats 52 (private rooms 24). Open 1200-1600, 2100-2400. Closed D mid Apr–mid Oct), 2 weeks mid Aug. Public parking. Amex, Diners, Mastercard, Visa.*

ATHENS   St George Lycabettus   48,000DRS

Tel: (1) 7290 711   Fax: (1) 7290 439
2 Kleomenous, 106 75 Athini

The public rooms and half the bedrooms of this 1970s hotel have recently been completely renovated and the final stage of refurbishment is now under way. Ornately decorated mirrors and ragged shell-coloured walls are features of the modern interior while the bedrooms now have chintzy bedcovers and curtains. The hotel is 30 minutes from the airport and ten minutes from the railway station. The Grand Balcon restaurant and roof garden have great views over Athens. *Rooms 162. Room service limited. Garage parking 2000drs. Banqueting facilities 250. Conference facilities 200. Secretarial/translation services on request. Air-conditioning. Satellite TV. Swimming pool. Amex, Diners, Mastercard, Visa.*

Meal prices for 2 are based on à la carte menus. When set menus are available, prices will often be lower.

Tel: (1) 4112043
Deligiorgi Street 14, 185 33 Athíni

This restaurant has developed a novel reputation in Athens for serving almost nothing but monkfish. Chef-owner Mr Lazarou has a passion for the fish and cooks it in a variety of ways: grilled, steamed, fried, on skewers. A particular speciality is steamed monkfish with celery and onion, filleted and served in front of the diner. If you are lucky, you might find a couple of other fish on the menu, perhaps sea bass baked in salt or flaked in a gazpacho. Reservations are essential. *Seats 50 (terrace 30). Open 2030-0130. Closed Sun, 10 Aug-10 Sep. Public parking. Amex, Visa.*

Tel: (1) 8960 211 311 Fax: (1) 8962582
Apollonos Street 40, 166 71 Vouliagmeni

A 30-minute drive from Athens and 15 minutes from the airport, this extraordinary resort complex consists of three luxury hotels, each with its own private beach, swimming pool and lagoon. All three hotels are currently undergoing a staggered renovation. The Arion is the showpiece of the resort, decorated in a cool, classical style. Leisure amenities are superb, and include four tennis courts, a health and fitness centre, a nearby golf course, a marina for yacht charters and deep-sea fishing, and all the water sports you could wish for. Business facilities are also impressive with four conference rooms (and a further ten in the other two hotels) and have attracted top-level clients, such as the EU and peace negotiators in the Bosnian conflict, who make use of the on-site helipad. ***Rooms** 152 (560 in resort). Room service 24hr. Private parking. Banqueting facilities 450. Conference facilities 600. Secretarial/translation services on request. Garden. 4 swimming pools (3 outdoor, 1 indoor). Tennis. Gym. Sauna. Massage. Hair salon. Amex, Diners, Mastercard, Visa.*

THE APARTMENT SERVICE

Tel in UK (0181) 748 4207   Fax (0181) 748 3972

The Apartment Service will find you the right apartment worldwide to suit your needs, whether you are on a short or long-term stay. A 96-page colour catalogue is free on request. All budgets are catered for.

THE INDEPENDENT

INDEPENDENT
ON SUNDAY

Your truly
independent
guides to life

Hungary

Currency Hungarian Forint **Exchange Rate** £1=approx Ft 165
International dialling code 00 36 (Budapest+1)
Passports/Visas No visa required by British passport holders for stay
of up to 6 months.
British Embassy in Budapest Tel 1-266 2888   Fax 1-266 0907

TRANSPORT

Airports
Budapest-Ferihagy Tel 1-157 9123
Railway Stations
Keleti Tel 1-113 6835 **Nyugati** Tel 1-149 0115 **Déli** Tel 1-155 8657
State Railways central ticket & information office
Tel 1-122 7860 (inland) 1-122 4052 (international)
Car hire in Budapest
Tel Nos. **Europcar** 1-113 1492/113 0207 **Hertz** 1-122 1471
(airport 1-157 8618/157 8606) **Avis** Tel (airport) 1-147 5754/147 8470 /
Budget 1-138 4205 (airport 1-157 9123)
Speed Limits 120 km/h on motorways, 100 km/h major roads, 80 km/h
other roads, 50 km/h in built-up areas.

OPENING HOURS

Banks 8am-3pm Mon-Thu (Fri till 1pm).
Shops Food shops in general Mon-Fri 7am-7pm (Sat till 1pm). Other
shops 10am-6pm Mon-Fri (Sat till 1pm). There are now some convenience stores open around the clock.

National Holidays

New Year's Day, 15 Mar, Easter Monday, 1 May, Whitsun Monday,
20 Aug, 23 Oct, Christmas Day & Boxing Day.

Tourist Offices

Hungarian Tourist Board in **London** Tel 0891 171200
Tourist Board in **Budapest** Tel 1-117 9800
American Express Travel Service Offices or Representative (R)
Budapest   American Express Hungary Ltd
              Deak Ferenc U.10
              1052
              PO Box 698 (PO Box Post Code 1365)
              Tel 1-2668680/2668671 #

Budapest

Tel (1) 266 1234　Fax (1) 266 9101
Roosevelt tér 2, Budapest 1051

One of the big three hotels in the very centre of the city, this one is on the Pest bank of the River Danube, next to the Chain Bridge, a famous tourist attraction. The facilities are as excellent as the location. Bedrooms are air-conditioned and come with all the comforts one would expect of an international hotel: mini-bar, safe (in most rooms), satellite television, in-house movies. The seventh and eighth floors, respectively, are the Gold Passport and Regency Club floors; both with their own lounges, the former offering free beverages in the morning and the latter also a complimentary breakfast. These rooms, and the 27 suites, also have additional telephone lines for modems or fax machines. Room rates are set in Deutschmarks (DM442 in the summer of 1995) so the local currency price quoted above will vary with the exchange rate. *Rooms 355. Room service 24hr.*
Parking Ft1600 per 24hr. Conference facilities 350. Business centre. Indoor swimming pool. Sauna. Sun beds. Fitness room. Beauty salon. Amex, Diners, Mastercard, Visa.

Tel: (1) 351 6395　Fax: (1) 342 2917
Állatkerti út 2, Budapest 1146

In the same building (and under the same ownership) as *Gundel* (qv), Bagolyvár is the Hungarian version of the *cucina mamma*: you will find home-style cooking (mostly Hungarian specialities), friendly service and an intimate, yet elegant atmosphere. Bagolyvár means Owl's Castle and refers to the fanciful Transylvanian style of the building, whose interior design evokes the feel of a turn-of-the-century Budapest home. In addition to the dishes on the menu, there are daily specials listed on a blackboard. Old-fashioned chicken and beef broth with shell-shaped noodles would be a good starter, or in the summer, have chilled fruit soup with sour cream. Goose dishes are especially good here: roasted goose with braised cabbage and potatoes is superb. If you prefer a lighter dish, have pan-fried breast of turkey with green salad. Home-made poppy-seed noodles are worth trying, or if you want to stay on more familiar ground, have a cottage cheese pancake with vanilla sauce, or a strawberry torte for a dessert. In summer eat outside in the attractive garden that is attached to the Japanese garden of the Zoo next door. *Seats 70 (+ 200 garden)*
Open 1200–2230. Public parking. Amex, Diners, Mastercard, Visa.

Tel: (1) 118 4576
Vigadó u 2, Budapest 1052

The restaurant is in the same building as the Casino Vigadó and diners get a free entry to the Casino plus a complimentary drink. The food is good and prices are reasonable, and this is the only restaurant open till 4am. Its central location also makes this a convenient place for a light lunch; in summer on one of their two terraces perhaps. For dinner, try the goose liver roulade with sesame seeds as an appetiser before a main course such as pike-perch Carpathian-style (with mushrooms and dill sauce), beefsteak à la matgeas, and stuffed quails with almond sauce. For dessert the Casino pancakes, filled with fresh fruit and served with a marzipan sauce, are a good bet. *Seats 70 (+ 200 terrace). Open 1000-0400.*
Public parking. Amex, Diners, Mastercard, Visa.

Tel: (1) 266 3096　Fax: (1) 118 4991
Kristóf tér 7-8, Budapest 1052

The inspiration for the name is a large chandelier that featured in the film Cyrano de Bergerac, filmed in Budapest, but which now hangs in the beautiful old Baroque building that is home to this restaurant opened by a group of young people in 1993. The building itself is located in the pedestrianised part of the city (off Váci Street and Vörösmarty Square) where young artists, most of them students at the Budapest Academy of Arts, sit in rows, drawing portraits of the passers-by. The cuisine is a mix of Hungarian and international dishes with the regular menu supplemented by a list of some seven or eight daily specials written up on a blackboard. Starters range from Russian caviar, goulash soup and bouillabaisse to prosciutto with melon and blue cheese-stuffed peach. Mains are equally varied: penne Napoli, crayfish in Campari sauce, paella, veal stew with noodles, pike-perch Kárpáthy. There are always vegetarian dishes on the menu. *Seats 60 (+40 terrace)*
Open 1100-2330. Closed 24 Dec. Amex, Diners, Mastercard, Visa.

Tel: (1) 112 2825
Bank utca 5, Budapest 1054

Steaks are the mainstay of this restaurant founded by Tamás Rádi and Oszkár Pölös in 1989. Their secret is to use beef from cattle kept in the open air all year round and then to marinade the meat for three days before grilling. There are over 20 different steaks to choose from served in a variety of ways: with green sauce, cheese sauce, peppered, flavoured with cumin; and with accompaniments such as Texan beans, various salads and potatoes. 30 wines from Hungary, Italy and France plus over 30 varieties of whisky to drink. The name Fehér Bölény means White Buffalo. *Seats 48. Open D only 1800-0130. Closed Sun, 3 days Christmas & 2 days Easter. Amex, Mastercard.*

Tel: (1) 342 6549
Kertész utca 36, Budapest VII

Fészek is an artists' club which has been going since the turn of the century. The restaurant is on the main floor and between spring and autumn meals are also served in the large courtyard garden with its flowers and mature trees. The cuisine is international but includes traditional Hungarian dishes. *Seats 350 (+ 300 garden). Open 1200-0030. Amex.*

Tel: (1) 117 8088   Fax: (1) 117 9808
Apaczai Csere utca 12-14, Budapest 1052

With an excellent location right on the bank of the River Danube and very near the business and financial centre, the 1981-built Forum provides every modern comfort. Air-conditioned bedrooms come with safe, mini-bar and satellite television and English-speaking secretaries are on hand in the well-equipped business centre (open 7am-8pm Mon-Fri). Room rates are set in Deutschmarks (DM470 in the summer of 1995) so the local currency price quoted above will vary with the exchange rate. *Rooms 400. Room service 24hr. Parking Ft2000 per 24hr. Conference facilities 250. Business centre. Indoor swimming pool. Sauna. Sun beds. Gym. Beauty salon. Hairdressing. Massage. Amex, Diners, Mastercard, Visa.*

Tel: (1) 185 2200   Fax:(1) 166 6631
Szent Gellért tér 1, Budapest 1111

Built in the early 1920s as a spa hotel, the Gellért is redolent of a more leisured European age: use of the thermal baths is still included in room prices (as are parking and breakfast). Bedrooms vary considerably both in outlook, some have great views over the Pest bank of the Danube, and comfort; so take care when booking. There are 40 single rooms with shower and WC only and no mini-bar and a further 68 singles with both bath tub and mini-bar but it is only the 13 suites and some of the double rooms that have the benefit of air-conditioning. Room rates are set in Deutschmarks (DM338 for a mid-priced double in the summer of 1995) so the local currency price quoted above will vary with the exchange rate. *Rooms 233. Room service 24hr. Free parking (guarded). Conference facilities 160. Business centre. Thermal baths. Indoor & outdoor swimming pools. Turkish baths. Sun beds. Health and beauty treatment. Amex, Diners, Mastercard, Visa.*

A first-floor dining-room with art-deco interior and a magnificent view of the river. Between the two World Wars, it was managed by the famous restaurateur, Károly Gundel, and some of the gourmet specialities he created are still to be found on the menu of the present chef, Ferenc Novák. Try cold fogas (pike-perch) with a mixed salad and yoghurt dressing to start followed perhaps by a chilled fruit soup in summer or gulyás (goulash) soup in winter. Main dishes include veal Gellért-style (in which the meat is sautéed and covered with slices of ham and bacon, a ragout of green peas, cream and egg yolks before being topped with grated cheese and baked in the oven), and a vegetarian option of tokaji mushrooms (wild mushrooms filled with mushroom paté, breaded, fried in olive oil and served with a Madeira sauce). *Seats 200 (+terrace) Open L 1200-1600, 1900-2330. Closed 2 days Christmas.*

Tel: (1) 321 3550   Fax: (1) 342 2917
Állatkerti út 2, Budapest 1146

This historic restaurant is in a century-old palace in the romantic City Park, with a view of the lake and Vadjahunyad Castle. It was Károly Gundel who, between the two World Wars, made the restaurant world famous and George Lang, the American-Hungarian restaurateur, who took over in 1991 and brought back its refined cuisine and elegance. Start with the *ujházy* (home-style) fowl soup (made by boiling a whole chicken with a selection of vegetables) and go on to George Lang's goose liver dish. You should also try one of Károly Gundel's classical creations: pike-perch and crayfish *pörkökt* or *Gundel Tokány*, which mixes fillet of beef with various kinds of mushrooms, marjoram, green peas and white asparagus, all garnished with crisp shoe-string potatoes in a nest of scrambled eggs. For dessert, Gundel pancakes are a must: filled with a mixture of raisins, candied orange peel and rough-ground walnuts, and covered with a chocolate-rum sauce. The House of Gundel owns vineries at Tokaj and Eger – for a white wine, Gundel Tokaji Furmint would be a good choice and for red, Gundel Bull's Blood of Eger. After dessert, a glass of Gundel Tokaji Aszu or Gundel Tokaji Aszu Essence would round things off perfectly. In summer head for their huge garden. *Seats 180 (+ 400 garden) Open 1200-1500, 1900-2400. Public parking. Amex, Diners, Mastercard, Visa.*

Tel: (1) 175 1000   Fax: (1) 156 0285
Hess András tér 1-3, Budapest 1014

On the spectacular Castle Hill in Buda, overlooking the beautiful city with its graceful bridges spanning the wide Danube, this tastefully-built modern Hilton has the old chapel and cloisters of a medieval Dominican monastery within its grounds (where open-air concerts are held in the summer). Bedrooms have satellite TVs, mini-bars and air-conditioning. Bathrooms have recently been refurbished. Room rates are set in Deutschmarks (DM503 in the summer of 1995) so the local currency price quoted above will vary with the exchange rate. *Rooms 323. Room service 24hr. Parking Ft2600 per 24hr. Conference facilities 600. Amex, Diners, Mastercard, Visa.*

With scenes from Hungarian folk tales around the walls and a gypsy violinist wandering around among the tables there can be no doubt that despite being in an international hotel you are also in Hungary. The menu has a distinct national flavour too: goulash soup (served in a cup), frogs' legs with Tokaj sauce, mignon of veal with goose liver and a paprika and dill sauce, sauerkraut cooked with cubes of meat and sour cream, venison with herb sauce and cranberries, wiener schnitzel, leg of mutton with garlic sauce and lentil purée. Desserts also have a distinctly mid-European slant with the likes of pancakes stuffed with poppy-seed cream and served with a red wine plum ragout, sour-cherry strudel with cinnamon sabayon and pistachio ice cream and hot apple cake with calvados sauce. *Seats 60. Open D only 1900–2330. Closed Aug.*

Tel: (1) 266 1000   Fax: (1) 266 2000
Erzsébet tér 7-8, Budapest 1051

Perhaps the most impressive of Budapest's small collection of luxury `Western' hotels. The large, airy lobby extends to two floors in height and with glass walls on two sides it is full of natural light. The Corvinus Bar is a sophisticated spot to take cocktails to the accompaniment of a pianist each evening. Air-conditioned bedrooms are stylishly decorated and furnished with quality freestanding wooden pieces. All have mini-bars, safes and satellite televisions. Extensive conference facilities are supported by a large business centre with secretarial and translation services. The hotel is conveniently located in the heart of the business district. Room rates are set in Deutschmarks (DM540 in the summer of 1995) so the local currency price quoted above will vary with the exchange rate. *Rooms 367. Room service 24hr. Valet parking Ft1500 per 24hr. Conference facilities 450. Business centre. Indoor swimming pool. Sauna. Steam room. Gym. Sun beds. Amex, Diners, Mastercard, Visa.*

Tel & Fax: (1) 176 1896
Kenyeres utca 34, Budapest 1021

Alice Mezõdy's restaurant is located in a charming old place in Old Buda. Furnished with turn-of-the-century furniture, old clocks and portraits, it successfully evokes the atmosphere of a 19th-century Old Buda home. There's a large garden for summer eating. Begin with garlic soup, the chef's *pièce de résistance*, before such tasty, filling mains as chicken à la Kugler – breast of chicken with some exotic seasoning. Cottage cheese dumplings are a popular dessert. The day here begins at 9am with breakfast. A less formal sister restaurant, *Remiz* (Tel: (1) 275 1396), is located in the depot for trams commuting between Moszkva Square and the Buda Hills and offers the likes of soups, steaks and fish plus things like jumbo prawns, spare ribs and chicken that you cook on a hot lava stone brought to your table. *Seats 70 (+ 300 garden). Open 0900-2400, Amex.*

BUDAPEST   Kispipa Restaurant   Ft2500

Tel: (1) 342 2587   R
Akácfa utca 38, Budapest VII

Lots on a menu that runs to nearly 200 dishes both Hungarian and international. If sticking to the former, try pheasant soup cooked in 'housewife-style', followed by either veal paprikás Bakony-style (with wild mushrooms and sour cream), or medallions of pork Vintners-style (filled with plum and apple). A pianist accompanies dinner. Set L (till 3pm) Ft250. *Seats 70. Open 1200-0100. Closed Sun & Aug. National Holidays. Amex.*

BUDAPEST   Liget Hotel   Ft18,200

Tel: (1) 269 5300   Fax: (1) 269 5329   H
Dozsa Gyorgy ut 106, Budapest 1068

Overlooking Heroes Square, on the edge of City Park, this is a modest hotel offering friendly service from staff who speak excellent English. Facilities in the bedrooms include mini-bar, TV and direct-dial phones; bathrooms all have both tub and shower. There is no restaurant other than for the breakfast that is included in the room price. The hotel was built just six years ago. Room rates are set in Deutschmarks (DM202 in the summer of 1995) so the local currency price quoted above will vary with the exchange rate. *Rooms 139. Room service all day. Parking Fts1080 per 24hr. Conference facilities 10. Sauna. Sun bed. Massage. Amex, Diners, Mastercard, Visa.*

BUDAPEST   Marriott   Ft32,000

Tel: (1) 266 7000   Fax: (1) 266 5000   H
Apaczai Csere Janos utca 4, Budapest 1364

Alongside the Danube, of which all the bedrooms have a view, this 25-year-old hotel has just benefited from a $23 million, top-to-toe refurbishment. Air-conditioned bedrooms come with all the usual modern conveniences including multi-channel, multi-lingual televisions that also offer no less than 25 in-house movies. All rooms have their own private balconies. The top three floors of executive rooms and suites share their own business lounge, where a complimentary breakfast is available, and separate check-in and check-out facilities. The refurbishment included the creation of a smart new health club. Room rates are set in Deutschmarks (DM355 in the summer of 1995) so the local currency price quoted above will vary with the exchange rate. *Rooms 362. Room service 24hr. Parking Ft2000 for 24 hours. Conference facilities 800. Squash. Gym. Sauna. Sun beds. Massage. Amex, Diners, Mastercard, Visa.*

BUDAPEST   Mátyás Pince Restaurant   ★   Ft8000

Tel: (1) 118 1693   Fax: (1) 118 1650   R
Márcus 15 tér 7, Budapest V

The restaurant Mátyás Pince (Matthias Cellar) was founded in 1904 by the renowned restaurateur, Mátyás Baldauf, who commissioned the artist Jen Haranghy to decorate the walls with scenes from the life of his namesake, the Hungarian Renaissance King Matthias. Inside it is attractive and typically Hungarian, with frescoes, stained-glass windows, folk embroideries and carved furniture. A gypsy orchestra plays both at lunchtime and during the evening. The food is good, with traditional Hungarian dishes and more modern European influences. Fresh-water fish comes from the Tisza River. Order the Mátyás platter as a cold appetiser (cold duck, pork, beef and goose liver) before carp Dorozsma-style (sautéed with smoked bacon and ham, a ragout of mushrooms and sour cream poured over the top, all seasoned with paprika and served with home-made noodles). An absolute must for dessert is their raspberry strudel, a house speciality. *Seats 300. Open 1200-0030. Public parking. Amex, Diners, Mastercard, Visa.*

Tel: (1) 322 3849   Fax: (1) 322 3849
Erzsébet krt 9-11, Budapest VII

Opened in 1894, this splendid art nouveau building (under repair and surrounded by scaffolding in the summer of 1995) quickly became a haunt–almost a club–for writers, painters, musicians, actors and directors; some of them virtually lived here, as it was then open day and night, seven days a week. Some actually used it as their postal address. The day it opened, a solemn procession led by Franz Molnár went to the banks of the Danube and threw the keys into the river demonstrating that the place would never close. Visit the basement restaurant (called mélyvíz, 'deep water', by the regulars) for a menu of Hungarian and international dishes (accompanied by gypsy musicians at night), or just have coffee or tea with snacks and sweets in the coffee house. There's also a gallery with caricatures of writers and journalists. No parking. *Seats 450. Open 0900-2400 (coffee house); 1200-1530, 1830-2330 (restaurant). Amex, Diners, Mastercard, Visa.*

Tel: (1) 118 3608   Fax: (1) 266 5240
Pesti Barnabás u 2, Budapest 1052

The name, '100 Years Old', has remained unchanged over the years although the restaurant has in fact been going for more than 160 years and the Baroque house it occupies is about 300 years old. With its three separate dining-rooms, the atmosphere is cosy and intimate. The menu, written in five different languages, offers a good range of dishes from starers like goose liver risotto with cheese, beef tea, French onion soup and vegetable strudel with a dill-flavoured crayfish ragout, to such mains as salmon with almonds, braised haunch of venison in burgundy sauce, wiener schnitzel, Hungarian veal stew with dumplings and flambée dishes like sirloin steak with Bull's Blood and breast of turkey with hazelnut and soya. Desserts include pancakes filled with curd cheese, and apple strudel. *Seats 75. Open 1200-2300. Closed 24 Dec. Amex, Diners, Mastercard, Visa.*

Tel: (1) 212 3746
Maros utca 16, Budapest

If you want to eat good, simple food in a family restaurant, join the locals in the Radegast Beer Hall where breakfast, lunch (from noon) and dinner can be taken sitting in high-backed, dark-stained wooden booths or, in summer, out in the tree-shaded courtyard. Instead of appetisers, have one of the salads such as thinly sliced cucumber, or tomato and onion, both served with a sugared vinegar dressing (there are Roquefort and yoghurt dressings too if you ask). The menu includes Hungarian specialities like pork fillet with peas, mushrooms and slices of onion in a creamy paprika sauce. For dessert go for the cottage cheese-filled pancakes. Somlói galuska (a rich, rum-soaked multi-layered sponge) is not for those on a diet. *Seats 70. Open 0700-2300. Amex, Diners, Mastercard.*

Tel: (1) 343 0955   Fax: (1) 343 3776
City Park Lake-side, Budapest 1146

Wild ducks swim almost under your feet at this restaurant that juts out over the City Park Lake. The creation of young restaurateur Árpád László, the cooking is as appealing as the location with dishes such as braised goose liver with French toast, chilled fruit soup, *fogas* (pike-perch) grilled with rosemary and served with a crayfish ragout, medallions of pork with calvados sauce, chicken stuffed with wild mushrooms and garnished with peaches and blueberries, charcoal-grilled pork ribs and Robinson's special pancakes filled with fruit and accompanied by vanilla sauce, showing a very un-Hungarian lightness of touch. A comfortable restaurant with friendly, personable service and occasional entertainment (music, ballet) on a stage built out over the lake. *Seats 50. Open 1200-2330. Amex, Diners, Mastercard, Visa.*

Meal prices for 2 are based on à la carte menus. When set menus are available, prices will often be lower.

Tel: (1) 138 4999   Fax: (1) 118 7188
Vaci utca 20, Budapest 1052

Ten-year-old hotel in the pedestrianised part of the city but with private parking beneath the building. Various public areas include a Champagne Bar and two lanes of ten-pin bowling. There is a surcharge for the two (out of seven) floors of bedrooms which have recently had air-conditioning installed. All rooms come with mini-bar, room safe, and multi-channel, multi-lingual television. Room rates are set in Deutschmarks (DM222 in the summer of 1995) so the local currency price quoted above will vary with the exchange rate. *Rooms 227. Room service 24hr. Parking Ft2000 for 24 hours. Conference facilities 200. Sauna. Sun bed. Fitness room. Massage. Amex, Diners, Mastercard, Visa.*

Tel: (1) 188 6921
Hármashatárhegyi út 2, Budapest 1037

This restaurant, on a hilltop, Hármasmatárhegy, about 15km from the centre of the town (15 minutes by taxi), enjoys splendid views of the city and the Buda Hills from its large terrace, which is the place to head for in summer. The main dining-room is large, making this a popular eating place with tour groups. Dishes are mostly Hungarian but there are also some more generally European choices. Gypsy music plays every evening and folklore dance-shows are regularly staffed. *Seats 400 (+ 150 terrace). Open 1100-2300. Closed Mon in winter. Own parking. Amex, Diners, Mastercard, Visa.*

Tel: (1) 135 1118   Fax: (1) 115 004
Pentelei Molnár u 15, Budapest 1025

Set in a former well-to-do family residence on the Hill of Roses (Rózsadomb), an elegant residential district, this restaurant still gives diners the feeling of being in a private house. Solid wooden walls, a crystal chandelier, soft piano music, fresh flowers and amiable service all combine to create a relaxed, friendly atmosphere. Start with the appetiser platter (goose liver, served either cold or grilled, with caviar and steak tartare) before a consommé and follow with perhaps fillet of fogas (pike-perch) with tartare sauce, or for a meat dish, the lecsó lamb that is grilled and served with a mixture of tomatoes, onions and paprika–one of the most delightful Hungarian dishes. Desserts include pancakes filled with puréed walnuts and flambéed with chocolate liqueur. *Seats 100. Open 1200-1500, 1900-2400. Closed 23-27 Dec & 2 weeks Jul. Amex, Mastercard, Visa.*

Your Guarantee of Quality and Independence

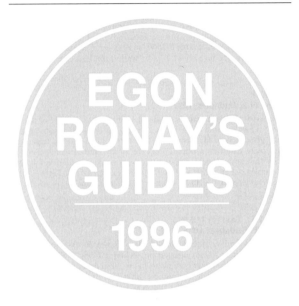

EGON RONAY'S GUIDES 1996

- ● Establishment inspections are anonymous
- ● Inspections are undertaken by qualified Egon Ronay's Guides inspectors
- ● The Guides are completely independent in their editorial selection
- ● The Guides do not accept advertising, hospitality or payment from listed establishments

Titles planned for 1996 include

Hotels & Restaurants ● Pubs & Inns ● Europe
Ireland ● Just A Bite
And Children Come Too ● Paris
Oriental Restaurants

Egon Ronay's Guides are available from all good bookshops or can be ordered from: Leading Guides, 35 Tadema Road, London SW10 0PZ
Tel 0171 352 0172

Ireland

Currency: Irish Punt **Exchange Rate** £1=approx Pt 0.95
International dialling code 00 353 (Dublin+1 Cork+21)
Passports/Visas No visa required by British passport holders.
British Embassy in Dublin Tel 1-269 5211

TRANSPORT

Airports
Dublin Tel 1-844 5039 **Cork** Tel 21-313 131
Railway Stations
Dublin-Heuston Tel 1-836 6222 Cork Tel 21-504 777
Car hire
Tel Nos. **Dublin Budget** 1-837 9802 (airport 1-837 0919/842 0793)
Hertz 1-660 2255 **Europcar** 1-668 1777 (airport 1-844 4179)
Avis 1-844 4466 **Cork Budget** 21-274 755 (airport 21-314 000)
Hertz 21-965 849 **Europcar** (airport) 21-966 736
Speed Limits 55 mph on trunk roads, 70 mph on motorways, 30 mph in
towns.

OPENING HOURS

Banks Mon-Fri 10am-5pm (can vary 10am-12.30pm & 1.30-3pm, Thu
till 5pm).
Shops Mon-Sat 9/9.30am-6pm.

National Holidays

New Year's Day, 2 Jan, 17 Mar, Easter, 5 Jun, 7 Aug, 30 Oct, Christmas
Day, Boxing Day & 27 Dec.

Tourist Offices

Irish Tourist Board in **London** Tel 0171-493 3201
In **Ireland** Dublin Tel 1-284 4768 / Cork Tel 21-273 251
American Express Travel Service Offices or Representative (R)
Dublin   116 Grafton Street
          PO Box 1184
          Dublin 2
          Tel 01-6772874 #
Cork   Heffernan's Travel (R)
          Pembroke House
          Pembroke Street
          Tel 021-271081

Cork

CORK   Arbutus Lodge   IR£80

HR

Tel: 021 501237   Fax: 021 502893
Montenotte Cork Co Cork

Considerable improvements and refurbishments have taken place in all the bedrooms at this former home of a Lord Mayor of Cork, high above the city with views of the River Lee and the surrounding hills. The hotel gets its name from the Arbutus tree, one of the many rare trees and shrubs growing in the spectacular terraced gardens. The house is full of genuine antique furniture (note the four-poster in the Blue Room) and some marvellous art, both old and new, the modern paintings by Irish artists much in demand by galleries and museums. Declan and Patsy Ryan, here since 1962, extend a warm welcome to all their guests, ably backed up by the charming staff. Whether you choose to relax in the cosy lounge or the panoramic bar with its own terrace, you'll feel at home and the cleverly designed and smartly decorated bedrooms, utilising all possible space, provide both comfort and tranquillity. Bathrooms boast best quality towels, bathrobes and toiletries and you'll start the day with as good a breakfast as you'll find anywhere. *Rooms 20. Garden. tennis. Closed 24-29 Dec. Conference facilities 150. Amex, Diners, Mastercard, Visa.*

Restaurant   IR£80

Alongside Myrtle Allen (see entry for *Ballymaloe House*), Declan Ryan has trained and brought on more chefs in this country than anyone. His restaurant has remained loyal to its roots-no stylish copying of French trends but a reliance on local produce including herbs and soft fruit from the hotel's own garden and traditional Cork dishes. Game in season and the freshest of fish are also a feature (inspect the seafood tank in the bar) and always a fine example of the kitchen's style is the nightly-changing, seven-course tasting menu-no tasting portions, but enough to satisfy the hungriest of souls-spiced beef and mushroom filo parcels, nage of fresh prawn tails, medallions of monkfish with mussels and saffron, very tender roast mallard with elderberry sauce, finishing with chocolate and rum log or gargantuan floating islands. Ask for the ingredients of the 'fence reducer sorbet', sometimes served as a palate cleanser! Service is as caring and professional as you'll find anywhere, the cheeseboard promotes Irish cheeses in top-top condition, and the sweet trolley will tempt even the faint-hearted. The wine list is not the easiest to find your way around, but what quality! Every wine has been carefully chosen, many personally by Declan himself. Prices are very fair, the choice vast in both France and the New World. A variety of breads is baked on the premises daily. *Seats 50. Open 1300-1400, 1900-2130. Closed Sun, 1 week Christmas.*

CORK   Clifford's   ★   IR£70

R

Tel: 021 275333
18 Dyke Parade Cork Co Cork

Style and quality are the keynotes here, in terms not only of cooking but also of service and decor. The building itself, once the civic library, is Georgian but the whole place has been elegantly modernised, and Michael and Deirdre Clifford's collection of contemporary Irish art adorns the walls. The dining area is striking in its simplicity, with comfortable high-back chairs, high-quality linen and single flowers floating in glass bowls. Michael's cooking is controlled and confident, with inventive use of the best of local produce. The dinner menu changes monthly, although some specialities put in regular appearances. Typifying his style are pan-fried scallops with lemon grass jus, Clonakilty black pudding with poached free-range egg, cabbage and smoked kassler, loin of venison in light cream sauce and medallions of monkfish in white wine sauce. There's always a fresh fish of the day, plus game in season and hard-to-resist chocolate desserts. The wine list is relatively short, but writ large! There are inexpensive house wines, but few half bottles. *Seats 45. Open 1230-1430, 1900-2230. Closed L Sat, all Sun & Mon, National Holidays, 1 week Aug, 1 week Christmas. Amex, Diners, Mastercard, Visa.*

THE APARTMENT SERVICE
Tel in UK (0181) 748 4207   Fax (0181) 748 3972
The Apartment Service will find you the right apartment worldwide to suit your needs, whether you are on a short or long-term stay. A 96-page colour catalogue is free on request. All budgets are catered for.

Tel: 021 294909   Fax: 021 508568
Churchyard Lane off Well Road Douglas Cork Co Cork

Dermod Lovett continues to make guests feel welcome in the cosy bar and reception area of this well-established restaurant and to keep a close eye on proceedings throughout and, while Margaret Lovett and Marie Harding's extensive and carefully sourced menus for the main restaurant remain, their new brasserie opened recently and is understandably claiming the limelight. Chargrills are the speciality there, with limited but carefully selected regulars – chicken, gammon, steak and salmon – cooked in front of diners and served with salad and potatoes; limited starters/soups and desserts, plus a keen pricing policy complete the formula. Bar lunches (soups, pasta, stir-fries, quiches, casseroles); times as restaurant. *Seats 45. Open 1230-1400, 1900-2145. Closed L Sat, all Sun, National Holidays, 23-30 Dec. Amex, Diners, Mastercard, Visa.*

Tel: 021 276887
4 Mardyke Street Cork Co Cork

Situated next door to Michael Clifford's eponymous restaurant (see entry), with its entrance around the corner and in its own separate (but communicating) kitchen under the supervision of Michael, the new bistro's colour scheme alone, with its violets, pinks and black, would alert aficionados to the common ownership. The air-conditioned Bistro is smaller and more intimate, however, seating a couple of dozen on smart black chairs at rather small tables plus an extra four on stools at a little bar by the door (better for a drink while waiting for a table); prints of food photographs from Michael's cookery book line the walls and the menu is much more informal, incorporating starters like casserole of wood pigeon, shallots and bacon, a stew of Clonakilty black pudding, flageolet beans and home-made sausages or a daily soup. Main courses are homely, typically Michael's 'gourmet' Irish stew served with boiled potatoes, or braised chicken with cabbage and onions on a puréed potato bed, home-made hamburger or good steaks; seafood and game feature when they're at their best. Desserts might include a nicely gooey caramelised banana crepe with butterscotch sauce, chocolate roulade with fresh fruit or an Irish cheese plate. *Seats 25. Open 1200-1500, 1800-2230. Closed Sun, Mon, National Holidays, 1 week Aug, 1 week Christmas. Mastercard, Visa.*

Tel: 021 772209   Fax: 021 774268
3 Pearse Street Kinsale Co Cork

Serious fishermen and trenchermen alike should head for the cosy Blue Haven hotel near the quay, where not only is there a 36ft ocean-going angling boat for hire, but also good food and comfortable accommodation after a hard day's sport. Bedrooms are all in a new wing, and all are neat with smart white furniture and pictures by local artists. All have en-suite facilities, some with baths, some with just showers. The bar serves a wide choice of imaginative food and is very attractive, with wood panelling, natural stone and a log fire, and has many snug corners. It opens on to a cane-furnished conservatory which, in turn, leads on to a patio. The entrance has recently been upgraded and a new wine shop and delicatessen opened just off the lobby. No dogs. ***Rooms** 18. Bar & conservatory (1030-2130), teas and light snacks (1500-1700). Sea fishing. Amex, Diners, Mastercard, Visa.*

The diner is left in no doubt as to the specialities of the characterful restaurant, which has a strong maritime theme and overlooks an attractive courtyard garden. Chef Stanley Matthews kicks off with starters of seafood chowder, garlic mussels or baked Rossmore oysters, followed by Oriental seafood Kashmiri, brill and scallop bake or scallops on a skewer with bacon and mushrooms. Seafood is balanced by dishes like Stanley's chicken liver paté, warm goat's cheese salad, Michelstown venison or prime fillet steaks. Good local farmhouse cheeses, including Carrigaline. A very fairly priced and comprehensive wine list has many 'wild geese' Bordeaux; perhaps light in half bottles, but compensated by the New World offerings. *Seats 80. Open 1230-1500, 1830-2230. Closed 25 Dec.*

KINSALE · Chez Jean-Marc · IR£55

Tel: 021 774625   Fax: 021 774680
Lower O'Connell Street Kinsale Co Cork

A cheerful yellow outside, beamed and country cosy within, this is a warm, welcoming place offering excellent food and efficient service. Jean-Marc Tsai's cooking is traditional French with Oriental accents (Sunday nights see a Chinese menu). From the classic repertoire come French onion soup, garlicky baked mussels, duck à la bigarade and roast pheasant with shallots and brandy sauce and pommes darphin. Striking a more exotic note are warm salade paysanne, Thai stir-fry and millefeuille of salmon and lobster ravioli. Desserts are simple and delicious. The wine list includes a good choice of house bottles. Upstairs from the restaurant Jean-Marc has now opened Time Out, a 60-seater piano bar/brasserie serving bistro-style fare-dishes range from black tiger prawn cocktail, beef and trotters salad and Vietnamese barbecue pork to pizza, steak and fish and chips. *Seats 60. Open 1900-2200. Closed all Mon Sep-Jun, 5 Feb-5 Mar. Amex, Diners, Mastercard, Visa.*

KINSALE · Man Friday · IR£55

Tel: 021 772260
Scilly Kinsale Co Cork

A popular and convivial restaurant housed in a series of little rooms high above the harbour. Seafood is the natural speciality, with oysters cold or poached crab au gratin, sweet and sour scampi, black sole (grilled or Colbert) and monkfish with a prawn sauce among the wide choice. That choice extends outside the fishy realms to the likes of Robinson Crusoe's warm salad (mixed leaves, croutons and bacon), deep-fried brie with a plum and port sauce, Swiss-style veal escalope and roast rack of lamb with rosemary and a red wine sauce. Strawberry crème brulée, chocolate terrine, grape pudding or home-made ice cream rounds things off. Consistency is the keynote here, and it is owner-chef Philip Horgan (in charge since 1978) who maintains it. *Seats 80. Open 1830-2230. Closed Good Friday, 24-26 Dec. Amex, Mastercard, Visa.*

SHANAGARRY · Ballymaloe House · IR£120

Tel: 021 652531   Fax: 021 652021
Shanagarry Co Cork

Part of an old castle that became a farmhouse, modernised through the centuries, but with the 14th-century keep remaining in its original form. The hotel is situated in the middle of a 400-acre farm, both owned and run by Ivan and Myrtle Allen, and part of a group of family enterprises that includes a cookery school, craft shop and the Crawford Gallery Café in Cork city. Two miles from the coast, near the small fishing village of Ballycotton, the main house provides the day rooms, a large drawing room with an open fire and a TV room, complete with video recorder. Throughout, there's an interesting collection of modern Irish paintings with works by Jack B Yeats in the dining-room. Thirteen bedrooms in the main building are traditionally furnished, and a further five modern garden rooms open on to a lawn. Another eleven rooms, more cottagey in character, surround the old coachyard, with some at ground level suitable for wheelchairs. Teenagers especially will appreciate the self-contained 16th-century Gatehouse, which has its own small entrance hall and a twin-bedded room with its bathroom up a steep wooden staircase. Ballymaloe is a warm and comfortable family home, especially welcoming to children of all ages (high tea is served at 5.30pm), who can rely on the Allen (grand)children to relay the latest news from the farm or share the sandpit and pool. For the delightful breakfasts, all the ingredients are local or home-made, with even the oatmeal used for porridge ground in an old stone mill down the road. *Rooms 29. Garden. Croquet. Outdoor swimming pool. Tennis. Golf (5-hole). Children's outdoor play area. Closed 24-26 Dec. Amex, Diners, Mastercard, Visa.*

Restaurant · IR£80

Perhaps more than anyone else in the country, Myrtle Allen has nurtured, encouraged and cajoled chefs from her kitchen to spread their wings further afield after first achieving high standards here. Wherever you go in Ireland, you're likely to come across an individual who at some time has cooked alongside this doyenne of Irish chefs. There are several smallish interconnecting dining-rooms, any of which may be used privately, all furnished with antiques, and a conservatory with a black-and-white tiled floor, Lloyd Loom furniture and lots of greenery. With the bread home-baked, the fish caught locally (sometimes the menu is deliberately late to see what the fishing boats have brought in), and the salads and vegetables picked that day, you can certainly rely on the ingredients being fresh and wholesome-indeed, much produce comes from their own farm. With Irish and French as the main influences, the cooking is simple, enhancing the quality of the raw materials. Typically, nightly-changing menus might feature Ballycotton fish soup, hot buttered oysters on toast, baked plaice with hollandaise sauce, a selection of patés, hot buttered lobster, cod à la dieppoise, grilled chicken with two sauces or fillet of pork en croute with apple and celery sauce. Try some Irish cheeses before the dessert (perhaps an apricot tart or praline gateau) and linger awhile over some excellent cafetière coffee. Ivan Allen has built up a fine wine cellar over many years: it's strong in France but light elsewhere and there are few half bottles; the spelling on the handwritten wine list is decidedly eccentric! *Seats 40*. *Open 1230-1400, 1900-2130 (Sun buffet at 1930)*.

Dublin

DUBLIN   **Hotel Conrad**   **IRE230**

Tel: 01 676 5555   Fax: 01 676 5424
Earlsfort Terrace Dublin 2

In the city's business district opposite the National Concert Hall, yet just a short walk away from the fashionable Grafton Street for shopping and St Stephen's Green for a stroll in the park, the hotel is blessed with wonderful staff, who are both courteous and friendly, efficient and professional, an important asset to a hotel of distinction. It has an impressive array of facilities and a staffed business centre, and thus caters largely to a corporate clientele, though at weekends, when very attractive rates are available, it serves as a good base to explore the delights of Dublin. Public areas are contemporary in style, though you'll find all the atmosphere of a traditional pub in Alfie Byrne's. Well-planned bedrooms are models of good taste and offer all the necessary comforts, from large beds and easy chairs to plenty of work space and good lighting, as well as air-conditioning. There are three telephones in each room (one in the bathroom), a fax socket, remote-control satellite TV and mini-bar, while the bathrooms have large tubs and good showers, decent toiletries and towelling, and generously-sized bathrobes. At night there's a full turn-down service with a bottle of Irish mineral water and hand-made Irish chocolate left beside the bed. *Rooms 191. Patio. Beauty/hair salon. Gift shop/news kiosk. Brasserie (0700-2330). Banqueting facilities 250. Conference facilities 300. Amex, Diners, Mastercard, Visa.*

DUBLIN   **Le Coq Hardi**   ★   **IRE100**

Tel: 01 668 9070   Fax: 01 668 9887
35 Pembroke Road Ballsbridge Dublin 4

John and Catherine Howard run a classic restaurant in a classic Georgian building at the end of a terrace. Inside are high ceilings and handsome mirrors, brasswork and ornate plasterwork, and the immaculately set tables put the seal on a setting that's entirely fitting for John's serious French-based cooking. Many of his dishes are from the traditional repertoire-terrine of foie gras with brioche, cod boulangère, Venetian-style lamb's liver, entrecote with a shallot and bone marrow sauce. Le Coq Hardi is a breast of chicken fillet filled with potato, wild mushrooms and herbs, wrapped in bacon, oven-roasted and finished with Irish whiskey sauce. Other dishes are more contemporary in style: Dover sole fillets poached in red wine, paprika and cream, strudel of vegetables on a light curry sauce with mint, or breast of duck and fresh asparagus salad with a light truffle oil dressing. Bread-and-butter pudding with Irish whiskey custard is a favourite dessert. *Seats 50. Open 1200-1430, 1900-2300. Closed L Sat, all Sun, 1 week Christmas, 2 weeks Aug. Amex, Diners, Mastercard, Visa.*

DUBLIN   **Jurys Hotel and Towers**   **IRE168**

Tel: 01 660 5005   Fax: 01 660 5540
Pembroke Road Ballsbridge Dublin 4

Flagship hotel of the Jurys Hotel group. With its close proximity to Lansdowne Road (rugby and soccer) ground, the main hotel can get seriously busy on match days with fans clamouring to gain access to the bars. The traditional Dubliner Pub to the right of the bright and airy foyer has a comfortable raised seating area, while the other, the Pavilion Lounge, is to the rear under a glass pyramid with rockery, greenery and trickling water. In addition, the hotel has two restaurants, a long-hours Coffee Dock and from May-October 2½ hours of sparkling Irish cabaret that has played to well over 2 million people during the last 30 years. Most of the bedrooms in the main hotel, including four rooms (two in each part of the hotel) specially adapted for the disabled, provide decent comfort and facilities. Away from all this hustle and bustle, The Towers is a separate hotel within a hotel! With its own security, hospitality lounge, boardroom and reading room you can escape the scrum

See over

and relax in total peace and tranquillity. Here, the superior bedrooms (£225) and suites, with their own dressing-room, and furnished to a high standard, even offer a modern rocking armchair, as well as fresh fruit and chocolates on arrival. There are well-stocked 'robo' bars that charge you at a touch, several telephone extensions, and a turn-down service at night. Smartly-tiled bathrooms have good toiletries, bathrobes and an overhead (and sometimes overpowering) shower above the bathtub. Children under 14 stay free in their parents' rooms. Extensive banqueting (600) and conference (850) facilities. Ample parking. No dogs. *Rooms 390. Garden. Indoor/outdoor swimming pools. Spa bath. Beauty/hair salons. Masseuse. Shop. Airline desk. Coffee shop (0630-0430, Sun to 2245). Amex, Diners, Mastercard, Visa.*

DUBLIN   Langkawi Malaysian Restaurant   IR£40

Tel: 01 668 2760
46 Upper Baggot Street Dublin 4

Decorated throughout with a batik theme, Langkawi offers a selection of Far-Eastern dishes with Malay, Chinese and Indian influences. Chef Alexander Hosey brings street credibility to his mee goreng 'hawker' style-the type of popular food sold cheaply in outdoor markets in Malaysia and Singapore-as well as subtlety to some of his more exotic dishes. Choose from mild satay to 'devil's curries' for fireproof palates: *ayam* (chicken breast) and *daging babi* (pork). The inspiration for the latter comes from 'a blending of locally produced spices and seasoning of Portuguese influence in the region of the city of Malacca'. *Seats 60. Open 1230-1400, 1800-2345. Closed L Sat & Sun, 24-27 Dec, Good Friday. Amex, Diners, Mastercard, Visa.*

DUBLIN   Patrick Guilbaud   ★   IR£100

Tel: 01 676 4192   Fax: 01 660 1546
46 James Place off Lower Baggot Street Dublin 2

Approaching this purpose-built restaurant, you might wonder if you are in the right street, so unprepossessing does the building look from a distance. But once inside there's no mistake-a comfortable reception lounge with several striped sofas, lots of greenery in both the plant-filled atrium and high-ceilinged dining room, decent art (mostly abstract paintings) and, above all, very smartly attired and professional staff. For well over a decade this has been the place in which to enjoy classic French cuisine with a light, modern approach. The seemingly ageless Patrick is on hand to offer advice on the menus as well as engaging customers in conversation, whether on golf-one of his passions-or France's chances in the Five Nations rugby championship, especially against Ireland at Lansdowne Road! For an eponymous restaurant, somewhat unusually Patrick is not the chef-patron – the cooking is entrusted to a team of French chefs, led by Guillaume le Brun and visible in a glass-fronted kitchen; indeed, most of the staff are French. The ingredients, naturally, are mostly Irish, notably as in seafood dishes such as pan-fried king scallops served with seasonal salad and bacon, Dublin Bay prawns in crisp pastry cases served with mango and capers, or sea bass with wild mushrooms and truffles. Also highly recommended as starters are carrot soup with thyme and game torte with pepper sauce, while game dishes in season (roast wild venison with red wine sauce or breast of pheasant with wild mushrooms) are eagerly awaited by regulars. The table d'hote lunch and dinner menus (both exclusive of a service charge of 15%, as is the carte) are particularly good value, and though there's a somewhat limited choice at dinner (four courses and coffee), lunch offers four selections among both starters and main courses. And for a table whose occupants cannot make up their minds, the menu surprise at £45 per person could be tempting. Desserts (a tart lemon mousse, berry cheesecake or poached pear in red wine) and French cheeses are quite splendid, as are the numerous breads offered, the amuse-gueule, the coffee and the petits fours. Service is impeccable. As you would expect, the wine list is predominantly French, but not exclusively so and-for a restaurant of this class-prices are reasonable; note the old classics in the 'Specialist Cellar'. The restaurant is air-conditioned. *Seats 60. Open 1230-1415, 1930-2200. Closed Sun & Mon, National Holidays. Amex, Diners, Mastercard, Visa.*

Meal prices for 2 are based on à la carte menus. When set menus are available, prices will often be lower.

Tel: 01 668 2611   Fax: 01 660 8535
7 Ballsbridge Terrace Ballsbridge Dublin 4

The combination of proven individuals-restaurateur Roly Saul and chef Colin O'Daly – makes for a successful restaurant, deservedly popular since opening. Of the two floors, upstairs perhaps has a more authentic bistro atmosphere, while the ground floor is a little more sedate, and there's a real buzz about the place, so much so that staff can sometimes become distracted and unobservant, especially when you're trying to attract their attention! First comes an excellent variety of breads, followed by an eclectic selection of dishes from prawn bisque and warm salad of duck breast with caramelised apple and clementine to roast pork with apple sauce and pan-fried monkfish with almonds, honey, dates and whiskey. Good accompanying salads and vegetables as well as the puddings (super orange crème brulée), coffee and inexpensive wines-many are between £10 and £15 a bottle *Seats* 100. *Open 1200-1445, 1800-2200. Closed Good Friday, 25 & 26 Dec. Amex, Diners, Mastercard, Visa.*

Tel: 01 676 6471   Fax: 01 661 6006
St Stephen's Green Dublin 2

Situated on St Stephen's Green, Europe's largest garden square, the Shelbourne has been at the centre of Dublin life since opening its doors early in the 19th century. The Irish Constitution was drafted in what is now one of the many function rooms. The hotel has retained much of its original grandeur, with a magnificent faux-marbre entrance hall and a sumptuous lounge where morning coffee and afternoon tea are taken. The famous Horseshoe Bar and the newer Shelbourne are among the favourite gathering places for Dubliners, especially on a Friday night, and many a scandal has originated within their walls. Spacious, elegantly furnished superior and de luxe bedrooms and suites have traditional polished wood furniture and impressive drapes, while standard rooms in a newer wing are smaller. All rooms are well appointed, with bathrobes, mini-bars and three telephones as standard. Valet parking. 12 function rooms can cater for up to 400 for a reception. Children up to 16 stay free in parents' room. Forte Grand. *Rooms 164. Beauty salon. Men's hairdressing. News kiosk. Amex, Diners, Mastercard, Visa.*

Tel: 01 677 8611   Fax: 01 677 3336
35 Dawson Street Dublin 2

If only more cities had a restaurant like this: bold, lively and fun-a place where the food really does complement the surroundings. And what a room-high-ceilinged, huge mirrors adorning the walls with shelves interspersed by candelabra, lamps, urns, plants and the odd bust at either end of the dining-hall (indeed it is more hall than room). The plain wood floor emphasises the clatter and bustle, and (if you can hear it above the din) the music is often loud and uplifting. The entrance seems cosier than in the past, with comfortable banquettes, marble-topped tables and lots of art-a mixture of the old and the new. All the staff are terrific, but why don't the lady members get to wear the same colourful waistcoats as the chaps? Kick off with decent bread (brown soda or focaccia perhaps) and scrutinise Paul Flynn's monthly-changing menu. There's an eclectic mix of dishes, with lobster bisque (topped with a frothy garlic cream) sitting happily alongside Thai crab risotto and perhaps goat's cheese pizza, escalope of veal milanaise or daube of beef with cabbage, bacon, carrots and mash; you could follow with bread-and-butter pudding (served with a light, raspberry-infused custard) or blackberry crème soufflé. Good local cheeses such as Abbey Blue, Cooleeney and Gubbeen, plus excellent coffee. The wine list is both inexpensive and cheerful. Downstairs, the bistro serves a slightly different and shorter menu, perhaps a feuilleté of mushroom and onions, pan-fried sea trout with a citrus beurre blanc and a praline cheesecake. Three courses and coffee in the bistro will set you back just £20. *Seats 200. Open 1230-1430, 1830-2315. Closed L Sat, Sun & National Holidays, all 25 & 26 Dec. Amex, Diners, Mastercard, Visa.*

Your Guarantee of Quality and Independence

EGON RONAY'S GUIDES 1996

- Establishment inspections are anonymous
- Inspections are undertaken by qualified Egon Ronay's Guides inspectors
- The Guides are completely independent in their editorial selection
- The Guides do not accept advertising, hospitality or payment from listed establishments

Titles planned for 1996 include

Hotels & Restaurants ● Pubs & Inns ● Europe
Ireland ● Just A Bite
And Children Come Too ● Paris
Oriental Restaurants

Currency Italian Lire **Exchange Rate** £1=approx 2450 Lire
International Dialling Code 00 39 (Rome+6, Milan+2, Florence+55,
Naples+81, Turin+11, Venice+41, Genoa+10, Pisa+50)
Passports/Visas No visa required by British passport holders.
British Embassy in Rome Tel 6-482 5441   Fax 6-487 3324

TRANSPORT

Airports
Rome Ciampino Tel 6-794941 Fiumicino Tel 6-65951
Milan Linate Tel 2-74852200 Malpensa Tel 2-74852200
Turin Caselle Tel 11-5778362 **Venice** Tessera Tel 41-2606111
Genoa Sestri Tel 10-2411 **Naples** Capodichino Tel 81-7896111
Pisa San Giusto Tel 50-500707
Railway Stations
Rome Termini Tel 6-4775 **Milan** Centrale Tel 2-67500
Venice Santa Lucia Tel 41-715555 **Turin** Porta Nuova Tel 11-517551
Genoa Porta Principe Tel 10-284081 **Florence** Santa Maria Novella
Tel 55-278785 **Naples** Centrale Tel 81-553418
Car hire Contact UK international branches for information
Tel Nos. **Avis** 0181-848 873 **Budget** 0800 181181
EuroDollar 01895 233300 **Hertz** Tel 0181 679 1799.
Speed limits 110 km/h on trunk roads, 90 km/h on secondary roads,
130 km/h on motorways, 50 km/h in towns.

OPENING HOURS

Banks 8/8.30am-1.30pm & 3pm-4pm Mon-Fri (check locally, times
may vary).
Shops 8.30/9am-12.30pm & 3.30/4-7.30/8pm Mon-Sat (Closed Monday
am)

NATIONAL HOLIDAYS

New Year's Day, 6 Jan, Easter Mon, 25 April, 1 May, 15 Aug, 1 Nov,
8 Dec, Christmas Day & Boxing Day.

Tourist Offices

Italian Tourist Board in **London** Tel 0171-408 1254 Fax 0171-493 6695
In **Italy** Rome Tel 6-4881851 Milan Tel 2-809662
American Express Travel Service Offices or Representative (R)

Rome	Piazza Di Spagna 38 00187 Tel 6-67641 #	**Florence**	Via Dante Alghieri 22R PO Box 617 50125 Tel 55-50981 #
Milan	Via Brera 3 20121 Tel 2-809410 #	**Florence**	American Express Co. S.P.A Via Guicciardini 49/R
Naples	Every Tour Srl (R) Piazza Municipio 5-6 07026 Tel 81-5518564 #		PO Box 617 50125 Tel 55-288751 #
Genoa	Viatur Srl (R) Piazza Fontane Marosa 3 16123 Tel 10-561241 #	**Venice**	1471 San Marco San Moise PO Box 271 30124 Tel 41-5200844 #

Capri

Tel: (081) 8370732   Fax: (081) 8376990
Via Le Botteghe 12-14 80073 Capri

A rather well-known and long-established family-run restaurant. Like most of the food on Capri, the menu is heavily weighted towards fish, including fish soup, linguine in a sauce of scorpion fish, calamari stuffed with a mixture of cheese, capers and breadcrumbs as well as ravioli filled with a local cheese, marjoram and raisins with a tomato and basil sauce. The two rustic but elegant dining rooms have marble floors and walls hung with pictures by local artists. Most of the wines are from Capri. Also in the same ownership is a splendid gourmet deli, *La Capannina Più*, where you can purchase salami, cheeses and Capri's speciality-lemon liqueur. *Seats 110. L 1200-1500 D 1930-2400. Closed Wed, 6 Nov-24 Mar. Amex, Mastercard, Visa.*

Tel: (081) 8377642   Fax: (081) 8377642
Via Le Botteghe 46 80073 Capri

The cooking here is traditional, specialising in local dishes and, in particular, all manner of seafood, caught in the warm, blue waters around the island. The secret of the restaurant's success is the simple methods of preparation and cooking. There's squid with fresh tomatoes and garlic, shrimps with rocket, oil and lemon, sea bream or bass in white wine among the fish dishes. Meat dishes include hunter-style rabbit, veal with prosciutto and artichokes and fillet steak with a sauce of Marsala and porcini mushrooms. Home-made pasta is a house speciality with *gnocchetti verdi ai ricci di mare* (spinach dumplings with sea urchins); *pennette Casanova* (small macaroni with clams, garlic and cream) and *linguine portofino* (noodles with cherry tomatoes, shrimps and garlic). Simple sweets include a local speciality, a delicious chocolate and almond torte. Their cellar is as indigenous as their kitchen. *Seats 60. L 1200-1500 D 1900-2330. Closed Thu & Oct-Jun. Amex, Diners, Mastercard, Visa.*

Tel: (081) 8370788   Fax: (081) 8376080
Via Camerelle 2 80073 Capri

Converted in 1878 from a rather grand private residence whose previous occupants include Sicilian nobility, this splendid hotel attracts a mix of the smart set as well as businessmen, the latter making use of the vast conference capacity of up to 550 people seated theatre-style and the availability of secretarial and translation services. The other facilities are equally up to date, with an indoor and outdoor swimming pool, two tennis courts, a gym and sauna. The rooms have that stylish simplicity found in the Mediterranean, with cool whitewashed walls and slabbed ceramic floors, but still have satellite TV and a host of modern conveniences. *Rooms 150. Room service all day. Garden. Indoor and outdoor swimming pools. Gym. Sauna. Steam bath. Hydromassage. Closed 5 Nov-end Mar. Amex, Diners, Mastercard, Visa.*

A very stylish and elegant dining-room with a classical decor of antiques and beautiful paintings of the marine life that abounds round the island. A fine terrace, is available for alfresco dining. The kitchen and menu were designed by Gualtiero Marchesi, one of the top Italian chefs (see *Gualtiero Marchesi L'Albereta* under Around Milan). The carte offers a varied and imaginative choice of modern, well-balanced dishes. A typical meal could begin with fish and vegetable fritters with a sweet and sour sauce, cold spaghetti with caviar and chives or rabbit salad with potatoes and crispy parmesan. For a second course the choice could be lobster with macaroni, risotto with saffron and mussels or fish soup with garlic bread. Fish main courses could be sole with black truffles, artichokes and a light lemon sauce or roasted sea bass with a vegetable compote and an olive sauce, while breaded veal cutlet milanese, roast rack of lamb with an aubergine mould and grilled rib of beef with a red wine sauce, glazed onions and potatoes are among the meat offerings. Splendid desserts round off a superb experience. *Seats 80. Open D only 1930-2300.*

An alfresco lunch here is a very relaxed and enjoyable affair. The chef, who is a relation of Marchesi, prepares typically Mediterranean dishes which are simpler than those he offers in the main hotel restaurant. There's grilled fish and meat and light pasta, pizza and rice dishes. There is also a daily buffet of salads and hot dishes. The wine list is dominated by Italian whites. *Seats 150. L only 1230-1430.*

Tel: (081) 8370433   Fax: (081) 8377459
Viale Matteotti 3 80073 Capri

A very smart and chic establishment with a relaxed and informal ambience that achieves a perfect balance between those very different aspects. The views are breathtaking as the hotel is perched on a cliff, overlooking the sea. The old-fashioned rooms have period furniture and cool ceramic floors plus air-conditioning. Capri is a relaxing place and here it is especially quiet, close to an ancient monastery as well as the Giardino d'Augusto. Guests can leave their cars at a garage in Sorrento while they are on Capri. Most people take a taxi or the funicular railway from the port to the hotel, but if guests do want to walk up, reception can organise for a porter to come down to carry their baggage. *Rooms 54. Room service 24hrs. Satellite TV. Outdoor swimming pool. Closed Nov-Easter Sun. Amex, Diners, Mastercard, Visa.*

Tel: (081) 8370844   Fax: (081) 8377790
Via Tragara 57 80073 Capri

A short distance from the centre of Capri, the hotel has a friendly, inviting atmosphere. Popular with holidaymakers (but do note that children under 12 are not allowed), it has some good health facilities including a beauty salon, hydromassage in the outdoor swimming pools as well as a large garden. The rooms are spacious, with a small sitting-room on a separate level from the bedroom and bathroom. The price quoted is for rooms without a balcony and view. *Rooms 43. Closed end Oct-Good Fri. Room service all day. Garden. Sports facilities. Amex, Diners, Mastercard, Visa.*

Tel: (081) 8370633   Fax: (081) 8378291
Via Tragara 10 80073 Capri

An exclusive hotel aimed primarily at the upper end of the tourist market. Such is its reputation that it doesn't produce a brochure. This is a tranquil retreat, with large gardens and plenty of gentle sporting activities. The rooms are well equipped, with cool ceramic floors and 16th-century furniture. There are no conference facilities and it must be noted that children are considered unwelcome in these elegant surroundings. *Rooms 30. Closed 30 Oct-28 Mar. Room service all day. Satellite TV. Outdoor swimming pool. Tennis. Gym. Amex, Visa.*

Tel: (55) 222402   Fax: (55) 222403
Via Romana 34, 50125 Firenze

This quiet pensione occupies the first floor of a large 15th-century palazzo, formerly belonging to the Orlandini family. It is near to Palazzo Pitti and the Boboli gardens and provided shelter for many Jews and other refugees during the last war. Rooms are simply but comfortably furnished and all the more charming for their lack of clutter. *Rooms 20. Room service limited. Public parking L20,000. Terrace. Amex, Diners, Mastercard, Visa.*

Tel: (55) 216237   Fax: (55) 280947
Via della Scala 6, 50123 Firenze

This 14th-century palazzo formerly belonged to the Medici family. Owner Valeria Succoni Cantini opened the Aprile 40 years ago with a handful of rooms and has gradually expanded the hotel by buying extra floors. The interior is traditionally decorated, with high ceilings, polished, rug-strewn floors and paintings on the walls. The courtyard garden is a lovely place to take breakfast. Air-conditioning is installed in seven rooms and only ten have televisions, but then you don't stay here to watch MTV. *Rooms 29. Room service limited. Public parking L40,000. Garden. Amex, Mastercard, Visa.*

Tel: (55) 288621   Fax: (55) 268272
Piazza San Firenze 29, 50122 Firenze

When Florence was briefly capital of the new Kingdom of Italy (1865-70), Parliamentarians met in the marvellous fresco-decorated, vaulted main room at the Bernini Palace. You can now eat a superb buffet breakfast there when you stay at this fine hotel. All bedrooms have satellite TV and air-conditioning. Ask for one of the five rooms with splendid views over the city. *Rooms 86. Room service 24hr. Private parking L40,000. Conference facilities 25. Terrace. Amex, Diners, Mastercard, Visa.*

Tel: (55) 562068   Fax: (55) 219653
Piazza Santa Elisabetta, 50122 Firenze

The Brunelleschi is one of the most unusually constructed hotels in the city. It is made up of several different buildings squeezed together around a tiny square, not far from the Duomo. The Byzantine Torre Pagliazza, which dominates the piazza, has been incorporated into the design. Despite the higgledy-piggledy internal plan there is plenty of space and every comfort has been considered. Rooms are decorated in pale tones and have air-conditioning, satellite TV and mini-bars. Those on the top floor have fine views and one suite has its own sun terrace. Breakfast in the tower is not to be missed. PCs, fax and photocopier are at the disposal of business guests. Because of the eccentric nature of the building, it is not suitable for the disabled. *Rooms 96. Room service limited. Banqueting facilities 170. Conference facilities 110. Terrace. Amex, Diners, Mastercard, Visa.*

Tel: (55) 688345   Fax: (55) 6580841
Angolo Ponte da Berrazzana, 50126 Firenze

In the days before the Arno became polluted, small fish from the river were grilled and sold in wooden *capannine* (huts) along the banks. One such hut stood on the site of this popular fish restaurant, which has a lovely flower-filled garden. The chef Sante Collesno trained with Lorenzo Borni at San Lorenzo in London and tailors his menu to the best the market has to offer each day. He brings some of the traditions of his native Sicily to dishes such as *pepata di cozze* (peppered mussels). As only the freshest seafood is used, very little ornamentation is necessary to serve it at its best. Lobster, sea bass and red mullet are lightly grilled, sturgeon and halibut are smoked, and pasta dishes such as *tagliatelle con aragosta* (lobster) are simplicity itself. *Seats 40 (garden 40). Open 2000-0130. Closed Sun, 10-20 Aug. Amex, Diners, Mastercard, Visa.*

Tel: (55) 2341100   Fax: (55) 244966
Via Andrea del Verrocchio 8 rosso, 50122 Firenze

Fabio Picchi opened this restaurant with some friends in 1979 but soon bought them out and is now sole owner and chef. His short but continually changing menu features typically earthy Tuscan food such as *coniglio ripieno* (stuffed rabbit), *agnello arrosto* (roast lamb) and *fegato di vitello* (calf's liver). Fabio favours tradition and simplicity over trendiness and elaboration. He is also justifiably proud of his 10,000 bottle cellar which, not surprisingly, consists mainly of Italian wines. The restaurant has recently been extensively restructured with a new kitchen and rest rooms, including a disabled toilet. *Seats 60. Open 1250-1430, 1930-2315. Closed Sun, Mon, 26 Jul-4 Sep, 1 week Jan. Amex, Diners, Mastercard, Visa.*

Tel: (55) 241452   Fax: (55) 241368
Via Ghibellina 51 rosso, 50122 Firenze

Set in a former Renaissance monastery, this family-run restaurant serves traditional Tuscan food. Chef Renza Casali changes her menu fortnightly but certain specialities will usually be available: risotto della Renza, for instance, flavoured with seven types of aromatic herb. Other favourites include eels (*anguille*) and *ravioli Mugellani* (potato-filled ravioli from Mugelli). *Seats 100. Open 1200-1430, 1930-2230. Closed D Sun, all Mon, Aug. Amex, Diners, Mastercard, Visa.*

Tel: (55) 475430   Fax: (55) 485305
Via Ridolfi 4r, 50129 Firenze

A short walk north-west of the city centre into this residential district near to the Piazza della Indipendenza will be amply rewarded if you choose to eat at Don Chisciotte. The decor is airy and elegant. Look out for the paintings of the quixotic Spaniard who gave the restaurant its name. Although only ten years old, it has built a formidable reputation for ambitious, creative, delicious food. Head chef Paolo Pasquini has worked at Orso in London and his cooking is described as Italiana regionale revisionata. The seasonal menu may include *fiore di zucca ripiene di pesce* (courgette flowers filled with fish, cooked in a fresh tomato sauce) or *ravioli ripieni de barbero e ricotta con fonduta di formaggio e tartufo* (ravioli filled with beetroot and ricotta with melted cheese and truffles). Another sublime dish is veal in breadcrumbs with aromatic herbs, rocket and parmesan. Desserts are of an equally high standard, usually delicate and subtle-for example, *bavarese di fragole con salsa di limone* (bavarois of strawberries with a lemon sauce). Chiantis are the focus of the 400-bottle wine list. There is also an excellent selection of malt whiskies. The friendly, attentive staff crown a superlative dining experience. *Seats 45. Open 1300-1430, 2000-2230. Closed L Mon, all Sun, Aug. Amex, Diners, Mastercard, Visa.*

Tel: (55) 242777   Fax: (55) 244983
Via Ghibellina 87, 50122 Firenze

In a splendid 15th-century building, east of the Palazzo Bargello, Georgio Pinchiorri, his wife Annie Feolde and head chef Italo Bassi have created one of the world's top restaurants. Everything is in harmony: the two dining areas have slightly differing ambiences with the smaller, split-level, room offering a more intimate, candle-lit atmosphere. The larger room is decidedly grand. A huge Murano crystal chandelier is the centrepiece, fine paintings hang from stucco walls and flowers in silver vases sit on every table. In summer, though, the best place to eat is the inner courtyard. And as for the food... The secret of Enoteca's success is restraint. There is nothing flashy about the food here and, for this, we must be thankful for the commonsense simplicity of Tuscan rustic cooking upon which the menu is based. For instance, the success of *composizione di coniglio con sedano brasato e tartufo nero* (rabbit with braised celery and black truffle) is in combining just three elements to perfection. Similarly, with *scorfano arrosto, servito con timballo di bietole all'origano* (roasted red snapper, served with a timbale of beetroot purée with oregano). Other superb combinations include monkfish flavoured with anchovies and rosemary and garnished with fennel, beef tenderloin in a red wine and marrow sauce with a crispy potato tart, and spicy duck breast with caramelised pears. Desserts are also a treat. Try *zuccotto e biscottini di Prato* (chocolate cream and candied fruit semifreddo with dry almond biscuits). Georgio estimates that his wine cellar contains an extraordinary 80-100,000 bottles, of which 5-7000 are different. *Seats 70 (courtyard 45). Open 1200-1400, 1930-2200. Closed L Mon & Wed, all Sun, Aug. Public parking L10,000. Amex, Mastercard, Visa.*

Tel: (55) 2298451   Fax: (55) 229086
Viale Machiavelli 18, 50125 Firenze

The Villa Cora has been described as "the most beautiful villa in Florence on the most beautiful street in the world" and it is not difficult to understand why. Built in neo-classical style by Baron Oppenheim in 1865 in honour of his wife, its mosaic floors, marble statuary, fabulous *trompe l'oeil* frescos and stucco friezes are truly breathtaking. Emperors and dignitaries from all over the world have been welcomed in its salons, hung with Venetian glass chandeliers. The bedrooms are similarly plush, furnished with antiques (but also air-conditioned and with satellite TV). Winner of our Best Hotel Western Europe award 1995. *Rooms 48. Room service 24hr. Valet parking. Banqueting facilities 120. Conference facilities 150. Garden. Terrace. Outdoor swimming pool. Solarium. Children's playroom. Amex, Diners, Mastercard, Visa.*

The decor in the cantine (marble floors, vaulted ceilings) is considerably simpler than in the Villa and the food is also unpretentious. Staples include spaghetti with tomato and basil sauce, Florentine chargrilled steak with stewed mushrooms, and roast sea bass *aux fines herbes*. In summer the entire restaurant decamps to around the swimming pool, where an American-style bar is set up. *Seats 100 (terrace 100). Open 1230-1430, 1945-2300.*

Tel: (55) 287814   Fax: (55) 288353
Via dei Pesconi 2, 50123 Firenze

Stravinsky, Pirandello and De Chirico are among the many luminaries who have stayed at the Helvetia e Bristol, which, in a city of fine hotels, stands out for the unique charm of its decor and welcome. The building dates back to the end of the 19th century but it was not until 1987 that a three-year renovation began to restore its original interior. All rooms are individually decorated with rich fabrics and antiques, yet are cosy and comfortable, and some have jacuzzis. The plant-filled Winter Garden was a meeting place for intellectuals and artists during the 20s and 30s and is now the hotel bar. Situated between the Via Tornabuoni and Piazza Strozzi, the hotel is in a fine position in the heart of the city. *Rooms 52. Room service 24hr. Private parking. Amex, Diners, Mastercard, Visa.*

Tel: (55) 210916   Fax: (55) 289794
Via dei Palchetti 61, 50123 Firenze

The Narciso family have run this immensely popular restaurant since 1950. Everything about it is relaxed and friendly, from the long trestle tables to the shared wine and bread that cheery waiters deposit in front of you. The building dates from the 1450s and formerly belonged to the Ruccellai family. The food is traditional no-nonsense Tuscan, with starters including *zuppa di fagioli con farro* (bean soup with farro, a wild grain, flavoured with garlic and rosemary). Main dishes are mainly simply grilled, fried and stewed beef, rabbit and lamb. If you can't make up your mind which to go for you can have a piatto misto, a selection of all of them. *Seats 110. Open 1230-1430, 1930-2030. Closed Mon, 3-4 weeks in Aug. Amex, Diners, Mastercard, Visa.*

Tel: (55) 289592   Fax: (55) 289595
Piazza SS Annunziata N3, 50122 Firenze

The square on which the hotel stands is one of the loveliest in the city, bordered on three sides by two colonnades and the church of SS Annunziata, with Giambologna's commanding statue of the Grand Duke Ferdinand I in the centre. The building which houses the hotel is a twin of the more famous Hospital of the Innocents across the way and was built for the Serviti fathers around 1527 by Antonio Sangallo "Il Vecchio". The Loggiato Dei Serviti fits perfectly in this marvellous setting, offering superb standards of comfort and service. Furnishings and furniture have been chosen with care to complement the stucco walls, polished stone floors and vaulted ceilings. The intrusions of modern life are discreetly incorporated into the rooms: all have air-conditioning, TV, safe and mini-bar. The nature of the building means that bedrooms and bathrooms come in all shapes and sizes. *Rooms 29. Room service 24hr. Public parking L40,000. Amex, Diners, Mastercard, Visa.*

Tel: (55) 294566   Fax: (55) 295318
Via Delle Terme 23r, 50123 Firenze

Abstract art hangs from the walls, contrasting with the otherwise traditional decor of this smart but unpretentious restaurant north of the Ponte Vecchio. The seasonal menu may include *pesce spada alla mediterranea* (swordfish fried with green vegetables), *tagliolini alla salvia con funghi porcini* (tagliolini with sage and porcini mushrooms) or *cotoletta di vitello farcita con rughetta e fagiolini bianchi* (veal cutlet stuffed with rocket and white beans). The home-made desserts are excellent. Tuscan, Piedmontese and Venetian wines feature strongly on the list. The name means 'by candlelight' although 'by lamplight' would be more appropriate, and it is a great place for a romantic dinner. *Seats 35. Open 1930-2245. Closed Sun, Aug. Amex, Mastercard, Visa.*

Tel: (55) 2479751   Fax: (55) 2479755
Borgo Pinti 27, 50121 Firenze

St Philip Neri, founder of the Oratorian order, was born in this magnificent palazzo in 1515 (probably in room 19, you may be interested to know). It was already an old building at that time, part of it dating from before 1300, and is now a wonderfully atmospheric hotel, packed with antique furniture and fine works of art. These include Giambologna's first model for his *Rape of the Sabine Women* and neo-classical sculptures and drawings by Giovanni Dupré, from whom the current owner's family is descended. All the bedrooms are decorated differently and are fully air-conditioned. There is a splendid, enclosed garden at the rear. *Rooms 35. Room service limited. Garden. Private parking L20,000. Amex, Diners, Mastercard, Visa.*

Tel: (55) 220053   Fax: (55) 2336183
Via Pian de' Giullari 11r, 50125 Firenze

This typical Tuscan trattoria was formerly a grocer's shop and, set in the Vecchio Borgo hills, is now a favourite bolthole for Florentines wishing to escape the city heat and enjoy simple rustic cooking. A typical meal might start with *prosciutto, salame e finocchiona con crostini* (crostini of three types of cured meat), followed by *ribollita*, a typically sturdy vegetable soup enriched with chopped dried bread, white beans and olive oil, or perhaps penne 'al Omero' (pasta with a meat and tomato sauce). There is also plenty of offal and rabbit on offer. Wines are almost exclusively Tuscan. *Seats 150 (garden 40).*
Open 1230-1430, 1930-2230. Closed Tue, Aug. Public parking. Amex, Diners, Mastercard, Visa.

Tel: (55) 245247   Fax: (55) 2346735
Piazza Massimo d'Azeglio 3, 50121 Firenze

The Regency is the sister hotel to the Lord Byron (qv) in Rome and is located in a quiet square opposite a park. This area was developed in the 1865-70 period when Florence was briefly capital of the new Kingdom of Italy. The hotel is smart and the decor graceful but it has the intimate atmosphere of a private home with big, comfy sofas and light wallpapers. Bedrooms are air-conditioned and nine are set aside for non-smokers. Snacks can be taken in the garden. *Rooms 35. Room service 24hr. Private parking L45,000. Conference facilities 20. Garden. Amex, Diners, Mastercard, Visa.*

Depending on your mood, you can choose to eat in the plushly-carpeted, wooden-ceilinged dining-room or in the lighter, cheerier conservatory. The food is more imaginative and less resolutely earthy than in many Florentine restaurants with plenty of interesting fish dishes. For instance, *filetti caldi di pescatrice con fonduta di gamberoni ed erbette di campo* (fillets of monkfish with prawn and herb fondue). Desserts include *budino di amaretti alla cannella con salsa fragole* (amaretti pudding with cinnamon and strawberry sauce). *Seats 40. Open 1230-1430, 1930-2230. Closed Sun (except for hotel guests).*

Tel: (55) 240951   Fax: (55) 240282
Via di Mezzo 20, 50121 Firenze

A haven from the tourist bustle, this building dates from the 16th century and was formerly a monastery. The ambience is intimate and friendly and, although there are concessions to modernity (air-conditioning, satellite TV, minibar), the wooden floors and frescoed ceilings, the arched bedrooms and cloistered reception rooms, feel wonderfully old. If you need secretarial services, a hire car or a babysitter, the owners, James and Jacqueline Cavagnali, will be happy to arrange them for you. *Rooms 19. Room service limited. Public parking L25,000. Conference facilities 50. Courtyard. Amex, Diners, Mastercard, Visa.*

Tel: (55) 282802   Fax: (55) 210293
Via Panzani 94, 50123 Firenze

This famous restaurant, not far from the station, has been open for over 70 years and is as popular now as it ever was. Chef Rosario Santoro (who is also one of the owners) offers typical Tuscan fare to a local and international crowd. Antipasto alla Sabatini, a selection of marinated salmon, sturgeon and vegetables, is the perfect appetiser, followed perhaps by *sformatino di spinaci o carciofi* (little spinach or artichoke soufflé) and rounded off with the delicious *cosciotto di agnello al forno* (roast leg of lamb with sage and rosemary). All the desserts and and ice-creams are home-made. There is a vast choice of Tuscan wines as well as some good French bottles. *Seats 180. Open 1230-1430, 1930-2230. Closed Mon. Amex, Diners, Mastercard, Visa.*

FLORENCE   Torre di Bellosguardo   L380,000

Tel: (55) 2298145   Fax: (55) 229008
Via Roti Michelozzi 2, 50124 Firenze

Dante's friend, the poet Guido Cavalcanti, was so enraptured by the view of Florence from this hill that he built a villa here and called it *Bellosguardo* (beautiful view). Successive generations of literati have stayed in the house, soaking up the history. Elizabeth Barrett Browning was moved to verse, and, more recently when it was an American college, Erica Jong became inspired to write about Europe. The cool, frescoed ballroom leads out on to the veranda and in summer lunch can be taken by the pool in the huge garden which tumbles down the hillside in a series of terraces. No two bedrooms are alike. The ceilings may be beamed or rosette-studded, some have gilded four-poster beds, others contain 15th-century chests of drawers. Some will be dismayed to know that most rooms are not air-conditioned, few have TVs and there's not a mini-bar in sight. *Rooms 16. Room service 24hr. Garden. Outdoor swimming pool. Amex, Diners, Mastercard, Visa.*

FLORENCE   Villa Carlotta   L240,000

Tel: (55) 220530   Fax: (55) 2336147
Via Michele di Lando 3, 50125 Firenze

A Florentine knight used to own the building housing this elegant hotel and his stables are now a restaurant. Inside, there are fine stuccoed ceilings and lots of 19th-century furniture, floral patterns and pale colours. Rooms are air-conditioned and have satellite TV and, should you empty your mini-bar, you will be pleased to know that the hotel bar is almost permanently open. A cottage with five rooms is currently being built in the garden. The villa is only a few minutes walk away from most of Florence's best-known sights. *Rooms 27. Room service 24hr (for drinks). Private parking. Banqueting facilities 80. Conference facilities 60. Garden. Amex, Diners, Mastercard, Visa.*

FLORENCE   Villa Le Rondini   L240,000

Tel: (55) 4000081   Fax: (55) 268212
Via Bolognese Vecchia 224, 50139 Firenze

If you are looking for a quiet hotel, away from the tourist log-jam of the city, then the Villa Le Rondini, 7km south of Florence, could be the place for you. It consists of three 17th- and 18th-century villas, set in their own 22-hectare park of cypress and fruit trees. The decor is simultaneously simple yet luxurious with hand-painted antique furniture, marble floors and carved bedheads. One room is specially equipped for disabled guests. The Reali familly, who have owned the hotel for 27 years, produce their own wine and olive oil on the property and you can sample both in the restaurant. *Rooms 43. Room service limited. Private parking. Banqueting facilities 250. Conference facilities 150. Park. Outdoor swimming pool. Tennis. Gym. Amex, Diners, Mastercard, Visa.*

Around Florence

BORGO SAN LORENZO   Il Feriolo   L90,000

Tel: (55) 8409928
Via Faentina 32, 50032 Borgo San Lorenzo

If you want a change from overpriced, tourist-packed restaurants in Florence, head north out of the centre on the Via Faentina. On the other side of the village of Olmo, follow the road for a further 2km and then turn right at the sign to Il Feriolo. This former monastery is on a small hill at the end of a lengthy, winding road, but is worth the effort of getting there. The views from the veranda over wooded countryside are wonderful and the food is traditional Tuscan cooking at its best. Prosciutto, *salame e finocchiona* (a type of local sausage) is a typical starter, or try the intriguing *ravioli nudi* which the chef describes as "pasta without pasta"-vegetables and ricotta rolled in flour and cooked to resemble gnocchi. Main dishes reflect the riches of the surrounding country, for instance, *tagliatelle al cinghiale* (wild boar) and *capriolo con panna e brandy* (wild deer in a stew of cream and brandy). There are also tempting desserts such as torta della nonna made with pastry, custard and almonds. Most of the wines are, somewhat inevitably, Tuscan. *Seats 100 (veranda 20). Open 1230-1500, 1930-2200. Closed Tue. Private parking. Amex, Diners, Mastercard, Visa.*

Tel: (55) 594512   Fax: (55) 598734
Via Doccia 4, 50014 Fiesole

The beautiful village of Fiesole looks down over Florence and provides the setting for this fabulous hotel. A former monastery, its facade was designed by Michelangelo and its reception area was the original chapel. A fresco of The Last Supper by Tito da Titi decorates the dining area. Despite the refreshing simplicity of the decor-whitewashed walls, curved archways-all rooms have air-conditioning and satellite TV. The popularity of San Michele has been such that the owners, Orient Express Hotels, constructed a further eight rooms last year. The restaurant moves out on to the loggia for the summer, and guests can eat there, looking out towards Florence, surrounded by cypress and olive trees and vines.
Rooms 36. Closed Dec, Jan, Feb. Room service 24hr. Banqueting facilities 50. Conference facilities 40. Garden. Terrace. Outdoor swimming pool. Amex, Diners, Mastercard, Visa.

Tel: (577) 749483   Fax: (577) 742969
Gaiole in Chianti, 53013 Siena

From Florence follow the very winding S222 through Grassina, Greve and the very heart of Chianti Classico country, turning on to the S408 to find this imposing ancient hill-top fortified monastery now owned by Seamus de Pentheny O'Kelly, who is also the chef. In fine weather the characterful inner courtyard is used for alfresco dining, otherwise the lofty, galleried dining-room with its huge open fireplace is the setting for some true and very fine Tuscan country cooking. The menu features a series of well-balanced set menus as well as a comprehensive carte. Typical dishes from a very meat- and vegetable-orientated menu include crostini with chicken livers, *pappardelle* (wide pasta ribbons) with a rich duck and wild fennel sauce, venison with a juniper sauce and roast leg of lamb with rosemary. Virtually all the vegetables are organically grown on the premises and wine list majors on excellent local vintages. There's a wine cellar in the basement where wine tastings are a regular feature and it's here too that snacks and light lunches are served. Set meals from L68,000. *Seats 80. Open 1230-1430, 1930-2230. Closed L Mon, L Tue (open for residents), 20 Nov-20 Mar. Private parking. Amex, Diners, Mastercard, Visa.*

The splendid rooms, all quite different in shape and size, are furnished to a high and very comfortable standard. Located on the upper floors, they have polished quarry-tiled floors, heavy-beamed ceilings and colourful fabrics creating considerable character and good taste. Many have fine views over the surrounding hills and all are well equipped, having mini-bars, televisions and air-conditioning. Bathrooms, too, are immaculate and modern. Guests have the use of a beautifully located outdoor swimming pool, while on the ground floor next to the dining-room is a simple lounge for the relaxation of both residents and diners.
Rooms 21. Room service limited. Closed as restaurant. Outdoor swimming pool.

Tel: (2) 416886   Fax: (2) 48302005
Via Montecuccoli 6, 20147 Milano

This restaurant's location in a quiet residential area isn't central but even without private transport it is easily accessible via Line 1 of the underground and using the Primaticcio stop. Aimo Moroni started working here as manager in 1964 and is now the owner. He has created a delightful establishment with an attractive, modern appearance and a clean, simple yet elegant decor. It comprises two smallish dining-rooms whose otherwise plain walls are hung with bold, colourful artwork. Well-spaced tables have their own multi-hued splashes of colour in the form of pretty flower posies. The menu takes Italian cooking into a realm of fantasy where imagination and cooking skills are combined to create dishes of superb quality. Even the breads are excellent, particularly the one with pine nuts. For lunch there's a good value three-course set menu which includes two glasses of wine. There is also the full à la carte and *menu degustazione*. Changing daily, typical fare could begin with slivers of marinated raw sea bass dressed with olive oil, basil and curly lettuce. A pasta course could be dainty filled bows flavoured with watercress, served with thin fingers of fresh ewe's milk ricotta, tomato and basil-a wonderfully light and very cooling dish on a hot

See over

summer's day. Sea bream fillets are carefully wrapped round a mixture of the fish and herbs then placed on a bed of very finely diced aubergines, tomato and capers. Veal rump from Piedmont has a filling of layers of prosciutto and quartirolo-a particularly fine version of taleggio cheese. This is served with a very delicate honey-flavoured onion purée. A typical sweet is jellied cherry terrine with a chilled plum mould and an apricot sauce as well as a refreshing fresh mint sorbet. A charming family-run establishment with booking essential in the evening. *Seats 35. Open 1230-1430, 2000-2230. Closed L Sat, all Sun, Aug, 1-6 Jan. Amex, Diners, Mastercard, Visa.*

MILAN   L'Ami Berton   ★   L260,000

Tel: (02) 713669
Via Nullo 14 20129 Milano

R

Now well-established, the restaurant is east of the city centre close to Piazza Novelli. It boasts a very elegant and classy decor with a beautiful sage green and pale grey interior. As well as the expected fine ornaments and decorations, walls have glass-shelved cabinets displaying an extensive selection of Scotch whiskies and rare brandies. The menu is a relatively short one, featuring classics presented in a very attractive and modern fashion. Cooking is first-rate, with superbly defined flavours adding to the visual appeal of the food. Dishes are uncomplicated, this simplicity very positively demonstrating the excellent quality of the raw materials. Starters from a late spring menu include a moreish courgette flower fritter, a puff pastry case with wild salmon and caviar, pan-fried prawns with artichokes and a fish terrine with wild rice. Fish is a speciality here appearing in such creations as swordfish with potatoes flavoured with thyme, sea bream with ginger and saffron and lightly poached sea bass with tomato. Those with a penchant for meat are able to enjoy the likes of lasagne with duck ragù, breast of guinea fowl with blackcurrants and beef with porcini mushrooms. There are extremely good desserts, too, such as hot cherries with vanilla ice cream, apple millefeuille with crème chantilly, peach poached in moscatel and served with a strawberry sauce or a lime semifreddo with citrus ragù. Smooth, accomplished service. No parking *Seats 50. L 1200-1430 D 2000-2300. Closed L Sat & Sun, 3 weeks Aug, 1 week Xmas. Amex, Mastercard, Visa.*

MILAN   Antica Trattoria della Pesa   L160,000

Tel: (2) 6555741   Fax: 2(2) 6555741
Viale Pasubio 10, 20100 Milano

R

The quaintly rustic trattoria has existed here since the 1880s and today, under the direction of the Fassi family, the cooking continues to produce good Milanese dishes such as osso buco with risotto, cabbage leaf rolls stuffed with meat, guinea fowl with greens, oil and vinegar and a house speciality, *cotoletta alla milanese* – the famous breaded veal escalope. *Seats 80. Open 1200-1430, 1930-2300. Closed Sun, end Jul-end Aug. Public parking. Amex, Diners, Mastercard, Visa.*

MILAN   Biffi Scala Toula   L180,000

Tel: (2) 866651   Fax: (2) 866653
Piazza della Scala, 20121 Milano

R

New owners have refurbished this restaurant which stands next to the renowned La Scala Opera House. The original style remains intact but there are improved facilities. In the kitchens head chef Nuncio Alibrandi, who has been here since 1988, continues to produce mainly southern Italian and Venetian cooking. Typical dishes are marinated salmon with fennel, squid-ink risotto, Venetian pasta and bean soup, and fillet of turbot with spinach and tomato. Try a catalana, a type of crème brulée with a caramelised crust, or the pistachio bavarois with a strawberry sauce, for dessert. Set meals are available from L40,000 (lunch) and L50,000 (dinner). *Seats 140. Open 1230-1445, 1930-2330. Closed L Sat, all Sun, 24 Dec-7 Jan. Amex, Diners, Mastercard, Visa.*

MILAN   Boeucc   L160,000

Tel: (2) 76020224   Fax: (2) 796173
Piazza Belgioioso 2, 20121 Milano

R

Occupying the 18th-century Piermarini building in a small, quiet square, the restaurant is a Milanese institution. The decor is grand, including splendid antique chandeliers which are suspended from the high ceilings. The food represents all that is good in Italian cooking combining traditional and modern influences in quite simple dishes such as ravioli of lobster and scampi, potato gnocchi with gorgonzola and courgette flowers and a salad of prawns, rocket and artichokes. There are luxury ingredients aplenty including caviar, oysters and porcini mushrooms. The choice of grilled fish is excellent and there are good meat dishes too, as in saltimbocca alla romana, chateaubriand with béarnaise sauce and osso buco with *risotto alla milanese*. Seats 140 (under the portico 60). ***Open** 1240-1430, 1940-2240. Closed L Sun, all Sat, Aug, Christmas. Private parking. Amex.*

Tel: (2) 8843   Fax: (2) 804924
Via Baracchini 12, 20123 Milano

A well-maintained hotel built in the 50s but modernised in 1988 that enjoys a good central location and smart, modern and well-equipped bedrooms, some of which have small balconies. ***Rooms** 128. Public parking L25,000. Banqueting and conference facilities 60. . Amex, Diners, Mastercard, Visa.*

Tel: (02) 2046003
Via Stoppani 5 20129 Milano

A stylish, modern, split-level dining-room whose stark white walls (even the windows have wide floor-to-ceiling translucent white screens) are hung with huge misty blue pictures of the Lipari islands, after one of whose islets the restaurant takes its name. The cooking, under the direction of Renato Carnevale, captures the simple, sunny character of the islands. There is no menu proper, the choice being explained at the table. For a starter, there could be a warm slice of moist lobster tart perhaps followed by a most unusual aubergine dish: the vegetables are sliced paper-thin and baked with a stuffing of herbs and cheese and served with a tomato sauce made solely from pulped and reduced fresh tomatoes. If it's available try the most wonderful risotto-of scampi and orange, which Dr Carnevale created for the occasion of the wedding of his eldest son. It is an outstanding combination of flavours. Conchiglia del pescatore evokes the sea coming in a giant clam shell packed with linguine in a rich tomato sauce with baby clams and scorfano (scorpion fish). There are a few meat dishes but the restaurant puts more emphasis on fish. A speciality is involtini of three fish each with its own character and meant to be eaten in a particular order-first baked sole fillets wrapped around lettuce, pecorino and parmesan, next grilled swordfish folded around a pine nut mixture and served on orange slices and finally fried red mullet with a filling of capers, and a little pounded red mullet. A simple rocket salad accompanies. Sweets could include a magnificent almond semifreddo, served with the darkest and richest of hot chocolate sauces. Stunning cannolichi (dainty little cream-filled pastries) precede the desserts and wonderful coffee ends a truly memorable meal. ***Seats** 45. Open 1230-1430, 2000-2230. Closed L Sat, all Sun. Diners, Visa, Mastercard.*

Tel: (2) 867651   Fax: (2) 866609
Via Hoepli 6, 20121 Milano

Situated a short distance from the Duomo, the hotel offers classic comforts with elegant rooms filled with antique furniture. Renovations have created a gleaming hall featuring cherrywood and most of the bedrooms have been given a facelift and are equipped with cable and satellite TV and a mini-bar. The new restaurant offers a menu of Milanese cooking, with the added perk of a vegetarian menu. ***Rooms** 104. Room service limited. Banqueting facilities 50. Conference facilities 50. Amex, Diners, Mastercard, Visa.*

Tel: (2) 29513404   Fax: (2) 201072
Viale Piave, 20129 Milano

The jewel in the crown of Milan's Belle Epoque, this is the oldest hotel in the city, dating back to 1905. Viale Piave is very conveniently on the circle route of the 29 and 30 trams but it might be advisable to avoid the bedrooms that face on to it. Instead, choose one of the quieter rooms overlooking the garden and terrace where you can have breakfast and lunch on a terrace in the summer. The hotel interior is chic, with huge original art deco windows, marble floors and fine, old pieces of furniture. ***Rooms** 94. Room service limited. Private parking. Conference facilities 50. Garden. Amex, Diners, Mastercard, Visa.*

Opening times are often liable to change at short notice, so it's always best to book.

Tel: (2) 6598006 Fax: (2) 6555413
Viale Monte Grappa 7, 20124 Milano

R

Pictures of the Italian hero adorn the white walls of this restaurant north of the city centre. The front room is more of a rendezvous place for locals, so choose the rear room in which to eat the good, solid cooking. The frequently-changing menu might include mini-lasagne with herbs and ricotta, fish casserole with asparagus or rabbit and courgette flower stew. The three-chocolate terrine with mocha sauce is an example of the fine desserts. The wine list include the raw, blackcurranty Franciacorta reds from east of Milan. *Seats 95. Open 1230-1430, 2000-0100. Closed L Sat, all Fri, 3 weeks in Aug, National Holidays. Valet parking. Amex, Diners, Mastercard, Visa.*

Tel: (2) 5462930 Fax: (2) 55195790
Via A Sciesa 8, 20135 Milano

R

The Milanese love the old-style grandeur and flamboyance of this restaurant. Patrons arriving by car enter to the side with secured parking available, while those using the main entrance proceed down a long, wide hallway past open-plan kitchens visible behind glass screens and rack upon rack of fine wines and huge, bubbling lobster tanks. In summer the place to eat is in the splendid winter garden with its caged, singing canaries and cool, leafy arbour. The interior dining-rooms are characterised by resplendent Murano crystal chandeliers and fine furniture. The lengthy menu is very traditional and the food is competently prepared. The charcoal grill renders a good selection of meats and seafood while the restaurant's own classic dishes include risotto with saffron and courgette flowers, the traditional breaded veal cutlet milanese and osso buco with gremolata. When in season, fresh porcini mushrooms are delicious served baked with a sprinkling of parsley, breadcrumbs and garlic. Booking is advisable. *Seats 400 (garden 200). Open 1230-1500, 1900-2400. Closed Sun, 7-20 Aug. Private parking. Amex, Diners, Mastercard, Visa.*

Tel: (2) 877120 Fax: (2) 877035
Via San Raffaele 2, 20121 Milano

R

For those unable to travel to Gualtiero Marchesi's L'Albereta in the beautiful and remote hilltop setting between Bergamo and Brescia, the city-based bistrot is a splendid place to sample the cooking of one of Italy's foremost chefs. Located at the top of the La Rinascente department store, the conservatory-like skylight takes full advantage of a unique view of the Duomo with its 135 marble spires and 2,200 sculptures. The food is simple but well prepared. Three set menus-vegetarian, Milanese and fish-offer excellent value and each comes with a small carafe of wine and half litre of mineral water per person. The carte consists of a choice of very enjoyable dishes, some traditional, others modern. Typical are *vitello tonnato* (veal with a creamed tuna sauce), Milanese risotto and *branzino arrosto con fave e piselli* and *tagliata di manzo alla rucola*. A house speciality is the *cotoletta di vitello alla milanese con insalata verde*. Delicious sweets such as *semifreddo allo zabaglione, salsa al Marsala* complete a memorable experience. Set meals from L46,000. *Seats 120. Open 1230-1430, 1900-2200. Closed L Mon, all Sun, 13-20 Aug, also closed for dinner 31 Jul-18 Oct. Amex, Diners, Mastercard, Visa.*

Tel: (2) 8321481
Piazzale Cantore, 20123 Milano

R

Not far from Porta Genova station, Al Porto stands alone on an island at the southern end of a large square. What little remains of Milan's canal system comes to a head in a small dock very close by and large black anchors either side of the entrance give a suitably nautical theme to this good fish restaurant. Typical offerings include seafood salad, *totanetti* (baby squid) stuffed with fish and breadcrumbs, classic seafood risotto, gilt-head bream with red peppercorns and baked sea bass with white Ligurian wine and black olives. Simple desserts to finish and excellent coffee. Service can be quite fast. *Seats 90. Open 1230-1430, 1930-2230. Closed L Mon, all Sun, Aug, 23 Dec-3 Jan. Amex, Diners, Mastercard, Visa.*

Tel: (2) 76023132   Fax: (2) 798565
Via Sant' Andrea 23, 20121 Milano

Located close to some of the city's top couture boutiques, the restaurant's interior retains a English club-like atmosphere reminiscent more of the 70s than the 90s. Walls are clad in dark brown leather with a polished mahogany strip ceiling and comfortable black leather chairs. The carte, available in several languages, is lengthy, offering all the elements of traditional luxury international and Milanese cuisine. Starters include a small lobster salad or warm smoked trout. Among the pasta dishes are risotti such *alla milanese* or *alla champagne* and spaghetti with caviar. Main dishes major on beef: chateaubriand with béarnaise sauce, tournedos and beef Wellington head the list. Other choices include grilled lamb cutlets and sole véronique. *Seats 70. Open 1300-1530, 2000-0030. Closed Sun, Aug. Valet parking. Amex, Diners, Mastercard, Visa.*

Tel: (02) 33610333   Fax: (02) 3317399
Via Messina 10 20100 Milano

The restaurant of the Hotel Hermitage is located north-west of the city centre, a few streets from the very splendid Monumental cemetery. The hotel was built two years ago and the restaurant is decorated in pretty shades of pink and red with soft lighting and attractive table settings. It's much favoured by a well-heeled, conservative clientele who come for the fish, which is all they serve here. It is of the freshest and finest quality and includes a delicious starter of steamed *cannochie* and *totani* (Adriatic shrimps and squid from the Ligurian sea). Other typical dishes from a menu which changes twice yearly are scallops sautéed with vegetables and a superb fritto misto of all manner of beautifully cooked fish. The wine list is predominantly white and Italian but with a few French vintages and very few reds. *Seats 80. Open 1200-1430, 2000-2230. Closed Aug, 27 Dec-5 Jan. Amex, Diners, Mastercard, Visa.*

Tel: (02) 782010   Fax: (02) 76014691
Corso Venezia 3 20121 Milano

A very fashionable and elegant restaurant close to Milan's top designer boutiques. From the street entrance with its uniformed doorman a long passageway leads into a splendid ante-room and bar with the stylishly appointed restaurant beyond. Decor is a cool combination of glittering whites and creams. The menu is modern and also Venetian including some excellent fish and shellfish such as salt cod *(baccala)* with polenta, scallops and baby squid. Tagliolini come with fresh crab, to be followed perhaps by a mixed grill of Adriatic seafood, or the classic calf's liver Venetian style, carpaccio or lamb cutlets in a sweet and sour sauce. Set L55,000. Set D L24,000. There are two sister restaurants in London, *Santini* and *L'Incontro*. *Seats 130. Open 1230-1430, 1730-2300. Closed 1 week Christmas. Amex, Diners, Mastercard, Visa.*

Tel: (2) 72003433   Fax: (2) 86461060
Galleria Vittorio Emanuelle II, 20121 Milano

This restaurant, in the very heart of Milan, opened in 1867 and for a long time was renowned as being the city's most fashionable, exclusive and expensive dining place. Prices are still high but the plush decor and glittering chandeliers create an elegant setting for a menu that remains loyal to largely traditional Milanese cooking. This is a good place to try the ubiquitous *risotto alla milanese* or fish dishes such as turbot with tomato and thyme. Unruffled, polished service. Set meals L65,000 at lunch and L85,000 at dinner, including wine. *Seats 100. Open 1245-1500, 1945-2230. Closed L Sat, all Sun, 3 weeks Aug. Amex, Diners, Mastercard, Visa.*

Tel: (2) 8831   Fax: (2) 8057964
Piazza Fontana (Duomo), 20122 Milano

A modern city-centre hotel a few hundred yards from the Duomo and occupying one side of an attractive square with a central fountain. The trompe l'oeil facade, in the style of the surrounding buildings, has much improved the exterior appearance. Bedrooms, all air-conditioned, are smart and comfortable and some of those on the top floors have good views over the cathedral's spires. Bathrooms, all with bidets, have both bath and shower facilities and are bright and well maintained. *Rooms 185. Room service limited. Banqueting facilities 150. Conference facilities 120. Amex, Diners, Mastercard, Visa.*

Around Milan

Tel: (02) 9420034   Fax: (02) 9420610
Piazza G Negri 9 Cassinetta di Lugagnano 20081 Abbiategrasso

In the heart of a sleepy village 20-odd kms south west of Milan, the characterful 15th-century stone inn that stands next to a small bridge over the Milan canal is the exalted domain of Renata, Maurizio and Ezio Santi, Ezio being in charge of what is one of the very best kitchens in Italy. To get here, either take a taxi the whole way from Milan (very expensive), or else take one of the hourly trains from Porto Genova in the direction of Montara, an easy and pleasant 25-minute journey. Be sure, however, to arrange when booking your table, to order a taxi to pick you up at the station to take you the short, but circuitous 2kms from Abbiategrasso to Cassinetta. In fine weather, the only place to eat is on the terrace, sheltered by a heavily beamed roof and a surrounding wall of lush greenery with a trickling waterfall in one corner. Even the tables are fresh and summery, with bold, colourful napery and pretty floral posies. At other times you dine in very elegant simplicity inside, under more beams, with thick, white-painted walls all around. The menu descriptions are short and exact; choice isn't extensive but is varied enough to be sufficient. Dishes, while not complex, display a great degree of refinement and immense attention to detail. This is food of the very highest order, ably demonstrating the style and quality of a tip-top restaurant. After a complimentary glass of sparkling wine and a tiny, delicious pre-appetiser, the menu offers such delights as a terrine of aubergines, peppers and courgettes with a tiny tomato and basil tartlet, brandade of dried cod with new Ligurian olive oil and fresh goose foie gras with spices and jelly as starters. It is customary in Italy to take a pasta course prior to the main dish. Here the choice includes tagliolini with red mullet, small ravioli with a shellfish mixture and lobster broth and cannelloni filled with ewe's milk ricotta and vegetables and served with a light pepper sauce. Main dishes range from sea bass with an olive purée and Ligurian pesto and John Dory with a sauce of broad beans to guinea fowl with green peppercorns, cherries and balsamic vinegar and noisettes of veal with orange powder and spices with a baked custard of foie gras and a basil sauce. Desserts such as a wild strawberry millefeuille served with an almond sauce are the culmination of an experience well worth the trip out of Milan. Staff couldn't be kinder. *Seats 45. Open 1200-1400, 2000-2200. Closed Sun, Mon & Aug. Amex, Diners, Mastercard, Visa.*

Tel: (030) 7760550   Fax: (030) 7760573
Via Vittorio Emanuele II 25030 Erbusco (Brescia)

Gualtiero Marchesi's splendid villa is 1½ kilometres from the centre of Erbusco in an area very aptly named Bellavista. The hotel is perched on a hilltop overlooking lush vineyards, wooded slopes, a lake and, beyond, the distant Alps. Built in 1880, but completely remodelled and brought bang up to date, the hotel fits perfectly into its setting and offering almost every conceivable modern comfort, from spacious, elegantly appointed day rooms including several smart, comfortable lounges and a library, to fabulous bedrooms and bathrooms all decorated in the best possible taste. Exemplary standards of service complement superb housekeeping. Every room is fully air-conditioned and furnished with antique, country-style furniture which fits in well with the thick, white walls and polished floors. Some rooms have balconies and some spa baths. In the winter of 94/95 a new wing of bedrooms was added which are in keeping with the style of the original building. Not only is the whole place beautifully furnished and immaculately maintained but there are exemplary standards of service too. All the bedrooms are fully air-conditioned and are furnished with antique furniture in a heavy, traditional country style which fits in well with the thick white walls and polished floors. Five bedrooms, with twin beds, have balconies and the best rooms have jacuzzi baths and separate showers. There's a well-placed indoor pool on the lowest level of the hotel with patio doors that open on to a sunny south-facing terrace overlooking the gardens. Breakfasts are a real treat, taken in the breakfast room to the accompaniment of the early morning sun. ***Rooms 44***. *Closed 3 weeks Jan. Room service all day. Satellite TV. Indoor swimming pool. Sauna. Keep-fit equipment. Theatre-style conferences for up to 50. Amex, Diners, Mastercard, Visa.*

If you're not staying in the hotel, it's still well worth the 60-odd kilometre journey out of Milan to eat here. There's no public transport to this establishment, so it's case of hiring a car or chauffeur and heading straight up the Viale Zara from the centre of Milan, ignoring pointers to Bergamo, until you reach the A4 Autostrada and head in the direction of Venice. After passing Bergamo take the Rovato exit. Turn left after the tollgate and continue through Erbusco heading for Sarnico. In the village centre a sign for the hotel and restaurant on the right points up a narrow lane which eventually leads into the hills. Once you arrive you can see why the Marchesis exchanged their first restaurant in central Milan for this idyllic spot. Surrounded by the Franciacorta vineyards, it is at the summit of a hill commanding magnificent views northwards towards Lake Iseo and the Italian Alps. The dining-room has a splendid enclosed terrace with the most wonderful view. The rear wall has a splendid fresco in muted colours and the roof is supported by huge beams providing a rustic touch in contrast to the chandeliered elegance of the internal dining-room. Gualtiero Marchesi's reputation is for advancing the cause of Italian gastronomy into the realm of studied innovation. Working with the wealth of first-class produce so readily at hand he fashions the simplest of dishes that capture the living essence of the ingredients. The cooking is light and fresh, delicately seasoned and with everything in perfect balance. The use of differing, sometimes contrasting, constituents produces new and unusual taste sensations. A typical meal begins with a complimentary glass of sparkling wine, here of exceptional Franciacorte spumante, then a super pre-appetiser before such delicacies as a salad of sturgeon with caviar, saffron risotto with a gold leaf (completely edible), an open raviolo with scallops and ginger, turbot with a salt crust, fried fillets of sole with a sweet and sour sauce and rib of beef steamed with vegetables and served with mustard fruits and salsa verde. Desserts include a delicious panettone soufflé or an omelette surprise. Set L L50,000 (Tue-Fri). *Seats 50. Open 1230-1430, 2000-2230.*

Meal prices for 2 are based on à la carte menus. When set menus are available, prices will often be lower.

Tel: (081) 7648684
Via Cuma 42 Lungomare di Santa Lucia Napoli

The veranda, with its rattan chairs and white linen-clothed tables, commands a superb view looking out over the Bay of Naples to Vesuvius and Sorrento. This is a wonderful setting for the food, which is based on the regional cuisine of the area, mainly fish, but with a few meat dishes (for some of which Angus beef is specially imported from Scotland). The fish dishes include old fishermen's recipes such as *cozze acqua pazza* (mussels baked with cherry tomatoes, though natural sea water used to be added by the fishermen in the past). Other dishes are *penne alla cantinella* (pasta quills with fresh tomato, aubergines and mozzarella), *linguine Santa Lucia* (home-made pasta with baby squid, octopus, clams and large prawns), *spigola alla mediterranea* (sea bass) and *bracciole con ripieno di pinoli, prezzemolo e aglio* (veal with a pine kernel, parsley and garlic stuffing). There are delicious Neapolitan sweet pastries to finish. The international wine list is one of the most extensive and interesting in Italy. Next door there is now a piano-wine bar (The Cantinella Club) open from 5pm to 2am. *Seats 120. Open 1230-1530, 1930-0030. Closed 24-26 Dec. Amex, Mastercard, Visa.*

Tel: (081) 8780026   Fax: (081) 5330226
Piazza Sant'Agata sui due Golfi 80064 Napoli   R

1890 was the year that family members of the present owner, Livia Iaccarino, opened this restaurant. She has been running it and cooking here since 1973. The combination of original 19th-century recipes and a fresh interpretation of regional dishes makes for an interesting menu. The menu sways towards fish and shellfish dishes like *astice al vapore* (steamed crayfish with a tomato and basil jelly and extra virgin olive oil) and *linguine con vongole e zucchini* (ribbon pasta with baby clams and baby marrows), but also includes *costoletta di agnello alle erbe fresche mediterranee* (lamb cutlets with Mediterranean herbs). The speciality is rib of veal with raisins, pine nuts and tomato. They grow and use all their own organic herbs and vegetables. They even have their own olive groves from where the delicious extra virgin olive oil used in the cooking comes from. *Seats 40. Open 1230-1430, 2000-2230. Closed Mon, also Tue Oct-May, all 10 Jan-25 Feb. Private parking. Amex, Mastercard, Visa.*

Tel: (081) 5756002
Via Ferdinando Russo 13 Capo Posillipo 80123 Napoli   R

Established in the early 80s, Antonio di Martino's restaurant offers cooking with an international slant which he prepares along with a selection of Mediterranean dishes. Fish is mostly featured, though the odd meat dish also appears. Both are quite simply treated, generally plain grilled or roasted with a dribble of olive oil. The lemon profiteroles to finish are refreshingly different. The setting, overlooking the Bay of Naples, is a splendid one and the restaurant, on a seaside road above a beach, makes the most of the location. *Seats 160. Open 1230-1600, 1730-2300. Closed Mon & 1st 2 weeks days Aug. Private parking. Amex, Diners, Mastercard, Visa.*

Tel: (081) 7612474   Fax: (081) 663527
Corso Vittorio Emanuele 135 80121 Napoli   H

A grand hotel in every sense of the word. Built in 1860 and lavishly refurbished a few years ago, it stands high up on a hillside above the seashore and communal gardens. The panoramic views from the front-facing bedrooms and public rooms over the Bay of Naples are magnificent, with Vesuvius clearly visible on the left, Capri in the centre and Ischia on the right. Each of the six bedroom floors is in a different style, the decor ranging from classic Louis XVI to smart, modern furniture. All are well equipped and have splendid bathrooms with marble floors. The public areas are particularly elegant with a well-balanced mix of French period-style furniture and a few more modern pieces. *Rooms 83. Room service all day. Theatre-style conference facilities for up to 250. Secretarial/translation services. Private parking. Amex, Mastercard, Visa.*

Tel: (081) 7611051   Fax: (081) 664186
Via Orazio 116 80122 Napoli   R

The setting and food are very classically Southern Italian, with a garden of orange and lemon trees surrounding a beautiful 19th-century villa. Original religious frescos decorate the ceilings of the stylish and very ornate restaurant, which also features windows and furniture taken from an old church. The light regional cooking takes every advantage of the fresh seafood available, for example tender baby squid with capers, as well as offering specialities such as *bottarga* (a dried tuna roe delicacy). A good local dish is *polpettone alla napoletana* (a chunky meat loaf with ham, cheese, sultanas and pine nuts). In summer the terrace is a great place to eat, sitting looking over the garden. *Seats 120. Open 1300-1530, 2000-0030. Closed Mon & Aug, also Sun in Jul, Amex, Diners, Mastercard, Visa.*

Tel: (081) 5705422   Fax: (081) 5701546
Via Beccadelli 41 80125 Napoli   R

Neapolitan cooking with lashings of seafood is very much the order of the day in a grand hotel restaurant on the outskirts of the city on the road to Pozzuoli. The seafood pasta is definitely worth looking out for. The menu changes seasonally, but always has a predominance of fish. Wines are mainly Italian, with no house bottles. *Seats 150. Open 1230-1430, 1930-2130. Closed Aug, 24 Dec-7 Jan. Private garage. Amex, Diners, Mastercard, Visa.*

Tel: (6) 5818668   Fax: (6) 5884377
Piazza San Cosimato 40, 00153 Roma

Alberto Ciarla's elegant fish restaurant, regally decorated in red and black, is in the leafy Trastevere district across the Tiber from the centre of the city. His lifelong love of the sea and lively personality have inspired his team of cooks to produce seasonal menus (written in Roman dialect) which combine tradition with experimentation to great effect. Examples include *tagliolini cò le cozze er baccalà* (tagliolini with mussels and salt cod) and *salmone al gingembre* (gingered salmon). Alberto offers a fine list of Italian, French and New World bottles. His own wine from Castelli Romani is available by the glass. Although it's normally closed at lunchtime, the restaurant will open, on request, for large bookings. Parking is fearsomely difficult, even for Rome, and you should come by taxi or on foot. *Seats 70. Open 2000-0100. Closed Sun, 1-15 Jan, 15 days mid Aug. Amex, Diners, Mastercard, Visa.*

Tel: (6) 3223993   Fax: (6) 3221435
Via Ulisse Aldrovandi, 00197 Roma

Formerly one of the most expensive girls' colleges in Rome, this recently renovated hotel is excellently situated on the edge of the Borghese Gardens and close to the Via Veneto and Spanish Steps. The building dates from the end of the last century and among the elegantly decorated rooms are 12 suites furnished with antiques. Horse riding, tennis and swimming pool are available nearby. Service is attentive and friendly. ***Rooms** 130. Room service limited. Private parking. Banqueting facilities 600. Conference facilities 600. Piano bar. Amex, Diners, Mastercard, Visa.*

Tel: (6) 4821891   Fax: (6) 4828151
Via Sardegna 28, 00187 Roma

Federico Fellini used to be a regular at Andrea, at the top of the fashionable Via Veneto, and it retains an air of panache and elegance from the Dolce Vita days. The international cooking of the two chefs, one from Lazio and one from Sardinia, includes dishes such as *rombo con carciofi al forno* (turbot baked with artichoke) and *stinco di vitello con funghi porcini* (shin of veal with porcini mushrooms). Among the wines are Biondi-Santi, the original producer of one of Italy's most celebrated reds, Brunello di Montalcino. *Seats 100. Open 1230-1500, 1930-2300. Closed L Sat, all Sun, 2 weeks mid-Aug. Amex, Diners, Mastercard, Visa.*

Tel: (6) 6873233   Fax: (6) 6872300
Via Vitelleschi 34, 00193 Roma

This family-run hotel near to the Vatican is furnished in an eclectic modern style and offers facilities that seem too good to miss. If you can afford a suite you are invited to "relax in a maxi-jacuzzi: not as a guest but as a master of undiscovered pleasure". Half the rooms are smoke-free zones. There are wonderful views of the city from the roof-garden terrace. ***Rooms** 70. Room service 24hr. Valet parking L40,000. Banqueting facilities 180. Conference facilities 75. Terrace. Secretarial service. Amex, Diners, Mastercard, Visa.*

Tel: (6) 6874927   Fax: (6) 6865244
Piazza Farnese 50A, 00186 Roma

The wonderful building which houses Camponeschi dates from 1400 and its garden, bordering the piazza, is a great spot to eat and admire the surroundings. Chef Luciano Latorre has been here since the restaurant opened eight years ago and his menu changes daily. He claims that many of his dishes are original creations and, if you are lucky, you might sample *piccione farcito alle prugne con salsa di arzente ai mirtilli* (pigeon stuffed with prunes in a myrtle brandy sauce) or *astice caldo con salsa di aceto lamponi con tartufo nero* (warm lobster with a raspberry vinaigrette and black truffle). There are also some fine desserts such as *souffle alla vaniglia con salsa di bosco* (vanilla soufflé with a fruits of the forest coulis). You will find most Italian regional wines on the list. Although it is usually open only for dinner, office lunches can be accommodated on request. *Seats 70 (40 garden). Open 2000-0030. Closed Sun. Valet parking. Amex, Diners, Mastercard, Visa.*

Tel: (6) 5746318   Fax: (6) 5743816
Via Monte Testaccio 30, 00153 Roma

A certain enterprising Signorina Fermania once used offal from the slaughterhouse across the road to provide the first meals at the trattoria she opened in 1887. She went on to invent many dishes and Checchino remains true to its earthy roots in providing excellent, simple, meaty fare such as *coda all vaccinara* (oxtail) and *l'abbachio* (milk-fed lamb) *alla cacciatora and insalata di zampe di vitello* (leg of veal salad). The chef and owner Ninetta Ceccacci-Mariani is a descendant of the founder and manages to temper the gutsy food with a lightness of touch that produces exquisite flavours. Many of the classic dishes are permanently on the menu but look out for interesting seasonal variations. The cheeseboard includes *pecorino romano* (served from the block), goat's cheese from the Orvieto region and even good old Stilton. Virtually every wine produced in Lazio is on the 400-bottle list. *Seats 65 (20 outside). Open 1230-1500, 2000-2300. Closed D Sun (all Sun Jun-Sep), all Mon, Aug, Christmas week. Amex, Diners, Mastercard, Visa.*

Tel: (6) 6865435   Fax: (6) 6864874
Via della Conciliazone 33, 00192 Roma

The Della Rovere family, whose marvellous 15th-century palazzo is now occupied by the Columbus, supplied Cardinals and Popes to the Vatican. They didn't have far to walk to work: St Peter's is only 100 metres away. Recently refurbished, the decor is a happy blend of the old and the new. The colonnaded hall is decorated with wonderful frescoes (reputedly by Pinturicchio) and three of the rooms contain 16th-century furniture. All have air-conditioning and four are specially equipped for disabled guests. The three reception rooms (one of which opens on to a walled garden) make magnificent backdrops for entertaining. **Rooms** 97. *Room service limited. Private parking. Banqueting facilities 500. Conference facilities 200. Garden. Amex, Diners, Mastercard, Visa.*

Tel: (6) 6861105   Fax: (6) 6832106
Via del Portico d'Ottavia 21A-22, 00186 Roma

In 1923, Luigi Ceccarelli (nicknamed 'Giggetto') and his wife Ines brought back to life an old inn in the Jewish quarter and established a restaurant which has become an institution. It is now in the third generation of the family and Franco Ceccarelli continues to cook high-quality but simple Roman and Jewish dishes such as *carciofi all Giudea* (artichokes cooked the Jewish way-deep fried in olive oil). Other specialities are *filetti di baccalà spinati* (fried salt cod fillets) and *fiori di zucchini ripieni* (fried courgette flowers filled with mozzarella and anchovies). If you are feeling brave, try *fritto di cervello, funghi, carciofi, zucchine* (fried brain, mushrooms, artichokes, courgettes). Wines from Piedmont and Tuscany are the most popular. **Seats** 200 (outside 100). *Open 1230-1530, 1930-2300. Closed Mon, 1st 2 weeks Aug. Amex, Diners, Mastercard, Visa.*

Tel: (6) 67331   Fax: (6) 6784213
Via Sistina 67-69, 00187 Roma

Hungarian architect Jozef Vago designed and rebuilt this stylish hotel in 1925 (and was also one of those responsible for the League of Nations building in Geneva) although the main part of the building dates from the 1700s. Situated at the top of the Spanish Steps, it affords wonderful views over the city from the terrace. Rooms are a successful blend of the antique and modern furnishings. The restaurant is located in a lovely inner courtyard. **Rooms** 192. *Room service limited. Banqueting facilities 100. Conference facilities 110. Terrace. Hair salon. Shopping arcade. Bureau de change. Amex, Diners, Mastercard, Visa.*

Tel: (6) 6780441   Fax: (6) 6840689
Piazza della Rotonda 63, 00186 Roma

Looking out over the small piazza to the mighty Pantheon beyond, you will experience the same sense of existential well-being that must have been felt by Sartre and de Beauvoir when they stayed at this hotel. The loveliness of the location is matched by the quality of the accommodation. Comfort and simplicity are combined with white marble and terracotta floors creating a clean, airy atmosphere. All rooms are air-conditioned and have carved wooden beds. This is one of the oldest hostelries in Europe (the first inn opened here in 1476) but the present hotel was extensively modernised a few years ago. The inner courtyard is a lovely spot for taking breakfast. *Rooms 26. Room service 24hr. Bureau de change. Amex, Diners, Mastercard, Visa.*

Tel: (6) 8804503   Fax: (6) 8804495
Via Salaria 1223, 00138 Roma

With his own interpretation of classical Roman cuisine, the chef at L'Elite has carved out a niche for this charming restaurant. Opened in the 50s, the building with its 5m-high bow windows and indoor pyramid-shaped fountain, was designed by the owner and a renowned architect and has been written about in several architectural magazines. Inside, the two dining-rooms – the aquarium room and the mermaid room - are decorated with sea-blue fabric wallpaper with painted waves and aquaria full of weird and wonderful fish. Classic Roman dishes like *rigatoni con la pajata* (pasta with calf's offal in tomato sauce) and *coda alla vaccinara* (oxtail) are served along with some outstanding fish dishes: *leone marino* (steamed shellfish served with six different sauces, *minestra all'antica civitavecchia* (a secret fisherman's recipe – bean and seafood soup) and *tagliolini alla vesuviana* (pasta with shellfish and molluscs flambéd in front of the customer).They even smoke and marinate their own salmon. Wines are almost exclusively Italian, with an emphasis on Sicily and Lazio. *Seats 150. Open 1230-1500, 1930-2300. Closed Sun, 8-28 Aug, 23 Dec-7 Jan. Private parking. Amex, Diners, Mastercard, Visa.*

Tel: (6) 6792446   Fax: (6) 6786479
Via Tor de' Conti 25, 00184 Roma

There are reminders of the Imperial past all around this hotel. There is a fine view over the magnificent old Forum from the fifth-floor roof garden. The ancient disused baths Terme di Caracalla nearby are ideal for jogging and strolling. Although the hotel is only just over 30 years old the building dates back to the 16th century. Rooms are decorated classically with much Louis XVI-style furniture in evidence, and half of them are designated non-smoking. *Rooms 78. Room service limited. Private parking L40,000. Banqueting facilities 100. Conference facilities 60. Roof garden. Bureau de change. Amex, Diners, Mastercard, Visa.*

Tel: (6) 6782651   Fax: (6) 6789991
Piazza Trinità dei Monti 6, 00187 Roma

The Hassler enjoys a wonderful location at the top of the Spanish Steps, next to the Trinità dei Monti. It has been run by the Swiss Wirth family since before the Second World War and they have successfully created a stylish yet friendly and personal atmosphere. If you are making an occasion of it, stay in the Penthouse Suite with its 18th-century writing desk, paintings, Venetian mirrors, hand-cut crystal chandeliers, silk curtains and Louis XV chairs. There is a fine view over the city from the roof restaurant. Requisitioned by US forces during the war, the Hassler remains particularly popular with American visitors. *Rooms 101. Room service limited. Private parking. Banqueting facilities 100. Conference facilities 100. Hairdresser. Amex, Diners, Mastercard, Visa.*

Tel: (6) 3220404   Fax: (6) 3220405
Via Giuseppe de Notaris 5, 00197 Roma

The district to the north of the Borghese Gardens is one of the most exclusive in the city. It is a fitting setting for this wonderful villa, which feels more like a private house than a hotel. Bookcases, antiques and oil paintings line the public rooms and the air-conditioned bedrooms (and nine apartments) are decorated in soothing tones with hand-painted Florentine-style white furniture. Although recreational facilities are limited there is a sports centre nearby and private tours of Rome can be arranged on request. The piano bar is open until 2am and is famed for its 'Le Jardin' champagne cocktail. *Rooms 37. Room service limited. Banqueting facilities 100. Conference facilities 80. Bureau de change. Amex, Diners, Mastercard, Visa.*

This marvellous restaurant serves some of the most exquisite food in the city. The surroundings, in keeping with the hotel, are plush but personal. Elaborate flower arrangements, green tablecloths, white napkins, silverware and marble columns help to create the atmosphere of a grand private house. Antonio Sciullo has been presiding over his team of assistants in the kitchen for ten years and has perfected a highly personal cuisine.

See over

The menu changes with the seasons but could begin with a salad of rabbit stuffed with beetroot and cherries or lobster salad with bottarga vinaigrette. Pasta dishes include ravioli filled with ricotta and aubergine with a tomato and basil sauce, and risotto of duck strips, asparagus and provolone cheese. The market dictates which fish will be served but examples are turbot in a potato crust with a purée of white beans, and fried prawns in a sesame batter. Meat dishes are similarly appetising: pork fillet with honey and ginger and a green pea ravioli, for instance. Desserts are also superb. If you get a chance, try the soufflé of cream and prunes in armagnac with whole-wheat bread ice-cream and Gianduia sauce. The wine cellar boasts an extraordinary 50,000 bottles. As you might expect, virtually every major producer is represented, with a particular strong showing of local produce. An example is wine from Colle Picchioni south of Rome, where the best Marino white is made. *Seats* 60. *Open 1230-1430, 2000-2230. Closed Sun (except for residents), 3 weeks in Aug, Easter week, Christmas week.*

ROME   Majestic   L600,000

Tel: (6) 486841   Fax: (6) 4880984
Via Veneto 50, 00187 Roma

The Majestic is proud to have been the first hotel built on the fashionable Via Veneto, in 1889. A century later the ever-popular architect Sturchio completely stripped it down and revamped it, enhancing the original marble and wood with art deco fittings and furniture. The Ninfa bar, one of Rome's best known, has recently opened again after almost ten years of refurbishment. *Rooms* 100. *Room service limited. Valet parking L40,000. Banqueting facilities 150. Conference facilities 150. Terrace. Bureau de change. News kiosk. Amex, Diners, Mastercard, Visa.*

ROME   Quinzi Gabrielli   L130,000

Tel: (6) 6879389   Fax: (6) 6874940
Via delle Coppelle 5, 00187 Roma

You expect Italians to take their food seriously. This restaurant owns two boats which fish exclusively for them, one on the Lazio coast, one on the Tuscan. If they aren't able to fish or the catch isn't up to standard, the restaurant closes. That is taking food seriously. Oysters are caught off France, crustaceans off Sardinia. The short menu changes seasonally and might feature orata in crosta di sale marino (gilt-head with a sea-salt crust). Wines include the excellent Franciacorta Bellavista from Lombardy. The walls are painted to represent the terrace of a villa looking out to sea. *Seats* 40 *(garden 25). Open 2000-2400. Closed Sun, Aug. Amex, Diners, Mastercard, Visa.*

ROME   Rosetta   L260,000

Tel: (6) 6861002   Fax: (6) 6872852
Via della Rosetta 8-9, 00186 Roma

The Riccoli family opened Rome's first fish-only restaurant 35 years ago and Massimo Riccoli continues to cook a superb range of imaginative seafood dishes. Specialities include asparagus and scampi salad, *insalata di piccoli calimari al aceto balsamico* (salad of baby squid in balsamic vinegar) and *spaghetti con scampi, fiori di zucca e peccorino* (spaghetti with scampi, courgette flowers and pecorino cheese). Don't miss out on the home-made desserts such as ricotta and honey tart. The restaurant is in a 19th-century house, decorated in cosy French bistro style, close to the Pantheon. *Seats* 50. *Open 1300-1500, 1930-2330. Closed L Sat, last 3 weeks Aug. Private parking. Amex, Diners, Mastercard, Visa.*

ROME   Sabatini   L170,000

Tel: (6) 5818307   Fax: (6) 5898386
Vicolo Santa Maria in Trastevere 18, 00153 Roma

Head Chef Pio de Castro has worked at this famous restaurant since it opened and is nearing 40 years of service. Although often considered a tourist trap because of its excellent location, Sabatini is also patronised by the Italians, glitterati and business folk alike. Set menus range in price from L75,000 to L105,000 and, although not particularly imaginative, include such Italian classics as *saltimbocca alla romana* (veal and parma ham in Marsala sauce) and *spaghetti alle vongole* (clams). Parking is very difficult in this area. There is a toilet for the disabled. *Seats* 200 *(outside 140). Open 1230-1400, 1930-2400. Closed 1-20 Aug, 23-27 Dec. Amex, Diners, Mastercard, Visa.*

ROME   Sans Souci   L240,000

Tel: (6) 4821814   Fax: (6) 4821771
Via Sicilia 20, 00175 Roma

This hip restaurant, with its wooden panelling and 17th-century oils, is a favourite for well-heeled, well-connected locals. The food is a melding of Italian and French with an emphasis on the finest ingredients. Lamb is imported from Normandy, Aberdeen Angus beef from Scotland, and fresh fish comes direct from the Mediterranean. All the pasta is home-made and soufflés, both savoury and sweet, are a speciality (try the cheese and truffle soufflé if it's available). The fish terrine is also excellent. Wines include good French, Australian and Californian bottles. *Seats 80. Open 2000-0130. Closed Mon, 6-31 Aug. Valet parking. Amex, Diners, Mastercard, Visa.*

ROME   Ai Tre Scalini di Rossana e Matteo   L140,000

Tel: (6) 7096309   Fax: (6) 7002835
Via dei Santi Quattro 30, 00184 Roma

The head chef, Rossana, never had any formal training as a chef (she studied for an engineering degree instead) but back in 1968 she decided to open this restaurant near the Colosseum, with some close friends. Her menu is varied and imaginative, ranging from classical Italian and regional dishes to international specialities, all based on the pick of the day's market. One fixed price menu at L30,000. Wines from Tuscany, Piedmont and Lazio are most prominent. *Seats 35. Open 1230-1500, 1930-2400. Closed Mon, last 3 weeks Aug. Amex, Diners, Mastercard, Visa.*

ROME   Valadier   L270,000

Tel: (6) 3611998   Fax: (6) 3610559
Via della Fontanella 15, 00187 Roma

Respectability has only come lately to the building that is now the Valadier hotel. From 1652 to 1950 it enjoyed a colourful history as a brothel with an up-market clientele. In 1991 it was extensively redesigned, rebuilt and refurbished in art deco style and now attracts a rather more respectable, still up-market clientele. The piano bar is open until 2am. **Rooms** *38. Room service 24hr. Valet parking L40,000. Banqueting facilities 80. Conference facilities 40. Secretarial service. Roof garden. Amex, Diners, Mastercard, Visa.*

THE APARTMENT SERVICE
Tel in UK (0181) 748 4207   Fax (0181) 748 3972
The Apartment Service will find you the right apartment worldwide to suit your needs, whether you are on a short or long-term stay. A 96-page colour catalogue is free on request. All budgets are catered for.

Turin

TURIN   Del Cambio   L205,000

Tel: (011) 546690   Fax: (011) 535282
Piazza Carignano 2 10123 Torino

This is one of the oldest restaurants in Italy, dating from the 18th century, and rather appropriately is opposite the Renaissance museum in a quiet city square. The decor reflects some of the building's ancient character, with a stylish mix of classical and baroque with much rich velvet in evidence as well as polished wood, old gilt-framed mirrors, and beautiful frescos on the ceilings. Every Friday there is music from a string quartet. Specialising in the cooking of the region, the menu offers a daily-changing choice of dishes such as spinach lasagne with a walnut and marjoram sauce, sole grilled with Piedmont herbs, lamb cutlets coated in sesame seeds, warm carpaccio with parmesan and veal kidneys in brandy. The pasta is home-made and delicious. Desserts could include the very special Muscat jelly with wild strawberries and zabaglione. The excellent wine list features mainly Piedmontese wines wtih Barbaresco vintages going back to 1947. Set meal L90,000. *Seats 90. Open 1200-1430, 1945-2230. Closed Sun, 28 Jul-28 Aug. Public parking. Amex, Diners, Mastercard, Visa.*

Tel: (011) 8179380   Fax: (011) 887260
Via Carlo Alberto 45 10123 Torino

Converted from a wine shop 50 years ago, the restaurant is located in a beautiful 17th-century palazzo. The chef, Carlo Bagatin, is loyal to his Piedmontese roots, but has been heavily influenced by the time he spent working at the Bristol in Paris. The menu revolves around a selection of specialities of the locality. There is plenty of choice and the dishes, though traditional in character, have modern touches including very attractive presentation. Artichoke tart with melted cheese, lightly-curried risotto with prawns and a number of super home-made pasta dishes are offered as first courses. Main dishes begin with a classic bollito misto served with a selection of Piedmontese sauces and garnishes and continues with excellent renditions of civet of hare with polenta and Provençal lamb cutlets. Other dishes include a slice of salmon with pink peppercorns and paprika, steamed fillets of sole with fresh tomato, duck breast with a Barbaresco sauce. Finanziera torinese con piccole quenelle di carne (small beef quenelles) is a house speciality. Wines are healthily split between well-known Italian and French names, with a very palatable French house Chardonnay. *Seats 80. Open 1230-1430, 1930-2300. Closed Sun. Amex, Diners, Mastercard, Visa.*

Tel: (011) 5627483   Fax: (011) 543610
Piazza San Carlo 157 10123 Torino

This is a restaurant whose specialities are very much the dishes of the surrounding Piedmont region, which are presented on a short, seasonal carte. Begin with a terrine of lobster tails with baby spring vegetables and a shellfish sauce or a plate of Tyrolean cured meats with herb-flavoured wild boar and fresh broad beans. To follow, choose from
a middle course of Saltena asparagus spears on a risotto of Selezione Tenuta Castello rice or snail-filled pasta with a wonderful pesto sauce. Main dishes include duck breast with stuffed pears in mulled wine, wild turkey roulades and farm-reared veal in a white stock with caramelised onions. For dessert there's lemon meringue tart, orange terrine with Grand Marnier jelly and a chocolate mousse flavoured with rum. *Seats 65. Open 1230-1430, 2000-2230. Closed L Sat, all Sun, 10-25 Aug. Amex, Diners, Mastercard, Visa.*

Tel: (011) 5625511   Fax: (011) 5612187
Via Sacchi 8 10128 Torino

The hotel is located near the main railway station and has been in the same family ownership since 1872. Built in the last century, the building retains some of its original and very stylish decor. Early 18th-century French furniture with silks and other fine fabrics on the walls create a refined and luxurious ambience. Bathrooms are spacious and beautifully appointed with white marble. *Rooms 123. Room service limited. Cable/satellite TV. Amex, Mastercard, Visa.*

Tel: (011) 3179657   Fax: (011) 3179191
Corso Unione Sovietica 244 10125 Torino

An excellent restaurant to sample the region's typical dishes. The menu offers a very good choice of Nothern Italian specialities given a light, modern treatment. Begin with, for instance, warm carpaccio of grouper with sunflower seeds, artichokes with pistachios and parmesan, stuffed courgette flowers or a pastry case filled with tripe and barley. For pasta and soup there's tagliolini with peas and bacon, pasta stuffed with borage and served with cherry tomatoes and a broth of spelt and beans. Main dishes range from a swordfish chateaubriand and sea bass with artichokes, potatoes and olives to herbed lamb cutlets and rib of beef with coarse salt and rosemary. Desserts are no less interesting, with warm apple tart with a chocolate mousse and warmed strawberries with cream among the possibilities. *Seats 70. Open 1230-1500, 1930-2330. Closed Mon, 1st 3 weeks Aug. Amex, Diners, Mastercard, Visa.*

Opening times are often liable to change at short notice, so it's always best to book.

Tel: (011) 537047   Fax: (011) 530391
Corso Re Umberto 21 10128 Torino

An elegant and stylish restaurant with a quiet, romantic ambience located overlooking Piazza Solferino. It is decorated in warm, muted colours with 19th-century Murano crystal chandeliers suspended from the ceilings and fine oil paintings on the walls. There's a smart American bar (with occasional live music entertainment) where pre-dinner drinks and orders are taken. The family who own the restaurant have been in the business for three generations and took over the running of this place in 1970. The father is the chef and offers a menu that combines a classical repertoire with some regional specialities. Noteworthy dishes are *insalata alla langarola*, a salad with beef fillet, hazelnuts and toma d'Alba cheese, flaky pastry with melted cheese and asparagus tips, pasta with duck ragù, veal tournedos with a Barolo sauce and, for dessert, a champagne torte with an orange sauce. There are usually three menus to choose from-a seasonally-changing carte, a fish menu and a *menu degustazione* (tasting menu). Occasionally they also offer a special menu of a well-balanced selection of the dishes of a particular region of Italy. The wine list is mainly Italian though with a few French and German vintages too. *Seats 45. Open 1200-1500, 2000-2400. Closed L Sat, all Sun, 10-20 Aug. Amex, Mastercard, Visa.*

Tel: (0141) 966012   Fax: (0141) 966012
Piazza Umberto I 27 Costiglione D'Asti

Lidia Alciati cooks in the kitchen now helped by one of her sons while husband, Guido, oversees the dining-room. She never had any formal training; instead she learnt the art of cooking from her mother and today offers superb examples of traditional Piedmontese food in a fine restaurant which as well as being in a quiet square has a glass frontage overlooking a wooded park. Decor is mainly classical, with antique furniture, but there are a few abstract paintings on the walls. This, perhaps, reflects the nature of the menu, which incorporates modern influences with the classic cuisine of the region. Menus change with the seasons. From a late spring and summer menu come starters such as agnolotti-a local variant of ravioli, here served with a ragù from shin of ham-or baked courgette flowers with a tomato mayonnaise, followed perhaps by a rabbit galantine with herbs while in the colder seasons you might well find stracotto, braised beef in red wine. To finish there are fine local cheeses as well as dainty petits fours and a fruit compote with cherries. From mid-September to December a speciality to look out for here are the dishes using the splendid white truffles from the region. *Seats 50. Open D only 2000-2200. Closed 20 Dec-10 Jan, 1-20 Aug. Amex, Diners, Mastercard, Visa.*

> Meal prices for 2 are based on à la carte menus. When set menus are available, prices will often be lower.

Tel: (041) 5224121   Fax: (041) 5289857
Campo San Fantin 1983 Venezia

Housed in an old and historic palace, the restaurant was established in 1720 and has been in the same family ownership since 1921. The menu appears lengthy but is in four languages. It mixes international and local dishes, with liver paté flavoured with port and consommé with sherry alongside Venetian bean and pasta soup, spaghetti with lobster and breast of duck with black truffles. The fish and seafood risotto is a popular dish for two people and takes 20 minutes to prepare. To finish, a selection of home-made desserts as well as crepes Suzette with Grand Marnier. Also featured are a number of good set menus priced from L66,000. *Seats 120. Open 1200-1430, 1900-2400. Closed L Wed, all Tue. Amex, Diners, Mastercard, Visa.*

Tel: (041) 5265921 Fax: (041) 5260113
Lungomare Marconi 17 30126 Lido di Venezia   H

Occupying a splendid location on the Lido, this is a grand hotel in every sense of the word.
The rooms are luxurious, with lavish curtains, high ceilings and fine furniture. The
receptions rooms too, are elegant in the style of the Belle Epoque. There are splendid
views from the terrace, down on to the hotel's own private beach. The sports facilities,
especially water sports, golf and riding are excellent. Thomas Mann immortalised the hotel
in his book, Death in Venice, which was subsequently made into a film by Visconti who,
as in the book, set the action around the hotel. *Rooms 191. Room service all day.*
Theatre-style conference facilities for up to 400. Outdoor swimming pool. Tennis. Golf. Riding.
Waterskiing. Windsurfing. Beach. Beauty salon. Sauna. Massage. Closed Oct-Mar.
Private parking. Amex, Mastercard, Visa.

Tel: (041) 5208901 Fax: (041) 5207131
Calle Larga 22 Marzo 2397 Venezia   R

This is the restaurant of the Hotel Saturnia-International, which has been in the same
family ownership for three generations. Both are housed in a building which dates from the
early 14th-century, when it was the private home of Doge Pisani. The restaurant's decor is
unusual, themed on Christopher Columbus and boats, with a wooden floor and walls, even
a rudder. Illuminated by soft candle-light and soothed with gentle background music, the
place has a warm, romantic atmosphere. In summer the garden provides a beautiful location
for alfresco dining. The menu is lengthy, with a mix of international dishes as well as
Venetian specialities. The latter include squid ink risotto, calf's liver with polenta, bigoli
(large pasta) with anchovies and onion sauce and Adriatic sea bass. A speciality is their
filetto alla Caravella – beef fillet with mustard, cognac and cream. Sweets include the
familiar but delicious zabaglione as well as a nougat semifreddo with Grand Marnier.
Seats 80. Open 1200-1500, 1900-2400. Amex, Mastercard, Visa.

Tel: (041) 5207744 Fax: (041) 5203930
Giudecca 10 30133 Venezia   HR

A short vaporetto trip across from St Mark's Square, the Cipriani is almost as much
a Venetian landmark as the Doge's Palace or the Rialto Bridge. Located on the Giudecca
island, the hotel has views in all directions: of the lagoon, the Palladian San Giorgio
Maggiore, the vineyards and the doomed Redentore. Giuseppe Cipriani opened it in the
late 50s with the Guinness family and apart from the having up-to-date facilities little has
changed since those early days. Almost unrivalled standards of service, luxury and comfort
are provided in this tranquil and beautiful setting. The beige-pink stucco, terracotta-tiled
roofs and deep green shutters have a soft, worn and uniquely Italian look; while the rooms
have been classically redecorated in keeping with the building itself. Meals are still normally
eaten alfresco, on three terraces spread alongside the waterfront. In the Palazzo Vendramin
next door, also owned by the Cipriani, guests can stay in one of the nine apartments.
Rooms 104. Closed Nov-Feb. Room service 24hrs. Satellite TV. Theatre-style conference
facilities for up to 100. Olympic-sized swimming pool. Tennis. Sauna. Yacht. Amex, Diners,
Mastercard, Visa.

An elegant restaurant that offers a selection of modern and sophisticated interpretations of
Venetian classics with plenty of choice to fire the palate.The antipasti include the world-
famous carpaccio invented at Harry's Bar, one of owner Arrigo Cipriani's other landmark
restaurants. The menu also features creations such as ravioli filled with artichokes and
mascarpone served with sizzling butter, small penne sautéed with rosemary-scented lamb
ragù, sautéed fillets of John Dory with asparagus tips and Adriatic shellfish and sliced fillet
of beef with a spicy spinach purée. The large wine list is predominantly Italian, with a good
house red and white. *Seats 130. Open 1230-1500, 2000-2230.*

Meal prices for 2 are based on à la carte menus. When set menus are
available, prices will often be lower.

Tel: (041) 5226480   Fax: (041) 5200208
Castello 4196 Venezia

The Danieli opened as a hotel at the beginning of the last century. The original building dates back to the late 14th century when Doge Dandolo built it as a palazzo for visiting dignitaries. It now comprises three distinct but connected buildings. The central one is the original palazzo, and retains its beautiful facade, while on the inside it is furnished in great style with colourful mosaics, a columned entrance hall with a gold frieze and splendid antique Venetian furniture. To one side is an 18th-century building furnished with handsome painted furniture while on the other is the Danielino, built in the 40s and therefore lacking some of the style and character of the other two. Conferences for up to 130 are held in a beautiful room lined with red damask – the same colour as a doge's hat. *Rooms 231. Room service all day. Theatre-style conference facilities for to 200. Secretarial/translation services. Amex, Mastercard, Visa.*

Tel: (041) 5260201   Fax: (041) 5267276
Lungomare Marconi 41 30126 Lido di Venezia

Very much a de luxe resort hotel, the Excelsior is also a major conference venue as well as being the central location of the annual Venice film festival. Built at the turn of the century it has splendid gardens, a swimming pool, and 2km of sandy beach dotted with hundreds of beach huts. Being on the beach does, of course, make the atmosphere more relaxed, but this hotel is still rather grand with its '1001 nights-style' Moorish decor. Everything is on a vast scale, with theatre-style conference facilities for up to 500, in a new conference centre with nine halls. The rooms are light and cool, reflecting the colours of the Italian summer, the Arab influences extending to the style of furniture, and the room decor. Facilities are superb, with everything from air-conditioning and safes to multilingual information services available. *Rooms 197. Room service 24hrs. Satellite TV. Tennis. Swimming pool. Water sports. Beach. Closed Nov-Mar. Private parking. Amex, Diners, Mastercard, Visa.*

Tel: (041) 5205844   Fax: (041) 5228217
Calle Larga 22 Marzo 2283/a 30124 Venezia

Family-owned and run, the hotel lives up to its name, having a lovely, flower-filled garden and a very traditional ambience that is both relaxed and friendly. Decor throughout is attractively old-fashioned but quite simple. There are few modern amenities, some rooms having TVs and hairdryers, all are air-conditioned. Bathrooms, with bidets, have either bath-tubs or showers. Although it is off one of the main routes west of St Mark's Square the hotel enjoys a surprisingly quiet location. *Rooms 44. Room service 24hrs. Garden. Amex, Diners, Mastercard, Visa.*

Tel: (041) 5289299   Fax: 3 (041) 5208041
Piazza San Marco 121 30100 Venezia

A truly historic café where Mr Quadri served the first cup of coffee in 1725, the café proper opening some 40 years later. It wasn't until after the First World War that it became a restaurant as well. This is a grandiose and splendid room with mirror and burgundy damask lined walls, gilt beamed ceilings from which hang Murano crystal floral chandeliers. The furniture in the café is Baroque and paintings from the Tintoretto school hang on the pale green stucco walls. The barman here-Massimo Barnabei can compose any cocktail. Food is limited to six lunchtime dishes including carpaccio, blinis with brie and walnuts and spaghetti with tomato and basil. The restaurant, the only one in St Mark's Square, offers a selection of well-prepared, sophisticated classic Italian dishes including Venetian specialities. Typical items from a seasonally changing menu are marinated swordfish with dill and coriander seeds, tagliatelle with peas, shrimps and basil, seafood risotto, squid-ink spaghetti, calf's liver with onions and stewed cuttlefish with grilled polenta. Desserts include a hazelnut ice cream baked under a meringue crust and delicios fresh fruit confections. A few French and German wines supplement a comprehensive Italian list. *Seats 80. Café Open 1000-2400. Closed Mon. Nov-mid May. Restaurant L 1030-1500 D 1930-2315. Closed Mon, L mid Jun-mid Aug. Amex, Mastercard, Visa.*

Tel: (041) 794611   Fax: (041) 5200942
Campo Santa Maria del Giglio 2467 30124 Venezia

Located just five minutes from St Mark's Square in the heart of the city, the hotel enjoys an incomparable view of the Grand Canal. This is another CIGA hotel and one of their most splendid. The Doge Andrea Gritti built it in the 15th century as his private residence. Since it became a hotel in 1948, Queen Elizabeth II has stayed and Hemingway has lived here and there's a suite bearing his name. Public rooms are beautifully decorated with very fine artwork on the walls including a large portrait of the Doge. The bedrooms are elegantly traditional with 18th-century antiques, and original Venetian floors have been retained in some. Modern amenities include air-conditioning, satellite TV and a mini-bar in the rooms and full secretarial services from the hotel's business centre. There is also a private beach with sporting facilities and an outdoor swimming pool at the Venice Lido. *Rooms 84. Theatre-style conference facilities for up to 120. Secretarial/translation services. Amex, Mastercard, Visa.*

Tel: (041) 5285777   Fax: (041) 5208822
Calle Vallaresso 1323 30124 Venezia

Arrigo Cipriani's world-renowned restaurant is a must on any gourmet's itinerary to this magical city. The champagne and peach juice cocktail, Bellini, was invented here as was another favourite, currently very much in vogue, carpaccio of beef. Traditional Venetian cooking is the mainstay of the kitchen, with risotto dishes being one of the house specialities, notably, squid ink risotto. Other specialities include Venetian-style calf's liver, and scampi thermidor. Light snacks and some truly excellent cocktails are served in the bar. There's also a splendid wine list featuring a fine selection, mostly from the north of Italy. *Seats 90. Open 1030-2300. Closed Mon (Nov-Feb). Amex, Diners, Mastercard, Visa.*

Tel: (041) 5200533   Fax: (041) 5225032
Riva degli Schiavoni 30122 Venezia

Originally there were two hotels, the Londres and the D'Angleterre, built in 1858. They were merged to become the Londra Palace just after the last World War. One of the bedrooms features a collection of Tchaikovsky memorabilia as it was in that room that he stayed and composed his Fourth Symphony. Other rooms are furnished in 19th-century Biedermaier style and are full of character, with a fine collection of pictures, fragments of antique fabrics, letters and photographs of other famous guests. Most of the bathrooms have jacuzzis. *Rooms 54. Room service all day. Theatre-style conference facilities for up to 80. Amex, Mastercard, Visa.*

Tel: (041) 5260227   Fax: (041) 5260726
Via Quattro Fontane 16 30126 Lido di Venezia

Looking for all the world like a Dolomite chalet, the hotel occupies a secluded position among a wealth of shrubs and acacia trees. It was originally a Venetian family's summer home and it still retains much homely charm; indeed the majority of guests come here for the tranquillity of the surroundings. The rooms are rather old-fashioned, though they do have TVs. All are furnished with beautiful chintzy fabrics. Most of the staff, including the concierge, have been here a great number of years, and organise the place as they would their own home. The hotel doesn't have a lift and there are 66 steps up to the third floor, from where there are excellent views. Accessible only by small cars which can come over on the ferry. No room service. *Rooms 60. Closed Nov-Apr. Private parking. Amex, Mastercard, Visa.*

Tel: (041) 730150   Fax:(041) 735433
Piazza Santa Fosca 30012 Torcello

Take the vaporetto from Fondamenta Nuove on the north shore for the 45-minute crossing to this island in the Venetian lagoon. The restaurant, an offshoot of *Harry's Bar* (qv), has been going since 1938. One of its finer features is the opportunity for alfresco dining in the large, well-tended garden. As well as a selection of well-balanced and reasonably priced fixed menus (from L70,000) there is a comprehensive carte of modern Venetian dishes. Seafood dominates, ranging from gratinated scallops with hollandaise, crab dressed with olive oil and lemon, and squid ink risotto to grilled bream, monkfish flavoured with thyme and curried scampi with pilaff rice. The few simple meat dishes include fillet of beef with green peppercorns and veal escalope with peas. The wine list specialises in carefully selected vintages from Northern Italy and excellent coffee concludes an enjoyable experience. *Seats 250. Open 1200-1500, 1900-2100. Closed Tue, Jan-mid Feb. Amex, Visa.*

There are six smart bedrooms,the three with double beds each with a fine sitting-room. While no TV is provided there are books and on sunny days one can amble round the gardens. All rooms are air-conditioned and bathrooms are up-to-date, all with bath, shower and bidet. *Half-board terms only.

Tel: (0543) 767471   Fax: (0543) 766625
Via Matteotti 38 47011 Castrocaro Terme Forli

Here, in a popular and ancient spa town in the Apennine foothills, Gianfranco Bolognesi, his wife Bruna and head chef Marco Cavallucci have together created one of Italy's very best restaurants. In summer, you dine alfresco under a cool, leafy canopy-hence the name La Frasca (leafy, evergreen bough), a sign used once upon a time by inns. Otherwise, the bar and dining-rooms of the solidly-built stone house offer cosy, traditional splendour. The best of local produce – game, white and red meats, truffles (predominantly white), diverse mushrooms, all manner of cheeses from the region and country aplenty as well as seafood direct from the coast, 40-odd kilometres away, and not forgetting the specially hand-made breads and pasta – is all fashioned into the most sublime dishes. The cooking follows the principles of Artusi, but with modern, lighter touches and shorter cooking times, the elimination of heavy sauces and a reduction and variation in the quantity of fats and seasonings used. This is cooking of the very highest level, where flavours and textures are so carefully married that the palate and senses are transported almost into a state of rapture. Yet all is so unbelievably simple and straightforward. As well as a short carte there are fixed-price menus including il Sapore della Tradizione (the taste of tradition) – a meat menu, and il Profumo del Mare e dell'Orto (the perfumes of the sea and garden) an exquisite seafood menu of unsurpassable quality. Each comprises six beautifully-balanced courses. For lunch there's a relatively inexpensive three-course set meal-the cheaper menus are only available to the whole table. A shortish carte is also offered. A meat menu from late spring began with rabbit terrine with an onion marmalade flavoured with balsamic vinegar followed by a cream of asparagus with *passatelli* (a local pasta speciality), then a dish of ravioli of an unusual sheep's cheese (one-month-old cheese is sealed and buried in truffle holes during August and then dug up in November). The ravioli were served with a yellow pepper sauce. Main course was truffled lamb cutlets with a gratin of potatoes and leeks. Dessert was a William pear pastry with an Amaretto mousse which together with a marvellous selection of petits fours with fine coffee made a perfect ending to a perfect meal. Mr Bolognesi, a top sommelier, has amassed an amazing wine cellar including a superb selection of the finest Italian vintages. *Seats 60. Open 1215-1430, 2000-2200. Closed Mon, 1st 2 weeks Aug, 1st 3 weeks Jan. Amex, Diners, Mastercard, Visa.*

There are two truly magnificent apartments some 200 metres away in a converted ancient fortress which have been fitted out in a truly luxurious manner. One is furnished in great style with furniture by some of Italy's top designers, while the other features beautiful 19th-century pieces from Romagna. Both have every conceivable comfort, with private terraces, spacious lounges, phone, radio and TV as well as modern kitchens. Bathrooms have jacuzzi tubs and are well-equipped and very up-to-date.

Scotch Beef Club Members: Italy

VAL D'AOSTA
AOSTA: Hotel Ristorante Europe
COURMAYEUR: Ristorante Hotel
Cresta et Duc
SAINT VINCENT: Ristorante
Le Grenier

PIEMONTE
BIELLA: Ristorante Prinz Grill
Da Beppe E Teresio
CUORGNE: Hotel Astoria
TORRE CANAVESE: Italia
TURIN: Jolly Hotel Il Ligure Rist.
Il Birichino
TURIN: Jolly Hotel Principi di
Piemonte Rist. Il Gentilom
TURIN: Jolly Hotel Ambasciatori
Rist. Il Diplomatico
TURIN: Ristorante Neuv Caval 'D
Brons

LOMBARDIA
ABBIATEGRASO: Ristorante
Napoleone
MEXXANINO: Ristorante
Dell'Angelo
MILAN: Jolly Hotel President Rist.
Il Verziere
MILAN: Jolly Hotel Touring Rist.
Amadeus
MILANO 2 SEGRATE: Jolly Hotel
Rist. I Papaveri
MILANOFIORI ASSAGO: Jolly Hotel
Milanofiori Rist. Quadrifoglio
MIRABELLO DI CANTU: Ristorante
La Querce
OLGIATE OLONA: Ristorante Idea
Verde
PAVIA: Locanda Vecchia Pavia
RHO: Al Rhotaia

FRIULI V.G.
CORNO DI ROSAZZO: Il Mulino
FONTANAFREDDA: Fassina
MAGNANO IN RIVERA: Hotel
Green
OPICINA (TS): Diana
PORDENONE: Hotel Palace
RAGOGNA: Locanda Vuanello
TARVISIO: Italia

TRIESTE: Hosteria Bellavista
TRIESTE: Jolly Hotel Rist. Cavour

TRENTINO
ARCO: Hotel Villa delle Rose
GAVAZZO DI TENNO: Albergo
Stella d'Italia
MOENA: Ristorante Ja Navalge
TRENTO: Chiesa

LIGURIA
CHIAVARI: Antica Osteria da U Dria
GENOVA: Jolly Hotel Plaza Rist.
Villetta di Negro
MONTEROSSO AL MARE: Hotel
La Spiaggia
LA SPEZIA: Jolly Hotel Rist.
Del Golfo

VENETO
ALTAVILLA VICENTINA:
Al Passeggio/Essevi
CADEGLIOPPI: Casa di Valle
CORNEDO: 2 Platani
CORTINA: Ristorante Grill Bahia
FOLLINA: Al Caminetto
GIAVERA DEL MONTELLO:
La Baita
MIANE: Da Gigetto
MOSSANO: Antica Trattoria
Agli Olmi
NERVESA DELLA BATTAGLIA:
Da Roberto Miron
ODERZO: Ristorante al Boschetto
Da Toni
SCHIO: For a Man
SOLIGHETTO: Locanda da Lino
TREVISO: Albergo Beccherie
VALDAGNO: Al Pezzo
VERONA: Torcoloti
VICENZA: Remo

EMILIA ROMAGNA
BELLARIA: Azienda Agrituristica
Chretien a Pippo
BOLOGNA: Jolly Hotel Rist.
Amarcord
BOLOGNA: Ristorante La Terrazza
CASADIO: La Grigliata
CORTEMAGGIORE: Antica Corte

GRAGNANO: Luna Nuova
RAVENNA: Jolly Hotel Rist.
  La Veranda
REGGIO EMILIA: Ristorante 5 Pini
  da Pelati
REGGIO EMILIA: Il Pozzo
RONCOPASCOLO: Il Gufo
SORBOLO: Spiga d'Oro

TOSCANA

AULLA: Il Rigoletto
FLORENCE: Ristorante Le Fonticine
FLORENCE: Jolly Hotel Rist.
  Carlton
PISA: Jolly Hotel Rist. Il Cavaliere
SAB CASCIANO VAL DI PESA:
  Ristorante La Calcinaia
SIENA: Jolly Hotel Rist. La Rotonda

MARCHE

ANCONA: Jolly Hotel Rist. Miramare

LAZIO

RIVIGNANO: Ristorante Dal Diaul
ROME: Ristorante Bacco
ROME: Harry's Bar
ROME: Jolly Hotel L da Vinci
  Rist. Giovannini
ROME: Jolly Hotel Midas Rist.
  Baiocco
ROME: Jolly Hotel V Veneto Rist.
  Il Giardino
ROME: Osterio L'Antiquario
FIUGGI FONTE (FR) Hotel Gran
Palazzo della Fonte Fiuggi

CAMPANIA

AVELLINO: Jolly Hotel Rist.
  Ippocampo
CASERTA: Jolly Hotel Rist.
  La Reggia
ISCHIA: Jolly Hotel Ischia

NAPLES: Jolly Hotel Rist.
  Il Grattacielo
NAPLES: Sale e Pepe
SALERNO: Jolly Hotel Rist.
  La Scaglio
SAN GIORGIO DEL SANNIO:
  Dante's Restaurant

PUGLIA

BARI: Executive restaurant S.t.l.
BARI: Jolly Hotel Rist. La Tiella
BARI: Piccinni
BARI: Ristorante Le Stagione
FOGGIA: Hotel Cicolella
LAMA (TA): Le Vecchie Cascine
TRANI: Ristorange Il Pirate

CALABRIA

CROTONE: Hotel Costa Tiziana

SICILIA

AGRIGENTO: Jolly Hotel Rist.
  Il Buon Gustaio
CASTELBUONO: Albergo Milocca
CATANIA: Ristorante La Siciliana
CATANIA: Jolly Hotel Rist. Gourmet
ERICE: Il Cortile di Venere
MESSINA: Jolly Hotel Rist.
  Dello Stretto
MODICA: Locanda Piccolit
MONTRELEPRE:
  Ristorante Orchidea
PALERMO: Jolly Hotel Rist.
  I Paladini
SIRACUSA: Jolly Hotel Rist.
  Il Giardinetto
TAORMINA: Jolly Hotel Diodoro

SARDEGNA

QUARTU s ELANA (CA):
  Pizzeria Sant'Andrea

THE INDEPENDENT

INDEPENDENT
ON SUNDAY

Your truly
independent
guides to life

Currency Latvian Lat ** **Exchange Rate** £1=approx Lts 0.85
**Not obtainable in UK. Travellers cheques/US dollars/DM
recommended.
International dialling code 00 371 (Riga+2)
Passports/Visas No visa required by British passport holders for stay
of less than 30 days.
British Embassy in Riga Tel 1-733 8126/31

Airports
Riga-Skulte Tel 2-207 661/207 009
Railway stations Enquire on arrival
Car hire in Riga
Tel Nos. **Hertz** (airport) 2-207 980 **Avis** 2-225 876
(airport 2-78 20 441)
Speed limits 70 km/h on trunk roads, 110 km/h on motorways, 60 km/h
in towns.

Banks Hours vary, but banks are generally open between 10am & 6pm.
Exchange bureaus may stay open later.
Shops Hours vary, shops but are generally open between 9am & 6pm
(some later) and many close for lunch.

New Year's Day, Easter, 1 May, 2nd Sunday in May, Jun 24, 18 Nov,
Christmas Day.

Latvian Embassy in **London** Tel 0171-312 0040
Tourist Board in **Riga** Tel 2-229 945 / 2-213 011 / 2-327 542
American Express Travel Service Offices or Representative (R)
Riga   Latvia Tours (R)
             Grecinieku iela 22/24
             Tel 2-213652/220047

Riga

Tel: (02) 882 00 50 Fax: (02) 882 00 59
Kalku iela 28, LV 1050 Riga

HR

In the 1920s, Riga was called the 'Paris of the East' and this hotel was the glamorous Grand Hotel. Today, it still aims to keep that stylish image and is the venue for local fashion shows and exhibitions. Now, most of the guests are German, with links to the new Latvian-German business initiatives being forged here. There are seven floors and the rooms, some of which look over the Opera House and public gardens opposite, were renovated in 1991 and are decorated in a smart, contemporary style. All have satellite TV, mini-bar and fax point. The reception area also has a stylish appearance, with a huge sculptured pyramid on one wall and a splendid display of flowers. **Rooms 90.**
Room service 24hr. Theatre-style conference facilities for up to 80. Translation services. Gym. Sauna. Solarium. Coffee shop (0900-2100). Amex, Diners, Mastercard, Visa.

The head chef is from North Germany and his cooking is traditional Latvian with German influences. The set menus offer good value though there is no choice. Typical dishes from a daily changing selection begin with carpaccio of beef with caviar and sour cream followed by a consommé of mushrooms, then salmon in a champagne sauce. Lemon sorbet precedes a main course of breast of chicken with a tarragon butter sauce. To finish there's strawberry ice cream in a chocolate basket. The dining-room is panelled with heavy, old, carved mahogany and there are views over Riga's rooftops. Set meals from LS30. **Seats 70.**
Open 1100-2400.

Lithuania

Currency Lithuanian Lita** **Exchange Rate** £1=approx 6.2Lт
**Not obtainable in UK. Travellers cheques/US dollars/DM recommended.
International dialling code 00 370 (Vilnius+2)
Passports/Visas No visa required by British passport holders for stay of less than 90 days.
British Embassy in Vilnius Tel 2-227 071

TRANSPORT

Airports
Vilnius Tel 2-669 481/630 201
Railway Stations
Vilnius Tel 2-356 225, 2-623 044
Car hire in Vilnius
Tel Nos. **Eva Car Rental** 2-642 880 **Balticar** 2-460 998
Hertz 2-227 025 **Avis** 2-733 005 (airport 2-291 131) 2-733 226
Speed limits 70 km/h on trunk roads, 110 km/h on motorways, 60 km/h in towns.

OPENING HOURS

Banks Hours vary, but banks are generally open between 10am & 5pm. Exchange bureaus may stay open later.
Shops Hours vary, but shops are generally open between 9am & 6pm (some later) and many close for lunch.

NATIONAL HOLIDAYS

New Year's Day, 16 Feb, Easter, first Sunday in May, 6 July, 1 Nov, Christmas Day & Boxing Day.

Tourist Offices

Lithuanian Embassy in **London** Tel 0171-938 2481
In **Lithuania** State Tourism Dept. 2-226 706
(further information available from **Intourist London** Tel 0171-538 8600/538 5965)

American Express Travel Service Offices or Representative (R)
Vilnius   Lithuanian Tours (R)
                Seimyniskiu Str. 18
                2005
                Tel 2-727 921/722 363 #

Tel: (02) 62 66 59   Fax: (02) 62 78 34
Subacius g. 3, 2001 Vilnius

A grand piano resounds through the upstairs restaurant, where the more formal tables are arranged; downstairs, there are tables surrounding a busy bar. This being in the centre of the city, the scene is equally lively outside. The menu is extensive and offers a choice of traditional Lithuanian dishes beginning with asparagus soup with meatballs, salted salmon, lobster cocktail and smoked eel. Main dishes include fried sturgeon with red caviar and a butter sauce, chicken breast with a sparkling wine sauce and veal in a grape sauce. For dessert there are blueberry dumplings with sour cream. They serve Western European wines (French, Italian and Spanish). No parking. *Seats 32. Open 1200-0100. Closed 1st Mon of each month. Amex, Mastercard, Visa.*

Tel: (02) 35 60 16   Fax: (02) 29 00 20
Ulitsa Ukmerges 20, 2600 Vilnius

This 22-storey, state-owned hotel is just across the river from the old town. It opened in the early 80s and the bedrooms are simple and functional, each with a telephone and satellite TV. *Rooms 350. Room service all day. Theatre-style conference facilities for up to 250. Translation services. Sauna. Hair salon. Chemist. Post office. Coffee shop (0800-2000). Private parking. Amex, Diners, Mastercard, Visa.*

Tel: (02) 22 23 18   Fax: (02) 22 38 70
Ulitsa Gaono 7, 2300 Vilnius

The first privately-owned company to open in Lithuania, this place has been run by a co-operative since 1987. The 17th-century building is sandwiched between two lively, winding streets right in the heart of the old town which became a Jewish ghetto during World War II. It is close to the university as well as the Presidential Palace. There are four separate eating areas with a further restaurant specialising in French cuisine due to open in early 1996 (at about the same time as a new 20-bedroom hotel - Hotel Sticklai - all of whose rooms will be equipped with satellite TV and air-conditionig). A beer bar and wine cellar with a capacity for 40 and 20 respectively while the café seats 150. These offer Lithuanian dishes such as potato blinis with salmon in the bar and potato dumplings stuffed with meat ususally, though sometimes mushrooms, and served with a sour cream dressing. The chefs trained at Lenotre cookery school in Paris and have introduced vegetarian choices onto the menu of the restaurant, which features more European dishes such as chicken Kiev, roast pork with oranges, and seafood including lobster, stuffed crab and moules marinière. A speciality is veal stiklai - roasted and served with mushrooms and cheese and a wine sauce. Another restaurant under the same ownership is *Pomiu Laime* (Lady's Happiness), open 0900-0100, at Gedimino 31, the main street of Vilnius' New Town. Both café and restaurant, it originally opened as a meeting place for gentlewomen and still offers a good selection of cakes and pastries in the café as well as a range of restaurant dishes similar to those at *Restaurant Stiklai. Seats 80. Open 1000-2400. Visa.*

Currency Luxembourg Franc **Exchange Rate** £1=approx 50 FLux
International dialling code 00 352 (for whole country)
Passports/Visas No visa required by British passport holders.
British Embassy in Luxembourg 14 Boulevard Roosevelt, L-2450
Luxembourg, Tel 22 98 64

Airports
Findel Airport Tel 47 98 2315
Railway Stations
Gare Centrale Tel 49 24 24
Care hire in Luxembourg
Tel Nos. **Europcar** 48 76 84 (airport 43 4588) **Avis** 48 95 95/6
Budget 44 19 38 (airport 43 75 75)
Speed limits 90 km/h on trunk roads, 120 km/h on motorways, 50 km/h
in towns.

Banks Mon-Fri 8.30/9am-12/12.30pm & 1.30-4.30pm.
Shops Mon-Sat 9am-6pm. Many shops are closed Monday mornings.

New Year's Day, 19 Feb, Easter Mon, 1, 16 & 27 May, 24 Jun, 15 Aug,
2 Sep, 1 Nov, Christmas & Boxing Day.

Luxembourg Tourist Board in **London** Tel 0171-434 2800
Fax 0171-734 1205
In **Luxembourg** (City) Tel 48 11 99 / 22 28 09 / 40 08 08-1
American Express Travel Service Offices or Representative (R)
Luxembourg City 34 Avenue De La Porte Neuve
                 L-2227
                 Tel 228555

Luxembourg

Tel: 46 22 11   Fax: 47 08 21
9 place de Clairfontaine, 1341 Luxembourg

With its salmon-coloured walls and wood panelling, this restaurant near the Foreign Ministry is particularly popular with the politicians and civil servants who work in the area. Chef-owner Tony Tintinger makes good use of luxury ingredients such as the house foie gras which comes in five different guises, including one with apples and calvados; each is accompanied by a glass of Gewürztraminer. Main courses include pan-fried fillets of red mullet *(rouget)* with stuffed courgette flowers and a red mullet liver sauce, and breast of guinea fowl *(pintadeau)* roasted *à la crème de truffes*. Iced passion fruit soup with cocoa sorbet is an appetising dessert. Wines, including some from Luxembourg, are stored in a nearby 11th-century tower. Set menus 1840FLux (lunch) and 3100FLux (dinner). *Seats 60 (terrace 25). Open 1200-1530, 1900-2130. Closed L Sat, all Sun, last 2 weeks Aug, National Holidays. Private parking. Amex, Diners, Mastercard, Visa.*

Tel: 4 16 16   Fax: 22 59 48
12 boulevard Royal, 2449 Luxembourg

This centrally-located modern hotel overlooks a park and offers an excellent range of amenities. Decor is contemporary and relatively plain apart from the marble-floored lobby with its reproduction furniture. Rooms are well equipped, with air-conditioning, mini-bar and satellite TV. The piano bar has a sleek black and gold Oriental theme and the terrace restaurant is a pleasant spot for alfresco eating. *Rooms 180. Room service 24hr. Valet parking. Banqueting facilities 340. Conference facilities 350. Terrace. Indoor swimming pool. Gym. Sauna. Solarium. Beauty treatment. Hair salon. News kiosk. Amex, Diners, Mastercard, Visa.*

Tel: 34 05 71   Fax: 34 02 17
Route de Trèves, 1019 Luxembourg

Located 1km from the airport and 8km from the city centre, this modern hotel is surrounded by peaceful woodland. It offers comfortable accommodation and good facilities, particularly for business, with six fully-equipped conference rooms. A neighbouring 18-hole golf course can be used by guests. *Rooms 146. Room service limited. Valet parking. Banqueting facilities 180. Conference facilities 150. Secretarial/translation services on request. Terrace. Amex, Diners, Mastercard, Visa.*

Around Luxembourg

Tel: 72 85 04 1   Fax: 72 85 08
47 route du Luxembourg, 6450 Echternach

The success of their restaurant *(see below)* persuaded owners Claude and Josette Phal to open this hotel in the pretty town of Echternach, 30 minutes from the airport and Luxembourg City. The bedrooms have modern, unfussy decor and the ornamental garden and sun terrace are lovely spots for relaxing. A shuttle service runs between the hotel and the restaurant. *Rooms 15. Closed 15 Jan-15 Feb. Private parking. Sauna. Solarium. Amex, Diners, Mastercard, Visa.*

Tel: 79464   Fax: 79771
62515 Geyershaff

This lovely 200-year-old farmhouse in the countryside is actually part of *La Bergerie* hotel in Echternach 6.5km away. Claude Phal and his son Thierry cook excellent French food and their specialities include roast Canadian lobster in a warm herb vinaigrette, brill soufflé with basil sauce, and fillet of lamb with almonds. Their sweet soufflés are also excellent or you could settle for a simple *tarte fine aux pommes*. The wine list is impressive and lengthy. Set menu 1800FLux (lunch) and six-course *menu dégustation* 2650FLux. *Seats 35. Open 1200-1400, 1900-2100. Closed D Sun, all Mon, 15 Jan-15 Feb. Private parking. Amex, Diners, Mastercard, Visa.*

Tel: 46 86 87   Fax: 48 55 05
274 route de Thionville, 5884 (Howald) Hesperange

Only a handful of smartly decorated bedrooms are available so you will need to book well in advance. The location, 5km outside Luxembourg City, is leafy and peaceful. *Rooms 5. Closed mid Jul-mid Aug. Room service limited. Private parking. Banqueting facilities 150. Conference facilities 50. Amex, Diners, Mastercard, Visa.*

The splendid Louis XV-style dining-room is an appropriate setting for classic French cooking. Starters on the seasonal carte could be fricassee of langoustines with courgettes and aubergines, and foie gras with a compote of onions and red wine. Main courses are balanced evenly between fish and meat and include red mullet cooked with basil and crème d'olives, and roast pigeon with morel mushrooms and asparagus meunière. Set menus from 1600FLux to 3200FLux. *Seats 30. Open 1200-1400, 1900-2130. Closed Sun & Mon, mid Jul-mid Aug.*

Tel/Fax: 34 00 39
90 rue Andethana, 6970 Hostert

Classic French dishes are served to a largely business clientele. An appropriately named starter is *salade riche*, consisting of foie gras, smoked salmon, langoustines and magret of duck). Fish and meat are simply cooked: *sandre* (pike-perch) is steamed and served with a *caviar* of vegetables, and noisettes of lamb come with a St Emilion sauce. Desserts are similarly straightforward. Set menus 920FLux (lunch) and 1100FLux and 2300FLux (dinner). *Seats 55. Open 1200-1400, 1900-2100. Closed L Sat, all Sun, 2 weeks in Aug, 25 Dec. Private parking. Diners, Mastercard, Visa.*

Tel: 22 64 99   Fax: 40 40 11
40 route de Bettembourg, 1899 Kockelscheuer

In as remote a setting for a restaurant as you could imagine, Michel Berring's Patin d'Or is hidden away in the middle of a forest. His superb cooking owes much to the 15 years he spent working with Roger Vergé in France. The menu changes weekly but might include *turbot à la mouginoise* (baked with mushrooms), *pied de porc farci à l'ancienne et sa fricassée de lentilles* and *filets de rougets de roche poelés, pates à l'huile de homard* (fried red mullet on a bed of home-made pasta with lobster-flavoured olive oil). Game is a speciality in season. *Seats 35. Open 1200-1330, 1900-2100. Closed Sat & Sun, National Holidays. Private parking. Amex, Diners, Mastercard, Visa.*

Tel: 47 22 59   Fax: 46 43 89
138 rue Albert Unden, 2652 Limperstberg

Christian Bouzonviller's restaurant stands on the edge of the Alzette valley, and much of the game for his kitchen is caught in the woods nearby. His cooking is French-inspired and includes dishes such as *rösti de tartare de saumon au caviar*, pigeon sausages with a mixed green salad, and smoked salmon trout with leeks. The wine list includes a good selection of Luxembourg Moselles. *Seats 30. Open 1200-1400, 1930-2200. Closed Sat & Sun, 1st 3 weeks Aug, 24 Dec-2 Jan. Mastercard, Visa.*

Tel: 31 36 66   Fax: 31 36 27
140a route d'Areon, 8008 Strassen

A well-equipped and spacious modern hotel in a quiet location yet only 3km from Luxembourg City and a ten-minute drive from the airport. It's surrounded by fields, and the terrace is a lovely spot to enjoy the regular summer barbecues. *Rooms 46. Room service limited. Private parking 300FLux. Banqueting facilities 250. Conference facilities 40. Terrace. Amex, Diners, Mastercard, Visa.*

Meal prices for 2 are based on à la carte menus. When set menus are available, prices will often be lower.

Scotch Beef Club Members: Luxembourg

CHAMPLON: Hostellerie de la Barrière de Champlon
DURBUY: Hotel de Prévot
LACUISINE: La Roseraie
NASSOGNE: Beau-Séjour

Currency Maltese Lira **Exchange Rate** £1=approx LM 0.54
International dialling code 00 356 (for whole island)
Passports/Visas No visa required by British passport holders for stay
of less than 3 months.
British High Commission in Malta Tel 233 134/8

Airports
Luqa airport Tel 243 455
Railway Stations
(None; buses from Valletta main terminal)
Car hire in Malta
Tel Nos. **Avis** (Msida) 246 640/225 986 **Hertz** (Gzira) 314 630/314 636
Budget (Marsa) 247 111/241 517
Budget, Europcar, Hertz & Avis at Luqa airport Tel 249 600
Speed limits 64 km/h on trunk roads, 40 km/h in towns
(no motorways).

Banks Mon-Fri 8.30am-12.30pm (to 11.30am Saturdays).
Shops 9am-7pm Mon-Sat (closed 3-4 hours at lunchtime).

New Year's Day, 10 Feb, 19 & 31 Mar, Good Friday, 1 May, 7 & 29 Jun,
15 Aug, 8 & 21 Sep, 8 & 13 Dec, Christmas Day.

Malta Tourist Office in **London** Tel 0171-292 4900
In **Malta** Luqa Airport Tel 239 915 Valletta Tel 224 444/5 or 225 048/9
Sliema Tel 313 409 Gozo Tel 556 454
American Express Travel Service Offices or Representative (R)
Sliema   A & V Von Brockdorff Ltd (R)
               Rocklands
               Windsor Terrace
               Slm
               Tel 339549/345369 #
Valletta   A & V Von Brockedorff Ltd (R)
               14 Zachary Street
               Vlt 10
               PO Box 494
               Tel 232141/230517/230763 #

Gozo

Tel: 56 04 55   Fax: 55 75 89   HR
2Mgarr, Gozo

There are wonderful views over the old fishing village and harbour of Mgarr from this
luxurious hotel, which was built in 1992. The air-conditioned bedrooms were individually
designed and furnished in low-key modern styles that aim to recreate the atmosphere and
character of an old farmhouse. On the terrace you can enjoy a drink, sunbathe or cool off
in the swimming pool. *Rooms 74. Room service 24hr. Private parking.*
Banqueting facilities 260. Conference facilities 250. Secretarial services on request.
2 outdoor swimming pools. Keep-fit equipment. Sauna. Massage. Shop. Amex, Diners,
Mastercard, Visa.

Restaurant   LM30

With the fishing boats of Mgarr literally a stone's throw away, it is no surprise that
wonderfully fresh seafood is a speciality of the restaurant. Italian chef Guido Perisinotto
changes his table d'hote menu daily. During summer you might be able to try tagliatelle
gratinate al prosciutto, freshly grilled fish of the day and Gozitan rabbit stew. Local fresh
fruit is as good a way as any to end a meal. Unusually, vegetarians and people on a gluten-
free diet have their own separate menus. Maltese and Gozitan wines feature on the list.
Every Friday there is a grand buffet consisting of salads, soups, cheeses, and two or three
pastas, meat and fish dishes plus a welcome drink and canapés on the terrace. *Seats 160.*
Open 1300-1430, 1930-2200.

Tel: 55 68 19   Fax: 55 81 99   HR
Sannat, Gozo

Guests enjoy wonderful views from this hotel, located on the highest point of the island,
surrounded by peaceful farmland, and 200m from the Gozo cliffs. Built in 1971, it has since
been thoroughly renovated and now offers superb standards of comfort and service.
Bedrooms are decorated in a traditional farmhouse style with patterned furnishings and
wooden furniture, and all have air-conditioning and satellite TV. A private beach with its
own bar is available for the exclusive use of guests and lunch can be ordered from there
and delivered to you as you sunbathe. For those with a passion for water sports, the hotel
has its own diving shop and speed boat for hire. *Rooms 82. Room service 24hr.*
Private parking. Banqueting facilities 300. Conference facilities 100. Secretarial/translation
services on request. Garden. 2 outdoor swimming pools. News kiosk. Amex, Diners,
Mastercard, Visa.

Carruba Restaurant   LM28

The food in the hotel restaurant varies according to the time of year. In summer, the chef
is an Italian and dishes are mainly from his native land while, in the low season, a Maltese
chef takes over and local specialities (heavily Italian-influenced anyway) are more to the
fore. The simple stone walls and marble floors are an appropriate setting for the unfussy,
straightforward cooking. Aljotta alla Gozitana (Gozitan-style fish soup), farfalle pasta with
tuna and capers, and roast chicken with aromatic herbs are typical high season dishes.
A daily set menu is available at lunch or dinner for Lm10.50. *Seats 150 (terrace 150).*
Open 1300-1430, 1930-2130.

Valletta

Tel: 22 52 41   Fax: 23 52 54   HR
The Mall Floriana, Valletta

It is worth paying the small supplement to get a room with a harbour view in this plush
Forte Grand hotel. Built in 1947, it has been tastefully modernised to introduce modern
comforts without spoiling a reassuringly traditional atmosphere, with the fan-vaulted
lounge, painted in pastel shades, an architectural highlight. The hotel stands outside the
main gates to the citadel and, although there is no direct access to the beach or harbour, it
is pleasant just to wander in the seven acres of lovely landscaped gardens, surrounded by
bastions, or swim in the year-round swimming pool. There is also a paddling pool and

crazy golf to keep children amused. Business customers will be impressed by excellent conference facilities, including six meeting rooms. *Rooms 136. Room service 24hr. Private parking. Banqueting facilities 200. Conference facilities 350. Secretarial/translation services on request. Garden. Outdoor swimming pool. Amex, Diners, Mastercard, Visa.*

Phoenix Restaurant   Lm28

Irish chef Paul Patterson arrived from the Balmoral Hotel in Edinburgh in 1994 and has established a reputation for cooking imaginative international food. The influence of Italy is, as ever on Malta, strong but Patterson finds some original combinations of ingredients, such as risotto of shrimps and tiger prawns surrounded by a Thai herb cream, pan-fried duckling with rösti potato and candied chestnuts and artichokes, and parfait of game with a plum and pear salsa. Desserts include 'Queen of Hearts', fine layers of shortbread with sweet cheese and strawberry coulis. *Seats 100 (terrace 60). Open 1230-1430, 1930-2230.*

VALLETTA   The Carriage   ★   Lm25

Tel: 24 78 28   Fax: 22 30 48
22/5 Valletta Buildings, South Street Valletta

The views from this modern fifth-floor penthouse are spectacular taking in the whole of the bay, the capital Valletta and Manoel Island. The restaurant used to be on The Strand in nearby Sliema but the owner, who trained with Alastair Little at London's *L'Escargot*, moved to Valletta in 1993 where he vowed to serve lunches only. Since then he has continued to update his innovative modern cooking, with dishes showing Mediterranean and Oriental influences: warm seafood salad with roast garlic, basil and lemon, ravioli of mixed mushrooms with truffle butter, parmesan and clams, miso broth with udon noodles and bonito flakes and bamboo-steamed fish are examples. The main menu changes seasonally and there is also a Menu of the Week (Lm6.25). A small but select wine list offers European and New World wines, with burgundy and champagne served by the glass. *Seats 50 (terrace 35). Open 1200-1500, 2000-2300. Closed D Tue-Thu, L Sat, all Sun, Aug. Amex, Diners, Mastercard, Visa.*

Elsewhere in Malta

MARSASCALA   Christopher's   Lm35

Tel: 82 91 42   Fax: 82 91 42
29 Marina Street, Marsascala

The quality and inventiveness of the food at Christopher's might come as a surprise until you realise that chef-owner Christopher Farrugia has worked in London at the Savoy Grill and at Harvey's with Marco Pierre White. He describes his cooking as "new Mediterranean" and supplements his seasonal menu with daily specials. Typical summer starters from the carte are millefeuille of frog's legs with oyster mushrooms, and game terrine with a red onion marmalade. Main courses such as Balinese prawn curry, quail with juniper berries and crème de cassis, and stuffed pig's trotters Pierre Koffmann (his culinary hero) display a wide range of influences. Marsascala is a small fishing village on the east side of Malta and the restaurant is small and unpretentious, with pale brick walls and wooden furniture. *Seats 32. Open 1930-2230, also L Tue-Sat from Sep-May. Closed Sun. Amex, Mastercard, Visa.*

Tel: 57 34 36
113 Gorgborg Olivier, Melleiha

It's easy to spot the long, grand facade of this restaurant on the main street of Melleiha. Inside, a splendid staircase leads to the elegant dining-room with its wooden floor and full-length arched windows, reminiscent of an orangery. Owner Joseph Vella opened The Arches 25 years ago and both his chefs have been with him almost as long. He describes the food as nouvelle cuisine "with bigger portions" and offers a weekly menu and a seasonal carte. Old classics such as fillet of beef strogonoff appear alongside more unusual dishes: sea bream and avocado mousse with a light saffron sauce, grilled salmon steak on a purée of leeks and basil sauce. There are also a few simple pasta and fish dishes. Once guests have ordered food, they are invited to descend to the wine cellar and choose their tipple from the mainly French selection. Although the echoing wooden floors can make the restaurant rather noisy, the atmosphere is relaxing and the service friendly. The owner hopes to re-open a terrace in 1996 for a further 50 diners. *Seats 80. Open 1900-2230. Closed Sun, 2 weeks in Feb. Amex, Diners, Mastercard, Visa.*

ST JULIAN'S   Peppino's   LM24

Tel: 37 32 00
31 St George's Road, St Julian's

From the day it opened five years ago, the oak and marble ground-floor bar at Peppino's has been a popular meeting place for locals. Upstairs, Maltese chef Philip Cianter cooks a wonderful range of local fish and Italian-influenced dishes such as fresh lobster soup, mushrooms with parmesan, port, garlic and cheese, octopus in white wine, and chicken breast with orange and apricot sauce. The home-made desserts are delicious. The building is a conversion of the last house in a terrace and regular exhibitions of works by contemporary Maltese painters adorn the restaurant walls. Note that parking is difficult in this area. *Seats 60. Open 1200-1500, 1900-2300. Closed Sun, 1-20 Jan. Amex, Diners, Mastercard, Visa.*

SAN ANTON   Corinthia Palace Hotel   LM77

Tel: 44 03 01   Fax: 46 57 13
De Paule Avenue, San Anton

Palace by name and palatial by design, this superb, collonaded, villa-style hotel is surrounded by its own lush gardens, and located next to the Presidential Palace. Facilities are excellent and firmly aimed at the business market, with fully-equipped conference rooms, and secretarial and translation services. The air-conditioned bedrooms are furnished simply but comfortably. The Athenaeum Centre offers 58 different body- and mind-soothing treatments from simple massage to Reiki, the ancient healing therapy from Tibet. You can also drain your lymphs, reshape your eyebrows and have a photo taken of your aura. Guests can use the centre's indoor pool and jacuzzi without charge but therapies are not included in the room price. **Rooms 155.** *Room service 24hr. Banqueting facilities 500. Conference facilities 500. Business centre. Outdoor swimming pool. Tennis. Squash. Health spa. Diners, Mastercard, Visa.*

Currency French Franc **Exchange Rate** £1=approx 7.68F
International dialling code: 00 33
British Consulate in Monte Carlo Tel 93 50 99 66

Airports
Nice Cote-D'Azur (General enquiries) Tel 93 21 30 30
(Flight enquiries) 93 21 30 12
Railway Stations
Monte Carlo (Passenger information) 93 25 54 54
(reservations) 93 30 74 00
Car hire in Monte Carlo
Tel Nos. **Avis** city 93 30 17 53 airport 93 21 36 33
Budget city 92 16 00 70 **Hertz** city 93 50 79 60 airport 93 21 36 72
Europcar city 93 50 74 95 airport 93 32 36 55
Speed limits: 75km/h on voie rapide (by-pass), 53km/h in built-up
areas.

Banks Mon-Fri 9am-12pm & 2-4.30pm (except afternoons preceeding
legal Bank Holidays).
Shops Daily from 9am-12pm & 3-7pm (except Sundays and Bank
Holidays).

2 & 27 Jan, 28 Feb, 17 April, 1 & 25 May, 5 Jun, 15 Aug 1 & 19 Nov,
8 Dec, Christmas Day, New Year's Day.

Monaco Tourist Board in **London** Tel 0171-352 2103
In **Monaco** (Direction du Tourisme et des congres) Tel 92 16 61 16.
American Express Travel Service Offices or Representative (R)
Monte Carlo
  35 Boulevard Princesse Charlotte
  Mo 98000
  Tel 93 25 74 45 #

Monaco

Tel: 92 16 30 00   Fax: 93 25 59 17
Place du Casino MC, 98000 Monaco

This palatial 19th-century hotel oozes glamour, especially during the Grand Prix weekend when the jetset stay in harbourside suites, with all the trappings of luxury. An ongoing refurbishment programme over the last couple of years has seen the redecoration of all the bedrooms in the old and new parts of the building. Satellite TV and mini-bars are now standard in all rooms, some eighty rooms have fax lines, and many have panoramic views. July 1995 saw the opening of the *Centre Thalassothérapie de Thermes Marins*, a magnificent spa centre built beneath the road between the hotel and the beach; a project which has taken 18 months to complete. The stunning indoor swimming pool has heated seawater and a shuttle takes you to an outdoor pool at the beach. Apart from the Louis XV restaurant (see below), there's the rooftop Grill with its sliding roof and sensational views of the Principality, and the Terrasse-Empire, only open during the season and at Christmas/New Year. *Rooms 200. Room service 24hr. Garage parking 120F. Banqueting facilities 500. Conference facilities 100. Secretarial/translation services on request. Gym. Sauna. Spa centre. Steam bath. Indoor swimming pool. Amex, Diners, Mastercard, Visa.*

Restaurant Louis XV   ★★   2400F

Chef Alain Ducasse began his career with Alain Chapel, who as his maitre spirituel has undoubtedly had a huge influence on his cooking. Ducasse was brought in in 1987 to breathe new life into the opulent and grand dining-room, with its ornately-painted ceiling, luxuriously decorated in classical Louis XV style. The result has been to produce cuisine which lives up to the breathtaking surroundings - classical but with very definite Mediterranean overtones. Expect to see all the dishes described at length, for example *légumes des jardins de Provence mijotés à la truffe noire écrasée, un filet d'huile d'olive Aroïno, vinaigre balsamique et fleur de sel* (Provence vegetables simmered with crushed black truffle with a dribble of olive oil, balsamic vinegar and salt). Other specialities are *pigeonneau des Alpes de Haute-Provence et foie gras de canard sur la braise* (breast of pigeon and chargrilled duck foie gras). You can choose à la carte or from the various suggestions. The two menus, the vegetarian Les Jardins de Provence (760F) and the Gourmet menu (850F) change daily, The dessert menu comes in two parts: fruit-based for example *gelée de citron du pays, tranche de pamplemousse rose confite et givrée fine tartelette au citron vert* (lemon jelly with a confit of frosted pink grapefruit and a lime tartlet) or chocolat/coffee/caramel-based, *truffé au caramel, beurre aux noisettes torrifiées* (caramel truffles with roasted hazelnut butter). From an enormous cellar with around 250,000 bottles there are gems like a Dom Pérignon 1962 and a Pétrus 1945. *Seats 70 (terrace 30). Open 1230-1400, 2000-2245. Closed Tue, Wed (but open D Wed in summer), Dec, 2 weeks Feb. Amex, Diners, Mastercard, Visa.* 🐂

MONACO: Chez Gianni

MONACO: Cote Jardin (Hotel de Paris)

MONACO: La Coupole (Hotel Mirabeau)

MONACO: Fuji

MONACO: Le Jardin (Hotel Métropole Palace)

MONACO: Les Quatre Saisons

MONACO: Le Salle Empire (Hotel de Paris)

MONTE CARLO: La Terrasse (Hotel Beach Plaza)

Netherlands

Currency Dutch Guilder **Exchange Rate** £1=approx 2.5HFL
International dialling code 00 31
(Amsterdam+20 Hague+70 Rotterdam+10)
Passports/Visas No visa required by British passport holders.
British Consulate in Amsterdam Tel 20-676 4343 Fax 20-676 1069
British Embassy in The Hague Tel 70-364 5800

Airports
Amsterdam-Schiphol Tel 20-601 9111 **Rotterdam-Zestienhoven**
10-446 3444 **Eindhoven** 40-524 255 **Maastricht-Beek** 43-666 444
Railway Stations
For **rail information** Tel 30-354652
Car hire
Tel Nos. **Amsterdam Avis** 20-683 6061 (airport 20-604 1301)
Europcar 20-590 9111 (airport 20-604 1566) **Budget** 2503-71222
(airport 20-604 1349) **Rotterdam Budget** 10-411 3022
(airport 10-427 8196) **The Hague Budget** Tel 70-382 4386/382 0609
Speed limits 50 km/h on secondary roads, 80 km/h on trunk roads,
120/100 km/h on motorways, 30 km/h in towns

Banks 9am-4pm Mon-Fri (Thu from 5pm-8pm). Some close at 5pm.
Shops Mon 1-6pm, Tue-Fri 9am-6pm, Sat 9am-5pm. Some stores in
main cities stay open until 9pm one night a week.

New Year's Day, Easter, 30 Apr, 5 & 16 May, 26 & 27 Jun, Christmas
Day & Boxing Day.

Dutch Tourist Board in **London** Tel 0891 200277
In Holland **Amsterdam** Tel 20-551 2512 **Rotterdam** Tel 10-402 3200
The Hague Tel 70-361 8888
American Express Travel Service Offices or Representative (R)

Amsterdam	Van Baerlestraat 38
	1071 AZ
	Tel 20-6714141 #
Amsterdam	American Express
	Damrak 66
	1012 LM Amsterdam
	PO Box 762 (PO Box Post Code 1000 At)
	Tel 20-5207777 #
Rotterdam	Meent 92
	3011 JP
	Tel 10-4330300 #
The Hague	Venestraat 20
	2511 AS
	Tel 70-3701100 #

Amsterdam

Tel: (20) 626 23 33   Fax: (20) 624 53 21
Herengracht 341, 1016 AZ Amsterdam

The nine 17th-century merchant's houses that make up the Ambassade boast a wonderfully romantic setting by the Herengracht canal. Unsurprisingly, the bedrooms come in all shapes and sizes, and are decorated in a tasteful, restrained modern style. Ask for one with a view over the canal. All the city's main sites are a few minutes walk away. *Rooms 52. Room service 24hr. Public parking 24hfl. Amex, Diners, Mastercard, Visa.*

Tel: (20) 624 53 22   Fax: (20) 625 32 36
Leidsekade 97, 1017 PN Amsterdam

The wonderful art deco café-restaurant is a major attraction at this large 19th-century hotel. The bar and hall have recently been redecorated in blue and pink and the comfortable bedrooms are clad in soothing, soft colours. Its city-centre site next to the Stadschouwberg theatre, near the bustling Leidseplein, is ideal for sightseeing. *Rooms 188. Room service 24hr. Banqueting facilities. Conference facilities. Gym. Solarium. Children's play room. Public parking 50hfl. Amex, Diners, Mastercard, Visa.*

Tel: (20) 622 60 60   Fax: (20) 622 58 08
Professor Tulpplein 1, 10018 GX Amsterdam

A favoured haunt of visiting celebrities and royalty, the 19th-century Amstel is rather more stylish and elegant than many Inter-Continental hotels. Following a major renovation a couple of years ago it is now back to its full, classical glory. All bedrooms are tradionally furnished but are air-conditioned and have TV, video, CD player and even fax with voice mail. Facilities at the health club are excellent. The hotel terrace leads down to the edge of the canal. *Rooms 79. Room service 24hr. Private parking 60hfl. Banqueting facilities 120. Conference facilities 180. Terrace. Indoor swimming pool. Sauna. Solarium. Beauty treatments. Hair salon. Amex, Diners, Mastercard, Visa.*

The restaurant re-opened in 1992 following refurbishment and chef Robert Kranenborg had, in little over a year, earned a Michelin star for his inspired cooking. He is currently "fighting for a second". Chef Robert Kranenborg's food is French with an accent on fish. Some dishes are startlingly inventive: grilled brochette of sweetmeats and macaroni gratinéed with aged Dutch cheese served with a parsley sauce, or asparagus and Breton lobster glazed with carrots and citronella and curry mayonnaise. Others are relatively simple such as salted and lightly smoked salmon with potato salad and caviar. The 200-bottle wine list includes the Dutch Apostelhoeve Riesling, made near Maastricht. There are lovely views over the Amstel and it is even possible to arrive here by boat. *Seats 115. Open 1200-1400, 1830-2230. Closed L Sat & Sun.*

Tel: (20) 664 01 55   Fax: (20) 664 01 57
Emmalaan 25, 1075 AT Amsterdam

A quiet residential district is the setting for this laidback brasserie serving excellent French/Mediterranean food. The menu changes every six weeks but you might find snails in garlic butter or pastrami of pigeon marinated in balsamic vinegar and coriander with a nut salad listed as starters. Typical main dishes are poached medallion of veal with marinated morel mushrooms, and asparagus with ham, egg and melted butter. There is also a good range of tempting desserts: sherbet of hibiscus with crystalline apple, for instance. The menu brasserie is good value at 55hfl. The wine list specialises in burgundy, both white and red. An unusual feature of Beau Bourg is that one table for ten people is in the kitchen where diners are served by the chef and can watch the team of cooks in action. *Seats 60. Open 1200-1500, 1800-2330. Closed L Sat & Sun, all 31 Dec. Amex, Diners, Mastercard, Visa.*

Tel: (20) 625 08 07   Fax: (20) 638 91 32
Leliegracht 46, 1015 DH Amsterdam

Jean-Christophe Royer's elegant restaurant is a celebration of the cooking of southern France. Using only the best and freshest ingredients, his dishes range from the extravagance of warm oysters with saffron and caviar to the simpler, but no less striking, aubergine and cumin terrine. Specialities include roasted monkfish with bacon and pipérade, émincé of veal kidneys and sweetbreads with truffled noodles, and grilled red mullet with artichokes en barigoule. A sublime dessert to conjure up the sun of Provence is roasted fresh figs with thyme ice cream. You will only find French wines on the list. The restaurant is only open for dinner. *Seats 45. Open 1900-2300. Closed Sun, 1-3 Jan. Amex, Diners, Mastercard, Visa.*

Tel: (20) 626 77 21   Fax: (20) 625 89 86
Prinsengracht 444, 1017 KE Amsterdam

The Italian Fenice group recently took over this hotel and have carried out substantial refurbishments. The lobby is luxurious with ochre walls, a black and white marble floor and big, brown chesterfields. All the bedrooms have also been redecorated. Ask for one with a view over the canal. *Rooms 25. Room service 24hr. Public parking 30hfl. Banqueting facilities 30. Conference facilities 30. Secretarial services on request. Amex, Diners, Mastercard, Visa.*

Tel: (20) 623 48 36   Fax: (20) 624 29 62
Nieuwe Doelenstraat 2-8, 1012 CP Amsterdam

Vast swathes of marble cover the floor of the reception area in this fine 19th-century hotel. Luxurious facilities abound, from the indoor swimming pool to the staffed business centre. Rooms are decorated in a variety of styles, some sleekly modern, others cosily Victorian, but all have air conditioning and some enjoy views over the Amstel. *Rooms 100. Room service 24hr. Private parking 45hfl. Banqueting facilities 180. Conference facilities 500. Business centre. Terrace. Indoor swimming pool. Gym. Sauna. Solarium. Massage. News kiosk. Coffee shop. Amex, Diners, Mastercard, Visa.*

This smart restaurant (jacket required) is usually filled with diners enjoying Jean Jacques Menanteau's excellent French cooking against a background of live piano music. The menu is dictated by the seasons and may include lobster-stuffed cannelloni with saffron sauce or vegetable terrine with truffle and chervil butter as starters, alongside main dishes such as grilled fillet of turbot with mustard sauce, and loin of veal with sage and shallots. Desserts include chocolate tart with sour cherries. There is a separate vegetarian menu. The set meals are good value, starting at 62.50hfl and rising to 165hfl for the menu alliance arrangement royal at dinner which includes five courses, four glasses of wine, coffee and chocolates. The huge wine cellar contains 30,000 bottles of 800 different types, mostly French. *Seats 90 (terrace 60). Open 1230-1400, 1900-2300. Closed L Sat.*

Tel: (20) 664 21 21   Fax: (20) 679 93 56
Dijsselhofplantsoen 7, 1077 BJ Amsterdam

This small luxury hotel is situated in Amsterdam's green belt, not far from the Concertgebouw and Vondelpark, but also close to the RAI Congress and the World Trade Centre. Decor is modern but restrained with bedrooms decorated in green, grey, pink or lilac. All have marble bathrooms with jacuzzi baths, as well as air-conditioning, cable TV and safes. The staff are extremely helpful and welcoming. *Rooms 98. Room service 24hr. Valet parking. Banqueting facilities 350. Conference facilities 120. Secretarial service on request. Amex, Diners, Mastercard, Visa.*

> Meal prices for 2 are based on à la carte menus. When set menus are available, prices will often be lower.

Tel: (20) 555 31 11   Fax: (20) 555 32 22
Oudezijds Voorburgwal 197, 1012 EX Amsterdam

The 16th-century building was the City Hall of Amsterdam for 200 years and its magnificent banqueting rooms survive from that time. Two canals run through the courtyard gardens and the hotel enjoys the twin advantages of being centrally located yet secluded. The bedrooms and public areas were designed by Monique Roux (wife of Albert) who aimed to create a cosy, partly English, partly French environment. Public facilities are excellent with opportunities to relax in the pool, sauna, spa, and Turkish bath. *Rooms 182. Room service 24hr. Valet parking 30hfl. Banqueting facilities 200. Conference facilities 300. Garden. Indoor swimming pool. Sauna. Spa bath. Turkish bath. Beauty treatments. News kiosk. Amex, Diners, Mastercard, Visa.*

Even though the excellent Admiralty restaurant closed a couple of years ago, the influence of Albert Roux on the brasserie that took its place is still immense. Why not start your meal with oeuf froid Albert (cold poached egg with smoked salmon in a globe artichoke with tomato-flavoured mayonnaise) or perhaps gateau de crabe et tomates. Continue with a simple grilled entrecote and béarnaise sauce, or something more typically local such as fillet of veal with mature Gouda and deep-fried sage. To finish, try crispy apple tartlets with creamy calvados sauce and caramel ice cream, or even an English summer pudding. The wine list includes a good selection of red and white Bordeaux. *Seats 65. Open 1200-1530, 1800-2300.*

Tel: (20) 554 91 91   Fax: (20) 662 86 07
Dam 9, 1012 JS Amsterdam

This large and luxurious hotel, five minutes from the Lido Casino, has grown from Krasnapolsky's original Polish café. In April 1995 the Royal Wing opened, adding a further 100 rooms. Facilities are excellent and particularly well suited to large conferences. One floor is reserved for non-smokers. *Rooms 429. Room service 24hr. Private parking hfl30. Banqueting facilities 800. Conference facilities 1500. Business centre. Garden. Beauty treatment. Hair salon. Bureau de change. News kiosk. Amex, Diners, Mastercard, Visa.*

Tel: (20) 644 32 06   Fax: (20) 644 17 77
Van Leyenberghlaan 20, Buitenveldert, 1082 GM Amsterdam

This resolutely modern restaurant, all aluminium and glass, was designed by prominent Dutch architect Alexander Boron. Inside it has a sleek elegance with a green and yellow colour scheme, white table-cloths and a wooden floor. John Halvemaan's imaginative cooking is a hybrid of local and French cuisine. Interesting starters include foie gras brulé (caramelised goose liver with black pepper and balsamic vinegar) and "sea and earth": scallops, lobster, octopus, potato, mushroom, leek and garlic with a ginger soy sauce. Main dishes are equally ambitious: for instance, turbot with pan-fried mushrooms and a broad bean risotto with Noilly Prat and cream sauce, and fillets of sole with asparagus, salsify, blood orange and hollandaise sauce. How about crème brulée with grapefruit, black pepper and honey for an arresting dessert? Set menus from 80hfl to 125hfl. Red Bordeaux and burgundy are well represented on the list. *Seats 65. Open 1200-1430, 1800-2230. Closed Sat, Sun, 24 Dec-7 Jan. Private parking. Amex, Diners, Mastercard, Visa.*

Tel: (20) 678 07 80   Fax: (20) 662 66 88
Apollolaan 138-140, 1077 BG Amsterdam

Still best known for being the venue of John Lennon and Yoko Ono's 'Bed-in for Peace' in 1969, the Hilton invites you to 'fulfil your fantasy' in the same airy, white suite where The Ballad of John and Yoko was composed. The decor of the rest of the hotel is sleek and modern, and the restaurant, lounge and some of the bedrooms have recently been refurbished. The Amstel runs by the hotel (which is out of the city centre) and you can cruise the canals on boats rented from the Hilton Marina. One floor is designated for non-smokers. *Rooms 271. Room service 24hr. Public parking 25hfl. Banqueting facilities 380. Conference facilities 600. Secretarial services on request. Marina and yacht club. Hair salon. Shopping arcade. News kiosk. Amex, Diners, Mastercard, Visa.*

Tel: (75) 165629   Fax: (75) 162476
Kalverringdijk 15, 1509 BT Amsterdam

This restaurant enjoys a fine location, ten minutes outside Amsterdam, amongst the 17th-century wooden houses of an old whaling village. The menu fuses French and Dutch cuisine, offering dishes such as De Huisman creamy mustard soup, poached fillets of sole with a white wine and tomato sauce, and fillet of beef with foie gras and Madeira sauce. Desserts might include cherry pie with macaroon ice cream. There are seven set menus ranging from 90hfl to 135hfl. *Seats 100 (terrace 50). Open 1200-1430, 1800-2130. Closed Sun. Private parking. Amex, Diners, Mastercard, Visa.*

Tel: (20) 641 13 78   Fax: (20) 645 91 62
Amsterdamseweg 104a, 1182 HG Amstelveen

A 17th-century windmill, ten minutes outside Amsterdam, is home to this friendly French restaurant. The polished red stone floors and Dutch paintings provide a rustic backdrop for excellent-value cooking. Set menus range from 55hfl to 85hfl while three courses from the carte cost 55hfl. The latter might consist of the restaurant's own smoked salmon with horseradish, then fried fillet of guinea fowl with cashew nuts and rye bread, and, lastly, a plate of local cheeses. *Seats 124 (terrace 80). Open 1200-1500, 1800-2200. Closed L Sat & Sun. Private parking. Amex, Diners, Mastercard, Visa.*

Tel: (20) 662 07 78   Fax: (20) 673 73 53
Van Baerlestraat 96, 1071 BB Amsterdam

Every four weeks a different exhibition of paintings from an up-and-coming artist lines the walls of this cosy, bohemian restaurant. The menu changes monthly but usually features six meat and six fish dishes which are simply prepared and might include Dover sole, local lamb chops, sweetbreads, grilled salmon and game in season. The international wine list features red and white Bordeaux as house wines. *Seats 140 (80 outside). Open 1100-2330. Closed Sun, Easter, 25 Dec. Amex, Diners, Mastercard, Visa.*

Tel: (20) 624 18 31   Fax: (20) 627 61 53
Spuistraat 247, 1012 VP Amsterdam

Simply prepared fish, oysters and other shellfish are the house specialities of this restaurant in a 19th-century newspaper warehouse. In addition to the carte, there is an Italian fish menu at 75hfl, featuring dishes such as tagliatelle salad with pesto and cockles, and red perch with thyme and radicchio. The three-course set menu at 47.50hfl is excellent value with the choice of five or six starters, mains and desserts. These might include "sea salad" (shrimps, seaweed, fish roe with oyster dressing), fried swordfish with cayenne, mustard and lemon sauce served with fried potatoes and vegetables, and a simple fruit salad to finish. Look out for the daily specials. Although it is normally only open for dinner, lunches can be arranged on request. *Seats 75. Open 1700-2400. Closed Sun, 31 Dec, National Holidays. Public parking. Amex, Diners, Mastercard, Visa.*

Tel: (20) 626 93 27   Fax: (20) 627 72 81
Regulierdwarsstraat 35, 1017 BK Amsterdam

An excellent restaurant, complete with fresh lobster tank and (purely ornamental) aquarium, known particularly for its Peking Duck. Other specialities include fresh oysters stir-fried with ginger and spring onions, Sichuan (gong bau) spicy chicken with cashews and, depending on the market, steamed sea bass and fresh abalone. Alsace whites are prominent on the list. Set menus from 75.50hfl to 82.50hfl. *Seats 35. Open 1700-2300. Closed 31 Dec. Public parking 4hfl. Amex, Diners, Mastercard, Visa.*

Opening times are often liable to change at short notice, so it's always best to book.

Tel: (20) 624 65 89   Fax: (20) 620 38 67
Kattengat 4-6, 1012 SZ Amsterdam

The beautiful restaurant terrace looks out on to "the Montmartre of Amsterdam", as this pleasant area of the city is known. Spieghel, one of the city's first mayors, built the house for his daughters in 1614 and it claims to be Amsterdam's oldest restaurant. Fresh fish comes three times a week direct from two North Sea boats belonging to friends of the chef. He grills monkfish with a tomato and olive oil dressing, steams skate and serves it in a red wine sauce, sautés sea bass in a paprika sauce, and serves steamed fillets of sole stuffed with lobster and a Noilly Prat sauce. Local ingredients are used whenever possible: Texel island lamb, chickens from north Holland, steak from Friesland. Most of the 300-plus wines on the list are French. *Seats 100 (terrace 50). Open 1200-1400, 1800-2200. Closed Sun (except for groups), 1 Jan. Amex, Mastercard, Visa.*

Tel: (20) 556 48 85   Fax: (20) 624 33 53
Prins Hendrikkade 59, 1012 AD Amsterdam

The setting of this restaurant, in three restored 17th-century canal houses within the Hotel Barbizon Palace, is not unlike the luminous interiors of Vermeer's paintings. Copies of his works hang on the walls and the atmosphere, enhanced by antiques and original wooden panelling, is cosy. The cooking is international with a French bias. An Italian influence is also evident in dishes such as langoustines with ham risotto, and tatin de veau with truffles and parmesan. Entrecote of beef with a truffle purée is a speciality, as is a wonderful hot mascarpone soufflé. Set dinner menus are available at 85hfl for four courses and 125hfl for five, in addition to an excellent value lunch menu at 48.50hfl. Most of the wines are French. There is a separate lounge with an open fireplace. *Seats 55. Open 1200-1500, 1830-2230. Closed L Sat, all Sun, mid Jul-mid Aug, 25 Dec-1 Jan. Private parking. Amex, Diners, Mastercard, Visa.*

Tel: (229) 214752   Fax: (229) 214938
Duinsteeg 1, 1621 ER Hoorn

The Fonk family run this cosy restaurant in a 17th-century building in the centre of Hoorn, north of Amsterdam. The son, Constant, presides over the kitchen and takes his French cooking very seriously: his motto is "l'art de la cuisine c'est toute ma vie". One of his specialities is profiteroles filled with foie gras but less rich fare, such as mango salad and white Limburg asparagus au gratin, is also often available on his daily-changing menu. Main dishes may include baked sea bass with tomato and basil, and baked turbot with red wine sauce and mushrooms. Four to six-course set menus range from 95hfl to 135hfl while the petit faim grand plaisir menu is particularly good value at 19.50hfl per course. The house wines change monthly. *Seats 35. Open 1800-2130. Closed Thu, Mon in winter, 2 weeks Aug depending on local fair. Amex, Diners, Mastercard, Visa.*

Tel: (23) 263600   Fax: (23) 273143
Zeeweg 53, 2051 EB Overveen, Haarlem

Eating out on the terrace of this fine restaurant, deep in dune country on a remote corner of a lake, the bustle of Amsterdam seems a million miles away. The chef, Mr Riva, cooks imaginative French food, often using local ingredients. The carte changes every two months but you will find different dishes on the menu every day. Appetising starters include asparagus aux coquilles St Jacques with a caviar vinaigrette, and salad of calf's sweetbreads with morel mushrooms and a mustard and apple dressing. Arresting main dishes such as roasted duck with a ragout of poultry organs sit alongside more delicate concoctions such as goujonettes of sole with lobster and asparagus in a lavender cream sauce, for instance. The house wines are an Alsace riesling and a red from Provence. *Seats 45. Open 1200-1430, 1800-2130. Closed L Sat, all Mon, 5 Dec, 24 Dec, 31 Dec-9 Jan. Valet parking. Amex, Diners, Mastercard, Visa.*

Tel: (1751) 19232   Fax: (1751) 10969
Stoeplaan 27, 2243 CX Wassenaar-Zuid, Den Haag

This hotel, in a smart district of The Hague, used to be a typical Dutch farmhouse. Following the building of two more storeys, the lower floors have now been redecorated in light colours. Rooms are fairly plain but some have fine antique furniture. There is a theatre and two boardrooms for the use of businessmen. The staff are very friendly and helpful. **Rooms** 24. *Rooms service limited. Private parking. Conference facilities. Garden. Amex, Diners, Mastercard, Visa.*

The functional simplicity of the Auberge is matched by the plain decor of its restaurant. The food, broadly French in slant, is good, with set menus starting at 39.50hfl. These change every two months but might include grilled salmon steak with dill sauce and duck à l'orange, while the carte features more ambitious creations: sautéed monkfish with onion confit and fennel, for example. The international wine list is biased towards France. **Seats** 80 (outside in summer 80). *Open 1200-1430, 1800-2200.*

Tel: (70) 363 79 30   Fax: (70) 361 57 85
Buitenhof 39-42, 2513 AH Den Haag

This cheery hotel enjoys a central location in a pleasant, leafy street next to the Binnenhof (the Dutch Parliament buildings). The decor is light and the rooms comfortable. The terrace is opened up during the summer for diners. **Rooms** 26. *Room service limited. Private parking 20hfl. Banqueting facilities 100. Conference facilities 100. Terrace. Amex, Diners, Mastercard, Visa.*

Tel: (70) 346 49 77   Fax: (70) 362 52 86
Noordeinde 196, 2514 GS Den Haag

Roberto De Luca's city centre restaurant was modernised and redecorated in early 1995. Now it is air-conditioned and the colour scheme of pale green and pastels creates a fresher and more intimate atmosphere to complement the traditional Italian food. Starters from the carte include veal in a creamed tuna sauce with peppers and warm carpaccio with pesto, while grilled turbot with truffle oil and potato patties and fillet of beef with basil and tomato pesto make satisfying main dishes. Set menus start at 57.50hfl for three courses. **Seats** 38. *Open 1200-1400, 1800-2200. Closed L Sat, all Sun, 2 weeks end Aug. Amex, Diners, Mastercard, Visa.*

Tel: (70) 347 55 14   Fax: (70) 381 95 96
Zijdelaan 20, 2594 BV Den Haag

De Hoogwerf is in an old Dutch farmhouse surrounded by a park near the Queen's Palace. Head chef Hans Bakx changes his menu of French food daily but typical dishes are lamb in a dill sauce and beef strogonoff. Oenophiles might be intrigued to find the little-known Dutch wine industry represented on the largely French list. **Seats** 40. *Open 1200-1500, 1800-2130. Closed Sun, Easter. Amex, Diners, Mastercard, Visa.*

Tel: (70) 363 29 32   Fax: (70) 345 17 21
Lange Voorhout 54-56, 2514 EG Den Haag

The Inter-Continental group took over this historic hotel five years ago and are continuing their extensive renovation plan. The banqueting rooms were being refurbished at the time of going to press. Decor is simple and elegant, with light colours and fabrics complementing reproduction furniture. In more glamorous days, the ballerina Pavlova stayed here, and Mata Hari practised the second oldest profession within these walls. If you are a fan of the exquisite paintings of Vermeer then Des Indes would be an ideal place to stay. A major exhibition of works by the enigmatic Dutchman will be taking place in the Mauritshuis opposite the hotel during 1996. Hotel guests have free use of a gym across the street. **Rooms** 76. *Room service 24hr. Private parking 25hfl. Banqueting facilities 120. Conference facilities 80. Secretarial/translation services on request. Amex, Diners, Mastercard, Visa.*

Tel: (70) 416 26 36   Fax: (70) 416 26 46
Gevers Deynootweg 30, 2586 CK Scheveningen, Den Haag

This famous hotel in the beach resort of Scheveningen was formerly the Grand Municipal Bathing House and is now part of the German Steigenberger chain. In the 1890s the gaming club here was a favourite haunt of the rich and frivolous. The casino re-opened in 1979 but is due to move to a building across the street at the end of 1995. Guests will still have free entry. The hotel is also the venue for monthly concerts, with music ranging from classical to Dionne Warwick. It's not all fun and games though: the conference facilities here are excellent, with 14 air-conditioned meeting rooms available. *Rooms 448.*
Room service 24hr. Public parking 21hfl. Banqueting facilities 300. Conference facilities 450. Gym. Casino. Amex, Diners, Mastercard, Visa.

The sleek, modern decor of the restaurant (complete with four signed lithographs by Kandinsky) sits comfortably with the adventurous French/Italian food cooked by Koos Vannoort. The carte features dishes such as lobster mousseline and an olive oil sauce perfumed with saffron and dill, and a trio of sweetbreads, veal medallion and calf's kidneys with polenta and a sherry sauce. The menu du marché at 87.50hfl changes monthly but might include salad of asparagus and quail's breast with truffle vinaigrette, and grilled turbot served on potato puree with asparagus and shrimp and a lobster sauce. French wines are the most popular on the international list. *Seats 55. Open 1230-1500, 1800-2230. Closed L Sat (L every day Jul/Aug), all Sun.*

Around The Hague

Tel: (70) 327 74 60   Fax: (70) 327 50 62
Veursestraatweg 104, 2265 CG Leidschendam

The Matarazzi family have run this substantial 18th-century mansion as a restaurant for 23 years. The arrival of a new chef six years ago shifted the balance of the menu from traditionally French towards more rustic Italian cooking as shown in salmon lasagne, spinach and ricotta ravioli and a *dégustation di carpaccio* (wafer-thin slices of various raw meats and fish). Some traditional French dishes remain, like *chevreuil aux mures et au poivre* (venison with blackberries and pepper) and traditional calf's sweetbreads in a white wine sauce. There are various different set menus, including a vegetarian menu at 75hfl. A large, but cosy place, with rich, red carpeted floors and wooden tables. The wine list focuses mainly on Italy. *Seats 80 (private room 65). Open 1200-1430, 1800-2200. Closed first 2 weeks Aug. Private parking. Amex, Diners, Mastercard, Visa.*

Tel: (70) 387 20 81   Fax: (70) 387 77 15
Oosteinde 14, 2271 EH Voorburg

Formerly known as Vreugd en Rust, the restaurant, set in a 17th-century mansion in its own park, has a serene, civilised atmosphere. Mr Savelberg returned early in 1995 after a two year absence to become chef and sole shareholder and he has not brought many changes to the excellent but straightforward French dishes on the seasonal menu. Starters might include a simple lobster salad or sautéed duck liver in a raspberry vinaigrette. Grilled turbot with chanterelles and tournedos Rossini are classic main courses. Some desserts are more adventurous: passion fruit soufflé with yoghurt sorbet, for example. Set menu 87.50hfl. The wine list is excellent with a good showing of Californians. Prices for one of the 14 bedrooms start at 250hfl. *Seats 80 (terrace 50). Open 1200-1530, 1900-2400. Closed Sun, Mon (only open for parties), 24 Dec-1 Jan. Amex, Diners, Mastercard, Visa.*

Meal prices for 2 are based on à la carte menus. When set menus are available, prices will often be lower.

Tel: (120) 436 03 44   Fax: (10) 436 78 26
Rochussenstraat 20, 3015 EK Rotterdam

The big wheels of Dutch industry have been eating, drinking and clinching deals in the restaurant and its Bodega Bar since it was rebuilt after World War II. As is so often the case in the Netherlands, the menu is a meld of Dutch and French cuisines. Seafood is the main speciality, particularly lobster, turbot and sole. Lobster bisque is finished at the table. There is also a good selection of meat dishes, including saddle of lamb with honey and thyme sauce, and crisp-fried veal sweetbreads served au gratin with small lobster tails and lavender sauce. The menu marché matinal changes weekly and is 62.50hfl for four courses, 77.50hfl for five. South African wine is the most popular newcomer on the list. *Seats 75. Open 1130-2400. Closed Sat, Sun (open for parties). Valet parking. Amex, Diners, Mastercard, Visa.*

Tel: (10) 436 05 30   Fax: (10) 436 71 40
Heuvellaan 21, 3016 GL Rotterdam

There is a fine view over the harbour through the large window of this cosy restaurant. Owner and chef Cees Helder's Dutch/French cooking includes dishes such as terrine of Dutch herring with potatoes, gherkins and dill, halibut with a mushroom ragout and mousseline of anchovy, and breast of duck with fried apples and onions. A three-course set lunch costs 67.50hfl and set dinners range in price from 78.50hfl to 137.50hfl for the five-course menu prestige. *Seats 60. Open 1200-1500, 1800-2200. Closed L Sat, all Sun, 25 Dec-1 Jan. Valet parking. Amex, Diners, Mastercard, Visa.*

Tel: (10) 4121 72 44   Fax: (10) 411 97 11
Kruishade 72, 3012 EH Rotterdam

The location of this Indonesian restaurant, in the middle of a shopping centre in the heart of the city, is not exactly picturesque. However, it is worth seeking out for the excellent Indonesian food. The menu is long and contains a number of unusual dishes. Starters include wild oyster or goat satay and baked lobster with marinated walnuts. If you are feeling brave you could go on to try wolf-fish in Balinese sauce, or perhaps the special "Chef's lamb" grilled in soya sauce, served with fruit. The wine list is mainly French with good selections of Pauillac and Margaux. There is live music every night from a singer/pianist. Set menus from 59.50hfl to 105hfl. *Seats 120. Open 1200-2230 (1600-2230 Sat & Sun). Public parking 3hfl. Amex, Diners, Mastercard, Visa.*

Tel: (10) 413 92 80   Fax: (10) 404 57 12
Hoogstraat 81, 3011 PJ Rotterdam

This formal but friendly hotel near to the harbour was built in the early 60s. It is modern and functional with a beige, pink and green colour scheme throughout. Rooms are plain but light and double-glazing successfully keeps the noise of the city at bay. Although the majority of guests are businessmen, there are no conference facilities. Health-conscious visitors can use the sports centre across the street. *Rooms 94. Closed 24 Dec-1 Jan. Room service limited. Amex, Diners, Mastercard, Visa.*

Tel: (10) 413 47 90   Fax: (10) 412 78 90
Willemsplein 1, 3016 DN Rotterdam

The hotel has been thoroughly renovated since becoming part of the Norwegian Rainbow chain. Decor is colourful but simple with lots of pale wood, and all bedrooms have cable TV, safe and mini-bar. Its position is lovely, on the banks of the Niewe Maas river, and Rotterdam railway station is 2km away. *Rooms 104. Closed 24 Dec-2 Jan. Room service 24hr. Conference facilities 60. Private parking. Amex, Diners, Mastercard, Visa.*

Around Rotterdam

Tel: (10) 455 13 33   Fax: (10) 456 80 23
Martin Luther Kingweg 7, 3069 EW Rotterdam

A convivial restaurant housed in a cosy old farmhouse decorated with antiques. The food is international with heavy Gallic leanings. Frogs' legs and snails sit alongside salmon with sesame in a ginger soy sauce and fillet of suckling pig with a honey and thyme sauce. Set menus range from the simple fare of the 39.50hfl menu sympathique to the carpaccio, duck liver, and lamb with strawberry sauce of the menu dégustation at 89.50hfl. The mainly French wine list of around 600 bottles is one of the most extensive in the country. *Seats 90 (terrace 30). Open 1100-2200. Closed 24 Dec, 31 Dec. Private parking. Amex, Diners, Mastercard, Visa.*

Tel: (10) 426 40 96   Fax: (10) 473 00 08
Korte Dam 8-10, 3111 BG Schiedam

The auberge was built in 1547 on the foundations of a 12th-century convent. The owners, the Hosman family, also run the adjoining bistro and a thriving wine importing business. The menu of French food is short but carefully chosen. Soups include bouillabaisse and cream of asparagus with tomato ravioli, while quail stuffed with Dutch asparagus is a fine main course in season. Desserts are simple. Try fresh mango with mango sorbet or a plate of Dutch cheeses. The lively bistro next door serves similar food but at cheaper prices. *Seats 50. Open 1200-1400, 1800-2200. Closed L Sat, all Sun & Mon. Amex, Diners, Mastercard, Visa.*

Tel: (10) 426 46 26   Fax: (10) 473 25 01
Maasboulevard 9, 3114 HB Schiedam

The success of this restaurant on the banks of the Meuse has been such that the owners, the Van Bruggens, have successfully opened another, Beau Bourg (qv), in Amsterdam. Asparagus, herring and the excellent Dutch Texel lamb are specialities of the house, but most of the imaginative dishes on the long menu are French. A typical meal might begin with sautéed duck liver with sweet asparagus and a port and ginger sauce, followed by lasagne with fillet of brill and smoked salmon in a lobster sauce, and ending with a tower of pears and spun sugar with a Sauternes sauce. House wines are from Georges Duboeuf. Set menus from 65hfl to 105hfl. *Seats 80. Open 1200-1500, 1800-2230. Closed L Sat, all Sun. Private parking. Amex, Diners, Mastercard, Visa.*

OUDESCHANS: De Piekenier

FRIESLAND
APPELSCHA: La Tourbe
BAKKEVEEN: De Slotplaats
BOLSWARD: De Doele
DRACHTEN: De Wilgenhoeve
HEERENVEEN: Sir Sebastian

BLOKZIJL: Kaatje bij Sluis
DALFSEN: Pien
DE LUTTE: De Wilmersberg
ENSCHEDE: Het Koetshuis
  Schuttersveld
ENTER: De Twentsche Hoeve
OOTMARSUM: De Wiemsel
ZWOLLE: Barbara

ARNHEM: De Menthenberg
BRUCHEM: Landgoed Groenboven
EDE: Het Pomphuis
GARDEREN: De Bonte Koe
's HEERENBERG: Le Loup
NUNSPEET: Het Roode Wold
OLDENBROEK: Herkert
WAGENINGEN: Steakhouse

HARMELEN: De Kloosterhoeve
HOUTEN: De Hofnar
MONTFOORT: De Schans
UTRECHT: Jean d'Hubert
VINKEVEEN: Le Canard Sauvage
WOERDEN: De Schutter

AMSTERDAM: Bartholdy
AMSTERDAM: Beddington's
AMSTERDAM: De Boekanier
AMSTERDAM: Chez Georges
AMSTERDAM: Forte Crest Apollo
AMSTERDAM: The Grand
AMSTERDAM: Intermezzo
AMSTERDAM: SAS Royal Hotel
AMSTERDAM: Swissotel Ascot
AMSTERDAM: Teppan Yaki
  Hosokawa

AMSTERDAM: De Trechter
AMSTERDAM: Het Tuynhuys
BENTVELD: Blanje Bleu
BEVERWIJK: 't Gildehuys
BEVERWIJK: In'd Hooge Heeren
CALLANTSOOG: De Vijverhut
HAARLEM: Peter Cuyper
HEEMSKERK: De Vergulde Wagen
HEEMSTEDE: Le Cheval Blanc
HEERHUGOWAARD: De Zandhorst
HILVERSUM: Chablis
HOORN: Portofino
KUDELSTAART: De Kempers Roef
LISSERBROEK: Het Oude Dijkhuys
MONNICKENDAM: Nieuw
  Stuttenburgt
SCHAGEN: Igesz
SCHIPHOL: Hilton Airport
SCHOORL: Merlet
TEXEL DEN HOORN: Het Kompas
ZANDVOORT: Riche
Z.O. BEEMSTER: La Ciboulette

BERGAMBACHT: Onder de Molen
DELFT: L'Orage
DEN HAAG: Julien
DEN HAAG: Rousseau
DEN HAAG: Sauvage
DEN HAAG: Sequenza
DEN HAAG: Shirasagi
HOEK VAN HOLLAND: De
  Blaasbalg
LEIDEN: Holiday Inn
LEIDERDORP: Elckerlyc
MIDDELHARNIS: De Hooge
  Heerlykheid
OEGSTGEEST: De Beukenhof
OOSTVOORNE: Parkzicht
OUDDORP: Beau Rivage
ROTTERDAM: Hilton
ROTTERDAM: Parkheuvel
SPIJKENISSE: 't Ganzegors
WADDINXVEEN: 't Baarsje
WARMOND: De Stad Rome

BREDA: Le Canard
DEN BOSCH: Chalet Royal
EINDHOVEN: Holiday Inn

EINDHOVEN: De Luytervelde
ETTEN-LEUR: De Zwaan
OIRSCHOT: La Fleurie
UDEN: De Druiventros

LIMBURG
HIEJEN: Mazenburg
MAASTRICHT: 't Plenske
NUTH: Pingerhof
VAALS: Ambiente
VAALS: Gillissen

VALKENBURG: Les Cupidos
VALKENBURG: Eduards
VALKENBURG: 't Hooght-
  Thermaetel
VALKENBURG: Lindenhorst
VALKENBURG: Prinses Juliana
WEERT: l'Auberge

ZEELAND
SCHUDDEBEURS: Schuddebeurs
SLUIS: Oud Sluis

Norway

Currency Norwegian Krone **Exchange Rate** £1=approx NKʀ 9.82
International dialling code 00 47 (Oslo+22)
Passports/Visas No visa required by British passport holders.
British Embassy in Oslo Tel 22-55 2400

Airports
Oslo-Fornebu (international & regular flights) Tel 67-53 8566
Oslo-Gardemoen (charter flights) Tel 63-97 8448
Railway Stations
Oslo Central Station Tel 22-36 8000 (reservations internat 22-36 8111
domestic 022-36 8085) **National theateret Station**
(tel information service) Tel 22-17 70 30
Norwegian State Railways (central office) Tel 22-83 8850
(Reservations 22-17 1400)
Car hire in Oslo
Tel Nos. **Hertz** 22-20 0121 (airport 67-53 3647) **Avis** 22-83 5800
(airport 67-53 0557) **Budget** 22-17 1050 (airport 67-7924)
Speed limits 80 km/h on trunk roads, 90 km/h on motorways, 50 km/h
in towns.

Banks Winter hours Mon-Fri 8.15am-3.30pm (Thu till 3pm). Summer
hours (15 May-15 Sep) Mon-Fri 8.15am-3pm (Thu till 5pm).
Shops Mon-Fri 9am-4/5pm, Thu till 6/8pm, Sat till 1/3pm.

New Year's Day, 9 & 13 Apr, Easater, 1, 17 & 25 May, 4 & 5 June,
Christmas Day & Boxing Day.

Norwegian Tourist Board in **London** Tel 0171-839 6255
In **Oslo** (main office) Tel 22-83 0050 (Central Station) Tel 22-17 1124
American Express Travel Service Offices or Representative (R)
Oslo   American Express
              Karl Johansgatan 33/35
              PO Box 1705
              0121
              Tel 2-2861300 #

Tel: 22 44 18 35   Fax: 22 44 47 91
Camilla Colletts vei 15, 0258 Oslo 2

Part of the American Best Western chain, the Ambassadeur is located in a pleasant residential district behind the Royal Palace. The hotel's decor breaks with the usual Norwegian minimalism, and bedrooms follow a variety of themes including 'Amsterdam', 'Rome', 'Shanghai' and 'Captain's Cabin'. If you want to explore the beautiful country around Oslo, cross-country skiing facilities are 15 minutes drive away. *Rooms 41. Conference facilities 25. Indoor swimming pool. Sauna. Amex, Diners, Mastercard, Visa.*

Tel: 22 41 64 64   Fax: 22 44 25 07
I Rådhuspassasjen, 0160 Oslo 1

The restaurant is justifiably proud of inspiring Karen Blixen's book Babette's Feast, subsequently made into an enchanting film. The chef is Bavarian which may explain why meat dishes receive equal billing with fish on the international menu. The choice is small but tempting, with specialities such as cold bell pepper soup with fresh langoustine, followed by garlic marinated rack of lamb in rosemary sauce, served with baked squash and aubergines. Desserts are straightforward but delicious: vanilla and chocolate parfait served with fresh strawberries, for instance. *Seats 40. Open 1600-2230 (1700-2230 Sat). Closed Sun, 5 days at Easter, 23 -27 Dec. Amex, Diners, Mastercard, Visa.*

Tel: 22 44 63 97   Fax: 22 43 64 20
Bygdøy Alle 3, 02257 Oslo 2

Chef Eyvind Hellstrøm's restaurant (open for dinner only) is one of Scandinavia's finest. He trained with Girardet among others and in 1982 bought this building, where he has made his reputation creating superb classic French food from the best Norwegian raw materials. Typical starters are grilled crayfish with tarragon, and cream of artichokes with mussels and celery. Main courses include sole steamed in seaweed, loin of veal with sage, and reindeer fillet with wild mushrooms. Soufflés are a feature of the dessert menu. Try the warm passion fruit soufflé if you get the chance. Set menus change daily and range in price from NKr375 to NKr750. The long wine list of over 600 bottles includes a magnificent selection of burgundies and Bordeaux. The modern Norwegian art on the walls and abundant flowers imbue the restaurant with a peaceful, civilised air. *Seats 75. Open 1800-2300. Closed Sun, Christmas Day, Easter, National holidays. Amex, Diners, Mastercard, Visa.*

Tel: 22 42 95 30   Fax: 22 41 94 37
Rosenkrantzgate 8, 0159 Oslo 1

This homely hotel in the centre of Oslo is another member of the Best Western chain. However, the welcome and decor are typically Norwegian, with stylish pine furniture in the bedrooms and restrained, restful colour schemes. Rustic souvenirs are available from the hotel's own craft shop. The central location means that it is best to ask for a room at the back overlooking the courtyard to be assured of complete peace. *Rooms 76. Closed Easter, Christmas. Room service 24 hrs. Sauna. Solarium. Amex, Diners, Mastercard, Visa.*

Tel: 22 82 60 00   Fax: 22 82 60 01
Kristian IV's gate 7, 0164 Oslo 1

The 1920s-style Bristol is well located in the centre of the city near the Royal Palace. It is part of the Norwegian Inter Nor chain and staff are very friendly and helpful. Facilities are not extensive but all bedrooms have cable TV and mini-bars. The library bar is a pleasant place to drink and browse. *Rooms 141. Room service limited. Public parking NKr120. Banqueting facilities 300. Conference facilities 120. Garden. Amex, Diners, Mastercard, Visa.*

Tel: 22 43 40 28   Fax: 22 55 65 65
President Harbitzgate 4, 0259 Oslo 1

Le Canard has recently moved (300m up the street) into a huge villa dating from 1900 with its own garden and private parking spaces. Not surprisingly, duck is one of chef Lucien Mares' specialities: canard roti aux olives is particularly fine. Other dishes on the menu of traditional French food are roti de turbot stuffed with aromatic herbs and vegetables, served with a Noilly Prat sauce, and fillet of veal à la hongroise. Desserts include chocolate mousse, sorbets and prune and armagnac ice cream. *Seats 80. Open 1700-2300 (1800-2300 Fri, Sat). Closed Sun, Easter. Amex, Diners, Mastercard, Visa.*

Tel: 22 41 90 60   Fax: 22 42 96 89
Stortingsgaten 24, 0117 Oslo 1

This family-run hotel enjoys an excellent location between the City Hall and the Royal Palace. Much modernisation has taken place in recent years and bedrooms are now smartly furnished and have cable TV and mini-bars. Some rooms are currently being refurbished with 'English-style' wallpapers. Conference facilities have been expanded and updated and there are now nine meeting rooms as well as more audio-visual equipment available. *Rooms 163. Closed 23 Dec-2 Jan. Room service limited. Private parking NKr100. Banqueting facilities 200. Conference facilities 9 rooms. Bureau de change. News kiosk. Amex, Diners, Mastercard, Visa.*

A sense of history and continuity pervades this wonderful Belle Epoque restaurant, with its high, ornate ceiling, columns and glittering chandeliers. Swiss chef Willi Wissenbach has been cooking here since 1956 and the head waiter arrived two years later. The classic French food is of a consistently high standard. The seasonal menu might include minestrone de coquilles Saint Jacques (minestrone with grilled scallops) or warm mousse of trout with langoustines and a champagne sauce, followed by lotte (monkfish) with creamed onions and red wine sauce, or rack of lamb with fettucine of vegetables and a thyme sauce. If you cannot make up your mind which dessert to order, try a little of everything with the Annen Etage dessert plate. A fine seven-course dégustation menu is NKr580. The wine list is international. *Seats 80. Open 1700-2230. Closed Sat, Sun, Jul.*

Tel: 22 41 50 62   Fax: 22 42 77 41
Øvre Slottsgate 16, 0157 Oslo 1

Chef Freddie Nielsen has always been fascinated by Dumas' heroic tales and vowed that when he opened his own restaurant it would bear the name of his favourite musketeer. His culinary heroes are Michel Guérard and Raymond Blanc and, following a training in France and Copenhagen, he opened here in the late 70s and has been successfully creating fine French food ever since. Baked sole and foie gras are among the specialities on his seasonal menu. Other fine dishes are vichyssoise with bell pepper sauce, marinated salmon with lime and pepper, gateau of halibut with truffles and armagnac, and (the more traditionally Norwegian) reindeer fillet with blueberry sauce. A selection of French cheeses or a fine chariot des desserts will supply the finishing touch to your meal. The restaurant is on the first floor while the bistro A Touch of France, under the same ownership, is at street level. *Seats 55. Open 1630-2300. Closed Sat (except Oct-Dec), Sun, 2nd week Jul-1st week Aug. Amex, Diners, Mastercard, Visa.*

Tel: 22 44 17 77   Fax: 22 56 11 39
Balchensgate 5, 0265 Oslo 2

Chef Jorn Lie is part of Norway's national culinary team and will be in action in the unofficial cooks' Olympics in Berlin in 1996. Back at home he uses many local ingredients to create French food of a very high standard. Fish and shellfish play a prominent role and his fresh marinated salmon (laks) with goat's cheese, avocado, Swedish orange caviar and creamy herb dressing is particularly outstanding. Brill, sole, turbot and monkfish are all cooked imaginatively. The last is grilled and served with steamed spinach, sauteed mushrooms, creamy morel sauce and red wine butter. A speciality meat dish is rack of lamb baked with veal sweetbreads, herbs and mustard, served with tarragon-glazed vegetables and creamed spring onions. Desserts make use of the multitude of seasonal local berries. A good range of French and international wines is available. The restaurant has recently been redecorated but retains the warm reds and dark greens which give it a relaxed, comfortable atmosphere. *Seats 70. Open 1630-2230. Closed Sun, 23 Dec-2 Jan, Easter, last 3 weeks Jul. Amex, Diners, Mastercard, Visa.*

Tel: 22 55 22 60   Fax: 22 44 27 30
Gabelsgate 16, 0272 Oslo 2

Agathe Riekeles has been running this relaxed hotel, 15 minutes walk from the centre of Oslo, for 50 years. She is constantly upgrading and redecorating although at the moment only the 15 bedrooms in the extension have bathrooms; the others have showers. In the summer breakfast can be taken in the small garden. *Rooms 45. Closed 22 Dec-3 Jan, Sun before and 3rd day after Easter. Room service limited. Private parking. Banqueting facilities 100. Conference facilities 100. Garden. Amex, Diners, Mastercard, Visa.*

Tel: (22) 42 93 90   Fax: (22) 12 25
Karl Johansgate 31, N-0159 Oslo 1

An impressive, palatial building right in the middle of Oslo's main street. One of the pleasures of staying here is that everything is a short stroll away: the sights, the theatre, the park and Parliament. The conference facilities are unusually large and well equipped for Oslo. Note that there are major reductions on the rate quoted above for longer stays during the Summer. *Rooms 289. Room service limited. Private garage 120NKr. Banqueting facilities 100. Conference facilities 300. Secretarial/translation services on request. Beauty treatment. Gym. Mini-bar. Satellite TV. Sauna. Solarium. Indoor swimming pool. Amex, Diners, Mastercard, Visa.*

Tel: 22 43 44 67   Fax: 22 55 48 72
Bygdøy Alle 18, 0262 Oslo 2

An informal restaurant in rustic style. International food comes in large portions with the monthly menu including dishes such as fried skate with tiny vegetables, lime-marinated salmon with basil-steamed cabbage, and veal chop with pasta terrine and pesto sauce. Fruit soups are popular in Scandinavia and one is usually on the dessert menu: for example, rhubarb soup with fresh strawberries and vanilla ice cream. *Seats 55. Open 1800-2300. Closed Sun, 9 Jul-24 Jul. Amex, Diners, Mastercard, Visa.*

Tel: 22 83 05 79   Fax: 22 83 20 09
Bryggetorget 1, Aker Brygge, 0250 Oslo 2

If you want a change from the French cooking favoured by virtually all Oslo's top restaurants, the Kyoto offers top-class Japanese food in a lively, colourful environment. A team of internationally-trained Japanese chefs create authentic sushi, sashimi, teppanyaki, teriyaki and tempura. Most of the fish and meat is Norwegian but, unsurprisingly, the majority of specialist dry ingredients are imported. The melding of the two cultures results in such delicacies as reindeer teriyaki. Set menus from NKr215 to NKr428. *Seats 176 (outside 75). Open 1130-2330. Closed 23 Dec-2 Jan. Amex, Diners, Mastercard, Visa.*

Tel: 22 44 79 90   Fax: 22 44 92 39
Bygdøy Alle 53, 0265 Oslo 2

Now in the third generation of the same family owners, the Norum was purpose-built in 1912. It stands in a quiet part of Oslo near the Vigeland Park and the greenery outside is reflected inside with lots of plants. Four years of renovations were completed in 1994 and all rooms have been been modernised and equipped with satellite TV and mini-bars. Small conferences can be accommodated. *Rooms 59. Closed 22 Dec-2 Jan, Easter week. Conference facilities 60. Garden. Amex, Diners, Mastercard, Visa.*

Tel: 22 44 39 60   Fax: 22 44 67 13
Frederik Stangs gate 3, 0272 Oslo 2

This family-run Ritz franchise is in a residential area not far from the Royal Palace. The building, dating from 1915, was formerly an inn and has a small garden at the front. Rooms are comfortable but facilities are limited. There is a bar and lounge area but no restaurant. *Rooms 50. Closed 23 Dec-3 Jan, Easter week. Room service limited. Private parking. Conference facilities 60. Garden. Amex, Diners, Mastercard, Visa.*

Tel: 22 83 33 00   Fax: 22 83 09 57
Munkedansveien 45, 0250 Oslo 1

This modern business hotel, part of the Rainbow chain, is situated on a busy street near the harbour. Inside, though, the atmosphere is tranquil. Rooms are comfortable and well equipped and business facilities, limited at present, are being upgraded. *Rooms 91. Private parking NKr100. Gym. Solarium. Amex, Diners, Mastercard, Visa.*

Tel: 67 54 57 00   Fax: 67 54 27 33
Sandviksveien 184, 1300 Oslo 2

Only minutes away from a fjord and a 15-minute drive from the centre of Oslo, the hotel is well placed for both business and leisure. Its design is modern and slick with a fine atrium and the works of Norwegian artists hung throughout. All rooms are air-conditioned (unusual, and usually unnecessary, in Norway) and ten are specially adapted for disabled guests. Conference facilities are superb, and have been utilised by NATO among others. If you fancy cruising the fjords, the hotel can rent a yacht for you. *Rooms 242. Room service limited. Private parking. Conference facilities 400. Gym. Steam room. Spa bath. Night club. Amex, Diners, Mastercard, Visa.*

THE APARTMENT SERVICE
Tel in UK (0181) 748 4207   Fax (0181) 748 3972
The Apartment Service will find you the right apartment worldwide to suit your needs, whether you are on a short or long-term stay. A 96-page colour catalogue is free on request. All budgets are catered for.

Your Guarantee of Quality and Independence

EGON RONAY'S GUIDES
1996

- Establishment inspections are anonymous
- Inspections are undertaken by qualified Egon Ronay's Guides inspectors
- The Guides are completely independent in their editorial selection
- The Guides do not accept advertising, hospitality or payment from listed establishments

Titles planned for 1996 include

Hotels & Restaurants ● Pubs & Inns ● Europe
Ireland ● Just A Bite
And Children Come Too ● Paris
Oriental Restaurants

Egon Ronay's Guides are available from all good bookshops or can be ordered from: Leading Guides, 35 Tadema Road, London SW10 0PZ
Tel 0171 352 0172

Currency Polish Zloty ** **Exchange Rate** £1=approx ZLT 3.8
** Not usually obtainable in UK. Travellers cheques recommended.
International dialling code 00 48
(Gdansk+58 Poznan+61, Krakow+12, Wroclaw+71, Warsaw+22(6fig)
+2(7fig), Bydgoszcz+52)
Passports/Visas No visa required by British passport holders for stay
of less than 6 months.
British Embassy in Gdansk Tel 58-628 1001/5   Fax 58-621 7161

Airports
Warsaw Tel (International) 22-461 731/22-465 603
(Domestic) 2-650 1750/2-650 1953
Railway Stations
Warsaw Tel (International) 22-204 512/22-259 942
(Domestic) 22-200 361/369
Car hire in Warsaw
Tel Nos. **Avis** 2-630 7316 (airport 2-650 4872) **Budget** 2-630 7280 (air-
port 22-467 310) **Europcar** (airport) 22-249 772
Speed limits 90km/h on trunk roads, 110 km/h on motorways, 60 km/h
in towns.

Banks 8am-noon Mon-Fri (varies from town to town).
Shops (for groceries) 6am-6/7pm (Sat 7am-1pm), some shops stay
open for late-night shopping and on Sundays and holidays. Other shops
10/11am-6/7pm, department stores generally 9am-8pm.

New Year's Day, Easter Sunday & Monday, 1 & 3 May, movable feasts,
Corpus Christi, 15 Aug, All Saints Day, 11 Nov, Christmas Day & Boxing
Day.

Polish National Tourist Office in **London** Tel 0171-580 8811
In **Poland** Warsaw Tel 2-635 1881/22-316 356
Gdansk Tel 58-314355/316637 Krakow Tel 12-226091
Poznan Tel 61-526156 Bydgoszcz Tel 52-228432
Wroclaw Tel 71-443111
American Express Travel Service Offices or Representative (R)

Gdansk	Orbis Travel (R)
	22 Heweliusza Street
	80-890
	Tel 58-314054/312132 #
Krakow	Orbis Travel (R)
	Cracovia Hotel
	1,F. Focha Ave
	30-111
	Tel 12-224632/219880 #
Warsaw	Dom Bez Kantow Krakowskie
	Przedmiescie 11
	PI-34500
	PO Box 159
	Tel 22-6352002 #

Gdansk/Gdynia/Sopot

GDANSK   **Hotel Hevelius**   ZLT185

Tel: (58) 31 56 31   Fax: (58) 31 19 22
Ul Heweiusza 22, 80-890 Gdansk

This hotel is ideal if you want an old city location, although it is a rather unimaginative, unappealing modern tower block. Rooms have no air-conditioning or mini-bars but do feature satellite TV with channels in both English and German. Half the bathrooms have recently been refurbished. Room rates are set in Deutschmarks (DM138 in the summer of 1995) so the local currency price quoted above will vary with the exchange rate.
Rooms 286. Room service all day. Parking in nearby public car park Zlt17 for 24 hours. Conference facilities 120. Hairdressing. Sun bed. Amex, Diners, Mastercard, Visa.

GDANSK   **Hotel Marina**   ZLT240

Tel: (58) 53 20 79   Fax: (58) 53 04 60
Ul Jelitkowska 20, 80-341 Gdansk

Modern, functional hotel built in the mid-80s. No air-conditioning or mini-bars in the rooms, but the hotel does boast a good range of leisure facilities and a location handy for the beach and marina. Room rates are set in Deutschmarks (DM140 in the summer of 1995) so the local currency price quoted above will vary with the exchange rate.
Rooms 147. Room service all day. Secure parking Zlt10 for 24 hours. Conference facilities 120. Tennis. Indoor swimming pool. Sauna. Sun bed. Gym. 10-Pin bowling (2 lanes). Amex, Diners, Mastercard, Visa.

GDANSK   **Pod Lososiem**   ZLT120

Tel (58) 31 76 52   Fax: (58) 31 56 48
Szeroka 54, 80-835 Gdansk

Situated right in the old town, with its magnificent squares of burghers' houses and historic docks, is this up-market and expensive restaurant, which specialises in grilled salmon, though other fish and meat dishes are also available. Credit cards not accepted for parties of more than four. *Seats 120. Open 1100-2300. Amex, Diners, Mastercard, Visa.*

GDANSK   **Tawerna**   ZLT200

Tel & Fax: (58) 31 41 14
Powroznicza 19-20, 80-828 Gdansk

Fish and duck (including a classic dish of duck with apples) are the specialities of this restaurant in the historic heart of the old city. *Seats 60. Open 1100-2300. Amex, Diners, Mastercard, Visa.*

GDYNIA   **Hotel Gdynia**   ZLT238

Tel: (58) 20 66 61   Fax: (58) 20 86 51
Ul Armii Krajowej 22, 81-372 Gdynia

This comfortably modern hotel is close to the marina and beach. Facilities include a small business centre (if it's a working trip) as well as boutiques, galleries and various leisure amenities. No air-conditioning. Mini-bars in the two suites only. Room rates are set in Deutschmarks (DM140 in the summer of 1995) so the local currency price quoted above will vary with the exchange rate. *Rooms 297. Room service all day. Private parking. Conference facilities 200. Indoor swimming pool. Sauna. Sun bed. Boutiques. Amex, Diners, Mastercard, Visa.*

SOPOT   **Grand Hotel Sopot**   ZLT255

Tel: (58) 51 00 41   Fax: (58) 51 61 24
Ul Powstancow Warszawy 12-14, 81-718 Sopot

Built in 1926, in the grand style of the period, this hotel enjoys a fabulous location being in the centre of Sopot but also right by the beach (there's a beach bar just to hand). A programme of bathroom refurbishment was almost half complete in mid-1995. Room rates are set in Deutschmarks (DM150 in the summer of 1995) so the local currency price quoted above will vary with the exchange rate. *Rooms 112. Room service 24hr. Parking free. Conference facilities 160. Casino. Billiard room. Fitness room. Amex, Diners, Mastercard, Visa.*

Tel (12) 37 50 44   Fax (12) 37 59 38
Ul Armii Krajowej 11 30-111 Krakow

Part of the Orbis chain. *Rooms 306. 24hr room service. Theatre-style conference facilities up to 250. Satellite TV. Air-conditioning. Indoor swimming pool. Sauna. Solarium. Massage. Hair salon. Bureau de change. Shop.*

Tel (12) 22 86 66   Fax (12) 21 95 86
Ul Marszalka Focha 1 30-111 Krakow

Part of the Orbis chain, this hotel is centrally located 10 mins from the city centre, close to the Krakowskie Blonia walking promenade. *Rooms 361. Theatre-style conferences for up to 90. Satellite TV. Hair salon. Bureau de change. Coffee shop 0700-2200. Closed 3 days November. Amex, Diners, Mastercard, Visa.*

Tel & Fax (12) 21 80 25 & (12) 21 86 89
Ul Szpitalna 28 31-024 Krakow

This hotel, located in the centre of the old town, offers accommodation in suites or single rooms only. *Rooms 15. Room service till to 0000. Satellite TV. Minibar. Amex, Diners, Mastercard, Visa.*

Tel: (12) 22 32 79   Fax: (12) 21 28 80
Rynek Glowny 17, 31-008 Krakow

Italian food has considerable cachet in Poland, and this establishment offers a comprehensive selection in a lively setting. *Seats 100. Open 1200-2400. No parking. Amex, Diners, Mastercard, Visa.*

Tel: (12) 66 95 00   Fax: (12) 66 58 27
Ul M Konopnickiej 28, 30-302 Krakow

Modern, five-storey hotel opposite the Royal Castle and about a 15-minute walk from the city centre. Air-conditioned bedrooms (of which two floors are reserved for non-smokers) are well-equipped with mini-bars, safes, and satellite television. There are fine views from the roof-top coffee shop. Room rates are set in Deutschmarks (DM250 in the summer of 1995) so the local currency price quoted above will vary with the exchange rate.
Rooms 277. Room service 24hr. Parking Zlt17 for 24 hours. Conference facilities 600. Indoor swimming pool. Sauna. Sun bed. Fitness room. Beauty salon. Hairdressing. Casino. Night club (disco). Amex, Diners, Mastercard, Visa.

Tel: (12) 22 51 22   Fax: (12) 22 52 70
Ul Pijarska 13, 31-015 Krakow

Built in 1912, this is a particularly handsome 'town house' example of the Polish art nouveau style of architecture. Comfortable and traditional, the public areas were renovated, along with the whole hotel, about four years ago. No air-conditioning but all rooms have mini-bar and satellite television. The hotel is located just 200m from the main market square. Room rates are set in Deutschmarks (DM190 in the summer of 1995) so the local currency price quoted above will vary with the exchange rate. *Rooms 42. Room service all day. Conference facilities 30. Amex, Diners, Mastercard, Visa.*

Opening times are often liable to change at short notice, so it's always best to book.

Tel: (12) 221 72 55   Fax: (12) 21 83 60
Slawokowska 507, 31-016 Krakow

One of a growing band of privately-owned hotels in Krakow, this delightful art nouveau house is ideally located in the centre of the city, just 50m from the main square. The whole hotel was completely refurbished about six years ago. Air-conditioning and mini-bars are only to be found in the six suites. Room rates are set in US dollars ($169 in the summer of 1995) so the local currency price quoted above will vary with the exchange rate. No parking. *Rooms 56. Room service all day. Conference facilities 18. Amex, Diners, Mastercard, Visa.*

Tel: (12) 22 47 53   Fax (12) 22 58 64
Rynek Glowny 34, 31-010 Krakow

Set within a burgher's house in the main market square, this up-market, first-floor restaurant has a light, contemporary decor. The menu includes both Polish and more generally European dishes: caviar with blinis, borsch with ravioli, roast duck with apple, pork tenderloin with prunes, roast veal, fruit strudel, walnut pancake. There is a less expensive all-day (1000-2200) eaterie on the ground floor and a café/wine bar in the cellar. *Seats 50. Open 1200-1600, 1800-2300. Amex, Diners, Mastercard, Visa.*

Tel: (12) 21 98 94
Rynek Glowny 25, 31-008 Krakow

Set in a 14th-century cellar with exposed stone and brick work and Louis XIV-style chairs, the restaurant comprises five separate rooms, the smallest with just one table for two, the largest seating up to 25. The menu features Polish specialities (two staples from the menu are onion soup and pork cutlet) along with more international dishes. *Seats 55. Open 1300-2300. Closed Sun (Jun-Aug), Mon (possibly) from Sep to May, 24-26 Dec & 2/3 days Easter. Amex, Diners, Mastercard, Visa.*

Tel: (12) 22 98 96   Fax: (12) 22 12 96
Rynek Glowny 15, 31-008 Krakow

This is one of Poland's best known restaurants-not surprising, as it dates back,in one form or another, to 1364. In a burgher's house in the main square, the mellow decor includes ancient timbered ceilings, a creaking wooden staircase and suits of armour. Particular specialities, from a menu that features suitably traditional Polish fare, include borsch with meatballs, roast duck with apples, collops of pork 'Radziwill', zander (pike-perch) à la polonaise, sautéed trout, and game dishes. *Seats 250. Open 1200-2400. Closed 25 Dec & 1 Jan. Amex, Diners, Mastercard, Visa.*

Poznan

Tel & Fax (66) 86 22 11
Ul Mostowa 24 Oboniki Wielkopolskie 64-600 Poznan

Small, friendly and modern hotel, usefully located away from the city centre. *Rooms 30. 24hr room service. Satellite TV. Air-conditioning in some rooms. Closed 2 days Christmas. Amex, Diners, Mastercard, Visa.*

Tel (61) 41 12 01   Fax: (61) 47 34 41
Ul Litewska, 60-605 Poznan

An inspiring setting on the edge of the Solacki Park, within an attractive country-style building with modern interiors. The service is excellent, as is the menu, which combines local, and national as well as French characteristics. *Seats 100. Open 1300-0100. Amex, Diners, Mastercard, Visa.*

Tel: (61) 77 00 11   Fax: (61) 77 36 54
Ul Warszawska 64-66, 61-028 Poznan

Modern low-rise hotel set within the Malta Lake Park and offering good, practical accommodation. No air-conditioning. Room rates are set in Deutschmarks (DM115 in the summer of 1995) so the local currency price quoted above will vary with the exchange rate. *Rooms 150. Room service all day. Parking Zlt14 for 24 hours. Conference facilities 250. Outdoor swimming pool. Sun bed. Amex, Diners, Mastercard, Visa.*

Tel: (61) 55 80 00   Fax: (61) 55 89 55
Ul Rossevelta 20, 60-829 Poznan

Only a few minutes walk from the international fair venue in the centre of the city, this 30-year-old hotel is undertaking a programme of bedroom refurbishment. The work includes the addition of air-conditioning, a rare luxury in Poznan, and 20 rooms had been completed in the summer of 1995. Room rates are set in Deutschmarks (DM120 in the summer of 1995) so the local currency price quoted above will vary with the exchange rate. Prices also rise when there are major trade fairs in town. *Rooms 314. Room service all day. Public (guarded) parking ZLt17 for 24 hours. Conference facilities 250. Business centre. Night club (disco). Amex, Diners, Mastercard, Visa.*

Tel: (61) 69 91 41   Fax: (61) 52 37 62
Aleja Niepodleglosci 36, 61-714 Poznan

Modern high-rise hotel, though bedrooms are without air-conditioning or mini-bars, conveniently located for the old town. Room rates are set in Deutschmarks (DM118 in the summer of 1995) so the local currency price quoted above will vary with the exchange rate. Prices also increase considerably when there is a major trade fair in town. *Rooms 407. Room service all day. Parking Zlt10 for 24 hours. Conference facilities 200. Sauna. Sun bed. Amex, Diners, Mastercard, Visa.*

Large restaurant with a long menu that includes, for example, no fewer than 14 soups (tomato, borsch, goulash, French onion), so there is going to be something on offer to suit most tastes. Omelettes, grills, poultry, game, fish and meat all get their own sections on the carte. *Seats 300. Open 1300-2300.*

Tel: (61) 33 20 81   Fax: (61) 33 29 61
Pl W Andersa 1, 61-898 Poznan

The city's largest hotel, this 18-year-old high rise is just 500m from the venue for the international trade fairs for which Poznan is well known. Bedrooms come with multi-language, multi-channel TVs but no air-conditioning or mini-bars. The night club features a cabaret. Room rates are set in Deutschmarks (DM118 in the summer of 1995) so the local currency price quoted above will vary with the exchange rate. Prices increase significantly when there is a major trade fair in town. *Rooms 495. Room service all day. Public parking. Conference facilities 500. Sauna. Sun bed. Night club. Amex, Diners, Mastercard, Visa.*

Lots of choice on the menu here with starters ranging from caviar and smoked salmon to zander in aspic, galantine of chicken, escargots au gratin and deep-fried camembert. Main dishes are equally varied: trout with almonds and sesame, sole parisienne, tournedos Rossini, beef stroganoff. Polish specialities include roast pork rib with plums and duck stew with apples plus some dishes from the local region like dumplings made from grated potatoes with bacon and onions, and roast shoulder of pork with boiled potato noodles and sautéed red cabbage. There are also grills, omelettes, vegetarian dishes (mostly salads) and two dishes especially for children. *Seats 240. Open 1300-2300.*

Tel: (61) 52 17 76
Stary Rynek 37-39, 61-772 Poznan

R

Fortunately prices aren't as high as the quality of the food, with plenty of native classics such as hare with prunes, turkey, sausage in batter and buckwheat pancakes. Poignant old Market Square location. *Seats 56. Open 0900-2200 (to midnight during trade fairs). No credit cards.*

Warsaw

Tel: (22) 625 99 61
Matejki 2, 00-478 Warsaw

R

The 'ambassadorial' name of this restaurant is probably more appropriate to its location, near the American Embassy (and, incidentally, within walking distance of the Lazienki Park), rather than being considered an ambassador for Polish cuisine. However, it's fine for straightforward staples, such as meat platters, though presentation can seem rather passé, particularly to Western diners who have long said good-bye to the 'radish flower' school of garnishing. The staff are warm and friendly, the colour scheme bright, with traditional, decorative panels, and there's plenty of greenery springing out from baskets and pots. For an alternative vista look out of the long picture window overlooking the street. Next to the dining room is the restaurant's coffee house, which is worth visiting for ice cream and patisserie, particularly if it's taken in the charming garden. Entrance in Aleje Ujazdowskie 8. *Seats 70. Open 1100-2300. Amex, Diners, Mastercard, Visa.*

Tel & Fax: (22) 31 63 47
Rynek Starego Miasta 3-7, 00-950 Warsaw

R

Walk straight past the snack bar (salads, vegetarian food, 40 different beers), on the ground floor of this distinguished burgher's house on the old town square, and continue up to the first floor, where Bazyliszek offers an altogether more substantial experience. Interconnecting dining-rooms with double wooden doors and period-style furniture have more of the air of a hunting lodge than a city-centre restaurant. Medieval armour, curved swords, cross-bows and other aggressive accessories decorate the walls. A pianist accompanies dinner. Game dishes are prominent on the menu, together with many long-standing favourites of native cuisine. Presentation can sometimes be a bit extravagant and over-elaborate but dishes are full of flavour and consistently impressive. In summer the large garden/terrace is popular and it is here, and on the ground floor, that the set-price (Zlt25) Business Lunch is served. All the French wine regions are covered on the wine list along with some Italians' and the odd bottle or two from Germany, Spain and the USA. Attentive service combines smoothly with all the other elements to make this one of Warsaw's best restaurants. *Seats 150 (+ 150 garden/terrace). Open 1200-2400. Amex, Diners, Mastercard, Visa.*

Tel: (22) 41 48 06   Fax: (22) 41 71 35
Lazienki Krolewskie Park, 00-460 Warsaw

R

Romantically set in a park that includes the magnificent Palace-on-the-Isle, an Egyptian temple and an amphitheatre as well as this Orangery restaurant. The Belvedere's menu takes its inspiration from both classic Polish sources and modern European cooking. Dishes like old Polish borsch with egg and chives, veal baked with apple and dumplings, and a Polish-style apple pie typify the former, while the latter might include carpaccio with parmesan, olive oil and lemon juice, turbot with balsamico sauce, warm chicken liver salad with raspberry vinaigrette, Scottish lamb chops with apricots and dumplings, and fillet of beef with foie gras and truffles. Desserts include tiramisu and a selection of soufflés. There is a French bias to the wine list but other European countries and the New World are also represented. When booking specify a table in the greenery-filled Orangery (or its terrace in summer) and dine to the accompaniment of a classical trio; the alternative is the adjoining neo-classical room where a pianist plays each evening. Poland's last king, Stanislaus Poniatowski, used to hold 'Thursday Dinners' for artists, writers and politicians at his nearby summer residence and the Belvedere revives the spirit of these occasions on the last Thursday of each month with special evenings when the staff dress up in historical costume and entertainment is laid on. The price for these evenings depends upon the entertainment but it's generally about Zlt200 per head. Book well in advance. In summer the business lunch is a daily-changing no-choice barbecue. Take the Parkowa Street entrance to The Lazienki Park to find the restaurant's own secure car park. Set L Zlt44 (business). *Seats* 120. *Open 1200-2330. Closed 25,31 Dec & 1 Nov. Private parking. Amex, Diners, Mastercard, Visa.*

Tel: (2) 625 25 25   Fax: (2) 625 25 77
Ul Krakowskie Przedmiescie 42-44, 00-325 Warsaw

Re-opened in December 1992 (officially five months later by Lady Thatcher), having been restored to its former art nouveau glory, the Bristol can once again be counted among the grand hotels of Europe, fully deserving of our award this year Hotel of the Year, Eastern Europe. Listed as a national monument, it is a short walk from the Old Town, the Royal Castle and the Opera and is situated on 'King's Walk', Warsaw's most fashionable street. It now boasts all the modern comforts in its air-conditioned bedrooms and suites *(Paderewski* and *Presidential* being the finest and grandest), each individually furnished and traditionally elegant, providing satellite TV, mini-bar and 24hr room service. In addition to the main à la carte restaurant (see below) an Italian restaurant *(Marconi)* and the Viennese-inspired *Café Bristol* offer further eating choices, while the magnificent Column Bar is where everyone meets. Room rates are set in US$ ($317 in the summer of 1995) so the local currency price quoted above will vary with the exchange rate. Conference facilities for up to 100. Business centre. **Rooms** 206. *Indoor swimming pool. Steam room. Sauna. Spa bath. Fitness room. Amex, Diners, Mastercard, Visa.*

'Malinowa' translates as 'raspberry' in Polish. New chef Bernard Lussiana presides over a restaurant at the forefront of 'new wave' Polish cuisine - witness his innovative dish of young wild boar stew flavoured with juniper and bison grass, a herbal grass from the Bialowieza forest in the North East of Poland, previously used for flavouring vodka, now partnering food for the first time. For the most part, the style of cooking is French with a native influence, thus a sturgeon fillet is stuffed with its caviar and served with a vodka sabayon and braised sweetbreads are served with a clove jus. Other dishes from the carte might include starters such as Russian caviar with seaweed waffles; warm goose liver salad with raspberry dressing, and a barley consommé with smoked game mousse before main dishes like roasted rack of lamb with a marjoram crust or lobster stew with bacon and wild mushrooms. There are weekly-changing market-inspired specialities in addition to the à la carte, and if you have difficulty in choosing, go for the six-course, no-choice 'Discovery' menu (Zlt155). *Seats 45. Open D only 1800- 2300. Closed Aug.*

Tel: (2) 628 54 72
Ujazdowskie 47, 00-536 Warsaw

Simple, unpretentious restaurant and café (one can drop in just for home-made cake and coffee) in the building of the Polish-Israeli Friendship Society, which provides the theme for a changing art exhibition around the walls. The menu is basically Polish but with other European influences picked up by owners Stash and Alekszandra Pruszynski whilst on their travels. Herring smothered in onions and sour cream, cold cherry soup with noodles, several pierogi (dumpling) dishes, and carp cooked with almonds and raisins in a sweet and sour sauce are all very Polish but there's also wiener schnitzel, filet mignon Lithuanian-style and, among the desserts, tarte au citron, peach melba and a walnut tart from Denmark. The café menu includes both quiche lorraine and croque monsieur. Located in the embassy district of the city, it is particularly popular with diplomats, politicians and journalists, yet the atmosphere is informal, with casual dress perfectly acceptable. About twenty wines on the list, half French and half Hungarian. *Seats 60. Open 1000-2230. Closed D 24 Dec, all 26,27 & 31 Dec & 2 days Easter. Street parking. Amex, Diners, Mastercard, Visa.*

Tel: (22) 26 50 51   Fax: (22) 26 11 11
Krakowskie Przedmiescie 13, 00-061 Warsaw

One of the city's oldest hotels, built in 1857 in a handsome, classical style, it is now somewhat in need of refurbishment and restoration. The location is good however, overlooking the Saxon gardens and only a few minutes walk from the Royal Castle and the old part of town. Room rates are set in Deutschmarks (201DM in the summer of 1995) so the local currency price quoted above will vary with the exchange rate. **Rooms** 200. *Room service all day. Parking at secure public car park next door. Conference facilities 200. Amex, Diners, Mastercard, Visa.*   *See over*

Europejski-Lux   ZŁT100

A colonnaded dining-room that harks back to the hotel's former splendour. At lunchtime the menu concentrates on traditional Polish cuisine while at night things take on a more international flavour. *Seats 120. Open 1000-2400*.

Tel & Fax (22) 49 44 34
Ul Pulawska 43 02-508 Warsaw

Situated near the Japanese embassy, this charming restaurant serves traditional Polish and international dishes. Specialities include blinis with caviar, sour cream, eggs and onions and pig's knuckle in beer. A smörgåsbord is offered everyday from 12.30-6pm. The less formal Garden restaurant downstairs offers dishes from the grill. *Seats 70. Open 1200-2400. Amex, Diners, Mastercard, Visa*.

Tel: (22) 226 53 37   Fax: (22) 27 87 16
Ul Foksal 3-5, 00-366 Warsaw

Once a journalists' club, this centrally located restaurant is now ultra-modern, with a 'river' and water garden featuring as part of a sophisticated decor along with marble and flowers. The cooking is a mix of French and Polish. Starters include no less than 13 different ways with snails (with sweet and sour sauce, deep-fried in batter, covered with hollandaise sauce, baby snails in a cream soup) but there is much else besides from foie gras, carpaccio of smoked and marinated salmon, and breaded frogs' legs with apples and strawberry sauce, to Polish pierogi stuffed with meat, mushrooms and sauerkraut. Mains are no less varied: sole normande, grilled salmon steak, saddle of venison with wild mushroom sauce, stuffed goose drumstick with Polish macaroni and sweet red cabbage, duck with orange, stuffed turkey with apricot sauce. The wine list runs to about 50 bins, mostly French and Italian. *Seats 50. Open 1200-2230. Private parking for ten cars. Amex, Diners, Mastercard, Visa*.

Tel: (22) 31 10 13
Rynek Starego Miasta 27, 00-272 Warsaw

Within one of the burgher's houses in the Old Town market square, this restaurant is resplendent with high-vaulted ceiling, chandeliers, oak panelling and period-style furniture; the grandeur is emphasised by the addition of some folk art. The cooking is 'new wave' Polish in which traditional dishes like bigos (hunters' stew) are given an up-to-date treatment. In summer you can dine alfresco in Fukier's patio courtyard. *Seats 160 (+ terrace). Open 1200-0100. Diners, Mastercard, Visa*.

Tel: (22) 29 40 51   Fax: (2) 621 97 24
Ul Krucza 28, 00-522 Warsaw

A rather stark and unappealing example of post-war socialist architecture but with a good central location close to the business district, the shops and the old part of town. Bedrooms do not have air-conditioning and there are no mini-bars but complimentary soda water is provided and there is a choice of six channels on the satellite TV. All rooms are en suite but about 80 have shower and WC only, however these were the first rooms to benefit from an on going programme of redecoration so might be the best bet at the moment. Room rates are set in Deutschmarks (131DM in the summer of 1995) so the local currency price quoted above will vary with the exchange rate. Room rates drop significantly at weekends. *Rooms 319. Room service 24hr. Own parking, Zlt15 for 24 hours. Conference facilities 100. Amex, Diners, Mastercard, Visa*.

Tel: (2) 620 03 41   Fax: (22) 30 05 68
Zlota Ul 48-54, Warsaw 00-120

Conveniently located in the city centre, the hotel is close to both business and shopping areas and just 200m from the main railway station. Rooms have all the usual facilities such as satellite television and mini-bar and it is planned to install air-conditioning during the winter of 1995/96. Room rates are set in US dollars ($227 from the beginning of 1996) so the local currency price quoted above will vary with the exchange rate. *Rooms 336. Room service 24hr. Parking Zlt24 for 24 hours. Conference facilities 100. Gym. Sauna. Sun beds. Amex, Diners, Mastercard, Visa*.

Tel: (2) 658 44 44   Fax: (2) 659 88 28
Plac Artura Zawiszy 1, 02-025 Warsaw

Something of a cause célèbre when it opened in 1992, the Jan III Sobieski's design was considered so avant-garde that locals streamed in to check it out for themselves. One traditional element is a stately portrait of the 17th-century Polish King after whom the hotel is named but modern design dominates, with variously coloured marbles and wood animating the open plan lay-out. Strangely, for such a modern hotel, only about three quarters of the bedrooms are air-conditioned but all come with mini-bar and satellite TV and those on the 7th (top) floor have a second telephone line to accommodate a fax. The hotel is only moments from the central railway station and the Palace of Culture. Room rates are set in US dollars ($235 in the summer of 1995) so the local currency price quoted above will vary with the exchange rate. *Rooms 403. Room service 24hr. Secure garage parking Zlt25 for 24 hours. Conference facilities 250. Business centre. Gym. Amex, Diners, Mastercard, Visa.*

Three restaurant areas (Arkadia, Chopin & Marysienka) share the same open-plan, atrium 'restaurant landscape' complete with greenery and a fountain bubbling down marble steps. The same menu operates throughout offering a good, varied selection of dishes ranging from warm shrimp salad with balsamic vinegar dressing, beef carpaccio, salmon hollandaise, pasta (mix and match between various shapes and classic sauces), veal florentine and beef shaslac with rice to sweet and sour pork. There is also a short menu of traditional Polish dishes. For afters it's either desserts like Sacher torte, strawberry mousse in pastry, and Viennese apple strudel, or something like deep-fried ice cream with apricot sauce or banana split from a tempting list of ice cream specialities. *Seats 190. Open 1200-2230.*

Tel: (2) 630 63 06   Fax: (2) 630 52 39
Al Jerozolimskie 65-79, 00-697 Warsaw

Soaring above central Warsaw, this Marriott, a joint venture with LOT (the Polish Airline), is always abuzz with life and activity. The various public areas include the well-named Club Panorama (on the 40th floor, for desserts as well as cocktails), O'Hare (pubby with pizzas), Vienna Café (self-explanatory), and Orpheus (disco night club). Restaurants include the all-day Lilla Weneda with Polish specialities, and Parmizzano's, Italian cooking and live music, as well as the Chicago Grill detailed below. Bedrooms are air-conditioned, as is the whole hotel, and come with everything one might expect, from mini-bar to multi-channel, multi-lingual TV. Marriott's American style has translated very successfully, with the local employees being friendly and attentive. Facilities include an American Express Travel desk and a Business Centre, with secretarial and translation facilities, that is manned around the clock. The hotel is located opposite the central railway station and the Palace of Culture, close to the main shopping and business districts. Room rates are set in US dollars ($285 in the summer of 1995) so the local currency price quoted above will vary with the exchange rate. *Rooms 521. Room service 24hr. Limited free parking. Conference facilities 1200. Business centre (24hr). Indoor swimming pool. Sauna. Sun beds. Spa bath. Gym. Massage. Hairdressing. Beauty salon. Casino. Florist. Amex, Diners, Mastercard, Visa.*

The special steak menu proudly states that all the beef comes from the USA, and includes the exhortation to "Eat and Drink American", so this is not perhaps the place for local colour or cuisine. In addition to the T-bone, New York striploin and US prime rib steaks, options include honey-glazed roast duck, veal medallions with morel mushrooms in a cream sauce, lamb Wellington, and roast wild boar on a bed of linguine with a chanterelle and paprika ragout. *Seats 64. Open 1800-2330.*

Tel: (2) 620 02 01   Fax: (2) 620 87 79
Al Jana Pawla II, 00-133 Warsaw

Friendly staff, for whom nothing is to much trouble, are a big plus at this modern mid-rise hotel near the business district. Air-conditioned bedrooms come with mini-bars and satellite TV and all have loos separate from the bathroom. A pianist entertains each evening in the bar. Room rates will be set in Deutschmarks from Jan '96 (when the double rate will be DM280) so the local currency price quoted above will vary with the exchange rate. *Rooms 250. Room service 24hr. Secure garage parking Zlt25 for 24 hours. Conference facilities 220. Business centre. Gym. Sauna. Spa bath. Massage. Amex, Diners, Mastercard, Visa.*

Tel: (22) 27 51 00   Fax:(22)27 23 47
plac Emila Mlynarsklogo 2, Warsaw 00-009T

Set within the National Philharmonic Building, faithfully rebuilt after being destroyed in the war, the menu here is broadly East European with a slight Polish bias. Game, often the product of owner Otto Stohl's own hunting trips, features in season. **Seats** *100 (+60 terrace). Open 1200-2400. Closed 4 days Christmas & 4 days Easter. Amex, Diners, Mastercard, Visa.*

Tel: (22) 31 56 34
Ul Jezuicka 6-8, Warsaw

Charming cellar restaurant in the old town market square. The mellow, candlelit atmosphere is rather more appropriate for dinner than for lunch perhaps. Booking is also advisable. Although technically a club, you don't need to worry about membership. Swietoszek's long-established reputation rests on a friendly, though sometimes over-eager staff, and a menu that accommodates well-presented and well-prepared Polish staples, such as zurek (sour rye soup) and pike-perch as well as international flourishes like chateaubriand and fondues. No parking. **Seats** *70. Open 1300-1130. Closed 25 & 26 Dec. Amex, Diners, Mastercard, Visa*

Tel: (22) 26 51 27   Fax: (22) 26 52 27
Foksal 16 00636 Warsaw

Warsaw's first Japanese restaurant (there are now two others), where the decor is as pleasing as the food. A long menu covers sushi, tempura, noodle and rice dishes plus much else besides like suki-yaki and shabu-shabu. There are various set meals, which are particularly good value at lunchtime when they start at Zlt25; there is a special selection of set lunches for children at Zlt15. Dishes are well presented in authentic Japanese style. They also do take-away and have a home delivery service. The drinks list includes some 40 cocktails and a variety of fruit juices as well as the usual selection of spirits but just a handful of wines. **Seats** *60. Open 1200-2300. Closed 25 Dec & Easter Mon. Street parking. Amex, Diners, Mastercard, Visa.*

Tel: (2) 657 80 11   Fax: (22) 27 98 56
Ul Krolewska 11, 00-065 Warsaw

More welcoming and friendly inside than the modern concrete-block-style exterior would suggest. The location is good too, overlooking the Ogrod Saski (Saxon Gardens) and only a short walk from the Old Town. Bedrooms are air-conditioned and come with mini-bars among other comforts. Room rates are set in Deutschmarks (395DM in the summer of 1995) so the local currency price quoted above will vary with the exchange rate. **Rooms** *363. Room service 24hr. Own parking, Zlt35 for 24 hours. Conference facilities 800. Indoor swimming pool. Sauna. Keep-fit equipment. Amex, Diners, Mastercard, Visa.*

Canaletto Restaurant   Zlt260

Two reproductions of the artist's views of Warsaw give this restaurant its name and are the main feature of an otherwise rather plain room. Polish specialities, especially game, take their place alongside more international dishes on the menu. Dinner is accompanied by a harpist. **Seats** *80. Open 1200-1600, 1800-late.*

Wroclaw

Tel & Fax (71) 356 17
Ul Rynek 20/21 50-101 Wroclaw

The elegant menu at Belle Epoque offers classical French and international cuisine such as magret de canard à l'ornage et au miel, truite sautée aux amandes and fondue bourguignonne. Leave room for the Grand dessert "Belle Epoque". **Seats** *50 (+50 outside). Open 1200-2400. Amex, Diners, Mastercard, Visa.*

Tel: (71) 370 41   Fax: (71) 351 03
Ul Modrzejewskiej 2, 50-071 Wroclaw

An enchanting art nouveau hotel, completed in 1892, with a central city location that's as handy for business as visiting the historic Old Town. No air-conditioning or mini-bars in rooms but all have satellite television. There are a book shop and an antique shop within the hotel. *Rooms 70. Room service all day. Parking at nearby secure public park Zlt90 for 24 hours. Amex, Diners, Mastercard, Visa.*

Tel: (71) 61 46 51   Fax: (71) 61 66 17
Ul Powstancow Slaskich 7, 53-332 Wroclaw

Modern, 12-storey hotel about 15 minutes walk from the city centre. Air-conditioned bedrooms come with mini-bars and satellite television. The public areas include a florist, a small art gallery and several boutiques, among them a jewellery shop. *Rooms 300. Room service 24hr. Parking Zlt15 for 24 hours. Conference facilities 200. Business centre. Swimming pool. Sauna. Sun beds. Hairdressing. Boutiques. Amex, Diners, Mastercard, Visa.*

Tel: (52) 22 18 61   Fax: (52) 22 89 88
Aleja Gdanska 14, 85-006 Bydgoszcz

1996 is centenary year for this hotel set in delightful public gardens in the centre of the city. The architecture is art nouveau and this style still distinguishes the public rooms although bedrooms, having been refurbished within the last few years, are more modern. Mini-bars and numerous satellite TV channels add to the comfort. Bathrooms are equally modern but about 12 of them have shower and WC only. There are four full suites. *Rooms 74. Room service all day. Private parking Zlt15-20 for 24 hours. Conference facilities 60. Sauna. Sun bed. Gym. Amex, Diners, Mastercard, Visa.*

THE APARTMENT SERVICE

Tel in UK (0181) 748 4207   Fax (0181) 748 3972

The Apartment Service will find you the right apartment worldwide to suit your needs, whether you are on a short or long-term stay. A 96-page colour catalogue is free on request. All budgets are catered for.

THE INDEPENDENT

INDEPENDENT
ON SUNDAY

Your truly
independent
guides to life

Currency Portuguese Escudo **Exchange Rate** £1=approx 233 Esc
International dialling code 00 351 (Lisbon+1, Oporto+2)
Passports/Visas No visa required for British passport holders.
British Embassy in Lisbon Tel 1-396 1191/396 1122

Airports
Lisbon-Portela Tel 1-841 5000
Oporto-Pedras Rubras Tel 2-948 2291
Faro International Tel 89-80 0801
Railway Stations
Lisbon Tel Rossio (local/Lisbon Coast) 1-346 5022
Santa Apolonia (international) 1-888 4181
Oporto Tel Campanha 2-565 645 / Sao Bento 2-200 2722
Car hire
Tel Nos. **Lisbon Avis** 1-356 1176 **Hertz** 1-579 027 (airport 1-80 1496)
Budget 1-53 7717 (airport 1-80 3981)
Oporto Avis 1-32 5947 **Hertz** 2-31 2387 (airport 2-944 9400)
Budget (airport) 2-948 5714 **Faro Avis** (airport) 89-81 8625
Speed Limits 90 km/h on trunk roads 120 km/h on motorways, 60 km/h
in towns.

Banks 8.30am-3pm Mon-Fri.
Shops Mon-Fri 9am-1pm & 3-7pm, Sat till 1pm (in December shops stay
open until 7pm on Saturdays). Shopping Centres 10am-11pm 7 days.

New Year's Day, 21 Feb, Easter, 1 May, 10 & 15 Jun, 15 Aug, 5 Oct,
1 Nov, 1 & 8 Dec, Christmas Day.

Portuguese Tourist Board in **London** Tel 0171-494 1441
In **Portugal** Lisbon Tel 1-352 5800 (airport 1-849 3689)
Oporto Tel 2-317 514 (airport 2-941 2534)
Faro Tel 89-80 0400/80 3604 (airport 89-81 8582)
American Express Travel Service Offices or Representative (R)
Lisbon Top Tours (R)
Av.Duque De Loule 108
1000
Tel 1-3155885 #
Oporto Top Tours (R)
Rua Alferes Malheiro 96
4000
Tel 2-6000861 #

Lisbon

Tel: (01) 886 60 02   Fax: (01) 87 77 83
Calçada do Monte 39, 1100 Lisboa

Looking down from the hill on which the hotel is built, you can see St George's Castle and the River Tagus. All the other tourist attractions are within walking distance of this small, friendly hotel. Dating from the 60s, this is still a fairly modern-looking building whose decor is up-to-date with pretty pastel colours and designs. All are air-conditioned and have TV . *Rooms 28. Room service 24hr. Amex, Mastercard, Visa.*

Tel: (01) 342 83 43   Fax: (01) 342 34 12
Rua do Alegrim 117, 1200 Lisboa

A lively, buzzy atmosphere with friendly, helpful staff and the simplest of menus characterises this modern, wood-panelled, informal brasserie. Good-quality sirloin steaks with a Café de Paris butter is all that is available, accompanied by excellent home-made French fries and a green salad with walnuts and a vinaigrette dressing. To finish there are desserts such as apple pie, hazelnut torte and chocolate cake. *Seats 94. Open 1230-1500, 2000-2400 (Sun till 2300). Closed 25 Dec. Mastercard, Visa.*

Tel: (01) 388 91 30   Fax: (01) 387 51 32
Travessa das Amoreiras 1, 1200 Lisboa

The plant-filled courtyard is a great attraction here, making it an ideal fine-weather dining spot. The chef, here since the restaurant first opened, prepares a wide-ranging selection of mostly fish dishes with a smattering for carnivores. The *mariscada* (shellfish) are a favourite dish and a speciality so begin perhaps with hot prawns fried in garlic or crab au gratin and continue with lobster in champagne. Other choices could be asparagus with a mousseline sauce, turbot in a green pepper sauce and monkfish with a lemon sauce. The meat selection includes roast kid with *fines herbes*, duck with wild mushrooms and game in season too. The exclusively Portuguese wine list has a good house red, Carvalho Pubeiro. *Seats 55. Open 1230-1500, 1930-2400. Amex, Diners, Mastercard, Visa.*

Tel: (01) 887 59 62   Fax: (01) 887 63 29
Castelo de São Jorge, 1100 Lisboa

The restaurant is inside the 800-year-old St George's Castle, one of Lisbon's main attractions. There's a terrace for summer dining from a menu that features traditional Portuguese cuisine. Casseroles and grilled fish dishes are very much the order of the day; but more adventurous dishes are also on offer: prawns with ginger and garlic, chicken risotto and fried kid. Monkfish in a light lemon sauce, clams served with potatoes, garlic and olive oil and *Cataplana* (a medley of seafood served with tomatoes, potatoes and garlic) are other good choices. All the wines are Portuguese, with an enjoyable Southern Portuguese house wine. Set meals from 4500esc. *Seats 100. Open 1230-1530, 2000-2230. Amex, Diners, Mastercard, Visa.*

Tel: (01) 342 59 31   Fax: (01) 343 12 13
Rua da Rosa traversa Poco de Cidad 60, 1200 Lisboa

A varied and well-prepared selection of classic Italian dishes is to be found on the extensive menu of this popular restaurant. A few more unusual dishes too, make an appearance, such as salmon carpaccio, tagliolini with lemon and vodka and trout stuffed with porcini mushrooms, ham and mozzarella. *Seats 45. Open 1230-1430, 2000-2330. Closed Mon, 10 days Christmas. Mastercard, Visa.*

Opening times are often liable to change at short notice, so it's always best to book.

Tel: (01) 388 78 11
Rua Rodrigo da Fonseca 87, 1200 Lisboa

A pleasant pub-styled place given a British name and decor to draw in the locals. However, the daily menu changes are a better reason to come here. Dishes of the day, like chargrilled sea bass and grilled beef steak served in a garlic sauce with sautéed potatoes, are deservedly popular. The carte is very meat orientated with typical dishes being Oriental-style lamb kebabs, mixed grill and veal escalopes. Look out for the good selection of vinhos verdes. Set meals 5000esc. *Seats 45. Open 1200-1500, 1900-2230. Closed Sun, 25 Dec. Amex, Diners, Mastercard, Visa.*

Tel: (01) 885 30 53   Fax: (01) 885 20 82
Campo dos Mártires de Pátria 49, 1150 Lisboa

This elegant, 100-year-old private house next to the Pombelino district was converted into a restaurant back in 1980 by Francisco Pimpista and his daughter Celia. The menu is a varied mix of Portuguese and international dishes including starters such as smoked swordfish, asparagus with hollandaise sauce, fish soup and poached eggs florentine. For a main course the choice extends from a selection of excellent seafoods such as monkfish and prawn brochette, lobster pancakes, grilled stone bass *(grouper)* with a shellfish butter and *bacalhau* (salt cod) to a good choice of meat dishes. These include saddle of lamb with mint sauce, fondue bourguignonne and roast duck breast with fruit. There are enjoyable desserts to finish. All the wines are Portuguese. A pianist entertains nightly and valet parking is offered. *Seats 75. Open 1200-1600, 1900-2400. Closed L Sat & National Holidays, all Sun. Amex, Diners, Mastercard, Visa.*

Tel: (01) 796 63 80   Fax: (01) 797 41 44
Avenida da República 38, 1100 Lisboa

An elegant restaurant converted from a 19th-century town house and offering a mix of French, and Portuguese and international cooking. Fish soups, fruit cocktail and smoked salmon starters, followed by dishes like grilled salmon with green peppers, rich partridge and pheasant casseroles and the traditional salted cod cooked Lisbon-style, with tomatoes, parsley, garlic and white wine are all found on the menu. In the piano bar next door, music and dancing goes on until dawn. *Seats 60. Open 1200-1500, 1900-2130. Private parking. Amex, Mastercard, Visa.*

Tel: (01) 60 91 96
Plaça das Flores 45, 1200 Lisboa

In the old quarter of Lisbon, this place started life as a humble bakery and has risen the world since. It was converted into a restaurant in the early 1980s and now businessmen and politicians fill the wooden tables and chairs, as the building is opposite the Houses of Parliament. Plain, traditional Portuguese cooking comes out of the kitchen prepared by just one chef. The set menus, which include wine and coffee, represent good value. A typical meal could be coriander cream soup followed by duck in a rich champagne sauce or a corn and shrimp salad with a cheese sauce and a gratin of sea bass with asparagus. *Seats 70. Open 1230-1500, 1930-2300. Amex, Diners, Mastercard, Visa.*

Tel: (01) 346 44 29   Fax: (01) 346 37 58
Rua das Portas de Santo Ant_o 47, 1100 Lisboa

The building, with its Portuguese-tiled walls, is as traditional as the cooking. Not surprisingly, fish predominates, with fresh swordfish, sole and bacalhau (salt cod), chargrilled lobster and *parrilhada de mariscos* (a mix of chargrilled shellfish with two sauces). A few international dishes are also thrown in: beef stroganoff and paella are two worth looking out for. Set menu 6000esc. *Seats 65. Open 1200-1530, 1900-2400. Closed L National Holidays. Amex, Diners, Mastercard, Visa.*

Tel: (01) 301 73 73   Fax: (01) 363 26 92

Avenida de Brasilia Edificio Espelho D'Agua, 1400 Lisboa

West of the city centre close to the Belém Tower and almost by the banks of the Tagus, the the restaurant occupies its own building by a small artificial lake. The decor is attractively modern and there's a delightful terrace for alfresco dining. The menu is based on typical Portuguese specialities which have been prepared for the past fifteen years by a small family team. They mostly serve fish and seafood: grilled salmon, lobster, prawns, squid, sea bass and sole are a few examples. The wines are conservative, with a good Portuguese red and white house wine. *Seats 70. Open 1230-1500, 1930-2230. Amex, Diners, Mastercard, Visa.*

Tel: (01) 342 14 66   Fax: (01) 346 50 32

Rua das Portas de Santo Anto 25, 1150 Lisboa

Four friends opened this lively restaurant in 1936. The place was last refurbished in the 60s and old leather upholstery and tapestries depicting the four seasons form part of the characterful decor. This place is filled with businessmen during the day and party-goers late at night. Classic Portuguese food features on the menu and includes *creme de mariscos* (shellfish soup), turbot cooked in clarified butter and pork cutlets with a spicy sauce. A speciality here is the national dish of suckling pig roasted on a spit. The wine list is quite lengthy with a choice of some 420 Portuguese wines. *Seats 120. Open 1200-0200. Closed 1 May. Amex, Mastercard, Visa.*

Tel: (01) 395 00 05   Fax: (01) 395 06 65

Rua do Pau de Bandeira 4, 1200 Lisboa

The original 17th-century palace has been restored and converted into a charming hotel with a new wing having been added. There are only suites or de luxe doubles in the older building, all decorated in different but tasteful styles: colonial, Arabian, or Portuguese, and filled with antique furniture; while the bedrooms in the new wing have a smart, modern decor. Rooms are air-conditioned and have all the usual amenities. The delightful wooded grounds contain a waterfall and swimming pool. *Rooms 94. Room service 24hr. Conference facilities for 250. Secretarial/translation services. Garden. Indoor/ Outdoor swimming pools. Sauna. Steam room. Solarium. Beauty treatment. News Kiosk/ Shop. Private parking. Amex, Diners, Mastercard, Visa.*

An elegant and stylish restaurant offering an imaginative and modern menu with some traditional Portuguese dishes that have been skillfully reworked to create a selection of well-prepared and fashionable items. The choice from a short but varied carte includes starters such as an escabèche of fresh sardines with a mousseline of tomato and sweet peppers, potato 'ravioli' filled with salt cod and served with a Malvasia wine sauce and grilled lobster medallions with a garlic vinaigrette. Main dishes range from poached sole fillets with Muscatel wine and beetroot and potato chips and bass baked with Indian spices to duck magret flavoured with Ivory Coast coffee and accompanied by a risotto of the giblets and beef tournedos with Jamaican peppers and gratin dauphinois. Desserts are equally innovative with hot mango tart with cinnamon ice cream and a mille feuille of exotic fruits both needing to be ordered 20 minutes in advance. A few French vintages supplement the list of Portuguese wines. On very warm evenings, opt, if possible, for a poolside table. Set meal 7800esc. *Seats 60. Open 1230-1500, 1930 -2300.*

Tel: (01) 69 04 00   Fax: (01) 69 32 31

Rua Castilho 149, 1070 Lisboa

The Meridien Group opened this centrally-located hotel in the mid-1980s. It's a popular conference venue, with a capacity of up to 550 in the largest room, or up to 30 in one of the smaller boardrooms. The bedrooms, described as 'modern executive', have smart, stylish, and up-to-date furniture and the usual amenities such as air-conditioning, mini-bar, satellite TV. *Rooms 330. Room service 24hr. Sauna. Beauty treatments. Hair salon. News kiosk. Boutique. Coffee shop (0700-2300). Secretarial/translation services. Private parking. Amex, Diners, Mastercard, Visa.*

La Brasserie des Amis   12,000ESC

The menu is a mix of Portuguese and classic French dishes. Grilled sea bass with a béarnaise sauce, rolled fillets of salmon in a saffron butter sauce and sirloin steak are typical of the style. House specialities are generally Portuguese in origin, with suckling pig and roast cod served with onions, potatoes, olive oil and garlic. A well-laden buffet is available for both lunch and dinner at 4000esc per person. Wines are French and Portuguese. *Seats 145. Open 1200-1500, 1900-2300.*

LISBON   Hotel Ritz Inter-Continental   38,000ESC

HR

Tel: (01) 69 20 20   Fax: (01) 69 17 83
Rua Rodrigo da Fonseca 88, 1093 Lisboa

Part of the Inter-Continental Hotel group, the Ritz offers sophisticated and stylish levels of accommodation. Built in the 50s, the hotel still retains many of the original members of staff as well as some of the elegant furnishings it began with. Bedrooms keep pace with modern tastes and now have smart Italian furniture and a host of up-to-date conveniences such as satellite TV, air-conditioning, fax point and mini-bar. Guests also have the use of a gymnasium and there are conference facilities for 600, theatre style. Breakfast is served in the Varanda restaurant from 0730 to 1130. *Rooms 303. Room service 24hr. Garden. Gym. Hair salon. News kiosk/shop. Coffee shop (1200-0130). Amex, Diners, Mastercard, Visa.*

Varanda   19,000ESC

The terrace offers a super location for alfresco dining whether it is for the splendid buffet luncheon or the à la carte dinners. The latter offers cooking of an accomplshed and very classical standard with a choice of sliced duck breast with apricot vinegar and wild mushroom consommé among the starters. Poached turbot, fillets of sole and scallops with a lobster sauce, fillet steak with smoked ham and garlic and pork escalopes with mustard grains feature among the main dishes. The desserts include crème brulée, chocolate mousse or iced ginger and pineapple soufflé. *Seats 80. Open 1230-1530, 1930-2230.*

LISBON   Senor Vinho   18,000ESC

R

Tel: (01) 397 26 81   Fax: (01) 396 20 72
Rua do Meio-à-Lapa 18, 1200 Lisboa

Housed in an ancient building, the restaurant is thoroughly Portuguese in character. This is a popular establishment and one where you come to enjoy the traditional music of Portugal (fado) as well as a menu which offers a selection of well-prepared fish and meat dishes. Grilled lobster and prawns served with rice are two of the chef's specialities. **Seats** 120. D only 2000-2400. *Closed Sun. Amex, Diners, Mastercard, Visa.*

LISBON   Sheraton Lisbon Hotel and Towers   42,000ESC

H

Tel: (01) 57 57 57   Fax: (01) 54 71 64
Rua Latino Coelho 1, 1069 Lisboa

Located some 500 metres east of Edward VII Park, this Sheraton has been here since the early 70s; the concierge has been here since 1972 as well, and is a great source of local information. The majority of guests are on business and the rooms are modern, with good facilities. All the rooms are doubles, and there are seven suites. All have satellite TV, mini-bar, fax point and air-conditioning. The Panorama bar on the 35th floor, as its name suggests, has great views over the capital, as do many of the bedrooms. The meeting rooms can open up into one large room for 350 people. *Rooms 384. Room service 24hr. Secretarial/translation services. Outdoor swimming pool. Gym. Sauna. Beauty treatment. Massage. Hair salon. News kiosk & shop. Amex. Diners. Mastercard. Visa.*

LISBON   Tagide   16,000ESC

R

Tel: (01) 342 07 20   Fax: (01) 347 18 80
Largo da Academia Nacional de Belas Artes 18, 1200 Lisboa

If possible book a table on the terrace or an internal one with a view, as the restaurant is located in the historic heart of Lisbon and there is much to admire. The decor is classically inspired with a fountain dating from 1677 in one corner, and 18th-century blue and white tiles on some walls, while others are painted with Greek mythological figures. Overlooking St George's Castle and the Tagus, the restaurant has, on the whole, stuck loyally to Portuguese dishes, but there are also a few French standards among the offerings. Smoked swordfish, cold shrimp vichyssoise, monkfish with spinach and cream, baked saddle of lamb, hare with a red wine sauce and duck with a bigarade sauce show the style. Look out for the occasional house specialities like pork and clams marinated in garlic and coriander. There is a choice of 200 different bottles on the Portuguese and French wine list. *Seats 70. Open 1230-1500, 1930-2230. Closed L Sat, all Sun, National Holidays. Private parking. Amex, Mastercard, Visa.*

Tel: (01) 342 11 12   Fax: (01) 347 81 25
Rua da Misericórdia 37, 1200 Lisboa

Opened in 1784 and housed in a splendid 16th-century building, the restaurant has an elegant and beautifully classical decor, featuring long Empire-style mirrors and chandeliers, which create a glitzy, glamorous ambience. The lengthy menu offers a selection of familiar French dishes which sit alongside traditional Portuguese favourites. Fish dishes include fillets of sole in a champagne sauce, supreme of sea bream florentine, prawns in a garlic sauce and spider crab soufflé. Meat dishes range from entrecote with red wine, chateaubriand and veal cutlet cordon bleu to quail with cherries and duck with orange. Bordeaux and burgundy wines complement the Portuguese list (with some good vinho verde). Set meals 6300esc. *Seats 50. Open 1230-1530, 1930-2300. Closed L Sun, all Sat & National Holidays. Amex, Diners, Mastercard, Visa.*

Tel: (01) 396 25 44   Fax: (01) 397 27 93
Rua das Janelas Verdes 32, 1200 Lisboa

Formerly a convent, and then a private residence, this house was rebuilt by the Marquis of Pombal after an earthquake destroyed the old part of the city. The building is on three levels, divided by low stone steps and surrounded by beautiful courtyard gardens and pathways. The simple, old-fashioned rooms are in keeping with the building, with stone floors, spartan decor and floral curtains. All have satellite TV. This is, without doubt, a real find, but for laid-back tourists, not busy businessmen. *Rooms 34. Room service none. Garden. No parking. Amex, Diners, Mastercard, Visa.*

Restaurant   12,000ESC

Eugénia Cerqueira, the chef, has been here since the mid-70s and offers a short menu of modernised classic Portuguese dishes. Begin with sautéed wild mushrooms with garlic, an assortment of Portuguese fried hors d'œuvres including bacalhao (salt cod) croquettes, fried green beans and shrimp rissoles or a fricassée of scallops. Main courses range from pan-fried sole with wild mushrooms and roasted almonds, grilled tuna with pink peppercorns and octopus sautéed with olive oil and garlic to roast capon with fresh rosemary, sautéed duck breast with grapes, marinated partridge and grilled venison loin steaks. To finish there are super desserts such as hazelnut tart, egg and almond pudding or apple pie with cinnamon ice cream. Portuguese wines, from tawny ports to vinho verde. On Sundays they offer only a buffet spread of fish, meat and salads. In fine weather the restaurant moves out on to the patio. *Seats 40. Open 1230-1500, 1930-2200.*

Around Lisbon

Tel: (01) 483 28 21   Fax: (01) 484 48 27
Rua Frederico Arouca 100, 2750 Cascais

Built as a palace in 1873 by the Duke of Loulé and known as his `Almond Box', it became an inn in the 60s and then, in 1983, it was re-opened after major refurbishment as a modern hotel. A few of the 11 rooms in the original house overlook Cascais Bay and the beach. The majority are still decorated in an elegant 19th-century style, while the 29 rooms in a new wing have a more contemporary appeal. Bedrooms have a range of modern facilities including air-conditioning, satellite TV and mini-bar. *Rooms 40. Room service 24hr. Outdoor swimming pool. Private parking. Amex, Mastercard, Visa.*

Restaurant   14,000ESC

The impressive Cascais and Estoril coastlines are visible from the windows of this quiet, traditional restaurant. The à la carte menu changes seasonally and offers a short selection of well-prepared meat and seafood. Start with cold, stuffed crab or baked potato filled with smoked salmon caviar and cream and follow with poached salmon with hollandaise, lobster thermidor or pork fillet cooked in a cockle sauce. Champagne is the only alternative to Portuguese wine. *Seats 50. Open 1230-1500, 1930-2200.*

Meal prices for 2 are based on à la carte menus. When set menus are available, prices will often be lower.

Tel: (01) 486 92 39   Fax: (01) 486 92 27
PO 197 Estrada do Guincho, 2750 Cascais

Right out on the coast near Cascais, with a magnificent view of the sea, this place is far away from the noise and bustle of the Cascais resort. Originally, it was an old family inn, which underwent a major renovation and became a hotel. The bedrooms are well equipped, with air-conditioning, mini-bars and satellite TV. Other facilities include a seawater-fed swimming pool. There are conference facilities for 80 delegates. Sea-facing rooms are very desirable but attract a supplement. *Rooms 43. Room service all day. Garden. Outdoor swimming pool. Solarium. Coffee shop (1000-2000). Private parking. Amex, Diners, Mastercard, Visa.*

Sitting on the terrace overlooking the sea you can enjoy a splendid selection of fresh seafood including baked sea bass, poached salmon with hollandaise and clams with garlic and olive oil. There are also a couple of steak dishes. Inside the old inn, diners eat in characterful surroundings, still with good sea views. Every lunchtime there's a good buffet of salady items and on a Friday or Saturday evening each week they hold a barbecue. *Seats 65. Open 1300-1500, 1930-2200.*

Tel: (01) 923 29 23   Fax: (01) 923 43 29
Estrada de Monserrate, 2710 Sintra

Thirty minutes from Lisbon for modern travellers, the building was a retreat, in the 16th century, for monks. Some of the original hand-painted ceilings are still to be seen. Mrs Braddell, whose family has been here since 1932, greets guests more as friends than clients; this place is run very much as a family home. A set five-course candle-lit dinner is available to those lucky enough to be either resident or manage to book a table (note, the restaurant doesn't open for fewer than four diners). Good home cooking is what's on offer with menus changing daily according to what the market provides. Diners are all seated together on long treste tables in the small dining-room and the food is a mix of French, Spanish and Portuguese dishes. Vichyssoise, spinach soufflé, sole meunière, steaks, pork with apricot stuffing are featured as well as plain-grilled local seafood. Afterwards there's a cheese platter and to round off a fine meal, prune soufflé, strawberries in Chablis or trifle, with fresh fruit as an alternative. At night the gardens are illuminated, just right for a post-prandial stroll. *Seats 26. D only by arrangement 2000-2130. Private parking. No credit cards.*

A quiet location and beautiful setting make this an ideal retreat. Public rooms are filled with fresh flower arrangements and the eight bedrooms offer simple, homely comforts.

Tel: (02) 200 81 01   Fax: (02) 31 49 37
Praça Dona Felipa de Lancastre 62, 4000 Porto

The same family have run this relaxed, informal hotel in the centre of Oporto since the early 50s; and it is small, relaxed and informal. The bedrooms are neat and attractively decorated and there are six spacious suites. All the rooms are equipped with satellite TV and mini-bars. There is also a conference and banqueting room for up to 120 people, though this is not a businessman's hotel. *Rooms 74. Room service 24hr. Garden. Own free parking. Amex, Diners, Mastercard, Visa.*

Tel: (02) 208 13 19   Fax: (02) 202 26 38
Rua do Outeirinho 13, 4000 Porto

A late-night eating spot that is also renowned for its music. The set menus offer good value, dinner being served in the early part of the evening with a nightly show starting at 2130. Both the food and the music are typically Portuguese, with *fado* (traditional folk songs) accompanying specialities such as *bacalhau* (salt cod), hake and sole as well as roast veal, steaks and barbecued pork. *Seats 65. Open 2030-2400. Closed Sun, 25 & 26 Dec. Private parking. No credit cards.*

Tel: (02) 57 07 17   Fax: (02) 57 02 06
Rua da Alegria 598, 4000 Porto

HR

Named after the two towns on either side of it, Oporto and Cale, the hotel occupies the top five floors of a tall, modern building. Bedrooms are neat and well equipped, each with 12- channel satellite TV, mini-bar and air-conditioning. Breakfasts come with fresh orange juice and a good selection of cheese and ham. **Rooms 30**. *Room service all day. Amex, Diners, Mastercard, Visa*.

Restaurant   18,0000ESC

An attractive room on the 13th floor enjoying excellent views over Oporto and out to sea. The menu includes traditional specialities among a long list of dishes: *bacalhau* (salt cod) with scrambled eggs, artichoke hearts and bacon, fillets of wild boar with apple purée and stewed kid in red wine. Plenty of grilled, fresh fish is also served. The wine list is extensive, but typically Portuguese. Set meals 6500esc. **Seats 60**. *Open 1230-1430, 1930-2200. Closed 1 May, 25 Dec. Private parking. Amex, Diners, Mastercard, Visa*.

Romania

Currency Romanian Leu ** **Exchange Rate** £1=approx LEI 2616
** Not obtainable in UK. US dollars/Cash recommended.
International dialing code 00 40 (Bucharest+1)
Passports/Visas Visa required by British passport holders. Full 10 year
passport required, with at least 6 months remaining before expected
departure from Romania.
(Romanian Embassy 4 Palace Green W8 4QD Tel 0171-937
9666/Consulate 937 9667)
British Embassy in Bucharest Tel 1-312 0303

TRANSPORT
Airports
Bucharest-Otopemi Tel 1-615 2747 (flight info) 1-212 0122 (general info)
Railway Stations
Contact Romanian Tourist Board Tel 0171-224 3692.
Car hire in Bucharest
Hertz 1-611 4365 (airport 1-212 0040) **Avis** 1-223 2080
(airport 1-212 0011)
Speed Limits 80 km/h on trunk roads, 60 km/h in towns (no
motorways).

OPENING HOURS
Banks Mon-Fri 9.30am-12pm (Fri to 12pm) for business transactions,
open until 4.30pm for exchange transactions.
Shops 9.30am-5pm Mon-Sat (variable).

NATIONAL HOLIDAYS
16 Apr, 1 & 2 May, 1 & 2 Dec, Christmas Day.

Tourist Offices
Romanian Tourist Board in **London** Tel & Fax 0171-224 3692
In **Bucharest** Tel 1-614 5160
American Express Travel Service Offices or Representative (R)
Bucharest   National Tourist Office
            Carpati (R)
            Boulevard Magheru Nr.7
            Tel 1-3122596/3122594

Bucharest

Tel: (1) 617 3402
53 Strada Turda, Bucuresti 1
R

Not the best part of town and not the smartest of restaurants, although tables do come with linen cloths and napkins, but this is the place to experience real Romanian cooking and local colour. Established in the late 19th century, 'La Gogosaru' (it's old-fashioned Romanian for sweet peppers) has been returned to family ownership since the revolution. Eating options are in the front room with its booth seating down each side and a TV at each end, a slightly smarter back room (still with TV) or, best bet when the weather is fine, outside on the green patio. Most of the dishes are translated into some sort of English. For starters, for a whole table, try the 'hot-plate' that will probably include little spicy sausages from the Oktana region, mici (a mixture of minced pork and beef grilled), chicken livers, mushrooms and deep-fried cheese in batter-the other one in batter could be calf's brain. If this does not fill you up, try the tochitura (mixed meat stew served with a mould of soft polenta topped with a fried egg). Customers are mostly local so prices are low. The address is not helpful as the restaurant is actually in a small back street called L'Autaru that runs parallel to Strada Turda at its southern end. *Seats 80. Open 1200 (Mon from 1400)-0200. No credit cards.*

Tel: (1) 222 8120   Fax: (1) 311 0567
13 Piata Aviatorilor, 7000 Bucuresti 1
H

Smallish modern hotel close to the Aviatorilor Metro Station, a couple of stops to the north of the city centre. The exterior is white marble, and the same stone covers the floor of the reception area which, with some stools at a bar counter and a couple of leather armchairs, provides the only public space apart from the restaurant. Air-conditioned bedrooms vary in size but all have double beds, a couple of easy chairs, coffee table and low chest of drawers. There is no desk or other usable work space but a collapsible table can be provided on request. All the bathrooms have tubs, except two rooms with showers only, and also hand-held showers. The rooms do not have mini-bars. Room prices are fixed in US dollars ($235 for a standard double in mid-1995) so the local currency price quoted above is liable to vary. *Rooms 30. Room service 24hr. Free open parking for 10 cars. Amex, Diners, Mastercard, Visa.*

Tel: (1) 210 7330   Fax: (1) 312 0486
4 Boulevard Nicolae Balcescu, 70121 Bucuresti 1
HR

In the summer of 1995 work was underway on refurbishment of the main lobby area of this 70s-built, high-rise hotel in the centre of the city; work on bedrooms was to follow. Even without refurbishment the spacious bedrooms, though a little drab, were still acceptable and offered all the usual amenities, including air-conditioning, mini-bar, room safe and multi-channel TV (with BBC World Service television). There are a pool and gym on the top floor (but don't count on an early morning dip, as it doesn't open until noon) with fabulous views. Excellent concierge service. Room prices are fixed in US dollars ($223 for a standard double in mid-1995) so the local currency price quoted above is liable to vary. *Rooms 423. Room service 24hr. Free open parking (not owned by the hotel) for 30 cars. Conference facilities 500. Indoor swimming pool. Sauna. Sun bed. Keep-fit equipment. Hairdressing. Beauty salon. Casino. Night club. News kiosk. Amex, Diners, Mastercard, Visa.*

Restaurant Balada   LEI85,000

Of the hotel's two restaurants this one is billed as offering Romanian cuisine but there is actually much that is familiar on a carte written in a mixture of French and Romanian but with good clear English translation: spaghetti milanese, cheese soufflé, sole meunière, tournedos Rossini, chicken Kiev, beef stroganoff, chateaubriand béarnaise. There are some Romanian dishes like turkey in jelly, minced pork wrapped in cabbage leaves with sauerkraut and Romanian-style soft polenta, and pheasant with mushrooms. Desserts include peach melba, profiteroles and pineapple fritters. The restaurant is located on the 21st floor so the views are splendid, and a five-piece band, featuring a rather good violinist, provides the entertainment. Attentive, friendly service. *Seats 180. Open 1200-1600, 1900-2400. Closed Sun.*

Tel: (1) 212 2998   Fax (1) 211 5688
2 Boulevard Expozitiei, Bucuresti 1

Far and away the best place to stay in Bucharest, this French-managed hotel is part of the new World Trade Centre, on the outskirts of the city centre towards the airport. Airy, spacious reception rooms have a touch of style and young Romanian staff are as keen as mustard to provide good service. Well-designed, air-conditioned bedrooms are of international standard. A shuttle bus runs to the airport (about 10 minutes away) and to the hotel's own sports centre which is located next to a lake in a nearby park. Back at the hotel there is a night club, fitness centre and direct access to the World Trade Centre with its meeting rooms, offices to rent and shopping arcade. Excellent buffet breakfast includes both pain au chocolat and real marmalade. Room prices are fixed in US dollars ($275 for a standard double in mid-1995) so the local currency price quoted above is liable to vary. *Rooms 203. Room service 24hr. Ample free garage and open parking. Indoor swimming pool. Gymnasium. Sauna. Turkish bath. Spa bath. Sun beds. Squash. Indoor and outdoor tennis courts. Hairdressing. Amex, Diners, Mastercard, Visa.*

Not only the best place to stay but a pretty good bet for eating too with a genuine French chef (Jean-Luc Baguerau) providing some sound and sophisticated Gallic cooking. Dover sole terrine with spring vegetables, fondant à la tomate de Joël Robuchon, magret of duck with lemon and honey, braised monkfish with horseradish sauce, medallions of pork with two sauces and a wild mushroom mousse, and paupiettes of veal stuffed with apples show the style of dishes that are attractively presented if sometimes rather nouvelle-ish in size. There is also a list of Romanian specialities. For dessert try a marjolaine aux fraises, coulis de fruits rouges or something from the pastry trolley. The setting is cool and comfortable and the staff very willing. There's a short wine list on which the most acceptable Romanian wines provide the best value. *Seats 60. Open 1230-1445 (Sun 'brunch' 1100-1500), 1900-2300.*

Tel: (1) 615 9241   Fax: (1) 312 7004
2-4 Strada Stirbei-Voda, Bucuresti 2

One of the smartest restaurants in town, a comfortable, air-conditioned basement with gilt-edged crockery, crystal glassware and attentive service. The menu is essentially international, with dishes such as salad niçoise, frogs' legs with tomato sauce, seafood salad, pike-perch meunière, steak au poivre, breast of duck bigarade and pork escalope with lemon sauce, all acceptably prepared by chef Dobre Doru, who puts a lot of effort into attractive presentation. The sweet trolley offers just a few desserts, like fruit tart, chocolate gateau and cheesecake, that come from the kitchens of the nearby Inter-Continental Hotel (qv). Good espresso coffee. There's a comfortable bar on the ground floor and meals are served on a small patio when the weather allows. *Seats 80 (+ 35 patio). Open 1200-1700, 1900-0200. Closed L Sat. Amex, Diners, Mastercard, Visa.*

THE APARTMENT SERVICE

Tel in UK (0181) 748 4207   Fax (0181) 748 3972

The Apartment Service will find you the right apartment worldwide to suit your needs, whether you are on a short or long-term stay. A 96-page colour catalogue is free on request. All budgets are catered for.

Your Guarantee of Quality and Independence

EGON RONAY'S GUIDES 1996

- Establishment inspections are anonymous
- Inspections are undertaken by qualified Egon Ronay's Guides inspectors
- The Guides are completely independent in their editorial selection
- The Guides do not accept advertising, hospitality or payment from listed establishments

Titles planned for 1996 include

Hotels & Restaurants ● Pubs & Inns ● Europe
Ireland ● Just A Bite
And Children Come Too ● Paris
Oriental Restaurants

Russia

Currency Russian Rouble ** **Exchange Rate** ** Not obtainable in UK.
Travellers cheques/US dollars recommended.
International dialling code 00 70
(Moscow area+96 Moscow city+95 St Petersburg+812)
Passports/Visas Visa required by British passport holders.
(Russian Consulate 5 Kensington Palace Gdns W8 4QS
Tel 0171-229 8027)
British Embassies in Russia Moscow Tel 95-231 8511
St Petersburg Tel 812-312 0072

TRANSPORT
Airports
Moscow-Sheremetyevo Tel 95-578 5753
St Petersburg-Pulkova Tel 812-104 3180/104 3444
Railway Stations
Main information centre for Russian railways Tel 95-292 3786/292 2111
Car hire
Tel Nos. **Moscow Avis** Tel 95-240 9863 (airport 95-578 5646)
Hertz 95-284 4391 (airport 95-578 7532) **Innis** 95-599 9222
St Petersburg Avis (airport) 812 235 6444 **Innis** 812-210 5858
Speed limits 90 km/h outside cities, 60 km/h in built-up areas.

OPENING HOURS
Banks Russian State banks are usually open 9.30am-1pm. Many of the
new private banks open from 10am to 6pm, and private exchanges in
hotels are generally open 9am-6pm (sometimes to 8pm). Most banks
are closed for lunch 1-3pm.
Shops Hours are variable. Food stores generally from 8/9am to 8/9pm
(often closed between 2 & 3pm). Department stores generally
9am-8pm; others till 6pm.

NATIONAL HOLIDAYS
New Year's Day, 8 Mar, 1, 2 & 9 May, 7 Oct, 7 & 8 Nov.

Tourist Offices
Russian Embassy in **London** Tel 0171-229 3628
Tourist Board in **Russia** Moscow Tel 95-923-5765/203 6962
St Petersburg Tel 812-210 0905/210 0990/104 3465
(further information available from **Intourist London**, Tel 0171-538
8600/538 5965)
American Express Travel Service Offices or Representative (R)

Moscow	21a Sadovaya-Kudrinskaya
	103001
	Tel 95-956 9000/9004 #
St Petersburg	Grand Hotel Europe 1/7 Ul.
	Mikhailovskaya St
	191073
	Tel 812-1196009 #

Moscow

Moscow   Azteca $80

Tel: (095) 956 84 89   Fax: (095) 972 05 11

R

3/5 Intourist Hotel Ulitsa Tverskaya 3/5, Moscow

A tiny Mexican restaurant, which first opened in December 1993 with just five tables and
a bar, crammed into a corner of the 20th floor of the Intourist Hotel. There is now a
second room with a spectacular view over the city. The lively atmosphere provided by the
Latin-American dance music ensures a full house, so get here early as they do not take
reservations. A wide variety of Mexican food is served, ranging from prawn quesadillas and
enchiladas, to beef marinated in tequila, all well prepared and presented. Cocktails and
Corona beer as well as various wines are available. *Seats 60. Open 1700-0600, (Sat & Sun
from 1200). Private parking. Amex, Diners, Mastercard, Visa.*

Moscow   Hotel Baltschug Kempinski Moskau $450

Tel: (095) 230 65 00   Fax: (095) 230 65 02

HR

Ulitsa Balchug 1, 113035 Moscow

For clearer reception on long distance calls use the following satellite connection numbers:
phone (007) 501 230 95 00, fax (007) 501 230 95 02. In 1992 the building's Soviet-style
interior was hollowed out, leaving only the 19th-century facade and making way for the
latest Kempinski hotel-the first in Eastern Europe. Splendid views of the Kremlin and Red
Square can be seen from the windows with Stalin's 1930s 'Wedding Cakes' and the five
towers that dominate the Moscow skyline also clearly visible. The hotel staff are mostly
Western European and the rooms match up to Western standards with marble bathrooms
and elegant furnishings. Each room has a safe and is double-glazed and insulated against the
extremes of Moscow's climate. A major advantage is a number for reservations based in
London for hassle-free booking-0800 86 85 88 (toll free). *Rooms 234. Room service 24hr.
Conference facilities for up to 220. Business centre. Indoor swimming pool. Gym. Sauna.
Spa bath. Solarium. Massage. Night club. Bureau de change. Boutique.
Coffee shop (1000-2300). Amex, Diners, Mastercard, Visa.*

Restaurant Le Romanoff $270

Here, traditional Russian specialities are given a new contemporary twist, served with finer,
much lighter sauces. Starters include Balic salmon with truffled hash brown potatoes and
crème double, grilled prawns with mango salad and quail's breast with a sour cherry foam.
Follow with medallions of gratinated monkfish with mushrooms and a paprika sauce,
grilled salmon steak with a basil béarnaise or sautéed lamb medallions in a potato wrapping
with a rosemary and mustard sauce. There are traditional dishes too: their Beluga Malossol
caviar comes on crushed ice, while the Siberian ravioli are solid pastry ravioli filled with
meat and cabbage. *Seats 50. Open D only, 1800-2300. Closed Sun.*

Moscow   Carousel $100

Tel: (095) 200 57 63   Fax: (095) 250 95 98

R

Ulitsa Pervaya Yamskaya 7, Moscow

Opened in early 1994, the restaurant offers a lengthy selection of classic Italian and Russian
dishes prepared with care under the direction of an Italian chef. Dishes offered include
starters such as penne with an arrabbiata sauce, baked aubergines Parmigiana and lobster
soup with garlic croutons. Main courses range from sautéed swordfish Sicilian style (with
tomatoes, onions and capers) and saltimbocca to roast suckling pig with buckwheat
porridge and baked sturgeon with tomatoes, potatoes and sour cream. The wine list is long
and mainly Italian, but does include some French, Californian and South American bottles.
A modest bottle of Pinot Grigio costs $30. *Seats 60. Open 1200-0600. Amex, Diners,
Mastercard, Visa. Roubles.*

Moscow   El Rincón Español $100

Tel: (095) 292 28 93

Ulitsa Okhotny Ryad 2, Moscow

Though located just inside the entrance of the Hotel Moscow, this restaurant is run quite
independently from it. A wide variety of imported Spanish dishes is served, with
particularly good starters of which there is a long list, including Spanish omelette, smoked
ham, chorizo, and pickled herrings. Main courses range from standards such as zarzuela and
paella to sautéed lamb in a red wine sauce with spices and baked potatoes and pork chops
with a garlic sauce. The atmosphere is lively, without being deafening. Service is fast by
Moscow standards. *Seats 120. Open 1200-2400. Private parking. Amex, Diners,
Mastercard, Visa. Roubles.*

Tel: (095) 956 83 01 Fax: (095) 956 83 56
3/5 Intourist Hotel, Ulitsa Tverskaya, Moscow

A good Chinese restaurant is hard to find in Moscow and this is one of the best. Its exotic Oriental decor is unequalled in the city and it also enjoys a central location, in the Intourist Hotel. The chefs are all from Hong Kong, and the food is authentic, with dishes from Canton, Peking, Shanghai and Szechuan all featuring on the lengthy menu. Starters include spring rolls, prawn and sesame toasts, crispy won ton and scallops in a black bean sauce. Soups range from crab and sweetcorn to shark's fin with shredded chicken. Among the main courses are dishes like Szechuan prawns (with chili and spring onion), crispy duck, Mongolian lamb (crispy lamb with lettuce and a spicy plum sauce), pork with cashew nuts and fillet steak Cantonese style (sliced and marinated in wine and served with a fruity sauce). *Seats 120. Open 1200-2400. No parking. Amex, Diners, Mastercard, Visa. Roubles.*

Tel: (095) 927 60 00 Fax: (095) 92 76 01
Teatrainy Proyazd 1/4, Moscow

For clearer reception on long distance calls use the following satellite connection numbers: phone (007) 501 927 60 00, fax (007) 501 927 60 10. Originally built in 1903, the hotel was fully restored to its former art nouveau grandeur in 1991 by the Inter-Continental Group. It's just a short walk from Red Square, and many of the rooms look out on to the Bolshoi Theatre. All the rooms are well equipped, with a mini-bar and satellite TV with 24 channels. The excellent conference facilities also make this an ideal place for businessmen. Cars can be rented and all the cultural events going on in the city can be booked from here. For a little relaxation after the conferences, try the nightclub or fitness centre with its sauna and swimming pool. *Rooms 403. Room service 24hr. Conference facilities for 300. Business centre. Indoor swimming pool. Sauna. Beauty treatment. Hair salon. Casino. Night club. Bureau de change. News kiosk/shop. Travel agency. Coffee shop (1000-2000). Secure private parking. Amex, Diners, Mastercard, Visa.*

Tel: (095) 213 90 00 Fax: (095) 213 90 01
Leningradsky Prospekt 37 Korpus 9, 125167 Moscow

For clearer reception on long distance calls use the following satellite connection numbers: phone (007) 502 213 90 00, fax (007) 502 213 90 01. Opened as a joint Russian-Canadian venture on May Day 1991 the hotel is a ten-minute drive from the Kremlin on the main thoroughfare to Sheremetievo II International airport. Buses, trams and Dynamo metro station (three stops to the centre) are all within walking distance. Bedrooms are well equipped, each with satellite TV and a movie channel, voice-mail, air-conditioning and fax point. The de-luxe rooms have a mini-bar too. Apart from comprehensive conference facilities for up to 400 there is also a health club with sauna, massage, aerobics and gym as well as an American medical centre. *Rooms 415. Room service 24hr. Conference facilities. Business centre. Sports facilities. Bureau de change. News kiosk/shop. Coffee shop (1800-0400). Private parking. Amex, Diners, Mastercard, Visa.*

Tel: (095) 931 90 00 Fax: (095) 931 90 76
Olympiski Prospekt 18/1, 129110 Moscow

For clearer reception on long distance calls use the following satellite connection numbers: phone (007) 502 223 90 00, fax (007) 502 223 90 76. Located outside Moscow's Garden Ring Road, near the Olympic Stadium, the hotel is well served by public transport, and the Prospekt Mira metro station is nearby. There's a well-equipped business centre and excellent sports facilities including a 22m indoor swimming pool along with tennis courts, a gym, sauna and solarium. The hotel was built in 1991, so the rooms are modern and equipped with air-conditioning, satellite TV and mini-bar. *Rooms 500. Room service 24hr. Business centre. Conference facilities for up to 300. Sports centre. Beauty treatments. Hair salon. Bureau de change. News kiosk/shop. Coffee shop (0900-2100), Private parking. Amex, Mastercard, Visa.*

MOSCOW · Pirosmani · ★ · $100

Tel: 095 247 19 26   Fax: 095 246 16 38

R

Novodevichy Prospekt 4, 119435r Moscow

This cosy restaurant with its Georgian-style decor is the best of its kind in Moscow, as illustrated by its predominantly Georgian clientele. Violinists provide the musical entertainment in the evenings. Classical Russian dishes such as cheese suluguny (fried cheese and served with sour cream) and shashlyk (skewered pieces of meat with mushrooms) are accompanied by freshly baked lavash (Georgian bread). Georgian and French wines are available, but the choice is limited. It is best to arrive here by taxi as suspicious-looking characters lounge around outside offering to guard diners' cars – at a price. Pay, or tyres may not remain intact. *Seats 113. Open 1200-1600, 1800-2230. Amex.*

St Petersburg

ST PETERSBURG · Bella Leone · $100

Tel: 812 113 16 70   Fax: 812 113 16 73

R

Vladmirisky Prospekt 9, St Petersburg

The Swiss-trained chefs at this smart and sophisticated restaurant produce a combination of traditional Russian fare with European influences. Home-marinated sea trout (in lemon, orange, cognac, dill, salt and sugar), scrambled egg with red caviar and smoked eel with parsley sauce could precede rack of lamb with gratin potatoes, veal à la diplomate, fish shashlik with a prawn sauce or lobster fricassee with a pernod sauce. The house specialities are Russian caviar (most caviar these days comes from Iran) and grilled lobster. Wines are Italian, French, German and Moldavian (very aromatic). This is one of the few restaurants in St Petersburg with a quiet ambience. *Seats 40. Open 1300-2300. Amex.*

ST PETERSBURG · Grand Hotel Europe · $365

Tel: 812 119 60 00   Fax: 812 119 60 01

HR

Ulitsa Mikhailovskaya 1-7, 191073 St Petersburg

For clearer reception on long distance calls use the following satellite connection numbers: phone–(007) 812 329 60 00, fax–(007) 812 329 60 01. On the corner of Nevsky Prospekt right in the heart of St Petersburg, near the Gostini Dvor metro station, this 19th-century hotel is owned and run by a Swedish hotel group. In 1991 the building was renovated and the Benois stained-glass window, the front façade by Carlo Rossi and the glass-roofed ballroom were restored. The facilities are very good, the health club has a gym, sauna and spa bath and there are excellent boardroom-style conference facilities for up to 250. The traditional features of the rooms have also been restored and reproduction period furniture arranged elegantly in them. *Rooms 301. Room service 24hr. Business centre. Secretarial/translation services. Indoor swimming pool. Leisure centre. Sauna. Solarium. Massage. Hair salon. News kiosk/shop. Coffee shop (0900-2200). Amex, Diners, Mastercard, Visa.*

Restaurant Europe · ☆ · $100

Jean-Michel, son of Michel Lorain (of La Cote St Jacques at Joigny) trained with his father and also served an apprenticeship with Troisgros at Roanne. As a result he was invited to the hotel when it opened and created a new style of cooking, now known in Russia as the 'Renaissance of Russia' cuisine. This combines traditional dishes with modern influences. A British and a Russian chef have now taken over. Traditional raw ingredients, like beetroot, pearl barley, mushrooms and caviar are used more imaginatively than before in a Russian menu, while a European-influenced menu brings even more innovation. Begin with warm duck salad with honey and cognac-marinated prunes and a tea dressing or cabbage and wild mushroom consommé flavoured with garlic and served with pelmenis (little meat-filled parcels) and a delicate cabbage pastry. Main courses could be grilled medallions of salmon on a bed of peas with a port wine and goose liver butter sauce or fillet of veal filled with a mixture of crayfish and spinach and baked in brioche. The 19th-century, building, featuring stained-glass windows and formerly used by the Tsars, makes an elegant and fitting setting for the fine food. The wine list is international. *Seats 90. Open 1200-1500 (Sun only), 1800-2300. Closed D Sun.*

ST PETERSBURG   Restaurant Troika $90

Tel: 812 113 53 43   Fax: 812 310 42 79
Zagorodny Prospekt 27, St Petersburg

R

Until the October Revolution, this place south of the city centre was an old-style drinking house, but after 1917 it became a restaurant. The cooking is traditional, with most of the dishes originating from old Polish recipes. The menu lists smoked sturgeon, baked pike – with mushrooms, beef stroganoff and chicken Kiev. There is an enormous list of *zakuski* (cold appetisers). White French and Spanish red wines are served. The tables rise up around a stage, where traditional Russian dancing and European cabaret provide a lively, nightly variety show, Moulin Rouge-style. *Seats 160. Open D only 2000-2400. Closed Mon. Mastercard, Visa.*

Elsewhere in Russia

SOCHI   Radisson Hotel Lazurnaya $213

Tel: (862) 297 59 74   Fax: (862) 661 59 98
Kuroitny Prospekt 103, 354024 Sochi

H

For clearer reception on long distance calls use the following satellite connection numbers: phone (0035) 815 661 59 99, fax (0035) 815 661 59 98. A well-equipped 19-storey hotel that sits on a bluff overlooking the Black Sea, in what is an up-and-coming holiday resort which Russians visit to escape the cold and to enjoy the healing powers of the hot Matsesta Springs. Some of the bedrooms have balconies which look out across to the hotel's private beach. All the the rooms have satellite TV and phone, mini-bar and air-conditioning. The sports facilities are excellent. *Rooms 300. Room service 24hr. Conference facilities for up to 300. Business centre. Water sports. Indoor and outdoor swimming pools. Gym. Tennis. Russian and Turkish baths. Massage. Hair salon. Casino. Night club. Bureau de change. Boutiques. Coffee shop (0800-2200). Amex, Mastercard, Visa.*

THE INDEPENDENT

INDEPENDENT
ON SUNDAY

Your truly
independent
guides to life

Spain

Currency Peseta **Exchange Rate** £1=approx Pts190
International dialling code 00 34
(Madrid+1, Barcelona+3, Malaga+5, Seville+5, Valencia+6)
Passports/Visas No visa required by British passport holders.
British Embassy in Madrid Tel 1-319 0200   Fax 1-319 0423

Airports
Barcelona Tel 3-478 5000 **Madrid** Tel 1-305 8343
Malaga Tel 5-224 0000 **Seville** 5-444 9000 **Valencia** Tel 6-370 9500
Railway Stations
Renfe Madrid Tel 1-563 0202 **Renfe Barcelona** Tel 3-490 0202
Car hire
Tel Nos. **Madrid Avis** 1-530 0168 **Hertz** (airport) 1-305 8452
Budget 1-5716660 (airport 1-747 7427)
Barcelona Avis 3-209 9533 **Budget** (airport) 3-322 9012
Malaga Avis (airport) 5-223 3096/230 855
Budget 5-244 7078 (airport 52-239 449)
Speed limits 120 km/h on motorways, 100 km/h on trunk roads, 90
km/h on secondary roads, 50 km/h in towns.

Banks 8.30am-4.30pm Mon-Thur, 8.30am-2pm Fri, 8.30am-1pm Sat
(main branches only). 8.30am-2pm June-Sept.
Shops 10am-8pm (most are closed at lunchtime between 1-4pm).

New Year's Day, 6 Jan, Good Friday, 1 May, 15 Aug, 12 Oct, 1 Nov,
6 & 8 Dec, Christmas Day.

Spanish Tourist Board in **London** Tel 0171-499 0901 (0891 669920 - for
brochures). In **Spain** Madrid Tel 1-429 4951 Barcelona
Tel 3-478 4704 Malaga Tel 5-221 3445
American Express Travel Service Offices or Representative (R)

Barcelona	Paseo De Gracia 101
	Corner of Rosellon
	08008
	Tel 3-217 0070/217 0556 #
Madrid	Plaza De Las Cortes 2
	28014
	Tel 1-322 5500 #
Malaga	Viajes Alhambra (R)
	Calle Especerias 10
	29005
	Tel 5-221 3744 #

Barcelona

Tel: (3) 221 10 00   Fax: (3) 221 10 70
HR

Calle de la Marina 19-21, 08005 Barcelona

The Hotel Arts enjoys a wonderful position by the Mediterranean next to the Olympic Marina, ten minutes away from El Prat international airport yet only a few minutes walk from the historical and commercial centre of the city. Luxurious facilities abound, from marble bathrooms, satellite TV, fax and PC connections to an honour bar in every room. The Japanese owners, SOGO, keen to attract businessmen, offer extensive conference facilities, 14 meeting rooms and a fax and secretarial service. Decor is unobtrusively modern. *Rooms 455. Room service 24hr. Private parking. Conference facilities 900. Fitness centre. Hair salon. Outdoor swimming pool. Sauna. Amex, Diners, Mastercard, Visa.*

In a country as fiercely nationalistic in culinary matters as Spain, it can be difficult to find a restaurant serving food that isn't a variation on local, regional or national specialities. The Newport Room at the Hotel Arts is an exception. Head chef Tony Bombaci spent many years in San Francisco and has imported a Californian style of cuisine which shows clear Oriental influences, from Thai-style smoked lobster to crispy teriyaki duckling. Fashionable ingredients such as bone marrow (with seared loin of tuna and Oakland sauce) also find a place on the fixed-price menu. As might be expected, the wine list has a strong Californian component. *Seats 100 (terrace 40). Open 2000-2400. Closed Sun, Aug.*

Tel: (3) 417 01 15   Fax: (3) 212 24 82
R

Avenida del Tibidabo 31, 08022 Barcelona

This large restaurant, on a hill in a residential area of the city, is most lively at weekends when families crowd in to enjoy its excellent traditional Castilian cooking. The menu is enigmatically minimalist with no description of the food. Items such as *el caldo* (broth), *los riñones* (kidneys), *la morcilla* (black pudding) and the brutally frank *la asadurilla* (entrails) leave plenty to the imagination. Spit-roasts and lamb cooked in wood ovens are specialities. No more is given away on the dessert menu with *las natillas* (custards) and *el hojaldre* (puff pastry) vying with the somewhat more specific *la tarta de whisky* (whisky tart). The *menu de la casa* costs Pts4000. *Seats 250. Open 1300-1600, 2100-2400. Closed Sun, Easter week, National Holidays. Valet parking. Amex, Diners, Mastercard, Visa.*

Tel: (3) 451 19 14   Fax: (3) 415 00 49
H

Calle Mallorca 216, 08008 Barcelona

This modern hotel, built five years ago, is centrally located. It provides all the facilities necessary for a comfortable stay: air-conditioned rooms, a restaurant, bar and an outdoor swimming pool for relaxing beside at the end of the day. Business facilities are limited. *Rooms 100. Room service limited. Private parking Pts2500. Conference facilities 30. Outdoor swimming pool. Solarium. Amex, Diners, Mastercard, Visa.*

Tel: (3) 237 75 88   Fax: (3) 237 95 26
R

Córcega 286, 08008 Barcelona

Fish is the the the speciality of this restaurant in the centre of Barcelona, just off Diagonal. The *paella parellada* is particularly good. Other dishes include *pimientos al piquillo rellenos de mariscos* (baby peppers stuffed with seafood) and *gratin de rape con setas a las hierbas aromaticas* (monkfish gratin with mushrooms and aromatic herbs). Meat-eaters can console themselves with the beef fillet with gorgonzola. *Seats 120. Open 1300-1600, 2100-2400. Closed Sun. Amex, Diners, Mastercard, Visa.*

Tel: (3) 215 30 24   Fax: (3) 487 00 81
R

Calle Mallorca 275, Centresvelos, 08008 Barcelona

Wood panelling and displays of china decorate this elegant, up-market restaurant. The owner-chef combines the culinary traditions of his native Basque country with those of Catalonia. Lobster and game dishes are particularly fine, as is the selection of old Riojas on the wine list. *Seats 88 (terrace 25). Open 1345-1530, 2045-2330. Closed L Sat, Sun, 2 weeks at Christmas, 2 weeks mid Aug. Amex, Diners, Mastercard, Visa.*

Tel: (3) 218 42 30   Fax: (3) 415 58 48
Gran de Gràcia 81, 08012 Barcelona

Owner José-Ramón Neira describes his clientele as 'mixed' although few of us would fall into the category between 'the President of France and the King of Spain'. Botafumeiro has certainly grown from humble beginnings in the early 70s to become one of the city's best places for eating simply prepared fish. Why, for instance, adulterate fresh grilled anchovies with anything more than a little olive oil and squeeze of lemon? Head chef Moncho Neira varies his menu daily, depending on what is available at market, but his lobster and seafood salad is renowned. Galician wines, such as the aromatic Albariño, are a feature of the 270-strong list. *Seats 350. Open 1300-0100. Closed 3 weeks Aug. Valet parking. Amex, Diners, Mastercard, Visa.*

Tel: (3) 428 03 01   Fax: (3) 428 19 17
Calle Jorge Manrique, 08035 Barcelona

This 17th-century building was formerly a country house-cum-gentleman's club. It is now a huge Catalan restaurant which doubles in capacity during the summer when its terrace is in use. The menu is fish-biased with dried salt cod (*bacalao*), monkfish (*rape*), hake (*merluza*), John Dory (*dorada*) and several types of shellfish appearing in a variety of traditional preparations: *suprema de rape a la mousselina*, for example. There are also interesting meat dishes such as *albóndigas con sépia* (meatballs with cuttlefish), and, unusually for Spain, some noteworthy desserts. *Helado de higos con tulipa y coulis de fresones* (fig ice cream with a strawberry coulis) sounds particularly intriguing. *Seats 200 (terrace 200). Open 1300-1630, 2030-2400. Closed D Sun. Valet parking. Amex, Diners, Mastercard, Visa.*

Tel: (3) 301 14 04   Fax: (3) 317 29 15
Avenida de la Catedral 7, 08002 Barcelona

A mixed clientele are attracted to a friendly hotel in the heart of the city, opposite Barcelona Cathedral. All rooms have balconies (seven have terraces) and are equipped with satellite TV, mini-bar and air-conditioning to ward off the blistering summer heat and humidity. The terrace bar is a pleasant spot to relax with a long drink. Room rates are at their cheapest at weekends. *Rooms 147. Room service 24hr. Banqueting facilities 150. Conference facilities 120. Amex, Diners, Mastercard, Visa.*

Tel: (3) 484 86 00   Fax: (3) 487 14 42
Passeig de Gràcia 73-75, 08008 Barcelona

Although the hotel only celebrated its tenth birthday in 1996, one of its fine buildings dates from the end of the last century. There is a minimalist elegance about the decor with an imaginative use of wood, metal and glass. The needs of business are fully catered for with a range of function rooms, secretarial and translation services, photocopying and fax facilities. And after a hard day clinching deals there is a swimming pool with wave machine and jacuzzi in which to relax and a garden terrace where one can sit, sip drinks and enjoy the late afternoon sun. Lovers of architecture can eat a Catalan breakfast while looking out admiringly at Gaudi's superb "La Pedrera" across Barcelona's busiest street. All rooms have satellite TV and three rooms are specifically adapted for disabled guests. *Rooms 183. Room service limited. Garage parking Pts2000. Banqueting facilities 200. Conference facilities 300. Secretarial/translation services. Outdoor swimming pool. Jacuzzi. Solarium. Bureau de change. Amex, Diners, Mastercard, Visa.*

THE APARTMENT SERVICE

Tel in UK (0181) 748 4207   Fax (0181) 748 3972

The Apartment Service will find you the right apartment worldwide to suit your needs, whether you are on a short or long-term stay. A 96-page colour catalogue is free on request. All budgets are catered for.

Tel: (3) 202 06 86   Fax: (3) 200 72 99
Avenida Diagonal 423, 08036 Barcelona

R

You will be as delighted by your surroundings as by the food when you dine at La Dama. Its sweeping, organic lines and opulent glass, wood and gold decoration are typical of the Catalan art nouveau movement. The food, however, is more internationally inclined with old favourites such as chateaubriand and duck à la orange making appearances on the menu. Of course, no Spanish restaurant worth its salt would fail to also offer four or five types of fish. Chef Josep Bullich includes fillets of sole *(lenguado)* with king prawns *au parfum d'estragon* (tarragon) and baked turbot with garlic and onions within his repertoire. In addition to the seasonal carte there are two *dégustation* menus priced at Pts5975 and Pts7500. *Seats 80. Open 1330-1545, 2030-2400. Valet parking. Amex, Diners, Mastercard, Visa.*

Tel: (3) 439 55 76   Fax: (3) 439 99 41
Avenida Diagonal 469, 08036 Barcelona

R

Catalan and international classic dishes are the speciality of this plush restaurant in the centre of Barcelona. Fish features heavily on the carte (there are no set menus), mostly baked and served with simple sauces. Paella, cannelloni and black rice are also popular choices. The extensive wine list features around 120 Riojas, dating back almost to the Second World War. *Seats 80. Open 1300-1600, 2100 -2400. Closed Sat & Sun in Jul & Aug. Valet parking. Amex, Diners, Mastercard, Visa.*

Tel: (3) 430 00 29   Fax: (3) 439 29 50
Provença 88, 08029 Barcelona

R

Jaime Burgués has combined the traditional Catalan cooking he learned from his mother with techniques and ideas from French cuisine to create an imaginative, individual style. The fruits of the sea are exploited to the full with dishes such as *salmonettes con salteado de chipirones, vinagreta de anchoas* (red mullet sautéed with baby squid and an anchovy vinaigrette) and *terrina de centolla al Jerez seco* (terrine of spider crab in dry sherry). Wines include whites from Catalonia, rosés from Navarra and reds from Rioja. This is a restaurant for a quiet, civilised meal rather than a raucous knees-up. *Seats 60. Open 1300-1600, 2100-2330. Closed D Sun, all Mon, Easter week, Christmas week, Aug. Amex, Diners, Mastercard, Visa.*

Tel: (3) 371 00 09   Fax: (3) 372 84 00
Avenida Països Catalans 58, Esplugues de Llobregat, 08950 Barcelona

Salvador Dali used to eat at this long-established restaurant on the outskirts of Barcelona. Although businessmen make up the bulk of the customers during the week, La Masía is taken over at the weekend by families who relax in the garden and enjoy Pedro Peran's cooking. This restaurant, like so many in the area, combines traditional Catalan with French cuisine and the menu changes weekly to reflect what is available at market. House favourites include cream of shellfish soup with fennel and salad of grilled peppers and shrimps dressed in olive oil. The decor, featuring old lamps, lots of wood and carpets, is more elegantly Bohemian than typically Catalan. *Seats 80 (garden 40). Open 1200-1600, 2030-2330. Closed D Sun. Amex, Diners, Mastercard, Visa.*

Tel: (3) 203 84 08   Fax: (3) 205 63 69
Beltrán i Rózpide 16 bis, 08034 Barcelona

Jean-Louis Neichel's ultra-trendy restaurant, 4km outside Barcelona, is one of the places to be seen in. Its interior is plain and light and affords a view into a garden strewn with lemon trees. Neichel trained under Alain Chapel in France and his cooking manages to be simultaneously luxurious and healthy. Examples of main dishes are *merluza de palangre gratinada con hierbas del campo, arroz negro de sepias y tomate confitado* (hake au gratin with country herbs, squid ink-blackened rice and a confit of tomatoes) and *pichón asado con bacon y especias suaves, su jugo aromatizado al vinagre agrodulce* (pigeon baked with bacon and served with its own stock spiced with a sweet and sour vinaigrette). There is a good-value lunch menu at Pts4700 and an excellent gourmet menu for Pts7200 per person which, for an extra charge of Pts1500, can include a tasting of six different wines. *Seats 50. Open 1300-1530, 2030-2330. Closed L Sat & Sun, Aug, Easter week. Valet parking. Amex, Diners, Mastercard, Visa.*

Tel: (3) 201 32 82   Fax: (3) 414 44 17
Santalo 54, 08021 Barcelona

The 80s saw an explosion of new restaurants in Barcelona and this purpose-built restaurant in a quiet tree-lined street just above Plaza Calvo Jatelo remains one the best and attracts quite a fashionable crowd. The cooking is simple Catalan fare like *espinacas a la catalana* (Catalan-style spinach salad), *pimientos del piquillo rellenos de merluza* (baby peppers stuffed with hake), *buñuelos de bacalao* (salt cod fritters) and *rodaballo al horno con cebollitas tiernas* (baked turbot with shallots). As well as the numerous fish dishes there are also some typical meat and offal dishes like *butifarra a la parilla* (chargrilled black pudding) and *higado de cabrito ecebollado* (kid's liver with onions). The wine list is dominated by regional bottles like Rueda and Rioja but there are also a few token French clarets. *Seats 140. Open 1300-1600, 2030-2400. Closed D Sun. Valet parking. Amex, Mastercard, Visa.*

Tel: (3) 419 31 81   Fax: (3) 419 18 99
Avenida Diagonal 593-595, 08014 Barcelona

Pictures of the legendary comedy duo hang from the walls of a trendy restaurant which caters mainly for businessmen at lunchtime, entertains a wider clientele for dinner and becomes a piano bar after midnight. Fish and shellfish feature heavily on the menu. *Lenguado relleno de frutos de mar al cava* (sole stuffed with seafood in Cava), *bogavante en hojaldre con espárragos trigueros y salsa de trufas* (lobster encased in puff pastry with wild asparagus and a truffle sauce), *chuletitas de cabrito a la parrilla* (grilled kid chops) are typical main dishes although the menu changes daily. The restaurant is situated in an upmarket business and shopping district. *Seats 70 (terrace 50). Open 1330-1600, 2130-0100. Closed L Sat, all Sun. Valet parking. Amex, Diners, Mastercard, Visa.*

Tel: (3) 371 10 84   Fax: (3) 371 65 12
Laureá Miró 202, Esplugues de Llobregat, 08950 Barcelona

Two kilometres outside Barcelona, Quirze has been in the Giralt family for six generations. It is now a light, airy, modern place serving a particularly fine selection of game – wild boar, wild duck, partridge – depending on the season. Other specialities include supreme of sea bass with garlic mousseline, morel mushrooms stuffed with foie gras in a cream sauce and monkfish with artichokes. The wine list features white from the Penedés region west of Barcelona, rosés from Navarra and Catalan Cavas. *Seats 90 (terrace 60). Open 1300-1600, 2100-2330. Closed D Sat & Sun, all Sun in Jul/Aug. Private parking. Amex, Mastercard, Visa.*

Tel: (3) 209 75 59   Fax: (3) 209 79 18
Sant Eliés 22, 08006 Barcelona

El Racó d'En Freixa will be celebrating its 10th birthday in 1996 but its owner, José Maria Freixa, has been working in restaurants since he was a teenager. He describes the cooking as "creative Catalan" and features seasonal *dégustation* menus priced between Pts5500 and Pts6850: truffles in February and March, a 'blossom' menu in May and June, 'bread, oil and wine' menu in October and November and a special 'classical' selection at Christmas. Fish is particularly fine here, as is the cheese trolley, which features a wide range of Spanish cheeses including *severeido garocha* and *cabrales*. Catalonian wines are strongly represented on the wine list. *Seats 50. Open 1300-1600, 2100-2330. Closed D Sun, all Mon, Aug, Easter week. Parking Pts125. Amex, Diners, Mastercard, Visa.*

Tel: (3) 200 91 29   Fax: (3) 414 41 14
Tuset 27, 08006 Barcelona

Reno is in the Sant Gervasi area and prides itself on the sober, classical "English-style" elegance of its decor with plenty of wood panelling and leather. Consequently, it attracts a generally up-market clientele of business executives at lunchtime and the wealthier breed of tourist in the evening. Chef Pedro Gonzalez's creative blending of Catalan and French cooking has won plaudits and includes such dishes as artichoke hearts stuffed with seafood with cardinale sauce, roast cutlet of lamb *aux fines herbes* and filet mignon with potato soufflé. The vast wine list (400 different bottles) is pan-European with a particularly fine selection of burgundies. There are fixed-price lunch menus from Pts5500 upwards and a gourmet menu at Pts6500. *Seats 190. Open 1300-1600, 2030-2330. Closed L Sat. Valet parking. Amex. Diners. Mastercard. Visa.*

Tel: (3) 318 52 00   Fax: (3) 318 01 48
La Gran Via de las Cortes Catalanas 668, 08010 Barcelona

Located in the bustling heart of Barcelona, the Ritz is a traditional, formal hotel built in 1919 to a classical design and decorated in a manner redolent of its London namesake. With thirteen function rooms, it is well equipped to host any type of event, from cocktail parties to conferences. All rooms have satellite TV and safes and, although the avenue on which the hotel stands is one of the city's busiest, double-glazing effectively keeps out the street noise. *Rooms 161. Room service 24hr. Private parking Pts1200. Conference facilities 300. Amex, Diners, Mastercard, Visa.*

Tel: (3) 209 01 25   Fax: (3) 209 12 95
Via Augusta 201, 08021 Barcelona

This restaurant, ten minutes outside Barcelona, has recently become independent from the Paradis chain, but the cooking is still Mediterranean. Starters include Jabugo ham, gazpacho Andaluz and lobster salad with truffle vinaigrette. The ubiquitous salt cod bacalao appears several incarnations, including cooked in a green sauce with clams, while a wide variety of fresh fish is simply prepared, perhaps grilled with a little salt and garlic. Meat-eaters have richer fare: fillet of veal in a black truffle sauce, for instance. A *menu gastronomico* is available at Pts3500. *Seats 500. Open 1300-1600, 2100-2400. Closed D Sun. Valet parking. Amex, Diners, Mastercard, Visa.*

Tel: (3) 319 30 33   Fax: (3) 319 30 46
Paseo Isabel Sugunod 14 (Planta Baja), 08003 Barcelona

You're as likely to be surrounded by Russians and Japanese as Spaniards or Catalans if you dine in this vast, 150-year-old restaurant in the cosmopolitan port area south of Barcelona. Head chef José Lladonosa formerly ran a cookery school and wrote several cookery books before taking over the helm five years ago. His menu features no-nonsense Catalan cuisine: paella, mixed grills, pot pourri of seafood, rice blackened with squid ink. All the top Spanish wines are listed (with a good range of Catalan Riojas and Penedés whites) as well as a fine French selection. *Seats 325. Open 1300-0100. Parking Pts200. Amex, Diners, Mastercard, Visa.*

Tel: (3) 302 22 21   Fax: (3) 485 27 48
Rambla de Catalunya 5, 08002 Barcelona

Tikal is a good place to try Jabugo, the best-known type of Spanish ham, cured by the cold air of the sierras. Other specialities include seafood salad and vichyssoise, peppered entrecote and turbot with tender garlic cloves and clams. The chef was previously at the Barcelona Hilton and his cooking is a blending of international and Catalan. Prices are low considering the quality of the food. *Seats 60. Open 1300-1600, 2000-2330. Closed Sun, National Holidays. Amex, Diners, Mastercard, Visa.*

Tel: (3) 487 01 96   Fax: (3) 487 19 16
Pasaje de la Concepción 5, 08008 Barcelona

This original art nouveau building with its glass ceiling, designed by architect Pepe Cortez, was converted into a restaurant five years ago and is a popular hangout, situated near the intersection of Diagonal and Paseig de Gracia. The famous Catalan designer Moriscal, who also designed the logo for the Olympics, collaborated on the project and everything inside, from the plates to the different shaped fish on the walls, is designed by him. The cooking is less typically Catalan than it once was – moving more towards international and Mediterranean styles - although the traditional fish dishes remain like *merluza* (hake), *gambas de Palamos* (prawns from the Costa Brava), lobster, clams and shrimps. Game is also served in season. There is one set menu, the *menú degustación* at Pts6500 per person. The well-thought-out wine list with regional Riojas, Ribera del Dueros, and Catalan Penedés, also, unusually, has some Californian wines. *Seats 150. Open 1330-600, 2030-2400. Closed Sun, National Holidays. Valet parking. Amex, Diners, Mastercard, Visa.*

Tel: (3) 200 72 44   Fax: (3) 201 60 95
Calle Ganduxer 10-12, 08021 Barcelona

This up-market restaurant in a quiet residential district is justly famous for sublime original food based on Catalan classics. Traditional favourites such as *patatas con butifarra de perol troceada al huevo frito* (potatoes with boiled black pudding chopped with fried egg) find a place alongside more delicate dishes like *flores de calabacín rellenas de brandada de bacalao sobre salsa romesco* (courgette flowers filled with salt cod in a garlic, almonds, hazelnuts and chili sauce). Chef José Moniesa cooks all the fish and meat over a charcoal grill. You should not miss out on his delicious home-made desserts. Wines include a fine selection of Cavas. *Seats 80. Open 1230-1600, 2030-2400. Closed L Sat, all Sun, Aug. Valet parking. Amex, Diners, Mastercard, Visa.*

Around Barcelona

Tel: (3) 867 28 51   Fax: (3) 867 38 61
Sant Joan 6, San Celoni, 08470 Barcelona

Owner and chef Santi Santamaria was born in the *mesía* (a typical Catalan country home) that is now his restaurant in the town of Sant Celoni, 45km from Barcelona. A former technical draughtsman, he taught himself cooking and his kitchen produces broadly Mediterranean dishes with a leaning towards mushrooms and truffles (the latter available on a special Pts12,500 menu during February only). Specialities include prawn-filled ravioli with ceps oil, fricassee of cod, tripe with black pudding and spicy sausage, and hake cooked with fennel. Home-made sorbets and ices of seasonal red berries are dessert highlights. A gourmet menu is available at Pts9500 per person. More than 200 wines are stocked, including many local varieties. *Seats 40. Open 1330-1530, 2030-2230. Closed D Sun, all Mon. Private parking. Amex, Diners, Mastercard, Visa.*

Tel: (3) 589 21 21   Fax: (3) 674 21 00
Rambla Mossen Jacinto Verdeguer 41, 08190 Vall Doreix

The Monzos converted their family home into a hotel and restaurant in the wake of the 1992 Olympics in Barcelona. Set in its own spacious grounds (5,000m2) up in the hills, it is a haven from the noise of the city yet only ten minutes drive away from the centre. An outdoor swimming pool and tennis courts are at the disposal of guests and the air-conditionied rooms have TVs, mini-bars, safes and air-conditioning. One room is specially equipped for disabled guests. Señora Monzo cooks local fare in the hotel restaurant Los Leones. A disco has recently opened under the hotel which is free for residents. *Rooms 16. Closed Aug. Room service 24hr. Banqueting facilities 300. Conference facilities 30. Garden. Outdoor swimming pool. Tennis courts. Amex, Diners, Mastercard, Visa.*

Madrid

Tel: (1) 431 64 56   Fax: (1) 575 54 91
Callejón de Puigcerdá 8, 28001 Madrid

Located in the elegant Barrio de Salamanca district, close to Plaza de Colon, this chic restaurant is set around a courtyard in a former stables. Dining is on three floors overlooking an open atrium and the majority of the clientele are businessmen, making the atmosphere quite formal. Basque chef Martin Perasitagoe cooks dishes typical of his native San Sebastian but has a highly individual touch, with an emphasis on colour and presentation. His specialities include *rollitos de langosta con salsa de soya* (rolls of lobster in a soya sauce), *huevos escalfados con salmón y caviar* (poached eggs served with salmon and caviar) and *pichones deshuesados a las dos pimientas* (baby pigeon served with two types of pepper). The excellent wine list features 600 plus bottles. *Seats 70. Open 1330-1530, 2100 -2330. Closed L Sat, all Sun, Aug. Valet parking. Amex, Visa.*

MADRID   **Bajamar**   ★   **Pts10,000**

Tel: (1) 548 48 18   Fax: (1) 559 13 26
Gran Vía 78, 28013 Madrid

Diners are encouraged to tour the open-plan kitchen before eating at this immensely popular restaurant in the city centre, near the Plaza España metro stop. Despite its size, Bajamar is comfortable and airy and the atmosphere laid-back and friendly. Seafood is the house speciality: try *camarones* (baby shrimps), *ostras* (oysters) or, if you fancy something a bit different, *percebes* (goose barnacles). Hake, salmon, turbot, monkfish, sole and sea bass are regular favourites as well as more unusual dishes such as *angulas de Aguinaga* (baby eels from Aguinaga). The paella is renowned throughout Madrid. Wines include the fine whites of Albariño and rosés from Perelada on the Costa Brava, in addition to a large selection of Riojas. *Seats 280. Open 1300-1600, 2100-2400. Amex, Mastercard, Visa.*

MADRID   **El Bodegón**   **Pts10,000**

Tel: (1) 562 88 44   Fax: (1) 562 97 25
Pinar 15, 28006 Madrid

Traditional regional cooking with a touch of luxury is the speciality of head chef José Machado. A typical meal from the seasonal menu might start with sautéed foie gras in *caldo de garbanzos y panes fritos* (a chick pea soup with croutons), followed by sea bass with carrot juice and shallot oil or *manitas de cerdo rellenas de cordero al grano de mostaza* (pig's trotters stuffed with lamb and mustard seed), and, to finish, caramelised pineapple with a scoop of warm chocolate. The decor is elegant and plush. *Seats 85. Open 1330-1600, 2100-2400. Closed L Sat, all Sun, Aug, National Holidays. Valet parking. Amex, Diners, Mastercard, Visa.*

MADRID   **Cabo Mayor**   ★   **Pts12,000**

Tel: (1) 350 87 76   Fax: (1) 359 16 21
Calle Juan Ramón Jiménez 37, 28036 Madrid

Pedro Luarumbe has made a name for himself in the capital since coming from his native Cantabria 15 years ago and opening this excellent restaurant. His chef Miguel Jiménez's fine Cantabrian cooking makes full use of the rich fishing grounds off the northern coast: salmon is grilled with lemon and green asparagus, hake is baked with red peppers, monkfish is cooked Santander style with beltxa mushrooms, even the gazpacho contains lobster. There are also simple meat dishes such as rack of lamb and roasted semi-wild duck with mango sauce. The dessert menu is unusually long for Spain and, in addition to the popular creamy puddings, includes fresh fruit salad and a plate of Cantabrian cheeses. Recommended wines include reds from Rioja and Ribera del Duero, and whites from the Navarra and Penedés regions. Each of the five dining-rooms is decorated like a different part of a ship, from hull to cabin. Unusually for Spain, where smoking is virtually the national pastime, a separate room is provided for non-smokers. *Seats 300 (terrace 40). Open 1330-1530, 2100-2400. Closed Sun, National Holidays. Amex, Diners, Mastercard, Visa.*

MADRID   **Café de Oriente**   **Pts13,000**

Tel: (1) 541 39 74   Fax: (1) 547 77 07
Plaza de Oriente 2, 28013 Madrid

This restaurant enjoys one of the best settings in Madrid, on the site of a 17th-century monastery, in a square amid some of the city's oldest buildings. Its success, since it opened in the early 80s, has spawned a chain that has spread as far as the USA. The cooking is imaginative and, although broadly Basque in slant, includes more unusual dishes such *filetes de lenguado al vapor suave y salsa de anis* (fillet of sole gently steamed in an aniseed sauce), *carpaccio de pez espada al eneldo* (wafer-thin slices of raw swordfish with dill) and *muslo de conejo relleno de ciruelas pasas* (leg of rabbit stuffed with prunes). *Seats 90. Open 1300-1600, 2100-2400. Amex, Diners, Mastercard, Visa.*

Meal prices for 2 are based on à la carte menus. When set menus are available, prices will often be lower.

Tel: (1) 365 32 52   Fax: (1) 366 48 66
Calle Cava Baja 35, 28005 Madrid

Near the Plaza Mayor in a bustling, central area, this place started as a simple neighbourhood tavern and has become one of Madrid's most popular restaurants. The owner was formerly a waiter here before taking it over and opening his own place in 1974. With his chef, Aurelio Calderón, he has created a menu of typically robust, rich Castilian dishes such as *callos a la madrileña* (tripe cooked Madrid-style', with a rich tomato and garlic sauce) and more subtle Basque specialities like *merluza a la bilbaína* (hake served 'Bilbao-style', served in a clam sauce). There are also plenty of succulent red meats and earthy peasant stews. The decor – dark wood, beams – is also typically Castilian, as is the relaxed, friendly service. A few French bottles fight it out with the Riojas on the wine list. Set menu at Pts5,000. *Seats 125 (terrace 15). Open 1300-1600, 2100-2400. Closed L Sat, Aug. Valet parking. Amex, Diners, Mastercard, Diners.*

Tel: (1) 416 44 55
Calle Emiliano Barral 14, 28043 Madrid

The simple pleasures of Galician cooking are celebrated at this restaurant owned by the Ortega family who moved to the capital from Santiago de Compostela 30 years ago. Most items on the short menu are cooked a *la gallega* (Galician-style). *Merluza a la gallega* is hake cooked with potatoes, served with its own stock and a little paprika. *Empanada de gallega* are typical Galician flat pies or fritters. It is no surprise to find a good selection of German-style whites from Galicia on the list. The relaxed, friendly atmosphere of the restaurant is popular with families. *Seats 45. Open 1400-1530, 2130-2300. Closed Sun, National Holidays. Mastercard, Visa.*

Tel: (1) 553 63 05   Fax: (1) 553 32 98
Calle General Ibáñez de Ibero 5, 28003 Madrid

This centrally-located restaurant is an excellent venue for a romantic *diner à deux*. Chef Francisco Vicente is confident enough of his cooking to offer only a short à la carte menu featuring Catalan favourites such as *merluza* (hake) and *arroz negro con chipirones* (black rice with baby squid) alongside more unusual dishes, of which *medallones de rape y endivias gratinadas* (medallions of monkfish and endive gratin) is an example. The restaurant will be celebrating its 15th anniversary in 1996 so look out for a special birthday menu or choose from one of the three fixed-price options which start at Pts3950. *Seats 110. Open 1330-1600, 2100-2400. Closed L Sat, all Sun, Aug. Valet parking. Amex, Diners, Mastercard, Visa.*

Tel: (1) 570 20 04   Fax: (1) 571 85 84
Calle Orense 64-66, 28020 Madrid

A marvellous variety of fish and shellfish is available at this busy restaurant in a modern building. Anchovies, whitebait, baby squid and spiny dogfish are simply grilled or fried and served with a sweet pepper and tomato salad. Bass, sole, red mullet and gilthead are baked in a salt crust *(a la sal)*. Swordfish, bream, turbot, grouper and angler fish are oven-baked. *Seats 200. Open 1300-1700, 2000-2400. Closed Sun. Valet parking. Diners, Mastercard, Visa.*

Tel: (1) 531 45 00   Fax: (1) 522 0307
Plaza de Santa Ana 4, 28012 Madrid

The Reina Victoria has gained a reputation as the favoured hotel of bullfighters and their followers. During the annual April San Isidro (Madrid's patron saint) bull fights, the hotel fills up with devotees of the ring. The plant-filled interior has been refurbished in sleek 1920s-style and all rooms are air-conditioned and have mini-bars, safes and satellite TV. *Rooms 201. Room service. Private parking Pts1600. Conference facilities 500. Amex, Diners, Mastercard, Visa.*

Tel: (1) 319 24 35   Fax: (1) 319 24 35
Calle Amador de Los Rios 6, 28010 Madrid

Jockey is an unusual restaurant, and not simply for its decor of mahogany panelling and
racing pictures and paraphernalia. To describe the lengthy menu as eclectic scarcely does it
justice. Almost every national cuisine is represented in at least one dish although the
combination of ingredients is highly imaginative, even startling, at times: anyone for
ensalada de arenques noruegos al curry (salad of curried Norwegian herring)? Spanish
dishes are not neglected with some good, rustic offal such choices as *sesos de ternera a la
manteca negra* (calf's brains in black butter). The wine list is comprehensive. *Seats 90.
Open 1300-1600, 2100-2400. Closed L Sat, all Sun, Aug. Valet parking. Amex, Diners,
Mastercard, Visa.*

Tel: (1) 319 40 29   Fax: (1) 319 40 29
Calle Génova 19, 28004 Madrid

It is a joy to eat amongst the flowers and fountains in the garden of this 19th-century
mansion, formerly home to the great Spanish liberal, Sagasta. A new Belgian chef, Nicolas
Pecquereau, arrived in 1995 and it is likely he will continue to cook the broadly French
food with a Mediterranean slant for which Lúculo is known. Lobster and sirloin steak,
prepared in a variety of ways, are house favourites. Unusually, in addition to the à la carte,
there are six fixed-price menus (ranging from Pts5000 to Pts7500) featuring dishes such as
foie de pato y espárragos de jardin con vinagreta de trufas (duck's liver and asparagus with
a truffle vinaigrette) and the unusual *salmón a la flor de lavanda* (salmon with lavender
flowers). The wine list is small but perfectly formed. *Seats 75 (garden 50). Open 1330-1630,
2130-2400. Closed L Sat, all Sun, National Holidays. Valet parking. Amex, Diners, Mastercard,
Visa.*

Tel: (1) 548 29 14   Fax: (1) 541 65 98
La Calle Hileras 4, 28013 Madrid

The chain, Patanovo A.A., opened this Galician and traditional Spanish restaurant back in
1970 and the three chefs have been here since it opened. On the menu is the set dish of
the day and a speciality dish, not normally on the à la carte menu. *Jamón iberico* (cured
slices of ham, like Parma ham, wrapped in Galician pastry), *gazpacho* (cold Andalusian
soup made from vegetables), and smoked salmon are typical dishes. There is also a wide
selection of seafood: large and small crabs, lobster, king prawns, mussels, eels and oysters.
The restaurant is named after their speciality: *bacalao Moaña* (cod cooked in
breadcrumbs). It is right at the epicentre of Madrid, yet the small dining-rooms here are
quiet and relaxed, with simple wooden tables and chairs. *Seats 100. Open 1300-1600,
2100-2230. Private parking. Amex, Mastercard, Visa.*

Tel: (1) 359 15 35   Fax: (1) 345 91 83
Calle General Gallegos 1, 28036 Madrid

Not only is the olive tree the symbol of Andalusia, but it is the star which guides the
cooking of Bordeaux-born chef and owner Jean-Pierre Vandelle. Many of his dishes are
prepared in olive oil from the Andalusian town of Baena, such as the wonderfully simple
starter of cod and salmon marinated in Baena oil. Although many of the dishes are typically
Mediterranean there are plenty of individual flourishes to distinguish the food. There is the
intriguing *nuestro surtido de bacalao* (cod prepared in four different ways) and *foie gras
caliente con uvas pasas al Pedro Ximénez* (foie gras with Pedro Ximenez raisins). Despite
an extensive wine list, sherry is the speciality of the house and diners can take part in
a tasting before eating if they wish. *Seats 80. Open 1300-1600, 2100-2400. Closed Sun, Mon,
Aug. Valet parking. Amex, Diners, Mastercard, Visa.*

Meal prices for 2 are based on à la carte menus. When set menus are
available, prices will often be lower.

Tel: (1) 576 86 92
Calle Jorge Juan 39, 28001 Madrid

Offal is a firm favourite at this restaurant, with *manitas de cerdo con salsa de trufas* (pig's trotters in a truffle sauce) a particular delicacy. Or how about sea urchin au gratin if you're feeling racy? Chef Segundo Alonso was formerly at the prestigious El Amparo and has brought some of that restaurant's sophistication to the traditional country cooking associated with La Paloma. Riojas feature heavily on the wine list. La Paloma is decorated in a simple style with plenty of greenery and wood and is a haven of calm from the hectic shopping streets outside. *Seats 70. Open 1330-1630, 2100-2345. Closed L Sat, all Sun, Aug, National Holidays. Valet parking. Amex, Mastercard, Visa.*

Tel: (1) 402 12 90
Calle José Ortega y Gasset 75, 28006 Madrid

Evaristo García Gomez not only owns two of the best fish restaurants in Madrid (also O'Paza) but is proud of supplying most of Madrid with fish and shellfish caught off the Cantabrian coast. His chef, Damian Alonso, has been cooking at El Pescador for 20 years and employs the simplest preparations to enhance the flavour of a wonderful variety of seafood. Sea bass and grouper are grilled or baked, red mullet fried, monkfish cooked 'Basque-style', squid cooked in its own ink and stuffed with seafood, mussels steamed, lobster boiled, shrimps fried with garlic. Other specialities include El Pescador soup, made with lobster, sea bream, sole and baked turbot, and creamy puddings such as crème caramel and rice pudding. There are no fixed-price menus. Cavas are well represented on the short wine list. The restaurant is in the Barrio de Salamanca district, near the airport. *Seats 90. Open 1330-1600, 2030-2400. Closed Sun, Aug. Valet parking. Mastercard, Visa.*

Tel: (1) 457 15 49   Fax: (1) 457 52 83
Calle Manuel de Falla 5, 28036 Madrid

Located in a cul-de-sac opposite the Ministry of Defence, this plush restaurant is a favourite haunt of businessmen and politicians. The owner is the famed restaurateur Jesús María Oyarbide (also owner of Zalacaín (qv)) and his son Javier is chef here, cooking excellent dishes from Navarre and the Basque Country. Inevitably, the emphasis is on seafood, with specialities including prawn and cod croquettes in a tarragon sauce, hake in a garlic and herb sauce, and salmon cooked with green peppers. Look out also for the daily specials. *Seats 80 (terrace 30). Open 1315-1600, 2100-2400. Closed L Sat, all Sun, Aug. Valet parking. Amex, Diners, Mastercard, Visa.*

Tel: (1) 457 28 52   Fax: (1) 458 86 76
Calle Serrano 240, 28016 Madrid

Much has been made of the benefits of a diet based on olive oil, but it is rare to find a Spanish restaurant that consciously attempts to cook healthy, low-cholesterol food. Principe y Serrano is an exception. Fish is lightly grilled and simply served without any heavy sauces. The house lobster salad is excellent and *bacalao* (salt cod) is a speciality. A pianist tinkles the ivories every night. *Seats 180. Open 1330-1600, 2100-2400. Closed L Sat, all Sun, Aug. Valet parking. Amex, Diners, Mastercard, Visa.*

Tel: (1) 521 28 57   Fax: (1) 532 97 76
Plaza de la Lealtad 5, 28014 Madrid

César Ritz himself oversaw the building of this fabulous hotel which was the first of its class in Spain and is now owned by Forte plc. It was opened in 1910 by King Alfonso XIII and ever since has been synonymous with style and luxury. Pink marble columns, glittering chandeliers, hand-made carpets, specially commissioned objets d'art, embroidered linen sheets, no expense has been spared, and the quality of personalised service matches the decor: some of the staff have been here 40 years. Facilities are, of course, excellent and the location, close to the stock exchange, galleries and 300-acre Retiro Park, is ideal for business and pleasure. *Rooms 156. Room service 24hr. Valet parking. Banqueting facilities 280. Conference facilities 300. Business centre. Garden. Gym. Sauna. Solarium. Beauty treatment. Hair salon. Bureau de change. News kiosk. Coffee shop. Amex, Diners, Mastercard, Visa.*

Tel: (1) 345 16 96   R
Avenida de Alberto Alcocer 1, 28036 Madrid

The unimposing exterior of this restaurant, in a quiet street, does not prepare you for the dark, heavy furniture and hunting lodge paraphernalia inside. The proprietor Doroteo Martín has developed an excellent Basque/Navarre menu which includes clams with rice in a salsa verde, black pudding and chorizo. French wines feature on the list as well as good selections from Rioja and Ribera del Duero. *Seats 80. Open 1300-1600, 2100-2400. Closed Sun, Aug, National Holidays. Amex, Mastercard, Visa.*

Tel: (1) 573 48 14   R
Alcalde Sainz de Baranda 80, 28007 Madrid

The 'Little Bull' restaurant is, not surprisingly, filled with big fight souvenirs and pictures but the menu eschews meat in favour of fish. A bewildering variety is offered including bracceta of hake, Galician prawns and *navajas* (razor clams). Most dishes are simply prepared and a gourmet menu is available at Pts5000. *Seats 60. Open 1330-1640, 2030-2330. Closed Sun, Aug, National Holidays. Valet parking. Amex, Mastercard, Visa.*

Tel: (1) 576 05 75   Fax: (1) 575 06 31   R
Calle Lagasca 60, 28001 Madrid

Miguel Garcia-Gomez's La Trainera is celebrating its 30th anniversary in 1996 and head chef Matias Fuentes has been cooking distinctive Cantabrian seafood there all this time. Hake, trout, salmon, sole, red mullet and sea bream dominate the menu with *salpicón de mariscos* (seafood salmagundy – a type of fish stew) a speciality. There are also four variations on lobster and a handful of crayfish, crab and prawn dishes. The wine list, to reflect the cuisine, consists mainly of whites. Although the restaurant is in Salamanca, the most elegant area of the city, decor is simple with fishing paraphernalia scattered around and it attracts a disparate clientele ranging from politicians to artists to families. *Seats 300. Open 1300-1600, 2000-2400. Closed Sun, Aug. Valet parking. Amex, Mastercard, Visa.*

Tel: (1) 576 75 00   Fax: (1) 575 95 04   HR
Paseo de la Castellana 22, 28046 Madrid

Located in the heart of Madrid's banking area, this hotel's fine conference facilities mean that it is constantly bustling with businessmen and politicians. The staffed business centre can provide secretarial, translation and fax services and the eight meeting rooms accommodate from ten to 350 people. Bedrooms are plush and include 16 suites and 2 Presidential suites. All are equipped with air-conditioning, satellite TV, video and safe. *Rooms 182. Room service 24hr. Private parking Pts2000. Banqueting facilities 225. Conference facilities 350. Business centre. Terrace. Sauna. Hair salon. Amex, Diners, Mastercard, Visa.*

Considering the location, it's no surprise that suits predominate in this restaurant at lunchtime, but in the evening, when tables are laid out on the terrace, the atmosphere becomes more relaxed. The short international menu changes weekly but might include starters such as smoked capon and lettuce salad with mango sauce or fettuccine with a basil and chicory sauce. Typical mains are angler fish medallions in batter with green peppers and spring onions, and guinea fowl breast stuffed with vegetables and sautéed prawns with a foie gras sauce. *Seats 65 (terrace 20). Open 1300-1600, 2030-2400.*

Tel: (1) 523 44 78   Fax: (1) 532 42 74   R
Calle Juan de Mena 14, 28014 Madrid

As with all the best Spanish restaurants, the menu at Viridiana each day depends on what is best at market each morning. Abraham Garcia and his wife Marjouve conjure up a wide range of specialities in the kitchen such as *risotto de bacalao* (risotto of dried salt cod) with spring mushrooms and baby leeks, and oxtail steeped in oloroso sherry. Puddings include a mouthwatering papaya filled with *flor de naranja* (orange blossom) in green melon sauce. The wine list of 400 bottles is as admirable as the food with a particularly fine selection of Tinto Fino reds from the Ribera del Duero region east of Valladolid. Buñuel's film Viridiana gave the restaurant its name and stills from the film adorn the walls. *Seats 70. Open 1330-1600, 2100-2400. Closed Sun, Aug. Public parking. Amex, Visa.*

Tel: (1) 561 47 32   Fax: (1) 561 47 32
Calle Alvarez de Baena 4, 28006 Madrid

You will need deep pockets if you are to join the Madrid glitterati in Jesús María Oyarbide's celebrated restaurant, but if you want a superlative meal with top-class service then you will consider the expense entirely justified. Head chef Benjamin Urdiaín is one of the country's best and his cooking is heavily influenced by the traditions of his Basque homeland but French cuisine and techniques have added considerable sophistication and subtlety to the menu. River salmon is a speciality, as is lobster salad, and the lasagne layered with asparagus, foie gras and hollandaise sauce must have been divinely inspired. Other excellent dishes are a fine gazpacho, pig's trotters stuffed with lamb and served in a mustard sauce, and green and white asparagus in a truffle vinaigrette. The wine list is enormous (600 bottles). Zalacaín was opened in 1973 to commemorate the centenary of the birth of the Spanish novelist Pio Baroja. *Seats* 100 (terrace 40). *Open 1300-1600, 2100-2400. Closed L Sat, all Sun, Aug, Easter week, National Holidays. Valet parking. Amex, Diners, Mastercard, Visa.*

Tel: (1) 857 77 22   Fax: (1) 857 77 80
Avenida de España 30, 28411 Moralzarzal

It's worth a journey into the mountains on the outskirts of Madrid to enjoy the friendly, family atmosphere of Salvador Gallego-Jiménez's grey stone restaurant. His chef, the renowned Pedro Olmedo Franco, produces an imaginative range of international dishes such as razor clam salad with sweetbreads, baked foie gras on a bed of artichokes and duck prepared in walnut oil. He also takes pride in his puddings: tart of apple and poire Williams, and chocolate soufflé being examples. The wine list includes the much sought-after Rioja Remélluri. There are few better places to enjoy good food in a relaxed environment. *Seats* 80 (terrace 80). *Open 1400-1630, 2100-0100. Closed D Sun, all Mon, 2nd week Oct. Valet parking. Amex, Diners, Mastercard, Visa.*

Tel: (5) 222 50 43   Fax: (5) 260 38 64
Calle Vélez 8, 29106 Malaga

Set one street back from the seafront, the wooden Café de Paris is built in replica Moorish style. Chef José Garcia-Cortez is proud of the fact that his four seasonal menus have not changed since 1975. If you visit at the right time of year you can sample sirloin steak with foie gras and grapes, piquillo peppers stuffed with seafood and duck marinated in *pinot negro*. Champagne and lemon sorbet makes a classy and refreshing end to a meal. Unusually, there is a special children's menu at Pts1700 and a wonderful seven-course *dégustation* menu priced at Pts5675. There is a sizeable bodega, which specialises in old vintages. *Seats* 60. *Open 1330-1600, 2030-2400. Closed Sun, 15-31 Jul. Amex, Diners, Mastercard, Visa.*

Tel: (5) 277 43 18
Avenida Cánovas del Castillo 52, 29600 Marbella

Cenicienta is the Spanish name for Cinderella. The food at this restaurant, in a tranquil part of Marbella, is more French than Spanish. Plats du jour supplement a menu which changes every fortnight and might include avocado with river crab, the ever-popular paté de foie gras, and duck. Most tastes can be accommodated and many dishes are available on request. The clientele is largely English and German. Note that it is only open for dinner. *Seats* 40 (terrace 40). *Open 2000-0100. Closed Jan. Amex, Mastercard, Visa.*

Opening times are often liable to change at short notice, so it's always best to book.

Tel: (5) 277 25 12   R
Plaza de Santo Cristo 9-10, 29600 Marbella

A varied clientele is attracted to the restaurant in this lovely 1830s Andalusian house in the old part of Marbella. There is nothing fancy about the cooking, which concentrates on fish and is broadly international in slant. Several regional specialities, such as baked gilthead, lamb with tarragon and roast potatoes and tricolore salad with marinated sardines and local white cheese with dill, are also served. Note that La Fonda is only open for dinner. *Seats 60 (terrace 50). Open 2000-2400. Closed Sun (except Aug). Valet parking. Amex, Diners, Mastercard, Visa.*

Tel: (5) 283 12 67   Fax: (5) 283 33 28   R
Hacienda Las Chapas, 29600 Marbella

Teresa Schiff has taken over the running of this famous restaurant (20 minutes from Fuengirola) since her husband Paul's death and their daughter Cati and Francisco Galvez now preside over the kitchen. The cooking is creative, witness lamb's brain and scampi salad with fresh fennel cream. In addition to some excellent fish dishes, beef, guinea hen, veal, duck, rabbit and pigeon are often also available. A gastronomic menu (Pts6715) includes salmon and dried salt cod tart with basil and red onion sauce. Most of the red wines on the list originate from the Ribera del Duero region north of Madrid. Diners are also treated to wonderful views of the mountains and the sea. *Seats 150 (garden 70). Open 1330-1530, 2030-2330. Closed Mon all year, Tue (except Jul/Aug), Easter week. Private parking. Amex, Diners, Mastercard, Visa.*

Tel: (5) 277 13 00   Fax: (5) 282 98 84   H
Boulevard Principe Alfonso Bon Hohanlohe, 29600 Marbella

You can follow in the glittering footsteps of the rich and famous and sojourn at the extravagant Marbella Club. Bedrooms are individually-decorated and the hotel is surrounded by its own tropical gardens. It is well equipped to cope with a sudden influx of Heads of State: there are 11 Presidential suites among the 28 new luxury rooms recently built. *Rooms 129. Room service 24hr. Private parking. Banqueting facilities 140. Conference facilities 140. Garden. Terrace. 2 outdoor swimming pools. Massage. Sauna. Night club. Bureau de change. Amex, Diners, Mastercard, Visa.*

Tel: (5) 277 03 00   Fax: (5) 277 99 54   HR
José Meliá, 29600 Marbella

A wealth of leisure facilities complements excellent business services at this popular hotel, which is set in its own extensive sub-tropical gardens only 200m from the beach. All rooms are air-conditioned and have satellite TV and three are equipped for disabled guests. There is live music every night until 3am. *Rooms 204. Room service 24hr. Private parking. Banqueting facilities 350. Conference facilities 350. Terrace. 4 swimming pools. Gym. Solarium. Turkish bath. Hair salon. Children's playroom. Piano bar. Bureau de change. News kiosk. Amex, Diners, Mastercard, Visa.*

Grill La Farola   Pts14,000

There are more concessions to international tastes here than you would find in a neighbourhood restaurant, but still plenty of good-quality maritime specialities: *paella valenciana,* for instance. Veal *(ternera)* is prominent on the menu, cooked in a variety of ways including with sherry. Inevitably, there are also a healthy number of seafood dishes. Swordfish, monkfish and red pepper kebabs are particularly mouth-watering. The wine list includes bottles from all the major Spanish wine regions including the stupendous and stupendously overpriced Vega Sicilia from Ribera del Duero (Pts27,600-Pts37,400). *Seats 60. Open 2000-2400.*

Meal prices for 2 are based on à la carte menus. When set menus are available, prices will often be lower.

Tel: (5) 277 61 90   Fax: (5) 282 60 24
Camino de la Cruz, 29600 Marbella

Chef Esebio Checa previously worked at Madrid's famed Jockey restaurant and has been equally successful since his move down south 16 years ago. His cooking is eclectically Mediterranean. Starters include warm magret of duck salad with foie gras and sour cherry vinaigrette while grilled sea bass with thyme and fresh tomatoes, and beef stroganoff with rice are excellent main courses. Look out for interesting specialities such as brains and sweetbreads fritura with artichokes and sauce tartare. The Pts6600 *dégustation* menu includes white and green asparagus with watercress butter. If you can afford a meal here you may as well splash out on a bottle from the extensive Cava and champagne selection. The restaurant is on a tree-lined road leading out of Marbella. *Seats 80. Open 1330-1500, 2000-2400. Closed 9 Jan-9 Feb. Valet parking. Amex, Diners, Mastercard, Visa.*

Tel: (5) 277 17 00   Fax: (5) 282 58 46
Carretera de Cádiz, 29600 Marbella

Subtropical gardens surround this traditional hotel situated a few kilometres from Marbella, just off the motorway to Málaga. Los Monteros has a star-studded visitor's book and boasts a loyal following of big stars, Michael Jackson being just one famous face to seek seclusion here. For the active guest, there are extensive sports facilities: as well as three swimming pools, five squash courts and ten tennis courts, guests have free use of the hotel's 18-hole golf course. *Rooms 169. Room service 24hr. Private parking. Banqueting facilities 240. Conference facilities 80. Air-conditioning. Golf. Gym. Hairdresser. Massage. News kiosk. Night club. Satellite TV. Sauna. Squash. Indoor and outdoor swimming pools. Tennis. Amex, Diners, Mastercard, Visa.*

Tel: (5) 282 09 00   Fax: (5) 277 57 66
Carretera de Cádiz, 29600 Marbella

The traditional Andalusian *casitas* (cottages) that make up the Puento Romano make a refreshing change from high-rise modern hotels, particularly as they are set in lush gardens that lead down to their own beach. Water sports are an obvious attraction, as are the ten courts of the tennis centre which is run by former Wimbledon champion Manolo Santana. The hotel also claims to have the most famous disco on the Costa del Sol where you can pour yourself a drop of happiness, mix it with the latest beat, add ice and drink it down to the last drop. Business facilities are not neglected but the atmosphere is supremely relaxed and the staff friendly. *Rooms 220. Room service 24hr. Private parking. Banqueting facilities 250. Conference facilities 160. 2 swimming pools (1 indoor, 1 outdoor). Gym. Sauna. Squash. Hair salon. Night club. Bureau de change. Amex, Diners, Mastercard, Visa.*

Tel: (5) 277 17 99   Fax: (5) 282 47 72
Carretera de Cádiz, 29600 Marbella

As can be inferred from the name, Italian food is prominent on the menu of the Villa Tiberio, next door to the Marbella Club hotel. It seems impossible, though, for any restaurant in Spain to ignore native specialities entirely and gazpacho sits alongside insalata tricolore. There are ten or so pastas to choose from including home-made pappardelle (wide ribbons) with chunks of fresh lobster. For once, there are more meat dishes than fish on the menu although the selection is not particularly inspiring. Simple is often best. Try calf's liver with sage lightly pan-fried in butter or rabbit baked with herbs. The restaurant has a large terrace which looks out on to the spectacular 5,000m^2 gardens, complete with waterfalls, pools and mock statuary. *Seats 150 (terrace 200). Open 1930-0230. Closed Sun (except summer). Private parking. Amex, Mastercard, Visa.*

Around Malaga/Marbella

FUENGIROLA — Byblos Andaluz — Pts30,300

Tel: (5) 247 30 50   Fax: (5) 247 67 83   H
Mijas Golf Apartado 138, 29640 Fuengirola

The cool, clean lines of Arabic architecture and decor blend with a more rustic Roman/Andalusian style to pleasing effect at the Byblos Andaluz. It is part of the Concorde group and, if you are a golf-lover, will be your idea of heaven. Surrounded by two 18-hole par 72 international standard courses designed by Robert Trent Jones, it runs three- and seven-night golf packages. If putting a small ball into a hole leaves you cold then you can work up a sweat in the gym or ease away your troubles in the thalassotherapy centre. *Rooms 144. Room service 24hr. Private parking. Banqueting facilities 300. Conference facilities 300. Garden. Terrace. 3 swimming pools (1 indoor, 2 outdoor). 2 18-hole golf courses. Gym. Beauty treatments. Hair salon. Children's playroom. News kiosk. Helipad. Amex, Diners, Mastercard, Visa.*

SOTOGRANDE — Cabo Mayor — Pts12,000

Tel: (5) 679 03 90   Fax: (5) 679 03 89   R
Puerto Sotogrande, 11310 Sotogrande (Cádiz)

You will be under no illusion about the importance of the sea at Cabo Mayor, 12km from Gibraltar. The terrace affords marvellous views of the harbour and there is a jaunty nautical decor inside. Pictures of yachts line the blue and white walls and the floor is hand-painted with 'waves'. Husband and wife Paco Teodoro and Manoli Gonzalez-Bernal run the restaurant, which is part of the Cabo Mayor group. Manoli cooks and fish predictably fills much of her menu. It changes monthly but look out for *milhojas de pimientos asados en leña con bacalao y espuma de tomate* (millefeuille of oven-roasted peppers with bacalao and tomato 'froth') and *ensalada de jamón y foie gras con pasas y piñones al aceite virgen* (salad of ham and liver with raisins and pine nuts in virgin olive oil). An excellent-value lunch menu is available during July and August at Pts3000. Unusually, the needs of disabled diners have been fully considered. *Seats 50 (terrace 120). Open 1300-1600, 2000-2400. Closed Sun (except Aug). Private parking. Amex, Diners, Mastercard, Visa.*

Seville

SEVILLE — Alfonso XIII — Pts44,100

Tel: (5) 422 28 50   Fax: (5) 421 60 33   H
San Fernando 2, 41004 Sevilla

This exquisite hotel in the centre of Seville was bought by the Sheraton Group from the Italian Ciga chain in 1995. Although it dates only from the late 1920s, its opulent architecture and decor shows strong Moorish influence. Despite the *bullicio* (hubbub) of the city all around, the Alfonso XIII has a wonderfully peaceful cloistered courtyard and cocoons its guests within its formal gardens. Facilities are all you would expect in a top-quality hotel. *Rooms 146. Room service 24hr. Private parking Pts2000. Conference facilities 500. Garden. Outdoor swimming pool. Hair salon. Bureau de change. Amex, Diners, Mastercard, Visa.*

SEVILLE — El Burladero — Pts12,000

Tel: (5) 422 29 00   Fax: (5) 422 09 38   R
Canalejas 1, 41001 Sevilla

If you object to bullfighting then you will probably want to give El Burladero a wide berth, dedicated as it is to the glories of the ring. The walls are decorated with pictures of famous matadors and toreadors and the heads of some of the unfortunate beasts whose demise they caused. All things big and beefy are favoured here. Oxtail (*rabo de toro*) is particularly popular, but such mild-mannered dishes as hake with potatoes and onions also find a place on the menu. The restaurant is part of the Hotel Trip Colón and is near the Plaza Magdalena. *Seats 100. Open 1330-1545, 2100-2300. Closed Aug. Private parking Pts2000. Amex, Diners, Mastercard, Visa.*

Tel: (5) 422 72 54   Fax: (5) 421 04 29
San Fernando 41, 41004 Sevilla

José Maria Egaña-Egaña migrated from his native Basque country via Madrid down to Spain's deep south, bringing with him the culinary traditions and techniques of the north east. Terrine of foie gras with honeyed shallots and millefeuille of smoked salmon with a sea urchin sauce are typical starters. Main courses include hake served *au naturel* with a garlic sauce and rump steak with foie in a truffle salsa. In addition to the predictable Riojas and Ribera del Dueros, the wine list includes local Andalusian whites. *Seats 170. Open 1330-1600, 2100-2400. Closed L Sat, all Sun, Aug. Amex, Diners, Mastercard, Visa.*

Tel: (5) 453 35 00   Fax: (5) 453 23 42
Hotel Occidental Portacoeli, Avenida Eduardo Dato 49, 41018 Sevilla

Although Florencia is part of the Occidental hotel, 85% of its clientele are locals, a sure sign that the food is well above average. Chef Juan-Martin Ruiz cooks imaginative, and often complex, international food with great flair. For example, the *grandiose sinfonía de pato, venado y ternera en sus diferentes sabores con puré de castaña* (symphony of duck, venison and veal flavoured individually and with a chestnut purée), or how about *obleas de patatas rellenas de lubina, rape y bogavante al aroma del vino oloroso sobre salsa de pimientos rojos* (wafer-thin potatoes filled with bass, monkfish and lobster flavoured with oloroso wine over a red pepper sauce), a mouthful in more ways than one. The classic white and salmon decor adds to the tranquil atmosphere. *Seats 48. Open 1330-1600, 2100-2400. Closed Aug. Private parking. Amex, Diners, Mastercard, Visa.*

Tel: (5) 427 84 17
Farmacéutico Murillo Herrera 10, 41010 Sevilla

Pello Roteta-Sagarzazu's eponymous restaurant is in the unglamorous working-class Triana district. Inside, though, it is anything but ordinary with enormous bookcases stuffed with cookery books dividing the two dining-rooms. Customers are encouraged to browse before eating and can also admire the crockery collection. Pello cooks specialities from his native Basque country: hake stuffed with seafood, for instance. He also brings an original stamp to imaginative dishes such as seaweed salad with sea urchin roe and, a Malagan speciality, anchovies arranged into a fan and grilled with fresh tomato and a green pepper coulis. Desserts may include the fancifully romantic perfecto of coffee in a tulip of almonds. Excellent-value light menus are available in the spring and autumn at Pts2000. Valencian and Catalan wines feature on the list. *Seats 40. Open 1330-1600, 2100-2330. Closed Sun, Easter week, 10-31 Aug. Amex, Diners, Mastercard, Visa.*

Tel: (5) 456 06 37   Fax: (5) 456 36 66
Zaragoza 20, 41001 Sevilla

You would not guess from the antique-filled rooms and wooden furniture in the 17th-century mansion that houses this restaurant, that it is actually part of a Madrid-based chain. The chef was formerly at the Marbella branch and cooks a range of international and Spanish dishes according to season. His specialities include baby peppers stuffed with oxtail and sirloin cooked in Rioja. There are also seven compact but luxurious suites, classically furnished with modernist touches, and all have jacuzzis (double Pts12,000). *Seats 170. Open 1330-1600, 2000-2400. Closed Aug. Private parking. Amex, Mastercard, Visa.*

Around Seville

CARMONA   Casa de Carmona   Pts22,000

Tel: (5) 414 33 00   Fax: (5) 414 37 52

Plaza de Lasso 1, Carmona 41410 Sevilla

Carmona, an unspoilt Andalusian town of Roman and Moorish origin, is full of the most charming paradors and this 16th-century palace is a splendid example. It took five years for the Medina family to complete the arduous task of converting the building into a hotel after they bought it in 1986; previously, it had been in the hands of the Lasso de Lavega family for four centuries. The antiques and original furniture remain but they have introduced Laura Ashley-style printed furnishings and new mahogany furniture. The rooms are spacious there and one of the suites is a grand 200 square metres. The excellent sports facilities at the hotel are rather a surprise in such a sleepy town: there's a swimming pool, gym, sauna and massage parlour and horse-riding can be arranged. *Rooms 30.*

Room service 24hr. Private parking. Banqueting facilities 40. Conference facilities 100. Secretarial/translation services on request. Air-conditioning. Gym. Massage. Sauna. Swimming pool. Amex, Diners, Mastercard, Visa.

SANLÚCAR LA MAYOR   Hacienda Benazuza   Pts36,200

Tel: (5) 5702 33 44   Fax: (5) 570 34 10

Valle de las Nieves, 41800 Sanlúcar la Mayor, Sevilla

If you are frustrated by the hassle of landing your Learjet at a commercial airport and catching a limo to your hotel, the Hacienda Benazuza, with its own landing strip, could be the place for you. If you also have a passion for golf, billiards and hunting wild boar then you will be in heaven in this luxurious retreat on a hill overlooking the Guadiamar valley. Naturally, you will have to pay for the privilege of staying in 'Andalusia's most exclusive hotel' but the facilities on offer are of the highest order. Rooms are furnished elegantly but without ostentation and manage to combine the needs of the modern world (satellite TV, safe, mini-bar) with the simplicity of the old. The Doñana nature reserve, western Europe's largest and home to over 250 species of animal, is on the doorstep and can be explored on the hotel's own Andalusian and Arabian horses. *Rooms 44. Closed 15 Jul-1 Sep.*

Room service 24hr. Private parking. Banqueting facilities 350. Conference facilities 500. Garden. Terrace. Outdoor swimming pool. Pitch & putt. Real tennis. Helipad. Landing strip. Bureau de change. Amex, Diners, Mastercard, Visa.

Valencia

VALENCIA   Eladio   Pts12,000

Tel: (6) 384 22 44

Chiva 40, 46018 Valencia

All the best restaurants depend upon the supplies of the market but Eladio Rodríguez's menu is even more unpredictable than most and varies daily. If this means that you can never be sure what you will find, it also means that it will be hard to find fresher food anywhere in Valencia. Eladio's sons Ramón and Manolo are the chefs and cook largely simple Galician fare with some international and French touches. For instance, salmon or turbot are prepared either a *la parrilla* (open-grilled) or *al horno* (baked). Crisp Galician wines from Rías Baixas complement the food. The decor is described as "English classical" with lots of wood and marble and the clientele is largely businessmen at lunch and romancing couples in the evening. Chiva is 15 minutes from the centre of the city near the motorway from Madrid. *Seats 70. Open 1230-1600, 2030-2400. Closed Sun, Aug.*

Amex, Diners, Mastercard, Visa.

Tel: (6) 380 94 73   Fax: (6) 380 06 54
Marvá 28, 46007 Valencia

There is an aura of old-fashioned solidity and luxury about Galbis, with its hand-made wooden furniture and still lifes hanging from thick walls. The Galbis family have run inns and restaurants in the region for generations and Juan Carlos opened this place five years ago. He is also the chef and cooks largely traditional Valencian cuisine based on what is best at market each week. Specialities include pan-fried young goat with sweet garlic gloves, salad of baked peppers with beans pickled in red wine and *suquet* of fish with prawns and asparagus. The fixed-price menu valenciana is good value at Pts2500. **Seats** *90.*
Open 1300-1630, 2030-2330. Closed L Sat, all Sun, 8 Aug-8 Sep. Amex, Visa.

Tel: (6) 142 01 00   Fax: (6) 142 21 68
Urbanización Monte Picayo, Puzol, 46530 Valencia

The Monte Picayo is a beautiful 17th-century *parador* (grandiose, formerly state-run hotel) perched on a hillside 18 km outside Valencia in the direction of Barcelona. All the air-conditioned rooms have terraces which afford views of the sea and the orange groves which surround the hotel. If you want a taste of the high life, ask for one of the five rooms which have their own outdoor swimming pools, or enjoy the superb leisure facilities which include mini-golf, riding and tennis. If you have money to burn, why not play the tables at the casino, one of the most prestigious in Spain. **Rooms** *83. Room service limited.*
Private parking. Banqueting facilities 150. Conference facilities 1000. Garden.
Outdoor swimming pools. Riding. Tennis. Mini-golf. Children's playground. Sauna. Hair salon.
Casino. Bureau de change. Amex, Diners, Mastercard, Visa.

Tel: (6) 373 29 49
Dr Sumsi 4, 46005 Valencia

The Ruzafa area is one of Valencia's most charming and home to Oscar Torrijos' eponymous restaurant. His superb blending of French and Spanish cooking makes particular use of fresh fish, foie gras and rice. Other imaginative dishes include *ensalada de bacalao ahumado con habas y guisantes* (salad of smoked cod, broad beans and peas) and hake in a nut vinaigrette. You should finish your meal with the wonderful home-made *pasteleria* (patisserie). Señor Torrijos boasts a bodega (cellar) containing 1800 bottles of wine including a fine selection of Riojas and reds from the Ribera del Duero region. There is an excellent-value Pts3500 lunch menu. **Seats** *45. Open 1200-1545, 2000-2300. Closed Sun, 15 Aug-15 Sep. Amex, Diners, Mastercard, Visa.*

Tel: (6) 357 20 07
Matemático Marzal 11, 46007 Valencia

Alfredo Alonso Nuñes and his wife Concha are rightly proud of their family-run Galician restaurant. You will not find any hired hands working here, only relatives, and the clientele is fiercely loyal. The cooking reflects the robust, earthy flavours of the Nuñes' homeland. For instance, *entrecote de buey con queso de cabrales y pimientos verdes* (entrecote of beef with *cabrales*, a strong blue Asturian cheese, and green peppers), hake with clams from Caril (a small Galician town) and *rodaballo a la gallega* (turbot with potatoes and salsa rossa). There are plenty of reservas and grand reservas on the wine list but one of the most popular bottles is produced by a neighbour. **Seats** *70. Open 1300-0130. Closed Sun, Aug.*
Private parking. Amex, Diners, Mastercard, Visa.

Tel: (6) 337 5037   Fax: (6) 337 5532
Paseo de la Alameda 32, 46023 Valencia

This centrally located hotel was opened two years ago. It is part of the Sol International chain and offers a full range of facilities which should appeal particularly to the sporty. Work up a sweat in the gym and then relax in the sauna, massage room or by the pool. The needs of business are also fully catered for with excellent conference facilities. Two bedrooms are specially equipped for the disabled. **Rooms** *199. Room service 24hr. Banqueting facilities 250.*
Conference facilities 600. Secretarial/translation services on request. Outdoor swimming pool.
Sauna. Gym. Sauna. Jacuzzi. Massage. Amex, Diners, Mastercard, Visa.

Elsewhere in Spain

Tel: (72) 15 04 57/25 76 51   Fax: (72) 15 07 17

Cala Montjoi 17480 Rosas

Closer to the French border (Perpignan is only 65km away) than, say, Barcelona (155km), the restaurant is just as popular with the French as it is with the Spanish. It is accessible via a terrible road along the Costa Brava, a road whose pitfalls are somewhat alleviated by stunning views of the Meidterranean and the intoxicating smells of eucalyptus trees that grow down to the sea. Once a smugglers' house, its rustic interior is eccentrically furnished with statues and ornamental bulldogs (after which the restaurant is named) – these dogs are the passion of co-owners Julio Soler (front-of-house) and chef Fernando Adriá. Inveterate travellers (the restaurant closes in winter), they bring back many cooking ideas from around the world, though the cuisine here is true to its Catalan origins, albeit with some strange combinations, for instance chop suey of clams; pears in wine with langoustines; house tagliatelle with sardines and five spices; mussels with saffron beneath a light fish jelly, served with a sort of apricot sorbet; and octopus sashimi with a confit of chicken served with pumpkin. More orthodox is a chicken curry or lemon sole served with fresh herbs (garlic, thyme, bay and rosemary). Coconut mousse with wild strawberries or a pineapple and fennel soup provides a fitting finale. *Seats 45 (Terrace 24). Open 1300-1500, 1930-2300. Closed Mon, Tue (except in summer), mid-Oct-mid-Mar. Amex, Diners, Mastercard, Vias.*

Tel: (43) 27 84 65   Fax: (43) 27 27 53

Alto de Miracruz 21, 20015 San Sebastian

Juan-Maria Arzak describes his cooking as Basque de autor, and is justifiably proud of the personal touch he brings to the traditions of north-east Spain. His daughter Elena now works with him in the kitchen and their continually-changing menu features a wealth of excellent fish dishes alongside some interesting original conceptions such as *pichon asado con jegibre y patatas horneadas con manzana y curcuma* (pigeon with ginger and potatoes baked with apple and turmeric). Carrots are used in a variety of innovative ways: for instance, *foie gras natural con pan de zanahoria y gelatina de vino de uvas pas* (foie gras with carrot bread and a raisin wine jelly). There is a *dégustation* menu priced at Pts7600 which may include such delicacies as *espuma de bacalao con zumo de pimientos rojos y aceite de nuez con queso fresco* (mousse of dried salted cod with the juice of red peppers, nut oil and fromage frais). Wines include some of the best riojas. *Seats 70. Open 1300-1500, 2030-2300. Closed D Sun, all Mon, 17-30 Jun, all Nov. Valet parking. Amex, Diners, Mastercard, Visa.*

Sweden

Currency Swedish Kronor **Exchange Rate** £1=approx SEK10.9
International dialling code 00 46 (Gothenburg+31, Stockholm+8)
Passports/Visas No visa required by British passport holders for stay
of less than 3 months.
British Embassy in Stockholm Tel 8-671 9000

TRANSPORT

Airports
Stockholm-Arlanda Tel 8-797 6000
Stockholm-Bromma Tel 8-797 6874
Railway Stations
Gothenburg Tel 31-10 3000
Stockholm Tel (international) 8-696 7509 (domestic) 8-696 7540
Car hire in Stockholm
Tel Nos. **Budget** 8-33 4383 (airport 8-593 62100) **Avis** 8-34 9910
Speed limits 70 km/h on trunk roads, 90-110 km/h on motorways, 50
km/h in towns.

OPENING HOURS

Bank Mon-Fri 9.30am-3pm (& 4-5.30pm on Thursdays). Some banks
stay open till 5.30pm daily.
Shops Generally 9am-6pm (1-4pm Sat). Some stores stay open till
8/10pm in large cities + 12-4pm some Sundays.

NATIONAL HOLIDAYS

New Year's Day, 6 Jan, 5, 7 & 8 April, 1,16 , 26 & 27 May, 22 Jun,
2 Nov, Christmas Eve, Christmas Day, Boxing Day & New Year's Eve.
NB TO BE CHECKED

Tourist Offices

Swedish Tourist Board in **London** Tel 0171-935 9784
In **Stockholm** Tel 8-725 5500/789 2400 Gothenburg Tel 31-81 8200
American Express Travel Service Offices/or Representative (R)

Stockholm	Birger Jarlsgatan 1
	PO Box 1761
	S 111 87
	Tel 8-6795200/6797880 #
Gothenburg	American Express TFS
	C/O Ticket
	Ostra Hamngatan 35
	S 40121
	Tel 31-130712 #

Gothenburg

Tel: (31) 40 93 00   Fax: (31) 18 98 04   H
Mässans Gata 24, 402 26 Göteborg

The hotel is in the same building (and ownership) as the Svenska Mässan Exhibition and Congress Centre, which opened in 1984; not a particularly quiet location, since the Lisebergs Amusement Park is next door. A programme of bedroom refurbishment that includes the installation of air-conditioning is currently under way, with 20 having been completed in the summer of 1995 and a further 100 due by the year end. *Rooms 290. May close 2 weeks Christmas. Room service morning and evening. Parking (reserved spaces in nearby multi-storey) SEK70 for 24 hours (SEK130 for valet parking). Conference facilities 1500. Sauna. Amex, Diners, Mastercard, Visa.*

Tel: (31) 16 03 33   Fax: (31) 16 78 54   R
Arkivgatan 7, 411 34 Göteborg

There's a choice of dining within this 100-year-old building. In the smaller Gourmet dining-room chef Olle Larsson offers a short carte of interesting dishes like green minestrone with spring chicken and duck liver ravioli; grilled crayfish with horseradish brulée, dill, salted cucumber and crayfish sauce; cod with morels, spring onion and lobster sauce, and Swedish suckling lamb with fresh garlic and a thyme gravy. There is also a five-course *menu dégustation* at SEK595 (or SEK895 with a different glass of wine specially chosen to complement each course). For less formal dining there is the larger Bakfickan room (it means 'back pocket') with a longer menu that includes the likes of garlic-fried snails in brioche, shrimp salad on rye bread, hamburger, entrecote with barbecue sauce and French fries, rack of lamb baked in garlic and thyme with a sour cucumber salad and mustard sauce, honeyed chicken cooked on a skewer with ginger sauce and peanut butter, fudge cake, apple tart and a wicked-sounding Toblerone parfait served with an almond muffin. *Seats 25 (Gourmet) 100 (Bakfickan). Open D only 1800-2400. Closed 25 Dec (Gourmet also closed Sun & mid Jun-end Jul). Street parking. Amex, Diners, Mastercard, Visa.*

Tel: (31) 10 12 00   Fax: (31) 13 08 66   H
Stora Badhusgatan 26, 411 21 Göteborg

A large international hotel, but with the advantage of still being family owned and run, the Riverton stands in the city centre and offers glitzy, 60s-style public areas and good standardised bedrooms that include mini-bars and satellite TV (the latter at an extra charge). *Rooms 191. Room service morning and evening (mornings only in summer). Free open parking for 60 cars. Conference facilities 300. Sauna. Sun beds. Spa bath. Amex, Diners, Mastercard, Visa.*

Tel: (31) 80 60 00   Fax: (31) 15 98 88   H
Södra Hamngatan 59-65, 401 24 Göteborg

Two hotels in one here with, for a premium to the regular room rate, the Tower rooms offering that little bit more luxury and free use of the leisure centre; other guests pay a SEK50 entrance fee. All bedrooms come with air-conditioning, mini-bars and satellite TV and 25 have fax machines. Located close to the main railway station. *Rooms 344. Room service 24hrs. Valet parking SEK195 for 24 hours. Conference facilities 450. Indoor swimming pool. Gymnasium. Sauna. Spa bath. Sun beds. Amex, Diners, Mastercard, Visa.*

Tel: (31) 24 65 10   Fax: (31) 24 55 39   R
Klippans Kulturreservat, 414 51 Göteborg

Set in a converted shipping warehouse in the oldest part of town, Sjömagasinet is a large restaurant specialising in fish and shellfish. Chef Lies Mannerström's menu ranges from starters like oysters with vinaigrette, carpaccio of salmon and angler-fish with a basil and rice noodle salad, and a lobster and asparagus fricassee flavoured with tarragon and parsley to mains such as fillet of salmon under a blanket of pasta with mussels and a rosemary and French mustard sauce, seafood casserole with a classic white wine sauce, and oven-baked turbot with Caesar salad and chive sauce. There's always something for meat-eaters: spring lamb with a zucchini, aubergine and mozzarella cake on a recent menu. Desserts might include rhubarb soup with fresh berries and home-made vanilla ice cream, tiramisu and crème brulée. The price of the Chef's menu of the day (three courses, no choice) varies according to market prices. In summer head for the large veranda, where there is seating for an additional 300 diners (150 eating à la carte and 150 self-service), who get the best of a gorgeous view over the River Gota Alv and the harbour. *Seats 300. Open 1130-2300. Closed 24, 25 Dec & 1 Jan. Amex, Diners, Mastercard, Visa.*

GOTHENBURG   Victors Hotel   SEK1150

Tel: (31) 17 41 80   Fax: (31) 13 96 10
Skeppsbroplatsen 1, 411 18 Göteborg

Three women own and manage this small, friendly hotel right in the city centre by the harbour. Rooms feature good-quality Swedish wood furniture of modern design and all have mini-bars and satellite TV. *Rooms 44. Room service 24hrs. Parking in nearby public car parks. Conference facilities 40. Sauna. Spa bath. Amex, Diners, Mastercard, Visa.*

GOTHENBURG   Westra Piren   ★ SEK1400

Tel: (31) 51 95 55   Fax: (31) 23 99 40
Dockepiren, 41764 Göteborg

This was an old service house for the floating docks before being converted into a restaurant; two restaurants actually as in addition to the main gourmet affair on the 2nd floor there is a ground-floor brasserie (summer only 1130-2000, Sat & Sun from 1300, Sun till 1900) where prices are lower and there is a terrace. Back upstairs the sophisticated, French-orientated carte might include open ravioli with fresh asparagus, morels and a watercress mousseline; 'bouillabaisse' in the form of a saffron-flavoured terrine with fish roe mousse; grilled fillets of sole with an armagnac-flavoured lobster sauce and garlic confit; Bresse pigeon with a sauce of juniper berries and fresh figs, and (for two persons) a Black Angus porterhouse steak with small baked potatoes. Desserts are typified by iced melon and peach soup flavoured with mint, hazelnut and pistachio parfait with almond flakes, and a selection of chocolates from the patissier. At night, and for whole parties only, there is a menu dégustation at SEK640 per person. Located about ten kilometres from the city centre; ask directions when booking. *Seats 80. Open 1130-2300, 1800-2200. Closed L Sat, all Sun & National Holidays. Amex, Diners, Mastercard, Visa.*

Solna

SOLNA   Ulriksdals Wardshus   SEK1200

Tel: (8) 85 08 15   Fax: (8) 85 08 58
Ulriksdal, 170 71 Solna

If you arrive early for dinner you can witness a traditional Swedish ceremony as the blue and yellow national flag is lowered in front of the dining-room veranda. Within a royal park, this lovely old country inn has been transformed into a first-class restaurant by its owner-host Lauri Nilsson and chef Karl-Heinz Krücken. The centrepiece of the dining-room at lunchtime (when there is also a short à la carte) is a lavish Swedish smörgåsbord featuring many different herring preparations and other Swedish fish dishes. Follow this with ham and beef, patés and meatballs and finally a variety of cheeses. The perfect drink to accompany this is chilled Swedish aquavit with a beer chaser. The evening à la carte might include a terrine of shellfish and pickles flavoured with curry, seasonal salad with truffles, cold breast of ptarmigan Lucullus, prawn-stuffed turbot wrapped in lettuce, angler fish with tomato sauce and fresh green noodles, roast fillet of beef provençale, and noisettes of reindeer in calvados. The wine cellar is one of the finest in Sweden and is the venue for regular tasting sessions conducted by Mr Nilsson. His personal collection includes almost every vintage since 1900 of each of the five 1er crus of Bordeaux; unfortunately most are not included in the, almost exclusively, French list but it does run to 35 pages with all except the most expensive wines available by the glass. Set L (smörgåsbord) SEK250. Set D SEK450. *Seats 140. Open 1200-2200 (Sat from 1230, Sun 1230-1830). Closed D Sun & all 24-26 Dec. Amex, Diners, Mastercard, Visa.*

Opening times are often liable to change at short notice, so it's always best to book.

Stockholm

Tel: (8) 614 07 00   Fax: (8) 611 51 75
Näckströmsgatan 8, Berzelii Park, 111 47 Stockholm

An ideal location right in the centre of the city, almost opposite the Halwyl Museum. Fronted by a large restaurant, the 1863 building was completely refurbished inside in 1989 but retaining the original Italian art deco style with cedarwood furnishings and marble and wooden floors. It's an extremely pleasant and hospitable hotel, geared-up for the business traveller with a good selection of conference facilities, a business centre and second telephone/fax line in all the bedrooms. All air-conditioned, rooms range from singles and smaller doubles through standard rooms (the price of which is quoted above), de luxe rooms and various suites. *Rooms 65. Closed 23 Dec-3 Jan.*
Room service 24hrs. Valet parking SEK260 for 24 hours. Conference facilities 1000. Amex, Diners, Mastercard, Visa.

Tel: (8) 23 85 00   Fax: (8) 796 60 69
Österlånggatan 17, 111 31 Stockholm

Eriks is found in the remarkably well-preserved old town of Stockholm, dating back to the 14th and 15th centuries. The restaurant - along with a small hotel - occupies elegant premises three minutes walk from the Royal Palace. The building itself, the Green House, is a converted 15th-century inn. Chef-patron Erik Lallerstedt is widely-regarded in Sweden as one of the country's finest chefs and now runs no less than three restaurants in Stockholm. He is usually to be found at Eriks, his flagship restaurant, where standards of service are a match for the excellent cooking. The restaurant is on two floors: the ground floor is informal, with a bar area and a few tables, while the second floor has comfortable booths and private dining-rooms. The six-course *dégustation* menu demonstrates Erik's talents with dishes such as casserole of scallops and shiitake mushrooms or grilled halibut with stuffed onions and creamed truffled potatoes. On the à la carte menu, a typically Swedish starter is trout roe served with blinis and sour cream. Another first course we liked was pigeon soup with fried duck liver - most unusual. The main courses included poached filet of brill and fried duckling *en deux services*. The dessert menu introduces a unique Swedish berry, the Arctic brambleberry, reddish-brown in appearane and very sweet. Alternatively there is a chocolate biscuit dessert with buckthorn coulis. The wine list is excellent but, as always in Sweden, is highly-priced. *Seats 60 (+ 20 at the bar).*
Open 1130-2300. Closed Sun, Jul & Public Holidays. Amex, Diners, Mastercard, Visa.

Tel: (8) 663 07 40   Fax: (8) 662 59 92
Strandvägen 7A, 114 56 Stockholm

Informal but smart family B&B hotel in a good residential area just a few minutes from the city centre. A few rooms have a very good view but most face a quiet courtyard. The decor is art nouveau in style. Bedrooms are comfortable and well maintained and all have multi-channel TV and mini-bar: most of the bathrooms have shower and WC only.
Rooms 33. No room service. Amex, Diners, Mastercard, Visa.

Tel: (8) 674 35 00   Fax: (8) 611 86 86
Södra Blasieholmshamnen 8, 103 27 Stockholm

When the Nobel prize-winners come to Stockholm to receive their awards from the King of Sweden, they always stay here, in Sweden's grandest and premier hotel, our winner of this year's Best Hotel Western Europe. The privately-owned hotel is set on the waterfront, facing the Royal Palace, and if you are lucky enough to have a room at the front, you can watch the tourist boats come and go. Luxurious, individually furnished suites and bedrooms (some non-smoking and allergy-free), provide round-the-clock room service, satellite TV, PC and fax outlets, computerised message retrieval and check-out from your TV screen. Bathrooms are fitted with Italian marble and underfloor heating. The marvellous pillared lobby reflects the elegant and classical style throughout, exemplified in some of the exquisite meeting and banqueting rooms, which can accommodate up to 1000. The business centre includes the hire of portable phones. Valet parking (SEK260 for 24 hours). Management and services are of the highest class. *Rooms 300. Valet parking SEK260 for 24 hours. Room service 24hrs. Conference facilities 600. Amex, Diners, Mastercard, Visa.*

The name means French Dining Room and, with its 19th-century decor, beautiful wall-panelling and fine views across the water to the Royal Palace, it is an elegant and prestigious setting for chef Roland Persson's fine cooking which is based on classic French cuisine. Cannelloni with duck foie gras and ceps, sea urchin and scallop mousseline, filet of pike-perch and langoustines fried with saffron, and pot-au-feu of lamb with ginger and goat's cheese potatoes show the style. Afters might include a wild strawberry dessert and a 'Granny Smith' sorbet. Set D SEK625 (Scandinavian) & SEK825 (dégustation) plus à la carte. In the Grand Veranda restaurant, you can enjoy a typical simple Swedish smörgåsbord at both lunch and dinner for SEK200. Service is first-class and the wine list extensive. *Seats 70. Open D only 1800-2300. Closed July & 2 weeks Christmas.*

Tel (8) 24 97 60   Fax: (8) 21 38 70
Österlånggatan 51, 103 17 Stockholm

This historic restaurant with its stone steps and deep cellar vaults has an illustrious past; in the early part of the 18th century it was the most famous of the 790 taverns in old Stockholm. Den Gyldene Freden means 'The Guilded Peace' reflecting the peaceful days of 1720s Sweden. The good citizens of Stockholm enjoyed their ale and sausages in these cellars until recently, when the Swedish Literary Academy became the owners and the tavern became a restaurant. In the last few years, new kitchens have been installed and one of the country's best chefs, Ulf Kappen, has taken over the stoves. While sticking to Swedish food, he offers some interesting dishes such as lobster consommé with ravioli; grilled salmon with trout roe, spinach and Chablis sauce, and poached turbot with beetroot and sorrel. Meat dishes include roast reindeer with juniper berry sauce, veal with sweetbreads and a particularly popular dish of brisket with cubed potatoes. Set meals SEK175 (two small starters followed by game 'burger' with mushroom sauce), SEK285/SEK325 (two/three courses, no choice) plus à la carte. Difficult parking. *Open 1100-2300. Closed Sun & Jul. Amex, Diners, Mastercard, Visa.*

Tel: (8) 679 60 32   Fax: (8) 611 82 83
Smålandsgatan 7, 111 46 Stockholm

KB is a Stockholm institution and one of the most popular places in town for lunch: the central location and swift, relaxed service combine with good, mostly Swedish food to ensure a full house. Örjan Klein is the chef-patron responsible for dishes such as dill-cured Baltic herring; supreme of duck with onion and raisin confit; grilled scallops with chervil, lemon and a chicory salad, parsley-baked cod with shiitake mushrooms and rack of lamb with savoy cabbage. A notable dessert is the almond parfait with apricots and caramel sauce or there is a selection of Swedish cheeses. KB is a Swedish acronym for the Artists Buffé. Set L SEK280/330. Set D SEK455. *Seats 60. Open 1130-2400 (closed 2-5pm for 2 weeks in Aug). Closed L Sat, all Sun, 22 Jun-6 Aug & some Public Holidays. Amex, Diners, Mastercard, Visa.*

Tel: (8) 676 58 00   Fax: (8) 20 95 92
Operahuset, 111 86 Stockholm

Classified as a historic monument (it dates back to 1787), Operakällaren is part of the Royal Opera House. A complex of several restaurants at different levels of price and formality (the Café Opera becomes a night club after midnight) it is the main dining-room we describe here. Head chef, Swiss-born Werner Vögeli, is a culinary adviser to the King and Queen of Sweden and there is a magnificent view across the water to the Royal Palace from the main dining-room. As a visitor to Stockholm it is almost mandatory to sample the gigantic Swedish smörgåsbord (Mon-Fri 1130-1400, Sat till 1800) which you can visit as many times as you like-there are more than 50 dishes, hot and cold, fish and meat, cheese and fruit. A speciality is Janssons Temptation (baked layers of sliced potatoes, anchovies, minced onions and cream). There is a variety of other menu options with dishes like feuilleté d'asperges with stuffed morels and chervil sauce, a chaud-foid of quail, braised smoked salmon on a bed of spinach with a dill sauce, rack of lamb with herb crust and Provençal timbale, and wild strawberry parfait showing the style. The wine list is one of the best in the country. Set L SEK130, SEK172 & SEK235 (smörgåsbord) Set D SEK475/SEK695 (gastronomic). *Seats 200. Open 1130-1400, 1700-2330. Closed L Sun & all Jul. Amex, Diners, Mastercard, Visa.*

Tel: (8) 663 81 83
Strandvägen 9, 114 56 Stockholm

Located on the fashionable Strandvägen, this intimate restaurant (there are just nine tables) is home to some of the best cooking in Sweden. The restaurant is a partnership between Paul Beck and Norbert Lang, the former looking after front of house with urbane charm and the latter the talent in the kitchen. Tempting starters like creamed crawfish bisque with armagnac and grilled crawfish, noisette of goose foie gras with gooseberry chutney, and quail terrine with chanterelles and a cold cumin sauce precede main dishes ranging from a very Nordic juniper-stuffed reindeer rump with red wine sauce, and steamed and grilled noisettes of Fjord salmon with white wine and Noilly Prat sauce to crisp wild duck with a caramelised raspberry vinegar sauce, grilled lamb's liver with a creamed caper and Dijon mustard sauce and such creations as Pernod-flamed sweetbreads with paprika pie and paprika sauce. Swedish game features in season. Desserts include hot soufflés and there is always at least one chocolate dish. 10 or 12 quality wines available by the glass. Reservations are advisable. Fixed-price meals L SEK240/330, L & D SEK420 & SEK980 (dégustation) are all composed from the à la carte. *Seats 32. Open 1145-1430, 1730-2230. Closed Sat, Sun, Jul & 24 Dec-6 Jan. Amex, Diners, Mastercard, Visa.*

Tel: (8) 678 78 00   Fax: (8) 611 24 36
Nybrokajen 9, 103 27 Stockholm

Now part of the Radisson chain (hence the change of name), the SAS Strand enjoys a superb location by the pleasure harbour where the white boats from the Archipelago dock. Rooms are modern and well equipped, with mini-bars and cable TV, and most have in-room safes. About 20% also have air-conditioning. In summer the Italian-style patio is a very pleasant place to have breakfast or afternoon tea. Business-class passengers with the SAS airline can check in for their flights before leaving the hotel. Hotel guests can use the facilities of a nearby leisure at concessionary rates. *Rooms 148. Room service 24hrs. Valet parking SEK210 (open) SEK260 (garage) for 24 hours. Conference facilities 100. Sauna. Amex, Diners, Mastercard, Visa.*

Tel: (8) 22 66 00   Fax: (8) 21 50 70
Brunkebergstorg 9, 103 27 Stockholm

Built in 1971 as apartments and conference rooms for Swedish parliamentarians, this modern building in the centre of the capital was converted into a hotel in the mid-80s. A stunning atrium lobby, designed by Alberto Pinto, includes a piano bar. For the business traveller there is a 42-roomed Executive Floor with its own breakfast lounge. The hotel is particularly proud of its full concierge service. *Rooms 406. Room service 24hrs. Garage parking SEK190 per 24 hrs. Conference facilities 200. Sauna. Spa bath. Massage. Amex, Diners, Mastercard, Visa.*

Tel: (8) 663 05 71   Fax: (8) 663 05 73
Rosendalsvägen 8, Djurgården 115 21 Stockholm

The excellent location, in a park on the island of Djurgården only minutes from the centre of town, makes Ulla Winbladh the perfect place for a meal in the summer, when there are tables for an extra 70 diners out on the veranda (covered in inclement weather) but it's worth a visit at any time for some good, largely Swedish cooking: herring platter with Cheddar cheese, steamed lightly-salted cod with beetroot and sorrel mayonnaise, *beef Rydberg* (cubes of beef with sauté potatoes, minced onion, egg yolk and mustard), roast leg of reindeer with port-glazed vegetables and a blue cheese cream sauce. Particular specialities include smoked salmon with horseradish cream and tomato dressing and fried angler fish with lobster butter, mangetout and asparagus salad with Sauternes and herbs, and a light dessert of elder-blossom and blackcurrant mousse. The restaurant is named after the girlfriend and muse of the 18th-century Swedish poet and composer, Carl Mikael Bellman. There is a smallish (about 50 entries) but reasonably priced globe-trotting wine list with about eight wines, plus champagne, served by the glass. Public car parks nearby. *Seats 60. Open 1130-2300 (Sat & Sun from 1200). Closed 24 & 25 Dec. Amex, Diners, Mastercard, Visa.*

STOCKHOLM · Victory Hotel · SEK1870 · H

Tel: (8) 14 30 90   Fax: (8) 20 21 77
Lilla Nygatan 5, 111 28 Stockholm

Originally built in 1642 for Pastor Primarius Olav Laurelius, this is an elegant, stylish hotel in the old part of the city. The bedrooms are well furnished, and decorated with maritime and Swedish folk antiques. Their design is unfussy, but full of character. Swedish colour schemes are used and a typical room has exposed beams, pine floors and a blue-and-white-striped bedspread with a pine headboard. The sparkling white, well-equipped bathrooms have tiled floors and some have spa baths. The four suites, in contrast, are furnished with antiques and lit by chandeliers. All rooms have mini-bars and room safes. A courtyard with tables arranged around a fountain provides an excellent place to eat lunch on a summer's day. In chillier weather, head for the brick-vaulted bistro if the main restaurant seems too formal. A famous cache of silver coins was found in the building and can now be seen in the city museum. *Rooms 48. Closed 1 week Christmas/New Year. Room service all day. Valet parking SEK210 for 24 hours. Conference facilities 90. Indoor swimming pool. Cold water spa. Sauna. Amex, Diners, Mastercard, Visa.*

STOCKHOLM · Wedholms Fisk · ★ · SEK1100 · R

Tel: (8) 611 78 74
Nybrokajen 17, 111 48 Stockholm

As a Nordic country, Sweden has the advantage of cold-water lakes which provide some of the best fish available anywhere and what better place to sample Swedish fish than Wedholm's. Chef-patron Bengt Wedholm is famous for his mastery of the art of selecting and cooking the fish. The restaurant is fashionable but informal; a place to enjoy the food and relax. Located on the quayside, this bistro-style restaurant has simple decor and very friendly staff. From some of the tables you can actually see Bengt at work in the kitchen, probably preparing a superb lobster bisque or some Swedish speciality like smoked Baltic herring on sweet brown bread with a raw egg yolk or the unique Swedish red caviar –bleak roe – with red onions and crème fraiche. As a main course there is a choice between pike-perch, turbot, sole and salmon, prepared in various ways, with excellent sauces and in generous portions. Occasionally the patron manages to find and offer the rare red-bellied lake trout which comes from only one lake - the Vattern - in Sweden. It is a must. To finish, there are a few well-chosen desserts such as gratin of fruit with zabaglione and sorbet or pear poached in red wine with cinnamon. The wine list is limited but well chosen. *Seats 70. Open 1130-2300 (except Sat open 1400-2300). Closed Sun, National Holidays, may close 23 Dec-2 Jan. Amex, Diners, Mastercard, Visa.*

Around Stockholm

SOLLENTUNA · Edsbacka Krog · SEK1000 · R

Tel: (8) 96 33 00   Fax: (8) 96 40 19
Sollentunavägen 220, 19147 Sollentuna

Situated near a lake on the outskirts of Stockholm, this very attractive old inn dates back to 1626, when it was given the Royal Charter by King Gustavus Adolphus. In the last century, the inn closed and became a temperance restaurant which, not surprisingly, did not survive long. In 1983, after extensive rebuilding, Christer Lingström reopened Edsbacka as a first-class restaurant-cum-country inn in the original and beautifully-restored building. There are five intimate dining-rooms in which you can enjoy quality Swedish cuisine with French overtones. Christer Lingström is a very talented chef who has quickly built himself a reputation among Swedish gourmets. Among the many tempting starters are quenelles of Norwegian lobster tails with garlic-fried vegetables, terrine of duck liver with pig's cheek, artichoke, tomato, apple sauce and a leek and almond potato cream, flavoured with cheese and served with baked scallops and marinated herbs. Main courses worth mentioning are medallions of prime veal with artichoke in a pepper sauce served with potato-tomato galettes and, in season, partridge with apple and parsnip. If you want to sample a selection of the chef's unusual dishes, there is a seven-course dégustation menu. At lunchtime there is also a reasonably-priced business menu. Edsbacka Krog, in its unique setting, is a most welcome addition to the small group of top-quality restaurants in Stockholm. *Seats 60. Open 1130-1430, 1730-2200 (Sat 1830). Closed D Mon, L Sat, all Sun, 15 Jul-15 Aug. Private parking. Amex, Diners, Mastercard, Visa.*

Your Guarantee of Quality and Independence

- Establishment inspections are anonymous
- Inspections are undertaken by qualified Egon Ronay's Guides inspectors
- The Guides are completely independent in their editorial selection
- The Guides do not accept advertising, hospitality or payment from listed establishments

Titles planned for 1996 include

Hotels & Restaurants ● Pubs & Inns ● Europe
Ireland ● Just A Bite
And Children Come Too ● Paris
Oriental Restaurants

Switzerland

Currency Swiss Franc **Exchange Rate** £1=approx FR 1.82
International dialing code 00 41 (Zürich+1, Geneva+22, Basle+61)
Passports/Visas No visa required by British passport holders.
British Embassy in Zürich Tel 1-47 1520 Fax 1-252 8351

TRANSPORT
Airports
Geneva-Cointrin Tel 22-799 3111/717 7711
Zürich-Kloten Tel 1-816 2211/816 3511
Basle-Mulhouse Tel 61-325 2511
Railway Stations
Geneva Tel 22-738 5200 **Zürich** Tel 1-211 5010
Basle Tel (Swiss) 61-272 6767 (French) 61-271 5033
(German) 61-691 5511
Car hire
Tel Nos. **Geneva Hertz** 22-731 1200 **Avis** 22-732 2606
Budget 22-732 5252 **Zürich Hertz** 1-242 8484 **Avis** 1-242 2040
Europcar 1-432 2424 **Budget** 1-383 1747
Basle Hertz 61-325 2780 (airport 61-271 5822) **Avis** (airport)
61-325 2840 **Budget** (airport) 61-325 2936
Speed limits 80 km/h on trunk roads 120 km/h on motorways, 50 km/h
in towns.

OPENING HOURS

Banks Mon-Fri 8.30am-4.30pm
Shops Mon-Fri 8am-12pm & 1.30-5.30pm (Sat till 4pm). Many shops
close Monday mornings.

NATIONAL HOLIDAYS

New Year's Day, Easter, 16 & 27 May, 1 Aug, Christmas Day & Boxing Day.

Tourist Offices

Switzerland Tourism in **London** Tel 0171-734 1921
In **Switzerland** Geneva Tel 22-788 0808
Zürich Tel 1-211 1256
Basle Tel 61-261 5050
American Express Travel Service Offices or Representative (R)

Basle	Reisebüro Müller & Co (R)
	Steinenvorstadt 33
	4002
	Tel 61-2813380 #
Geneva	7 Rue Du Mont Blanc
	Ch-1211
	PO Box 1032 (PO Box Post Code 01)
	Tel 22-7317600 #
Zürich	Bahnhofstrasse 20
	PO Box 5231
	Ch-8022
	Tel 1-2118370 #

Basle

Tel: (61) 281 14 10   Fax: (61) 281 14 20

R

Bachlettenstrasse 1, 4054 Basel

This spacious, elegant and relaxed restaurant, hung with modern art, is ideal for business lunches, small parties or romantic tete-à-tetes. Since opening ten years ago, owner Gregory Holzmann and his French chef Luc Bourqui have developed a light but refined French style of cooking, grounded in the market freshness of top-quality ingredients. Warm duck foie gras with rhubarb ravioli, fresh noodles with roquefort and nut crumbs, and poussin roasted with balsamic vinegar are examples of their seductively subtle dishes. You will find Swiss wines from the Valais and the Vaud regions on the list. *Seats 70. Open 1130-1400, 1830-2200. Closed Sun, Sat (in winter), mid Jul-mid Aug. Private parking. Amex, Diners, Mastercard, Visa.*

Tel: (61) 261 52 52   Fax: (61) 261 21 53

HR

Blumenrain 8, 4001 Basel

The history of this old castle, in the centre of the city near the zoo, can be traced back to 1026. Napoleon and Dickens are among the many distinguished guests who have admired the splendour of the tapestries in the Salon des Gobelins, the unusual turquoise columns in the banqueting room and high-ceilinged reception area with its antique chandeliers and wood-panelled walls. Bedrooms are equipped with the essentials of modern life (TV, phone, safe, mini-bar) but antiques, thick carpets and rich fabrics create an atmosphere of timeless elegance. *Rooms 88. Room service limited. Private parking Fr25. Banqueting facilities 120. Conference facilities 100. Business centre. Amex, Diners, Mastercard, Visa.*

Rotisserie de Rois   FR220

Eating on the terrace overlooking the Rhine is a splendid experience in summer, while in cooler weather the Louis XV decor and open fires of the dining-room are equally enticing. French chef Guy Lutz combines the techniques of his homeland with Swiss touches to produce dishes such as sliced potatoes with caviar and lobster sauce, noisettes of lamb with garlic and basil, and classic desserts like crème brulée with raspberries, and chocolate terrine. *Seats 65. Open 1130-1400, 1845-2200.*

Tel: (61) 691 80 80   Fax: (61) 691 82 01

HR

Clarastrasse 35-43, 4058 Basel

This modern hotel in the heart of the city is ideally placed for the nearby Trade Fairs. Business facilities are currently being improved with the construction of a new banqueting and conference room to accommodate up to 200 (completion due April 1996). The bedrooms were refurbished a few years ago and are comfortable although the colour scheme, with lots of orange and brown, is stuck in the 70s. *Rooms 166. Room service 24hr. Private parking. Banqueting facilities 150. Conference facilities 150. Garden. Amex, Diners, Mastercard, Visa.*

Les Quatre Saisons   FR280

Chef Peter Mosar is German but his market-led seasonal menu is French with an Italian twist. Dishes are interesting without being over-elaborate: for instance, starters such as carpaccio of spring lamb with a rocket pesto and artichokes, and tarragon soup with lobster claws. Main courses include veal cutlet with asparagus and morel mushrooms, and brochette of angler fish on noodles with white tomato butter. *Seats 80. Open 1200-1430, 1830-2300. Closed Sun, mid Jul-4 Aug.*

Tel: (61) 271 28 33   Fax: (61) 271 29 19
Centralbahnplatz 1, CH-4002 Basel

Currently celebrating one hundred years of ownership by the same family, this small hotel is a stone's throw from the main railway station and within walking distance of the shops, museums and zoo. There is little cohesion in the decoration-some rooms are reminiscent of the 1960s while others feature original pieces from the 1860s-but the attentive staff are united in putting individual service at the top of the priority list. The marble-floored reception area, arranged like a cosy living room with sofas and armchairs, provides a relaxing space in which to unwind. Half of the rooms are air-conditioned. *Rooms 75. Room service limited. Private parking. Banqueting facilities 80. Conference facilities 100. Secretarial services on request. Amex, Diners, Mastercard, Visa.*

Tel: (61) 361 82 22   Fax: (61) 361 82 03
Bruderholzallee 42, 4059 Basel

From the hillside above the city of Basle, Hans and Susi Stucki welcome you to their restaurant set in an attractive 1920s villa. It is now 36 years since Hans Stucki took charge of the kitchen and began to offer some of the finest food in Switzerland to appreciative gourmets. In three elegant dining-rooms – and in the garden in summertime-you can choose between a well-balanced à la carte dominated by fish dishes and one of the *dégustation* menus, which comprise six or seven courses in smaller portions (although not that small). To accompany the attractively-presented food we suggest a light Swiss wine. Mr Stucki is famous for being one of the foremost proponents of his country's wines. Swiss white wines in particular are excellent and are underrated outside the Heimat. They complement Stucki's many fine fish dishes such as *gelée de crustacés aux primeurs* (shellfish in aspic with spring vegetables) or *fricassée de langoustines au curry* and *blanc de turbot poché aux fèves sauce beurre blanc*. Meat courses feature *pièce de boeuf double grillée au Merlot et à la moelle* and *pigeon de la Toscane roti aux vieux porto*. Not to be missed are desserts such as *soufflé au coulis de fruits de saison* and *blanc-manger aux amandes avec une soupe de cerises*. *Seats 70. Open 1200-1430, 1830-2130. Closed Sun, Mon, first 2 weeks Feb, 23 Dec-7 Jan. Private parking. Amex, Diners, Mastercard, Visa.*

Tel: (61) 261 10 10   Fax: (61) 261 10 04
Leonhardsgraben 47, Heuberg 30, CH-4051 Basel

Der Teufelhof is not just one of the country's best restaurants, it is, as it claims, a Kultur-und Gasthaus. This splendid 19th-century villa hotel is filled with contemporary art and incorporates two small theatres and a specialist wine shop. A husband-and-wife team bought and converted the building six years ago bringing in the renowned chef Michael Baader formerly of the Schweizer Stuben in Germany. Since then, the daily-changing menu has developed some strong French and international specialities. Start with a goose-liver mousse with asparagus in a sesame vinaigrette followed perhaps by *gegrillte Perlhuhn mit Pfifferling-Thymiansauce* (grilled guinea fowl with a thyme and chanterelle mushroom sauce). When available, the house speciality, *steinbuttfilet im Mangoldblatt mit Périgord-Trübchen in Chambertinjus* (fillet of turbot wrapped in Swiss chard with Périgord truffles) is not to be missed. The 450 wines come from Italy, France and Switzerland and the weinset supplement gives you a different glass of wine with each course. The Weinstube wine bar and the attractive café-cum-bar are worth a visit for a digestif-there are 50 different kinds of grappa to choose from. *Seats 50. Open 1200-1330, 1900-2230. Closed L Sat, all Sun, Mon, July. Amex, Mastercard, Visa.*

Every three years, eight new artists are given free rein to redecorate the eight bedrooms which make up the Teufelhof hotel – be warned, they are sometimes on the bizarre side. Due to expand in 1996 following the acquisition of an adjoining building, the Teufelhof will soon have another 24 rooms.

Around Basle

Tel: (61) 421 20 55　Fax: (61) 421 06 35
Schlossgasse 5, 4102 Binningen

R

An impressive 13th-century castle, 2km from Basle and once the stamping ground of wealthy noblemen, is now home to this splendid restaurant. It was converted into a restaurant back in 1895 and many of the original paintings, furniture and tables still exist. It may feel as if you are eating in a museum, but the menu is modern and imaginative, adapting French cooking techniques to Swiss seasonal produce. Highlights of a summer meal were an entrée of veal tripes with morels and tarragon followed by medallions of venison with elder sauce, vegetables and risotto with apple. There are lots of traditionally-prepared dishes based on lobster, salmon, turbot, crayfish and local game. The desserts, like the rest of the menu, change only seasonally but the mouthwatering choux filled with chocolate crème patissière and oranges marinated in 20 different spices are welcome staples. Unusually, all the wines on the wine list are available by the glass. *Seats 56. Open 1130-2130. Closed Sun, Mon, first 2 weeks Feb. Private parking. Amex, Diners, Mastercard, Visa.*

Geneva

Tel: (22) 311 13 44　Fax: (22) 311 13 50
34 quai Général-Guisain, 1204 Genève

R

Hotel Métropole, the 19th-century listed building which houses L'Arlequin, was restored after the people of Geneva vetoed its demolition in 1976. Although the original facade remains, the restaurant was completely rebuilt, keeping the high-ceilinged rooms, which provide an excellent setting for the modern French cooking. Inspired by the work of Georges Blanc and Joël Robuchon, chef Alain Jennings makes interesting use of herbs and spices: *carré d'agneau aux jus d'herbes* and *filet de boeuf avec une sauce au vinaigre balsamic* being two specialities. The Carte Des Mets offers numerous pasta and seafood combinations like *cannelloni de langoustines, lasagnes de homard et ravioli de homard sur gingembre* (ravioli of lobster with ginger). A particularly refreshing combination is the *filet de loup avec sauce au basilic et quenelles de crabe* (sea bass fillet with a basil sauce and very light crab dumplings).The two dégustation menus are good value at Fr90 and Fr110. *Seats 45. Open 1200-1400, 1900-2130. Closed Sat, Sun, Aug. Valet parking. Amex, Diners, Mastercard, Visa.*

Tel: (22) 321 00 28　Fax: (22) 381 31 15
4 quai de la Poste, 1204 Genève

R

This renowned stone and wood-fronted restaurant on the banks of the Rhone in the very heart of Geneva has been going for 50 years. Its two dining-rooms are very different: Empire has rich period furniture and glistening glass and cutlery, while Rustique is smaller, with simple wooden chairs and tables. Whichever you choose, the menus offered are the same: traditional French. The *Menu Printemps* offers *rillettes de tourteau et saumon d'Ecosse à l'émulsion de concombre.* An autumn speciality is *l'oursin de Bretagne fourré de coquilles St Jacques* (Brittany sea urchins stuffed with scallops) or alternatively there is *Le Mets de Chasse* game menu. 10 truffle specialities like soufflé de truffes fraiches dominate the winter carte. The wine list introduces some of the lesser-known vineyards from the Geneva area. Business lunch menu at Fr58. *Seats 65. Open 1200-1400, 1930-2200. Closed Sat (except D Oct-May), Sun, mid Jul-end Aug. Amex, Diners, Mastercard, Visa.*

Tel: (22) 731 50 50   Fax: (22) 732 19 89
33 quai des Bergues, 1201 Genève

For the last century and a half, this splendid neo-classical hotel has been a landmark on the quayside of Lake Geneva. Close to the business and shopping areas, the hotel has the added advantage of being only 6km from the airport and 500m from the railway station. The rooms are still decorated with original Louis Philippe furnishings and all have marble bathrooms; there are also ten spacious suites. One room is equipped for disabled guests. The reception hall, with its shiny grey marble, is dazzling and the Grande Salle makes an impressive conference venue. The hotel has no sports facilities of its own but residents are offered free use of a nearby health club. You can dine in the hotel's terrace restaurant or relax in the piano bar. *Rooms 123. Room service 24hr. Private garage Fr35. Banqueting facilities 290. Conference facilities 450. Secretarial/translation on request. Cable TV. Amex, Diners, Mastercard, Visa.*

Tel: (22) 311 42 42   Fax: (22) 311 40 65
17 place Longemalle, 1204 Genève

A real gem of a hotel set in adjoining houses on a quiet street in the old part of Geneva. From the entrance, a stone-flagged floor leads up to a lounge area with frescoed ceiling and walls. All the bedrooms were renovated and individually designed in 1985: some are furnished with Louis XV or XVI furniture, others with chinoiserie, and one particular room seems to be a tribute to Gaudi. The meeting room, though small, is almost medieval in style and features a *trompe-l'oeil* stained-glass skylight. The lakeside gardens are only about 100 metres away and watersports can be arranged on request. *Rooms 52. Room service 24hr. Public parking Fr30. Banqueting facilities 25. Conference facilities 15. Cable TV. Safe. Video. Amex, Diners, Mastercard, Visa.*

There is a clubby feel to this mahogany-panelled dining-room, which opened back in 1900 and was very fashionable during both World Wars. Over the last six years, it has seen a new lease of life with the arrival of chef Bernard Moreno, who worked with Guérard in Eugénie-les-Bains in France. His classical French culinary upbringing expresses itself in dishes like *fondant de caille et foie gras aux raisins blonds* (fondant of quail with foie gras and white grapes), *mille-feuille de pommes de terre et mignons de canard aux mousserons des prés* (wafer-thin potatoes and small fillets of duck with wild mushrooms), and *dos de cabillaud aux fèvettes et flan d'ail doux* (fillet of cod with baby broad beans and sweet garlic). The carte des mets changes seasonally and there are always about six *suggestions de la semaine.* Bordeaux and burgundies figure high on the wine list but there is also a good choice of Swiss wines. *Seats 36. Open 1200-1400, 1900-2200.*

Tel: (22) 792 04 11   Fax: (22) 792 05 46
28 chemin de la Vendée, Petit-Lancy, 1213 Genève

This small hotel in a residential suburb 3km out of Geneva is dedicated to all things gastronomic, with regular dégustations drawing in the guests. It was recently renovated and the bedrooms have modern, wooden furniture and pastel decor. Amenities are, however, limited, with no sports or extra conference facilities. But at only 5km from the airport and 3km from the railway station, the location is great. *Rooms 34. Room service limited. Private parking. Banqueting facilities 100. Conference facilities 60. Air-conditioning. Cable TV. Mini-bar. Amex, Diners, Mastercard, Visa.*

The chef of two years, Stéphane Taffonneau, has worked up through the ranks of this well-respected restaurant and the place still continues to attract the attention it has had since the 60s. The menu is faithfully French, traditional to its core. Staple dishes are daurade *royale poelée et artichauts en barigoule, beurre à l'oseille* (pan-fried gilthead) and *rouget entier désareté, tagliatelle de courgette et pistou aux saveurs d'anchois* (red mullet with courgette ribbons and an olive oil, lime, basil, anchovy and tomato sauce). The set business lunch menu changes every week, the à la carte seasonally. The finale is definitely grand with such desserts as *symphonie autour des fruits rouges* (a compote of red fruits served with strawberry mousse and red fruit ice cream). The owner, a Bordeaux aficionado, has included a fair number of Swiss labels on the 300-strong wine list. *Seats 30 (terrace 25). Open 1200-1345, 1900-2145. Closed L Sat, all Sun, 23 Dec-6 Jan.*

Tel: (22) 919 39 39   Fax: (22) 919 38 38
7 chemin du Petit-Saconnex, 1211 Genève

HR

This 18-storey 1960s skyscraper has an impressive penthouse conference centre. Try to get a room near the top if possible, where the views are breathtaking. Like all hotels in the group, they have a constant renovation policy and regularly update the rooms and the facilities. The hotel is only five minutes from the very centre of Geneva and the airport and near to the headquarters of the international organisations like the UN. *Rooms 358. Room service 24hr. Private/valet parking Fr25. Banqueting facilities 600. Conference facilities 450. Secretarial/translation services on request. Beauty treatment. Satellite TV. Sauna. Outdoor swimming pool. Amex, Diners, Mastercard, Visa.*

Restaurant Les Continents   FR250

The Irish chef, Tommy Byrne, has had a classical French training, but he likes to mix foods of different "status", in other words, luxury foods with humbler staples. Two good examples of this are *poelé de turbotin à la purée de pois chiches* (pan-fried turbot with a purée of chick peas) and filets de rouget (sautéed fillet of red mullet with potatoes, young leeks, truffles and carrots). Recent specialities include *gelée de bouillabaisse aux rouelles de homard* (bouillabaisse jelly with slices of lobster served with ratatouille and fresh basil) and *risotto de fruits de mer au fumet de crustacés* (seafood risotto with an aroma of shellfish). There's a good selection of Swiss wines as well as the best French crus and an international selection. *Seats 80. Open 1200-1430, 1900-2230. Closed Sat, Sun.*

Tel: (22) 731 79 35   Fax: (22) 731 49 79
128 rue de Lausanne, 1202 Genève

R

Set in a 1920s building on the left bank of Lac Leman and surrounded by a lovely flower garden, this piece of Swiss heritage is now entrusted to the City of Geneva. Christian Grenard heads a team of chefs who prepare a carefully thought-out and balanced carte and three set menus. The presentation is superb and there are some truly original dishes. Some of the rather daring aromatic combinations are *filet de daurade au laurier et zestes d'orange confits* (fillet of sea bream with bay leaves and orange zest preserve) and *filets mignons de veau au citron vert et gingembre* (small veal fillets with lime and ginger). There are also some more simple and traditional fish entrées like *fantaisie de saumon fumé au sevruga and ravioli de homard au beurre de thym citronné* (lobster ravioli with lemon thyme butter). Among their 300 different wines, there are some strong New World contenders which complement this cuisine most effectively. *Seats 45 (terrace 50). Open 1200-1400, 1900-2200. Closed Mon, Jan. Private parking. Amex, Diners, Mastercard, Visa.*

Tel: (22) 735 41 40   Fax: (22) 786 87 65
82 quai Gustave-Ador, 1207 Genève

R

In the heart of the lovely Parc des Eaux Vives on Geneva's rive gauche, the 18th-century building which houses this restaurant is owned, like so many others in Switzerland, by the City of Geneva. Nowadays it is run by a husband-and-wife team. Inside it is typically Swiss, with wooden tables and chairs, but the menu is more French. Chef Claude Legras came here from the *Auberge du Lion d'Or* (qv) in Cologny and is truly inventive, incorporating Mediterranean ingredients like sun-dried tomatoes, olives, parmesan and mascarpone in his French repertoire. The gourmet menu proposes *duo de lapin et canard aux courgettes fleurs confites et gnocchis aux céréales complètes* (duo of rabbit and duck with courgette flowers and wholemeal gnocchi). Red mullet comes pan-fried with artichokes and ginger, and the pan-fried *filet de boeuf Vallée d'Aosta* is served with aubergine lasagne. The *Menu Des Amis Du Parc* at Fr98, the *Menu Végétarien* at Fr85 and the *Menu Des Gourmets* at Fr145 all change weekly. The cellar is stacked with 1000 different wines, including an impressive array of Italian and Californian bottles. *Seats 250 (terrace 200). Open 1200-1400, 1930-2200. Closed Sun (but open L Sun Easter-Sept), Mon. Private/valet parking. Amex, Mastercard, Visa.*

> Opening times are often liable to change at short notice, so it's always best to book.

GENEVA   Hotel du Rhône   FR496

Tel: (22) 731 98 31   Fax: (22) 732 45 58

quai Turrettini, 1201 Genève

The Rafael Group owns hotels in Germany, France and the United States, as well as this large hotel in the heart of Geneva's commercial centre, only ten minutes from the airport, with superb views over Lake Geneva. Although this is a 1950s construction, once inside you feel as if you are stepping into the 1920s. The art-deco furnishings are luxurious and tasteful and no expense was spared during the refurbishment three years ago. The bedrooms are also decked out in 20s style, with plain bedcovers and curtains and marble bathrooms, and there is an attractive art nouveau marine fresco in Le Neptune restaurant. The Mont Blanc penthouse suite takes up the entire 7th floor and has a stunning view as far as the Alps. *Rooms 214. Room service 24hr. Private parking Fr30. Banqueting facilities 190. Conference facilities 250. Staffed business centre. News kiosk. Safe. Video. Amex, Diners, Mastercard, Visa.*

GENEVA   Hotel Le Richemond   FR682

Tel: (22) 731 14 00   Fax: (22) 731 67 09

Jardin Brunswick, 1201 Genève

Overlooking Lake Geneva with the Alps beyond, Le Richemond feels more like a private mansion than a hotel. The hotel has been under new management for the last year although still owned by the Armleder family, who have run it for the 120 years. It is the pinnacle of luxury with prices to match-but they stint on nothing. The public rooms feature carved, wood-panelled walls and moulded ceilings with sumptuous velvet and brocade furnishings in a Regency style. The bedrooms and suites are spacious and well equipped. Enjoy afternoon tea in the gracious lounge and hall, or sip a cocktail in the art deco Jardin Terrace, whilst waited upon by effusively helpful staff. Room service is second to none with a full gourmet menu served round the clock. *Rooms 98. Room service 24hr. Garage parking Fr35. Banqueting facilities 250. Conference facilities 200. Secretarial services on request. Beauty salon. Cable TV. Hairdresser. Limousine service. Massage. Amex, Diners, Mastercard, Visa.*

Around Geneva

BELLEVUE   La Réserve   FR551

Tel: (22) 774 17 41   Fax: (22) 774 25 71

301 route de Lausanne, 1293 Bellevue

This luxurious Florida-style hotel complex on Lac Léman is 10 minutes outside Geneva, just off the Lausanne motorway and only five minutes from the international airport. Surrounded by 10 acres of park, the hotel even has its own private beach and dock connected by an underground passage as well as a glittering outdoor swimming pool. American Presidents (landing their helicopters on the lawn) and even Davis Cup teams have stayed here-the latter, doubtless, because of the splendid keep-fit facilities available in the Business & Health centre. The conference facilities are also impressive with seven fully-equipped meeting rooms. The bedrooms are all quite alike: ultra-modern and decorated in light, creamy pastels. The American Bar is a striking spot for pre-dinner cocktails and there are no less than six restaurants from Chinese to Italian. *Rooms 114. Room service 24hr. Private parking for 150 cars. Banqueting facilities 200. Conference facilities 200. Beauty treatment. Hairdresser. Heliport. Laundry service. Private beach. Indoor and outdoor swimming pools. Tennis courts (1 indoor). Amex, Diners, Mastercard, Visa.*

Restaurant Tsé Fung   FR220

A formal setting, with its low lanterns and revolving tables, is the perfect place for the very refined Chinese cooking that the small kitchen produces. The menu with its inscription "Chinese cooking prevents and cures all body and soul troubles" promises the world and does not disappoint. There are in fact eight different menus (Fr80-125), each named after a precious stone. A regular and popular house speciality is *canard laqué péquinois* (Peking duck served with pancakes and a plum and black bean sauce). The *dégustation* menus have some interesting nibbles: *le potage de la longévité* (longevity soup), *le poulet ivre du Dragon* (drunken chicken of the Dragon) whose ingredients can only be guessed at, and the more familiar tiny egg rolls with mint and shrimps served with a spicy lime sauce and stuffed crab claws. A refreshing way to end your meal is with one of the various sorbets made with different fruit liqueurs. *Seats 60 (terrace 80). Open 1200-1430, 1900-2230.*

Tel: (22) 342 30 77 Fax: (22) 300 22 19
RR
33 chemin de Pinchat, 1227 Carouge

About half a kilometre outside the little town of Carouge, near Geneva, this early 20th-century beamed mansion is haven of tranquillity. The owners opened it as a hotel and restaurant in 1987, after their restaurant and club Le Curling in Geneva became too hard to manage. The chef was born and bred in Normandy and cites Escoffier's cookery book as his bible although his cooking is undoubtedly lighter than that of his mentor. Every three weeks he changes the menu, but his signature entrée is without doubt *foie gras de canard aux morilles fraiches en gelée au Beaumes-de-Venise* (duck foie gras with wild mushrooms and Beaumes-de-Venise, a sweet Rhone wine) served with a glass of Chateau les Justices 1990. Other specialities are langoustines served in various ways, *carré d'agneau roti à la diable* (rack of lamb roasted with white wine, shallots and chili) and *rognons de veau poelé au beurre de curry garniture de saison du marché* (calf's kidneys pan-fried with curry butter with a market-fresh seasonal garnish). The helpful suggestions de vins at the foot of the menu assure you of the perfect complement to your meal. *Seats 55. Open 1200-1330, 1930-2130. Closed last 2 weeks Oct, 20 Dec-10 Jan. Private parking. Mastercard, Visa.*

Needless to say, being able to stay here is principally a bonus for diners in the restaurant so accommodation is limited, with just four double rooms and one single (with showers and toilets but not baths). Nevertheless the rooms are comfortable and light, decorated in pastel colours and have cable TV No room service. *Rooms 5. Cable TV.*

Tel: (22) 736 44 32 Fax: (22) 786 74 62
R
5 place Pierre Gauthier, 1223 Cologny

For the last 18 years, Henri Large has been faithfully cooking French food at this delightful inn, filled with Louis XVI furniture and with large bay windows overlooking Lake Geneva. Large tends to concentrate on Mediterranean fish dishes: with *savarin de rascasse au coulis de homard* (savarin of scorpion fish with a lobster coulis), *raie aux capres beurre noisette* (skate with capers and brown butter), *filet de rouget aux nouilles fraiches* (red mullet cooked with noodles), and *turbot au four* (baked turbot). Lunch menu Fr70 and a dégustation menu at Fr170. All the Swiss labels are represented on the wine list as well as a big collection of Bordeaux. A separate bar seats 40 people and has a small, hearty menu. *Seats 70 (terrace 100). Open 1200-1400, 1900-2200. Closed Sat, Sun, 20 Dec-20 Jan, Easter Week, National Holidays. Private parking. Amex, Diners, Mastercard, Visa.*

Tel: (22) 753 15 11 Fax: (22) 753 1924
HR
16 chemin de Chateau, Peney-Dessus 1242

The 13th-century wood and stone castle was destroyed in the religious wars in Geneva in the 1800s. The old stones were kept and rebuilt into this farmhouse, which stands in a vineyard in the quiet countryside by the Rhone close to both Geneva and Satigny. The hotel is dotted with reproduction wood furniture and paintings and the bedrooms are decorated in Laura Ashley style with lovely fresh flower arrangements. *Rooms 20. Room service none. Closed 2 weeks Aug, 23 Dec-7 Jan. Private parking. Banqueting facilities 24. Conference facilities 15. Secretarial services on request. Cable TV. Amex, Mastercard, Visa.*

The kitchen has recently been enlarged and modernised and is now visible to diners through a large glass screen. Chef Philippe Chevrier, a trained patissier, has been here for eight years and produces superb *cuisine du terroir* using all local produce: *l'escalope de foie gras de canard sautée aux betteraves rouges et à la compote d'oignons nouveaux* (escalope of duck foie gras sauted with beetroot and a compote of spring onions), *la rascasse rotie entière au fenouil, le bouillon de crevettes royales à l'anis étoilé* (whole scorpion fish roasted with fennel in a prawn stock scented with star anise) and *les supremes de pigeonneau roti* (supreme of roasted squab with a mushroom fricassee, parsley and sweetcorn biscuits). There are some great cheeses including Stilton, served by the spoonful and accompanied by vintage port. The two set menus, *Le Gourmet* and *Le Fin Bec* are Fr120 and Fr150 per person respectively. Excellent wines. *Seats 60 (terrace 19). Open 1200-1400, 1900-2200. Closed Sun, Mon, 2 weeks Aug, 23 Dec-7 Jan.*

Tel: (21) 964 44 11   Fax: (21) 964 70 02
75 rue du Lac, 1815 Clarens

Etienne and Isabelle Krebs fulfilled their dream when they took over this late 19th-century house three years ago. Surrounded by flowery gardens which border on the lake, the house is decorated the light summery colours of "water and sunshine" and has stunning views of the Alps. The seven bedrooms are all en suite, with comfortable cane furniture and modern fabrics and the Hollywood-style chambre exotique has a real palm tree in the bathroom. Note on Sunday and Monday the hotel reception closes at 2100 hrs. *Rooms 7. Room service. Closed Sun, Mon, 23 Dec-19 Jan. Private parking. Banqueting facilities 20. Cable TV. Minibar. Private mooring (5 berths). Amex, Diners, Mastercard, Visa.*

Mr Krebs' cooking is earthy and unfussy, allowing the pure flavours of the ingredients dominate and he just loves to unearth old recipes: for example *la marinade de langoustine à l'huile de crustacés et pipérade au jambon* (langoustines with shellfish-infused oil and pipérade) or *escalope de ris de veau* (calf's sweetbreads served with summer truffles in a light parsley cream sauce). The mouth-watering *beignets d'abricots crème glacée à l'amande amère* (little apricot doughnuts with bitter almond ice cream) are a perfect conclusion to the meal. The wine list is international but there's a fine local vaudois selection. *Seats 60 (terrace 20). Open 1200-1345, 1900-2100.*

Tel: (21) 964 52 30   Fax: (21) 964 55 30
1817 Brent-sur-Montreux

With its Italian stucco walls, Louis XV furniture, marble floors and flowers, this is a grand restaurant for a tiny village outside Montreux. The refined French food lives up to the surroundings with starters such as risotto of veal sweetbreads and chanterelle mushrooms, and feuilleté of frog's legs and roquefort. Wild sea bass with olives and artichokes, and tournedos of rabbit with prunes are fine southern French main dishes, while the abundant local fruit is evident in desserts such as *macaron glacé aux fraises des bois.* Set menus Fr140 and Fr 165. *Seats 50. Open 1200-1400, 1900-2130. Closed Sun & Mon, last 2 weeks Aug, 2 weeks at Christmas. Private parking. Mastercard, Visa.*

Tel: (21) 963 31 31   Fax: (21) 963 13 51
1823 Glion-sur-Montreux

A little village on the sunny southern slopes of Lake Geneva overlooking the snow-capped peaks of the Alps is home to this wonderful hotel retreat. Sitting in its own shady 16-acre park at an altitude of 2300 ft, the hotel has good facilities of its own and easy access to others such as fishing, hiking, horse-riding and skiing. Montreux is just a few minutes by car and guests may also benefit from the funicular link between the hotel and the tram station. All the rooms are different, decorated in a turn-of-the-century style with reproduction antiques. *Rooms 60. Room service 24hr. Private parking Fr15. Banqueting facilities 120. Conference facilities 120. Secretarial services on request. Heated outdoor swimming pool. Tennis. TV. Amex, Diners, Mastercard, Visa.*

Zurich

Tel: (1) 251 26 26   Fax: (1) 252 50 62

R

Hottingerstrasse 5, 8032 Zürich

An elegant restaurant near the Schauspielhaus and the Kunsthaus, serving sophisticated French food. The decor is sleek and relatively plain with mirrors and a few oil paintings lining the walls and candles and silverware on the tables. Prices are high but this is a great place to linger all evening. Chef Martin Surbeck's *cuisine du marché* is imaginative and his specialities include terrines (*foie de canard* is exceptional), lamb consommé with spring vegetables and parmesan, and king prawns with tempura paste. Lamb ragout with wild herbs and glazed shallots and mignon of veal in a morel mushroom and sherry sauce with new potatoes and thyme are excellent main dishes. Refreshing desserts include mousseline of strawberries and fresh mint sorbet with pernod. There is no carte but a wide choice of set menus from Fr70 (lunch) and Fr140 to Fr170 (dinner). Unusually, there are also separate vegetarian menus. *Seats 45. Open 1200-1330, 1900-2130. Closed Sat & Sun.* *Amex, Diners, Mastercard, Visa.*

Tel: (1) 220 50 20   Fax: (1) 220 50 44

H

Talstrasse 1, 8022 Zürich

Set in beautiful gardens, the hotel boasts a fine location, on the shore of Lake Zürich and close to the exclusive Bahnhofstrasse shopping street. It has been owned by the Kracht family for over 150 years and offers elegant, individually decorated and air-conditioned bedrooms and a superb level of personalised service. At present, major construction and refurbishment work is taking place (due to be completed by autumn 1996) including the rebuilding of 80 bedrooms and suites and the creation of a fitness room, new restaurant and bar. At the time of going to press the management were unsure to what extent clientele might be affected. *Rooms 140. Public parking Fr25. Banqueting facilities 150. Conference facilities 250. Garden. Terrace. Hair salon. Night club. News kiosk. Amex, Diners, Mastercard, Visa.*

Tel: 01 251 62 31   Fax: 01 251 62 31

HR

Kurhausstrasse, 65 8032 Zürich

This hotel is architecturally unique: the architect, Jacques Gros, a famous exponent of the German Art Nouveau movement, *Jugendstil*, built it with spires and turrets, and nooks and crannies. The extraordinary building is set in an equally extravagant park, with 20 acres of woods and gardens. The rooms were renovated back in the 80s and are all painted and decorated in pale colours, with fitted furniture and fine curtains. Balconies look out over the park, Zürich and the lake. They are all very well equipped in the meticulous Swiss-style, with faxes, safes and satellite and cable TV in all the rooms. Conference facilities for up to 500. *Rooms 184. 24hr room service. Secretarial/translation/valet services on request. Hairdresser/doctor. Outdoor swimming pool. Tennis courts. Golf. Ice skating. Private garage. Amex, Mastercard, Visa.*

Restaurant La Rotonde   ⬛ Fr230

Long sash windows give diners a panoramic view over the park and across the lake. Inside, this large dining room is very light, with bronze furniture, white curtains and pale seasonal arrangements of flowers. Despite adhering to traditional French cooking, there are always interesting nuances and new ingredients to look out for. Home-made ravioli are filled with artichokes and pine nuts, brook char (salmon-trout) fillets are topped with morels and a Swiss white wine and walnut sauce and grilled fillets of sole come with a rich white butter and fennel seed sauce. Fresh peaches served with a vanilla almond parfait are an excellent way to end this feast. The wine list is sizeable, but still tends to concentrate on Swiss and French wines. *Seats 80. Open 1200-1430, 1900-2230.*

Meal prices for 2 are based on à la carte menus. When set menus are available, prices will often be lower.

ZÜRICH   Eden au Lac   FR570

Tel: (1) 261 94 04   Fax: (1) 261 94 09

HR

Utoquai 45, 8023 Zürich

The neo-classical facade of this lakeside hotel, 20 minutes drive from the airport, looks splendid when floodlit at night. Inside it is decorated in a plush and chintzy Regency style although the comfortable, air-conditioned bedrooms are more modern in design. There are fine views of the city, the lake and the mountains from the roof gardens. *Rooms 56.* *Room service limited. Private parking. Banqueting facilities 80. Conference facilities 30.* *Secretarial/translation services on request. Garden. Sauna. Amex, Diners, Mastercard,* *Visa.*

Restaurant   FR200

Although the smart restaurant with its chandeliers and oil paintings looks the epitome of tradition, the Swiss chef is by no means old-fashioned, so you might find a fine chicken madras alongside more conservative French dishes like roasted saddle of lamb. Other mains include roast duckling breast with mixed mushrooms, noodles with basil and a tomato filled with vegetables, and roast sea bass with a lime butter sauce and creole-style rice. Short but varied wine list. Set menus Fr 50 to Fr 60 (lunch) and Fr62 to Fr 100 (dinner). *Seats 50.* *Open 1200-2300.*

ZÜRICH   Hotel Europe   FR350

Tel: (1) 261 10 30   Fax: (1) 251 03 67

H

Dufourstrasse 4, 8008 Zürich

Close to the Bahnhofstrasse and the lake, this relaxed hotel is also not far from the Schauspielhaus so actors and opera singers are among the regular clientele. Decor is an eclectic mix of styles and colours with the individually-decorated bedrooms featuring heavy curtains and patterned carpets and wallpapers. *Rooms 40. Room service limited.* *Public parking Fr22. Amex, Diners, Mastercard, Visa.*

ZÜRICH   Wirtschaft Flühgass   FR165

Tel: (1) 381 12 15   Fax: (1) 422 75 33

R

Zollikerstrasse 114, 8001 Zürich

A picture-postcard 16th-century Swiss chalet with wonderful window boxes outside and traditional carved furniture within, situated a mere seven-minute drive from the centre of Zürich. Owner-chef Robert Haupt's cooking combines French and Swiss ideas to produce dishes such as veal steak with a calvados cream sauce and home-made noodles. A typical meal might start with rösti and smoked salmon, continue with rack of lamb with a parsley mousseline and truffle jus, and finish with a crisp pastry case (croustillant) filled with strawberries and raspberries. Set menus Fr51 (lunch) and Fr 96 (dinner). *Seats 50.* *Open 1130-1400, 1830-2130. Closed Sat & Sun, mid Jul-mid Aug. Private parking. Amex,* *Mastercard, Visa.*

ZÜRICH   Zunfthaus zur Schmiden   FR120

Tel: (1) 251 52 87   Fax: (1) 261 12 67

R

Marktgasse 20, 8001 Zürich

The magnificent 14th-century Blacksmiths' Guildhouse is the location of this excellent restaurant, although you will have to be attend a banquet to enjoy the hand-carved wood and panelled ceiling of the 16th-century dining hall. Wolfgang Kretschmer has been cooking here for 30 years and the wood-panelled restaurant is a fine setting for his Franco-Swiss dishes. Local specialities such as *Zürcher Leberspiessli auf grünen Bohnen* (calf's liver cooked on a skewer with green beans) and Obersee-Zanderfilets an Krebssauce (fillets of pike-perch from Lake Zürich with crayfish sauce) are well worth trying. No set menus. *Seats 70. Open 1130-1400, 1800-2200. Closed mid Jul-mid Aug. Amex, Diners,* *Mastercard, Visa.*

Opening times are often liable to change at short notice, so it's always best to book.

Around Zürich

GATTIKON   Sihlhalde   ★   FR150

Tel: (1) 720 09 27   Fax: (1) 720 09 25
Sihlhaldenstrasse 70, 8136 Gattikon

A 200-year-old farmhouse in a village 3km from Zürich is the setting for this fine restaurant, where the Smollensky family are justifiably proud of the French and Swiss food they prepare from the freshest ingredients. Typical starters are caramelised scallops (Jacobsmuscheln) with endives, and ravioli stuffed with black truffles. Mains include North Sea cod with scampi in a vermouth sauce and fillet of pork in a lemon sauce, while desserts are simple but delicious: rhubard strudel with a vanilla sauce is a fine example. *Seats 45 (terrace 45). Open 1100-1315, 1800-2130. Closed Sun & Mon, last week Jul-mid Aug. Private parking. Mastercard, Visa.*

KÜSNACHT   Restaurant Kunststuben   ★+   FR250

Tel: (1) 910 07 15   Fax: (1) 910 04 95
Seestrasse 160, 8700 Küsnacht

A pretty, flower-filled dining-room in a lakeside setting is a pleasant spot to sample Horst Petermann's imaginative market-based cooking. The short carte lists dishes such as roast langoustine tails with tarragon-scented asparagus and tartare of sea bass (loup de mer) in an aniseed cream sauce. His specialities include terrine of foie gras with oxtail and St Pierre piqué au lard fumé et laurier (John Dory larded with smoked bacon and laurel), and desserts such as a warm biscuit with bitter chocolate and raspberries. The cellar contains a good range of Swiss wines including the Merlot Sassi Grossi from Ticino, an Italian-speaking region of south Switzerland. Set menus Fr125, Fr160 and Fr185. *Seats 50 (terrace 20). Open 1200-1400, 1900-2200. Closed Sun, Mon, 2 weeks in Feb, 20 Aug-11 Sep. Private parking. Amex, Diners, Mastercard, Visa.*

UNTERENGSTRINGEN   Witschi's   ★   FR450

Tel: (1) 750 44 60   Fax: (1) 750 19 68
Zürcherstrasse 55, 8103 Unterengstringen

There is a Mediterranean feel to the decor and the food at Heinz Witschi's popular restaurant in a quiet residential suburb of Zürich. The clay-tiled floor, white walls hung with original works by Swiss artists and plenty of plants make a relaxing setting for enjoying starters such as lasagne of spring vegetables with foie gras and veal sweetbreads and pigeon with spring salad leaves and new potatoes. Superb main dishes include roast sea bream with a fondue of leeks and spring onions, and Challans duck with a sweet and sour cherry sauce and ginger. A simple dessert of seasonal fruits and sorbets is a refreshing way to end a meal. The mainly French wine list includes a *'trésors du patron'* section listing some fine Bordeaux and burgundies. Set menus from Fr69 to Fr190. *Seats 40 (terrace 30). Open 1100-1400, 1800-2200. Closed Sun, Mon, 1st week Jan, 2 weeks mid Jul, 2 weeks at Christmas. Private parking. Amex, Diners, Mastercard, Visa.*

Elsewhere in Switzerland

CRISSIER   Girardet   ★+   FR550

Tel: (21) 634 05 05
1 rue d'Yverdon, 1023 Crissier

Fredy Girardet is a culinary legend and his restaurant at the old Town Hall and Post Office in Crissier, near Lausanne, is widely considered to be one of the best in the world, let alone Switzerland. Girardet is the author of the book Cuisine Spontanée which encapsulates his aim of creating spur-of-the-moment dishes around the pick of the market. Monsieur Rochat, who has been here for 15 years under Girardet's tutelage, now does the bulk of the cooking and the all-time specialities remain: *saumon sauvage juste tiède à l'émulsion de fenouil et à l'huile de Maussane* (warm wild salmon coated with fennel and Maussane olive oil), *canard nantais cuit rose au vin de Brouilly* (duck cooked pink with red beaujolais) and *mignonnettes de rable de lapereau aux pistaches et fleurs de thym* (fillets of saddle of rabbit with pistachios and thyme flowers). The desserts are also exquisite: try the original *peche pochée au craquelin d'amandes, coulis de bigarreaux et crème de cannelle* (poached peach with almond cracknel, a coulis of cherries and cinnamon cream). Two set menus: Fr180 and Fr195. There is an excellent cellar featuring French and Swiss wines. *Seats 60. Open 1200-1315, 1900-2030. Closed Sun, Mon, first 3 weeks Aug, 23 Dec-12 Jan. Air-conditioning. No credit cards.*

Tel: (21) 802 21 91 Fax: (21) 802 22 40
CH-1134 Vufflens-le-Château

Bernard and Ruth Ravet opened this country retreat six years ago. Situated just outside the village of Vufflens-le-Chateau with its vineyards and rolling farmland, the grounds are spacious, with gardens and a lake and Lausanne is only fifteen minutes away by car. The house itself has two wings: one contains the rooms and suites while the other is dedicated to the kitchen and restaurant. Although he has uprooted himself from his native Burgundy, Bernard Ravet's cooking remains true to his origins. His imaginative French menu is fresh and seasonal-guests can marvel at the raw ingredients in his magnificent kitchen gardens. In his two old kitchens, which he has recently modernised, he also has a bakehouse where fresh bread is baked every day. His house speciality is fresh foie gras smoked along with meat and fish in their old-fashioned smokehouse: try the *dinette des quatre foies gras* selection of four different foies gras. The *omble chevalier de la cote vaudoise* (a delicate lake fish, similar to trout) and the *canette de Challens roti à la broche* (duckling roasted on a spit and served with a hint of grapefruit and gentian from Jura) are perennial favourites. The old stone wine cellar has over 30,000 bottles from all over the world and notably some rare local wines from the coteaux vaudois. *Seats 60. Open 1200-1330, 1900-2130. Closed Sun, Mon, first 3 weeks Aug, 23 Dec-10 Jan. Private parking. Diners, Mastercard, Visa.*

The rooms are really a resting place for satiated gourmets and are therefore for the exclusive use of diners. The six rooms and three suites in the petite maison des peintres (where various artists have their studios) have each taken on a character of their own. The beamed rooms are simply furnished in a homely style. ***Rooms** 9. Room service limited. Banqueting facilities 60. Conference facilities 15.*

THE INDEPENDENT

INDEPENDENT
ON SUNDAY

Your truly
independent
guides to life

Ukraine

Currency Ukrainian Karbovanets** **Exchange Rate** **Not obtainable
in UK. Travellers cheques/US dollars/DM recommended.
International dialing code 00 380 (Kiev+44)
Passports/Visas Visa required by British passport holders.
(Ukranian Embassy in London, 78 Kensington Park Road W11 2PL Tel
0171-727 6312)
British Embassy in Kiev Tel 44-228 0504

TRANSPORT
Airports
Kiev-Borispol (International) Tel 44-295 6701
Kiev-Zhulyany (Domestic) Tel 44-272 1201
Railway Stations
Kiev Vokzalmaya Ploscha Tel 44-223 3306
Car hire enquire at airport
Speed limits 90 km/h outside cities, 60 km/h in built-up areas.

OPENING HOURS
Banks Hours vary, but banks are generally open between 10am & 6pm.
Exchange bureaux may stay open later.
Shops Shop hours vary, but are generally open between 9am & 6pm
(some later) and many close for lunch.

NATIONAL HOLIDAYS
New Year's Day, 7 Jan, 8 Mar, Orthodox Easter, 1, 2 & 9 May, Holy
Trinity Day, 24 Aug, New Year's Eve

Tourist Offices
Ukranian Embassy in **London** (see above)
In **Kiev** Intourist Kiev Tel 44-225 3243
(further information available from **Intourist London** Tel 0171-538
8600/538 5965)
American Express Travel Service Offices or Representative (R)
None in the Ukraine

Kiev

Tel: (044) 229 86 29   Fax: (044) 229 86 29   **R**
Baresha Grechenko 7, Kiev

This restaurant, near one of the city's main squares, is a private co-operative. Its unexceptional facade belies a smart interior, with polished parquet flooring, crystal chandeliers and fine paintings. Regional dishes are the specialities of its Ukrainian chef: black or red caviar with butter, jellied sturgeon, Ukrainian borsch and chicken soup with noodles are among a plentiful choice of starters. Main courses include fish in batter, pork stewed with prunes, stuffed rissoles and Kiev-style chicken. There are simple desserts to finish. Only Ukrainian and Russian wines are available. *Seats 50. Open 1100-0000. No credit cards.*

Tel: (044) 220 42 55   Fax: (044) 220 43 96   **H**
Ulitsa Gospitalnaya 4, Kiev

The hotel is currently undergoing a major refurbishment which includes increasing the size of some of the bedrooms. A few rooms overlook the sports stadium where the 1980 Olympic Games were held. The de luxe rooms have a stocked mini-bar as well as a hairdryer and trouser press; the rest are more modestly equipped, with just a fridge but all have satellite television. Residents have use of the sports and recreational facilities at the Kievskaya Hotel, sister hotel to the Rus located at Gospitalnaya 12. These include an indoor swimming pool, sauna and massage. The hotel has a separate Congress Hall for large conferences. *Rooms 480. Room service 24hr. Garden. Conference facilities for 465. Amex, Diners, Mastercard, Visa.*

Currency Pound Sterling
Dialling code from overseas: 44
(prefix number differs according to country from which call is being made).
British Consulate in Vienna Tel 1-713 1575 Fax 1-712 7316

Airports
England London – Heathrow: Tel 0181-759 4321. Gatwick: 01293 535353 Stansted: 01279 680500 City: 0171 474 555.
East Midlands Tel 0121 767 5511.
N Ireland Belfast International 01849 422888
Wales Cardiff-Wales International: 01446 711111
Scotland Glasgow International: 0141 887 1111
Edinburgh International 0131 333 1000
Railway Stations (General Rail enquiries for UK)
England London Tel 0171-278 2477 (for King's Cross); 262 6767 (Paddington); 387 7070 (Euston, St Pancras, Marylebone & Kins Cross Thameslink); 928 5100 (for all other London terminals
N Ireland Belfast 01232 899411
Scotland Glasgow 0141 204 2844; Edinburgh 0131 556 2451
Wales Cardiff 01222 228000
Car hire
Tel Nos. **Avis** 0181-848 8733 **Hertz** 0181-679 1799 **Budget** 0800 181181 **Europcar** 01345 222525
Speed limits: 70mph on motorways,60mph on dual carriageways, 50mph on other main roads, 30 mph in built-up areas (unless otherwise indicated). Local speed limits.

Banks Standard hours 9.30-3.30pm Mon-Fri. Individual banks and branches may stay open later and some main branches are also open on Saturdays. Some banks in Scotland may stay open later on Thursdays (to 5/5.30pm, closing 12.30-2.30pm).
Shops 8am-6.30pm weekdays, 8am-1pm Sat, 8am-5pm first Sat every month. Many shops closed 2hrs midday.

New Year's Day, Good Friday, Easter Monday, 6 & 27 May, 26 Aug, Christmas Day & Boxing Day (some holidays in Scotland and N Ireland vary).

British Tourist Association & Tourist Board Tel 0181-846 9000
American Express Travel Service Offices or Representative (R)
London 6 Haymarket
          SW1Y 4BS
          Tel 0171-930 4411
          or 78 Brompton Road
          Knightsbridge
          SW3 1ER
          Tel 0171 584 6182 or 225 0055

Tel 01224 867355   Fax 01224 861283
South Deeside Road Blairs Grampian AB1 5YP

A few minutes' drive from the centre of Aberdeen, Ardoe House enjoys a secluded setting at the end of a winding drive. Its style is Scottish Baronial, and day rooms retain all their best original features, with carved oak panelling and handsome ceiling work. The drawing-room and cocktail bar are warm and inviting, and there's a choice of rooms available for conferences and banquets (for up to 300/200). Bedrooms are comfortable and well appointed, whether in the main building (some reached by a fine oak staircase past a stained-glass window) or in the sympathetically designed modern section, where the majority are located. Children stay free in parents' room. *Rooms 71. Garden. Croquet. Putting. Amex, Diners, Mastercard, Visa.*

Tel 01224 861000   Fax 01224 868860
North Deeside Road Pitfodels Aberdeen Grampian AB1 9PA

Aberdeen's latest and best hotel is set in six acres of landscaped grounds on the western outskirts of the city, newly built, but in traditional style, by experienced local hoteliers Stewart and Sheila Spence. Day rooms like the rug-strewn, flagstoned lobby and richly furnished lounge with its red walls, real fire and scattering of antiques, demonstrate Sheila's flair for interior design. Bedroom decor is particularly striking with innovative combinations of floral patterns, checks and colourful Mediterranean prints used to great effect. Well-designed and spacious, with quality furniture – antiques in the Master bedrooms that boast such extras as video machines and decanters of sherry – and comfortable armchairs, all rooms have desk as well as bedside phones, mini-bars with fresh milk for the discreetly hidden beverage kit (there's also 24hr room service) and trouser press incorporating iron and ironing board. Good bathrooms feature a third tap at the washbasin dispensing specially purified drinking water. Immaculate staff, kitted-out in the hotel's own tartan, are numerous and attentive, providing a high level of service. Good breakfasts include 'Aberdeen Rowies', a local speciality a bit like a flat croissant. Banqueting/conferences for up to 400/600. *Rooms 42. Garden. Croquet. Putting. Fishing. Games room. Snooker. Amex, Diners, Mastercard, Visa.*

A choice of eating here: the smart yet informal, split-level (divided by a stone balustrade) Conservatory with terrace offering a short but varied à la carte – fillet of lamb with a garden herb crust, medallions of monkfish with a wild mushroom mousse, chargrilled steaks – and the opulent, formal, dinner-only Invery Room. The latter, sporting a handsome antique sideboard, offers a fixed-price, four-course menu that shares some dishes with the Conservatory plus the likes of cream of curried parsnip soup with chicken and herb dumplings, ravioli of lamb's sweetbreads, salmon escalope on a bed of leeks with a tomato béarnaise and roast fillet of venison on a port and rowanberry sauce. Cooking generally is uncomplicated but not unsophisticated; and the raw materials are first-rate. Price quoted is for the no-smoking Invery Room. Good value house wines, imaginative New World section, France less so.
Invery Room: Seats 32. Parties 12. Private Room 24. Open D only 1900-2200. Closed Sun & Mon. Conservatory: Seats 74. Open 1200-1430, 1830-2200.

Tel 01224 576229
Pocra Quay North Pier Aberdeen Grampian AB2 1DQ

A French speciality 'barbecued seafood' restaurant overlooking the city and old port from the farthest point of the North Quay. Most of the fish is prepared in full view of diners through a large kitchen window, cooked on the barbecue and served with fennel, tomatoes and a herb butter sauce. Besides this there's a wide choice, from a soup of monkfish, mussels and smoked haddock flavoured with sorrel and a warm salad of scallops and Dublin Bay prawns with blueberry vinegar to sole, halibut and prawns poached on a bed of seaweed and fish stock finished with cream and saffron. Just three half bottles on the concise French-only wine list that includes extensive tasting notes. Set L £16.50. *Seats 35. Open 1200-1345, 1900-2145. Closed L Sat, all Sun & 2 weeks Christmas. Amex, Diners, Mastercard, Visa.*

Tel 01232 331532   Fax 01232 312093
Lesley House Shaftesbury Square Belfast Co Antrim BT2 7DB

Still the Belfast restaurant in which to see and be seen, with sunny yellow walls and the recent removal of a room divider (originally intended to make a more private dining area – but it seems that nobody wanted to be behind it) opening up its modern interior. Given the cachet of a well-known chef (Paul and Jeanne Rankin have a TV series and several books to their credit), slick service and quality cooking, the £21.50 fixed-price menu (three courses, coffee and petits fours) offers excellent value for money. With seven choices at each stage, the modern, weekly-changing menu offers something to suit most tastes: from the straightforward and familiar like warm salad of duck confit, sliced potatoes and green beans, rack of lamb with garlic and parsley crust, fillet of beef with leeks, shallots and red wine, dark chocolate truffle cake and tarte tatin to more adventurous options such as tagliatelle with sweetbreads, pancetta and fresh rosemary, roast haunch of venison with salsify and wild mushrooms, peppered monkfish with soy glaze and fresh coriander cream, and coconut crème brulée with fresh mango purée. As an alternative to the puds there's a good British/Irish cheese trolley. A bowl of olives and a selection of good home-baked breads give you something to nibble while looking at the menu. The shorter lunch menu is in similar style. New World wines are well represented on an interesting list that also offers half a dozen or so wines by the glass. Set L £14.50 Set D £21.50. *Seats 70. Open 1215-1415, 1830-2230. Closed L Sat, all Sun, 11 & 13 July, 25 & 26 Dec, 1 Jan. Amex, Diners, Mastercard, Visa.*

Tel 01232 658621   Fax 01232 480240
587 Upper Newtownards Road Stormont Belfast Co Antrim BT4 3LP

Way out of town on the Newtownards Road, opposite Stormont Castle, this modern hotel is always busy and bustling, having various function rooms in addition to the Confex Centre with its 10 purpose-built trade and exhibition rooms. Public areas centre around a sunken lounge (sometimes used as a conference 'break-out' area) off which is a cosy cocktail bar. A mezzanine lounge has huge glass windows overlooking the castle grounds. The majority of bedrooms have been completely refurbished in recent times and are spacious, comfortable and practical with good, well-lit work space and modern easy chairs. Good bathrooms feature marble tiling. All rooms are well equipped, with satellite TV etc. Smart, helpful staff offer attentive lounge service and there's a 24hr room-service menu. Good breakfasts are served in the informal all-day brasserie. *Rooms 106. Amex, Diners, Mastercard, Visa.*

Tel 0121-622 5669   Fax 0121-622 5860
16 Wrottesley Street Birmingham West Midlands B5 4RT

The Chinese flock to this well-established, traditionally appointed restaurant for its long Cantonese menu. The choice extends to well over 300 dishes, including more than 40 dim sum items and a 'special dishes' section with stuffed peppers, crabmeat on straw mushrooms, frog's legs and venison among the choice. Also of note are the casseroles and the Sunday lunchtime hot pots from which you help yourself. *Seats 220. Meals 1200-2330 (Sun to 2300). Closed 25 Dec. Amex, Diners, Mastercard, Visa.*

Tel 0121-643 1234   Fax 0121-616 2323
2 Bridge Street Birmingham West Midlands B1 2JZ

A canalside setting in the heart of Birmingham for the impressive, mirrored 25-storey Hyatt Regency, which has a direct link to the International Convention Centre next door. Inside, the huge glazed atrium is the epitome of style and elegance, bedecked with plants, and awash with marble. The luxuriously appointed bedrooms include 12 suites; all have quality modern furniture and fashionably uncluttered decor, plus equally splendid, marble-floored bathrooms. Three rooms are adpated for the disabled, one floor of 17 rooms is reserved for non-smokers and three floors make up the Regency Club of superior rooms; the latter has its own Club Lounge on the 22nd floor. Floor-to-ceiling windows afford fine views over the Second City. Excellent leisure facilities. Conference and banqueting facilities for up to 240. Children up to 16 stay free in parents' room. Parking £7 for 24 hours. *Rooms 319. Garden. Indoor swimming pool, Gym. Sauna. Solarium. Steam room. Spa bath. Business centre. Café (0630-2330). Amex, Diners, Mastercard, Visa.*

See over

Number 282   £80

Tagged as a Brasserie on Broad Street, though 'broadsheet' might be even more appropriate with the day's news headlines, weather, entertainment and even a personalised message on the paper place mat. The menu itself (on the same sheet) ranges from French onion soup, roasted monkfish tail wrapped in bacon and savoy cabbage with red wine sauce and a seafood medley to poached egg with bubble and squeak, and black pudding with mashed potato. Familiar puds like sherry trifle, bread-and-butter pudding and tarte tatin. Plenty of New World as well as European wines. Other eating venues include the all-day Court café and the Atrium itself. Set L £12.75 Set D £15. *Seats 75. Parties 16. Open 1230-1430, 1830-2300. Closed L Sat, all Sun.*

BIRMINGHAM   Swallow Hotel   £145

Tel 0121-452 1144   Fax 0121-456 3442   HR
12 Hagley Road Five Ways Birmingham West Midlands B16 8SJ

An imposing Edwardian building, strikingly transformed into a quality luxury hotel. The foyer features sparkling Italian marble floors, rich mahogany woodwork and crystal chandeliers; there is a refined drawing room elegantly decorated with oil paintings, a quiet, dignified library and a handsome bar with colourful floral displays throughout. The air-conditioned bedrooms are stylish, well-proportioned and comfortable; one room is well equipped for disabled guests. Beautiful fabrics are complemented by fine inlaid furniture and bathrooms are impressive, with marble tiling and a host of extras. An interestingly designed leisure club is based around an Egyptian theme. Attentive, professional staff. Parking for 70 cars. *Rooms 98. Indoor swimming pool. Gym. Spa bath. Steam room. Solarium. Hair & beauty salon. Amex, Diners, Mastercard, Visa.*

Sir Edward Elgar Restaurant   £100

High-class service fits comfortably into the luxurious surroundings – murals and fine fabrics covering the walls, pianist/singer six nights a week – of this split-level, Edwardian-themed restaurant. Luxury is not hard to find on the menu, either, with the likes of caviar blinis accompanying smoked salmon, foie gras and bean casserole under roast squab, more foie gras in the apple terrine, and truffles both in the spaghetti of vegetables starter and larded into a rib of beef. From the fixed-price menus Toulouse sausage and vegetable broth, warm scallop salad with leek and balsamic dressing, casserole of veal with winter vegetables and chump of lamb on a garlic and potato purée are typical. In addition to the à la carte and table d'hote menus there is a special £25 post-theatre supper served until 2245 by prior arrangement only. No smoking. Perfunctory tasting notes alongside each wine on a so-so list. Langtry's list is slightly shorter. Set L £17.50 (Sun £20.50) Set D £25 (not Sat)/£30.L 12.30-2.30 D 7.30-10.30 (Sun till 10). *Seats 60. Open 1230-1430, 1930-2230 (Sun till 2200). Parties 10. Private Room 20. Closed L Sat.*

Langtry's   £60

British cookery to traditional recipes produces daily lunchtime dishes from around the country: Lancashire hot pot on Wednesday, boiled ham with parsley sauce on Thursday and east-coast beer-battered cod and chips on Friday. Popular à la carte favourites include oxtail soup, English duck with cranberry and mint sauce, home-made fruit cake with Lancashire cheese and steamed treacle pudding. Outdoor seating for 16 in summer. *Seats 60. Parties 14. Open 1130-1500, 1830-2200. Closed Sun, Bank Holidays & 1 week Christmas.*

BRISTOL   Bristol Marriott   £105

Tel 0117 929 4281   Fax 0117 922 5838   H
2 Lower Castle Street Bristol Avon BS1 3AD

Overlooking the castle ruins, the hotel stands in the city centre and although a tall and distinctive building it is best to ask for directions when booking. The lobby, with polished stone floors and exotic plant-filled Ali Baba jars, is spacious and welcoming. The remainder of the public rooms are smartly furnished and inviting too. Bedrooms are up to date and comfortable; all have double beds, even in twin rooms. They are equipped with satellite TV, full air-conditioning and a host of useful extras including 24hr room service. The majority are designated as non-smoking rooms and top of the range Executive rooms have their own dedicated lounge. Three bedrooms are suitable for disabled guests. The hotel offers an excellent range of leisure facilities and it's definitely child-friendly. The Conference venue caters for up to 600 theatre-style. Free parking in an adjacent multi-storey car park. Half-price weekend tariff. *Rooms 289. Indoor swimming pool, Gym. Sauna. Spa bath. Steam room. Solarium. Beauty salon. Children's playroom. Games room. News kiosk. Coffee shop 0700-2300. Amex, Diners, Mastercard, Visa.*

Tel 0117 927 5034   Fax 0117 927 5003
12 Denmark Street Bristol Avon BS1 5DQ

The ancient cellars of Harveys Wine Merchants are home to a comfortable, air-conditioned restaurant featuring the accomplished cooking of chef-manager Ramon Farthing, who brings a contemporary touch to classic skills. Specialities include chicken and black olive sausage; sauté of fresh langoustines with sugar snap peas, truffle and radishes finished with a light hazelnut cream; breast of wood pigeon on a potato and bacon rösti with foie gras, sweet shallots and a game sauce finished with grenadine. Among the sweets look out for their special apple dessert and the hot soufflé, but also cast an eye on the magnificent British cheeseboard. The name Harveys is of course synonymous with sherry and port, but the rest of the wine list here ain't half bad! In fact, it's exceptional and fairly priced, bearing in mind that prices include service. Clarets really excel, but the entire list is thoroughly comprehensive with many wines from the New World too. Adjoining the restaurant is a fascinating wine museum. Set L £16 Set D £29 & £38. *Seats 120. Parties 14. Private Room 50. Open 1200-1345, 1900-2230. Closed L Sat, all Sun, Bank Holidays, 4 days Christmas & 2 days New Year. . Amex, Diners, Mastercard, Visa.*

Tel 0117 968 6456   Fax 0117 968 6943
9 Druid Hill Stoke Bishop Bristol Avon BS9 1EW

Martin Blunos combines natural talent with true dedication to produce the kind of dishes that makes the effort of finding this small restaurant (just seven tables) in suburban Bristol well worthwhile. The house is in a shopping arcade, and the surroundings do not immediately give a hint of the thought, skill and enterprise that go in to the cooking. Everything on the menus bears the Blunos stamp of individuality, like his starters of pan-fried scallops on parsnip purée, finished with chicken juices, duck and calvados terrine with toasted brioche or glazed pheasant with foie gras and sauerkraut. Main dishes show the same confidence with flavour combinations as in baked brill fillet with a caviar butter sauce, roast calf's sweetbreads with smoked bacon and a Noilly Prat cream sauce, rump of lamb with garlic fritters and a thyme leaf sauce or pig's trotter with a port sauce. As well as the cheeseboard there's goat's cheese tortellini with a lemon butter sauce and desserts such as chocolate marquise with a bitter orange sorbet and orange cream sauce or a vanilla and poppyseed parfait with macerated blueberries. The set menus offer two or three choices per course. Most wines on the modest list are French; practically all the classic clarets can only be found among the bin ends. Set L £17.95 Set D £23.50 (Tue-Thurs) & £39.50. *Seats 24. Open 1230-1400, 1900-2100. Closed Sun & Mon, 2 weeks Aug, 2 weeks Christmas. Amex, Mastercard, Visa.*

Tel 0117 925 5100   Fax 0117 925 1515
College Green Bristol Avon BS1 5TA

A Victorian hotel in one of the most favourable locations in Bristol next to the cathedral and overlooking the neat lawns of College Green. The original Victorian grandeur has been enhanced by a decor with firmly traditional leanings but which also has an elegantly fashionable touch. The polished red marble-floored foyer has beautiful lounges on each side furnished in a comfortable country house style with deep-cushioned settees arranged in well-spaced groups. Light refreshments and afternoon teas are served here. The cocktail bar features huge Oriental murals at either end and a bar with gleaming glass and silverware. All the bedrooms, apart from a few smaller, inward-facing rooms, are spacious, with two armchairs and a writing desk. Every room has a whole host of extras from mini-bars with complimentary mineral water and fresh milk to irons and ironing boards for those who must press to impress. Coloured marble bathrooms have super-strong showers and most have bidets though a few, where space is more limited, have large corner baths instead. There are ten small suites with cosy sitting rooms and spa baths in their bathrooms. *Rooms 242. Indoor swimming pool. Sauna. Sun bed, Spa bath. Beauty & hair salons. Keep-fit equipment. News kiosk. Amex, Diners, Mastercard, Visa.*

The grand Palm Court extends up through three floors lined in Bath stone with curved balustrades and topped by stained-glass skylights. The à la carte is modern in style, taking inspiration from numerous sources: seared langoustines and scallops on a carrot and soy dressing with sesame mangetout, osso buco of monkfish(!) with squid noodles and orange oil, and loin of venison with chive creamed potatoes and baby leeks. The day's 'concept'

See over

menu (priced for two, three or four courses) offers a choice only at the main dish stage and is designed to be a balanced meal showing off the creativity of the kitchen. Service is formal yet unfussy. Set D £21/£24/£27. *Seats 60. Parties 8. Open D only 1930-2230. Closed Sun & National Holidays.*

CARDIFF   **Copthorne Hotel**   £122

Tel 01222 599100   Fax 01222 599080
Culverhouse Cross Cardiff South Glamorgan CF5 6XJ

H

Leave the M4 at junction 33 to reach this very modern five-storey hotel near the HTV studios. Lots of wood panelling and rich autumnal colour schemes predominate in appealing public areas, some of which overlook the hotel's own small lake. All the good-sized bedrooms are well laid out, with large desks (to which the phone is easily movable) and comfortable armchairs in addition to breakfast table and proper armchair. Good bathrooms feature polished red-granite vanitory units. Rooms on the Connoisseur Floor get extras like bathrobes and slippers plus use of an Executive lounge with free soft drinks and Continental breakfast. Two rooms are equipped for disabled guests. Children up to 15 stay free in parents' room. Banqueting/conference facilities for 200/300; parking for 225 cars. *Rooms 135. Indoor swimming pool. Gym. Sauna. Spa bath. Steam room. Hairdresser. Amex, Diners, Mastercard, Visa.*

CARDIFF   **Le Monde**   £40

Tel 01222 387376
60 St Mary Street Cardiff South Glamorgan

R

One of a trio of dark, intimate restaurants-cum-wine bars, this one appeals primarily to fish-eaters with a wide array of shell, sea and freshwater fish. Its siblings are *La Brasserie* (01222 372164) specialising in grilled meats and seasonal game and offering a £5 set lunch, and *Champers* (01222 373363) with a Spanish slant to both decor, menu and wine list – over 100 Riojas! *Champers* is also open Sunday evening to 0015 and seats 150. *Seats 180. Open 1200-1430 D 1900-0015. Closed Sun, 25 & 26 Dec. Amex, Diners, Mastercard, Visa.*

CARDIFF   **Park Hotel**   £116

Tel 01222 383471   Fax 01222 399309
Park Place Cardiff South Glamorgan CF1 3UD

H

The Park's impressive stone-clad facade is a striking landmark on Cardiff's pedestrianised Queen Street and today's lack of traffic is a bonus for those occupying the best, front-facing bedrooms. All the bedrooms – singles, twins/doubles and top-of-the-range studios – have been refurbished, and attention has now turned to the public rooms, notably the reception area, the main restaurant (to be enlarged) and a new public bar. The lounge and residents' bar keep their traditional atmosphere. There are several conference and function suites, the largest accommodating 250. Thistle & Mount Charlotte. *Rooms 119. Amex, Diners, Mastercard, Visa.*

EDINBURGH   **Atrium**   £60

Tel 0131-228 8882
Cambridge Street Edinburgh Lothian EH1 2ED

R

Within the atrium of Saltire Court – a smart new office building next to the Usher Hall in Edinburgh's Theatre district – the restaurant's post-modern decor is quite stunning with railway sleeper tables, raw linen-draped chairs and glass torches based on an ancient glass drinking horn, set in wrought-iron sconces imparting an almost medieval atmosphere. Andrew Radford's short but truly eclectic twice-daily-changing menus utilise the best of Scottish produce to create dishes that ably demonstrate his culinary knowledge and skills. A typical winter's dinner could provide starters like a samosa of squat lobster and scallops, salmon fishcake with greens or wood pigeon with champ, Parma ham and lentils. To follow: monkfish tails with spring onion, coriander and leeks; Scottish beef, savoy cabbage with mushrooms and bacon; wild duck with roast roots and juniper or mackerel fillet with grilled endive, salsa and olive oil. Finish in great style with delectables like white truffle cake with a toffee sauce and praline, strawberry tart or poached pear with sablé and crème fraiche. There is also a short snack menu at lunchtime and for pre-theatre diners between 6-7pm. The wine list is imaginative, fairly priced and with some tasting notes, though seemingly there's no order to it at all! *Seats 70. Open 1200-1430 D 1800-2230. Closed L Sat, all Sun, 10 days Christmas. Amex, Diners, Mastercard, Visa.*

Tel 0131-556 2414   Fax 0131-557 3747
Princes Street Edinburgh Lothian EH2 2EQ

At the top of Forte's tree in Scotland, the Balmoral wears its total refurbishment from the early '90s very comfortably indeed. Opulence, comfort, courtesy, elegance are the watchwords here – definitely a place in which to be cosseted, and nothing is too much trouble for the very professional staff. Bedrooms (with marble bathrooms) and suites are excellently equipped and maintained, modern conveniences blending discreetly with traditional furnishings. We quote a standard price: there are superior, de luxe and suites above that. Public areas are of a similarly high standard, encompassing the Palm Court Lounge, coffee shop, bars, brasserie and the main restaurant, so that any style of refreshment can be provided. Room service is available around the clock. There are ten function suites, the largest holding 400. *Rooms 189. Gym. Sauna. Steam room. Sunbeds, Beauty & hair salon. Cashmere & crystal shop. Amex, Diners, Mastercard, Visa.*

Very much the grand hotel dining-room, where discretion and attention to detail (both in decor and in food presentation) are impeccable. On the à la carte menu the prices are written out as words not figures (slightly prolonging the shock), although the better value set lunch menus are expressed in a more straightforward manner. Many dishes are indicated with a thistle device as being a "Taste of Scotland". Try perhaps terrine of wild Crathie pigeon marbled with pistachio and oak-smoked peppers, galantine of quail served with yellow tomato chutney or grilled Oban scallops served with a broad bean salad and crispy bacon, then for main course saddle of rabbit with a farce of Scottish lamb with Lanark Blue cheese sauce and young vegetables. An extensive range of excellent quality fish and meat can be simply grilled, and with eight hours' notice two people can share pressed Rouennais duck, its preparation finished at table. The separate vegetarian menu is of similar style, and the lunch menus read more simply. Quite a comprehensive wine list, though prices are on the high side; best value is in the New World. Set L £17.50/£19.95 Set D £35. *Seats 45. Parties 8. Open 1200-1430 D 1900-2230. Closed L Sat & Sun..* 🐂

A brasserie in the Continental style, with an all-day menu of salads, snacks, appetisers (soup, fishcakes, paté) and main courses (fish and chips, pasta, charcoal grills). Also a wide selection of cakes and pastries, coffees and teas. Regular live music. The bar section is in traditional pub style. The hotel used to be called the North British, affectionately known as the NB, hence the name change from *Bridges*. Set L £8.50 Set D £20. *Seats 90. Parties 16. Open 0700-2300.*

Tel 0131-459 9988   Fax 0131-225 6632
Princes Street Edinburgh Lothian EH1 2AB

Built at the turn of the century by the Caledonian Railway Company, the 'Caley' is virtually a national monument. Traditional standards of hospitality and service have been maintained while moving with the times in terms of comfort and amenities. The carpeted foyer leads to the grand, elegantly proportioned lounge which is at the heart of the public areas; a popular place with both locals and visitors to Edinburgh to take afternoon tea seated on plush shot-silk sofas. Bedrooms, including 22 full suites, are individually styled, featuring traditional freestanding furniture and well-chosen fabrics. 43 Superior business bedrooms have large work stations, fax and computer points and a voicemail facility. De luxe rooms and those with a view of the Castle attract a supplement. Towelling robes are provided in all the bathrooms, some of which boast elegant antique-style fittings. Plus factors are the number of telephone extensions in each room, 24hr lounge service and an evening turn-down service. Families are particularly well catered for with children up to 16 staying free in parents' room. No dogs. Conference facilities for up to 300. Dedicated business centre. Free parking for 50 cars. *Rooms 236. Amex, Diners, Mastercard, Visa.*

Opened in 1925 and named after Louis XV's mistress, the Pompadour is elegant and formal; ornate plasterwork frames large wall-paintings of delicate flowers, a pianist plays soothing music and excellent staff provide impeccable service. Executive chef Tony Binks has been here since 1980 and, together with his young team, he continues to use the best of Scottish produce to good effect. The evening à la carte (also available on request at lunchtime) is sensibly short with dishes like Lanark Blue cheese mousse wrapped in cured ham and filled with creamed leeks finished with Sauternes sauce, fillet of young turbot layered with scampi mousseline in pastry, and medallions of wild fallow deer pan-fried and

See over

served with spiced curly kale and preserved cherry sauce supplemented by a list of 'classics': asparagus hollandaise, cognac-flavoured roulade of foie gras with toasted brioche, grilled Dover sole. There is also a no-choice, four-course Signature menu. The fixed-price lunch menu claims to represent the tradition and history of the national cuisine under the title 'Legends of the Scottish Table' but stretches credulity somewhat with dishes such as avocado and blood orange salad with ginger dressing, baked filo pastry of Parma ham, brie and basil with a cucumber and apple salad, and grilled lamb's liver with red pepper sauce and a courgette and onion chutney. A well-rounded wine list, though with no tasting notes. Set L £22.50 Set D £40. *Seats 60. Open 1230-1415, 1930-2215. Closed L Sat & Sun & D Sun in winter.* 🐂

Carriages Restaurant   £60

Retaining the redbrick former station entrance as an inside wall, Carriages is the hotel's informal eaterie, open for breakfast, lunch and dinner seven days a week. It offers a range of familiar, fairly straightforward dishes on à la carte and fixed-price menus: deep-fried mushrooms, mulligatawny soup, spaghetti bolognese, grills, mushroom and vegetable risotto, French apple tart, cheesecake. Scottish favourites include cock-a-leekie soup and haggis. Set L £14.75/£17.75 (Sun £16.25) Set D £24.50 & £28. *Seats 130. Open 1200-1430 1930-2200.*

EDINBURGH   Denzlers 121   £50
                                                                      R
Tel 0131-554 3268
121 Constitution Street Leith Edinburgh Lothian EH6 7AE

A Swiss/French reataurant located in externally forbidding former bank premises down amongst the bonded warehouses of Leith (5-minute taxi ride from the centre of Edinburgh); inside is bright and welcoming, while outside the parking is easy in the evening. Solidly traditional Swiss favourites like veal zurichoise, air-dried beef and ham (*bunderplattli*), cheese fondues (minimum 2 persons) and apfel strudel are favourites, along with fish soufflé in a smoked salmon 'chemise', duck with cherries and assiette Lucullus – a platter of sweets comprising profiteroles, meringue with ice cream and fruit tartlet. The set lunch offers very good value (soup, chipolatas with purée of peas, swordfish meunière, chicken pie) and includes a drink. Short, diverse wine list opens with three Swiss wines. *Seats 65. Parties 12. Open 1200-1400, 1830-2200. Closed L Sat, all Sun, Mon, 1st week Jan, 2 weeks end Jul, 2 days early Christmas. Amex, Diners, Mastercard, Visa.*

EDINBURGH   Malmaison Edinburgh   £90
Tel 0131-555 6868   Fax 0131-555 6999   HR
1 Tower Place Leith Edinburgh Lothian EH6 7BD

With tower and turrets, this imposing Scottish Baronial-style edifice was actually built in Victorian times as a seamen's mission in what is now the up-and-coming docks area of Leith across a dock basin from the new Scottish Office building. The first of Ken McCulloch's new Malmaison hotels to open (the second is in Glasgow qv), it offers spacious, stylish bedrooms, including six full suites, that feature high-tech music centres (for which CDs can be borrowed from reception) and two telephones among the amenities. What is not offered are things like luggage porterage or room service other than Continental breakfast with either tea or coffee. Start the day in the café, where cooked breakfasts are served. *Rooms 25. Amex, Diners, Mastercard, Visa.*

Brasserie   £60
Tel 0131-555 6969

On one side of the hotel entrance is the bar/café serving various sandwiches and baked potatoes at lunchtime, on the other this brasserie with an informal atmosphere and a menu of fairly standard dishes: eggs benedict, rocket and parmesan salad, seared salmon and hollandaise, steak frites, coq au vin. There are about ten main dishes in all, with puds like *pot au chocolat*, rice pudding with armagnac prunes and crème brûlée. In summer, food is served all day and tables spill out on to the cobbled quayside. Some 30 wines from around the world are on offer of which about a dozen (including two champagnes) are also available by the glass (large or small) and half-pint pot. Set L (Sat & Sun only) £7.50. *Seats 74. Open 1200-1430, 1800-2230 (meals all day in summer).*

Opening times are often liable to change at short notice, so it's
always best to book.

Tel 0131-225 6060   Fax 0131-225 8830
10 Randolph Place Edinburgh Lothian EH3 7TA

A sophisticated setting for the all-day service of Italian cooking with the emphasis on Tuscany. Good home-made pasta features in a dish like trenette with pesto sauce and pecorino cheese; other choices might include scampi risotto, fillet of lemon sole with watercress sauce, shinbone of veal with cannellini beans or grilled T-bone of veal with garlic and rosemary. Snacks in the wine bar next door. *Seats 60. Open 1215-2130 (Sat to 2230). Closed L Sat, all Sun, National Holidays. Amex, Diners, Mastercard, Visa.*

Tel 0141-204 5555   Fax 0141-204 5004
1 William Street Glasgow Strathclyde G3 8HT

A modern 20-storey city-centre landmark situated close to the M8 between junctions 18 and 19. The glass and granite exterior is complemented by an eyecatching and stylish interior with public rooms arranged off a well-lit and spacious central atrium. Air-conditioned standard bedrooms (with sealed windows) are not large and have a uniform up-to-date decor and furnishings, but an extra £25 on the room-only rate brings Executive status with extras like bathrobe and slippers, and use of the top-floor Executive lounge with complimentary Continental breakfast, afternoon tea and evening drink. One floor caters specifically to Japanese guests, with green tea added to the beverage tray and a yukata (Japanese pyjamas) provided as standard. A traditional Japanese breakfast is also available. Extensive 24hr room service and conference/banqueting facilities for up to 1100. Valet parking. *Rooms 319. Indoor swimming pool. Gym. Sauna. Steam room. Spa bath. Solarium. Beauty & hair salons. News kiosk. Coffee shop (0630-2300). Amex, Diners, Mastercard, Visa.*

Designed to resemble several interconnecting rooms from a grand Scottish hunting lodge, the decor here is among the most appealing of any modern hotel restaurant. There's plenty to like about the menu too with dishes like a potage of Loch Fyne oysters; foie gras encased in Tay salmon on crisp artichokes; *pot-au-feu* of Western Isles seafood with a Keta caviar sauce; chateaubriand of Angus fillet and poached fillet of Borders lamb with couscous on a rosewater jus, combining a light, modern style with the best of Scottish produce. The grape variety sometimes appears alongside a wine on the carefully compiled and comprehensive list, which includes many half bottles and a house selection under £15. Set L £16.95. *Set D £29.50. Seats 60. Private Room 25. Open 1200-1430, 1900-2230. Closed L Sat, all Sun.*

Tel 0141-221 6400   Fax 0141-221 6411
278 West George Street Glasgow Strathclyde G2 4LL

A new hotel concept (there are two so far, the other is in Edinburgh) created by Ken McCulloch of *One Devonshire Gardens*, qv. The idea is to offer stylishly designed, quality bedrooms (complete with high-tech music centres for which CDs can be borrowed from reception) along with traditional French brasseries/cafés in architecturally interesting buildings. Costs are kept down by not providing things like room service (except for Continental breakfast – full breakfast can be had in the Brasserie), luggage porterage or turning-down of beds at night. This one has been created within an early 20th-century, former non-conformist church designed by Charles 'Greek' Thompson. Local craftsmen have been used for the conversion, the furniture specially made to complement the style of the building and with a striking wrought-iron staircase leading to the upper floor of bedrooms (there's no lift). *Rooms 21. Amex, Diners, Mastercard, Visa.*

£60

Tel 0141-221 6401

Buzzy brasserie in vaulted basement where the menu (choice of about ten main dishes) covers familiar territory: eggs benedict, French onion soup, mussels with garlic and parsley, steak frites, coq au vin, salade niçoise, lamb's liver and bacon. Puds might include *pot au chocolat* or rice pudding with armagnac prunes. The café/bar area is open all day with coffee and croissants till midday and a bar menu of sandwiches, croque monsieur, salads and quiche between 11am and 4pm. Set L (Sat & Sun only) £7.50. *Seats 80. Open 1200-1430, 1800-2300.*

Tel 0141-339 2001   Fax 0141-337 1663

HR

1 Devonshire Gardens Glasgow Strathclyde G12 0UX

One Devonshire is one of a kind. Owned by Ken McCulloch and superbly run by Beverly Payne, this is a hotel of real style and distinction. It's an unusual spot at which to find such insulated comforts, situated as it is at the junction of the Great Western and Hyndland Roads; rooms at the rear are therefore quieter. Every creature comfort imaginable (within a hotel context!) seems to be available in bedrooms, bathrooms or public rooms as appropriate, creating an air of opulence and luxury that somehow doesn't overawe. Quality is evident throughout, whether it's the level of service provided (courteous porterage, immaculate housekeeping and cheerful turning-down of beds at night), the facilities offered in the bedrooms (hi-tech TV and CD player, mini-bar, fresh flowers, books, magazines, quality toiletries, and luxurious hooded bathrobes), or the standard and degree of comfort in the lounge and bar, where you can unwind and relax in splendour, surrounded by antiques and good paintings. You really feel valued and cosseted in a manner that only a truly professional hotelier and his staff can achieve. Up to 50 can be catered for conference-style in the boardroom, study or private dining-room. Children under 16 may stay free in their parents' room. *Rooms 27. Patio garden. Amex, Diners, Mastercard, Visa.*

Restaurant

£95

Sophisticated decor sees the crisp, spotlit whiteness of damask tablecloths set against a background of midnight blue with dense medieval-tapestry patterned drapes and wallpaper. The market-driven, fixed-price menu format offers a choice of five main dishes (four at lunchtime). Very much in the modern idiom, typical dishes might include a dodine of quail with a salad of winter endives, warm salad of globe artichoke with pleurottes on a walnut and truffle dressing, roasted king scallops with bean sprouts and crispy fried vegetables in a Thai-spiced sauce, pot-roasted poussin with braised flageolets and baby onions and mignons of pork fillet with potato and turnip gratin and glazed chestnuts; all are based on first-rate ingredients cooked with flair and skill. Puds range from lemon tart to iced aniseed parfait. Good selection of home-made breads. Sunday lunch comes with a glass of champagne and always includes prime roast joints of Scottish roast beef carved at your table. Fair section of half bottles on an enterprising, though pricey, wine list. Set L £25 Set D £37.50. *Seats 50. Parties 8. Private Room 32. Open 1230-1400, 1900-2230. Closed L Sat.* 🐂

Tel 0141-339 8444   Fax 0141-339 7666

R

11 Ruthven Lane Glasgow Strathclyde G12 9BQ

Venture down a narrow lane opposite Hillhead Metro station in Glasgow's West End to find one of the city's most chic restaurants. The first choice to make is whether to eat in the dark green, candle-lit, labyrinthine interior (one wall features a detail from the ceiling of the Sistine Chapel, another is mirrored, and there is an intimate padded booth) or the eccentrically-shaped conservatory to the rear of the early 19th-century building. The evening à la carte might include salad of roasted quail and pigeon; seared marinated beef fillet with radish, cucumber and roasted peanuts; baked monkfish with saffron risotto; calf's liver with lime and caramelised onions; duo of salmon with seared queenies and a creamy vermouth sauce. Puds range from the exotic – gateau of coconut ice cream, mango and banana – to a lemon tart with raspberries with cream. Just two dozen well-chosen wines on offer, almost all (except the fizz) at less than £20 a bottle. Set L £13.95/£16 (Sun £21) Set D £29/£34. *Seats 65. Private Room 26. Open 1200-1430, 1900-2300. Closed L Sat, all Mon, 25 & 26 Dec, 1 & 2 Jan. Amex, Mastercard, Visa.*

Tel 0141-248 4055   Fax 0141-248 2608

R

11 Exchange Place Glasgow Strathclyde G1 3AN

As much a part of Glasgow as Sauchiehall Street, the institution that is Rogano remains as popular as ever. The setting is ocean-liner art deco and the menu predominantly seafood: oysters, fish soup with rouille and parmesan croutons, feuilleté of mussels and scallops in a saffron cream sauce, grilled sardines with tomato and garlic concassé, grilled monkfish with red onions, crisp-fried salmon with orange and coriander. There are a couple of meat dishes such as an Angus steak with pink peppercorns and leeks, and liver and bacon with port sauce. Finish with the baked lemon tart or steamed toffee pudding with butterscotch sauce. With the cheapest bottle of champagne at £39, go for two halves at £18 each! Downstairs, the all-day Café Rogano is more informal. No smoking at lunch or dinner until 2pm and 9pm respectively. Set L £16.50 (Sat & Sun £15) *Seats 50. Private Room 16. Open 1200-1430, 1900-2230 (Sun till 2200) (Café 1200-2300, Fri & Sat till 2400. Sun till 2200). Closed 26 Dec. Amex, Diners, Mastercard, Visa.*

Tel 0171-734 5183

49 Frith Street Soho W1V 5TE

Foremost among Soho's eating places for its exceptional cuisine, the restaurant has a decor that leaves some cold, because of its stark modernity. The rows of tiny strip lights that decorate the ceiling illuminate a room whose pale walls are hung with abstract contemporary artwork. Tables and designer chairs are jet-black in contrast. The simplicity of the decor is a perfect foil for a style of cooking which gives the impression of being uncomplicated. Alastair Little's skills are in the assembly of top-rate ingredients into dishes with an often surprising complexity of well-married flavours and textures. Changing daily and continually evolving, the menus include starters such as a small, thin and very crisp pizza topped with slivers of mozzarella, with rocket and potato, houmus with a goat's cheese salad and flat breads or tagliatelle with morels, asparagus and peas. To follow, baked sea bass with a parsley salad and roast tomato sauce dribbled with olive oil, tournedos with a superb pesto on a nicely browned polenta base or a plump chicken breast stuffed with herbs under the skin and accompanied by a rich, creamy morel sauce. As a finale there's a creamy crème brulée, a very rich chocolate marquise with a ginger sauce or a superb rhubarb trifle studded with crunchy pistachios. Downstairs there's a bar where a simple £12.50 lunchtime-only fixed-price menu operates. Fair prices on a wine list that covers both Old World and New. Set L £12.50 (basement only) & £25. **Seats 38. Parties 8. Private Room 16. Open 1200-1500, 1800-2330. Closed L Sat, all Sun, Christmas & National Holidays. Access, Amex, Visa.**

Tel 0171-287 2057

41 Beak Street W1R 3LE

Originally there were artisans' workshops here, hence the name., and it was also once home to Canaletto. While the exterior retains some of the original character the interior has been completely updated, creating a stylish and very attractive restaurant decorated in warm, summery colours. Walls have a terracotta hue and down one side runs a series of large plain, curved, canvas screens. Place settings include very colourful handmade plates featuring quite life-like fruit and vegetables. Stephen Bulmer, the chef, and partner Joanna Shannon have both gained experience with Raymond Blanc at Great Milton and bring their resulting expertise to this venture. The short menu features a selection of truly delicious and very well-prepared dishes. The cooking style is simple with the emphasis on clear, well-defined flavours. Begin with a splendid plump and tender quail boudin served on a bed of spinach with a pea purée and delicate marjoram jus, chilled gazpacho with orange and thyme breadsticks or warm spinach mousse with white anchovies, tomato and parsley. For a main course there could be pan-fried tuna served on smooth saffron mash with a topping of pistou and a sauce of red peppers and coriander – a wonderful combination of Mediterranean flavours. Other choices are a salad of duck confit, duck ham and crispy skin, apple and celeriac with a walnut dressing, roasted lamb chump with basil-flavoured mashed potato, tomato fondue and rosemary jus and pan-fried monkfish with mussels, fresh linguine and a tarragon and mustard seed sauce. Only three desserts but they are not to be missed, particularly the exceptionally brilliant warm chocolate torte accompanied by a cherry compote subtly flavoured with cinnamon and kirsch and served with a nugget of chantilly cream. The set meals are very well balanced, no choice at lunch and two dishes per course for dinner. Set L & D from £14.50. **Seats 45. Parties 20. Private Room 16. Open 1200-1430, 1800-2245. Closed L Sat, all Sun, 2 weeks Jan, 2 weeks Aug. Amex, Diners, Mastercard, Visa.**

Tel 0171-352 3449   Fax 0171-351 1770

11 Park Walk SW10 0AJ

Chef-patron Gordon Ramsay's smart, yellow-themed restaurant goes from strength to strength, so much so that booking days if not weeks in advance is often necessary. The influence of one of his mentors, Marco Pierre White, is now less apparent, but that of Guy Savoy is visible in the delicious cappuccino soups sometimes appearing as amuse-gueule and sometimes as starters. The menus are written in a confusing mixture of English/French and some mid-channel patois; starters might include mosaique of rabbit with cabbage and ceps, salad of roasted langoustines with candied aubergine or an excellent terrine of foie gras and confit canard. Follow perhaps with pot-au-feu of Bresse pigeon with *choux farci*; caramelised calf's sweetbreads, etuvée of carrots jus sauternes with curry; or blanquette of turbot with ravioli of oyster and cucumber. Fish, in particular, is expertly handled and

See over

might appear as a wonderful selection of six varieties of the freshest morsels on a base of choucroute with a light coriander jus, the whole topped with a julienne of carrots whose flavour was so intense one imagines they came straight from a garden at the back! A splendid selection of French cheeses is offered, all in perfect condition. Desserts now scale the same heights, in both taste and display; and petits fours show the confectioner's art to the full. Service, under the charming direction of Jean-Claude Breton, is earnest but professional. A no-choice "Menu Prestige" is also offered for dinner, 6 courses for £44 – showing just what the kitchen can do. Fame has brought an increase in prices, but no more than the food deserves; but at lunchtime a short, daily-changing set menu is offered in addition to the main carte. At £19.50 for 3 courses and no skimping of standards this must be one of London's best bargains. An improved wine list, albeit denuded of any notes, and without sparkling wines, just champagne (quite steeply priced, except for a couple or non-vintage lesser *marques*). Set L £19.50 Set D £34/£44. *Seats 40. Parties 10. Open 1215-1430, 1900-2300. Closed L Sat, all Sun, Bank Holidays, first 2 weeks August, 23 Dec-1 Jan. Amex, Diners, Mastercard, Visa.*

LONDON   Bombay Brasserie   £70

Tel 0171-370 4040   Fax 0171 835 1669
Courtfield Close Courtfield Road SW7 4UH

The most glamorous Indian restaurant in town, and a hit since opening its doors in 1982. The handsome room, with its Raj pictures and paddle fans, is from a time past, evoking a grand hotel of a century ago. Entrance is to a roomy bar area where mango Bellini is a popular cocktail. One part of the restaurant proper is a large and flowery conservatory, which despite its lack of views manages to convey a garden feel. The kitchen garners its recipes from Northern and Western regions of the sub-continent and numbers Goan, tandoori and vegetarian dishes among its specialities. Some of the best dishes are Bombay seaside snacks (*sev batata puri*), *papri ma gosht* – a Parsee dish of lamb and flat bean stew with herbs and garlic, Goan fish curry, chicken biryani and lobster *hara masala* (pan-fried and flavoured with fresh green herbs). Meat and vegetarian thali provide tasting portions of many dishes. Lunchtime buffet. Evening pianist. *Seats 175. Parties 20. Private Room 100. Open 1200-1500, 1930-2400 (Sun to 2330). Closed 25 & 26 Dec. Diners, Mastercard, Visa.*

LONDON   Chez Nico at Ninety Park Lane   ★+   £150

Tel 0171-409 1290   Fax 0171-355 4877
90 Park Lane London W1A 3AA

The setting is an opulent dining room elegantly appointed with honey-coloured panelling and brightened by mirrors and discreet lighting. Menus are written in refreshingly straightforward English with no florid descriptions and the choice is long, with over 10 dishes at each stage. Sensational signature dishes remain, as in a warm salad of foie gras on toasted brioche with caramelised orange – a glorious combination of flavour and texture, though Nico's highly individual style of creativity continues to evolve. Dishes are constantly being reworked, often simplifying but also subtly refining them; but invention never takes a back seat. Delights such as a rosette of grilled scallops with baby spinach leaves, crispy salmon with ginger and teriyaki sauce and a salad of crisp guinea fowl with French beans in truffle oil and truffles are among the starters. The choice of fish main courses might include John Dory with a sweet and sour Oriental sauce and brill or turbot with a potato crust, while meat and offal dishes range from honey-roasted Bresse pigeon with cabbage and foie gras to saddle of lamb with a herb crust and fillet of Scotch beef with truffles, celeriac purée and foie gras. Sauces are simply sensational – glossy veal reductions that simply burst with flavour; there are no corners cut in these kitchens. A magnificent climax to a truly unforgettable meal is the grand plate of assorted mini-desserts (£6 supplement) – a tasting of many of the desserts, which include a slice of chocolate tart with pistachio ice cream, praline ice cream with glazed fruit and apricot sauce, lemon tart with cassis sorbet and cassis sauce and iced nougat with caramelised nuts. The thin apple tart with caramel sauce and vanilla ice cream is worth the advertised 20-minute wait – after all, a meal here is not one to be hurried. Consistency is of supreme importance in a restaurant that heads the Premier Division and Nico's watchful eye ensures that all is just as it should be. Around a couple of dozen wines are priced under £30, otherwise most wines on the very fine list are steeply marked up. Set L £29 Set D £48 (2 courses)/£57. *Seats 70. Parties 10. Private Room 20. Open 1200-1400, 1900-2300. Closed L Sat, all Sun, 4 days Easter, L National Holiday Mondays, 10 days Christmas/New Year. Amex, Diners, Mastercard, Visa.*

Tel 0171-823 3000   Fax 0171-351 6525
Chelsea Harbour SW10 OXG

Were it not for the uncertainty of the British climate the all-suite Conrad, with its glass-balconied, gleaming white-stoned exterior overlooking an exclusive marina, could well be mistaken for being in some sunny Mediterranean spot. The setting has the further advantage of being blissfully quiet. Designed by David Hicks, the tastefully furnished, double-glazed, air-conditioned suites offer every modern comfort: twin wardrobes, three telephones with two lines, multi-channel TV with video, mini-bar and many extras, such as fresh fruit, flowers, books and magazines, suit-carriers and even an umbrella. In the luxurious marble bathrooms you'll find a walk-in shower as well as a large tub, twin washbasins, bidet, separate loo (some suites also have a guest loo), bathrobes and quality toiletries. There's a cool and relaxing feel in the spacious marble-floored public areas, where uniformed and smartly-dressed staff are always on hand to offer a high standard of service, including valet parking. Drake's Bar, with its windy terrace, is a relaxing spot in which to enjoy a light snack, especially during the Wimbledon fortnight in front of a large TV screen. There's a free car service to Knightsbridge. Conference/banqueting facilities for up to 200. *Rooms 160. Terrace. Indoor swimming pool. Sauna. Solarium. Steam room. Gym. Beauty & hair salon. Kiosk. Amex, Diners, Mastercard, Visa.*

A plush dining-room with a pleasant outlook; a brasserie it is not! However, Peter Brennan's à la carte menu, supplemented by set menus both at lunchtime and in the evenings, features exciting modern dishes such as langoustine and smoked salmon salad with plum dressing, roasted pheasant breast with pumpkin, onion confit and port sauce, and hot pear and blueberry streussel. From the grill you could choose simple Dover sole or rack of lamb. Though there are tasting notes alongside each wine, the thin list is rather disappointing for a hotel of this class, though wines of the week and several available by the glass offer good value. Set L £17/£19 (Sun champagne brunch £31.50) Set D £22.50/£24.50. *Seats 45 (+40 on terrace). Parties 16. Open 1230-1500, 1800-2230.*

Tel 0171-629 8888   Fax 0171-409 0114
Park Lane W1A 2HJ

Since opening its doors in 1931, the Dorchester has been among the world's top hotels, renowned for its enviable standards of service, comfort and cooking. The grand oval foyer, with its rug-strewn black-and-white marble floor, bustles with the comings and goings of smartly attired porters, page boys and guests. The splendid, long Promenade, complete with enormous floral display at one end and rows of faux-marble columns with ornate gilt capitals, is very much the heart of the hotel and a wonderful place to take traditional English afternoon tea. Another focal point is the bar (see below). Bedrooms have an essentially English style with fine fabrics varying from striking floral prints and delicate damasks to heavy tapestries; the bed linen is, of course, real linen. All rooms are triple-glazed and have white Italian marble bathrooms with bidets and hand showers in addition to powerful showers over the bathtubs; many even have separate shower cubicles and twin washbasins, while most have natural light. Four superb roof garden suites, all restored to their original splendour, put the icing on the cake. Standards of service throughout the public areas are superlative and are matched on the bedroom floors following the implementation of the call button system for valet, maid and waiter room service (the hotel boasts an amazing ratio of three staff to each room). Breakfasts, as one can expect from a hotel with such an outstanding culinary history, are first-rate, covering English (a superior fry-up, poached haddock, grilled kippers, coddled egg with smoked salmon or chives), Continental (excellent baking includes croissants and apple scones) and low-fat and low-cholesterol options; served from 0700 (0730am Sun) in the Grill Room. Among the many elegant public rooms, opulent banqueting and conference facilities (for up to 550) feature over 1500 square metres of gold leaf gilding and are among London's finest. The Dorchester Spa offers thermal therapy as well as the more usual relaxations. *Rooms 247. Gym. Sauna. Steam room. Spa bath. Solarium. Beauty & hair salon. Shopping gallery. Amex, Diners, Mastercard, Visa.*

Here, in an elegant setting off the fabled Promenade, can be found a showcase for Willi Elsener's talents. The restaurant is open only on Friday and Saturday for dinner and it is essential to book in order to ensure a table in a room that is decorated with great style: there are mirrored columns, Chinese-inspired painted wall panels, a central gazebo where

See over

four couples can dine in relative seclusion, and a band which strikes up from mid-evening till late (around 0100hrs), the singer inviting diners to face the music and dance. The menu offers a fixed-price meal of either three or four courses. The choice is of imaginative, modern, sophisticated dishes. There is also a very extensive vegetarian menu, its dishes a very creditable and worthwhile alternative, and a result of increased demand. The orthodox menu begins with a super appetiser and might continue with carpaccio of scampi marinated in an orange vinaigrette, or a light guinea fowl timbale with morel mushrooms in a cream sauce. A granité follows and for a main dish the choice could be a beautifully fresh roasted centre cut of turbot, Oriental style, a trio of veal – the fillet, sweetbreads and liver served with a simple jus – or roast breast of chicken with a lemon grass-flavoured sauce. Examples of the desserts are brought to the table, making them irresistible. Service is superbly professional. There's a sommelier's selection and bin ends, both well worth perusing, in addition to the well-rounded list of wines from around the world. Most of the better known names are represented, prices are predictably on the high side. No children under 12. Set D £38/£42. **Seats** 81. *Parties 14. Open D only 1900-2330. Closed Sun-Thu, Aug.*

Grill Room   £130

Largely unchanged in style since the hotel first opened in 1931; although the decor is grand Spanish, the menu is firmly and splendidly English. Tables are widely spaced, which is just as well given the numerous trolleys that bring not just the traditional roast rib of beef and Yorkshire pudding and the side of smoked salmon – to be sliced at the table – but also the dish of the day (Monday's boiled silverside and caraway dumplings, Friday's Cornish fisherman's pie), the wide range of breads, salads, good desserts and the notably wide selection of British cheeses. The à la carte extends to just about every corner of the British Isles from Glamorgan sausages and cock-a-leekie soup to glazed South Coast scallops and prawns with a delicate mustard sauce. See Terrace Restaurant for the wine comment. Set L £24.50 Set D £32. **Seats** 84. *Parties 12. Open 1230-1430, 1900-2300 (Sun & Bank Holidays 1900-2230).*

Oriental Room   £120

London's most elegant and exclusive Chinese restaurant and almost certainly the most expensive, too. The mainly Cantonese menu features many luxurious items. Super dim sum are available at lunchtime and specialities from the carte include Peking duck, beef with lemon grass and steamed sea bass in black bean sauce. No monosodium glutamate is used in any of the dishes. Staff are smart, charming and knowledgable under a suave and accomplished manager. No children under 12. Lovely private rooms (Indian-themed, Chinese, Thai). See Terrace Restaurant for the wine comment. Set L £22.50/£24.50 Set D from £32. **Seats** 51. *Parties 16. Private Rooms 6/10/14. Open 1200-1430, 1900-2330. Closed L Sat, all Sun, Aug.*

Dorchester Bar   £70

Beautiful Delft-tiled panels alternating with mirrors in a carved, light-oak framework take the eye in this brightly lit, split-level bar. A baby grand piano covered in mirror mosaics, crisply-clothed tables, comfortable banquettes and light tan leather chairs complete a most elegant setting in which to enjoy excellent modern Italian cooking. A selection of antipasti (available only at lunchtime) is spread out next to the entrance. Other choices could be panzerotti filled with four cheeses and served with minted fresh tomatoes, tagliatelle with Beluga caviar, monkfish with a wild fennel sauce and veal cutlet with wild mushrooms. Delicious sweets too such as Amaretto parfait with prickly pear sauce or ice cream bombe round off an enjoyable experience. Service is first-class. Several well-chosen though pricey wines available by the glass. Booking is advisable. **Seats** 80. *Parties 8. Open 1200-2345 (Sun 1200-1430, 1900-2200).*

LONDON   Four Seasons Hotel   £331

Tel 0171-499 0888   Fax 0171-493 1895   HR
Hamilton Place Park Lane Mayfair W1A 1AZ

A small garden of sycamore trees at the front slightly obscures this hotel from the bustle of Park Lane and though several storeys high it is somewhat overlooked by its neighbours. Inside, the modernity of the exterior gives way to a stylish elegance firmly rooted in classic good taste. The lobby walls are clad in rich mahogany with a huge Venetian chandelier suspended from the ceiling, while underfoot is a floor of polished light brown and other matching coloured marbles. The lounge, as well as being a place to meet and relax, is also where all-day light meals and superb afternoon teas are served in gracious, supremely civilised surroundings with colourful, springy carpets and, as elsewhere in the public areas, Grecian-style urns of exquisite flowers in grandiose arrangements. Equally grand is the wide bifurcated staircase which leads to the bars, restaurants and banqueting rooms. Among the

finest of the splendid bedrooms are the 11 conservatory rooms which are especially bright and airy. There are 26 suites, including five grand apartment suites. The suites have CD players but all rooms have stereo televisions, video players and satellite broadcasts in six languages as well as a Reuters and an in-house channel, the latter showing first releases on video. There's also a library of 200 feature films available for guests' use. Not only are the rooms beautifully decorated in soft hues with fine furniture (some with marble tops), spacious, well-equipped, but the beds too are extremely comfortable – queen-size in single rooms and king-size or twin in double. Bathrooms in fine cream marble live up to expectations with every facility provided including bidets (not in single rooms), fine toiletries and ample thick towels. The Conservatory fitness club on the second floor is for the exclusive use of residents and is an up-to-date, light room with a comprehensive selection of the latest exercise equipment each with individual TV monitors and headphones. The hotel has fine banqueting suites including the magnificent Pine Room with its ornate 18th-century panelling. Breakfasts are, as one would expect, superb, not only for choice – a lengthy à la carte is supplemented by four set-price breakfasts including Japanese and healthy options – but also for quality. Staff are on the whole excellent, providing efficient, discreet and smiling service. Underground garage and valet parking.
Rooms 227. *Garden. Gym. Florist. News kiosk Valeting. Coffee shop (0900-0100). Amex, Diners, Mastercard, Visa.*

Four Seasons Restaurant   £120

Jean-Christophe Novelli is probably one of the country's most ambitious and innovative chefs. He is certainly the most artistic, and his creations, always visually stunning, are the flamboyant manifestation of a sharp eye for detail and the infinite patience required to execute the elaborately constructed and sometimes quite radical combinations. The menu comprises an extensive choice of dishes whose ingredients are in quite complex but well-thought-out and perfectly balanced compositions. Novelli's influences are those of Provence and the South West tempered with a few subtle flavours from further afield – notably the Orient. Dinner could begin with a tiny coffee cup of creamy sun-dried tomato soup and move on to an hors-d'oeuvre such as a skewer of mackerel and scallops, by themselves an unusual marriage, but whose accompaniments are also quite extraordinary. Having been marinated with orange zest and roast cardamon they are grilled on a lemon grass skewer and surrounded with a beetroot oil escabèche. The result is amazingly good. A slice of terrine composed of the ingredients of a traditional South Western cassoulet makes a rich and very satisfying starter too. Fish main dishes include a millefeuille of pan-fried Dover sole fillets interleaved with crisp paper-thin slices of aubergine and courgette with sun-dried tomato, anchovy and pistou creating the taste of sunshine so typical of the food here. Meat dishes include some much-favoured offal as well as the more conventional cuts. Roast fillet of beef is served on a piece of baked marrow-bone, surmounted by a crown of ultra-thin, crisp rounds of potato and a deep-fried bay leaf, a rich red wine sauce surrounding the meat. The cheese trolley features a small but superb collection of some of the best from Britain and France. Filip Tibos, the patissier, uses his considerable skills to produce desserts that are a fitting complement to Novelli's food. A tiramisu of the lightest creams comes on a fine pastry gondola on a rippled Kahlua sea. Other choices could be a banana tatin with rum and raisin ice cream and a caramel sauce or hot chocolate mould with a melted chocolate centre and white chocolate ice cream. Service is very much of the old school – which does have its charms. House wines (with tasting notes) apart, the list is on the expensive side though prices are inclusive of service and VAT. Comprehensive choice, good balance. The room, florally decorated in shades of charcoal and pink, has a discreet elegance and is on the first floor of the hotel. The main aspect is out over a small tree-filled garden whose summertime leaves screen diners from the hustle of Park Lane.
Set L £14.50/£25 (Sun £28) Set D £45. **Seats** 50. *Parties 8. Open 1230-1500, 1900-2230.*

Lanes Restaurant   £80

A stylish and smartly decorated restaurant; although windowless, the room has a splendidly light and contemporary decor and features a central buffet with wonderful displays throughout the day. Executive chef Eric Deblonde offers a choice of fixed-price three-course lunch menus all including wine. Dinner menus are well laid out and simply priced: your pick of the buffet as first or main course, ditto for pasta, grills, or other main courses like pan-fried spiced cod with squid and saffron-mashed potatoes, salmon escalope with a Sauternes and mango sauce and osso buco with tomato and orange, served with rice. Lanes' Alternative Cuisine offers light and vegetarian options. Superb breakfasts cover every almost choice from healthy to self-indulgent, from British to Japanese. The wine list attracts the same prices as in the main restaurant, but there's a shorter list; house wines have tasting notes. One half of the restaurant is reserved for non-smokers. Set L from £22.75 Set D £25.
Seats 75. *Parties 10. Open 1200-1500, 1800-2300 (Sun 1830-2230).*

Tel 0171-408 0881   Fax 0171-491 4387
43 Upper Brook Street Mayfair W1Y 1PF

In a restaurant long considered by others as the benchmark for quality and standards, head chef Michel Roux (jr only because he shares his forename with his uncle) continues to perform in top gear. Of course, his father Albert is still involved, but the style of cooking is very much Michel's, which he delightfully describes as "traditionally French with a Roux touch". However, Albert's signature dishes, such as *soufflé suissesse, l'assiette du boucher* and omelette Rothschild, which have played such a large part in the restaurant's success over the years, remain. The dining-room, orchestrated by manager Silvano Giraldin, so instrumental himself in the restaurant's achievements, is situated on the lower ground floor, reached via the street-level reception area where you can peruse the menus while nibbling exquisite canapés. On the lunch menu, a real bargain considering it includes service and a half bottle of excellent wine per person, there are three choices within each course, perhaps, respectively, *soufflé de homard parfumé à l'armagnac, mignonette de boeuf gratinée aux poivres* and *plateau de fromages* (these from Maitre Jacques Vernier in Paris). Alternatively, you can select from the à la carte menu, Michel's fixed-price menu, the six-course menu exceptionnel, for an entire table only, and additional daily-changing dishes, typical examples being *charlotte d'asperge et crabe en salade, ragout de langoustines et pied de cochon à la graine de moutarde, canon d'agneau et ragout de morilles,* ending with a *petite assiette du chef,* a tasting of several desserts. As you can see, everything is very French, though each dish is meticulously explained if required. The cooking is top notch, precise, imaginative and correct in all aspects; presentation is stunning. Service, like a well-oiled motor, purrs along, the staff almost unnoticeably at your side whenever appropriate. All the trappings of a luxury restaurant are there as well, from fine table settings and comfortable, elegant seating to well-baked bread and little stands of petits fours, almost a dessert in themselves, that accompany coffee. Evian mineral water is free. California (plus three from Spain) apart, the wine list is (fabulously) French. Expensive it may be, but the quality more than makes up for this fact, and remember that prices are inclusive of service. Minimum evening charge £50. Set L £37/£75 (six courses) Set D £55/£75. **Seats** 60. *Parties* 10. *Private Room* 20. *Open* 1200-1400, 1900-2300. *Closed Sat & Sun, National Holidays, 10 days at Christmas/New Year. Amex, Diners, Mastercard, Visa.*

Tel 0171-409 3131   Fax 0171-409 7460
1 Hamilton Place Hyde Park Corner W1V 1QY

Always popular with Americans both on business and on holiday, the hotel, located at Hyde Park Corner, has a vast, elegant foyer with highly polished, coloured marble floors leading to a stylish lounge well provided with supremely comfortable seating. It's also a fine conference and banqueting venue (up to 1000/850) and the fully equipped business centre has four private meeting rooms. There's also a purpose-built Video Conferencing Suite. Bedrooms, though not particularly large, are sleek and airy with seating areas, air-conditioning, double-glazing and mini-bars; bathrooms provide quality towelling and good toiletries. Rooms extend over eight floors, and those at the top enjoy fine views. The hotel offers a luxury airport service – the chauffeur will telephone ahead to advise reception of your arrival ensuring minimum delay when checking-in. There's underground parking for 100 cars. *Rooms* 460. *Gym. Sauna. Spa bath. Solarium. Beauty salon. Coffee shop (0700-2300). Amex, Diners, Mastercard, Visa.*

One of the most discreet and least known of London's top dining rooms, Le Soufflé has stylishly modern decor with a memory of 'Grand Hotel' style maintained by formally attired staff who provide exemplary old-fashioned standards of service. Hailed as a maestro by his peers, Peter Kromberg, the restaurant's chef-patron, keeps a low profile, avoiding publicity. He prefers to maintain a true hands-on approach in his kitchens, overseeing a dedicated and skilled team producing extraordinary food both for the restaurant and for the splendid banquets that are held in the hotel's function suites. As one would expect from the restaurant's name, soufflés both savoury and sweet are a feature of the menus. The carte has among its many delicious starters a soufflé of langoustines and fresh dill with a salad of spinach and scallops, a truffle and goose foie gras soufflé with lamb's lettuce and a rich truffle and foie gras sauce as well as tender Scottish lobster with asparagus, chives and ravioli of lobster and a risotto of cep mushrooms, asparagus and rocket. Main dishes follow in the same highly innovative and very accomplished style including a fillet of sole filled with lobster with a caviar and chive champagne sauce and fillets of venison wrapped in smoked bacon in a cherry sauce garnished with pommes dauphin and Belgian endive.

In making a decision full consideration should be given to the superlative *Le choix du Chef* menu which comprises seven outstanding, well-balanced courses. You must look carefully for value-for-money wines on the list here, many falling under the sommelier's suggestions. However, it is a good list, though the word 'fine' is somewhat overused. Gentlemen are requested to wear jacket and tie. Set L £27.50 (Sun £28) Set D £37.50/£43. **Seats** 80. *Parties 12. Open 1230-1500 D 1900-2230. Closed L Sat, D Sun, all Mon, August, 2 weeks Christmas.* 🐄

Tel 0171-491 8822
Stratton Street W1X 5FD

The legendary Langan's Brasserie, on two floors just off Piccadilly, remains one of London's most glamorous eating places. The long menu features around 80 dishes, from seafood salad, venison terrine and carpaccio with parmesan shavings to cold meats and coleslaw, braised knuckle of gammon with butter beans, grilled king prawns with pesto and a glazed vegetable and pasta bake. The mix covers both traditional English and French – spinach soufflé served with an anchovy sauce is the speciality on the ground floor, carré d'agneau roti aux herbes de Provence upstairs. Among the 25 or so desserts you might find apple strudel, blueberry tart, crepes des Alpes, and profiteroles with chocolate sauce. Traditionalists could be well pleased with a meal of cod and chips or bangers and mash with white onion sauce followed by rice pudding or trifle, washed down, of course, with a favourite champagne. The ground floor is always bustling (see and be seen!), while upstairs the Venetian room has its own quieter charm. **Seats** 220. *Parties 12. Open 1215-1500, 1900-2345 (Sat 2000-0045). Closed L Sat, all Sun, National Holidays, Easter weekend, Christmas. Amex, Diners, Mastercard, Visa.* 🐄

Tel 0171-229 4481
92 Kensington Park Road W11 2PN

A stylish and thoroughly modern interior now greets diners at this renowned and long-established restaurant. Bright, modern artwork and simple yet effective flower arrangments serve to bring colour to an otherwise uncluttered setting where Alex Floyd continues to produce innovative dishes which have a mainly British pedigree. To begin: a selection of hors d'oeuvre, now plated since the trolley has been discontinued, and a few other starters on the carte such as langoustine and crab salad and ravioli of foie gras and veal tongue in a light Scotch broth. Main dishes are like the rest, very carefully assembled, each a well-balanced synthesis of flavours as in pan-fried fillet of sea bass with a scallop and courgette galette and tomato and basil oil, best end of lamb with a grain mustard and herb crust and tarragon jus or feuilleté of roast pigeon with swede purée, wild mushrooms, braised cabbage and thyme. A superb selection of new British cheeses is available to follow and finally some unmissable desserts such as chocolate and chestnut soufflé with white chocolate ice cream or prune and marzipan parfait with bitter orange sauce. Vegetarians have the rare opportunity of enjoying food from their own well-thought-out and carefully constructed menu. The wine list is one of pure quality everywhere you look. For the most part prices are not unreasonable, though if you're prepared to spend, the bottles are there for you to choose from! Nick Tarayan prefaces each section with helpful tasting notes – note the Spanish section, which includes some cavas, an alternative to champagne. Set L £16.50/£19.50.
Set D £26.50/£36. **Seats** 70. *Parties 16. Private Room 40. Open 1215-1415, 1900-2330. Closed L Sat & Mon, all Sun. 2 weeks Aug, 2 weeks from Dec 24. Amex, Diners, Mastercard, Visa.*

Tel 0171-259 5380   Fax 0171-235 4552
66 Knightsbridge London SW1Y 7LA

Marco Pierre White's fuller figure looms larger than ever and his influence is expanding further to encompass some of London's premier and most modish establishments. A true genius, he is obsessed with his art and can always call upon a fresh flow of inspiration. He creates new dishes with the meticulousness of a scientist often working far into the night. The end results he presents in a stylish and elegant dining room beneath the Hyde Park Hotel. On offer is a fixed-price three-course menu which features a mouthwatering selection of starters followed by an almost too lengthy choice of exquisite main dishes and, finally, desserts which are so good that one is seriously tempted to order more than one. Begin with grilled scallops, which have a hint of curry and are accompanied by a confit of garlic and wonderful Sauternes jus, salad of lobster with tomato confit, vichyssoise of oysters with caviar chantilly or a galette of foie gras with elderberries. Fish is a forte – roast

See over

fillet of sea bass with olives, artichokes barigoule and tomato butter, tranche of salt cod with a thyme crust, young spinach and sabayon of grain mustard are typical. Meat dishes include braised pig's trotter 'Pierre Koffmann' with potato purée and morel essence; fillet of lamb with olives, a millefeuille of aubergine, couscous and the roasting juices with rosemary; and roast Bresse pigeon with ventreche, garlic ravioli, braised cabbage, fondant potatoes and thyme jus. Thierry Busset produces sybaritic confections such as a stunning tarte tatin of pears, omelette Rothschild and hot raspberry soufflé. The wine list is impressive, with carefully chosen wines from around the world. At first sight it seems expensive, but prices are inclusive and at around £30 per bottle you can drink very well. Spend more and you can drink exceptionally well – the food certainly deserves it! Set L £29.50 Set D £70. *Seats* 50. *Parties* 12. *Open* 1200-1430, 1900-2300. *Closed* L Sat, all Sun, National Holidays, first 2 weeks in Aug, 2 weeks Christmas. *Access, Visa.*

LONDON **Museum Street Café** £55

Tel 0171-405 3211
47 Museum Street Bloomsbury WC1A 1LY

R

A café by name but the atmosphere, albeit informal with its bright white walls and simple, dark furniture, is much more that of a restaurant. The choice is a short one but is imaginative and eclectic with inspiration for dishes depending on the availability of the fine ingredients that are essential to this simple, unfussy, contemporary style of cooking. Neal's Yard Dairy, Monmouth Coffee Company and Frances Smith (organic salad grower) are among the suppliers. Much use is made of the chargrill and this is Mark Nathan's domain, while Gail Koerber's task is preparing the breads, starters and desserts. What comes from the kitchen continues to captivate the palate with its delicacy and subtlety. Lentil, chestnut and red wine soup or a salad with bresaola, parmesan, roasted fennel and grilled courgette could be your starter choice, followed by lamb with tapénade, salmon with soy, ginger and coriander, or calf's liver with grilled sweet red onions. Desserts are every bit as appealing as the rest – try olive oil and Sauternes cake with blood oranges and crème fraiche. No smoking. Set L £12/£15 Set D £17/£21. *Seats* 37. *Open* 1230-1430, 1830-2130. *Closed Sat & Sun. Access, Visa.*

LONDON **Panda Si Chuen** £50

Tel 0171-437 2069
56 Old Compton Street W1V 5PA

R

Just outside the traditional heart of Chinatown, Panda Si Chuen is one of London's best Chinese restaurants. The cooking of Szechuan province is renowned for its generally spicy nature and here it has reached an exalted level which produces dishes of often exquisite flavour. Grilled dumplings to begin burst with succulent meats and juices while Szechuan tea-smoked duck (a speciality) is imbued with a distinct and delicious flavour reminiscent of Lapsang Souchong. Deep-fried oysters are large, with a moist, plump inside and crisp outside, kung-po chicken has the fieriness of chili and the sweet crunchiness of cashew nuts. Among the 'variety meats dishes' section are shredded pork with eggplant in sea-spiced sauce, home-style double-cooked pork and fried beef with seasonal vegetables. Staff are helpful, polite and friendly. *Seats* 63. *Parties* 18. *Private Room* 13. *Open* 1200-2300. *Closed Sun, National Holidays. Amex, Diners, Mastercard, Visa.*

LONDON **Le Pont de la Tour** £95

Tel 0171-403 8403   Fax 0171-403 0267
Butlers Wharf Building 36D Shad Thames Butlers Wharf SE1

R

Part of Sir Terence Conran's 'Gastrodrome' in a beautiful setting on the south bank of the Thames right by Tower Bridge and overlooking St Katharine's Dock across the water. In fine weather the large canopied terrace allows for alfresco dining with a very Continental air. Lunch is fixed-price with half a dozen or so starters and main dishes whilst in the evening a slightly more extensive à la carte applies, plus a pre- and post-theatre menu at £19.50 for three courses. Dishes are, as befits the cool, stylish elegance of the setting, very fashionable, with strong Mediterranean influences. Twice-cooked cheese soufflé with mustard and chives or wild mushroom tart with rocket and parmesan could precede sauté of scallops with grilled plum tomatoes and gremolata, grilled duck breast with confit of red cabbage or persillade of calf's liver with peppercorn sauce. Vegetables and potatoes are priced separately. Desserts are superb – steamed ginger sponge pudding or a stunning blueberry and vanilla millefeuille. An exceptional wine list with exceptional names at exceptional prices, though to be fair, there is plenty of choice under £20 as well – those on the house selection are accompanied by tasting notes. If you like what you drink here, all wines are available for sale and delivery at retail prices. Excellent espresso and chocolate coffee beans round off a splendid meal served by on-the-ball staff. In addition to the main restaurant there is a less formal bar and grill open noon to midnight every day; plateau de fruits de mer is the speciality there. Brunches on Saturday (in the bar) and Sunday are very popular. Park at the end of Curlew Street on the riverfront. *Set L £26.50*. **Seats 105**. *Parties 9. Private Room 22. Open 1200-1500, 1800-2330. Closed L Sat, Good Friday & 5 days Christmas. Amex, Diners, Mastercard, Visa.*

LONDON   Les Saveurs   ★ ✦   £120

Tel 0171-491 8919   Fax 0171-491 3658
37a Curzon Street Mayfair W1V 8EY

A change of personnel at front-of-house, where the service under new restaurant manager Frederic Serol continues to be correct and proper, while in the kitchen, chef Joël Antunès and his team continue to perform at the height of their powers, producing dishes of stunning complexity and visual appeal. The basement restaurant itself provides all the trappings of sophisticated luxury from the exquisite place settings and artistic floral arrangements to tasteful decor and comfortable seating. Further proof, if proof were needed, that you're dining at one of the country's top restaurants, comes with those special extras that define real excellence – savoury nibbles, quality bread rolls, an amuse-bouche, say, a tiny tart of salmon rillettes with cucumber sauce, a magnificent (French) cheese trolley with every offering in tip-top condition, and a tray of petits fours, almost a dessert in itself with a choice of four treats per person. The differing menus are all fixed-price, though too many dishes attract supplements, with the daily-changing table d'hote a steal at both lunch and dinner (£38 for four courses), particularly the former when you are offered a choice of four dishes in each section. A typical example is a delicate courgette flower filled with crab, roast lamb served with zucchini, and a gratin of red fruits in orange sauce, a perfect interpretation of a hot and cold dessert. Turning to the major menu, you'll encounter perhaps a chilled crab fondant with almond and herb mousse or terrine of duck foie gras and smoked pigeon with truffle oil, to be followed by roast sea bass on a bed of red sweet peppers and apricots or pan-fried sweetbreads in beetroot sauce. For dessert you could try the rather bizarre, but nevertheless delicious, fennel ice cream served with biscuit and red fruits, or peach and champagne soup with verbena ice cream (sometimes strawberry soup with tea sorbet), though the word soup is something of a misnomer. A very grand wine list for a grand restaurant, though most wines are on the expensive side. Best value obviously in lesser-known wines and sommelier Claude Douard's daily recommendations, and a surprisingly good New World selection for an oh! so French restaurant. Plenty of half bottles. Set L £17/£22.50 D £36/£42 & £38. **Seats 50. Parties 16**. *Private Room 10. Open 1200-1430, 1900-2300. Closed Sat & Sun, National Holidays, 2 weeks Aug, 2 weeks Christmas/New Year.*

LONDON   The Savoy   HR

Tel 0171-836 4343   Fax 0171-240 6040
The Strand WC2R 0EU

A household name for over one hundred years, The Savoy continues its fine traditions under new General Manager Duncan Palmer, as well as Group Managing Director Ramón Pajares, one of London's leading hoteliers for more than twenty years. Innovative when built, the hotel always seems to move with the times, introducing the latest technology without compromising its trademark standards of typically British sang-froid, efficiency and splendour. It is above all a hotel of grandeur, of contrasting styles, the marble-pillared Thames Foyer with a gazebo where a pianist or harpist plays during teatime and the cocktail hour, the imposing entrance hall, always a hive of activity with both guests and staff going about their business, the quiet drawing room, and the famous American Bar, one of London's favourite meeting places. Bedrooms, in styles ranging from traditionally English to art deco, benefit from having beds and mattresses made by the Savoy's own manufacturer, and boast such luxuries as real linen bedding, huge cosseting bath sheets, a nightly turn-down of beds and personal maid, valet and waiter bell service. River view rooms attract a supplement, and the much sought-after river suites are arguably the capital's finest. Even when originally built, bathrooms were huge and luxurious, and today, through constant renovation and refurbishment, they remain so. Another of the hotel's attractions is the Fitness Gallery, created when the adjoining Savoy Theatre was rebuilt. Favoured by natural daylight and fresh air, it is centred around the roof-top swimming pool, and includes his and hers saunas, steam rooms, warm-up and work-out rooms, and a massage room. Guests also have temporary membership of the renowned Wentworth golf and country club, a short drive from London, which has tennis courts and an outdoor pool in addition to several golf courses (proof of handicap required). Banqueting, without equal, is available for up to 500 in the Lancaster Ballroom, and theatre-style conferences can

See over

accommodate up to 600; smaller parties can take advantage of a number of elegant private rooms named after Gilbert and Sullivan operas. Own garage (£23 overnight charge). No dogs. **Rooms** 202. *Indoor swimming pool, Gym. Sauna. Steam room. Beauty & hair salon. Gift and flower shops. Valeting. Amex, Diners, Mastercard, Visa.*

River Restaurant   £130

This is a restaurant of two moods – at lunchtime busy and buzzy, at dinner, a more sedate affair with dancing to a live band (not Sunday) an additional attraction – in which to enjoy the grand setting (and the view if you're lucky enough to bag a window table overlooking the Thames). The chief protagonists, namely *maitre chef des cuisines* Anton Edelmann and restaurant manager Luigi Zambon, arrived here at the same time in the early '80s. Both are consummate professionals, orchestrating large brigades to provide admirable cooking and smooth service, no small feat given the number of guests fed each day. Long established as perennial favourites are the trolleys, whether accommodating oak-smoked Scotch salmon, 'roast of the day' under a silver dome, or desserts and puddings. Alternatively, choose à la carte (dishes, incidentally, are written in French with English translations), perhaps paupiettes of salmon filled with crab meat and topped with caviar; noisettes of lamb with truffle sauce, and peach Melba in an open sugar cage. A typical fixed-price menu, with several choices at each course, might offer home-made tagliatelle with foie gras, mignons of venison with wild mushrooms and juniper berry sauce, and chocolate terrine. In addition, there's a five-course dinner menu (£55) which includes a glass of wine, chosen by sommelier Werner Wissmann, to complement each dish, as well as a two-course (£27) theatre menu served until 1900 with first and main courses before the show, returning for coffee and pastries (add another £5) in the Thames Foyer afterwards. The health-conscious and vegetarians are not neglected – note the Régime Naturel options (artichoke and wild mushroom salad in pumpkin seed oil, or ratatouille wrapped in courgettes on a potato purée with garlic, leek and extra virgin oil, vegetable cannelloni and vegetable cage). An impressive wine list, claret especially, with wines from around the world, though unpatriotically none from this country! Set L £27.50 (Sun £24.50) Set D £32.90 (Fri/Sat £39.50) and £55. **Seats** 160. *Parties 50. Private Rooms 8/80. Open 1230-1430, 1800-2315 (Sun 1900-2230).*

Grill Room   £120

Regular diners consider this yew-panelled dining-room to be almost their own club, some expecting to be seated at their favourite table whenever they book (essential by the way), occasionally testing the diplomatic skills of *maitre d'hotel* Angelo Maresca. *Maitre chef de cuisine* David Sharland's menus rarely change, though he does add the odd modern nod to classic dishes: sweet pepper salsa with smoked eel and quail's eggs, wilted greens and carrot butter sauce with fish cakes, an onion marmalade with a herb butter sauce with pan-fried calf's liver. Otherwise, the day of the week dictates les plats du jour, which differ at lunch and dinner; for instance, on a Tuesday lunch either hocks of ham with lentils or steak and kidney pie with sweetbreads are served, while the evening sees fillet of beef Wellington. Sausage and mash-lovers pinpoint Monday lunch, while those who prefer roast chicken with calvados and apple black pudding choose Wednesday evening. If your choice is roast saddle of lamb, it's served every day. For dessert, the trolley carries the usual selection, but if you're feeling daring, try the banana mousse with a ginger snap and a light custard, or iced lemon parfait with a warm blueberry compote topped with praline. There's a theatre menu here too (see River Restaurant above, similarly the wine list). Service is polished, professional, and skilful with much emphasis on carving and flambéeing. Set D £29.75 (pre/post-theatre only). **Seats** 100. *Parties 8. Open 1230-1430, 1800-2315. Closed Sun, Aug.*

Upstairs at the Savoy   £60

You can sit either at the long marble bar counter or at small tables overlooking the courtyard for an informal meal, and enjoy seafood specials and fine wines by the glass from Le Grand Cruvinet. Each month there's a different champagne (by the glass or pint silver tankard) to wash down some oysters, dressed crab, fish cakes or cod and salmon kedgeree. If you're really hungry, 'Jaks Plate' consists of smoked salmon, crab meat, avocado, prawns, bacon, scrambled eggs and sweet pepper salsa. Finish with sherry trifle or crème brulée. **Seats** 38. *Parties 6. Open 1200-2400 (Sat from 1500). Closed Sun & National Holidays.*

THE APARTMENT SERVICE
Tel in UK (0181) 748 4207   Fax (0181) 748 3972
The Apartment Service will find you the right apartment worldwide to suit your needs, whether you are on a short or long-term stay. A 96-page colour catalogue is free on request. All budgets are catered for.

Tel 0171-836 9112   Fax 0171-836 1381
100 The Strand WC2R 0EW

The quintessential English restaurant opened its doors in 1848 and has become a veritable institution. Today it continues to offer a whole range of true British classics. Since 1994 it now starts business at 0700 (Mon-Fri) to serve a splendid selection of breakfast dishes. One of its traditions is the silver carving wagons which daily include roast Scotch beef with Yorkshire pudding, roast saddle of lamb with redcurrant jelly and roast Aylesbury duck with apple sauce and stuffing. Each day of the week also brings its own warming favourite: on Sunday there's Lancashire hot pot, Tuesday sees steak, kidney and mushroom pudding and on Thursday boiled silverside with pease pudding, carrots and dumplings is offered. Puddings will also delight Anglophiles with apple pie and cream, Spotted Dick and rhubarb crumble among the many offerings. Set L & D £10 (Sun L £17.50). **Seats 240. Parties 12.** *Private Room 145. Open 1200-1430, 1800-2300 (Sun till 2100). Closed 25 & 26 Dec, 1 Jan, Good Friday. Amex, Diners, Mastercard, Visa.*

Tel 0171-839 8787
32 King Street St James's SW1 6RJ

Just off St James's Square, the restaurant has a smartly contemporary decor of brightly coloured upholstery and cream-coloured walls which complements Philip Howard's menus. The daily-changing choice includes modern interpretations of Mediterranean as well as a smattering of British classics. Combinations of ingredients are excitingly original, producing food that truly excites the senses. Begin with a warm salad of game with port and raisins, oxtail soup with baked roseval potatoes and bone marrow, seared scallops with squid ink risotto and gremolata and parfait of foie gras and chicken livers with toasted granary bread. Main dishes include a sauté of John Dory with pesto noodles and sauce vierge, thinly sliced veal with a Jerusalem artichoke purée and fondant potatoes, roast Tuscan squab with a sauté of trompettes and balsamic jus and rump of lamb with tomato confit and rosemary. Desserts are no less innovative: witness a superb baked chocolate sponge with a chocolate and orange sauce, a soup of fruits served with an apple sorbet or *tarte bourdalou* with a pear sabayon. Improved lay-out of the wine list makes selection much easier, but choose carefully to avoid too deep a hole in your pocket. Set D £32/£38. **Seats 65. Parties 8.** *Private Room 20. Open 1200-1500, 1800-2345. Closed L Sat & Sun, most National Holidays. 8. Access, Visa.*

Tel 0171-352 6045   Fax 0171-352 3257
68 Royal Hospital Road SW3 4HP

One of the marks of a great restaurant is consistency, and there is no more consistent performer than the chef here, Pierre Koffmann. Since he opened his restaurant almost twenty years ago, he has been one of Britain's leading chefs. And yet he is the quiet man of the kitchen, rarely venturing out, hardly a TV appearance, little publicity or controversy, in short, a chef at his stoves. His dishes are much copied, but seldom, if ever, improved upon, and just about the only change this year is the very smart, bolder and brighter name above the restaurant's entrance. Inside, the elegant dining room is relatively small, but not uncomfortably so, as it's airy and tables are reasonably well spaced. There's a crisp look to the decor – some modern paintings, immaculate table settings, but certainly no clutter. Staff, under the guidance of restaurant manager Bruno Bellemère, are supremely professional and very, very French, and if sometimes they appear aloof, do not confuse this trait with unfriendliness. The atmosphere at lunchtime is usually more animated, while at dinner a hushed tone prevails, but then at lunch you can eat three courses for an almost giveaway £25. In fact, there are two table d'hote menus side by side, offering the likes of *mousseline de St Jacques au beurre d'herbes; tarte aux poireaux, moules et safran; filet de barbue aux graines de moutarde; magret de canard au poivre vert;* and *savarin au rhum* or French cheeses. Coffee and petits fours are included, as is service. Divert to à la carte, and seek out Pierre's specialities, such as *galette de foie gras au Sauternes et échalotes roties, pied de cochon aux morilles* and *croustade de pommes à l'armagnac*. Whatever you choose, this is cooking in the premier league, based on classical foundations and executed in exemplary fashion. Flavours, aromas, combinations of tip-top ingredients, precise timing – they all contribute to mouthwatering perfection, enhanced by presentation that positively invites you to enjoy. Perhaps surprisingly, but very commendably for a restaurant of this class, the wines (excusably French-only) are not priced beyond the reach of mere mortals. Set L £25. **Seats 43. Parties 10.** *Open 1230-1400, 1900, 2300. Closed Sat & Sun, National Holidays, 1 week Christmas, 3 weeks August. Amex, Diners, Mastercard, Visa.*

Tel 0161-236 3333   Fax 0161-228 2241

H

Peter Street Manchester Greater Manchester M60 2DS

A grand city-centre hotel (adjacent to the G-Mex centre) restored at great expense to its past glory with ornate ceilings, arches and pillars. The foyer area is vast, with a glass roof and hanging plants crowning white columns. Cane chairs and comfortable couches adorn the adjoining terrace lounge. The high-ceilinged Octagon, one of three bars, is decorated in similar style; there are also three restaurants. Corridors that lead to the bedrooms are wide and reminiscent of a former age of spacious and luxurious hotels. Bedrooms, all recently refurbished, are generously sized and have a high standard of decor, with tiled bathrooms throughout. Extensive conference and banqueting (including kosher) facilities for up to 700. Under-19s stay free in parents' room. No dogs. *Rooms 303.*
Indoor swimming pool. Sauna. Spa bath. Gym. Squash. Beauty & hair salon. Osteopath.
Coffee shop (1300-2230). Amex, Diners, Mastercard, Visa.

Tel 0161-834 3743

R

Edge Street/104 High Street Manchester Greater Manchester M4 1HQ

Close to the city centre, in what is now the garment district, Peter and Anne O'Grady's friendly, homely restaurant has enormous appeal. Decorwise it's like stepping back in time with everything from the crockery and green wicker chairs to the light fittings and background music dating back to the 1940s – even the wine carafes are old-fashioned milk bottles. The monthly-changing menu takes its inspiration from all over the place. Starters might include turnip and dill soup, Thai pork sausage with sweet chili and cucumber relish and Westphalian ham with celeriac rémoulade, while main courses span wild mushroom pancakes, salmon with a mousseline of hake baked in filo, breast of tuna with a redcurrant and port sauce and top rib of beef in a green peppercorn sauce. There are always a couple of interesting vegetarian choices. Puds are important here too, as is fitting for the home of the famous Pudding Club, whose members meet six times a year to indulge in a feast of desserts like steamed puddings, fruit pies, chocolate confection, syllabubs and the like all helped down with lashings of real custard and extra thick cream. For those with more savoury tastes there is also a Starters Society. Beers, even ciders, receive equally billing with wine on an inexpensive drinks list. *Seats 42. Private Room 24. Open D only 1800-2130 (Sat from 1900). Closed Sun, Mon, Tue, 1 week Easter, most of Aug, 1 week Christmas. Amex, Mastercard, Visa.*

Tel 0161-832 1188   Fax 0161-834 2484

HR

Water Street Manchester Greater Manchester M3 4JQ

Between their TV studios and the River Irwell, Granada's flagship hotel is a cleverly converted mid-19th-century warehouse. Original oak-timbered ceilings and cast-iron pillars feature in the smart galleried reception area, Watsons bar/lounge with its comfortable Victorian drawing room atmosphere and conservatory overlooking the river, and in the all-day French-style café/bistro. Bedrooms, which vary in size and shape, also boast timbered ceilings and some exposed brickwork; each is named after, and subtly themed with stills from, a different Granada TV drama or series. King- or queen-sized beds and a high level of equipment – the TV offers account review, quick check-out and breakfast ordering facilities – make for a comfortable stay aided by keen staff offering an above average level of service. Children under 12 years free in parents' room. Free Granada Studios tour. 24hr room service. No dogs. Conference facilities for up to 350. *Rooms 132. Garden. Keep-fit equipment. Sauna. Solarium. Café (2000-2400). News kiosk. Amex, Diners, Mastercard, Visa.*

Cooking alongside executive chef John Benson-Smith, Steve Chesnutt and his team cook with confidence and style. The menu might be a bit gimmicky, but the dishes, essentially British with Oriental influences, are always enterprising, starting perhaps with potted lobster and leeks with chicken livers or hot Thai-style pork with red onions, followed by a pot roast English duck with honey and bottled cherries or roast halibut set on a vegetable Italian stew. Plain and simple dishes (chicken liver paté, best end of English lamb) are also available. To end, try the toasted rice pudding or baked filo parcel of caramelised bananas with sticky toffee sauce. Fabulous British farmhouse cheeses from around the country, good selection of breads, and a variety of teas. Simple and balanced wine list. Set D £28.50. *Seats 70. Parties 8. Private Room 60. Open 1200-1400, 1900-2200. Closed L Sat & all Sun.*

MANCHESTER   **Yang Sing**   **£50**

Tel 0161-236 2200   Fax 0161-236 5934
34 Princes Street Manchester Greater Manchester M1 4JY

The class of cooking and the length of the menus make this the most appealing Chinese restaurant in town, and its popularity remains undiminished. Tanks of live carp, eels and lobsters testify to the importance chef-proprietor Harry Yeung places on freshness and quality of ingredients. Some 40 different dim sum (even more on Sundays) can be chosen from trolleys parked in the middle of the restaurant or ordered from the waiting staff. A selection of pastries (all from their own kitchen) or fresh fruit for afters. Banquets for up to 200 guests can be held in the largest of several private rooms. Booking advisable except for Sunday lunch when you just have to join the queue. Set meals from £28 for two. *Seats 140. Parties 40. Private Room 220. Open 1200-2300. Closed 25 Dec. Amex, Mastercard, Visa.*

Elsewhere in the UK

BRAY-ON-THAMES   **The Waterside Inn**   **★ ★   £170**

Tel 01628 20691   Fax 01628 784710
Ferry Road Bray-on-Thames Berkshire SL6 2AT

Michel Roux's delightful and celebrated restaurant lies right on the river bank; indeed you can sit outside on the terrace for a pre/post-prandial drink or coffee and almost touch the water. Since it opened in 1972, there have been many changes here, not least the addition of bedrooms (see below), so this is *un vrai restaurant avec chambres*. Michel has surrounded himself with an enviable team of dedicated professionals, none more so than head chef Mark Dodson and restaurant manager Diego Masciaga, recently joined by Louis Abdilla. The setting is spectacular, the dining-room elegant and bright, with, naturally, the tables alongside the picture windows enjoying the best views. Cooking is, of course, very, very French, based on classic principles, but with an added lightness of touch and a nod to modern practices. You really are spoilt for choice, since there are a number of menus and the carte to choose from: a £29.50 *menu gastronomique* at lunchtime during the week, £37 on Sunday; an evening *menu du printemps* at £49.50 between October and April; *menu exceptionnel*, five courses, including a sorbet, at £66, taken from à la carte, served in smaller portions for a minimum of two persons. A typical example from the latter might include *terrine de foie gras, vinaigrette de truffes; paillard de saumon fumé sur douillet d'aubergines; aiguillettes de caneton Challandais à la vie de vin, dés d'olives au parfum d'anchois; soufflé chaud aux framboises* (note the timing for last orders of hot desserts). The other fixed-price menus are simpler (don't stray or each course will be charged separately), typified by *gourmandise de lapereau aux noisettes caramélisées; supreme de turbot poelé; timbale de crustacés, au parfum de pesto; dome aux deux chocolats et framboises*. English translations probably do not do the dishes justice, so don't be afraid to ask! Add to these delights the dainty *canapés* and *amuse-bouche*, excellent rolls, fine French cheeses, exquisite petits fours and courteous service, and you have the complete package. Yes, for the most part the wine list is pricy, but remember prices are inclusive of service. France only, the best growers, the classic names, with some less expensive bottles. No children under 12. Electric launch *The Waterside Inn II* available for hire, as is the restaurant for private functions when closed.*Set L £29.50 (Sun £37)* Set D Oct-April £49.50, also Set L & D £66. *Seats 75. Parties 10. Private Room 8. Open 1200-1400 (Sun 1430), 1900-2200. Closed all Mon, L Tue, D Sun end Oct-mid April, National Holidays (open L 25 Dec), 26 Dec-end Jan. Diners, Mastercard Visa.*

Rooms   **£130**

A new suite (bedroom, drawing room and breakfast room) situated on the river a minute's walk from the restaurant has been added to the six existing bedrooms, two of which share a large terrace. Each, with a neat bathroom, is individually and stylishly decorated, and the obvious benefit of staying here, apart from not having to drive home, is the continental breakfast with the morning's baking.

EAST GRINSTEAD   Gravetye Manor   £200

Tel 01342 810567   Fax 01342 810080
Vowels Lane East Grinstead West Sussex RH19 4LJ

HR

Peter Herbert and his staff continue to provide an object lesson in how a country house hotel should be run. The care and attention to every last detail shows everywhere, both within the splendidly transformed Elizabethan stone mansion (built in 1598) and in the 1000 acres of grounds that incorporate the William Robinson English garden recently restored to its former glory. Flower displays fill the gracious day rooms, which include a really delightful sitting room with oak panelling and an ornate moulded ceiling, and the entrance hall with its carefully selected chair patterns. Bedrooms, with their comfortable beds, antique furniture and sumptuous fabrics, are models of good taste; books, magazines, post cards, bedside radios and TVs concealed behind tapestry screens are among a long list of thoughtful extras. The bathrooms, too, with his and her washbasins, bidet and power shower over the bath, provide for every conceivable need, and are havens of comfort. No children under 7, but babes in arms welcome – cots provided. Fly fishing on the lake between May and September. No dogs in the hotel; kennels at the head of the drive. This most civilised of hotels stands 5 miles south-west of East Grinstead off the B2110 at the West Hoathly sign. *Rooms 18. Garden. Croquet. Fishing. Mastercard, Visa.*

Restaurant   £105

A comfortable restaurant whose enviable reputation for consistently high standards is certain to be maintained by Mark Raffan, who returned to Gravetye's kitchen (he was head chef from 1989-91) in the summer of 1995 after spending, among other posts, three years as personal chef to King Hussain of Jordan. Ingredients are of the highest quality, with a walled kitchen garden providing much of the produce in summer, their own smokehouse the smoked salmon, duck breast and the like and the spring which has served the Manor from the start still providing water for the tables. Typical of Mark's dishes are seared Hebridean scallops and roasted lobster with a warm gazpacho and crispy basil; steamed courgette flower with roasted aubergine and goats' cheese soufflé; *millefeuille* of calf's liver with caramelised apple, lardons of bacon and a rich Dubonnet sauce; rib of beef with roasted beetroot and *jus nicoise*; and poached fruits with spices and aromatics and coconut crème caramel. The dining-room, with mellow oak panelling beneath a Tudor ceiling, is a lovely setting and service is silky smooth and attentive without being overbearing. Menu prices include service but not VAT. Sommelier Thierry Morigeon presides over a quite magnificent wine list that seems to get better and better each year. All the top names and growers are present, from classic clarets and burgundies to vintage champagnes and the very best the New World has to offer. Both Germany and Italy feature prominently too. No smoking. Set L £22 (+VAT) (Sun £28 +VAT) Set D £28 (+VAT). *Seats 42. Parties 8. Private Room 18. Open 1230-1400, 1930-2130 (Sun to 2100). Closed D 25 Dec to non-residents.*

GREAT MILTON   Le Manoir aux Quat'Saisons   £204

Tel 01844 278881   Fax 01844 278847
Church Road Great Milton Oxfordshire OX44 7PD

HR

Raymond Blanc's renowned and very special country house hotel is only a short drive from the M40. From London leave the motorway at Junction 7, approaching from the north at Junction 8. Imposing wide gates in the high surrounding stone walls lead up to a graceful 15th-century manor house built of mellow Cotswold stone. The 27 acres of carefully tended gardens include a three-acre kitchen garden and a newly created authentic Japanese tea garden. The flagstoned entrance hall leads into luxurious and comfortable lounges that are immaculately furnished with antiques, fine paintings and splendid flower arrangements and warmed in winter by open fires. The theme continues in the individually decorated bedrooms, which provide every conceivable luxury, from a decanter of Madeira to a bowl of fresh fruit. Several garden-wing rooms have their own private terrace with wrought-iron patio furniture, while the medieval dovecote has been converted into a romantic honeymoon suite. There are jacuzzi and whirlpool baths in the magnificent bathrooms, not to mention huge towels, generous bathrobes and exquisite toiletries. Of course, all this would be wasted without service and excellent housekeeping to match, and this, under the direction of General Manager Simon Rhatigan, proceeds smoothly and efficiently. Breakfasts, naturally, are quite delicious. Small conferences (40). Dogs in kennels. *Rooms 19. Garden. Croquet. Tennis. Outdoor swimming pool. Limousine. Amex, Diners, Mastercard, Visa.*

Restaurant   ★ ★ ★   £195

One of the country's premier country houses also has one of its leading restaurants – a true haven of comfort and gastronomy. Dining is in one of three stylish rooms which include the spacious conservatory, filled with greenery but also with splendid garden views, and the more intimate Loxton room decorated in summery yellows and blues. Chef-patron Raymond Blanc, who began in humbler surroundings in Oxford, is assisted by Clive Fretwell, who together with a strong kitchen brigade produces dishes that are both highly creative and technically superb. The grounds and kitchen gardens provide most of the quality produce used – whether it's organic herbs, vegetables or fruit – and head gardener Anne-Marie Owens gets a well-deserved mention on the menu. The style has changed little down the years – it has evolved, but still displays the lightest of touches, with influences from the Far East adding intriguing and exotic flavours to captivate the palate. A three-course *menu du jour* offers two choices in each section following an appetiser. The eight-course *menu gourmand* offers the opportunity of sampling a well-balanced selection of specialities while the carte offers a further exercise in studied perfection. Typical starters include ravioli of quail's eggs, spinach, parmesan and black truffles in a delicate chicken jus with meunière butter and Swiss chard or a trio of scallop tartare with shiso leaves, poached oyster in a cucumber butter and crab croustillant in seaweed. Main dishes range from a pan-fried fillet of gilt-head sea bream in a bouillabaisse jus with a fricassée of squid and herbs from the garden to a breast of *Landes* chicken in a white port wine sauce with leeks and truffles and pan-fried venison fillet with a bitter chocolate sauce, braised chestnuts and winter vegetables. Desserts (try Le Café Crème) and farmhouse cheeses, from both France and Great Britain, are a delight, petits fours and chocolates, mini-masterpieces. A fantastic wine list, yes, value for money, no!! Just over half a dozen wines are priced under £20, otherwise the list is hugely expensive. However, there's no doubting the quality – great names from France and Italy, fine wines from the New World. If you want to learn how to emulate the dishes here, ask for details of their cookery school. Set L £29.50 (not Sun) D £65. **Seats** 110. *Parties 10. Private Room 24/46. Open 1215-1415 (Sun to 1430), 1915-2215.*

Tel 01254 240555   Fax 01254 246568
Northcote Road Langho nr Blackburn Lancashire BB6 8BE

About ten miles from the M6 (Junction 31), the extended Victorian redbrick house looks down over the Ribble Valley, though not all the hotel's rooms enjoy this view. Inside, the atmosphere is almost 'olde worlde' with beams, oak panelling and roaring log fires (even in summer if the night is chilly). The entrance hall-cum-bar has two lounges leading off it and a fine staircase that ascends to the bedrooms. These are spacious and attractively decorated and furnished, retaining much of their original character, with good antiques, bric-à-brac, bold and colourful fabrics, and nice touches such as board games, magazines, music alarm and remote-control satellite TV. Bathrooms vary from modern to old-fashioned (with Victorian tiles and cast-iron tubs), all splendidly equipped, even boasting Nina Ricci toiletries. Under the direction of joint owners Craig Bancroft and Nigel Haworth (see below), service is of a high standard (for example afternoon tea and warm shortbread on arrival) with excellent housekeeping and maintenance. Improvements to the grounds continue with a new herb garden the latest project along with the planting of yet more trees. Breakfasts are sensational, with freshly squeezed juices, seasonal fruits, local yoghurt, home-made jams and marmalade, as well as farm eggs, local sausages and black pudding. Banqueting for 100, conferences for 40, with the boardroom ideal for small numbers up to 26. No dogs. **Rooms** 14. *Garden. Amex, Diners, Mastercard, Visa.*

£90

The main dining-room has an attractive bay window and a pair of gilt and crystal chandeliers with matching wall lights creating a suitably civilised setting for some quite splendid cooking. Nigel Haworth leads a gifted team (William Reid is credited on the menu as head chef) producing such carefully composed dishes as crisp duck confit with warm tarragon potato salad and a mustard dressing, and a risotto of forest mushrooms with Italian parsley and shavings of *tete de Moine* cheese among the starters and main dishes like a rack of Pendle lamb with coriander, chargrilled Mediterranean vegetables and olive'd potatoes; breast of Goosnargh duckling with chicken liver samosas on glazed winter vegetables, fondant potatoes and a mild pepper sauce, and steamed Scottish salmon with hollandaise. There are also a couple of regional dishes such as Bury black pudding and buttered pink trout served together with a mustard and watercress sauce. Desserts are equally delicious: banana custard with a caramel crust, sticky toffee pudding with butterscotch sauce, iced bread-and-butter pudding with apricots and raspberries. Good selection of British and Irish farmhouse cheeses too plus a special plate of Lancashire cheeses. Lunchtimes there's a limited choice table d'hote in addition to a shortened version of the evening à la carte and at night there is also a no-choice, six-course gourmet menu. Sunday lunch brings a short à la carte that always includes a traditional roast. A good all-round wine list notable for the number of half bottles available. Set L £18.95 Set D £35. **Seats** 80. *Parties 12. Private Room 40. Open 1200-1330 (Sun till 1400) 1900-2130 (Sat till 10).*

LONGRIDGE   Paul Heathcote's Restaurant   ★ +   £90

Tel 01772 784969   Fax: 01772 785713
104-106 Higher Road Longridge nr Preston Lancashire PR3 3SY

On the edge of the village, and dating back to the early 1800s, this row of three cottages had a chequered history (quarrymen's pub, café, Indian restaurant) before the arrival of Paul Heathcote in 1990 and its transformation into one of the very best restaurants in Britain. The interior retains something of a cottagey feel but with the elegance and style of a sophisticated restaurant. With impeccable culinary credentials gained in such eminent kitchens as those of *The Connaught, Sharrow Bay* and *Le Manoir Aux Quat' Saisons*, Paul has gone on to develop his own exciting brand of modern British cooking. Only one menu is available at lunchtime (Fri & Sun only except in December) but at the fixed price of only £22.50 for four courses plus coffee it's a real bargain. At night there are three menus to choose from, an à la carte; a six-course, no-choice Gourmet Menu (both of which are amended daily to take account of the market and seasonal produce); and Paul's ten-course Signature (tasting) Menu which rarely changes and includes such wonderful dishes as black pudding with crushed potatoes, lobster roasted with dried citrus fruit and herbs, wing of skate with a tartare of mussels and parsley, Goosnargh duckling with buttered potatoes, prunes and jasmine-scented juices, and a down-to-earth bread-and-butter pudding with apricot coulis and clotted cream. From the other menus dishes such as pig's trotters filled with ham hock and sage and served with a tartlet of pea purée and onion sauce; lightly poached oysters served with herb purée, braised leeks, ginger and a champagne sauce (both starters), roast sea bass with thyme potatoes, pan-fried scallops, a pistou of vegetables and red wine sauce, and fillet of beef garnished with braised oxtail and preserved and roasted winter vegetables, mashed potato, glazed button onions and ale sauce demonstrate Paul's sophisticated but robust style. Desserts receive as much thought as everything else here and if you go for Heathcote's Assiette you get a selection of seven, in suitably small-sized portions, all on one plate. Just as well that you'll receive sensible advice from sommelier Paul Wiltshire, since there are no tasting notes (apart from his own recommendations) on the youngish wine list on which the New World is prominently featured. Set L £22.50 Set D £35 & £50 (*dégustation*). **Seats** 55. *Private Room 18. Open 1200-1400 (Sun to 1430) 1900-2130. Closed L Tues, Wed, Thurs, Sat (but open those L in Dec), all Mon. Amex, Mastercard, Visa.*

Meal prices for 2 are based on à la carte menus. When set menus are available, prices will often be lower.

SHINFIELD   L'Ortolan   ★ +   £140

Tel 01734 883783   Fax 01734 885391
The Old Vicarage Church Lane Shinfield nr Reading Berkshire RG2 9BY

There are few better restaurants in the country than this one, and a more passionate and gifted chef than John Burton-Race you will not find, confirming that the British can compete on equal terms with, or even, dare we say, surpass the French. For, make no mistake, this is as near to a grand French country restaurant as you'll get, either side of the Channel! And yet it's but an hour's drive from London, and half that from Heathrow airport (five minutes from the M4, Junction 11). After crunching up the drive, you'll be warmly welcomed; a drink first in the plant-hung lounge/conservatory while considering the French-written menus with English translations, a dining-room decorated in apricot with bird and botanical prints, and another (dining) conservatory, leading onto a patio and overlooking a delightful garden, a great place for coffee (and a snooze after your meal). The whole operation is very much Anglo-French with a formidable British kitchen brigade alongside John: second-in-command Nigel Marriage, pastry chef Michael Taylor, and chef tournant James Race (John's brother). Front-of-house on the other hand is mostly French with John's wife Christine a charming and knowledgeable hostess, backed up by head waitress Olga Pailley and sommelier Jerome Debris, a team of premier division status. The quality of cooking continues to excite, flavours are intense, and combinations of ingredients both innovative and interesting: for instance *pommes de terre nouvelles fourrées aux escargots bourguignon*, new potatoes filled with snails cooked in red wine, garlic and herbs, served with an enriched red wine sauce, or *galette de foie gras aux figues*, a pastry case lined with sliced figs, topped with pan-fried fresh foie gras and served with onion confit with sherry vinegar. Fixed-price menus are now only available at lunchtime, perhaps *salade de coquilles St Jacques grillés et son gazpacho*, sliced grilled scallops on a gazpacho sauce garnished with a seasonal salad, *pigeon sauvage, soufflé de foie gras, fumet de Medoc*, wild pigeon breast topped with foie gras soufflé, wrapped in a 'crépinette' and roasted, and served with a red wine sauce, ending with a cappuccino framboise, a pastry case of various raspberry creations. From the à la carte you might select some of the restaurant's specialities: *gourmandise de la mer*, buckwheat pancakes, caviar, an oyster topped with a sweet and sour horseradish cream and a little crown of marinated salmon, *lasagne de langoustines à l'huile de truffe*, layers of langoustines in its mousse, between leaves of fresh pasta, then steamed and sprinkled with truffle oil, and *dome de mousse, caramel brulée*, caramel mousse served in a toffee dome. Alternatively, select from the cheeseboard, where there are never fewer than twenty-five varieties, each described in detail (if required) before serving. The excellent wine list, very carefully compiled under the watchful eye of Christine, does present the best from France; the New World is well represented by USA, reasonably by Australia, but hardly at all by New Zealand; however, of paramount importance is the quality of choice. Set L £28/£37. *Seats 60. Parties 10. Private Room 40. Open 1215-1415, 1915-2200. Closed D Sun, all Mon, last 2 weeks Feb, last 2 weeks Aug.*

Scotch Beef Club Members: United Kingdom

ENGLAND

BANBURY: The Moon and Sixpence
BOURTON-ON-THE-WATER:
  Lords of the Manor
BROADWAY: The Lygon Arms
BUCKLAND: Buckland Manor
COVENTRY: Nailcote Hall
EAST GRINSTEAD: Gravetye Manor
FAVERSHAM: Read's Restaurant
FLITWICK: Flitwick Manor
GRANGE-OVER-SANDS: The Old
  Vicarage
GRASMERE: Michael's Nook
GREAT MILTON: Le Manoir aux
  Quat'Saisons
HOCKLEY HEATH: Nuthurst Grange
KENILWORTH: Simpson's
LANGHO: Northcote Manor
LONDON: Café Royal
LONDON: The Capital
LONDON: The Connaught
LONDON: Guinea Grill
LONDON: Le Gavroche
LONDON: Hyatt Carlton Tower Rib Room

LONDON: Inter-Continental Hotel
LONDON: Langan's Brasserie
LONDON: Rotisserie Restaurant
LONDON: Turner's
LONDON: Tatsuso
LYMINGTON: Gordleton Mill
MAIDENHEAD: Boulters Lock
  Restaurant
MIDHURST: The Angel Hotel
SHINFIELD: L'Ortolan
ST LEONARD'S ON SEA: Rösers
  Restaurant
STORRINGTON: Manleys Restaurant
STORRINGTON: Old Forge
  Restaurant
TAPLOW: Cliveden
TUNBRIDGE WELLS: Thackeray's
  House
ULLSWATER: Sharrow Bay
WINTERINGHAM: Winteringham
  Fields
WISHAW: The Belfry

SCOTLAND

ABERFOYLE: Braeval Old Mill
ALEXANDRIA: Cameron House Hotel
ALYTH: Drumnacree House
ANSTRUTHER: The Cellar
  Restaurant
APPIN: Invercreran Country House
  Hotel
AUCHTERARDER: Auchterarder
  House
AUCHTERARDER: Gleneagles Hotel
AYR: Fouters Bistro
BALLATER: Tullich Lodge
DUNBLANE: Cromlix House Hotel
DUNKELD: Kinnaird House
EDINBURGH: Balmoral Hotel
EDINBURGH: Caledonian Hotel
EDINBURGH: Prestonfield House
  Hotel
EDINBURGH: Sheraton Grand Hotel
FORT WILLIAM: Inverlochy Castle
GLASGOW: Hilton International
GLASGOW: One Devonshire
  Gardens
GULLANE: La Potinière
INVERNESS: Bunchrew House Hotel

INVERNESS: Culloden House Hotel
INVERURIE: Thainstone House Hotel
ISLE OF SKYE: Kinloch Lodge
ISLE OF SKYE: Skeabost House
  Hotel
KELSO: Sunlaws House Hotel
KILFINAN: Kilfinan Hotel
KINCLAVEN: Ballathie House Hotel
KINROSS: Croftbank House Hotel
KIRKNEWTON: Dalmahoy Hotel
  & Country Club
LANGBANK: Gleddoch House
LINLITHGOW: Champany Inn
MARKINCH: Balbirnie House Hotel
MELROSE: Burts Hotel
NEWTON STEWART: Kirroughtree
  Hotel
OBAN: Isle of Eriska
PEAT INN: Peat Inn
PORT APPIN: Airds Hotel
SPEAN BRIDGE: Old Pines
  Restaurant with Rooms
SPEAN BRIDGE: Old Station
  Restaurant
TURNBERRY: Turnberry Hotel

Your Guarantee of Quality and Independence

- Establishment inspections are anonymous
- Inspections are undertaken by qualified Egon Ronay's Guides inspectors
- The Guides are completely independent in their editorial selection
- The Guides do not accept advertising, hospitality or payment from listed establishments

Titles planned for 1996 include

Hotels & Restaurants ⬤ Pubs & Inns ⬤ Europe
Ireland ⬤ Just A Bite
And Children Come Too ⬤ Paris
Oriental Restaurants

Egon Ronay's Guides are available from all good bookshops or can be ordered from: Leading Guides, 35 Tadema Road, London SW10 0PZ
Tel 0171 352 0172

FOR THE WIDEST RANGE OF SERVICED APARTMENTS WORLDWIDE

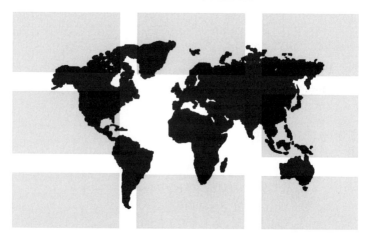

CALL THE SPECIALISTS

Serviced Apartments are the ideal alternative to hotel accommodation for holidays, business or as an interim housing solution.

Cost-effectively priced, all our apartments are serviced by maids, fully equipped and offer unrivalled luxury, space, privacy and security.

With over 25 international partners, The Apartment Service has unique representation in local markets who can help you choose the property that best suits your needs from the thousands of quality apartments throughout the World, from London to New York, from Paris to Sydney.

The Guide to Serviced Apartments containing details of over 3,000 apartments in Europe is available free of charge on request.

SERVICES APARTMENTS HAVE:-

- Lounges
- Kitchens
- Bathrooms
- Maid Service
- Baby Sitting Service
- Direct Dial Telephones

IDEAL FOR:-

- Holidays
- Training Courses
- Relocation
- Temporary Assignments
- Workbases
- Exhibitions
- Conference Presentations

Call today for more details of our
FREE service and our brochure

THE APARTMENT SERVICE

5-6 Francis Grove, Wimbledon, London SW19 4DT, UK.
Tel: 0181 944 1444   Fax: 0181 944 6744

Europe : West

Seagram

ATLANTIC OCEAN

NORTH SEA

BALTIC SEA

SWEDEN

NORWAY

DENMARK

GERMANY

POLAND

CZECH REP.

NETHER-LANDS

BELGIUM

UNITED KINGDOM

IRELAND

Shetland Islands

Orkney Islands

Hebrides

Channel Islands

Oslo

Gothenburg

Berlin

Prague

Dresden

Leipzig

Hanover

Hamburg

Frankfurt am Main

Cologne

Düsseldorf

Baden-Baden

Friedrichsruhe

Stuttgart

Luxembourg

Strasbourg

Brussels

Rotterdam

The Hague

Amsterdam

Paris

Joigny

Avallon

St-Père-sous-Vézelay

Reims

Lille

Edinburgh

Glasgow

Aberdeen

Longridge

Langho

Manchester

Birmingham

Great Milton

Bray

Bristol

Cardiff

London

Belfast

Dublin

Cork

1

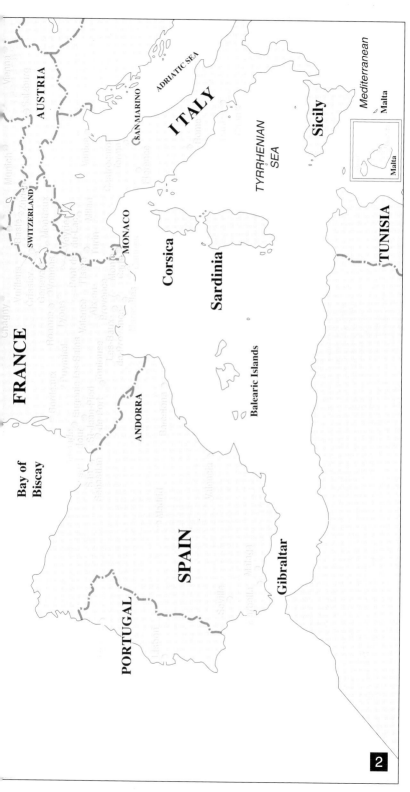

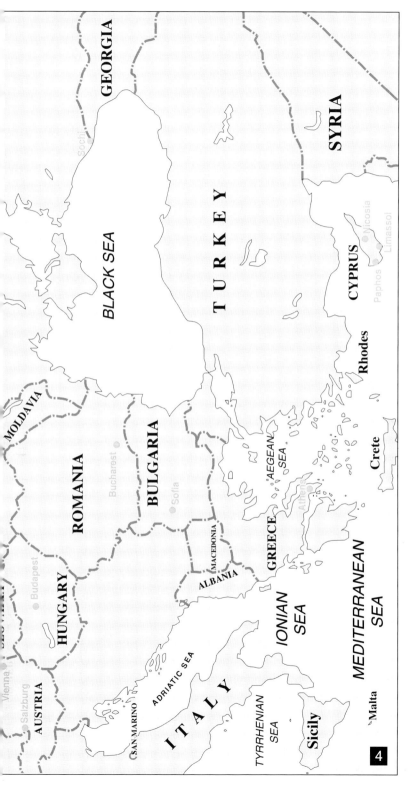

Index

GERMANY

GREECE

HUNGARY

Egon Ronay's Seagram Guide 1996 Europe concentrates on hotels and restaurants in major towns, plus others of note. Please let us know of any establishments you think should be in the next edition and let us have your comments (both good and bad) on those which are included in this year's Guide. *(Europe 1996).*

Name and address of establishment   **Your recommendation or complaint**

Name and address of establishment   **Your recommendation or complaint**

_____   _____

_____   _____

_____   _____

_____   _____

_____   _____

_____   _____

_____   _____

_____   _____

_____   _____

_____   _____

_____   _____

_____   _____

_____   _____

_____   _____

_____   _____

_____   _____

_____   _____

Your name and address *(BLOCK CAPITALS PLEASE)*

_____

_____

_____

_____

READERS' COMMENTS

Egon Ronay's Seagram Guide 1996 Europe concentrates on hotels and restaurants in major towns, plus others of note. Please let us know of any establishments you think should be in the next edition and let us have your comments (both good and bad) on those which are included in this year's Guide. *(Europe 1996)*.

Name and address of establishment	Your recommendation or complaint

Name and address of establishment   **Your recommendation or complaint**

_____   _____

_____   _____

_____   _____

_____   _____

_____   _____

_____   _____

_____   _____

_____   _____

_____   _____

_____   _____

_____   _____

_____   _____

_____   _____

_____   _____

_____   _____

Your name and address *(BLOCK CAPITALS PLEASE)*

_____

_____

_____

_____

Egon Ronay's Seagram Guide 1996 Europe concentrates on hotels and restaurants in major towns, plus others of note. Please let us know of any establishments you think should be in the next edition and let us have your comments (both good and bad) on those which are included in this year's Guide. *(Europe 1996).*

Name and address of establishment	Your recommendation or complaint

Name and address of establishment	**Your recommendation or complaint**

Your name and address *(BLOCK CAPITALS PLEASE)*

Egon Ronay's Seagram Guide 1996 Europe concentrates on hotels and restaurants in major towns, plus others of note. Please let us know of any establishments you think should be in the next edition and let us have your comments (both good and bad) on those which are included in this year's Guide. *(Europe 1996).*

Name and address of establishment	Your recommendation or complaint

Name and address of establishment

Your recommendation or complaint

Your name and address *(BLOCK CAPITALS PLEASE)*

Egon Ronay's Seagram Guide 1996 Europe concentrates on hotels and restaurants in major towns, plus others of note. Please let us know of any establishments you think should be in the next edition and let us have your comments (both good and bad) on those which are included in this year's Guide. *(Europe 1996).*

Name and address of establishment	Your recommendation or complaint
_____	_____
_____	_____
_____	_____
_____	_____
_____	_____
_____	_____
_____	_____
_____	_____
_____	_____
_____	_____
_____	_____
_____	_____
_____	_____
_____	_____
_____	_____
_____	_____
_____	_____
_____	_____

Name and address of establishment   **Your recommendation or complaint**

_____   _____

_____   _____

_____   _____

_____   _____

_____   _____

_____   _____

_____   _____

_____   _____

_____   _____

_____   _____

_____   _____

_____   _____

_____   _____

_____   _____

_____   _____

Your name and address *(BLOCK CAPITALS PLEASE)*

_____

_____

_____

_____